Film Sound

THEORY AND PRACTICE

Edited by Elisabeth Weis and John Belton

COLUMBIA UNIVERSITY PRESS   NEW YORK

Library of Congress Cataloging-in-Publication Data
Main entry under title:

Film sound.

"Annotated bibliography on film sound (excluding
music) / Claudia Gorbman": p.
Includes bibliographies and index.
1. Moving-pictures, Talking—Addresses, essays,
lectures.   2. Sound—Recording and reproducing—
Addresses, essays, lectures.   3. Moving-pictures—
Aesthetics—Addresses, essays, lectures.   I. Weis,
Elisabeth.   II. Belton, John.
PN1995.7.F53 1985   791.43'024   84-23117
ISBN 0-231-05636-2
ISBN 0-231-05637-0 (pbk.)

p 10 9

Columbia University Press
New York   Chichester, West Sussex

Contents

PREFACE   ix

PART I: HISTORY, TECHNOLOGY, AND AESTHETICS   1

INTRODUCTION   3

The Coming of Sound: Technological Change
in the American Film Industry
DOUGLAS GOMERY   5

Economic Struggle and Hollywood Imperialism:
Europe Converts to Sound
DOUGLAS GOMERY   25

Film Style and Technology in the Thirties: Sound
BARRY SALT   37

The Evolution of Sound Technology
RICK ALTMAN   44

Ideology and the Practice of Sound Editing and Mixing
MARY ANN DOANE   54

Technology and Aesthetics of Film Sound
JOHN BELTON   63

PART II: THEORY   73

SECTION 1: CLASSICAL SOUND THEORY   75

A Statement
S. M. EISENSTEIN, V. I. PUDOVKIN, and G. V. ALEXANDROV   83

Asynchronism as a Principle of Sound Film
V. I. PUDOVKIN   86

The Art of Sound
RENÉ CLAIR   92

Manifesto: Dialogue on Sound
BASIL WRIGHT and B. VIVIAN BRAUN   96

Sound in Films
ALBERTO CAVALCANTI   98

A New Laocoön: Artistic Composites and the Talking Film
RUDOLF ARNHEIM   112

Theory of the Film: Sound
BELA BALAZS   116

Dialogue and Sound
SIEGFRIED KRACAUER   126

Slow-Motion Sound
 JEAN EPSTEIN 143
SECTION 2: MODERN SOUND THEORY 145
 Notes on Sound
 ROBERT BRESSON 149
 Direct Sound: An Interview with
 JEAN-MARIE STRAUB and DANIÈLE HUILLET 150
 Aural Objects
 CHRISTIAN METZ 154
 The Voice in the Cinema: The Articulation of Body and Space
 MARY ANN DOANE 162

PART III: PRACTICE 177
 SECTION 1: PRACTICE AND METHODOLOGY 179
 Fundamental Aesthetics of Sound in the Cinema
 DAVID BORDWELL and KRISTIN THOMPSON 181
 On the Structural Use of Sound
 NOËL BURCH 200
 SECTION 2: PIONEERS 210
 The Movies Learn to Talk: Ernst Lubitsch, René Clair,
 and Rouben Mamoulian
 ARTHUR KNIGHT 213
 American Sound Films, 1926–1930
 RON MOTTRAM 221
 Applause: The Visual and Acoustic Landscape
 LUCY FISCHER 232
 Enthusiasm: From Kino-Eye to Radio-Eye
 LUCY FISCHER 247
 Lang and Pabst: Paradigms for Early Sound Practice
 NOËL CARROLL 265
 The Voice of Silence: Sound Style in John Stahl's Back Street
 MARTIN RUBIN 277
 SECTION 3: STYLISTS 286
 Orson Welles's Use of Sound
 PENNY MINTZ 289
 The Evolution of Hitchcock's Aural Style and Sound
 in The Birds
 ELISABETH WEIS 298
 The Sound Track of The Rules of the Game
 MICHAEL LITLE 312
 Sound in Bresson's Mouchette
 LINDLEY HANLON 323

Godard's Use of Sound
      ALAN WILLIAMS 332
SECTION 4: CONTEMPORARY INNOVATORS 346
Altman, Dolby, and The Second Sound Revolution
      CHARLES SCHREGER 348
Sound Mixing and *Apocalypse Now:* An Interview
with Walter Murch
      FRANK PAINE 356
The Sound Designer
      MARC MANCINI 361
Sound and Silence in Narrative and Nonnarrative Cinema
      FRED CAMPER 369
APPENDIX: A NARRATIVE GLOSSARY OF FILM SOUND
TECHNOLOGY
      Stephen Handzo 383
ANNOTATED BIBLIOGRAPHY
      Claudia Gorbman 427
NOTES ON CONTRIBUTORS 447
INDEX 449

PREFACE

This anthology derived from the joys and frustrations of teaching sound aesthetics. The joys came from really *hearing* films for the first time—from listening to films as intensively as we have all learned to look at them.

The frustrations came from inadequacies and gaps in the critical literature on sound. There were any number of books on film sound, but they were on one of two subjects: movie music or the birth of the sound era. Articles that went beyond these two areas were often untranslated, out of print, or in magazines not generally available. And some essays simply had yet to be written. Given the absence of a comprehensive book on sound aesthetics, we decided to put together an anthology that would serve not only in the classroom but for reference or general reading. Hence, *Film Sound* combines the historically important articles on sound, more recent articles that have appeared in relatively ephemeral sources, and finally several pieces that we commissioned to fill the gaps that remained once the book took shape.

As is suggested above, the literature on sound aesthetics seems to us a bit skewed. While we have not intended to rewrite the entire history of sound, we have tried to redress two imbalances, one aesthetic, the other historical.

The aesthetic imbalance has been toward film scoring. Any number of major composers have written for films; and there has been no shortage of specialists to write books or columns on the contributions of movie music. (See, for example, Irwin Bazelon's *Knowing the Score* or Tony Thomas's *Music for the Movies.*) It is somewhat problematic, however, that the term "sound track," used as the main title of another book on film music, should be taken by the general public to mean simply music—to the exclusion of sound effects, dialogue, or narration. And most writers, too, discuss scoring in isolation from these other elements. Our effort here has been not to undervalue the importance of scoring but to choose essays that situate music within the context of a film's other aural and visual components. The essays by Williams, Burch, Knight, Hanlon, Rubin, Mintz, Litle, and Fischer do just that.

The shape of our anthology is also determined by the unbalanced coverage of sound in traditional film sound histories. These histories have been dominated by a single era—the transition from silents to talkies—which generated the bulk of classical sound theory and which still continues to fascinate historians. Our anthology necessarily reflects that emphasis, but it also seeks to reshape sound history by suggesting that there are indeed some interesting sound tracks after 1932.

Our task is made easier by the rediscovery of sound during the last decade. More than fifty years after the birth of the talkies, sound is finally coming of age. There have always been isolated directors with good ears, but now there is a whole generation more aware of sound. This is particularly true in the United States among a number of filmmakers who became major figures in the seventies. Unlike earlier directors who began their careers making films or directing live television dramas, such directors as Coppola, Scorsese, and Lucas attended film schools, where courses on film recording and mixing would have made them more aware of sound's potential. The public, too, has become more sound conscious, partly owing to the recording industry's attempts to achieve better fidelity for home stereo systems.

The last decade has also seen a surge of interest in sound from the academic world. Conferences have been organized around the topic, and a number of magazines—ranging from scholarly publications like *Yale French Studies* to the more popular *Film Comment*—have devoted issues to the sound track. French and Italian scholars have written on the subject, and the British magazine *Screen* devoted its June 1984 issue to sound.

Yet there is much more to be done. One of the major shortcomings with all the present literature on sound has been the lack of a single, succinct explanation of the mechanics of sound that was comprehensive but addressed to aestheticians rather than technicians. Therefore, rather than expect our readers to understand sound techniques piecemeal from the usual alphabetical glossary, we asked Stephen Handzo to write what we call a "narrative glossary" that would cover the terms used in this book. The essay is structured to reflect the logical order by which film sound is recorded, mixed, and reproduced in the theater. At the same time, it documents historical developments within sound recording and reproduction technology. This appendix is the one section of the book, incidentally, where music is treated as a separate entity, but that separation represents the process by which film music is usually scored and edited.

All of the other essays in the anthology are introduced section by section. Our seven introductions are meant to suggest the relationships among articles and to provide a historical, aesthetic, or ideological context for some of the arguments. Nevertheless it might be useful to survey here the overall structure of the anthology.

Part I begins with an economic approach to the coming of sound in the American and European industries. Once the conversion takes place, however, the film style is inevitably affected by sound techniques, and so the last four pieces discuss the effect of sound technology on the aesthetics of film in general.

The articles on classical sound theory in Part II represent certain attitudes toward sound popular during the thirties and forties and address theoretical questions that continue to concern students of the cinema. Although this section stresses theory, there are nonetheless references to sound practice, especially as so many of the early theorists, such as Eisenstein, Pudovkin, Cavalcanti, Epstein, et al., were themselves filmmakers. The section on modern theory contains more recent articles by writers who reject classical theory's subordination of sound to the image and who explore its independent status. This section, too, often reflects certain pragmatic interests, as when Straub and Huillet, for instance, contrast the use of direct sound in their own films with the Italian practice of dubbing all sound after shooting is completed.

The articles in Part III, on sound practice, reveal the expressive possibilities of sound by analyzing the considerable achievements of specific films. Most of these pieces imply an aesthetic of film sound. For a more concrete approach to sound aesthetics, however, it may be useful to look at the introductory article by Bordwell and Thompson, who propose some descriptive terms and set forth a critical methodology that provides a solid basis for the analysis of the sound track.

Section 2 of Part III deals with films that appeared shortly after the conversion to sound and managed, often brilliantly, to overcome the extreme technological limitations. It includes a piece by Ron Mottram that disabuses us of some of the myths about those restrictions by looking at a number of lesser-known transitional-period films.

Section 3 focuses on directors we call sound "stylists" because their entire oeuvre reveals distinctive and expressive uses of sound. Section 4 presents developments in film sound during the last ten years. These include Altman's multitrack recording system, the expansion of the Dolby system, and the contributions of sound designers.

Finally, Claudia Gorbman's annotated bibliography of articles and books on the theory, aesthetics, and technology of film sound should prove useful to those readers who wish to pursue the study of sound further.

Our first criterion for the selection of articles on sound practice was to provide readers with the major texts on sound. At the same time, we also sought to choose case studies with approaches that might serve as models for future analyses of film sound. To set forth a single, definitive analytical methodology at this point in sound studies seems a bit restrictive. Instead, we let the variety of approaches represented in this book suggest the multiplicity of ways in which film sound may be discussed. Thus the reader will find articles that analyze a film's sound track as an aspect of a director's overall style and theme, as a text to be studied for what it reveals of technological possibilities at a given time, or for historical biases and trends that imply a hidden ideology.

The third criterion by which we chose articles that dwelt on one or two films was the accessibility of the films themselves—so that the longer essays can be assigned in conjunction with a course on sound aesthetics. As the titles of articles indicate, the anthology covers many key sound films, such as *Applause, Enthusiasm, M, Kameradschaft, Rules of the Game, Touch of Evil, The Birds, Mouchette, Apocalypse Now,* and major films by Clair, Godard, and Altman. Yet many other films and filmmakers are represented and the reader should check the index or skim the articles themselves in order to locate isolated discussions of specific works. The theory sections, especially those articles in which filmmakers discuss their own works, also include extensive references to specific films.

Given limitations of space, we chose to emphasize sound in feature-length narrative films. This is particularly true in our choice of case studies, which in part counterbalances the emphasis in some theoretical articles on the more overtly experimental uses of sound that is dialectical, asynchronous, and the like. The sections on film sound practice do include discussions of films by nontraditionalists, like Godard and Kubelka, both of whom were very much influenced by the earlier experimentation and theories of Eisenstein, Pudovkin, and Vertov. Hence, a more or less continuous line of reasoning emerges if one reads Pudovkin's essay on "Asynchronism as a Principle of Sound Film"; then the addendum to Lucy Fischer's article on Vertov's *Enthusiasm,* an interview with Peter Kubelka, who restored prints of Vertov's film; and finally Fred Camper's piece on avant-garde works, including Kubelka's own brilliant use of asynchronous sound in his short *Unsere Afrikareise.*

Finally, we would like to thank certain contributors whose names may or may not appear in this volume: sound recordist Mark Dichter, for his freely given and much appreciated advice and information; Claudia Gorbman, Fred Camper, and Steve Handzo, for their specially written articles; Jeanine Basinger, for her helpful counsel; editor William Bernhardt, for his unflagging enthusiasm and support at Columbia University Press; and, last, a number of Hollywood and New York filmmakers interviewed by Elisabeth Weis in 1975 who were extraordinarily generous in providing information and allowing her to sit in on mixes. We have not included those interviews here for lack of space, but would like to thank director Robert Wise; supervising editor Rudi Fehr; sound supervisors James G. Stewart, Murray Spivack, Gordon Sawyer, and Ed Scheid; music editors Ken Wannberg, Len Engel, Erma Levin, and Mimi Arsham; and the late cinematographer Lee Garmes.

New York
September 1984

ELISABETH WEIS
JOHN BELTON

PART I: HISTORY, TECHNOLOGY, AND AESTHETICS

Introduction

Traditional histories of the coming of sound focus on a handful of "Great Men"—mostly inventors and filmmakers—who single-handedly brought about the transition to sound. A linear course of events, seen as a natural evolution toward a preordained goal, leads inevitably to *The Jazz Singer*. Unfortunately, such histories tend to ignore the complex pressures of economics and ideological demand that play a role in shaping the evolution of the cinema. Douglas Gomery implicitly critiques such histories in his essays "The Coming of Sound" and "Economic Struggle and Hollywood Imperialism." Relying on neoclassical economic theory, Gomery situates technical change within a broader economic context. The coming of sound in Hollywood thus occurs in three distinct phases—invention, innovation, and diffusion. Exploring the roles played by Western Electric, Warner Bros., Fox, and RCA in the development of sound systems, Gomery argues for a history of sound that is economically determined, inspired by the desire to control patents and increase profits.

Gomery views the transition to sound in Europe in terms of the economic relations among advanced capitalist countries. Through the pooling of patents, cartels are formed. These patents trusts control competition, dividing world markets among themselves, instituting lucrative royalty systems, and establishing protective quotas. Drawing upon Marxist economic theory, Gomery connects the coming of sound to the complex systems of exchange developed among the European powers prior to and during the worldwide economic depression of the 1930s.

In "Film Style and Technology in the Thirties," Barry Salt constructs a history of technology that he then relates to cinematic forms of the 1930s. Salt bases his work on empirical evidence gathered from actually looking at the films of the period and on trade journals that concern themselves with technological matters. Unlike the histories of sound written by Sponable and Kellogg (see bibliography) which concern themselves solely with technology, Salt's survey of early sound cameras, editing practices, and sound recording techniques relates technology to industry practice and illustrates that relationship with specific examples from individual films.

Introducing an issue of *Yale French Studies* devoted to cinema sound, Rick Altman examines both the way in which film criticism and theory has privileged image over sound and the role that illusionism plays in the evolution of sound technology. For Altman, technology and practice seek to create the impression that sound and image are one and that sound is produced by the image when, in fact, they are separate from one another. At the same time, technological innovation is seen as motivated by the desire "to reduce all traces of the sound-work from the sound track."

Similarly, in "Ideology and the Practice of Sound Editing and Mixing," Mary Ann Doane relates the development of editing and mixing techniques to the attempts of bourgeois ideology to efface all signs of work. The "marriage" of sound and image, seen in various practices such as blooping and the use of sound to bridge cuts, conceals the fact that the sound track is constructed, thus naturalizing the artifice that has gone into its creation.

In "Technology and Aesthetics of Film Sound," however, John Belton argues that this artifice can never be quite concealed. The work of effacement is never totally successful; it reveals itself, in a somewhat transformed state, in the aesthetics and stylistic practices that grow out of that work. For Belton, sound technology, no matter how transparent it becomes, inevitably reveals its own presence in the form of a consciousness that intervenes between the spectator and the original sound.

The Coming of Sound: Technological Change in the American Film Industry DOUGLAS GOMERY

The coming of sound during the late 1920s climaxed a decade of significant change within the American industry. Following the lead of the innovators—Warner Bros. Pictures, Inc. and the Fox Film Corporation—all companies moved, virtually en masse, to convert to sound. By the autumn of 1930, Hollywood produced only talkies. The speed of conversion surprised almost everyone. Within twenty-four months a myriad of technical problems were surmounted, stages soundproofed, and theaters wired. Engineers invaded studios to coordinate sight with sound. Playwrights (from the East) replaced title writers; actors without stage experience rushed to sign up for voice lessons. At the time chaos seemed to reign supreme. However, with some historical distance, we know that, although the switchover to talkies seemed to come "overnight," no major company toppled. Indeed the coming of sound produced one of the more lucrative eras in U.S. movie history. Speed of transformation must not be mistaken for disorder or confusion. On the contrary, the major film corporations—Paramount and Loew's (MGM)—were joined by Fox, Warner Bros., and RKO in a surge of profits, instituting a grip on the marketplace which continues to the present day.

Moreover, sound film did not arrive Minerva-like on the movie screens of twenties America. Its antecedent reached back to the founding of the industry. We need a framework to structure this important thirty-year transformation. Here the neoclassical economic theory of technical change proves very useful. An enterprise introduces a new product (or process of production) in order to increase profits. Simplified somewhat, three distinct phases are involved: invention, innovation, and diffusion. Although many small inventor/entrepreneurs attempted to marry motion pictures and sound, it took two corporate giants, the American Telephone & Telegraph Corporation (AT&T) and the Radio Corporation of America (RCA), to develop the necessary technology. AT&T desired to make better phone equipment; RCA sought to improve its radio capabilities. As a secondary effect of such research, each perfected sound recording and reproduction equipment. With the inventions ready two movie companies, Warner Bros. and Fox, adapted telephone and radio research for practical use. That is, they innovated sound movies. Each developed techniques to produce, distribute, and exhibit sound motion pictures. The final phase, diffusion, occurs when the product or process is adopted for widespread use. Initially, the movie industry giants hesitated to follow the lead of Warners and Fox but, after elaborate planning, decided to convert. All others followed. Because of the enormous economic power of the major firms, the diffusion proceeded quickly and smoothly. During each of the three phases, the movie studios and their suppliers of sound equipment formulated business decisions with a view toward maximizing long-run profits. This motivation propelled the American motion picture industry (as it had other industries) into a new era of growth and prosperity.

Attempts to link sound to motion pictures originated in the 1890s. Entrepreneurs experimented with mechanical means to combine phonograph and motion pictures. For example, in 1895 Thomas Alva Edison introduced such a device, his Kinetophone. He did not try to synchronize sound and image; the Kinetophone merely supplied a musical accompaniment to which a customer listened as he or she viewed a "peep show." Edison's crude novelty met with public indifference. Yet, at the same time, many other inventors attempted to better Edison's effort. One of these, Léon Gaumont, demonstrated his Chronophone before the French Photographic Society in 1902. Gaumont's system linked a single projector to two phonographs by means of a series of cables. A dial adjustment synchronized the phonograph and motion picture. In an attempt to profit by his system, showman Gaumont filmed variety (vaudeville) acts. The premiere came in 1907 at the London Hippodrome. Impressed, the American monopoly, the Motion Picture Patents Company, licensed Chronophone for the United States. Within one year Gaumont's repertoire included opera, recitations, and even dramatic sketches. Despite initially bright prospects, Chronophone failed to secure a niche in the marketplace because the system, relatively expensive to install, produced only coarse sounds, lacked the necessary amplification, and rarely remained synchronized for long periods of time. In 1913 Gaumont returned to the United States for a second try with what he claimed was an improved synchronizing mechanism and an advanced compressed air system for amplification. Exhibitors remembered Chronophone's earlier lackluster performance, ignored all "advertised" claims, and Gaumont moved on to other projects.

Gaumont and Edison did not represent the only phonograph sound systems on the market. More than a dozen others, all introduced between 1909 and 1913, shared common systems and problems. Their only major rival was the Cameraphone, the invention of E. E. Norton, a former mechanical engineer with the American Gramophone Company. Even though in design the Cameraphone nearly replicated Gaumont's apparatus, Norton succeeded in installing his system in a handful of theaters. But like others who preceded him, he never solved three fundamental problems: (1) the apparatus was expensive, (2) the amplification could not reach all persons in a large hall, and (3) synchronization could not be maintained for long periods of time. In addition, since the Cameraphone system required a porous screen, the image retained a dingy gray quality. Therefore it was not surprising that Cameraphone (or Cinephone, Vivaphone, Synchroscope) could never be successfully innovated.

It remained for one significant failure to eradicate any further commercial attempt to marry the motion picture and the phonograph. In 1913, Thomas Edison announced the second coming of the Kinetophone. This time, the Magician of Menlo Park argued, he had perfected talking motion picture! Edison's demonstration on January 4, 1913, impressed all present. The press noted this system seemed more advanced than all predecessors. Its sensitive microphone obviated traditional lip-sync difficulties for actors. An oversized phonograph supplied the maximum mechanical amplification. Finally an intricate system of belts and pulleys erected between the projection booth and the stage could precisely coordinate the speed of the phonograph with the motion picture projector.

Because of the success of the demonstration, Edison was able to persuade vaudeville magnates John J. Murdock and Martin Beck to install the Kinetophone in four Keith-Orpheum theaters in New York. The commercial premiere took place on February 13, 1913, at Keith's Colonial. A curious audience first viewed and listened to a lecturer who praised Edison's latest marvel. To provide dramatic evidence for his glowing tribute, the lecturer then smashed a plate, played the violin, and had his dog bark.

After several music acts (recorded on the Kinetophone), a choral rendition of "The Star-Spangled Banner" stirringly closed the show. An enthusiastic audience stood and applauded for ten minutes. The wizard, Tom Edison, had done it again!

Unfortunately this initial performance would rank as the zenith for Kinetophone. For a majority of later presentations, the system functioned badly—for a variety of technical reasons. For example, at Keith's Union Square theater, the sound lost synchronization by as much as ten to twelve seconds. The audience booed the picture off the screen. By 1914, the Kinetophone had established a record so spotty that Murdock and Beck paid off their contract with Edison. Moreover, during that same year, fire destroyed Edison's West Orange factory. Although he quickly rebuilt, Edison chose not to reactivate the Kinetophone operation. The West Orange fire not only marked the end of the Kinetophone but signaled the demise of all serious efforts to unite mechanically the phonograph with motion pictures. (The later disc system would use electronic connections.)

American moviegoers had to wait nine years for another workable sound system to emerge—and when it did, it was based on the principle of sound on film, not on discs. On April 4, 1923, noted electronics inventor Lee De Forest successfully exhibited his Phonofilm system to the New York Electrical Society. De Forest asserted that his system simply photographed the voice onto an ordinary film. In truth, Phonofilm's highly sophisticated design represented a major advance in electronics, begun when De Forest had patented the audion amplifier tube in 1907. Two weeks later Phonofilm reached the public at large at New York's Rivoli theater. The program consisted of three shorts: a ballerina performing a "swan dance," a string quartet, and another dance number. Since the musical accompaniment for each was nonsynchronous, De Forest, whose brilliance shone in the laboratory rather than in showmanship or business, generated little interest. A New York *Times* reporter described a lukewarm audience response. No movie mogul saw enough of an advancement, given the repeated previous failures, to express more than a mild curiosity.

In fact, De Forest never wanted to work directly through a going motion picture concern, but instead to go it alone. Consequently legal and financial roadblocks continuously hindered substantial progress. De Forest tried, but he could not establish anywhere near an adequate organization to market films or apparatus. Movie entrepreneurs feared, correctly, that the Phonofilm Corporation controlled too few patents ever to guarantee indemnity. Still De Forest's greatest difficulties came when he attempted to generate financial backing. This brilliant individualist failed to master the intricacies of the world of modern finance. Between 1923 and 1925, Phonofilm, Inc. wired only thirty-four theaters in the United States, Europe, South Africa, Australia, and Japan. De Forest struggled on, but in September 1928, when he sold out to a group of South African businessmen, only three Phonofilm installations remained, all in the United States.

It took American Telephone & Telegraph (AT&T), the world's largest company, to succeed where others had failed. In 1912, AT&T's manufacturing subsidiary, Western Electric, secured the rights to De Forest's audion tube to construct amplification repeaters for long-distance telephone transmission. In order to test such equipment the Western Electric Engineering Department, under Frank Jewett, needed a better method to test sound quality. After a brief interruption because of World War I, Jewett and his scientists plunged ahead, concentrating on improving the disc method. Within three months of the armistice, one essential element for a sound system was ready, the loudspeaker. First used in the "Victory Day" parade on Park Avenue in 1919, national notoriety came during the 1920 Republican and Democratic national conventions. A year later, by connecting this technology to its long-distance telephone network AT&T broadcast President Hard-

ing's address at the burial of the Unknown Soldier simultaneously to over-
flowing crowds in New York's Madison Square Garden and San Francisco's
Auditorium. Clear transmissions to large indoor audiences had become a
reality. Other necessary components quickly flowed off Western Electric's
research assembly line. Significantly, the disc apparatus was improved by
creating a single drive shaft turntable using 33⅓ revolutions per minute. By
1924, the complete new disc system included a high-quality microphone, a
nondistortive amplifier, an electrically operated recorder and turntable, a high-
quality loudspeaker, and a synchronizing system free from speed variation.

In 1922, in the midst of these developments, Western Electric
began to consider commercial applications. Western Electric did advertise and
sell the microphones, vacuum tubes, and loudspeakers in the radio field, but
Jewett's assistant, Edward Craft, argued that more lucrative markets existed
in "improved" phonographs and sound movies. Employing the sound-on-
disc method, Craft produced the first motion picture using Western Electric's
sound system. To *Audion*, an animated cartoon originally created as a (silent) public relations film, he added a synchronized score. Craft premiered
Audion in Yale University's Woolsey Hall on October 27, 1922. He followed this first effort with more experiments. On February 13, 1924, at a
dinner at New York's Astor Hotel, Craft presented *Hawthorne*. This public
relations film made at Western Electric's plant in Chicago employed a perfectly synchronized sound track. By the fall of 1924, the sound-on-disc system seemed ready to market.

Laboratory success did not constitute the only criterion which
distinguished Western Electric's efforts from those of De Forest and other
inventors. Most importantly Western Electric had almost unlimited financial
muscle. In 1925, parent company AT&T ranked with United States Steel as
the largest private corporation in the world. Total assets numbered over $2.9
million; revenues exceeded $800 million. At this time America's national in-
come was only $76 billion, and government receipts totaled only $3.6 billion. Western Electric, although technically an AT&T subsidiary, ranked as
a corporate giant in its own right with assets of $188 million and sales of
$263 million, far in excess of even Paramount, the largest force in the mo-
tion picture industry at the time. If absolute economic power formed the
greatest advantage, patent monopoly certainly added another. AT&T spent
enormous sums to create basic patents in order to maintain its monopoly
position in the telephone field. Moreover, AT&T's management actively encouraged the development of nontelephone patents to use for bargaining
with competitors. For example, between 1920 and 1926 AT&T protected
itself by cross-licensing its broadcasting-related patents with the Radio Corporation of America (RCA). In turn, RCA and its allies agreed not to threaten
AT&T's monopoly for wire communication. Specifically in the cross-licen-

sing agreement of 1926 AT&T and RCA contracted to exchange information on sound motion pictures, if and when required. Thus by 1926 AT&T had control over its own patents, as well as any RCA created.

Using its economic power and patent position, Western Electric moved to reap large rewards for its sound recording technology. As early as 1925 it had aroused enough interest to license the key phonograph and record manufacturers, Victor and Columbia. Movie executives proved more stubborn, so Western Electric hired an intermediary, Walter J. Rich. On May 27, 1925, Rich inked an agreement under which he agreed to exploit commercially the AT&T system for nine months.

Warner Bros. Pictures, Inc. would eventually be the company to innovate sound motion pictures. However, in 1925 Warners ranked low in the economic pecking order in the American film industry. Certainly brothers Harry, Albert, Sam, and Jack had come a long way since their days as nickelodeon operators in Ohio some two decades earlier. Yet in the mid-1920s their future seemed severely constrained. Warners neither controlled an international system for distribution nor owned a chain of first-run theaters. The brothers' most formidable rivals, Famous-Players (soon to be renamed Paramount), Loew's, and First National, did. Eldest brother Harry Warner remained optimistic and sought help.

In time Harry Warner met Waddill Catchings, a financier with Wall Street's Goldman Sachs. Catchings, boldest of the "New Era" Wall Street investors, agreed to take a flyer with this fledgling enterprise in the most speculative of entertainment fields. Catchings correctly reasoned the consumer-oriented 1920s economy would provide a fertile atmosphere for boundless growth in the movie field. And Warner Bros. seemed more progressive than other companies. The four brothers maintained strict cost accounting and budget controls, and seemed to have attracted more than competent managerial talent. Catchings agreed to finance Warners, only if it followed his master plan. The four brothers, sensing they would find no better alternative, readily agreed.

During the spring of 1925, Harry Warner, president of Warner Bros., formally appointed Waddill Catchings to the board of directors, and elevated him to chairman of the board's finance committee. Catchings immediately established a $3 million revolving credit account through New York's National Bank of Commerce. Although this bank had never loaned a dollar to a motion picture company, not even the mighty Paramount, Catchings possessed enough clout to convince president James S. Alexander that Warners would be a good risk. Overnight Warner Bros. had acquired a permanent source for financing future productions. Simultaneously Warners took over the struggling Vitagraph Corporation, complete with its network of fifty distribution exchanges throughout the world. In this deal Warners also gained the pioneer company's two small studios, processing laboratory, and extensive film library. Finally, with another $4 million that Catchings raised through bonds, Warner Bros. strengthened its distribution system, and even launched a ten-theater chain. Certainly by mid-1925, Warners was becoming a force to be reckoned with in the American movie business.

Warners' expansionary activities set the stage for the coming of sound. At the urging of Sam Warner, who was an electronics enthusiast, the company established radio station KFWB in Hollywood to promote Warner Bros. films. The equipment was secured from Western Electric. Soon Sam Warner and Nathan Levinson, Western's Los Angeles representative, became fast friends. Until then, Walter J. Rich had located no takers for Western Electric's sound inventions. Past failures had made a lasting and negative impression on the industry leaders, a belief shared by Harry Warner. Consequently, Sam had to trick his older brother into even attending a demonstration. That screening, in May 1925, included a recording of a five-piece jazz band. Quickly Harry and other Warner Bros. executives reasoned as follows. If Warner Bros. could equip its newly acquired theaters with sound and present vaudeville acts as part of their programs, it could successfully challenge the Big Three. Then, even Warners' smallest house could offer (1) famous vaudeville acts (on film), (2) silent features, and (3) the finest orchestral accompaniments (on disc). Warners, at this point, never considered feature-length talking pictures, only singing and musical films.

Catchings endorsed such reasoning and gave the go-ahead to open negotiations with Walter J. Rich. On June 25, 1925, Warner Bros. signed a letter of agreement with Western Electric calling for a period of joint experimentation. Western Electric would supply the engineers and sound equipment; Warner Bros, the camera operators, the editors, and the supervisory talent of Sam Warner. Work commenced in September 1925 at the old Vitagraph studio in Brooklyn. Meanwhile, Warner Bros. continued to expand under Waddill Catching's careful guidance. Although feature film output was reduced, more money was spent on each picture. In the spring of 1926, Warner Bros. opened a second radio station and an additional film-processing laboratory, and further expanded its foreign operations. As a result of this rapid growth, the firm expected the $1 million loss on its annual income statement issued in March 1926.

By December 1925, experiments were going so well that Rich proposed forming a permanent sound motion picture corporation. The contracts were prepared and the parties readied to sign, but negotiations ground to a halt as Western Electric underwent a management shuffle. Western placed John E. Otterson, an Annapolis graduate and career Navy officer, in charge of exploiting nontelephone inventions. Otterson possessed nothing but contempt for Warner Bros. He wanted to secure contracts with industry giants

Paramount and Loew's, and then take direct control himself. Hitherto, Western Electric seemed content to function as a supplier of equipment. Catchings saw this dictatorial stance as typical of a man with a military background unable to adjust to the world of give-and-take in modern business and finance. Unfortunately for Warner Bros., AT&T's corporate muscle backed Otterson's demands.

Only by going over Otterson's head to Western Electric's president, Edgar S. Bloom, was Catchings able to protect the interests of Warner Bros. and secure a reasonable contract. In April 1926, Warner Bros., Walter J. Rich, and Western Electric formed the Vitaphone Corporation to develop sound motion pictures further. Warners and Rich furnished the capital. Western Electric granted Vitaphone an exclusive license to record and reproduce sound movies on its equipment. In return, Vitaphone agreed to lease a minimum number of sound systems each year and pay a royalty fee of 8 percent of gross revenues from sound motion pictures. Vitaphone's total equipment commitment became twenty-four hundred systems in four years.

As *Variety* and the other trade papers announced the formation of the alliance, Vitaphone began its assault on the marketplace. Its first goal was to acquire talent. Vitaphone contracted with the Victor Talking Machine Company for the right to bargain with its popular musical artists. A similar agreement was reached with the Metropolitan Opera Company. Vitaphone dealt directly with vaudeville stars. In a few short months it had contracted for the talent to produce the musical short subjects Harry Warner had envisioned. So confident was Vitaphone's management that the firm engaged the services of the New York Philharmonic orchestra. Throughout the summer of 1926, Sam Warner and his crew labored feverishly to ready a Vitaphone program for a fall premiere, while the Warner publicity apparatus cranked out thousands of column inches for the nation's press.

Vitaphone unveiled its marvel on August 6, 1926, at the Warner theater in New York. The first-nighters who packed the house paid up to $10 for tickets. The program began with eight "Vitaphone Preludes." In the first, Will Hays congratulated the brothers Warner and Western Electric for their pioneering efforts. At the end, to create the illusion of a stage appearance, Hays bowed to the audience, anticipating their applause. Next conductor Henry Hadley led the New York Philharmonic in the overture to *Tannhäuser*. He too bowed. The acts that followed consisted primarily of operatic and concert performances: tenor Giovanni Martinelli offered an aria from *I Pagliacci*, violinist Mischa Elman played "Humoresque," and soprano Anna Case sang, supported by the Metropolitan Opera Chorus. Only one "prelude" broke the serious tone of the evening and that featured Roy Smeck, a popular vaudeville comic-musician. Warners, playing it close to the vest, sought approval from all bodies of respectable critical opinion. The silent feature *Don Juan* followed a brief intermission. The musical accompaniment (sound-on-disc) caused no great stir because it "simply replaced" an absent live orchestra. All in all, Vitaphone, properly marketed, seemed to have a bright future.

That autumn the *Don Juan* package played in Atlantic City, Chicago, and St. Louis. Quickly Vitaphone organized a second program, but this time aimed at popular palates. The feature, *The Better 'Ole,* starred Charlie Chaplin's brother, Sydney. The shorts featured vaudeville "headliners" George Jessel, Irving Berlin, Elsie Janis, and Al Jolson. These performers would have charged more than any single theater owner could have afforded, if presented live. The trade press now began to see bright prospects for the invention that could place so much high-priced talent in towns like Akron, Ohio, and Richmond, Virginia. By the time Vitaphone's third program opened in February 1927, Warners had recorded fifty more acts.

As a result of the growing popularity of Vitaphone presentations, the company succeeded in installing nearly a hundred systems by the end of 1926. Most of these were located in the East. The installation in March 1927 of apparatus in the new Roxy theater and the attendant publicity served to spur business even more. Consequently, the financial health of Warner Bros. showed signs of improvement. The corporation had invested over $3 million in Vitaphone alone, yet its quarterly losses had declined from about $334,000 in 1925 to less than $110,000 in 1926. It appeared that Catchings's master plan was working.

John Otterson remained unsatisfied. He sought to take control of Vitaphone so that Western Electric could deal directly with Paramount and Loew's. To accomplish this he initiated a harassment campaign by raising prices on Vitaphone equipment fourfold, and demanding a greater share of the revenues. By December 1926, Western Electric and Warner Bros. had broken off relations. Simultaneously, Otterson organized a special Western Electric subsidiary called Electrical Research Products, Inc. (ERPI), to conduct the company's nontelephone business—over 90 percent of which concerned motion picture sound equipment.

Realistically Warners, even with Catchings's assistance, could not prevent Otterson from talking with other companies—even though exclusive rights were contractually held by Warners. However, only Fox would initial an agreement. The majors adopted a wait-and-see stance. In fact, the five most important companies—Loew's (MGM), Universal, First National, Paramount, and Producers Distributing Corporation—signed an accord in February 1927 to act together in regard to sound. The "Big Five Agreement," as it was called, recognized that since there were several sound systems on the market, inability to interchange this equipment could hinder wide distribution of pictures and therefore limit potential profits. These companies agreed to adopt jointly only the system that their specially appointed committee would certify, after one year of study, was the "best" for the industry. As further protection, they would employ no system unless it was made available to all producers, distributors, and exhibitors on "reasonable" terms.

Otterson needed to wrest away Warners' exclusive rights if he ever hoped to strike a deal with the Big Five. To this end, he threatened to declare Warners in default of its contractual obligations. Catchings, knowing such public statements would undermine his relations with the banks, persuaded Warner Bros. to accede to Otterson's wishes. In April 1927, ERPI paid Vitaphone $1,322,306 to terminate the old agreement. In May, after the two signed the so-called New License Agreement, Vitaphone, like Fox, became merely a licensee of ERPI. Warner Bros. had given up the exclusive franchise to exploit ERPI sound equipment and lost its share of a potential fortune in licensing fees.

Now on its own, Warners immediately moved all production to several new sound stages in Hollywood. While the parent company continued with its production program of silent features, Vitaphone regularly turned out five shorts a week, which became known in the industry as "canned vaudeville." Bryan Foy, an ex-vaudevillian and silent film director, now worked under Sam Warner to supervise the sound short subject unit. At this juncture, Vitaphone's most significant problem lay in a dearth of exhibition outlets for movies with sound. By the fall of 1927, ERPI had installed only forty-four sound systems in the six months since the signing of the New License Agreement. ERPI was holding back on its sales campaign until the majors made a decision. Warner Bros. would later charge that ERPI had not used its best efforts to market the equipment and had itself defaulted. This accusation and others were brought to arbitration and, in a 1934 settlement, ERPI was forced to pay Vitaphone $5 million.

As the 1927–28 season opened, Vitaphone began to add new forms of sound films to its program. Though The Jazz Singer premiered on October 6, 1927, to lukewarm reviews, its four Vitaphoned segments of Al Jolson's songs proved very popular. Vitaphone contracted with Jolson immediately to make three more films for $100,000. (The four Warner brothers did not attend The Jazz Singer's New York premiere because Sam Warner died in Los Angeles on October 5. Jack Warner took over Sam's position as head of Vitaphone production.) Bryan Foy pushed his unit to create four new shorts each week, becoming more bold in programming strategies. On December 4, 1928, Vitaphone released the short My Wife's Gone Away, a 10-minute, all-talking comedy based on a vaudeville playlet developed by William Demarest. Critics praised this short; audiences flocked to it. Thus Foy, under Jack Warner's supervision, began to borrow even more from available vaudeville acts and "playlets" to create all-talking shorts. During

Christmas week, 1927, Vitaphone released a 20-minute, all-talking drama, *Solomon's Children*. Again revenues were high, and in January 1928 Foy moved to schedule production of two all-talking shorts per week.

Warner Bros. had begun to experiment with alternative types of shorts as a cheap way to maintain the novelty value of Vitaphone entertainment. Moreover, with such shorts it could develop talent, innovate new equipment, and create an audience for feature-length, all-sound films. In the spring of 1928, with the increased popularity of these shorts, Warner Bros. began to change its feature film offerings. On March 14, 1928, it released *Tenderloin*—an ordinary mystery that contained five segments in which the actors spoke all their lines (for 12 of the film's 85 minutes). More part-talkies soon followed that spring.

Harry Warner and Waddill Catchings knew the investment in sound was a success by April 1928. By then it had become clear that *The Jazz Singer* show had become the most popular entertainment offering of the 1927–28 season. In cities that rarely held films for more than one week *The Jazz Singer* package set records for length of run: for example, five-week runs in Charlotte, North Carolina; Reading, Pennsylvania; Seattle, Washington; and Baltimore. By mid-February 1928 *The Jazz Singer* and the shorts were in a (record) eighth week in Columbus, Ohio, St. Louis, and Detroit, and a (record) seventh week in Seattle, Portland, Oregon, and Los Angeles. The Roxy even booked *The Jazz Singer* package for an unprecedented second run in April 1928, where it grossed in excess of $100,000 each week, among that theater's best grosses for that season. Perhaps more important, all these first-run showings did not demand the usual expenses for a stage show and orchestra. It took Warner Bros. only until the fall of 1928 to convert to the complete production of talkies—both features and shorts. Catchings and Harry Warner had laid the foundation for this maximum exploitation of profit with their slow, steady expansion in production and distribution. In 1929 Warner Bros. would become the most profitable of any American motion picture company.

As noted above, only the Fox Film Corporation had also shown any interest in sound movies. Its chief, William Fox, had investigated the sound-on-film system developed by Theodore W. Case and Earl I. Sponable and found it to be potentially a great improvement over the cumbersome Western Electric disc system. Theodore Case and Earl Sponable, two recluse scientists, worked in a private laboratory in upstate New York. In 1913 the independently wealthy, Yale-trained physicist Case established a private laboratory in his hometown of Auburn, New York, a small city near Syracuse. Spurred on by recent breakthroughs in the telephone and radio fields, Case, and his assistant Sponable, sought to better the audion tube. In 1917 they perfected the Thalofide Cell, a highly improved vacuum tube, and began to integrate this invention into a system for recording sounds. As part of this work, Case met Lee De Forest. For personal reasons—envy perhaps—Case turned all his laboratory's efforts to besting De Forest. Within eighteen months Case Labs produced an improved sound-on-film system, based on the Thalofide Cell. Naïvely, De Forest had openly shared with Case all his knowledge of sound-on-film technology. So as De Forest unsuccessfully attempted to market his Phonofilm system, Case quietly constructed—with his own funds—a complete sound studio and projection room adjacent to his laboratory.

In 1925 Case determined he was ready to try to market his inventions. Edward Craft of Western Electric journeyed to Auburn, and saw and heard a demonstration film. Craft left quite impressed. But after careful consideration, he and Frank Jewett decided that Case's patents added no substantial improvement to the Western Electric sound-on-disc system, then under exclusive contract to Warner Bros. Rebuffed, Case decided to solicit a show business entrepreneur directly. He first approached John J. Murdock, the long-time general manager of the Keith-Albee vaudeville circuit. Case argued that his sound system could be used to record musical and comedy acts—the same idea Harry Warner had conceived of six months earlier. Murdock blanched. He had been burned by Edison's hyperbole only a decade earlier, and by De Forest a mere twenty-four months before. Keith-Albee would never be interested in talking movies! Executives from all the "Big Three" motion picture corporations, Paramount, Loew's (MGM), and First National, echoed Murdock's response. None saw the slightest benefit in this latest version of sight and sound.

Case moved to the second tier of the U.S. film industry—Producers Distributing Company (PDC), Film Booking Office (FBO), Warner Bros., Fox, and Universal. In 1926 Case signed with Fox because Courtland Smith, president of Fox Newsreels, reasoned that sound newsreels could push that branch of Fox Film to the forefront of the industry. In June 1926 Smith arranged a demonstration for company owner, founder, and president William Fox. The boss was pleased, and within a month helped create the Fox-Case Corporation to produce sound motion pictures. Case turned all patents over to the new corporation, and retired to his laboratory in upstate New York.

Initially, William Fox's approval of experiments with the Case technology constituted only a small portion of a comprehensive plan to thrust Fox Film into a preeminent position in the motion picture industry. Fox and his advisers had initiated an expansion campaign in 1925. By floating $6 million of common stock, they increased budgets for feature films and enlarged the newsreel division. (Courtland Smith was hired at this point.) Simultaneously Fox began building a chain of motion picture theaters. At that time Fox Film controlled only twenty small neighborhood houses in the New York City environs. By 1927 the Fox chain included houses in Philadelphia, Washington, D.C., Brooklyn, New York City, St. Louis, Detroit, Newark, Milwaukee, and a score of cities west of the Rockies. To finance these sizable investments, William Fox developed close ties to Harold Stuart, president of the Chicago investment house of Halsey Stuart. Meanwhile, Courtland Smith had assumed control of Fox-Case, and, in 1926, initiated the innovation of the Case sound-on-film technology. At first all he could oversee were defensive actions designed to protect Fox-Case's patent position. In September 1926, exactly two months after incorporation, Fox-Case successfully thwarted claims by Lee De Forest and a German concern, Tri-Ergon. For the latter, Fox-Case advanced $50,000 to check the potential of future court action.

At last Fox-Case could assault the marketplace. Although Smith pushed for immediate experimentation with sound newsreels, William Fox, conservatively, ordered Fox-Case to imitate the innovation strategy of Warners and film popular vaudeville acts. On February 24, 1927, Fox executives felt confident enough to stage a widely publicized demonstration of the newly christened Movietone system. At 10:00 in the morning fifty reporters entered the Fox studio near Times Square, and were filmed using the miracle of Movietone. Four hours later these representatives of the press-corps saw and heard themselves as part of a private screening. In addition, Fox-Case presented several vaudeville sound shorts: a banjo and piano act, a comedy sketch, and three songs by the then popular cabaret performer, Raquel Meller. The strategy worked. Unanimous favorable commentary issued forth; the future seemed bright. Consequently, William Fox ordered sound systems for twenty-six of Fox's largest, first-run theaters, including the recently acquired Roxy.

However, by this time Warners had signed nearly all popular entertainers to exclusive contracts. Smith pressed William Fox again to consider newsreels with sound. Then, Smith argued, Fox Film could offer a unique, economically viable alternative to Warner Bros. presentations, and move into a heretofore unoccupied portion of the market for motion picture entertainment. Furthermore, sound newsreels would provide a logical method by which Fox-Case could gradually perfect necessary new techniques of camerawork and editing. Convinced, William Fox ordered Smith to adopt this course for technological innovation. This decision would prove more successful for Fox Film's overall goal of corporate growth than either William Fox or Courtland Smith imagined at the time.

Smith moved quickly. The sound newsreel premiere came on April 30, 1927, at the Roxy in the form of a four-minute record of marching West Point cadets. And despite the lack of any buildup, this newsreel elicited an enthusiastic response from the trade press and New York-based motion picture reviewers. Quickly Smith seized upon one of the most important symbolic news events of the 1920s. At 8:00 A.M. on May 20, 1927, Charles Lindbergh departed for Paris. That evening Fox Movietone News presented footage of the takeoff—with sound—to a packed house at the Roxy theater. Six thousand persons stood and cheered for nearly ten minutes. The press saluted this new motion picture marvel and noted how it had brought alive the heroics of the "Lone Eagle." In June, when Lindbergh returned to a tumultuous welcome in New York City and Washington, D.C., Movietone News cameramen also recorded portions of those celebrations. Both William Fox and Courtland Smith were now satisfied that the Fox-Case system had been launched onto a propitious path.

That summer Smith dispatched camera operators to all parts of the globe. They recorded the further heroics of aviators, beauty contests, and sporting events, as well as the earliest filmic records of statements by Benito Mussolini and Alfred Smith. Newspaper columnists, educators, and other opinion leaders lauded these latter short subjects for their didactic value. Fox Film's principal constraint now became a paucity of exhibition outlets. During the fall of 1927, Fox Film did make Movietone newsreels the standard in all Fox-owned theaters, but that represented less than 3 percent of the potential market. More extensive profits would come as Fox Film formed a larger chain of first-run theaters. In the meantime Courtland Smith established a regular pattern for release of Movietone newsreels, one ten-minute reel per week. He also increased the permanent staff and established a worldwide network of stringers.

In addition Smith and William Fox decided again to try to produce vaudeville shorts, as well as silent feature films accompanied by synchronized music on disc. Before 1928, Fox-Case released only one scored feature, *Sunrise*. (Two earlier features, *Seventh Heaven* and *What Price Glory?*, were rereleased with synchronized musical scores.) The two executives moved quickly. By January 1928 Fox had filmed ten vaudeville shorts and a part-talkie feature, *Blossom Time*. During the spring of 1928 these efforts, Fox's newsreels, and Warners' shorts and part-talkies proved to be the hits of the season. Thus in May 1928 William Fox declared that 100 percent of the upcoming production schedule would be "Movietoned." Simultaneously Fox Film continued to wire, as quickly as possible, all the houses in its ever-expanding chain, and draw up plans for an all-sound Hollywood-based studio. Fox's innovation of sound neared completion; colossal profits loomed on the horizon.

Only the Radio Corporation of America (RCA) offered Warner Bros., Western Electric, or Fox any serious competition. In 1919 General Electric and Westinghouse had created RCA to control America's patents for radio broadcasting. Like rival AT&T, GE conducted fundamental research in radio technology. The necessary inventions for what would become RCA's Photophone sound-on-film system originated when, during World War I, the U.S. Navy sought a high-speed recorder of radio signals. GE scientist Charles A. Hoxie perfected such a device. After the war, Hoxie pressed to extend his work. Within three years, having incorporated a photoelectric cell and a vibrating mirror, he could record a wide variety of complex sounds. In December 1921 GE executives labeled the new invention the Pallo-Photophone.

To test it, Willis R. Whitney, head of the GE Research Laboratory, successfully recorded speeches by Vice-President Calvin Coolidge and several Harding Administration Cabinet members. At this point GE executives conceived of the Pallo-Photophone as a marketable substitute for the phonograph. During 1922 and 1923, Hoxie and his assistants continued to perfect the invention. For example, they discovered that the recording band need not be 35mm wide. A track as narrow as 1.5mm proved sufficient, and thus freed sound to accompany a motion picture image. Simultaneously other GE scientists, Chester W. Rise and Edward W. Kellogg, developed a new type of loudspeaker to improve reception for the radio sets General Electric manufactured for RCA. Late in 1922, Whitney learned of Lee De Forest's efforts to record sound on film. Not to be outdone, Whitney ordered Hoxie and his research team to develop a sound reproducer that could be attached to a standard motion picture projector. In November 1923 Hoxie demonstrated such a system for GE's top executives in an almost perfect state. However by that time Whitney and his superiors sensed that De Forest's failure to innovate sound motion pictures proved no market existed for Hoxie's invention. Whitney promptly transferred all efforts toward the development of a marketable all-electric phonograph. GE successfully placed its new phonograph before the public during the summer of 1925.

One year later, because of Warners' success, Whitney reactivated the sound movie experiments. At this point he christened the system "Photophone." By the end of that year, 1926, GE's publicity department had created several experimental short subjects. Quickly GE executives pondered how to approach a sales campaign. However, before they could institute any action, Fox sought a license in order to utilize GE's amplification patents. Contemplating the request, David Sarnoff, RCA's general manager, convinced his superiors at GE that RCA should go out on its own, sign up the large movie producers, Paramount and Loew's, and not worry about Fox. The GE high brass agreed and assigned Sarnoff the task of commercially exploiting GE's sound movie patents.

Sarnoff easily convinced Paramount and Loew executives seriously to consider RCA's alternative to Western Electric's then monopoly, even though RCA had yet to demonstrate Photophone publicly. Presently the "Big Five Agreement" was signed. Sarnoff immediately went public. On February 2, 1927, Sarnoff demonstrated Photophone for the press and invited guests at the State theater in GE's home city of Schenectady, New York. Musical short subjects featuring a 100-piece orchestra impressed all present. Nine days later Sarnoff recreated the event for more reporters at New York's Rivoli theater. Here two reels of MGM's *Flesh and the Devil* were accompanied by a Photophone recording of the Capitol theater orchestra. Then three shorts featured the Van Curler Hotel Orchestra of Schenectady, an unnamed baritone, and a quartet of singers recruited from General Electric employees. A New York *Times* reporter praised the synchronization, volume, and tone. Sarnoff, in turn, lauded Photophone's ease of installation and simplicity of operation.

In private Sarnoff tried to convince the producers' committee of his company's technical and financial advantages. The producers had established three specific criteria for selection: (1) the equipment had to be technically adequate, (2) the manufacturer had to control all required patents, and (3) the manufacturer had to have substantial resources and financial strength. Only two systems qualified: RCA's Photophone and Western Electric's Vitaphone. At first, the producers favored RCA because it had not licensed any movie concern, whereas Western Electric had formal links to Warners and Fox. In October 1927 Sarnoff proposed an agreement which called for a holding company, one-half owned by RCA and one-half by the five motion picture producers. All of GE's sound patents would be vested in this one corporation. Sarnoff demanded 8 percent of all gross revenues from sound movies as a royalty. The producers countered. They sought individual licenses and fees set at $500 per reel. For a typical 8-reel film (90 minutes) with gross revenues of $500,000, the 8 percent royalty would be $40,000; at the new rate the amount came to $4,000, a savings of $36,000.

Sarnoff reluctantly acceded to the per reel method of royalty calculation, but stubbornly refused to grant individual licenses. On the other hand, the motion picture corporations held fast to their belief that they should play no role in the manufacture of the apparatus. Each wanted only a license to produce and distribute sound films. For two months the two parties stalemated over this issue. Late in November 1927 John Otterson of Western Electric stepped forward and offered individual licenses. Western Electric's engineers had made great progress with their sound-on-film system, and there no longer existed exclusive ties to Warner Bros. Consequently, in March 1928 the movie producers, with all the relevant information in hand, selected Western Electric. Each producer—Paramount, United Artists, Loew's, and First National—secured an individual license and would pay $500 per reel of negative footage. All four signed on May 11, 1928. Universal, Columbia, and other companies quickly followed. The movie producers had adroitly played the two electrical giants against each other and secured reasonably favorable terms.

Sarnoff reacted quickly as the tide turned toward Western Electric. First General Electric purchased (for nearly one-half million dollars) 14,000 shares of stock of the Film Booking Office (FBO) from a syndicate headed by Joseph P. Kennedy. This acquisition guaranteed Photophone a studio outlet. FBO was the only producer with national distribution which was not linked in talks with Western Electric. Next Sarnoff formed RCA Photophone, Inc. Sarnoff now controlled production facilities and the necessary sound technology. To generate significant profits, RCA needed a chain of theaters.

In 1928, the Keith-Albee vaudeville circuit controlled such a chain. Faced with declining business in vaudeville, Keith-Albee executives developed two approaches. First, they took over the Orpheum vaudeville chain, and thus merged all major American vaudeville under one umbrella. The new Keith-Albee-Orpheum controlled two hundred large downtown theaters. Second, Keith-Albee acquired a small movie company, Pathé, just to hedge its bets. When Sarnoff approached the owners of the new Keith-Albee-Orpheum they were more than ready to sell. Sarnoff quickly moved to consolidate his empire. FBO and Pathé formally acquired licenses for Photophone. FBO and Pathé executives supervised the addition of music-on-film to three features, *King of Kings*, *The Godless Girl*, and *The Perfect Crime*. Upcoming sound newsreels and vaudeville shorts were promised. However, these films would be useless unless Sarnoff could wire the Keith-Albee-Orpheum theaters with Photophone equipment. Warner Bros., Fox, and Western Electric had taken almost two years to eliminate all the problems of presenting clear sounds of sufficient volume in large movie palaces. As of this point Photophone had yet to be tested in a commercial situation. And Sarnoff and his staff would need at least six months to iron out technological problems. Promised first in April, then July, commercial installations commenced in October 1928. In the meantime, Sarnoff used a low installation price and sweeping prognostications of future greatness to persuade a shrinking number of prospective clients to wait for Photophone equipment.

That October Sarnoff legally consolidated RCA's motion picture interests by creating a holding company, Radio-Keith-Orpheum (RKO). Sarnoff became president of the film industry's newest vertically integrated combine. The merger united theaters (Keith-Albee-Orpheum), radio (NBC), and motion pictures (FBO and Pathé, subsequently renamed Radio Pictures in May 1929). Although late on the scene, RCA had established a secure place in the motion picture industry. RKO released its first talkies in the spring of 1929, and Photophone could battle Western Electric for contracts with the remaining unwired houses. Gradually during the 1930s RCA Photophone would become as widely accepted as Western Electric's system.

The widespread adoption of sound—the diffusion—took place quickly and smoothly, principally because of the extensive planning of the producers' committee. Since an enormous potential for profits existed, it was incumbent on the majors to make the switchover as rapidly as possible. Paramount released its first films with musical accompaniment in August 1928; by September its pictures contained talking sequences; and by January 1929 it sent out its first all-talking production. By May, one year after signing with ERPI, Paramount produced talkies exclusively and was operating on a level with Warners and Fox. In September 1929, MGM, Fox, RKO, Universal, and United Artists completed their transitions. Those independent production companies which survived took, on average, one year longer.

Elaborate plans had been laid by the industry to facilitate diffusion. In Hollywood, the Academy of Motion Picture Arts and Sciences was designated as a clearinghouse for information relating to production problems. The local film boards of trade handled changes in distribution trade practices. And a special lawyers' committee representing the major producers was appointed to handle disputes and contractual matters with equipment manufacturers. For example, when ERPI announced a royalty hike, the committee initiated a protest, seeking lower rates. Unions presented no difficulties. The American Federation of Musicians unsuccessfully tried to prevent the wholesale firing of theatrical musicians; Actors' Equity, now that professionals from the Broadway stage began to flock West, failed to establish a union shop in the studios. All problems were resolved within a single year; the industry never left an even keel.

ERPI's task all the while was to keep up with the demand for apparatus. It wired the large, first-run theaters first and then, as equipment became available, subsequent-run houses. Installations were made usually from midnight to nine in the morning. For example, in January 1930, ERPI installed more than nine systems each day. To facilitate the switchover, Western Electric expanded its Hawthorne, Illinois, plant, and ERPI established training schools for projectionists in seventeen cities and opened fifty district offices to service and repair equipment. Many smaller theaters, especially in the South and Southwest, could not afford ERPI's prices and signed with RCA, or De Forest. As late as July 1930, fully 22 percent of all U.S. theaters still presented silent versions of talkies. That figure neared zero two years later.

The public's infatuation with sound ushered in another boom period for the industry. Paramount's profits jumped $7 million between 1928 and 1929, Fox's $3.5 million, and Loew's $3 million. Warner Bros., however, set the record; its profits increased $12 million, from a base of only $2 million. A 600 percent leap! Conditions were ripe for consolidation, and Warner Bros., with its early start in sound, set the pace. It began by acquiring the Stanley Company, which owned a chain of three hundred theaters along the East Coast, and First National. In 1925, when Waddill Catchings joined the Warner Bros. board of directors, the company's assets were valued at a little over $5 million; in 1930 they totaled $230 million. In five short years, Warner Bros. had become one of the largest and most profitable companies in the American film industry.

Not content merely to establish RKO, David Sarnoff of RCA set out to sever all connections with General Electric and Westinghouse and acquire sound manufacturing facilities of his own. The first step in this direction was the acquisition in March 1929 of Victor Talking Machine Company and its huge plant in Camden, New Jersey. In the process, RCA secured Victor's exclusive contracts with many of the biggest stars in the musical world. By December 1929 Sarnoff had reached his goal. RCA was now a powerful independent entertainment giant with holdings in the broadcasting, vaudeville, phonograph, and motion picture industries.

William Fox had the most grandiose plan of all. In March 1929 he acquired controlling interest in Loew's, Inc., the parent company of MGM. Founder Marcus Loew had died in 1927, leaving his widow and sons one-third of the company's stock. Nicholas Schenck, the new president, pooled his stock and that belonging to corporate officers with the family's and sold out to Fox at 25 percent above the market price. The new Fox-Loew's merger created the largest motion picture complex in the world. Its assets totaled more than $200 million and an annual earning potential existed of $20 million. William Fox assumed a substantial short-term debt obligation in the process, but during the bull market of the late twenties he could simply float more stock and bonds to meet his needs.

Adolph Zukor, meanwhile, added more theaters, bringing Paramount's total to almost one thousand. He also acquired a 49 percent interest in the Columbia Broadcasting System. Then, in the fall of 1929, he proposed a merger with Warner Bros. that would create a motion picture and entertainment complex larger than Fox-Loew's and RCA combined. Catchings and Harry Warner were agreeable, but the new U.S. Attorney General, William D. Mitchell, raised the red flag. If that merger went through, the industry would have been dominated by three firms. As it happened, though, it was to be dominated by five. After the stock market crash, William Fox was unable to meet his short-term debts and had to relinquish ownership of Loew's. The oligopolistic structure of the industry, now formed by Warner Bros., Paramount, Fox, Loew's, and RKO, would continue to operate well into the 1950s. The coming of sound had produced important forces for industry consolidation, immediately prior to the motion picture industry's first crisis of retrenchment—the Great Depression.

Bibliographical Note

This article is based on a series of articles I wrote between 1976 and 1980. I refer the reader to the appropriate journal or book.

The innovative activities of Warner Bros. are best analyzed in "Writing the History of the American Film Industry," *Screen*, 17, No. 1 (Spring 1976): 40–53. Likewise there exists a separate discussion for the experiences of Fox and RCA. See "Problems in Film History: How Fox Innovated Sound," *The Quarterly Review of Film Studies*, 1, no. 3 (August 1976): 315–30, and "Failure and Success: Vocafilm and RCA Innovate Sound," *Film Reader*, 2 (January 1977): 213–21.

The reaction of the industry at large can be seen in two distinct stages. I treat the initial reluctance and waiting in "The Warner-Vitaphone Peril: The American Film Industry Reacts to the Innovation of Sound," *Journal of the University Film Association*, 28, no. 1 (Winter 1976): 11–19. General acceptance and prosperity form the core of yet another piece. See "Hollywood Converts to Sound: Chaos or Order?," in Evan W. Cameron, ed., *Sound and the Cinema* (Pleasantville, N. Y.: Redgrave, 1980), pp. 24–37.

A complete set of my publications on the coming of sound can be found in Claudia Gorbman, "Bibliography on Sound in Film," *Yale French Studies*, no. 60 (Winter 1980): 276–77. On other matters, persons should consult my earliest work, "The Coming of Sound to the American Cinema: The Transformation of an Industry," Ph.D. dissertation, University of Wisconsin–Madison, 1975. It should be noted that for nearly all questions the dissertation serves as only a base for the later articles.

Economic Struggle
and Hollywood Imperialism:
Europe Converts to Sound
DOUGLAS GOMERY

The coming of sound to world cinema has precipitated many important studies of its aesthetic, social, and cultural effects. Surprisingly, there exists very little systematic analysis of the consequences of this technological change for international trade of motion pictures. Film distribution presents few problems within a single nation; international commerce is not nearly so simple. Examining prior work for trade among the United States, United Kingdom, France, and Germany, one finds three types of analysis.[1] First, textbooks tell of world domination (and exploitation) by Hollywood, the success of film production in Britain in 1933, the disastrous effect of the world depression in France, and the rise of Hitler (and Goebbels) in Germany. No connections are made; the coming of sound simply happens.[2] Recent work makes stronger claims. On the one hand Thomas Guback examines the U.S. film industry's expansion into and takeover of European markets after World War I. By 1925 Hollywood products accounted for 95 percent of British movie revenues and 70 percent of French. When the United States film industry exported sound films, it utilized this change to solidify its hegemony, and maintain its dominant position in the world until after World War II. In contrast, Robert Sklar argues that in the late 1920s European countries, particularly Britain, France, and Germany, began to repel Hollywood expansion with a moderate degree of success. The addition of sound helped these countries because of the problems of the troublesome conversion of films for different language audiences.[3]

In this essay I shall argue that the full impact of the worldwide diffusion of sound cannot be understood in the simple terms Guback and Sklar suggest. We need an explicit theory of international exchange by which to structure our analysis. Marxist economics provides the most appropriate theoretical framework. Both Guback and Sklar (implicitly) utilize the neoclassical economic model: how did foreign quotas and tariffs disrupt free distribution of films? Combined with a dramatic narrative structure—how could a poor European country survive the onslaught of the Hollywood monopoly—their accounts make for compelling reading. Unfortunately their analyses gloss over complex issues and thus do not provide a systematic explanation of world exchange of motion pictures. The free-trade model ignores questions of imperialism and cartels; the Marxist model of international trade places expansion of trade to other countries at the core of the capitalist social formation. Marxist economists argue that during the late 1920s and early 1930s the United States moved from classical imperialism to a new category of international exploitation founded on the products of the second industrial revolution: steel, the internal combustion engine, and electricity—including motion pictures.[4]

1

For the coming of sound to Europe, the analysis must focus on the question of the nature of economic relations among advanced capitalist countries. One concept emerges as central: cartelization. During this period a small group of large powerful corporations in the United States, United Kingdom, France, and Germany sought dominance and consequently formed alliances to "control competition" on an international scale. Numerous pools, cartels, and trusts were formed. Such relationships were rarely static; each corporate giant sought to gain power from its rivals. Agreements would only last until one signatory felt strong enough to extract more surplus value. Cycles of truce . . . battle . . . truce . . . battle were common. Frequently the nation-state would assist resident corporations, using tariffs or quotas to gain temporary advantage.

 Pivotal in this new imperialism was the multinational corporation. After World War I a monopolist corporation rarely operated in a single nation-state. During the 1920s United States corporations began large-scale expansion into European markets, especially into those countries most damaged by war. The so-called new technology industries—usually associated with mass consumable products like automobiles or motion pictures—grew most rapidly. European corporations, the former imperialist powers, had to retreat and develop methods by which to respond to aggressive United States competitors.[5]

 Hollywood's multinational corporations (Warners, RKO, Fox, Paramount, Loew's, Columbia, United Artists, Universal) began to export sound movies late in 1928. At that time there were few theaters wired for sound; conversion of cinemas in Europe lagged far behind the United States. By the end of 1929 only 18 percent of European theaters could present talkies while nearly half the cinemas in the United States could. In all cases the most deluxe picture palaces (super-cinemas) in the biggest cities were wired first. Then cinemas with less revenue-generating potential converted. Very small houses (100-200 seats) came last, some as late as 1935. United Kingdom exhibitors wired most quickly (22 percent in 1929; 63 percent by the close of 1930). German theater owners moved more slowly; the penetration rate did not top 60 percent until 1932. French exhibitors proved even more recalcitrant. Consequently the United Kingdom became Hollywood's first important foreign market. Later, Hollywood would utilize experience gained in Great Britain to establish precedents which it would try to follow on the Continent. First, in conjunction with Western Electric and the Radio Corporation of America (RCA), the dominant U.S. suppliers of sound apparatus, the Hollywood monopolists gave preferential treatment to the owners of the deluxe (super) cinemas. Western Electric and RCA wired these theaters first; Hollywood provided the most popular talkies for exclusive first-runs. All technical problems of compatibility were easily eliminated. Native producers, importers, and owners of smaller cinemas simply had no choice but to acquiesce or lose the chance to capture a share of the surplus profits.[6]

However, Hollywood, RCA, and Western Electric could not utilize similar marketing strategies for the Continent because of language conversion difficulties. Initially, dubbing, subtitles, and native language narrators were tried—with little success. The most promising, dubbing, was fraught with technological limitations, and caused adverse audience reaction. Consequently the Hollywood monopolists began to produce foreign language versions of feature films and short subjects. In November 1929 Metro-Goldwyn-Mayer (MGM) took the lead by embarking on a two million dollar program to replicate, in at least three versions, nearly all of its feature films. With fully amortized sets, costumes, and scripts, additional versions rarely cost more than 30 percent of the original. MGM also filmed a few original foreign language films, usually based on previously successful silents. Early in 1930 Paramount established a huge studio at Joinville, six miles from Paris, to create foreign versions in five languages. By March 1930, this studio was in full operation, the equivalent of any lot in California. The other Hollywood monopolists joined Paramount and by the summer of 1930 Joinville functioned on a 24-hour-a-day schedule, creating films in twelve languages. Hollywood continued to make foreign versions in California. On a much smaller scale the British, French, and German film industries also produced their own foreign versions for export.[7]

Yet within one year, Hollywood would realize it had grossly miscalculated. Foreign versions could not generate a profit. Even sharing expenses at Joinville did not keep costs below the break-even point. Dubbing had greatly improved and become far less expensive. Late in 1931 the Hollywood monopolists, in order to minimize losses, turned completely to that alternative. The large revenues for MGM's dubbed versions of *Min and Bill* (in Italian) and *Trader Horn* (in French) convinced all concerned. MGM ceased production of separate versions early in 1932; the other Hollywood monopolists soon followed. Paramount converted Joinville into Hollywood's dubbing center for Europe. Special language versions had a short life (1930–31), and served only as the transition to the dubbing process, still in use today.[8]

As Hollywood worked to resolve its language conversion problem, a German cartel appeared to challenge the U.S. film industry's domination of European markets. Three German inventors had developed an alternative sound-on-film method which became known as Tri-Ergon. They unsuccessfully tried to innovate their system into the German film industry between 1922 and 1926. However in 1928, after realizing the threat of U.S. domination of world sound technology, the German government encouraged the formation of an alternative. The Tonbild Syndicate A.G. (Tobis), organized with German, Dutch, and Swiss money, acquired the Tri-Ergon patents and began to install sound equipment in German theaters. Simultaneously the two most important German electrical manufacturers, Siemens and Halske, and Allgemeine Elektrizitäts Gesellschaft (AEG) announced their own, jointly developed sound system. Quickly they formed Klangfilm. After some initial struggle, Tobis and Klangfilm agreed to unite against the anticipated U.S. "talkie-invasion."[9]

Tobis-Klangfilm set up formal operations during the spring of 1929. In May 1929 Warner Bros. brought *The Singing Fool* to Berlin; Tobis-Klangfilm sued and stopped the premiere. In July 1929 an appeals court upheld Tobis-Klangfilm's sole right to sound film patents within Germany; no U.S. films could be exhibited while the case continued to a higher court. Simultaneously Tobis-Klangfilm pressed for similar exclusivity in the United Kingdom and Switzerland. In reaction the Hollywood monopolists (represented by Will Hays) and Western Electric worked for an out-of-court settlement. The German company would not back down and thus late in 1929 Hollywood began to boycott the German market. Hays reasoned that German theater owners would not be anxious to forfeit the short-run profits they could expect from the new Hollywood talkies and would pressure Tobis-Klangfilm to agree to present films recorded on U.S. systems. In 1929 the Hollywood monopolists had used such a boycott quite successfully to force the French government to dilute a stiff quota law.[10]

Hays underestimated Tobis-Klangfilm's power. Within six months, with the support of the German government, Tobis-Klangfilm broke the Hollywood–Western Electric boycott. In fact Tobis-Klangfilm successfully secured (final) injunctions against Western Electric in Germany, Holland,

Czechoslovakia, Hungary, Switzerland, and Austria. Equally as important, early in 1930 Warner Bros. and RKO broke with their fellow monopolists, and began to rent films to exhibitors in the disputed markets. Warners had little incentive to cooperate with Western Electric; the two were in the middle of a six-year arbitration struggle concerning Warners' original contract. RCA had created RKO to provide a market for its sound equipment. Seizing on Western Electric's foreign problems, RCA's parent corporation, General Electric, acquired part-interest in AEG and thus became part-owner of Tobis-Klangfilm. Soon after RCA, RKO, and Tobis-Klangfilm initialed a cooperative agreement.[11]

The other Hollywood monopolists soon acquiesced. In mid-June 1930 representatives from Tobis-Klangfilm, Western Electric, RCA, and the U.S. film industry began to confer in Paris. An international cartel was the stated goal; the surplus profits were estimated to be a quarter of a billion dollars. Quickly all parties agreed to split up the world for patent rights and then charge film companies royalties for distribution within each territory. The negotiations lasted one month. On July 22, 1930, Western Electric, RCA, and Tobis-Klangfilm formed a loose cartel which divided the world into four territories. Tobis-Klangfilm secured exclusive rights for Europe and Scandinavia, while Western Electric and RCA obtained the United States, Canada, Australia, New Zealand, India, and the Soviet Union. For the valuable British market, royalties were split one-fourth for Tobis-Klangfilm, three-fourths for Western Electric and RCA. The rest of the world became open territory; no company held exclusive rights. All parties exchanged and pooled technical information. The royalty fees ranged from $500 to $5,000 per film, depending on how many countries were involved. The diffusion of sound seemed to be complete, the economic struggle over.[12]

In fact, the Hollywood monopolists never formally ratified the "Paris Agreement." Shortly after the conference, Germany instituted stiffer quota regulations. In protest Hollywood leaders refused to sign the pact, but would continue to make all necessary royalty payments. Western Electric, RCA, Tobis-Klangfilm, and the Hollywood monopolists began meeting informally to negotiate a final settlement. Finally in February 1932 they held a second Paris conference. French representatives also attended and bitterly complained because under the 1930 accord they had to pay Western Electric one fee to rent equipment and Tobis-Klangfilm a second fee for the right to distribute the same film in their own country. Other disputes surfaced and the cartel fractured. It endured a mere eighteen months.[13]

Consequently, patent disputes erupted in Europe and throughout the rest of the world. A typical challenge came in Denmark. In 1929 the dominant Danish producer, Nordisk, had acquired the rights to the Peterson-Poulson sound system. Eventually these patents became part of the

German group. With the world sound cartel in disarray, Nordisk began to reassert its exclusive rights for Denmark. First Nordisk petitioned a Danish court for the right to collect royalties for all foreign films presented in Denmark which were not recorded using the Peterson-Poulson system. In October 1933, the Danish Court ruled for Nordisk and issued an injunction preventing the exhibition of any film in Denmark unless it had been recorded (or rerecorded) on the Peterson-Poulson system. Quickly Nordisk instituted similar suits in Norway, Sweden, and Finland. Immediately tripartite negotiations opened among Western Electric, the Hollywood monopolists, and Nordisk. Tobis-Klangfilm ceded all rights. In November 1934, the Hollywood monopolists signed an agreement with Nordisk for Denmark. Because of court rulings, Hollywood had to agree to yet another pact for Sweden. Nordisk lost its suits in Norway and Finland.[14]

As Hollywood negotiated more and more individual compacts, Tobis-Klangfilm, Western Electric, and RCA lost a larger and larger percentage of the royalties guaranteed under the 1930 Paris Agreement. Consequently Tobis-Klangfilm pressured for a modified cartel. During 1935 in Europe and the United States, representatives from Western Electric, RCA, Tobis-Klangfilm, the Hollywood monopolists, and several European film industries met and negotiated a second "Paris Agreement." The producers settled all past royalty claims, and secured lower rates for the future. The agreement was signed on March 18, 1936, and would last longer than its predecessor, nearly three years. The outbreak of World War II made any cartel impossible.[15]

2

In sum, the second Paris Agreement and the complete conversion of cinemas signaled the end of the diffusion of sound for Europe. Evaluating its impact for United States, French, German, and British relations proves quite difficult. Language conversion problems did provide foreign countries a temporary advantage. When dubbing became universal, the advantage swung back to Hollwood. Patent warfare helped the United States and Germany. Throughout the ebb and flow of this economic struggle, U.S. and German firms dictated the terms of exchange; the British and French were simply exploited. Thus it is not surprising that, by 1936, the Germans had recaptured a major share of their own market from Hollywood. But so did the French and British! The Germans had reduced Hollywood's share (compared to 1929, pre-Depression levels) by 36 percent, the French by 24 percent, and the British by 20 percent. One is tempted to side with Sklar and find that the coming of sound *caused* the Germans, principally because of patent hegemony, to be able to ward off Hollywood's domination of German screen time. But this explanation cannot account for the success of the French and British. For too long the coming of sound to Europe has been treated as a single, isolated variable. I argue we must turn to other factors to help explain the reduction of Hollywood's power. Without a complete understanding of variations in economic exchange throughout the period of the coming of sound, we can never fully understand its impact.[16]

To keep this present analysis within manageable bounds, I will consider only the two additional factors which we should include in any new analysis: the effect of the state and the relative impact of the world depression. By 1928, Britain, France, and Germany all had state restrictions regarding the exhibition of foreign films within their respective countries. In France, the Quota Commission required that for every "French" film produced, seven U.S. films could come into France. German and British laws were stronger. The Germans required "import permits" and with year-to-year modification kept their numbers at levels lower than what Hollywood desired. The British law required that United Kingdom exhibitors and distributors reserve a certain portion of their business for British pictures. The Cinematograph Film Act of 1927 established initial minimums of 7½ percent for distributors and 5 percent for exhibitors. These lower bounds increased annually until both reached 20 percent for 1936. There was limited cooperative action. In 1930 the French and German film interests and governments agreed to drop quota restrictions for exchange between those two countries.[17]

This is how government control stood as Hollywood began to export its sound films. As with the late 1920s, the French government continued its passive stance during the early 1930s. Its quota law expired in October 1931 and, under much pressure from the U.S. film industry, the French government did not renew the law. U.S. talkies flowed into France with no impediments. After one year a revised law was passed (August 1933) which controlled the number of dubbed films which could be exhibited. Modeled on the successful German law, the French [ruling] initially set the number (140) much lower than what Hollywood desired (about 200). The effect was lost, however, because the government permitted so many loopholes. French cinema owners, assisted by the Hays office and the U.S. State Department, successfully lobbied for loose enforcement. By 1936, when the market consisted entirely of sound films, the U.S. film industry was able to export to France about 85 percent of what they would have desired had there been no quota. Thus, all other things being equal, the law helped abate U.S domination by about 15 percent. The British quota law also had a marginal effect. Like France, the internal struggle lay between British exhibitors who wanted more of the popular U.S. films and native producers who pushed for tighter control. Neither side gained; the law would not be rewritten until the original act expired in 1938. Gradually, however, throughout the 1930s the British did recapture 20 percent of the screentime lost to Hollywood during the prior decade.[18]

Germany proved the most successful against Hollywood. Each year Germany instituted a new quota, each equal to or stiffer than its predecessor. Early in 1933 Hitler took power and pushed for strong involvement in cinema but would not nationalize the film industry until 1942. In fact, just prior to the Nazi seizure of power, it seemed likely that U.S. film interests had succeeded in pressuring for a weaker quota law for 1933. The Nazis reaffirmed the strong traditional quotas and even added special provisions: all dubbing had to be done in Germany and the Minister of Propaganda, Joseph Goebbels, could refuse the showing of any foreign films with anti-Nazi themes. Even stricter censorship came in 1934. With the complete diffusion of sound in 1936, the Nazi government was gradually reducing the presentation of non-German motion pictures to zero. Franco-German "free-trade" lapsed in 1936.[19]

State action enabled Germany and France, and Britain to a lesser degree, to combat U.S. movie imperialism. So did the worldwide depression. This century's most severe economic crisis provided France, Germany, and Britain a distinct comparative advantage—in both the short and long run. As the depression spread throughout the world, exchange rates of foreign countries began to fluctuate significantly, usually against the U.S. corporations and in favor of their European counterparts. European governments either froze the currency holdings of foreign traders or used (deflated) currency exchange rates to assist native industries at the expense of foreign corporations. Thus, in real dollars Hollywood extracted from its overseas operations smaller and smaller revenues, despite the popularity of the early talkies. The U.S. government finally adjusted exchange rates in 1934, but not before U.S. multinational corporations suffered large losses abroad.[20]

Equally as important—in the longer run—was the relative effect of the Great Depression in the four countries of concern here. Germany and the United States experienced severe decline. Between 1929 and 1932 U.S. national income fell 38 percent, industrial production nearly 50 percent. Comparisons between nations are difficult, but by economists' best estimates Germany's slide matched that of the United States while the United Kingdom declined only half as much, and France three-quarters as much. I shall assume these gross declines matched those for relative consumer purchasing power, and thus potential cinema revenues. In fact, the available (albeit crude) cinema attendance data indicate such logic is acceptable; for example, U.S. attendance declined 35 percent. There also existed a significant difference in terms of recovery: strongest in Britain (24 percent *above* 1929 levels by 1937), next in Germany (17 percent above), and the United States (3 percent above). In contrast, in 1937 France remained 18 percent *below* 1929 levels. The French economy did not decline as severely as that of the United States or Germany, but it never did regain previous levels of economic activity during the coming of sound. Germany and the United Kingdom surged back strongly. The U.S. economy simply returned to pre-Depression levels.[21]

For cinema exhibition there were three very different reactions for the Germans, French, and British. Specifically in Germany the downturn for cinema attendance came in 1930. Numerous cinemas closed. In response, the Nazi government banned double features, in order to place the most popular films in the maximum number of theaters, and initiated an embargo on construction of new theaters. Attendance began to creep up in 1934 and rose dramatically in 1936. In France cinema attendance remained strong until 1933, declined severely for two years, and then stagnated at that lower level. During the Depression the United Kingdom experienced an increase in moviegoing. New cinemas opened; in 1932, at the nadir of the economic crisis, 150 new theaters were built, including several picture palaces. With rapid and strong recovery of the national economy, the British film industry grew stronger while Hollywood was weakest. The French made small gains until 1933; the Germans dissipated. Across the sea, U.S. movie admissions plunged; three of the Hollywood monopolists went bankrupt and had to be reorganized by the federal government: Paramount, Fox, and RKO. In 1936 Hollywood did regain its power and the potential strength to surge forward in foreign markets. Throughout the early 1930s, despite its patent position, Hollywood saw exports decline. In 1936 foreign revenues began to increase again, but not in the stronger European countries, only in weaker markets such as France and Latin America.[22]

In sum, the impact of the coming of sound to Europe cannot be properly separated from questions of the power of the state and the relative effect of the world economic depression. Guback and Sklar pose limited questions. Instead we should analyze the introduction of sound as part of a complete system of world film exchange. This article has suggested how such a study might begin. I have purposely excluded—for the sake of brevity—questions of production and industry structure, conduct, and finance for each separate country. Quite simply, we have much to learn, and should carefully reexamine the commonplace conclusions which dot our histories of the coming of sound.

Notes

1. I examine these particular countries because in economic terms they were the largest. This paper is a work-in-progress, the beginning of a larger study of the economic history of world cinema. In the future I shall examine Eastern and Third World countries. Moreover, this study lacks primary documents from the United Kingdom, France, and Germany, and so all conclusions for the present must be taken as only tentative.

2. See, for example, David Robinson, *The History of World Cinema* (New York: Stein and Day, 1973), pp. 170–75, 195, 201, or Arthur Knight, *The Liveliest Art* (New York: Macmillan, 1957), pp. 158–59, 201–2, 207, 222.

3. Robert Sklar, *Movie-Made America* (New York: Vintage, 1975), pp. 215–24, and Thomas H. Guback, *The International Film Industry* (Bloomington: Indiana University Press, 1969), pp. 8–10. These positions are typical of many others; I used Guback and Sklar because they are most accessible.

4. Harry Magdoff, "Imperialism: A Historical Survey," *Monthly Review*, 24, no. 1 (May 1972): 14–16; Michael Barratt Brown, *The Economics of Imperialism* (London: Penguin, 1974), pp. 48–72; James O'Connor, *The Corporations and the State* (New York: Harper & Row, 1974), pp. 153–96.

5. Paul Sweezy, *The Theory of Capitalist Development* (New York: Monthly Review Press, 1970), pp. 254–65, 301–9; Louis Turner, *Invisible Empires* (London: Hamish Hamilton, 1970), pp. 1–10; Mira Wilkins, *The Maturing of Multinational Enterprise*, vol. 2 (Cambridge, Mass.: Harvard University Press, 1974), pp. 101–92.

6. C. J. North and N. D. Golden, "Meeting Sound Film Competition Abroad," *Journal of the Society of Motion Picture Engineers*, 15 (December 1930): 751; *Variety*, 10/3/29, p. 6; Franklin S. Irby, "Recent and Future Economic Changes in the Motion Picture Field," *Journal of the Society of Motion Picture Engineers*, 15 (September 1930): 343; Martin Quigley, ed., *The Motion Picture Almanac—1931* (New York: Quigley Publications, 1932), pp. 302–9; *Variety*, 2/13/29, 8/21/29, 12/11/29, 12/18/29; United Artists Collection, O'Brien File, Manuscript Collection (Wisconsin Center for Film and Theater Research, Madison, Wisconsin), Box 84-4, letters, 1929.

7. *Variety*, 4/30/29, 8/7/29, 10/2/29, 10/16/29, 11/6/29; *Business Week*, February 9, 1930, p. 40; George Lewin, "Dubbing and Its Relation to Sound Motion Picture Production," *Journal of the Society of Motion Picture Engineers*, 16 (January 1931): 38–48; *Variety*, 3/26/30, 4/19/30, 4/30/30, 7/2/30, 9/10/30, 9/17/30, 10/22/30; M. S. Phillips, "The Nazi Control of the German Film Industry," *Journal of European Studies*, 1, no. 1 (1971): 42.

8. *Variety*, 3/19/30, 8/6/30, 9/30/30, 10/29/30, 12/24/30, 1/7/31, 9/15/31, 11/3/31, 4/12/32, 8/16/32, 6/20/33; Alfonso Pinto, "Hollywood's Spanish Language Films," *Films in Review*, 24 (October 1972): 474–83.

9. Franklin S. Irby, "International Relations in the Sound Motion Picture Field," *Journal of the Society of Motion Picture Engineers*, 15 (December 1930): 744–46; Douglas Miller, "Talking Syndicate Organizing in Germany," *Commerce Reports*, August 20, 1928, p. 496; Rudolph K. Michels, *Cartels, Combines and Trusts in Post-War Germany* (New York: Columbia University Press, 1928), pp. 128–39; Frank A. Southard, *American Industry in Europe* (Boston: Houghton Mifflin, 1931), pp. 17–37, 100–101; Douglas Miller, "Competing Talking Film Companies Organized in Germany," *Commerce Reports*, October 1, 1928, p. 53; *Variety*, 10/31/28, 1/9/29, 2/6/29, 2/13/29, 3/13/29.

10. *Variety*, 4/17/29, 6/12/29, 6/5/29, 6/19/29, 7/24/29, 8/28/29, 9/25/29; U.S. Federal Communications Commission, *Telephone Investigation Exhibits* (Pursuant to Public Resolution No. 8, 74th Congress, 1936–37), Exhibits 1813–14.

11. *Variety*, 7/31/29, 9/4/29, 11/6/29, 11/13/29, 12/4/29, 12/11/29, 1/8/30, 3/12/30, 4/9/30, 6/25/30; Douglas Miller, "Difficulties of the Spitzen Organization in Germany," *Commerce Reports*, November 18, 1929, p. 430.

12. New York *Times*, 5/17/30; *Variety*, 5/21/30; E. S. Gregg, *The Shadow of Sound* (New York: Vantage Press, 1968), pp. 61–62; New York *Times*, 6/18/30, *Variety*, 6/25/30, 7/2/30, 7/16/30; Ervin Hexner, *International Cartels* (London: Isaac Putnam and Sons, 1946), pp. 374–75; United Artists Collection, Box 86-2, Agreement, American-German Film Conference, July 22, 1930.

13. *Variety*, 7/23/30, 8/27/30, 9/10/30, 2/2/32, 3/29/32, 9/9/32, 8/11/33; United Artists Collection, Box 86-2, Memos, 1935.

14. *Variety*, 11/15/32, 2/12/35, 5/1/35; United Artists Collection, Boxes 84–7, 85-1, 86-2, and 87-7, letters 1933–35; New York *Times*, 11/11/32, 10/13/34.

15. *Variety*, 10/9/35; Gregg, *The Shadow of Sound*, p. 181; United Artists Collection, Boxes 85-3 and 86-2, contracts and letters, 1936–39.

16. William V. Strauss, "Foreign Distribution of American Motion Pictures," *Harvard Business Review*, 8, no. 3 (April 1930): 307–15; Jeremy Tunstall, *The Media Are American* (New York: Columbia University Press, 1977), p. 284; Jack Alicoate, ed., *Film Daily Year Book, 1931* (New York: Film Daily, 1931), pp. 1001, 1017, 1025–26, 1050; *Film Daily Year Book, 1936*, pp. 1124–30.

17. U.S. Bureau of Foreign and Domestic Commerce, *Trade Information Bulletin*, no. 694, May 1930, pp. 6–7; Howard T. Lewis, ed., *Harvard Business Reports*, no. 8 (New York: McGraw-Hill, 1930), pp. 452–72; Carlton J. H. Hayes, *France: A Nation of Patriots* (New York: Columbia University Press, 1930), pp. 190–95; *Film Daily Year Book, 1926*, pp. 858–59; U.S. Bureau of Foreign and Domestic Commerce, *Trade Information Bulletin*, no. 542, p. 4; Howard T. Lewis, *The Motion Picture Industry* (New York: D. Van Nostrand, 1933), pp. 399–404, 421–23; Political and Economic Planning, *The British Film Industry* (London: PEP, 1952), pp. 41–44; *Variety*, 10/6/28, 9/28/28.

18. Georges Sadoul, *French Film* (London: Falcon Press, 1953), p. 158; Lewis, *Motion Picture Industry*, pp. 417–19; *Film Daily Year Book, 1931*, p. 1017; *1933*, pp. 970–75, 986–87; *1934*, pp. 998–99, 1023–24; *1935*, pp. 1017–22, 1049–51; *1936*, pp. 1124–27, 1169, 1171; *1937*, pp. 1163–67, 1215–16; F. D. Klingender and Stuart Legg, *Money Behind the Screen* (London: Lawrence and Wishart, 1937), pp. 1–50; R. K. Neilson Baxter, "The Structure of the British Film Industry," *Penguin Film Review*, no. 8 (September 1948): 86–87; George Perry, *The Great British Picture Show* (New York: Hill and Wang, 1974), pp. 78–79; Michael Balcon, Ernest Lindgren, Forsyth Hardy, and Roger Manvell, *Twenty Years of British Film 1925–1945* (London: Falcon Press, 1947), pp. 18–22.

19. Lewis, *Motion Picture Industry*, pp. 403–4; Roger Manvell and Heinrich Fraenkel, *The German Cinema* (New York: Praeger, 1971), pp. 69–70; H. H. Wollenberg, *Fifty Years of German Film* (London: Falcon Press, 1948), pp. 35–37; Phillips, "Nazi Control," pp. 37, 53–54; David Stewart Hull, *Films in the Third Reich* (Berkeley: University of California Press, 1969), pp. 109–12; *Film Daily Year Book, 1932*, p. 1031; *1933*, pp. 972–73; *1934*, pp. 1000–1001, 1030; *1935*, pp. 1019–20, 1055; *1936*, pp. 1127–29, 1177, 1179; *1937*, pp. 1168–69, 1219–20.

20. Lester V. Chandler, *America's Greatest Depression, 1929–1941* (New York: Harper & Row, 1970), pp. 101–9, 161–69; Charles P Kindleberger, *The World Depression, 1929–1939* (Berkeley: University of California Press, 1973), pp. 177–98; William I. Greenwald, "The Motion Picture Industry: An Economic Study of the History and Practices of a Business," Unpublished Ph.D. dissertation, New York University, 1950, pp. 185–86; *Film Daily Year Book, 1932*, p. 1004; *1933*, p. 963.

21. Christopher H. Sterling and Timothy R. Haight, eds., *The Mass Media* (New York: Praeger, 1978), p. 187; W. Arthur Lewis, *Economic Survey, 1919–1939* (New York:

Harper & Brothers, 1949), pp. 52–69; Kindleberger, *World Depression*, pp. 128–45, 232–46.
        22. Georges Sadoul, *Le Cinéma Français* (Paris: Flammarion, 1962), pp. 141, 145;
Balcon et al., *Twenty Years*, p. 18; Perry, *The Great British Picture Show*, p. 73; Phillips, "Nazi
Control," p. 53; Ernest Betts, *The Film Business* (London: Allen and Unwin, 1973), pp. 75–
106; Political and Economic Planning, *British Film Industry*, pp. 55–78; *Film Daily Year Book,
1931*, pp. 1017, 1025–26, 1050–51; *1932*, pp. 1002–4, 1023, 1030–31, 1050–51; *1933*,
pp. 962–63, 970–75, 986–93, 1014; *1934*, pp. 998–1001, 1023–24, 1030–31; *1935*, pp.
1013–22, 1049–50, 1055–56, 1079–80; *1936*, pp. 1121–29, 1124–25, 1169, 1171, 1179,
1207; *1937*, pp. 116–69, 1215–21, 1253.

Film Style and Technology
in the Thirties: Sound   BARRY SALT

Now that some interest has arisen in the history of the influence of film technology on the forms of films, there has been an unfortunate tendency to exaggerate its importance, whereas in truth it appears that, as far as the more interesting aspect of movies are concerned, technology acts more as a loose pressure on what is done rather than a rigid constraint. For instance, one can connect the move toward faster cutting in the middle thirties with the introduction of "rubber numbering" (or "edge numbering") of the cutting copies of the sound and picture tracks, but an opposite tendency toward longer takes, which began at the end of the thirties, seems to be independent of any of the technical developments of the period. And a complex train of events involving aspects of sound recording and film stock development relate to the rise of background projection and total studio shooting that so distinguishes the later thirties from the early thirties.

So in this article these matters, and also other aspects of the general movement of the formal stylistic features in the mainstream cinema of the thirties, are considered in relation to the technological developments of the period. The emphasis is strongly on American practice, but the state of European developments is mentioned from time to time. The analytical approach to film style used here has already been demonstrated more fully in some respects in *Film Quarterly,* Vol. 28, No. 1, and since then extended somewhat, and the general attitude taken is that it is impossible to establish what is interesting about a particular film unless one knows the norms holding in general for other films of the same kind made at the same time and place. Ignoring this principle has led people to describe features of particular films as remarkable, when they are in fact quite commonplace in the context of their period, and although this error is much more common with early cinema, one instance in connection with sound editing can be mentioned here.

At the beginning of the thirties editors were beginning to realize the importance of what might be called the "dialogue cutting point" for making weak (i.e., smooth, unnoticeable) cuts when cutting from one speaker to another in a scene. In general the weakest cut from a speaker to the shot of his listener, who is about to reply in the succeeding shot, will be made while the last syllable of the last word of the speech is still being spoken. Some editors cut at the very end of the last syllable, which is almost equally acceptable, but virtually none cut in the middle of the pause between the two speeches, or just at the beginning of the reply. (Some uncertainty about this point is still visible in Capra's *Platinum Blonde* [1931].) Of course deviations from this point can be made for reasons of emphasis and expression in general, most notably cutting to a listener's reaction in the middle of a speech. Curiously enough this principle has never been written down in books on editing technique, and presumably it is passed on to apprentice assistants at the editor's knee, but in any case it should be immediately obvious to any would-be editor from watching a couple of films. But in a recent article by Raymond Bellour on *The Big Sleep* in *Screen*, Vol. 15, No. 4, p.17, several lines are spent in discussing one instance of this standard dialogue cutting point as though it were something unique and remarkable rather than the usual thing.

The picture of the technology situation has been put together from information obtained from complete runs of *The American Cinematographer* and *The Journal of the Society of Motion Picture Engineers*, together with *The Cinematographic Annual,* Vols. 1 and 2 (American Society of Cinematographers, Hollywood, 1930 and 1931), *Recording Sound for Motion Pictures* (ed. Lester Cowan, McGraw-Hill, 1931), and *Motion Picture Sound Engineering* (Research Council of A.M.P.A.S., Hollywood, 1938). Some several hundred films of the period have been considered in the light of this information, and also of the present author's filmmaking experience at the professional level, principally as a cameraman, but extending a little way into most other areas. . . .

Cameras

In 1930 Warners was the only studio still using the "icebox" type of soundproof booth containing both camera and operator for sound filming, and from 1931 all the studios were using Mitchell NC cameras in blimps of their own various handmade designs. So although Warners had fitted some of its booths with wheels, as had other studios during 1929, there was still during 1930 at that studio a strict limitation on the use of panning simultaneously with tracking, a limitation that no longer obtained elsewhere. (Cameras inside soundproof booths were naturally limited by the size of the booth window to pans of about 30 degrees on either side of the forward direction, whereas both unblimped and blimped cameras can obviously be pointed in any direction while the dolly they are mounted on is being tracked along.)

The prototype Mitchell BNC was produced in 1934, but this camera was not put into series production till 1938. However, Gregg Toland acquired and used one of the prototypes years before it was put on sale, but with no visible effect on the style of his camerawork at this point. In 1935 another silent camera was designed for Twentieth Century–Fox, and in 1939 several were produced for the sole use of that studio, but further production was prevented by the precision engineering requirements of World War II. Both the Fox camera and the Mitchell BNC were slightly easier than earlier cameras to get into extreme positions, and slightly easier to use in general, but this really had little significance as far as studio filming was concerned. What *was* important was that sync-sound shooting with lenses of wider angle than 25mm was now possible. (Blimped cameras had been restricted to using lenses of focal length longer than 25mm.) However, the effect of this was not to be realized till the forties. . . .

Editing

The basic tool for sound editing had already been introduced at the beginning of sound filmmaking, and this was the multiple synchronizer just as we know it today in its unadorned form without track reading heads. Originally its purpose had been to keep the several simultaneous picture tracks obtained from multiple cameras filming in synchronism with each other during editing, and hence finally with the sound-track disc, but by 1930 both multiple camera filming and sound-on-disc were abandoned. The synchronizer was then used just to manipulate the series of pairs of picture track and sound-on-film track, and keep them in synchronism during editing. This simple procedure gave no way of hearing the words on the sound track, was extremely inefficient, and was not conducive to scene dissection into a large number of shots.

But in 1930 the sound Moviola became available, and from 1931 the Average Shot Lengths in Hollywood films started to drop. The sound Moviola was a simple adaptation of the silent Moviola, with a continuously moving sprocket drive pulling the sound-track film under a photoelectric sound head identical to that in a sound projector, the whole unit being mounted beside the standard Moviola picture head, and driven from it in synchronism by a rigid shaft drive. Basically the machine was the same as the present

"Hollywood" Moviola, except that the picture was viewed through a magnifying lens, and not back-projected on to a tiny screen. The sound track could be moved slowly by hand under the sound head, and the exact position of any part of a sound identified.

The other development that facilitated the fast cutting (in both senses) of sync-sound shots occurred in 1932, with the introduction of "rubber numbering" (or "edge numbering") for sound and picture tracks. "Rubber numbers" are footage numbers stamped in ink down the outer edge of the picture and sound track for each shot. The numbers coincide at the points on the sound track and picture track where the corresponding image and its sound lie. After numbering has been carried out it is possible to shuffle about sections of picture and sound track in the editing knowledge that synchronism can be regained when necessary, purely "by the numbers."

As a result of the freedom provided by both these developments, the Average Shot Length in films of this period started to decrease in a way that can be exemplified by the work of William Wellman: *The Public Enemy* (1931) has an A.S.L. of 9 seconds, *Wild Boys of the Road* (1933) has an A.S.L. of 6.5 seconds, and Wellman stayed remarkably close to this latter figure for the rest of his career. Particular advantage of the possibility of speeding up the cutting rate was taken at the Warner Bros. Studio, and this effect can also be seen in Michael Curtiz's films; but the pressure was not absolute, as can be seen from the work of Mervyn LeRoy who stayed with a slower speed and some camera movement. (It is obviously difficult, though not impossible, to use camera movement in a large number of shots when the A.S.L. gets down to around 6 seconds.) The other extreme of cutting speed, which was commoner in 1930 than 1933, can be represented by John Stahl's *Only Yesterday* (1933), which has an A.S.L. of 14 seconds.

The trend toward faster cutting in many films in the middle thirties can be easily explained as a desire on the part of many people to return to the sort of cutting that had been usual in the majority of American silent films made in the late twenties, when Average Shot Lengths were usually down around 5 seconds. And once the restrictions on cutting sound had been removed by the sound Moviola and rubber numbering, they were free to return toward silent cutting speeds as far as the length of the average line of dialogue would let them. Then after some years of that sort of thing, many directors were ready for a new fashion which appeared, and which will now be discussed.

It was only in the middle thirties that the technical developments in editing procedures introduced prior to 1933 had their full effect. For the period 1934–39 the mean Average Shot Length for Hollywood movies was around 8–9 seconds. (This figure has been derived from a fairly random collection of over fifty films. Although there are not enough results to make a year-by-year estimate of the mean figure, it is fairly clear that the minimum was achieved round 1935. This means that most directors were taking advantage of the ease of making a large number of cuts in a scene, but there was still a wide spread of characteristic Average Shot Lengths from director to director.) But by 1939 a new tendency in the opposite direction was just beginning to appear, a tendency toward long takes that only became fully developed in the forties.

To give some examples, George Cukor moved from A.S.L.s such as 17 seconds for *Dinner at Eight* (1933) to an A.S.L. of 10 seconds in 1935 for *Sylvia Scarlett*, and then back to long takes for *Holiday* (1938) (A.S.L. of 14 seconds) and *The Women* (1939) (A.S.L. of 13 seconds) and subsequent films. Obviously this sort of movement with the trend was the most common (e.g., Wyler, Hawks), but there were also a number of directors who stuck with what they were doing at the fast cutting end of the spectrum. For example, Curtiz had already arrived at an A.S.L. of around 7 seconds in the early thirties, and he continued right through with the later thirties and into the forties in the same way: *Charge of the Light Brigade* (1936) has an A.S.L. of 7.5 seconds and *Dodge City* (1939) has an A.S.L. of 7 seconds.

On the other hand it was possible to go against the tide, as John Stahl quite remarkably did. From an A.S.L. of 13 seconds in *Imitation of Life* in 1934 he went on to use even longer takes in *Magnificent Obsession* (1935), which has many shots some minutes long, and an Average Shot Length of 26 seconds. Even more remarkably, these long scenes are mostly carried out in "profile two-shot," with two performers facing each other, and there is very little staging in depth in the manner used in Europe by Renoir, and to a lesser extent Marcel Carné and others who used long takes. But none went to such lengths in this period as Stahl did. However by 1939 Stahl had retreated from this extreme position (*When Tomorrow Comes* has an A.S.L. of 14 seconds), and by the forties he was working near the norm for those years.

It might be thought that Average Shot Lengths are related to the genre of the films concerned, and not specific to the directors, but this is only so to an extremely limited extent. The only important cases so far discovered after checking several hundred are those of the musical, where if one includes the musical numbers in the count, there is a definite tendency for a director to use longer takes than he would otherwise. This conclusion is of course dependent on the assumption that the way the musical numbers were shot was controlled by the named director, which probably is not always the case. Another rare instance of the genre of a film dominating the way it is shot is that of the Tarzan films. Here the necessity of faking all the animal stuff ensured that the A.S.L. was always close to 4 seconds, from the thirties through to the fifties, regardless of who directed the films. Regular

Tarzan directors such as Richard Thorpe never used such fast cutting on their later films.

On the other hand one finds consistency of Average Shot Length from comedies to dramas to action subjects in the work of directors such as Hawks and Wyler and so on throughout this (and other) periods.

Sound Recording

1930 saw the final triumph of sound-on-film recording; sound-on-disc was phased out. Starting at the beginning of the sound recording chain, we note that the microphones used continued to be of the "condenser" (capacitance) type. If several microphones were being used to record sound for a shot, their signals were mixed directly before being recorded photographically on the sound negative in the sound camera, in electrical synchronism with the film camera. The mixing of a set of film sound tracks subsequent to their intial recording to give a final combined recording was very rare at the beginning of the thirties; the extra film recording stage introduced a perceptible loss of quality. (This loss of sound quality can be studied in those Laurel and Hardy films from 1931–32 which have continuous background music mixed with the dialogue and effects.) Thus, although postsynchronization of voices to a film scene could be carried out from 1929, it was mostly not used in the early thirties, and location scenes involving dialogue were always shot with direct sound, which naturally ensured that both the voices *and* all the effects went into the right place. This was extremely difficult to do in one pass when postsynchronizing without remixing and rerecording.

In some location situations ultradirectional microphones were created by putting an ordinary microphone at the focus of a large (up to 6 feet) parabolic metal reflector. In this way *fairly* good recordings could be obtained at 15 feet or more from the actors. Since otherwise all the microphones in use were omnidirectional, picking up sounds equally whatever direction they came from, background noise could be a serious problem with location recording, and this was one of the pressures encouraging the change to the shooting of "exterior" dialogue scenes in the studio as soon as good background projection made this possible.

Throughout the thirties there were more or less continuous improvements in the performance of sound-on-film recording systems through attention to various aspects of their functioning: exposure and development control of the sound-track negative, amplifier circuit improvements, mechanical refinements of the sound cameras and printers, and so on. But the really audible advance in the quality of recording was largely due to the track noise suppression techniques introduced in 1931.

By 1933 it was possible to mix a separately recorded music track with the synchronous dialogue track recording after the editing stage without audible loss of sound quality at the extra film recording stage, and from this point on "background music" came to be used more and more extensively. (Up to 1932 there was, roughly speaking, either dialogue or music on the sound track, but never both together unless they had been recorded simultaneously. Which they sometimes were.) As the kind of improvements already mentioned continued into the late thirties, including then the important introduction of "push-pull" double sound tracks in the RCA system, it became possible to do multiple-channel music recording on One Hundred Men and a Girl (Henry Koster, 1938) and other subsequent musical films.

Putting the situation in another way, there was now full freedom to assemble as complicated sound tracks as could be desired, going through several recording stages if that was necessary.*

---

* Much more about these matters can be read in my book Film Style and Technology: History and Analysis (Starword, 1983).

The Evolution
of Sound Technology   RICK ALTMAN

More than half a century after the coming of sound, film criticism and theory still remain resolutely image-bound. Early filmmakers' skepticism about the value of sound has been indirectly perpetuated by generations of critics for whom the cinema is an essentially visual art, sound serving as little more than a superfluous accompaniment. In recent years the reasons underlying this hegemony of the visual have continued to multiply. With each new visually oriented analysis, with each new image-inspired theory, film study's exclusive image orientation gains ground.

The source of the image's current dominance is closely linked to the vocabulary developed by three-quarters of a century of film critics. With few exceptions film terminology is camera-oriented. The distance of the camera from its object, its vertical attitude, horizontal movement, lens, and focus all depend quite specifically on the camera's characteristics and provide the field of cinema studies with a basic language. Another set of terms concentrates on the noncamera aspect of the film's visual component: film stock, punctuation, aspect ratio, lighting, special effects, and so forth. While these terms and many others constitute part of any introductory film course, the corresponding audio terms remain virtually unknown. The type and placement of microphones, methods of recording sound, mixing practices, loudspeaker varieties, and many other fundamental considerations are the province of a few specialists.

This general situation has been strongly reinforced by the concerns evinced by influential film critics over the last half-century. To choose only a well-known pair of examples, we find that Eisenstein and Bazin, considered from the standpoint of the sound track, appear strikingly similar in their interests. Though Eisenstein stresses montage and Bazin prefers long takes and deep-focus photography, both constantly emphasize the visual component of filmmaking. Like its vocabulary, film criticism's problematics have remained consistently visual in nature. Outside of a spate of reaction to the coming of sound, the concerns of the sound track have remained excluded from the nodal points of film criticism. In recent years this situation has grown even more one-sided, due to the strongly visual emphasis of recent French film theory. The strain which analyzes the film apparatus (be-

ginning with the work of Jean-Louis Baudry and Jean-Louis Comolli) usually defines film apparatus as camera and projector, with the mechanics of
sound reproduction left on the margin. The justification for this approach is
said to lie in the Western world's privileging of vision over all other senses;
the cinema, it is claimed, is no more than a child of Renaissance perspective.
According to this approach the spectator is placed, within the film as well as
within the world at large, primarily by visual markers; even within the limits
of this method of handling spectator placement, however, it is surprising that
more emphasis has not been placed on the sound track's role in splitting
and complicating the spectator, in contesting as well as reinforcing the lessons of the image track. Recent theory has been pushed even further in a
visual direction by the adoption of Jacques Lacan's visual metaphors (first
by Baudry and Christian Metz, then by virtually the entire Paris school). Developing a fascinating and logical tie between the "mirror stage" as described by Lacan and the film-viewing experience itself, these critics find
themselves limited to visual language alone. Now, the mirror metaphor could
easily be applied to sound as well as to vision (the Narcissus myth includes
Echo as well, as I have pointed out in a recent review[1]), but, given the im-
age-consciousness already present in previous criticism and theory alike, the
mirror analogy has been restricted to visual experiences. As a result, the an-
cillary role previously played by the sound track has been diminished still
more. It is difficult to imagine how the auditory dimension of cinema might
at this late date be reinstated.

　　　　Perhaps the most important single requirement for a revival of
interest in the sound track is an increased sensitivity to problems of sound
technology. Paradoxically, book after book chronicles the technological,
economic, and artistic innovations which led to the coming of sound, yet
subsequent developments have been neglected by all but a minuscule group
of technicians. Everyone knows that Edison intended sound and image reproduction as a synchronized pair, and that various influences delayed for
decades the acceptance of his original concept. Stress has repeatedly been
placed on Lee De Forest's early invention of the audion tube and his later
collaboration with Theodore Case and Earl Sponable. Economic historians
have pointed out the importance of patent disputes with the German Tri-
Ergon group and, in a general way, the dilatory effects of the capitalist system's profit-consciousness. In fact, nearly every history of the cinema devotes an entire chapter to the period stretching from Warners' experiment
with sound-on-disc in *Don Juan* (August 1926) through Fox's highly successful use of sound-on-film in its *Movietone News* series to the supposed
landmark of Warners' *Jazz Singer* (October 1927). As a general rule, these
chapters go on to mention the 1928 *Lights of New York* ("the first completely dialogued full-length film") and the 1929 fascination with the musi-

cal, but in keeping with standard film history's preoccupation with "firsts" the chapter ends with no more than brief reference to the early experiments with sound conducted by King Vidor, Rouben Mamoulian, Ernst Lubitsch, and Walt Disney.

Though this is hardly the place for a full-fledged history of sound technology during the last half-century, it will nevertheless prove useful to provide an outline of major developments and concerns.[2] The early history of sound film is marked by the limitations of the carbon and condenser microphones then in use. Nondirectional, fragile, sensitive to wind and other ambient noises, needing an amplification stage very close to the microphone, these mikes required very special recording conditions. Providing these conditions heavily influenced image recording as well as sound. Simply put, the problem lay in the difficulties of producing a high quality and complex sound track (including dialogue, music, effects) with an unselective microphone at a time when the technology of sound mixing practically forbade postmixing of multiple tracks without audible loss of quality. In fact, until approximately 1933 it was extremely rare for music and dialogue to appear simultaneously on the sound track unless they were recorded simultaneously. The latter solution of course presents other difficulties. The amount of reverberation generally required for dialogue varies greatly from that which is appropriate for music (dialogue needs the fast and relatively limited reverberation of familiar upholstered interior spaces, while we expect orchestral music to have the slow reverb provided by a large auditorium); similarly, dialogue and music require different amplification and thus are difficult to record with the same microphone(s). The industry's solution to this problem, already generally operational by late 1929, was to record the music separately—in an atmosphere conducive to proper music recording—then to play the *recorded* music back while the scene was being acted and its dialogue recorded. This so-called playback system had the immediate effect of separating the sound track from the image—a primary factor in the constitution of film ideology. By facilitating the matching of a performer with a sound which he or she had not necessarily created, the playback permitted immediate capitalization on the sound film's fundamental lie: the implication that the sound is produced by the image when in fact it remains independent from it.

While the playback system serves as an early model of the prestidigitation characterizing the later multiple-channel mixing of effects, dialogue, and music (first perfected in the late thirties), it was not able to solve the problem of outdoor synchronized dialogue recording. The early mikes continued to pick up unwanted noises in all but the most carefully selected outdoor sites (the new directional ribbon or velocity mikes were even more sensitive to wind pressure than the familiar carbon and condenser mikes).

Simply to move indoors, however, deprived the filmmaker of location photography. Here again, the relatively primitive state of sound technology determined the development of major aspects of image technology. In order to benefit from the controlled atmosphere provided by the new heavily insulated sound studios, without giving up outdoor scenes entirely, research in the area of back projection was accelerated, with acceptable results achieved as early as 1932. That the technique of back projection is modeled on that of the playback seems incontrovertible. In both cases the material prerecorded under special conditions (music needing special miking in a proper room, location photography involving movement and distances inconsistent with current sound practices) is inserted in the final recording by virtue of a hidden reproduction device (the playback speaker, the back projector). It is thus on the model of sound-track practices that Hollywood's habit of *constructing* reality (as opposed to *observing* it) is based.

Throughout the thirties, nearly every important technological innovation can be traced back to the desire to produce a persuasive illusion of real people speaking real words. Not only sound stages but camera blimps, microphone booms, incandescent lights (replacing the noisier arc lamps), and the development of highly directional microphones derive from a felt need to reduce all traces of the sound work from the sound track. This effacement of work, commonly recognized as a standard trait of bourgeois ideology, provides the technological counterpart to the inaudible sound editing practices developed during this period (blooping, cutting to sound, carrying sound over the cut, raising dialogue volume levels while reducing the level of sounds which don't directly serve the plot). These technological and technical contributions to inaudible sound editing of course parallel the well-known standards of invisible image editing developed during the same period. The technical aspects of this visual practice have received regular comment—match-cutting, cutting on movement, 180° rule, 30° rule, and so forth—but the technological aspects deserve to be more widely recognized: finer grain film to reduce graininess, faster film to reduce degree of artificial lighting, color film to simulate natural vision, coated lenses to reduce distortion and glare, more mobile cameras to reproduce variety of human motion. Indeed, many of these innovations, usually mentioned only from the image-improvement standpoint, have corresponding effects on sound reproduction. To mention only a few, the experiments in film stock carried out by Eastman, Du Pont, and others immediately before the war resulted not only in the faster panchromatic films, permitting the cinematographers of the period to increase depth of field, but also in definite improvements in the quality of sound-on-film recording. Fine-grain film stock, like Eastman's No. 1302 and Du Pont's No. 222, contributed markedly, as did the new coated lenses, to the increase in quality of sound recording during and after the war. (It is too seldom remembered that sound technology during the thirties and forties is also image technology: all sounds, whether coded as variable density or variable area, were expressed in optical terms, and thus had to be recorded photographically on the film, and ultimately read by means of a lamp in the projector. Thus nearly every advance in image technology—film, lens, printer, lamp—resulted in a corresponding leap in sound quality.)

In terms of sound quality, the average film of the mid-forties, whether in Hollywood, France, or England, represented a significant improvement on the original efforts of the late twenties. In more general terms, however, the films of the forties remained the direct descendants of those earlier films. Every step of the process had been improved—from microphones to printers, from amplifiers to loudspeakers—yet the fundamental optical recording and printing technology remained basically the same. Not until after the war, thanks in part to German wartime technology, did the sound recording industry in general and the film sound track in particular take a quantum leap forward with the perfection of magnetic recording techniques. As with all important technological developments, however, the magnetic recording revolution met with immediate economic resistance. There was no question that magnetic recording was easier, used lighter, more mobile equipment, cost less, and produced decidedly better results; theaters, however, were not equipped to play films which substituted a magnetic stripe for the traditional optical sound track. Just as Hollywood delayed the coming of sound for years, it has for economic reasons delayed the coming of better sound for decades. Over a quarter of a century after the general availability of magnetic recording technology, very few theaters (usually only the high priced, first run, big city variety) are equipped with magnetic sound equipment. Ironically, for years the average amateur filmmaker working with super-8 sound equipment has possessed better and more advanced sound reproduction facilities than the neighborhood cinema.

Nevertheless, Hollywood was able to capitalize on the new technology in another way. Though filmmakers around the world continued to use optical sound for distribution prints, they very early began to do all their own recording in the magnetic mode (by the end of 1951, 75 percent of Hollywood's original production recording, music scoring, and dubbing was being done on magnetic recording equipment). Finishing what the playback had begun, magnetic recording divorced the sound track still further from the image and from the image's optical technology. Now, any number of sound sources could easily be separately recorded, mixed, and remixed independently of the image (thus simplifying the manipulation of stereophonic sound, now often coupled with the new wide-screen formats).

Ironically, the very technology that permitted Hollywood and other studio systems all over the world further to separate the production of sound and image tracks encouraged independent filmmakers to tie the recording of the two tracks more tightly together. As inexpensive as they are portable, magnetic recorders were soon made a part of the standard *cinéma vérité* kit. Perceiving the ideological roots of Hollywood's split between image and sound (re)production, the partisans of direct sound developed a theory of the naturalness of direct, unedited recording, of this method's ideologically uncontaminated nature. Though these theories are contestable on many grounds, they had an enormous effect, particularly in France. Jean-Luc Godard and other practitioners of the New Wave were soon abandoning Hollywood's characteristic directional microphones and selective amplification in favor of the direct transcription of all ambient sounds by means of a single omnidirectional centrally located mike. No doubt this approach neglects the extent to which the human ear selects sounds, but it certainly had the important effect of foregrounding the artificiality, i.e., the constructed nature, of sound practices in studio-produced classical narrative films the world over.

Of all those influenced by Godard and *le direct*, no one has had such an important technological influence as Robert Altman. Experimenting from the very first with multiple-channel mixing (e.g., *M.A.S.H.*), Altman has since *Nashville* adopted the eight-track technology developed by the popular recording industry. In many ways, this was an obvious development, since film sound has regularly profited from parallel developments in related sound industries (radio, phonograph, tape, etc.), yet this borrowing was longer in coming and promises to bear still more fruit than most of the others. Over the past quarter of a century the popular recording industry has been one of the most profitable in the entire entertainment complex, and thus has benefited from technological developments far surpassing those made available to the cinema over the same period. At present, it is not at all uncommon for twenty-four separate tracks to be used in the constitution of the final sound track for an inexpensive record or tape. The standards of mixing technology have thus grown rapidly, to the point where they far surpass those typical of the film industry. Whereas nearly all previous productions had necessitated a mechanical connection between the microphone and other sound apparatus (whence the sound boom required for sound takes since the early thirties), Altman introduced the use of radio mikes broadcasting to the separate tracks of an eight-track system, using two or three times the basic eight when necessary. This frees the actor entirely from the tyranny of the microphone, and also, thanks to microphone technology developed for other purposes, permits Altman to restrict each channel to a single, carefully controlled input (usually a single character's voice). Each track can then be dealt with separately in any of the ways in which sound signals have traditionally been handled (filtered, reverb added, amplified, etc.), so that the final mix can do anything from reproducing the exact sound actually heard from a specific point to constructing a highly contradictory set of signs which utterly splits the hearing subject. By manipulating his sound, whether through microphone location, signal deformation, or editing strategies, Altman—and the many others who now follow this system—is in a position to manipulate his auditor independently from his spectator. When the two sets of positioning signals are combined in the viewing/hearing subject, the full possibilities of cinema's audiovisual collaboration may clearly be sensed.

One final development deserves mention, because it represents the most recent progress in solving an old problem. When there was only one microphone input for the sound track, the problem of ground noise already existed. Indeed, throughout the thirties and forties, one of the main concerns of sound engineers was that of ground noise reduction. Many solutions were proposed and indeed put into effect, but none capable of solving the problems endemic to the multiple tracks and frequency ranges possible in current equipment. Recently, however, the Dolby system (not surprisingly, an innovation of the popular recording industry) has been applied to film sound with very favorable results. Basically, the Dolby system reduces distortion by artificially amplifying and then reducing low-volume sounds (compensating for differences in frequency range), thus returning the sounds to their original volume but in the process reducing ground noise. Used for the final track of *Nashville*, the Dolby system was first used throughout production in *Star Wars*, and since then for a number of other expensive Hollywood features, including Michael Cimino's *Deer Hunter*. Indeed, now that the film industry has at last begun to take its cue from the area which represents the state-of-the-sound-art—popular recording—it is to be expected that new technology will continue to be made available. Whether or not local theaters will ever be equipped with the sound systems necessary to use these innovations to their fullest must remain a separate—and economically problematic—question.

Just as attention to the technology of sound has largely been concentrated on the innovations leading up to the coming of sound, so reflection on the role of the sound track is concentrated in the years immediately following the sound revolution. . . .

In order to understand the source of early suspicion of sound, as well as the subsequent disenfranchisement of sound in the realm of theoretical speculation, we must consider the role which sound—and especially language—had played during the heyday of the silent film. The earliest days of the cinema were marked by a practical and all-consuming desire for simple survival, but as soon as the new art found the leisure to contemplate its own position it felt compelled to differentiate itself from its renowned parent, the theater. Hugo Münsterberg constantly opposes the virtues of the cinema to those of the stage, while Vachel Lindsay devotes a chapter of his *Art of the Moving Picture* to "Thirty Differences Between the Photoplays and the Stage."[3] Later we find Eisenstein and many others attempting to put away the threat to the cinema's individuality represented by theater.[4] Theories of montage in particular valorize the very areas in which cinema easily outshines the stage. Increasingly, self-conscious filmmakers attempted to reduce the effect of intertitles, shunning direct transcription of dialogue in favor of commentary whose graphic design often carried as important a message as its semantic content. The coming of sound could hardly have represented a welcome innovation to such a world, devoted as it was to surpassing film's competitor and parent, the theater.

For the coming of sound represents the return of the silent cinema's repressed. It is thus hardly surprising that sound should be seen by silent filmmakers more as a threat than as an opportunity. Repeatedly warning against the temptation to return to the theatrical model, represented by the dominance of synchronized sound and especially of dialogue, early critics of sound devised two strategies which lie at the root of nearly all subsequent reflection on the sound track. Eager to relegate language and theatricality once more to the shadows whence they came, these early critics initiated two fallacies whose power and durability are effectively grounded in their repressive function. The first of these I shall term the *historical fallacy*. A proper theory of sound cinema, one might expect, would begin with the observation that sound films are composed of two simultaneous and parallel phenomena, image and sound. Such, however, has rarely been the case. From the very first, critics who had lived through the coming of sound took the historical process (whereby an art which once lacked sound had the capabilities of sound reproduction added to it) as an adequate model for theoretical reflection. Instead of treating sound and image as simultaneous and coexistent, the historical fallacy orders them chronologically, thus implicitly hierarchizing them. Historically, sound was added to the image; *ergo* in the analysis of sound cinema we may treat sound as an afterthought, a supplement which the image is free to take or leave as it chooses.

By adhering to the historical fallacy, early critics succeeded admirably in marginalizing sound. With the rapid universalization of sound technology, however, the force of the historical argument necessarily subsided; once the silent era faded into the background the primacy of the silent image no longer appeared self-evident. Another argument was called for, a strategy tied not to film's history but to the medium's very essence. Thus was born the *ontological fallacy*. The version of the ontological fallacy regularly applied to cinema claims that film is a visual medium and that the images must be/are the primary carriers of the film's meaning and structure. Already present in capsule form during the early years of sound, this argument reaches its height in Arnheim's "New Laocoön" and Kracauer's *Theory of Film* ("films with sound live up to the spirit of the medium only if the visuals take the lead in them," p. 103). Today the primacy of the image continues to be taken as a given. Witness, for example, Gianfranco Bettetini: "The essence of the cinema is basically visual, and every sonic intervention ought to limit itself to a justified and necessary act of expressive integration."[5] Now, what is at issue here is not whether the image is essential to a definition of cinema but whether or not notions of a form's essence provide a proper and sufficient basis for legislation of that form's activity and for description of its structure. Instead of developing a logical method of describing the actual characteristics of a composite form, the ontological fallacy represents a clever strategy for dissembling sound film's composite nature—in short, for repressing yet again the scandal of theatrical language. No matter that the practice of fifty years of filmmaking has clearly established the dominant position of dialogue, along with the initial position of the screenwriter, no matter that the most characteristic practice of classical film narrative should be the normally redundant technique of pointing the camera at the speaker, no matter that critics commonly quote a film word-for-word but rarely illustrate their comments with frame enlargements (usually preferring the better quality but largely irrelevant production still).

In short, the historical and ontological fallacies are the prescriptive arguments of silent filmmakers intent on preserving the purity of their "poetic" medium. That such strategies should have been devised is understandable; that they should have provided the model for a descriptive theory is entirely unacceptable. By perpetuating an image-oriented stance, film criticism has failed to provide either the theory or the teminology necessary for proper treatment of sound cinema as it exists (and not as early theoreticians predicted it would develop—we must not forget that the same Arnheim who willingly invoked the authority of Lessing claimed that the future of sound film lay in animated cartoons!).

In order to deal intelligently with the sound track we need a new beginning. We need to start, for once, not with the self-serving pronouncements of silent film directors and fans but with the phenomenon of sound film itself, analyzing its practices and its possibilities rather than prescribing its supposed duties and drawbacks.

Notes

1. Charles F. Altman, "Psychoanalysis and Cinema: The Imaginary Discourse," *Quarterly Review of Film Studies*, 2, no. 3 (August 1977):257–72.

2. This summary is heavily dependent on many of the items listed in Claudia Gorbman's excellent bibliography, especially Edward W. Kellogg, "History of Sound Motion Pictures," repr. from *Journal of the Society of Motion Picture Engineers* in Raymond Fielding, ed., *A Technological History of Motion Pictures and Television* (Berkeley: University of California Press, 1967).

3. Hugo Münsterberg, *The Film: A Psychological Study* (New York: Dover, 1970; orig. 1916); Vachel Lindsay, *Art of the Moving Picture* (New York: Liveright, 1970; orig. 1915).

4. Sergei Eisenstein, *Film Form: Essays in Film Theory*, ed. and trans. Jay Leyda (New York: Harcourt, Brace, 1949), pp. 15ff.; René Clair, *Réflexion faite: Notes pour servir à l'histoire de l'art cinématographique de 1920 à 1950* (Paris: Gallimard, 1951), pp. 116 and *passim*; René Clair, *Cinéma d'hier, cinéma d'aujourd'hui* (Paris: Gallimard, 1970), pp. 33, 60, 78, and *passim*; Lev Kuleshov, *Kuleshov on Film: Writings by Lev Kuleshov*, trans. Ron Levaco (Berkeley: University of California Press, 1974), pp. 56ff.

5. Gianfranco Bettetini, *The Language and Technique of the Film* (The Hague: Mouton, 1973), p. 111.

Ideology and the Practice
of Sound Editing
and Mixing   MARY ANN DOANE

The practices of sound editing and mixing to be considered here are those developed within the Hollywood studio system. "System" should be understood in a rigorous sense as necessitating a certain amount of standardization (with respect to techniques and machinery) and a relatively strict division of labor. Nevertheless, these practices have become "normalized" to a large extent outside of that system—they have had enormous impact on the filmmaking industries of other countries, for instance, and on independent filmmaking activities as well. My assumption is that not only techniques of sound-track construction but the language of technicians and the discourses on technique are symptomatic of particular ideological aims.

It has become a cliché to note that the sound track has received much less theoretical attention and analysis than the image. Yet the cliché is not without truth value and isolates, but leaves unexplained, a fact. This lack of attention indicates the efficacy of a particular ideological operation which is masked, to some extent, by the emphasis placed on the "ideology of the visible." While it is true that, as the expression would have it, one goes to "see" a film and not to hear it, the expression itself consists of an affirmation of the identity (i.e., wholeness, unity) of the film and a consequent denial of its material heterogeneity. Sound is something which is added to the image, but nevertheless subordinate to it—it acts, paradoxically, as a "silent" support. The effacement of work which characterizes bourgeois ideology is highly successful with respect to the sound track. The invisibility of the practices of sound editing and mixing is ensured by the seemingly "natural" laws of construction which the sound track obeys.

The disregard of the sound track on the level of theory, however, does not have its counterpart on the level of practice. Hollywood has recognized the extent to which the "supplement," that is to say sound, can infiltrate and transform that which is supplemented. In an industry whose major standard, in terms of production value, might be summarized as "the less perceivable a technique, the more successful it is," the invisibility of the work on sound is a measure of the strength of the sound track. The publicity accorded to the activity of shooting a film is far more extensive than that given the "backstage" processes involved in building a track.

A concentration on the ideological determinants of sound editing practices does not necessarily entail a denial of the significance of the "ideology of the visible" stressed by Jean-Louis Comolli and others. In a culture within which the phrase "to see" means to understand, the epistemological powers of the subject are clearly given as a function of the centrality of the eye. Michel Marie has illuminated the degree to which the eye is posited as the ground of all knowledge in a discussion of the hierarchy of the senses established by Western civilization. Marie maintains that hearing is not as privileged as sight within that hierarchy—it is sight which becomes "the royal road to the apprehension of the external world."[1]

Nevertheless, bourgeois ideology cannot be reduced to a monolithic ideology of the visible. Behind the historical use of the cinema lies a complex of determinations whose very multiplicity guarantees the subtlety and pervasive nature of the ideology. While the notion that the eye is central places the subject in a certain position of knowing, the verb "to know" does not exhaust the function of the subject in bourgeois ideology. Or rather, the concept of knowledge is split from the beginning. This split is supported by the establishment and maintenance of ideological oppositions between the intelligible and the sensible, intellect and emotion, fact and value, reason and intuition. Roland Barthes explains that

bourgeois ideology is of the scientistic or the intuitive kind, it records facts or perceives values, but refuses explanations; the order of the world can be seen as sufficient or ineffable, it is never seen as significant.[2]

The ineffable, intangible quality of sound—its lack of the concreteness which is conducive to an ideology of empiricism—requires that it be placed on the side of the emotional or the intuitive. If the ideology of the visible demands that the spectator understand the image as a truthful representation of reality, the ideology of the audible demands that there exist simultaneously a different truth and another order of reality for the subject to grasp.

The frequency with which the words "mood" or "atmosphere" appear in the discourse of sound technicians testifies to the significance of this other truth. Most apparent is the use of music tracks and sound effects tracks to establish a particular "mood." In *The Technique of the Film Cutting Room*, Ernest Walter describes this practice:

Music is used to create an atmosphere which would otherwise be impossible. . . . Just as the sound editor assembles his sound effects to create an almost musical effect in some sequences, so the music composer creates the instrumental background, to become at times an additional sound effect in itself. Often, it is an augmented effect blending with a dialogue scene so that one is almost unaware of its musical presence, yet adding so much to the value of the scene.[3]

The "value" alluded to remains unexplained. On this question the writer must be mute, inarticulate—precisely because the concept is inaccessible to language, to analysis, or to intellectual understanding. Sound is the bearer of a meaning which is communicable and valid but unanalyzable. Its realm is that of mystery—but mystery sanctioned by an ideology which acknowledges that all knowledge is not subsumed by the ideology of the visible, allows a leakage, an excess which is contained and constrained by that other pole of the opposition which splits knowledge and emotion, intuition, feeling. However, one cannot deny the remarkable powers of sensuality and mystery attributed to the image as well as the sound track or the use of dialogue to guarantee intelligibility. The image and the sound track are both subject to an ideological overdetermination. Nevertheless, what sound adds to the cinema is not so much the intelligibility as the presence of speech—banishing its absence in the mode of writing, in the intertitles which separate a character's speech from his or her image. The techniques applied in the construction of a sound track do not partake of the neutrality of a "pure science." But neither do they function simply to reinforce a unitary ideology of the visible. While sound is introduced, in part, to buttress this ideology, it also risks a potential ideological crisis. The risk lies in the exposure of the contradiction implicit in the ideological polarization of knowledge. Because sound and image are used as guarantors of two radically different modes of knowing (emotion and intellection), their combination entails the possibility of exposing an ideological fissure—a fissure which points to the irreconcilability of two truths of bourgeois ideology. Practices of sound editing and mixing are designed to mask this contradiction through the specification of allowable relationships between sound and image. Thus, in the sound technician's discourse synchronization and totality are fetishized and the inseparability of sound and image is posited as a goal. The "joy of mixing," according to one sound editor, lies in watching the emergence of "something organic."[4] Editor Helen Van Dongen acknowledges the existence of similar goals in her own work:

Picture and track, to a certain degree, have a composition of their own but when combined they form a new entity. Thus the track becomes not only an harmonious complement but an integral inseparable part of the picture as well. Picture and track are so closely fused together that each one functions through the other. There is no separation of *I see* in the image and *I hear* on the track. Instead, there is the *I feel*, *I experience*, through the grand-total of picture and track combined.[5]

It is no accident that, in the language of technicians, sound is "married" to the image.

Symptomatic of this repression of the material heterogeneity of the sound film are the practices which ensure effacement of the work involved in the construction of the sound track. Cuts in the track are potential indicators of that work. In the editing of optical tracks, it was discovered that the overlapped lines of a splice caused a sharp noise in playback. The technique of "blooping" was developed to conceal what could only act as an irritating reminder that syntagmatic relationships are not "found" or "natural" but manufactured. Blooping is the process of painting or punching an opaque triangle or diamond-shaped area over a splice and results in a fast fade-in, fade-out effect. In the editing of magnetic film, it is paralleled by the practice of cutting on a diagonal. The ideological objective of these techniques doubles that of continuity editing—the effect desired is that of smoothing over a potential break, of guaranteeing flow. Abrupt cuts on music or sound effects are avoided in favor of the homogenizing effects of the fade or dissolve. Obviously repetitive sounds in loops are labeled "irritating."[6] Since the absence of sound would signal a break in an otherwise continuous flow, it has become a major taboo of sound-track construction. When there are no sound effects, music, or dialogue, there must be, at the very least, room tone or environmental sound. Ernest Walter's prescriptions for sound in the screening of rough cuts indicate the extent to which the values of continuity and fullness govern techniques:

It can be very disturbing to all concerned [in the screening of rough cuts] when the sound track of sequences incorporating mute shots suddenly goes dead on the cut. It is better to incorporate even a temporary sound effect to cover these shots so that the normal flow of sound is uninterrupted.[7]

"Normality" is established as a continuous flow, and the absence of sound, in the language of the sound technicians, is its "death." When a sound track goes "dead on the cut," the transgression is one of a theological nature. "Death" and "life" are consistently metaphors associated with sound. A room or stage with low reverberation potential is "dead" and in postsynchronization, reverberation must be added to give "life" to the recording. Sound itself is often described as adding life to the picture. And the life which sound gives is presented as one of natural and uncodified flow.

This illusion of an uncodified flow is also supported by the practice of staggering cuts. Only in exceptional cases are sound and image cut at exactly the same point. The continuation of the same sound over a cut on the image track diverts attention from that cut. Similarly, the process of mixing is characterized by "a work of unification, homogenization, of a softening and polishing of all the 'roughnesses' of the sound track."[8] All of these techniques are motivated by a desire to sever the film from its source, to hide the work of the production. They promote a sense of the effortlessness and ease of capturing the natural.

What is concealed is the highly specialized and fragmented process, the bulk and expense of the machinery essential to the production of a sound track which meets industry standards. Direct sound, the sound which is recorded during shooting, consists only of dialogue and some sound effects. Most of the sound effects and the music are recorded later and this necessitates the establishment of specialized departments within the studio structure. Dialogue which is not recorded on location or which is marred by background noise is postsynchronized. The stratification, the continual subdivision which the sound track undergoes, is aligned with the aim of sustaining a rigid hierarchy of sounds. Because the microphone itself, whether omnidirectional or unidirectional, is not sufficiently selective, because it does not guarantee that the ideological values accorded to sounds and their relationships will be observed in the recording, the expensive mixing apparatus which will enforce that hierarchization is standardized. Dialogue is given primary consideration and its level generally determines the levels of sound effects and music. Dialogue is the only sound which remains with the image throughout the production—it is edited together with the image and it is in this editing that synchronization receives its imprimatur as a neutral technique through the sanction of the Moviola, the synchronizer, the flatbed. Sound effects and music are subservient to dialogue and it is, above all, the intelligibility of the dialogue which is at stake, together with its nuances of tone. The hierarchy observed in mixing reinforces, in Comolli's terms, the identification of "discourse and destiny" in Hollywood fictions and the concept of the "individual as master of speech."[9] The notion that sound dissolves or fades applied to dialogue are "unnatural," expressed in a 1931 article on rerecording,[10] indicated a desire to preserve the status of speech as an individual property right—subject only to a manipulation which is not discernible.

The need for intelligibility and the practice of using speech as a support for the individual are both constituted by an ideological demand. Yet, it is an ideological demand which has the potential to provoke a fundamental rent in the ideology of the visible. This potential finds expression in the arguments concerning sound perspective which appear with regularity in the technical journals of the early 1930s. If sound is used simply to confirm the ideology of the visible, to reassert the notion that the world *is* the same as it looks, it necessarily encroaches upon that speech which *belongs* to the individual, defines and expresses his or her individuality, and distinguishes the individual from the world. In the arguments over sound perspective, "realism" (as an effect of the ideology of the visible) is viewed as conflicting with intelligibility. If the demands of sound perspective are respected (that is, close-up sound "matches" close-up picture, long-shot sound "matches" long-shot picture), at a certain apparent camera-subject distance intelligibility of dialogue is lost. The problem is similar to that of the relationship between dialogue and background sounds or sound effects. For instance, in a shot involving a couple conversing, in a large crowd, the mimetic power of the crowd noise is generally reduced in favor of the intelligibility of the dialogue. The compromises made in favor of intelligibility indicate an ideological shift within the rationale of "realism." The Hollywood sound film operates within an oscillation between two poles of realism: that of the psychological (or the interior) and that of the visible (or the exterior). (While it is true that interior states are often depicted through *mise-en-scène* as well as facial expression, this representation is less "direct" than that of speech— it must operate as displacement. And it is precisely the presence-to-itself of speech which is valorized.) The truth of the individual, of the *interior* realm of the individual (a truth which is most readily spoken and heard), is the truth validated by the coming of sound. It is the "talkie" which appears in 1927 and not the sound film.

The fact that sound perspective poses a significant problem in the early 1930s, however, requires further explanation. If the individual within the film is defined by his or her words, this does not automatically guarantee a position for that other individual—the spectator. Renaissance perspective and monocular vision organize the image which positions the spectator as the eye of the camera. But that position is undermined and placed in doubt if the apparent microphone placement differs from that of the camera and fails to rearticulate the position. In the first years of sound film production, a number of microphones were spread around the set and their signals mixed during shooting in a monitor room to attain consistent quality and intelligibility of speech. In 1930 a writer complains that this technique results in dialogue scenes in which

quality and volume remain constant while the cutter jumps from across the room to a big close-up. At such times one becomes conscious that he is witnessing a talking picture, this condition indicating that the illusion has been partially destroyed at that point.[11]

The effect of spatial depth conveyed by the image is destroyed, and it is this illusion of a certain perspective and a certain spectator position which is broken by the early sound films.

The astonishment at hearing actors speak and the captivation of the experience of the synchronization of word and image conceal for a time

the fragmentation of a position, the splitting of the senses which characterizes the spectator's reception of the spectacle. In a 1930 article entitled "The
Illusion of Sound and Picture," John Cass describes the body of the spectator posited by the early sound film:

When a number of microphones are used, the resultant blend of sound may not be
said to represent any given point of audition, but is the sound which would be heard
by a man with five or six very long ears, said ears extending in various directions.[12]

This confusion of the body is the consequence of another confusion on the
level of the different media. The realm of sound recording is initially that of
the radio industry, the phone industry, and of electricians. For the film technician and the director of the early thirties sound is the mysterious province
of a group of specialists. A writer in the *Journal of the Society of Motion
Picture Engineers,* Joe Coffman, places the blame for complex microphone
systems and the resultant lack of sound perspective on the intrusion of the
radio industry:

In some ways it is unfortunate that the radio industry supplied most of the sound
experts to the film industry. In radio broadcasting it usually is desirable to present all
sounds as coming from approximately the same plane—that of the microphone. And
so levels are raised and lowered to bring all sounds out at approximately the same
volume, the microphone being placed as near as possible to the source of sound.
But in talking picture presentations, it is very desirable to achieve space effects, and
dramatic variation of volume level.[13]

The crucial difference between radio and film is posited as the image—the
image which anchors the sound in a given space. Coffman makes a suggestion which is very close to that given in current handbooks of filmmaking:
use one microphone, position it, set the levels, and do not readjust them
during the recording. In 1930 Western Electric moving-coil microphones and
RCA velocity microphones were made available to the industry, simplifying
microphone boom construction.[14] The action on the set was more easily followed and the maintenance of sound perspective ensured. The presentation
of all sounds as being emitted from one plane could not be sustained. For
the drama played out on the Hollywood screen must be paralleled by the
drama played out over the body of the spectator—a body positioned as unified
and nonfragmented.

   The visual illusion of position is matched by an aural illusion of
position. The ideology of matching is an obsession which pervades the practice of sound-track construction and demands a certain authenticity of the
technique. A 1930 article on dubbing assures audiences that dubbing is not
faking, because no matter how many times the sound is reproduced it re-

mains "the actual voice of the person speaking in the picture." [15] The standard of authenticity is most intensively applied with the voice, and different standards restrict the uses of nonmotivated music and sound effects. Their validity is guaranteed by dramatic logic. Karel Reisz describes a scene from *Odd Man Out* in which the footsteps of men robbing a mill become louder as they get nearer their objective—despite the fact that they are further from the camera than in preceding shots. Reisz cites this scene as an example of the deviations from natural sound perspective which "are justifiable when the primary aim is to achieve a dramatic effect"; the rhythmic beat of the mill "makes the sequence appear intolerably long-drawn-out, almost as if we were experiencing it through the mind of a member of the gang." [16] Music as well is used to match the "mood" or action of a particular scene. When the principle of mimesis is not strictly observed on the level of the represented world (for instance, in the case of nonmotivated music or sound effects which are nonanalogical), that principle is carried over to the level of matching different material strata of signification. Sound and image, "married" together, propose a drama of the individual, of psychological realism. "Knowledge" of the interior life of the individual can be grounded more readily on the fullness and spontaneity of his or her speech doubled by the rhetorical strategies of music and sound effects (as well as *mise-en-scène*). The rhetoric of sound is the result of a technique whose ideological aim is to conceal the tremendous amount of work necessary to convey an effect of spontaneity and naturalness. What is repressed in this operation is the sound which would signal the existence of the apparatus. For it is the opposition of sound (audible vibrations of air which have a communication purpose) to noise (the random sounds of the machinery—these lack meaning) which has determined so many technical developments in sound recording. The techniques of sound editing and mixing make sound the bearer of a meaning—and it is a meaning which is not subsumed by the ideology of the visible. The ideological truth of the sound track covers that excess which escapes the eye. For the ear is precisely that organ which opens onto the interior reality of the individual—not exactly unseeable, but unknowable within the guarantee of the purely visible.

Notes

1. Michel Marie, "Son," in Jean Collet et al., *Lectures du film* (Paris: Albatros, 1975), p.206.

2. Roland Barthes, *Mythologies* (London: Cape; New York: Hill and Wang, 1972), p. 142.

3. Ernest Walter, *The Technique of the Film Cutting Room* (New York: Focal Press, 1973), p. 212

4. Walter Murch in an interview by Larry Sturhahn, "The Art of the Sound Editor: An interview with Walter Murch," *Filmmakers Newsletter,* 8, no. 2 (December 1974):25.

5. Helen Van Dongen, quoted in Karel Reisz, *The Technique of Film Editing* (London and New York: Focal Press, 1964), p. 155.

6. Walter, *Technique,* p. 208.

7. Ibid, p. 128.

8. Marie, "Son," p. 203.

9. Jean-Louis Comolli, "Technique et idéologie" (6), *Cahiers du cinéma,* no. 241 (September-October 1972):22.

10. Carl Dreher, "Recording, Re-recording, and Editing of Sound," *Journal of the Society of Motion Picture Engineers,* 16, no. 6 (June 1931):763.

11. John L. Cass, "The Illusion of Sound and Picture," *Journal of the Society of Motion Picture Engineers,* 14, no. 3 (March 1930):325.

12. Ibid.

13. Joe W. Coffman, "Art and Science in Sound Film Production," *Journal of the Society of Motion Picture Engineers,* 14, no. 2 (February 1930):173-74.

14. James R. Cameron, *Sound Motion Pictures* (Coral Gables: Cameron Publishing Company, 1959), p. 365.

15. George Lewin, "Dubbing and Its Relation to Sound Picture Production," *Journal of the Society of Motion Picture Engineers,* 16, no. 1 (January 1931):48.

16. Reisz, *Techniques of Film Editing,* p. 266.

Technology and Aesthetics
of Film Sound   JOHN BELTON

Contemporary Marxist and psychoanalytic film theory regards technology, the evolution of technology, and the evolution of technique as products of an ideological demand that is, in turn, constituted by socioeconomic determinants.[1] Neither techniques nor technologies are natural, nor do they evolve naturally. Contrary to André Bazin's idealist notions of the history of technology and of cinematic forms, their evolution is not natural but "cultural," responding to the pressures of ideology. These pressures suppress signs of technique and technology. For Jean-Louis Baudry, the technological apparatus of the cinema, i.e., the camera, transforms what is set before it but conceals the *work* of that transformation by effacing all traces of it.[2] Thus the basic apparatus reflects the actions of bourgeois ideology in general, which seeks to mask its operations and to present as "natural" that which is a product of ideology.

Recent studies of film sound by Rick Altman and Mary Ann Doane extend this argument to the study of the evolution of sound technology, viewing it as an ideologically determined progression toward self-effacement. For Altman, technological innovations "derive from a felt need to reduce all traces of the sound-work from the sound track."[3] And Doane argues that "technical advances in sound recording (such as the Dolby system) are aimed at diminishing the noise of the system, concealing the work of the apparatus."[4] Even though technological evolution performs an ideological function, I would argue that the work of technology can never quite become invisible. Work, even the work that seeks to efface itself, can never disappear. A fundamental law of physics tells us that energy, though it may change in form, can be neither created nor destroyed. Neither mass nor energy nor work is ever lost. Similarly, technology and the effects of technology—by which I mean the aesthetics and stylistic practices that grow out of it—remain visible, though to varying degrees, in every film. The work of sound technology, through its very efforts to remain inaudible, announces itself and, though concealed, becomes audible for those who choose to listen for it.

Russian Formalist notions of the "laying bare" of devices, whereby the work announces itself, are rooted in theories that view art as a perceptual process that derives its effects from a prolongation of the processes of

perception. Consideration of the perception of sound and of the prolongation of that process thus constitutes the first step in a study of the "audibility" of the sound track.

The perception of sound is necessarily bound up with perception of the image; the two are apprehended together, though sound is often
perceived *through* or *in terms of* the image and, as a result, acquires a "secondary" status. For this reason, the psychology of the image differs from
that of the sound track. The viewer perceives and regards the information
presented on the sound track differently from that on the image "track,"
though in both cases the viewer, through his/her response to visual and aural
cues, plays a decisive role in the realization of the events seen and heard on
the screen.

Sound recording and mixing lack the psychology of the photographic image, which guarantees the authenticity of the reproduction.[5] The
camera, recording the visible world set before it, produces images that—"no
matter how distorted"—remain directly motivated by that world, the automatic and mechanical nature of the process of their production generating
in viewers a "quality of credibility absent from all other picture-making."[6]
At the same time, the image possesses a wholeness that serves as further
testimony to its "integrity." The image, as Christian Metz points out, is a
unity that cannot be broken down into smaller elements.[7] The microphone,
however, records an invisible world—that of the audible—which consists of
different categories of sound—dialogue, sound effects, and music—and which
is regularly broken down into and experienced as separate elements. Not
only does sound in general possess a different psychology from that of the
image, but the psychology of each category of sound differs slightly. As Metz
argues, sound is experienced not as a concrete object or thing but as an
attribute or characteristic of it.[8] The voice (i.e., the dialogue category) is one
of several attributes of the human body, which also produces noises and
sounds that fall under the category of sound effects; sound effects, in turn,
are the attributes of the world and of the objects within it (and include the
body as object).

Sound lacks "objectivity" (thus authenticity) not only because it
is invisible but because it is an attribute and is thus incomplete in itself. Sound
achieves authenticity only as a consequence of its submission to tests imposed upon it by other senses—primarily by sight. One of the conventions
of sound editing confirms this. In order to assure an audience that the dialogue and/or sound effects are genuine, the editor must, as soon as possible
in a scene, establish synchronization between sound and image, usually
through lip-sync. Once that has been done, the editor is free to do almost
anything with the picture and sound, confident that the audience now trust

what they hear, since it corresponds to (or is not overtly violated by) what they see.

By the same token, dubbing, and especially the dubbing of foreign films in which one language is seen spoken but another heard, is "read" by audiences as false. As early as 1930, the industry noted "a public reaction against . . . voice doubling," forcing a discontinuation of that practice.[9] More recently, Jean Renoir, an advocate of realistic sound practices, wrote that "if we were living in the twelfth century . . . , the practitioners of dubbing would be burnt in the marketplace for heresy. Dubbing is equivalent to a belief in the duality of the soul."[10] The rather obvious intervention of technology involved with dubbing severely circumscribes our faith in both sound and image, provoking a crisis in their credibility.

This perceptual process of testing or attempting to identify sound can, through a system of delays that postpone the synchronism of sound and source, be manipulated to create suspense, both in the area of voice/dialogue and in that of sound effects, calling attention to sound *as a device* by playing with our perception of it. The identification of a voice with a body can be delayed, as in the case, say, of *The Wizard of Oz* (1939), in which the Wizard's unmasking occurs at the precise moment that synchronization is established; the achievement of synchronization creates a unity whose completeness spells the end of a hermeneutic chain within which an enigma is introduced, developed, prolonged, and resolved. Or in the more complex case of *Psycho* (1960), in which off-screen sound is employed to create a nonexistent character (Mrs. Bates), the particular revelation of the sound's source carefully avoids synchronism: we never see Bates speak in his mother's voice; even at the end, his/her request for a blanket comes from off-screen and his/her final monologue is interiorized. Image and sound here produce a tenuous, almost schizophrenic "synchronization" of character and voice, which precisely articulates the fragmented nature of the enigma's "resolution" and completes a "incompletable" narrative.

As for sound effects, their separation from their source can produce suspense that ranges from the familiar off-screen footsteps that stalk central characters, such as the helpless L. B. Jeffries trapped in his darkened apartment at the end of *Rear Window* (1954), to the mysterious noises and screeches throughout *The Haunting* (1963), whose effects, unlike the earlier example from *The Wizard of Oz*, remain unexplained and unidentified. Though off-screen diegetic sound—whether dialogue or sound effects—will, with few exceptions, ultimately be tied to seen (or unseen) sources and thus be "explained" or "identified," we experience that sound *through* what we see on the screen. It is an extension or completion (or even denial) of the images, but it operates on a plane that is less concrete than that of the images. One could argue that even our experience of on-screen sound involves, though in a much less extreme form, a recognition of a reality of a different order, a reality one step removed from that of the images. The sound track corresponds not, like the image track, directly to "objective reality" but rather to a secondary representation of it, i.e., to the images that, in turn, guarantee the objectivity of the sounds. The sound track, in other works, does not undergo the same tests of verisimilitude to which the images are subjected. Images attain credibility in the conformation to objective reality; sounds, in their conformation to the images of that reality, to a derivative reconstruction of objective reality. The rules the sound track obeys—for the spectator at least—are not those of the visible world or of external reality to which photographic images appear to correspond point by point but those of the audible world, which occupies part of the spectrum of phenomena that remain invisible. Paradoxically, the sound track can only duplicate the invisible by means of the visible. Thus sound defines itself in terms of the temporality and spatiality of the image, observing a synchronism and/or perspective dictated by the visuals. Its mimetic processes take as a model not the pro-filmic event but the recorded image of it. The sound track does not duplicate the world set before it; it realizes an imaginary world, endowing the space and objects within the story space with another dimension that complements their temporal and spatial existence *as representations.*

What the sound track seeks to duplicate is the sound of an image, not that of the world. The evolution of sound technology and, again, that of studio recording, editing, and mixing practice illustrate, to some degree, the quest for a sound track that captures an idealized reality, a world carefully filtered to eliminate sounds that fall outside of understanding or significance; every sound must signify. In other words, the goal of sound technology in reproducing sound is to eliminate any noise that interferes with the transmission of meaningful sound. As Mary Ann Doane points out, technical developments in sound recording, after the creation of the basic technology (which was in place by 1928–29), were inspired, in part, by attempts to improve the system's signal-to-noise ratio, to reduce noise and distortion introduced by recording, developing, printing, and projection or playback practices.[11] During 1929–30, blimps and "bungalows" are developed to encase and thus silence cameras. By 1930, electrical circuits for arc lighting systems are devised to eliminate hum, enabling cinematographers to return from incandescent to arc lighting. Materials used in the construction of sets and the design of costumes are changed to reduce excessive reverberation and rustling. Condenser microphones, which tend to "go noisy" in wet weather, are supplanted (ca. 1931) by the quieter dynamic microphone. By 1939, unidirectional microphones are designed, achieving a 10:1 ratio of "desired to undesired pickup" and effectively reducing "camera noise, floor squeaks,

dolly noises, and sounds reflected from walls and other reflecting surfaces."[12] Biased recording and printing (ca. 1930–31) and push-pull recording (ca. 1935) reduce ground noise and harmonic distortion.[13] Nonslip
printers (ca. 1934) further help control noise: by ensuring a more precise
registration between negative and print films, they reduce the loss of quality
formerly observed in the printing process. And throughout the thirties special fine-grain negative, intermediate, and print film stocks are developed,
along with ultraviolet recording and printing lights (ca. 1936), producing a
sharper, distortionless image on the sound track. Meanwhile, the frequency
characteristics of recording and playback systems are improved from a range
of 100 to 4,000 cycles per second in 1928–30 to that of 30 to 10,000 in
1938, expanding the range of the signal while holding the noise level down.[14]
The evolutionary process culminates in the Dolby noise reduction and stereo sound system introduced into the cinema in 1975 in such musical films
as *Tommy* and *Lisztomania*. By flattening, during recording, the response to
low frequencies and boosting the highs and by reversing this process in
playback, the Dolby system effectively masks out surface noise, producing a
sound that is clean and that permits louder playback in the theater without
increasing noise.

Yet the Dolby system also changes the characteristics of whatever sound it records, albeit only slightly. It cuts the very tops and bottoms
off the sounds, resulting in a sound that is somewhat "unnatural." At the
same time, the nearly total elimination of noise—the goal toward which sound
technology has evolved, like that of camera movement "noise" with the
perfection of the Steadicam in 1976 (see *Bound for Glory, Marathon Man,
Rocky,* etc.)—results in a final product that is too perfect, that is ideal to a
fault. In watching Claude Lelouch's Steadicamed opus *Another Man, Another Chance* (1977) or listening to Steven Spielberg's postrecorded and
Dolbyized *Raiders of the Lost Ark* (1981), one misses the rough, jittery camera
movements, floor squeaks, and unmixed, ambient sound of films like Jean
Renoir's *La Chienne* (1931). A certain amount of noise has become necessary to signify realism; its absence betokens a sound that has returned to
an ideal state of existence, to a point just before it enters into the world and
acquires the imperfections inherent in its own realization. The sound track
has become artificially quiet, pushing beyond the realism of the outside world
into an inner, psychological realism. The sound track duplicates what sound
recordist Mark Dichter and sound designer Walter Murch refer to as the sound
one hears in one's head,[15] a sound that has not been marked by any system
noise nor by transmission through any medium, such as air, that might alter
its fidelity to an ideal.

The technology and practice devoted to the duplication of sound's
spatial properties have undergone a similar evolution, becoming unreal in a

quest for realism. With the abandonment in 1927–29 of radio-style recording such as that in *The Lights of New York* (1928), in which performers speak into a stationary microphone and depth is "suggested" by changes in volume (e.g., when doors leading onto a dance floor open and close in the background), sound recording strives to model sound the way a cameraman models figures with light. The industry seeks to produce a track that reflects the space of the original scene. Carefully positioning the microphone to blend direct and reflected sound, soundmen record not only the informational "content" of an actor's speech or sound effects but also its spatial presence. The soundman, in effect, duplicates through sound the space seen on the screen: the microphone mimics the angle and distance of the camera, creating a sound perspective that matches the visual perspective of the image. The advent of wide-screen cinematography—whether the Grandeur system (1929–30), Cinerama (1952), CinemaScope (1953), or Todd-AO/70mm (1955)—provides a wider visual field for the sound track to duplicate, necessitating multiple track, stereo sound. In Fox's CinemaScope process, for example, four different tracks play on three separate speakers behind the screen and on one "surround" speaker.[16] The footsteps (or speech) of a character walking across the screen from right to left would originate first from the right horn, then from the center, and finally from the left, the source of the sound matching, point for point, the character's various positions on the screen. The final effect, however, is that of three sound perspectives rather than one. No matter how many speakers or tracks film technology develops, it can never quite duplicate the spatial qualities of the sound of the event seen on the screen. Every square inch of the screen would require a separate speaker and track to reflect the nearly limitless number of potential sources for sounds, while an infinite number of speakers and tracks would be needed to duplicate sounds emanating from off-screen space. Stereo systems that establish two, three, four, or even five sound sources, rather than creating a more perfect illusion of depth on the screen, call attention to the arbitrariness of their choice of sources. Instead of becoming better able to approximate the real and to efface its own presence, stereo sound remains marked by the nature of the system(s) it uses to create the illusion of real space. The infinite supply of original information has been *channeled* into a handful of tracks. We experience stereo sound tracks as a limited (rather than limitless) number of distinct sound sources. No matter how "noiseless" it becomes, the system never quite disappears.

At the same time, perspective undergoes stylistic as well as technological evolution. The careful correlation of aural and visual spaces achieved by Hollywood in the thirties gives way in the postwar period to the violation of perspective. Influenced in part by television sound, which tends to maintain constant close-up levels, ignoring the nuances of perspective, contemporary cinema frequently "mismatches" long shots with close-up sound, as in *The Graduate* (1967) and any number of other films that combine long shots of a car on a highway with close-up sound of its occupants conversing. The current fondness for radio mikes, seen in the work of Robert Altman and others, involves a similar disruption of traditional spatial codes in sound recording. Radio microphones pick up speech (and body tone) *before* it is projected—that is, before it can acquire spatial properties. Though it can be given some perspective during the mixing process, the quality of the sound differs from that recorded by traditional microphones hung just beyond the camera's field of view. Though it permits more freedom in shooting and ensures good sound coverage, recording with radio microphones, like mismatched perspective, lends a surfacy quality to the image, which may suit certain modern stylists such as Altman but which plays havoc with more traditional, illusionistic notions of space. By the same token, contemporary sound editing, in which the sound cut often precedes the picture cut by six to eight frames or more (e.g., *Somebody Up There Likes Me,* 1956; *The Loneliness of the Long Distance Runner,* 1962; *Jaws,* 1975; any number of contemporary Hollywood films; and even recent Robert Bresson films like *L'Argent,* 1983), violates the invisible cutting of the thirties in which the picture cut often precedes the sound cut by a frame or two, the sound bridging and thus concealing the picture cut.

It is perhaps useful to distinguish at some point between technological and stylistic evolution, which do not always share a single goal, and to acknowledge the coexistence of disparate stylistic uses of a single technology. Theories of technological evolution are shaped by Darwinian notions of advancement and self-perfection; the tools that an artist (or culture) uses become more and more perfect, developing from lower into higher forms. But theories of stylistic evolution such as Bazin's are informed, in large part, by the "mimetic fallacy," and are clearly more problematical. As Heinrich Wolfflin argues, "It is a mistake [for art history] to work with the clumsy notion of the imitation of nature, as though it were merely a homogeneous process of increasing perfection."[17] For that matter, can art or even artists themselves be said to possess goals that it/they seek to realize? Is not that notion the height of idealistic thinking? As Jean-Louis Comolli has shown, Bazinian theories of the evolution of cinematic forms are essentially idealistic reconstructions of film history that fail to account for delays, gaps, and contradictions in their development.[18] Given that cinematic forms do not necessarily evolve in the direction of qualities that enable "a recreation of the world in its own image,"[19] can they be said to improve, or to perfect themselves over time? Is the style of a Fassbinder better or even more evolved than that of a Griffith? Is that of Picasso better than that of Rembrandt? No; it is merely *different,* reflecting the different technological, socioeconomic, and cultural systems within which each artist worked. If development can be gauged at all, it is not to be found in the comparison of individual artists or works but in that of different schools, groups, or periods, as Wolfflin has demonstrated. It is only in the area of dominant practice—the point of intersection between the timeliness of technology and the timelessness of style, between tools and cultural/individual expression—that change can be charted and given a goal.

At each stage along the axis of technological development, recording, editing, and mixing practices change in response to linear changes in technology and to unpredictable shifts in stylistic concerns of a period, nation, or group of individuals. Thus dominant film practice conforms, more or less, to the direction taken by the technology that informs it, that is, toward self-perfection and invisibility, *and* to the attitudes of those who use that technology, attitudes that color its "invisibility."

Developments in the area of sound recording—especially in the use of radio microphones and Dolby—point, as we have seen, in the direction of the ideal: they culminate in the sounds one hears in one's head. Changes in editing and mixing practice reflect an increase in control over the sound track and in its ability to duplicate the sound not of the pro-filmic event but of that event's photographic image. The initial practice (ca. 1926–29) of mixing sound while it is being recorded and recording it (except for music that was often added later) at the same time that the image is recorded locks the sound indexically into the pro-filmic event of which it is the record, giving it an immediacy and integrity resembling that of the image. The introduction of rerecording and mixing in the early thirties breaks that indexical bond of sound to the pro-filmic event. Mixing now takes place *after* the film has been shot (and often even after it has been edited) during the phase of postproduction. At the same time, the sound track loses its wholeness: it is separated into dialogue, sound effects, and music tracks that are recorded at different times, dialogue and some sound effects being recorded during production, other sound effects, music, and even some dialogue during postproduction. Whereas initially the sound track was "recorded," now it is "built." Sound mixing no longer observes the integrity of any preexistent reality; it builds its own to match earlier recorded visual information. The growth of postproduction departments within the studio system institutionalizes the separation of sound and image that frees the former from its ties to the events that produced the latter. The building of the sound track, using the image rather than the pro-filmic event as a guide, now becomes a final stage in the "realization" of the image.

During the postwar period, even the recording of dialogue, which is traditionally tied, through concerns for synchronization, to the moment at which the image is recorded, is freed from its bonds to the pro-filmic event.

The use of wide-angle lenses (which provide a wide field of view and thus force the microphone further away from its target, resulting in a less acceptable sound) and the practice of shooting on location (where ambient noise cannot be controlled as well as in the studio) result in the use of the "production" sound track as a guide track to cue the actor's dialogue during looping sessions back at the studio. The original track, at times, functions merely as a blueprint for an entirely new track created on the sound stage to match an image that has already been assembled in rough cut form. Again, changing practice reveals that it is the sound of the image that Hollywood strives to recreate.

Neither the cinematic institution, seen in its practices, nor the cinematic apparatus possesses a single identity. Practice seeks to produce a more realistic sound track by "unrealizing" its recording and rerecording methods. Its final product is thus marked *as a product.* Although Baudry and others argue to the contrary, the cinema never quite succeeds in masking the work that produces it. This is due, in large part, to the very nature of the apparatus itself. The recording aspects of motion picture technology possess dual characteristics: they both transmit and transform. Though the cinematic apparatus becomes, decade by decade, a more perfect transmitter, reducing signs of its own existence by eliminating its system's noise, it inevitably reproduces not only the light and sound waves reflected and emitted by objective reality but also *its own presence,* which is represented by the perspective from which these waves are seen or heard. In the cinema, there is always present, in the positioning of the camera and the microphone(s), a consciousness that sees and (in the sound film) hears and that coexists with what is seen or heard. Even in the silent cinema, someone is always speaking and something is always spoken. In the sound cinema, we always see and hear events *through* images and sounds of them. The cinema remains the phenomenological art par excellence, wedding, if indeed not collapsing, consciousness with the world.

Notes

1. Jean-Louis Comolli, "Technique et ideologie (part 2: Depth of Field: The Double Scene)," *Cahiers du cinéma,* nos. 229–31 (1971): 2a.2, trans. Chistopher Williams.

2. Jean-Louis Baudry, "Ideological Effects of the Basic Cinematographic Apparatus," *Film Quarterly,* 28 (Winter 1974–75):40, trans. Alan Williams.

3. Rick Altman, "Introduction," *Cinema/Sound: Yale French Studies,* no. 60 (1980):4.

4. Mary Ann Doane, "The Voice in the Cinema: The Articulation of Body and Space," *Cinema/Sound: Yale French Studies,* no. 60 (1980):35.

5. See André Bazin, "The Ontology of the Photographic Image," *What Is Cinema?*, vol. 1, trans. Hugh Gray (Berkeley: University of California Press, 1967), pp. 13–14; and Christian Metz, "On the Impression of Reality in the Cinema," *Film Language: A Semiotics of the Cinema*, trans. Michael Taylor (New York: Oxford University Press, 1974), pp. 5–6.

6. Bazin, "Ontology," p. 13.

7. Metz, "The Cinema: Language or Language System," *Film Language*, pp. 61–63.

8. Christian Metz, "Aural Objects," *Cinema/Sound: Yale French Studies*, no. 60 (1980):26–27.

9. Jack Alicoate, ed., *The 1930 Film Daily Year Book of Motion Pictures* (New York: The Film Daily, 1930), p. 857.

10. Jean Renoir, *My Life and My Films*, trans. Norman Denny (New York: Atheneum, 1974), p. 106.

11. Mary Ann Doane, "Ideology and the Practice of Sound Editing and Mixing," *The Cinematic Apparatus*, ed. Teresa De Lauretis and Stephen Heath (New York: St. Martin's, 1980), p. 55.

12. G. R. Groves, "The Soundman," *JSMPTE*, 48, no. 13 (March 1947):223.

13. Biased recording effectively reduces the noise of film grain by reducing the amount of light that reaches the negative. As a result, the sound track on positive prints has a darker exposure. Thus less film-grain noise is reproduced during silent or low sound level passages. Push-pull recording involves doubling the width of the track, thereby increasing the useful area of modulated light and decibel output. One variety of push-pull recording splits the track into positive and negative parts of the sound waves. As a result, there is never any transparent or clear area on the track and, thus, ground noise is eliminated.

14. The frequency range of the human ear extends from 16 to 20,000 cycles per second. Thus evolution in this area might be said to have as its goal the range of the human ear. Unless otherwise noted, technological data in this paragraph derive from material in Groves (see note 12); Edward W. Kellogg, "History of Sound Motion Pictures, Parts I–III," *JSMPTE*, 48, nos. 6–8 (June-August 1955); Barry Salt, "Film Style and Technology in the Thirties," *Film Quarterly*, 30–31 (Fall 1976).

15. Mark Dichter, interview with Elisabeth Weis (March 1975). Walter Murch, interview with F. Paine, *University Film Association Journal*, 33, no. 4 (1981):15–20.

16. These tracks are narratively coded. The behind-the-screen tracks contain on-screen sound while the surround track contains off-screen sound and voice-over commentary. The authority of a voice-over track is partly the result of its spatial qualities. It occupies a space that is beyond or outside that of the film, thus it can be either privileged *(Apocalypse Now)* or disadvantaged *(Days of Heaven)* in terms of its knowledge of information on the picture "track."

17. Heinrich Wolfflin, *Principles of Art History* (New York: Dover, n.d.), 13.

18. Comolli, "Technique et ideologie," 1.7–1.17.

19. Bazin, "The Myth of Total Cinema," *What Is Cinema?*, vol. 1, p. 21.

Classical Sound Theory

Classical sound theory, like classical theory in general, is determined in part by a quest for cinematic specificity. That which distinguishes film from literature, theater, and the plastic arts defines the "essence" of the cinema. For theorists of the silent film, that essence lay in the image. The introduction of sound—or more particularly of talk, dialogue, or language—posed tremendous problems for the champions of pure cinema, who located the source of its artistry within the silent discourse of images that constituted a unique "language." Through expressionistic manipulation of the plastics of the image or through montage, the cinema could articulate anything. The addition of sound threatened the hegemony that the images had exercised over cinematic expression for more than thirty years.

Strangely enough, very few (if any) opponents of sound actually condemned sound as a whole. It was the talkies to which they objected; sound effects and music were rapidly appropriated by Chaplin, one of the most outspoken advocates of silence, and others as extensions of the natural (i.e., innate) expressiveness of the image.

Actual language posed a threat to a figurative language that had evolved to a state of near-perfection during the silent era. The various approaches taken toward dialogue in this period reflect early attempts to disarm, undermine, or banish it entirely from the screen. Certain Soviet theorists advocated contrapuntal use of sound, a position quickly embraced by a number of British filmmakers and writers. At the same time, certain French filmmakers independently arrived at similar conclusions involving the asynchronism of sound and image.

Eisenstein, Pudovkin, and Alexandrov

In August 1928, Soviet film directors S. M. Eisenstein, V. I. Pudovkin, and G. V. Alexandrov (Eisenstein's assistant on *Strike* and *Potemkin* and co-director and co-scenarist on *October* and *Old and New*) published a joint statement on the sound film in a Leningrad magazine. The statement does not, however, reflect the approach toward sound of *all* Soviet directors. Dziga Vertov, as Lucy Fischer points out in her essay on *Enthusiasm*, never advocated a purely contrapuntal interplay of sound and image. The manifesto does, however, reveal uniquely Eisensteinian concerns, especially that for "neutralization." According to this notion, a photograph of an object tends to neutralize that object by cutting it off from all surrounding reality, transforming "nature" into a block of material (or a complex sign, if you will), which the editor can use in assembling a work. The coincidence of sound and image threatens this process by restoring power and autonomy to the photographed object, increasing "the independence of its meaning" and thus "its inertia as a montage piece." A contrapuntal use of sound will prevent the sounds and images from further realizing the world from which they derive and enable them to function as neutral fragments of material whose potential meaning is realized in a montage sequence. The "Statement" dismisses talking films as naturalistic and speech, by implication, as nonaesthetic.

Pudovkin

Pudovkin, though a co-signer of the "Statement," holds a somewhat different view from that of Eisenstein. Writing in 1929, he sees asynchronous sound as a means of enriching rather than neutralizing the image. It reveals complexities within the image that were previously invisible. The result is "a more exact rendering of nature than its superficial copying."

For Pudovkin, sound cinema resembles human perception; it does not duplicate events but rather affects the way we perceive them. Out attention focuses first on one thing, then on another. When we see an object, we do not hear it as profoundly as we see it and vice versa. Contrapuntal manipulation of image and sound enables the director to duplicate the course of a character's or spectator's perceptions. While Eisenstein's sound theories remain staunchly dialectical, Pudovkin presents a program for associational approaches to sound and image.

Clair

An exponent of "pure cinema," director René Clair initially resisted the transition to sound, remaining inactive until 1930 when *Sous les toits de Paris* was released. During this period he visited London, saw the early sound films playing there, and reported back his reactions in a series of letters (excerpted here). Clair actively fought the *talking* film but just as actively celebrated the *sound* film, which, in such successes as *A nous la liberté* (1932) and *Le Million* (1931), provided him with a vehicle for the associationist imagery he perfected in his silent works.

Clair saw that an asynchronous use of sound would provide a new method for expression. Through a careful selection and organization of sounds, filmmmakers could liberate the cinema from the wordy theatricalism that threatened to engulf it and thus recapture some of the poetic energy that animated the silent cinema.

Wright and Braun

Influenced in part by the publication of Pudovkin's *Technique of the Film* in 1929, which was translated into English by Ivor Montagu, and by its theories of asynchronism, British filmmakers and critics actively debated the new role of sound in film. In their 1934 "Dialogue on Sound," Basil Wright, director of *Song of Ceylon*

(1934) and one of John Grierson's top directors at the G.P.O. Film Unit, and B. Vivian Braun, a contemporary critic, distinguished between sound films and talkies, dismissing the latter as filmed stage plays. De-emphasizing counterpoint as the sole device appropriate to sound aesthetics (but offering nothing in its place), they call for a more general "orchestration" of sounds accompanying images.

Cavalcanti

A colleague of Wright's at the G.P.O., Brazilian-born Alberto Cavalcanti exerted considerable influence on the approach to sound taken by the British documentary movement in the thirties. As seen in his 1939 survey of speech, music, and noise in "Sound in Films" and in the British films he directed, such as *Pett and Pott* (1934) and *Coalface* (1936), Cavalcanti advocated a nonnaturalistic use of sound.

Cavalcanti bases his advocacy of asynchronous sound on the different natures of images and sounds, especially as they function in the documentary. Images provide literal statements, while sounds introduce nonliteral suggestions. Film, for Cavalcanti, should not be content merely to reproduce reality. Like Pudovkin, Cavalcanti feels that sound can enable the cinema to achieve a more exact rendering of reality, in particular, of emotional reality. An asynchronous use of sound, as Cavalcanti's historically grounded argument demonstrates, enables the sound cinema to realize an affective potential that the silent cinema lacked. It can, through its suggestiveness, directly address the emotions of the spectator.

Arnheim

The most devastating attack on the talkies comes from Rudolf Arnheim in his 1938 "A New Laocoön: Artistic Composites and the Talking Films." In *Film* (reprinted in *Film as Art*), Arnheim, answering those who view film as a reproduction of reality and thus not as an art form, celebrates those aspects of the cinema that *limit* its reproductive potential and that call attention to film as a form. The addition of sound, which reduces the gap between film and reality, threatens the artistic status of the medium and is thus opposed by Arnheim. In challenging the talkies in "A New Laocoön," Arnheim goes even further than he did in *Film*, arguing that the talking film is not only a backward step in the course of film art but an aesthetic impossibility. Arnheim models his argument on that of Lessing, who in his *Laocoon* explores composite forms (e.g., a piece of sculpture based on a passage of poetry) and argues that each form possesses a medium-specificity that determines the means of its expression. Thus poetry is primarily a temporal medium, while painting and sculpture are primarily spatial media. Arnheim maintains that, in all composite forms, one medium must dominate the other. In the theater, which combines speech with visual spectacle, speech dominates, the text inspiring the staging of the action. If the cinema, which also combines speech and spectacle, is to differ at all from the theater, then the image (i.e., spectacle) must dominate speech.

Though the composite status of the theater is acceptable to Arnheim, that of the cinema is not. Its two voices drown out one another. The "voice" of the image, which is always present, conflicts with that of the sound track, which is (ideally) also always speaking. For Arnheim, the primacy of the image in the cinema is total: there is no room for anything else. Speech is either redundant or at odds with the image, preventing a true fusion of the two media and thus frustrating the aesthetic viability of the sound cinema.

In the last pages of "The New Laocoön," which are excerpted here, Arnheim argues that the addition of dialogue adds nothing to the already complete and perfected expressivity of the moving image. Sound, in fact, reduces the power of the images to express information by privileging human speech over that of objects, which were once as articulate as people, but which now must be mute. Rejecting techniques such as asynchronism, which makes sound and image separate but equal, Arnheim, playing counterrevolutionary to Eisenstein and other lobbyists for nonsync sound, calls for a restoration of silence and, with it, the golden age of the image.

Balazs

Hungarian theoretician Bela Balazs, author of the libretto for Bela Bartok's opera *Bluebeard's Castle* (1911) and co-scenarist for G. W. Pabst's *Threepenny Opera* (1931) and Leni Riefenstahl's *Blue Light* (1932), endorses the transition to sound as progress yet faults the sound film for its failure to realize its potential. In his response to progress, Balazs remains a figure of paradox. Though a Marxist, Balazs is skeptical of modern technology, believing it to be a threat to man's humanity. In his 1923 *Der sichtbare Mensch*, Balazs argued that with the development of the printing press and the resultant translation of all experience into the arbitrary medium of language, mankind lost the ability to read faces. Ironically, another technological innovation, the cinema, restores this lost ability, reeducating our senses so that we can once again decipher the visible world. Celebrating the cinema as a wordless language, Balazs sees the coming of sound and the introduction of speech as a second Tower of Babel that severely limits the universality of the cinema. Language itself, for Balazs, is always less expressive than the panlinguistic gestures that accompany it and that, along with the physiognomy of the face, constitute the visible "language" of the cinema.

In his 1945 *Theory of the Film*, Balazs's disenchantment with sound stems from its failure to produce more highly evolved forms or new themes. For Balazs the potential of the sound film lies in its ability to recover certain "lost" sensations for us, such as the sounds of objects or nature, the sounds of certain spaces, or the sound of silence, which can only be heard in the context of other sounds. Moreover, the sound cinema possesses the ability to restore our contact with the world in a direct rather than indirect way: what we hear are sounds themselves, not images or records of them. In the passages excerpted here, Balazs sees the role of the sound track as that of organizing sounds into a new language that will decipher the noises around us and give us "the speech of things." At the same time, Balazs stresses the spatial qualities of sound that prevent it from being isolated and that endow it with the timbre or color of the particular space in which it was recorded.

Kracauer

Like Balazs, theorist Siegfried Kracauer is also distrustful of the products of modern science that intervene between us and our environment and that, in the postwar nuclear age, threaten our very existence. For both theorists, we have come to understand the world through conceptualizations of it, thus losing actual touch with it. Kracauer sees the cinema as a means of redeeming physical reality for us, rendering visible what we did not or could not see before the advent of the cinema.

Language, a conceptualizing form par excellence, provides a system of signs that, like certain systematic beliefs, " 'cover' physical reality in both senses of the word," denying our access to it. A partisan of neither sync nor async sound, Kracauer favors a sound style that employs dialogue "cinematically." By this he means that the content of speech—i.e., what it refers to—should be de-emphasized and that the irrational, material qualities of speech should be stressed. Thus he favors Chaplin and the Marx Brothers who ridicule speech, and he singles out for praise the famous "Gettysburg Address" scene in *Ruggles of Red Gap* (1935) in which the meaning of the familiar speech yields in importance to the fact that this English manservant knows the text by heart. Stripped of its conceptual meaning, speech becomes the equivalent of sound effects and music, capable of recovering the expressive purity of man's prelinguistic utterances at the dawn of civilization.

Epstein

In writing of his own film, *Le Tempestaire* (1947), director Jean Epstein, former member of the French Impressionist group of filmmakers of the twenties and, like those directors, an advocate of "pure cinema," also emphasizes the nonliteral aspects of sound. Less interested in speech than in the sounds of nature and objects, Epstein seeks, through slow-motion processes, to reduce sounds to their essences. By discovering a common denominator among all sounds that enables them to "speak" equally, Epstein thus erases the hierarchy of sounds, in which speech has a more prominent "voice" than objects, a hierarchy that earlier had disturbed Arnheim.

What binds all these classical theorists together is neither their acceptance of sound nor their championing of a certain sound style, such as asynchronism, but rather their approach to speech, which they view with hostility. Perhaps, as Christian Metz suggests in "The Cinema: Language or Language System?" *(Film Language)*, the presence of verbal language threatens their notion of cinema as a kind of language. Concrete verbal structures call into question the figurative, pseudo-verbal systems in which classical theorists sought to ground the cinema as an art. Avoiding the bias of their predecessors, contemporary sound theorists, as we shall see in the next section, embrace speech as an essential element of the sound track. If classical theory legitimizes the sound film, then modern sound theory might be said to have discovered that the sound film talks. Speech is reintegrated into our notion of what the sound track is.

A Statement

S. M. EISENSTEIN, V. I. PUDOVKIN, and G. V. ALEXANDROV

The dream of a sound film has come true. With the invention of a practical sound film, the Americans have placed it on the first step of substantial and rapid realization. Germany is working intensively in the same direction. The whole world is talking about the silent thing that has learned to talk.

We who work in the U.S.S.R. are aware that with our technical potential we shall not move ahead to a practical realization of the sound film in the near future. At the same time we consider it opportune to state a number of principal premises of a theoretical nature, for in the accounts of the invention it appears that this advance in films is being employed in an incorrect direction. Meanwhile, a misconception of the potentialities within this new technical discovery may not only hinder the development and perfection of the cinema as an art but also threaten to destroy all its present formal achievements.

At present, the film, working with visual images, has a powerful effect on a person and has rightfully taken one of the first places among the arts.

It is known that the basic (and only) means that has brought the cinema to such a powerfully effective strength is MONTAGE. The affirmation of montage, as the chief means of effect, has become the indisputable axiom on which the worldwide culture of the cinema has been built.

The success of Soviet films on the world's screens is due, to a significant degree, to those methods of montage which they first revealed and consolidated.

Therefore, for the further development of the cinema, the important moments will be only those that strengthen and broaden the montage methods of affecting the spectator. Examining each new discovery from this viewpoint, it is easy to show the insignificance of the color and the stereoscopic film in comparison with the vast significance of SOUND.

Sound recording is a two-edged invention, and it is most probable that its use will proceed along the line of least resistance, i.e., along the line of *satisfying simple curiosity.*

In the first place there will be commercial exploitation of the most salable merchandise, TALKING FILMS. Those in which sound recording will proceed on a naturalistic level, exactly corresponding with the movement on the screen, and providing a certain "illusion" of talking people, of audible objects, etc.

A first period of sensations does not injure the development of a new art, but it is the second period that is fearful in this case, a second period that will take the place of the fading virginity and purity of this first perception of new technical possibilities, and will assert an epoch of its automatic utilization for "highly cultured dramas" and other photographed performances of a theatrical sort.

To use sound in this way will destroy the culture of montage, for every ADHESION of sound to a visual montage piece increases its inertia as a montage piece, and increases the independence of its meaning—and this will undubtedly be to the detriment of montage, operating in the first place not on the montage pieces but on their JUXTAPOSITION.

ONLY A CONTRAPUNTAL USE of sound in relation to the visual montage piece will afford a new potentiality of montage development and perfection.

THE FIRST EXPERIMENTAL WORK WITH SOUND MUST BE DIRECTED ALONG THE LINE OF ITS DISTINCT NONSYNCHRONIZATION WITH THE VISUAL IMAGES. And only such an attack will give the necessary palpability which will later lead to the creation of an ORCHESTRAL COUNTERPOINT of visual and aural images.

This new technical discovery is not an accidental moment in film history but an organic way out of a whole series of impasses that have seemed hopeless to the cultured cinematic avant-garde.

The FIRST IMPASSE is the subtitle and all the unavailing attempts to tie it into the montage composition, as a montage piece (such as breaking it up into phrases and even words, increasing and decreasing the size of type used, employing camera movement, animation, and so on).

The SECOND IMPASSE is the EXPLANATORY pieces (for example, certain inserted close-ups) that burden the montage composition and retard the tempo.

The tasks of theme and story grow more complicated every day; attempts to solve these by methods of "visual" montage alone either lead to unsolved problems or force the director to resort to fanciful montage structures, arousing the fearsome eventuality of meaninglessness and reactionary decadence.

Sound, treated as a new montage element (as a factor divorced from the visual image), will inevitably introduce new means of enormous power to the expression and solution of the most complicated tasks that now oppress us with the impossibility of overcoming them by means of an imperfect film method, working only with visual images.

The CONTRAPUNTAL METHOD of constructing the sound film will not only not weaken the INTERNATIONAL CINEMA but will bring its significance to unprecedented power and cultural height.

Such a method for constructing the sound film will not confine it to a national market, as must happen with the photographing of plays, but will give a greater possibility than ever before for the circulation throughout the world of a filmically expressed idea.

(signed by)

S. M. EISENSTEIN
V. I. PUDOVKIN
G. V. ALEXANDROV
(Translated by Jay Leyda)

Asynchronism
as a Principle of Sound Film
V. I. PUDOVKIN

The technical invention of sound has long been accomplished, and brilliant experiments have been made in the field of recording. This technical side of sound filmmaking may be regarded as already relatively perfected, at least in America. But there is a great difference between the technical development of sound and its development as a means of *expression*. The expressive achievements of sound still lie far behind its technical possibilities. I assert that many theoretical questions whose answers are clear to us are still provided in practice only with the most primitive solutions. Theoretically, we in the Soviet Union are in advance of Western Europe and [the] U.S.A.

Our first question is: What new content can be brought into the cinema by the use of sound? It would be entirely false to consider sound merely as a mechanical device enabling us to enhance the naturalness of the image. Examples of such most primitive sound effects: in the silent cinema we were able to show a car, now in sound film we can add to its image a record of its natural sound; or again, in silent film a speaking man was associated with a title, now we hear his voice. The role which sound is to play in film is much more significant than a slavish imitation of naturalism on these lines; the first function of sound is to *augment the potential expressiveness of the film's content*.

If we compare the sound to the silent film, we find that it is possible to explain the content more deeply to the spectator with relatively the same expenditure of time. It is clear that this deeper insight into the content of the film cannot be given to the spectator simply by adding an accompaniment of naturalistic sound; we must do something more. This something more is the development of the image and the sound strip each along a separate rhythmic course. They must not be tied to one another by naturalistic imitation but connected as the result of the interplay of action. Only by this method can we find a new and richer form than that available in the silent film. Unity of sound and image is realized by an interplay of meanings which results, as we shall presently show, in a more exact rendering of nature than its superficial copying. In silent film, by our editing of a variety of images, we began to attain the unity and freedom that is realized in nature only in its abstraction by the human mind. Now in sound film we can, within the same strip of celluloid, not only edit different points in space, but can cut into association with the image selected sounds that reveal and heighten the character of each—wherever in silent film we had a conflict of but two opposing elements, now we can have four.

A primitive example of the use of sound to reveal an inner content can be cited in the expression of the stranding of a town-bred man in the midst of the desert. In silent film we should have had to cut in a shot of the town; now in sound film we can carry town-associated sounds into the desert and edit them there in place of the natural desert sounds. Uses of this kind are already familiar to film directors in Western Europe, but it is not generally recognized that the principal elements in sound film are the asynchronous and not the synchronous; moreover, that the synchronous use is, in actual fact, only exceptionally correspondent to natural perception. This is not, as may first appear, a theoretical figment, but a conclusion from observation.

For example, in actual life you, the reader, may suddenly hear a cry for help; you see only the window; you then look out and at first see nothing but the moving traffic. But *you do not hear the sound natural to these cars and buses;* instead you hear still only the cry that first startled you. At last you find with your eyes the point from which the sound came; there is a crowd, and someone is lifting the injured man, *who is now quiet.* But, now watching the man, you become aware of the din of traffic passing, and in the midst of its noise there gradually grows the piercing signal of the ambulance. At this your attention is caught by the clothes of the injured man: his suit is like that of your brother, who, you now recall, was due to visit you at two o'clock. In the tremendous tension that follows, the anxiety and uncertainty whether this possibly dying man may not indeed be your brother himself, *all sound ceases* and there exists for your perceptions total silence. Can it be two o'clock? You look at the clock and at the same time you hear its ticking. *This is the first synchronized moment* of an image and its caused sound since first you heard the cry.

Always there exist two rhythms, the rhythmic course of the objective world and the tempo and rhythm with which man observes this world. The world is a whole rhythm, while man receives only partial impressions of this world through his eyes and ears and to a lesser extent through his very skin. The tempo of his impressions varies with the rousing and calming of his emotions, while the rhythm of the objective world he perceives continues in unchanged tempo.

The course of man's perceptions is like editing, the arrangement of which can make corresponding variations in speed, with sound just as with image. It is possible therefore for sound film to be made correspondent to the objective world and man's perception of it together. The image may retain the tempo of the world, while the sound strip follows the changing rhythm of the course of man's perceptions, or vice versa. This is a simple and obvious form for counterpoint of sound and image.

Consider now the question of straightforward dialogue in sound film. In all the films I have seen, persons speaking have been represented in one of two ways. Either the director was thinking entirely in terms of theater, shooting his whole speaking group through in one shot with a moving camera, using thus the screen only as a primitive means of recording a natural phenomenon, exactly as it was used in early silent films before the discovery of the technical possibilities of the cinema had made it an art form. Or else, on the other hand, the director had tried to use the experience of silent film, the art of montage in fact, composing the dialogue from separate shots that he was free to edit. But in this latter case the effect he gained was just as limited as that of the single shots taken with a moving camera, because he simply gave a series of close-ups of a man speaking, allowed him to finish the given phrase on his image, and then followed that shot with one of the man answering. In doing so the director made of montage and editing no more than a cold verbatim report, and switched the spectator's attention from one speaker to another without any adequate emotional or intellectual justification.

Now, by means of editing, a scene in which three or more persons speak can be treated in a number of different ways. For example, the spectator's interest may be held by the speech of the first, and—with the spectator's attention—we hold the close-up of the first person lingering with him when his speech is finished and *hearing* the voice of the commenced answer of the next speaker before passing on to the latter's image. We see the image of the second speaker only *after* becoming acquainted with his voice. Here sound has preceded image.

Or, alternatively, we can arrange the dialogue so that when a question occurs at the end of the given speech, and the spectator is interested in the answer, he can immediately be shown the person addressed, only presently hearing the answer. Here the sound follows the image.

Or, yet again, the spectator having grasped the import of a speech may be interested in its *effect*. Accordingly, while the speech is still in progress, he can be shown a given listener, or indeed given a review of all those present and mark their reactions toward it.

These examples show clearly how the director, by means of editing, can move his audience emotionally or intellectually, so that it experiences a special rhythm in respect to the sequence presented on the screen.

But such a relationship between the director in his cutting room and his future audience can be established only if he has a psychological insight into the nature of his audience and its consequent relationship to the content of the given material.

For instance, if the first speaker in a dialogue grips the attention of the audience, the second speaker will have to utter a number of words before they will so affect the consciousness of the audience that it will adjust its full attention to him. And, contrariwise, if the intervention of the second speaker is more vital to the scene at the moment than the impression made by the first speaker, then the audience's full attention will at once be riveted on him. I am sure, even, that it is possible to build up a dramatic incident with the recorded sound of a speech and the image of the unspeaking listener where the latter's reaction is the most urgent emotion in the scene. Would a director of any imagination handle a scene in a court of justice where a sentence of death is being passed by filming the judge pronouncing sentence in preference to recording visually the immediate reactions of the condemned?

In the final scenes of my first sound film, *Deserter*, my hero tells an audience of the forces that brought him to the Soviet Union. During the whole of the film his worst nature has been trying to stifle his desire to escape these forces; therefore this moment, when he at last succeeds in escaping them and himself desires to recount his cowardice to his fellow workers is the high spot of his emotional life. Being unable to speak Russian, his speech has to be translated.

At the beginning of this scene we see and hear shots longish in duration, first of the speaking hero, then of his translator. In the process of development of the episode the images of the translator become shorter and the majority of his words accompany the images of the hero, according as the interest of the audience automatically fixes on the latter's psychological position. We can consider the composition of sound in this example as similar to the objective rhythm and dependent on the actual time relationships existing between the speakers. Longer or shorter pauses between the voices are conditioned solely by the readiness or hesitation of the next speaker in what he wishes to say. But the image introduces to the screen a new element, the subjective emotion of the spectator and its length of duration; in the image longer or shorter does not depend upon the identity of the speaking man but upon the desire of the spectator to look for a longer or shorter period. Here the sound has an objective character, while the image is conditioned by subjective appreciation; equally we may have the contrary—a subjective sound and an objective image. As illustration of this latter combination I cite a demonstration in the second part of *Deserter;* here my sound is purely musical. Music, I maintain, must in sound film *never be the accompaniment*. It must retain its own line.

In the second part of *Deserter* the image shows at first the broad streets of a Western capital; suave police direct the progress of luxurious cars; everything is decorous, the ebb and flow of an established life. The characteristic of this opening is quietness, until the calm surface is broken by the approach of the workers' demonstration bearing aloft their flag. The streets clear rapidly before the approaching demonstration, its ranks swell with every moment. The spirit of the demonstrators is firm, and their hopes rise as they advance. Our attention is turned to the preparations of the police; their horses and motor vehicles gather as their intervention grows imminent; now their champing horses charge the demonstrators to break their ranks with flying hoofs, the demonstrators resist with all their might, and the struggle rages fiercest round the workers' flag. It is a battle in which all the physical strength is marshaled on the side of the police, sometimes it prevails and the spirit of the demonstrators seems about to be quelled, then the tide turns and the demonstrators rise again on the crest of the wave; at last their flag is flung down into the dust of the streets and trampled to a rag beneath the horses' hoofs. The police are arresting the workers; their whole cause seems lost, suppressed never to rearise—the welter of the fighting dies down—against the background of the defeated despair of the workers we return to the cool decorum of the opening of the scene. There is no fight left in the workers. Suddenly, unexpectedly, before the eyes of the police inspector, the workers' flag appears hoisted anew and the crowd is re-formed at the end of the street.

The course of the image twists and curves, as the emotion within the action rises and falls. Now, if we used music as an *accompaniment* to this image we should open with a quiet melody, appropriate to the soberly guided traffic; at the appearance of the demonstration the music would alter to a march; another change would come at the police preparations, menacing the workers—here the music would assume a threatening character; and when the clash came between workers and police—a tragic moment for the demonstrators—the music would follow this visual mood, descending ever further into themes of despair. Only at the resurrection of the flag could the music turn hopeful. A development of this type would give only the superficial aspect of the scene, the undertones of meaning would be ignored: accordingly I suggested to the composer (Shaporin) the creation of a music the dominating emotional theme of which should *throughout* be courage and the certainty of ultimate victory. From beginning to end the music must develop in a gradual growth of power. This direct, unbroken theme I connected with the complex curves of the image. The image succession gives us in its progress first the emotion of hope, its replacement by danger, then the rousing of the workers' spirit of resistance, at first successful, at last defeated, then finally the gathering and reassembly of their inherent power and the hoisting of their flag. The image's progress curves like a sick man's temperature chart; while the music in direct contrast is firm and steady. When the scene opens peacefully the music is militant; when the demonstration appears the music carries the spectators right into its ranks. With its batoning by the police, the audience feels the rousing of the workers, wrapped in their emotions the audience is itself emotionally receptive to the kicks and blows of the police. As the workers lose ground to the police, the insistent victory of the music grows; yet again, when the workers are defeated and disbanded, the music becomes yet more powerful still in its spirit of victorious exaltation; and when the workers hoist the flag at the end the music at last reaches its climax, and only now, at its conclusion, does its spirit coincide with that of the image.

What role does the music play here? Just as the image is an objective perception of events, so the music expresses the subjective appreciation of this objectivity. The sound reminds the audience that with every defeat the fighting spirit only receives new impetus to the struggle for final victory in the future.

It will be appreciated that this instance, where the sound plays the subjective part in the film, and the image the objective, is only one of many diverse ways in which the medium of sound film allows us to build a counterpoint, and I maintain that only by such counterpoint can primitive naturalism be surpassed and the rich deeps of meaning potential in sound film creatively handled be discovered and plumbed.

(Translated by Marie Seton and Ivor Montagu)

The Art of Sound
RENÉ CLAIR

London, May 1929. Today there is no individual, no company, no financial coalition capable of stopping the triumphant march of the talking film. The industrialists of the American cinema maintain that the public has clearly manifested its liking for talkies, and that they have done no more than meet the public's wishes.

But if the public suddenly got tired of its new toy, the same docile industrialists would certainly refuse to pander further to its whims. For meanwhile the talkies have become one of the biggest business undertakings of our age, to which banks and public utility companies with interests on an imperial scale have linked their fate. So many thousand million dollars have been invested in this enterprise that from now on any and every means will be used to ensure its success. The talking film exists, and those skeptics who prophesy a short reign for it will die themselves long before it's over.

It is too late for those who love the art of moving pictures to deplore the effects of this barbaric invasion. All they can do is try to cut their losses.

The talking film is not everything. There is also the sound film— on which the last hopes of the advocates of the silent film are pinned. They count on the sound film to ward off the danger represented by the advent of talkies, in an effort to convince themselves that the sounds and noises accompanying the moving picture may prove sufficiently entertaining for the audience to prevent it from demanding dialogue, and may create an illusion of "reality" less harmful for the art than the talking film.

However, we have grounds to fear that this solution will only half-satisfy the public. If there is almost universal agreement about the advantages of a mechanical musical accompaniment over the improvisations of a cinema orchestra, opinions vary as far as noises accompanying the action are concerned. The usefulness of such noises is often questionable. If at first hearing they are surprising and amusing, very soon they become tiresome. After we have heard a certain number of sound films, and the first element of surprise has worn off, we are led to the unexpected discovery that the world of noises seems far more limited than we had thought. . . .

. . . Although the talkies are still in their first, experimental stage, they have already, surprisingly enough, produced stereotyped patterns. We have barely "heard" about two dozen of these films, and yet we already feel that the sound effects are hackneyed and that it is high time to find new ones. Jazz, stirring songs, the ticking of a clock, a cuckoo singing the hours, dance-hall applause, a motorcar engine, or breaking crockery—all these are no doubt very nice, but become somewhat tiresome after we have heard them a dozen times in a dozen different films.

We must draw a distinction here between those sound effects which are amusing only by virtue of their novelty (which soon wears off), and those that help one to understand the action, and which excite emotions which could not have been roused by the sight of the pictures alone. The visual world at the birth of the cinema seemed to hold immeasurably richer promise. . . . However, if *imitation* of real noises seems limited and disappointing, it is possible that an *interpretation* of noises may have more of a future in it. Sound cartoons, using "real" noises, seem to point to interesting possibilities.

Unless new sound effects are soon discovered and judiciously employed, it is to be feared that the champions of the sound film may be heading for a disappointment. We shall find ourselves left with the "hundred per cent talkie," as they say here, and that is not a very exhilarating prospect. . . .

. . . Of all the films now showing in London, *Broadway Melody* is having the greatest success. This new American film represents the sum total of all the progress achieved in sound films since the appearance of *The Jazz Singer* two years ago. For anyone who has some knowledge of the complicated technique of sound recording, this film is a marvel. Harry Beaumont, the director, and his collaborators (of whom there are about fifteen, mentioned by name in the credit titles, quite apart from the actors) seem to delight in playing with all the difficulties of visual and sound recording. The actors move, walk, run, talk, shout, and whisper, and their movements and voices are reproduced with a flexibility which would seem miraculous if we did not know that science and meticulous organization have many other miracles in store for us. In this film, nothing is left to chance. Its makers have worked with the precision of engineers, and their achievement is a lesson to those who still imagine that the creation of a film can take place under conditions of chaos known as inspiration.

In *Broadway Melody*, the talking film has for the first time found an appropriate form: it is neither theater nor cinema, but something altogether new. The immobility of planes, that curse of talking films, has gone.

The camera is as mobile, the angles are as varied as in a good silent film. The acting is first-rate, and Bessie Love talking manages to surpass the silent Bessie Love whom we so loved in the past. The sound effects are used with great intelligence, and if some of them still seem superfluous, others deserve to be cited as examples.

For instance, we hear the noise of a door being slammed and a car driving off while we are shown Bessie Love's anguished face watching from a window the departure which we do not see. This short scene in which the whole effect is concentrated on the actress's face, and which the silent cinema would have had to break up in several visual fragments, owes its excellence to the "unity of place" achieved through sound. In another scene we see Bessie Love lying thoughtful and sad; we feel that she is on the verge of tears; but her face disappears in the shadow of a fade-out, and from the screen, now black, emerges a single sob.

In these two instances the sound, at an opportune moment, has replaced the shot. It is by this economy of means that the sound film will most probably secure original effects.

We do not need to *hear* the sound of clapping if we can *see* the clapping hands. When the time of these obvious and unnecessary effects will have passed, the more gifted filmmakers will probably apply to sound films the lesson Chaplin taught in the silent films, when, for example, he suggested the arrival of a train by the shadows of carriages passing across a face. (But will the public, and, above all, the filmmakers, be satisfied with such a discreet use of sound? Will they not prefer an imitation of *all* the noises to an intelligent selection of a few useful ones?)

Already in the films we are shown at present, we often feel that in a conversation it is more interesting to watch the listener's rather than the speaker's face. In all likelihood American directors are aware of this, for many of them have used the device quite often and not unskillfully. This is important, for it shows that the sound film has outgrown its first stage, during which directors were intent on demonstrating, with childish persistence, that the actor's lips opened at exactly the same moment as the sound was heard—in short, that their mechanical toy worked beautifully.

It is the *alternate,* not the simultaneous, use of the visual subject and of the sound produced by it that creates the best effects. It may well be that this first lesson taught us by the birth pangs of a new technique will tomorrow become this same technique's law. . . .

. . . Whenever the most faithful devotees of the silent cinema undertake an impartial study of talking films, they inevitably lose some of their assurance right at the start, for, at its best, the talkie is no longer photographed theater. It is itself. Indeed, by its variety of sounds, its orchestra of human voices, it does give an impression of greater richness than the silent cinema. But are such riches not in fact quite ruinous to it? Through such "progressive" means the screen has lost more than it has gained. It has conquered the world of voices, but it has lost the world of dreams. I have observed people leaving the cinema after seeing a talking film. They might have been leaving a music hall, for they showed no sign of the delightful numbness which used to overcome us after a passage through the silent land of pure images. They talked and laughed, and hummed the tunes they had just heard. *They had not lost their sense of reality.*

(Translated by Vera Traill)

Manifesto: Dialogue on Sound
BASIL WRIGHT and B. VIVIAN BRAUN

Wright: First we must realise that films have always been sound films, even in the silent days. The bigger the orchestra the better the film appeared.

Vivian Braun: Quite. And now that talk has been made possible, do you consider it as good an adjunct as music?

W.: No, because a good "talkie" is a stage play possibly improved by the mechanical advantages of the camera, e.g., pans, close-ups, [and] cutting.

V.B.: You mean that "talkies" are not films?

W.: "Talkies" are technically film, but cinematically they are not.

V.B.: Then the only thing to do is to separate "talkies" and sound films into different categories from the start.

W.: Yes, and so we need not discuss "talkies" any further, let's go on to sound film proper. To begin with, what do the aesthetes say about sound film?

V.B.: A great deal. Firstly they crack up contrapuntal sound and sound imagery as grand artistic effects.

I believe this was originally due to a typical aesthetic reaction when the talking film first came; they refused to recognize them, quite rightly, and then when a year had passed and talking films had not wilted under their disapproval they went to the other extreme.

W.: Yes, I remember the hanging scene in *The Virginian* came in for a lot of praise.

V.B.: Still the aesthetes (I am never quite clear as to who these folk are) have a good deal on their side.

W.: Of course they have; most of the opinions are good solid cinema theory, but the difficulty is that they are unaware of this. It doesn't harm the theory, but it vitiates the practice.

V.B.: Well perhaps we had better analyze the advantages of sound and in particular the advantages of sound imagery, if any, and counterpoint.

W.: But we must not forget that the film is visual, so much so that the perfect film should be satisfactory from every point of view without sound, and, therefore, shown in complete silence.

V.B.: BUT THIS IS NOT TO SAY THAT THE PERFECT FILM COULD NOT BE SUPER-PERFECTED BY THE USE OF SOUND AS AN ADJUNCT.

W.: The use of sound imagistically, the crosscutting of sound and visuals (counterpoint) can undoubtedly be effective, but this does not mean to say that good visuals could not get the same effect more legitimately—in fact I begin to wonder if sound has any advantage at all.

V.B.: Yes it has. It can and does undoubtedly intensify the effect of visuals. But it does not necessarily create that effect. The wrong sound (so powerful is sound) can kill the image.

W.: Yes, and I happen to have seen my pet sequence killed stone dead by the addition of Bach's music, which happens to be better than any film yet made. It killed my visuals because it was too powerful.

V.B.: Which reminds us that one of the most potent arts is sound.

W.: What do we mean by sound in connection with film?

V.B.: Before you start your film you have available every sound in the world from the lark's song to Mae West's voice, to the Jupiter symphony to the internal combustion engine.

W.: And the human voice is no greater in value than any other sound.

V.B.: When synchronizing your film you select, from all the sounds, those you require. If you put natural sound corresponding to visual image, and in particular concentrate on the human voice, you make a "talkie."

W.: If you put any natural sound which doesn't correspond with the visual action, you make a dull highbrow film!

V.B.: If you make a good visual film which is self-contained without any sound, you will find that the only sound which will really intensify your visuals is abstract sound.

W.: Music is abstract.

V.B.: But music confines itself, very rightly, to noises produced by a limited number of special instruments. You are at liberty to orchestrate any sound in the world.

W.: Once orchestrated they will become as abstract as music. Orchestrated abstract sound is the true complement to film.

It can intensify the value of, say, an aeroplane in flight in a way which natural aeroplane sound could not achieve—

V.B.: Because natural sound is uncontrolled. No art is uncontrolled. Abstract sound is completely controlled by the artist, in this case the director of the film.

The director must create his sound as well as his visuals, and as he cannot create natural sound he must orchestrate it for his own purpose.

W.: When he can do this as well as Cezanne orchestrated nature onto canvas, the first real film will have been made.

Sound in Films   ALBERTO CAVALCANTI

The subjects reproducible in the kinetoscope include the most rapid movements, such as quick dancers, blacksmiths hammering on the anvil, &c, or incidents of ordinary life involving much gesture and change of facial expression, and nothing can be more amusing than to see all these shown to the life by the images on the screen, or by the pictures viewed through the lens, especially if, at the same time, the phonograph is made to emit the corresponding sounds. *Discoveries and Inventions of the Nineteenth Century*, by Robert Routledge, B.Sc., F.C.S.

. . . The corresponding sounds.

Mr. Routledge is writing somewhere about 1900.

If I am to give any reasonable account of sound in film, I must begin at the beginning. The story of sound in film begins not, as many historians have presumed, with the introduction of the sound film, but with the invention of film itself. At no period in the history of films has it been customary to show them publicly without some sort of sound accompaniment. In other words, the silent film never existed.

As soon as films were invented, and long before there were such things as picture palaces, filmmakers and showmen began to employ devices to provide a sound accompaniment and complete the illusion. First they used the phonograph, to which Mr. Routledge refers in the extract quoted above. But not for long. Phonograph records are fragile, and synchronization of records has always been a chancy business. Furthermore, as films got longer and longer, they needed more records than it was convenient to make and maintain.

The next device to which showmen turned was the "barker." In those early times, the bulk of film distribution was in the fairgrounds, where barkers were easy to find. These early commentators had almost certainly many of the qualities of today's Pete Smith or [E. V. H.] Emmett. They went so far as to attempt synchronized speech: what he said to her, and what she said to him (the last in falsetto).

When the film started to move into special premises, called cinemas, the use of the barker in turn ceased to be a practical proposition. A man's voice could not be heard easily in a large hall. Besides, a running commentary was monotonous in a full-length show.

Barkers did not disappear all at once. I heard one myself in a provincial British cinema as late as 1910 or 1912. Indeed, as is well known, the barker is still to be heard in the East, in places where the audiences are illiterate and cannot read subtitles, and where sound versions dubbed in the native language are not available. Moreover in certain Eastern countries, I understand, the barker has evolved a very high degree of technique, and individuals have become stars and box-office attractions in their own right.

Let us leave these "atavisms" and get back to the main trend of cinema development.

As the barker went out, the intertitle came in to explain the action and comment upon it. I suppose that strictly speaking any discussion of intertitles is irrelevant in a disquisition upon sound in film, but I cannot resist digressing to give a brief résumé of the progress made by this device.

Ambitious filmmakers raided novels and stage successes for film subjects, without giving any thought to real filmic possibilities, and indeed without any real conception of the essentially kinetic nature of film itself. Before long, films consisted of a long series of elaborate and lengthy titles linked together by scenes.

Continuous development along these lines had its effect upon the actual methods of production. The intertitles took care of the continuity. Actors at this period spent the morning on the sets, having their photographs taken in long and in mid shot, and the afternoon sitting by turn in front of an immobile camera, having their photographs taken in close-up with appropriate "expressions," or appropriate mouthings of the lines quoted in the titles.

Intertitles, since they played such a large part in films, soon became arty. For some reason or other I have always remembered *Burning the Candle*, a story of moral degeneration and redemption, of which the intertitles all bore the picture of a candle behind the printed words. The length of the candle was the measure of the hero's moral status throughout the film. Perhaps I should not bore you with such a chance memory. No doubt you also have lively recollections of the lengths to which such symbolism was carried. Spiders' webs, books, lamps, and other bric-à-brac. A young friend of mine told me he always thought that the "art director" was so called because he drew the pictures which played such an important part in the film.

Moreover, title writing became quite a trade. Certain star title writers got a credit card all to themselves and became box-office attractions. In certain countries, the title writers reedited imported films to provide opportunities for cracks. I remember once seeing in a Belgian cinema a copy of Chaplin's *The Pilgrim* almost ruined by the insertion of hundreds of intertitles, mostly vulgar Flemish puns, each illustrated by cartoons which had nothing to do with the action.

So big a part did titles play in films, that when a German direc-

tor, Lupu Pick, made a film without any intertitles at all, the film was regarded as a sort of curio, and had its publicity arranged accordingly.[1]

Enough about intertitles. What was happening to the sound during the so-called silent period? Music came in. By acquiring a house of its
own, the moving picture rose from the status of the pedlar to a more bourgeois standard, to which the greater refinements of a musical accompaniment were appropriate.

At the beginning music was used for two very different purposes
at once: (a) to drown the noise of the projectors; (b) to give emotional atmosphere.

As cinema developed commercially, the music became more
elaborate and played a larger and larger part in the show as a whole. Cinema owners vied with each other to attract the public. The piano became a
trio. The trio became a salon orchestra. The salon orchestra became a symphony orchestra.

Not only the composition of the orchestra but also the technique
of musical accompaniment enjoyed, or suffered, continuous development.
The system of leitmotifs was introduced. Certain themes were associated with
certain characters, and played whenever they appeared on the screen. A
cinema musician's desk contained a thick bundle of music of every possible
kind—his music for the big picture. After every half-dozen pieces, or so, there
was a card inserted, bearing the legend Theme 1, Theme 4, Theme 3.
Throughout the whole of the feature, the orchestra kept breaking into these
themes, which the individual players kept open at the side of their desks, or
on the floor, or "carried in their heads."[2] So it came about that the music
kept hopping from Beethoven to Irish ballads, and back to Beethoven via
Moussorgsky. One could quite often hear portions of *Pique Dame, Londonderry Air, La Paloma*, the *Choral* Symphony, *Baby's Sweetheart*, and the
Mass in B Minor, all within a period of five minutes. And in the next five
minutes the *Death of Ase, Baby's Sweetheart* again, *L'Aube Radieuse, Kol
Nidrei, Londonderry Air* again, *Symphony Pathetique*. Such artistic purity
consorted well with the architectural features of the cinemas, which often
combined Moorish, Greek, and Gothic elements in varied splendor. It is not
unlikely that some future historian will call this the "surrealist" period in
modern art.

Meanwhile the small harmonium used in the orchestra to make
up for the lack of woodwinds had been supplanted by the cinema organ,
equipped with every device for rendering "effects." As we all know to our
cost, these organs survive, and in fact are used in most cinemas to provide
what a friend of mine calls "the musical interruption." Take a look at the
console of one of them next time you get the chance. In all probability (and
with certainty if the organ was built in the so-called silent days) you will see

a number of stops labeled train, chains, crockery, horse, siren, side drum, bass drum, cymbals, piano, airplane, child crying, and so on; this will give you some idea of the absurdity of referring to the "great days of the silent cinema."

In an incredible architectural setting, and in the midst of the most appalling noise, the so-called silent film expired.

The sound film came in. This was the time, this was the golden opportunity, for some brilliant analyst to come forward and work out then and there the principles which should govern the employment of the three sound elements: speech, music, and noise. For these elements, as we have seen, had been a part of cinema from the very beginning. Now the time had come when they could be organized properly within the fabric of the film itself, so that the creations of the director, in the domain of sound, could be made a permanent part of his film.

But alas, no analyst came forward. Film people, by and large, have never been given to constructive analysis, which is one reason why no proper "critique" of the film has ever been written. Film people, like the early scientists, prefer trial and error to any other method of investigation and construction.

The rest of my story, on the historical side, is thus a story of slow progress made with immense expenditure of time, money, and energy.

In the first place, many of the silent film directors, including some of the more intelligent of them, actually refused to believe that the sound film would ever establish itself at all. It would not last three months. (I notice that many film directors of the present day are making precisely the same mistake with regard to color.) Silence meant art. Sound was a new toy, of which the public would soon tire.

They were wrong about the public tiring. But they were right enough about the way in which sound was taken up. The public, and the producers alike, fastened upon the one thing which was apparently novel in the new invention—synchronized speech. The films went speech-mad.

While the recalcitrant silent film directors stood like Canute trying to stem the tide, a horde of theatrical people descended upon the studio in order to make films. Now that films can speak, they said, we are going to make them. They further confounded the situation, because they knew nothing about films, and started off with the absurd assumption that in order to make a sound film it is only necessary to photograph a play. Accordingly, as we shall see, the next few years saw millions of dollars poured into productions which were on the wrong lines, and which, after the first year or two, bored the public to such an extent that film producers were forced, in self-defense, to adapt their methods.

Here someone might have seen the possibilities of the other form of speech—nonsynchronized speech—commentary. But the naïveté of the public and producers alike was all against the exploitation and development of this excellent dramatic device. The people wanted to see the people speaking in sync. To my lasting regret, nonsync speech, i.e., commentary, was relegated to the comparatively minor role of providing continuity and "story" in travelogues, newsreels, and documentary. Yet even in this narrow field, on the rare occasions when commentary is used creatively, its value is at once apparent. Consider for instance the great effect produced by Pete Smith, or Emmett, wisecracking against the pictures. Consider more exalted uses of the device, in documentary. Think of Watt's *Night Mail,* Lorentz's *The River,* and Ivens's *Spanish Earth,* to take three recent examples. If you doubt that commentary, which the makers of dramatic theatrical films have thrown on one side, is a dramatic device of immense potentialities, think again about Ivens's *Spanish Earth.* The effect of this film, which no audience can resist, arises from the contrast between the cool, tragic dignity of Hemingway's prose on the one hand, and the terrors of the images on the other. One is reminded of Wordsworth's brilliant flash of insight expressed in his definition of poetry as "emotion recollected in tranquillity." In *Spanish Earth* as in *The River* and *Night Mail,* the direct emotional stimulus is in the images, while the commentary supplies in contrast the organized, universalized interpretation. The poetic effect is great. The emotion is on the screen, the tranquillity in the sound track. Out of the conflict between the objectiveness of the picture and the subjectiveness of the commentary comes a third thing, a dramatic feeling which is different in essentials from, and I think deeper in effect than, either of the two elements which are combined to create it.

But as I have said, the makers of dramatic films, at the beginning of the sound era, threw commentary on one side as being none of their business, and put all their energies into the production of photographed plays. Here the theatrical people felt that they were on ground they knew. They knew how to produce stage plays. But it never occurred to them that a film is not, and never can be, the same thing as a play. In order to reach this not very advanced conclusion they would have had to do some theoretical investigation, which as I said above was not their strong point.

They might have gone back twenty years, for instance, to the first dramatic silent films. If they had taken some of them out of the vaults and run them, they could have saved themselves a great deal of embarrassment. For the same mistake was being made in 1909 as they were proceeding to make over again in 1929. The early silent directors learned by a process of trial and error which lasted for many years, that [the] technique of stage acting is not the same as the technique of film acting. The gestures and attitudes are far too striking. By a long process, a technique of film acting was built up, in which the skillful actor employed restrained gestures, attitudes, and expressions which, magnified and emphasized on the screen, got him the effects he wanted. At the beginning of the sound period, when the actors from the theater poured into the studios, this lesson had to be learned all over again.

Further a simple analogy might have been drawn, which would have indicated at the outset that just as the screen required restraint in gesture, it also required restraint in delivery of speech. But this lesson had to be learned by trial and error. The microphone is a very searching instrument. The round-mouthed oratory of stage delivery becomes intolerable affectation when it is amplified by loudspeakers in the cinema (unless of course, as in some of the magnificent speeches of Paul Muni or Charles Laughton, the context justifies the use of rhetoric). A technique of voice delivery proper to the film was in the long run worked out, largely through the success of American Grade B pictures and the rise to fame of such actors as Spencer Tracy, James Cagney, and Gary Cooper. Film dialogue, it was discovered, was most effective and dramatic when it was uttered clearly, rapidly, and evenly, almost thrown away. Emphasis and emotional effect must of necessity be left to the care of the visuals.

But the difference between stage and screen goes far beyond such externals as the technique of miming and speaking. It is an organic difference. A play is all speech. Words, words, words. Now, when the early talkie directors put whole plays on the screen, they were forgetting the lesson which the barker had taught them—that the continuous utterance of words in the cinema is monotonous. More important, the preponderance of the speech element in the resulting film crushed out the other elements—visual interest, noise, and music. In a stage play there is no room for any sound but the telephone bells and taxi hooters, which for a long time were the exclusive embellishment of the talkie sound tracks and thus in due course became excessively fatiguing and ridiculous.

Moreover, films must move, or they become intolerable. Long stretches of dialogue inevitably cancel movement and visual variety, in spite of all that the most enlightened director can do (you may remember how in the early "trial" films the camera used to be spun round in quick pans from one face to another in the courtroom, just because the director, stifled by words, words, words, felt that he had to get his visuals moving somehow). In the years that have passed since the introduction of the sound film, film has fought for and won an ascendance over speech. In some of the most successful films, speech almost takes second place to visuals. In the trial scene of *Mr. Deeds Goes to Town,* for instance, the hero does not say a word during the first three-quarters of the scene. As a further example, consider the brilliant climax of *The Charge of the Light Brigade,* a film which in a sense represents the triumph of movie over stage.

So much for speech. Summing up: film producers have learned in the course of the last ten years that use of speech must be economical, and be balanced with the other elements in the film, that the style employed by the dialogue writers must be literal, conversational, nonliterary: that the delivery must be light, rapid, and offhand, to match the quick movements of the action, and the cuts from speaker to speaker.

It must not be thought that all films adhere to these principles. Far from it. But nine times out of ten it will be found that where a film is ponderous and boring, it owes this defect to bad handling of the speech element in respect of some of the principles mentioned above (I am thinking, for instance, of *Winterset*).

Music

Soon after the sound film was introduced, the "musical" film came into being. This was at first an exact analogy of the photographed stage play—only instead of a play, a big Broadway musical show was photographed. So great were the opportunities for spectacle and mass effects, that this kind of film had a big momentum at the beginning, and for some years such spectacles continued to be produced. But there was always something fundamentally wrong in them—something that the public gradually recognized and rejected. They were not films at all, in the pure sense of the word. Scenes stayed on the screen too long. "Numbers" dragged out their length on the track. The story was slight, and contained nothing exciting. The action did not advance—it flowed like an underground river to appear only between the "scenes" and disappear again. One of the last examples was *The Great Ziegfeld*—a huge, magnificent spectacle, but on the whole, a bore.

The "musical" film began to adapt itself.

Somehow or other, in the interreaction of public and producers, the musical melodrama was born. Sensing what was wanted, the producers called in the police. They built their film around a murder or a crime plot, and made the stage stuff a mere adjunct of the story. These backstage films had a great vogue.

Alongside the musical melodrama came the "hoofer" films—Astaire-Rogers, Eleanor Powell—the emphasis here was transferred to the personality of the stars. The story was strengthened, the films took shape, the stars and their adventures became more and more important, the spectacle less and less. "Film" was fighting back, against spectacle, in the "musical" film, just as it had fought back, and won, in the old "silent" days, during which the film people learned by trial and error that the public is interested in individuals and action, not masses and picture. Now they were learning that lesson all over again.

The prodigy performers, such as Shirley Temple, Judy Garland, Deanna Durbin, gave producers an excellent chance to put musical performance in its proper place in film. They combined in themselves performance-ability and a high degree of individual star-value. The public is far too interested in Shirley Temple's virtuosity in all departments to be content to watch a long series of songs sung by her in only one of her many capacities.

If you want to see *performed-music* used in films in a way that seems to me exactly right, consider the denouement of *Three Smart Girls Grow Up*. The technique here is amazing, and represents the musical film at its best. Deanna gets up on the dais to sing a song in honor of her sister, who is marrying the wrong man. The solution is to be as simple one—the substitution of bridegrooms, an old and respected device. Charles Winninger comes solemnly in with the bride on his arm, solemnly overshoots the parson, continues to the door, takes her out, comes back without her (but with his own hat, which her true lover offstage had appropriated early in the film) and as solemnly gives to the deserted bridegroom the girl he really wants. And all while Deanna is singing. The continued song translates the whole thing to a realm in which all things are credible, because one is loath to disbelieve anything while Miss Durbin is singing. The song also gives feeling-tone (as the orchestra did in the best days of the "silent" cinema). The song also keeps Deanna the star, although the action concerns only her supporters. The song also makes the action "silent," while it is being sung, and gives the director a chance to use a technique of suggestion (such as the excellent hat gag) which sound films had all but lost. It is a great piece of work—a triumph—for what? For silence? No. For music? No—for the creative combination of two elements, music and images. The unrelated song, the "silent" action—the fusion of these two creates a third element, a sort of dramatic excitement, in which both music and images are enhanced, and suspense, humor, sentiment, acquire almost sensational valency.

As it seems to me at present, that moment in Deanna Durbin's film (only the most obviously successful of many such moments) is the end of a period and the beginning of another. A musical performance is presumably worth *looking* at in a concert hall (because nearly everybody looks), but it is not worth looking at in a cinema. The screen is so selective and so emphatic and so commanding that things must happen on it—dramatic things—or the people get bored. Thus when musical performances came into the movies, they nearly wrecked them—but in the course of evolution, action has absorbed such music as it absorbed speech—conditioned it, em-

ployed, subjugated it, transcended it. In the Durbin films, this process is all
but complete.

So much for "performance" music. What about "incidental"
music?—accompanying music in speech films? Here there is no great progress to report. It is a sad story, but the sound film producers made the same
mistake with music, when they got their hands on it, as the cinema owners
made in the past, when the responsibility was theirs.[3] Let me mention in
turn their sins of commission and sins of omission.

They began with big orchestras playing big "symphonic" or-
chestrations—they began where the "silent" film left off, as far as the size of
the orchestra was concerned. And they have continued as they began. And
as for the idiom employed in film music, it has varied little in the last ten
years. It is an idiom suited to an atmosphere of pomp and display. In style,
the music of the cinema, by and large, represents a fixation at a stage of
development which the art itself left behind about thirty years ago. It is music of the late romantic period: Tschaikovsky, Rachmaninoff, Sibelius, are
the spiritual fathers of most cinema music.

Now there is nothing wrong with heavy romantic music (for those
who like it) just as there is nothing wrong with suet-pudding or plum-duff.
But I can scarcely suppress a smile when I hear the title music of a new film,
because nine times out of ten it is the same as the title music of the last film
I saw, no matter what the subject of the film may be. It is a great swelling
theme suggesting that the photoplay to be presented is the best, the weight-
iest, the most profound, that the world has ever seen. How pretentious and
self-conscious this music is, the general public does not seem to notice: perhaps because they don't listen to it, and because it generally stops when the
action begins. It did not always do so. In early talkies it ran under most of
the action and even went so far as to point it with synchronized effects which
were derived from the manner of the "silent" orchestra—and were just about
the last word in outrageous absurdity. Happily that period is over. Nowa-
days music is used as an advertisement at the beginning and at the end of
all films, and comes in during the film only at certain well-defined places—
a train journey, a pursuit, a transition.

It is the omissions of the film producers that are most interesting.
The main one is, as I have noticed above, their omission to recognize that
music is developing rapidly in modern times. The sonata was a structural
formula invented in order to give internal relevance to musical compositions,
so that they could be listened to at concerts in their own right, without a
"program" of events or a "story" in the form of a poem or a ballet. The
trend of music, in the course of the last fifty years, has been away from the
concert hall (sonatas and symphonies), toward the theater (opera, ballet),
and further out still into the world. You have only to think of Debussy's pictures, and Stravinsky's *Firebird,* and such things as Alban Berg's *Wozzek,*

and then to take some further examples, in order to realize that modern music is nearly all "descriptive," not "absolute." Anyhow, most "modern" music (Walton's *Façade,* for instance) is written for a dramatic context and much of it sounds bad in a concert hall. Now does it not seem absurd that while music is clamoring for dramatic contexts as opportunities for expression, and the film is in great need of means of vital expression and suggestion, there is no marriage between film and modern music? Instead, the filmmakers on the whole insist on giving us music in a style which was stale in 1895. But what opportunities there are—if only they would take them! The modern composer specializes in all that is "counter, original, spare, strange" in suggestions and moods, in terrors and nameless questionings, "fallings from us, vanishings"—excellent music for film. But most of the time we hear his music on the wireless, where it means nothing. In film, the modern music idiom, where it has been intelligently tried (as in France), is vital, immediate, and contributes much to the success of the production.

Consider in passing what happened to *Romeo and Juliet.* It is impossible to realize how bad this film was unless you reflect upon how good it might have been. The music—Tschaikovsky's—fitted the production perfectly—that is to say, it was music of the indoors, heavy with scent, unventilated, introverted, consorting well with the glorified seraglio that was the set designer's picture of ancient Verona. Tschaikovsky's main musical theme has since come out in its true colors as a crooner's nostalgic drag called "Our Love." This is the musical accompaniment, if you please, of a play by Shakespeare which presents one of the purest love-stories of all time—full of stark, sharp terrifying beauty. One can't represent such a love with Tschaikovsky's music. One might as well try to etch with a paintbrush. I would not have had any other music in that particular production, all the same. For that, it was perfect. But in another production, I should certainly like to entrust the music to a good modern composer. Shakespeare's strangely universal genius needs to be interpreted anew in every age—by the most modern means. The recent film *Romeo and Juliet* was thirty years out of date all the way through.

Not for the dignities of Shakespeare only, but also for all other dramatic presentations, I plead for modern music, mood-music, because I am sure that it has a great deal to contribute.

Noise

Finally, the third element, natural sound, or noise. Here it must be confessed that practically all natural sound used in films has been in synchronization: that is to say, the appropriate accompaniment of the thing seen. The door-bang, the telephone bell, the roar of the aero engine, the wheels of the train, the rushing of the waterfall. Such obvious sound images pass practically unnoticed. By now they are quite banal.

Yet there have been instances of the exceptionally skillful use of noise. To take a famous example. You remember in Fritz Lang's *M*—the murderer has the habit of whistling a few bars of Grieg's "Troll Dance." Lang, with his usual brilliance, built this up to the climax of his film, at which the murderer was recognized by a blind man. Now, quite apart from the fact that Lang made the tune part of the plot, do you remember anything noteworthy about the effect of the sound on the dramatic intensity of the film? I do. I seem to recollect quite clearly that this harmless little tune became terrifying. It was the symbol of Peter Lorre's madness and blood-lust. Just a bar or two of music. And do you remember at what points (toward the end) the music was most baleful and threatening? I do. It was when you could hear the noise, but could not see the murderer. In other words, when the tune was used "nonsync," as film people say.

Now let us go further. Have you ever heard a noise in the night—nonsync—i.e., without having any notion of what caused it? Of course. And you left your bed and went down to find out what caused the bang, or the thump.

These two examples—Lang's whistle and the bump in the night which you got up to investigate—lead us to consider two ways of using sound for dramatic effect, both methods based on suggestion. Lang's way was to use a recognized and identified sound. He used it to suggest the menacing nearness of his character—without showing the character. Suggestion is always more effective in drama than statement. This particular trick is capable of great development. A black screen, feet crunching on gravel: and so on. A friend of mine, making a comedy, made an amusing effect out of the tick of a clock in a dentist's waiting room; he speeded up the tick when the nurse came to claim the victim. I have a bit of dog-barking in my sound library which I sometimes stick into the track when I wish to suggest the open air, and a pleasant, gay atmosphere. It is almost essential that there should be no dog on the screen, or the effect is lost, because then suggestion becomes statement. The crying of seagulls was a sound-suggestion-device which became so common with film experimenters that it was laughed out of court.

The other device is the use of unrecognized and unidentified sound. Now, let us go back to the noise that got you out of bed. Had it been a voice, you could have recognized it as your wife's or your son's or your neighbor's, or an unknown, and it would not have disturbed you. But noises have this quality—they do not inevitably suggest what made them. This means that certain types of noise can be used "incognito." An example: when we

made *North Sea* we had to do a studio-crash, to represent a sudden catastrophe on board a ship. The sound staff approached the B.B.C. and everybody else, but they could not get a combination of sounds that would be
sufficiently terrifying. They asked me. I told them at once that they would
have to get a loud, unidentifiable sound to stick into the crash. They got it.
A horrid metallic squeal which suggested that the vessel had been squeezed
diagonally and had started all her seams. It was a wonderful noise—because
it was unrecognizable. To take an example from the so-called silent days.
An airplane was flying toward us. The music director "cut" the orchestra,
and a strange, frightsome sound began, and got louder and louder. It was
nothing like an airplane, but very frightening. When I got home I was still
wondering how this noise was done. Then I got it. It was a noise I had known
all my life—an open cymbal beaten with two soft-headed drumsticks. How
familiar! Yet it had lost its identity, and retained only its dramatic quality,
used in conjunction with the picture. Pictures are clear and specific, noises
are vague. The picture had changed a cymbal noise into an air-noise.

That is why noise is so useful. It speaks directly to the emotions.
Babies are afraid of loud bangs, long before they can have learned that there
is any connection between noise and danger—before they even know there's
such a thing as danger. Many dogs can be made to run away by beating a
tin tray. Pictures speak to the intelligence. Noise seems to by-pass the intelligence and speak to something very deep and inborn—as the instance of
the baby seems to show.

This last reflection leads to my conclusion.

The outstanding characteristic of the screen image is its literal-
ness. The cinema picture is a medium of literal statement. I have not the
space to prove my point, but I doubt if it will be disputed. If you have seen
a scene being shot, you will know what I mean. The scene looks like a studio set to you, because your "wide-angle" eyes take in a range of objects
which includes the roof and walls of the studio—in the morning when you
see the rushes, you find that the funnel-like gaze of the camera has somehow made it all look literally true. (Strangely enough, that is why costume
plays often fail to convince on the screen. The camera is so literal-minded
that if you show it actors dressed up, it *sees* actors-dressed-up, not characters.)

Now for sound.

I think that we have enough material in this review of sound to
conclude that, while the picture is the medium of statement, the sound is
the medium of suggestion. This is not to say that the picture cannot make
suggestions, or that the sound cannot make statements. That would be far
too much to say. But I think we can allow that the picture lends itself to clear
statement, while the sound lends itself to suggestion.

During what is called the "great silent days of the German cinema," we saw a great attempt to use visuals for suggestion rather than statement. While it cannot be denied that many startling effects were obtained, I think it must at the same time be admitted that this genre went out of fashion because the directors were attempting to use the camera in a way which is not proper to it. At this time the pictures got farther and farther away from reality, until a stage was reached at which they became ridiculous, because the credulity of the audiences was finally overstrained.

And I think that we can add that the present trend of visual[s] is toward a more and more faithful representation of reality. In my opinion this process is inevitable, because of the nature of the camera itself as an instrument (and perhaps also because of the nature of vision itself as a sense), but as I have said before I have not space to take this point up and try to prove it.

I now propose to run briefly over this ground we have covered, and see if we cannot reach a further conclusion about the technique of sound. I may as well give my own conclusions. I believe in the first place that suggestion is such a powerful device in presentation that film cannot be fully expressive if it allows itself to become primarily a medium of statement, and I believe that whenever the device of suggestion is required for dramatic or poetic purposes, the line to follow is the exploitation of the sound elements. I also think that we have discovered a clue, in our review of the history of sound in film. And I think this clue can be indicated simply, perhaps too simply, in the cryptic expression "nonsync."

It seems to me that all the most suggestive sound devices have been nonsync.

The commentator appeared on the scene in the nineties. He spoke nonsync, with an effect which we can only guess at, but which, arguing from an early historical parallel (the Greek chorus), was probably highly dramatic.

He allowed himself to transgress into sync speech, and I cannot help thinking that his efforts became absurd.

Then music came into the picture theaters. At first it was nonsync, and I do not think any of us are too old to remember how effective nonsync musical accompaniment could be. But then music in turn succumbed to the attraction of attempting synchronization (much more dangerous in the case of music than speech), and perished, by disrupting itself with bangs and whistles. Then came the great era of sync speech—which the public has found to be a bore, but which still continues. On the other hand nonsync speech (commentary), although it has not been exploited in dramatic films, is showing excellent dramatic results in the best short films and documentaries. I believe it is only a question of time until commentary comes into the dramatic films, at least in an experimental way. Indeed in *Confessions of a Nazi Spy*, the process may be said to have begun.

Finally, music and noise. I think I have indicated in my analysis of successful modern practice that the most suggestive way of employing these elements is to use them nonsync.

With noise, we must include silence. Even in the so-called silent days, a clever musical director would sometimes cut the orchestra dead at a big dramatic moment on the screen (producing an effect similar to Handel's general pause just before the end of the "Hallelujah Chorus"). Yet sound film directors do not appear to be aware of the possibilities of the use of silence. One brilliant early example, however, will remain always in my memory. It is in Walter Ruttmann's *Melody of the World*. He built up a big climax of guns in a war sequence, worked it up to a close-up of a woman emitting a piercing shriek, and cut at once to rows of white crosses—in silence.

In the hands of an artist of Ruttmann's caliber silence can be the loudest of noises, just as black, in a brilliant design, can be the brightest of colors.

Notes

1. This was *Scherben (Shattered)* produced in 1921 from a scenario by Carl Mayer. A comprehensive chapter on intertitles can be found in Eric Elliott's *Anatomy of Motion Picture Art* (Territet, Switzerland: Pool, 1928), pp. 74–82.—Ed. of *Films*.

2. The largest film companies themselves prepared and published complete ready-made musical scores and "cue-sheets" for distribution with the films.—Ed. of *Films*.

3. Largely because the composers of the old ready-made scores became the musical directors of the sound studios.—Ed. of *Films*.

A New Laocoön:
Artistic Composites and the
Talking Film   RUDOLF ARNHEIM

In the preceding sections we have worked out some fundamental concepts, which can be useful in judging the talking film. From what I have said it follows that, first of all, there should be a dominant medium. This part would fall to the moving image since predominance of the word would lead to the theater. The question is, then, whether the art of the animated image, which has been developed as the silent film, could use the kind of libretto through which the opera provides a skeleton of the dramatic action.

First of all, we must repeat here that by means of the opera libretto (as well as its predecessors in church music, etc.) music conquered a vast new realm, namely, that of dramatic music or the musical drama. In the case of the film, the dialogue does not give access to a new type of work. At best, it enlarges what exists. We have to remember that in silent film the dialogue, as given in the titles, was not at all the foundation and starting point of the work, from which the pictures were developed. They were a mere expedient added secondarily and for the purpose of explanation to works conceived and realized in images. Perhaps the spoken dialogue may not be able to fulfill even this humble function. What is useful for the opera, may be harmful for the film.

Will an artist, that is, a person guided by a sure sensitivity for the medium he employs, ever feel impelled to "set" a dialogue "to pictures" instead of creating in pictures? Since pictures are what attract him, he might be tempted by speech as a technical device that would sharpen the meaning of his scenes, save him the tortuous detours necessary to explain the plot, and open up a larger field of subjects. Now, in fact, dialogue makes possible an extensive development of the external action, and particularly also the internal action. No fairly complicated event or state of mind can be conveyed by pictures alone. Therefore, the addition of spoken dialogue has made storytelling easier. In this sense, film dialogue has been defined by some critics as a device for saving time, space, and ingenuity—a saving that would reserve the available limited length of the film and the creative energy of the maker for the truly relevant content of the work. It remains to be seen, how-

ever, whether there is, in the movies, any justification for the kind of involved plot that we find in the novel and the play.

We can easily understand why the large movie audience has applauded the introduction of the spoken word. What the audience wants is
to take part in exciting events as fully as possible. The best way of achieving
this is, in a certain sense, the mixture of visual action and dialogue: external
events are shown concretely to the eye, and at the same time the thoughts,
intentions, and emotions of the characters are communicated through words
in the directest and most natural way. Moreover the felt presence of the events
is enormously enhanced by the sound of voices and other noises. The audience will object only when the dialogue is cut down so much that it does
not explain the action or when, on the contrary, there is too little outer action, and all the talking becomes tiresome. In a crude way, these objections
to the talking film are the same as those of the connoisseur.

Dialogue Narrows the World of the Film

The example of the opera seemed to justify and recommend the use of dialogue. But not without caution can we compare the art of sound and the art
of pictures in their relation to the spoken word. One of the main characteristics of dramatic dialogue is that it limits the action to the human performer.
This suits music perfectly since, as we said, the opera was created precisely
in order to represent human beings in dramatic action musically. The image,
of course, does not need dialogue to present man, but in the visual world
the human kind does not enjoy the leading role it has on the stage. Granted
that in certain paintings human figures hold the foreground gigantically; but
just as often painting shows man as a part of his environment, which gives
meaning to him and to which he gives meaning. Man appears as a part of
the Creation, from which he can be isolated only artificially. The moving picture was from the beginning more concerned with the world animated by
man than with man set off against his world. Therefore, to be limited by
dialogue to the performances of the human figure was bound to seem intolerable.

The presentation of man's natural setting had been one of the
achievements that justified the existence of the movies next to the theater.
Naturally, the silent film also had often shown the actor in close-ups. But
more importantly, it had created a union of silent man and silent things as
well as of the (audible) person close-by and the (inaudible) one at a far dis-

tance. In the universal silence of the image, the fragments of a broken vase could "talk" exactly the way a character talked to his neighbor, and a person approaching on a road and visible on the horizon as a mere dot "talked" as someone acting in close-up. This homogeneity, which is completely foreign to the theater but familiar to painting, is destroyed by the talking film: it endows the actor with speech, and since only he can have it, all other things are pushed into the background.

Now there is a limit to the visual expression that can be drawn from the human figure, particularly if the picture has to accompany dialogue. Pure pantomime knows of three ways to overcome this limitation. It can give up the portraying of plots and instead present the "absolute" movement of the body, that is, dance. Here the human body becomes an instrument for melodic and harmonic forms, which are superior to mere pantomime, as music is superior to a (hypothetical) art of natural noises. Secondly, pantomime can adopt the solution of the silent film, namely, become a part of the richer universe in motion. And finally, it can become subservient to dramatic speech—as it does in the theater. But to the pantomime of the talking film all three of these solutions are inaccessible: it cannot become dance because dance does not need speech and perhaps does not even tolerate it; it cannot submerge in the huge *orbis pictus* of the silent film because of its tie to the human figure; and it cannot become the servant of speech without giving up its own self.

The Dialogue Paralyzes Visual Action

Not only does speech limit the motion picture to an art of dramatic portraiture, it also interferes with the expression of the image. The better the silent film, the more strictly it used to avoid showing people in the act of talking, important though talking is in real life. The actors expressed themselves by posture and facial expression. Additional meaning came from the way the figure was shown within the framework of the picture, by lighting, and particularly by the total context of sequence and plot. The visual counterpart of speech, that is, the monotonous motions of the mouth, yields little and, in fact, can only hamper the expressive movement of the body. The motions of the mouth convincingly demonstrate that the activity of talking compels the actor into visually monotonous, meaningless, and often ludicrous behavior.

It is obvious that speech cannot be attached to the immobile image (painting, photography); but it is equally ill-suited for the silent film, whose means of expression resemble those of painting. It was precisely the absence of speech that made the silent film develop a style of its own, capable of condensing the dramatic situation. To separate or to find each other, to win or to give in, to be friends or enemies—all such themes were neatly presented by a few simple attitudes, such as a raising of the head or of an arm, or the bowing of one person to another. This had led to a most cinegenic species of tale, which was full of simple happenings and which, with the coming of the talking film, was replaced by a theater-type play, poor in external action but well developed psychologically. This meant replacing the visually fruitful image of man in action with the sterile one of the man who talks.

As far as the opera is concerned, there is no objection to the dialogue centering the action around the human character; nor is there any to the visual paralysis of the actor. What the opera wants is, we said, the musical expression of man in action. It has little use for the expressive virtues of the animated image on the stage, which remains secondary, complementary, explicatory. The opera director does not hesitate to stop the stage action in favor of long arias. This gives the dialogue plenty of time, and in fact too much time: phrases have to be stretched and repeated to comply with the music. So that what hurts the film does not hurt the opera.

If after discussing the theoretical difficulties that lie in the way of the talking film we look around to see whether in practice the motion picture production has worked out satisfactory solutions, we find our diagnosis confirmed. The average talking film today endeavors to combine visually poor scenes full of dialogue with the completely different traditional style of rich, silent action. In comparison with the epoch of the silent film there is also an impressive decline of artistic excellence, in the average films as well as in the peak productions—a trend that cannot be due entirely to the ever-increasing industrialization.

It may seem surprising that mankind should produce in large number works based on a principle that represents such a radical artistic impoverishment if compared with the available purer forms. But is such a contradiction really surprising at a time at which in other respects, too, so many people live a life of unreality and fail to attain the true nature of man and its fitting manifestations? If the opposite happened in the movies, would not such a pleasant inconsistency be even more surprising?

There is comfort, however, in the fact that hybrid forms are quite unstable. They tend to change from their own unreality into purer forms, even though this may mean a return to the past. Beyond our blundering there are inherent forces that, in the long run, overcome error and incompleteness and direct human action toward the purity of goodness and truth.

Theory of the Film: Sound
BELA BALAZS

The Acoustic World

It is the business of the sound film to reveal for us our acoustic environment, the acoustic landscape in which we live, the speech of things and the intimate whisperings of nature; all that has speech beyond human speech, and speaks to us with the vast conversational powers of life and incessantly influences and directs our thoughts and emotions, from the muttering of the sea to the din of a great city, from the roar of machinery to the gentle patter of autumn rain on a windowpane. The meaning of a floorboard creaking in a deserted room, a bullet whistling past our ear, the deathwatch beetle ticking in old furniture, and the forest spring tinkling over the stones. Sensitive lyrical poets always could hear these significant sounds of life and describe them in words. It is for the sound film to let them speak to us more directly from the screen.

Discovery of Noise

The sounds of our day-to-day life we hitherto perceived merely as a confused noise, as a formless mass of din, rather as an unmusical person may listen to a symphony; at best he may be able to distinguish the leading melody, the rest will fuse into a chaotic clamor. The sound film will teach us to analyze even chaotic noise with our ear and read the score of life's symphony. Our ear will hear the different voices in the general babble and distinguish their character as manifestations of individual life. It is an old maxim that art saves us from chaos. The arts differ from each other in the specific kind of chaos which they fight against. The vocation of the sound film is to redeem us from the chaos of shapeless noise by accepting it as expression, as significance, as meaning. . . .

     Only when the sound film will have resolved noise into its elements, segregated individual, intimate voices, and made them speak to us separately in vocal, acoustic close-ups; when these isolated detail-sounds will be collated again in purposeful order by sound-montage, will the sound film have become a new art. When the director will be able to lead our ear as he could once already lead our eye in the silent film and by means of such guidance along a series of close-ups will be able to emphasize, separate, and bring into relation with each other the sounds of life as he has done with its sights, then the rattle and clatter of life will no longer overwhelm us in a lifeless chaos of sound. The sound camera will intervene in this chaos of sound, form it and interpret it, and then it will again be man himself who speaks to us from the sound screen. . . .

The Picture Forms the Sound

In a sound film there is no need to explain the sounds. We see together with the word the glance, the smile, the gesture, the whole chord of expression, the exact nuance. Together with the sounds and voices of things we see their physiognomy. The noise of a machine has a different coloring for us if we see the whirling machinery at the same time. The sound of a wave is different if we see its movement. Just as the shade and value of a color changes according to what other colors are next to it in a painting, so the *timbre* of a sound changes in accordance with the physiognomy or gesture of the visible source of the sound seen together with the sound itself in a sound film in which acoustic and optical impressions are equivalently linked together into a single picture.

In a radio play the stage has to be described in words, because sound alone is not space-creating.

Silence

Silence, too, is an acoustic effect, but only where sounds can be heard. The presentation of silence is one of the most specific dramatic effects of the sound film. No other art can reproduce silence, neither painting nor sculpture, neither literature nor the silent film could do so. Even on the stage silence appears only rarely as a dramatic effect and then only for short moments. Radio plays cannot make us feel the depths of silence at all, because when no sounds come from our set, the whole performance has ceased, as we cannot see any silent continuation of the action. The sole material of the wireless play being sound, the result of the cessation of sound is not silence but just nothing.

Silence and Space

Things that we see as being different from each other, appear even more different when they emit sounds. They all sound different when they do this, but they are all silent in the same way. There are thousands of different sounds and voices, but the substance of silence appears one and the same for all. That is at first hearing. Sound differentiates visible things, silence brings them closer to each other and makes them less dissimilar. Every painting shows this happy harmony, the hidden common language of mute things conversing with each other, recognizing each others' shapes, and entering into relations with each other in a composition common to them all. This was a great advantage the silent film had over the sound film. For its silence was not mute; it was given a voice in the background music, and landscapes and men and the objects surrounding them were shown on the screen against this common musical background. This made them speak a common silent language and we could feel their irrational conversation in the music which was common to them all.

But the silent film could reproduce silence only by roundabout means. On the theatrical stage cessation of the dialogue does not touch off the great emotional experience of silence, because the space of the stage is too small for that, and the experience of silence is essentially a space experience.

How do we perceive silence? By hearing nothing? That is a mere negative. Yet man has few experiences more positive than the experience of silence. Deaf people do not know what it is. But if a morning breeze blows the sound of a cock crowing over to us from the neighboring village, if from the top of a high mountain we hear the tapping of a woodcutter's axe far below in the valley, if we can hear the crack of a whip a mile away—then we are hearing the silence around us. We feel the silence when we can hear the most distant sound or the slightest rustle near us. Silence is when the buzzing of a fly on the windowpane fills the whole room with sound and the ticking of a clock smashes time into fragments with sledgehammer blows. The silence is greatest when we can hear very distant sounds in a very large space. The widest space is our own if we can hear right across it and the noise of the alien world reaches us from beyond its boundaries. A completely soundless space on the contrary never appears quite concrete, and quite real to our perception; we feel it to be weightless and unsubstantial, for what we merely see is only a vision. We accept seen space as real only when it contains sounds as well, for these give it the dimension of depth.

On the stage, a silence which is the reverse of speech may have a dramaturgical function, as for instance if a noisy company suddenly falls silent when a new character appears; but such a silence cannot last longer than a few seconds, otherwise it curdles as it were and seems to stop the performance. On the stage, the effect of silence cannot be drawn out or made to last.

In the film, silence can be extremely vivid and varied, for although it has no voice, it has very many expressions and gestures. A silent glance can speak volumes; its soundlessness makes it more expressive because the facial movements of a silent figure may explain the reason for the silence, make us feel its weight, its menace, its tension. In the film, silence does not halt action even for an instant and such silent action gives even silence a living face.

The physiognomy of men is more intense when they are silent. More than that, in silence even things drop their masks and seem to look at you with wide-open eyes. If a sound film shows us any object surrounded by the noises of everyday life and then suddenly cuts out all sound and brings it up to us in isolated close-up, then the physiognomy of that object takes on a significance and tension that seems to provoke and invite the event which is to follow. . . .

Sound-Explaining Pictures

Not only the microdramatics expressed in the microphysiognomy of the face can be made intelligible by the sound which causes it. Such a close-up-plus-sound can have the inverse effect. The close-up of a listener's face can explain the sound he hears. We might perhaps not have noticed the significance of some sound or noise if we had not seen its effect in the mirror of a human face. For instance we hear the screaming of a siren. Such a sound does not acquire a dramatic significance unless we can see from the expression on human faces that it is a danger-signal, or a call to revolt. We may hear the sound of sobbing, but how deep its meaning is will become evident only from the expression of sympathy and understanding appearing on some human face. Further, the acoustic character of a sound we understand is different too. We hear the sound of a siren differently if we know that it is a warning of impending deadly peril.

The face of a man listening to music may also show two kinds of things. The reflected effect of the music may throw light into the human soul; it may also throw light on the music itself and suggest by means of the listener's facial expression some experience touched off by this musical effect. If the director shows us a close-up of the conductor while an invisible orchestra is playing, not only can the character of the music be made clear by the dumbshow of the conductor, his facial expression may also give an interpretation of the sounds and convey it to us. And the emotion produced in a human being by music and demonstrated by a close-up of a face can enhance the power of a piece of music in our eyes far more than any added decibels.

Asynchronous Sound

In a close-up in which the surroundings are not visible, a sound that seeps into the shot sometimes impresses us as mysterious, simply because we cannot see its source. It produces the tension arising from curiosity and expectation. Sometimes the audience does not know what the sound is they hear, but the character in the film can hear it, turn his face toward the sound, and see its source before the audience does. This handling of picture and sound provides rich opportunities for effects of tension and surprise.

Asynchronous sound (that is, when there is discrepancy between the things heard and the things seen in the film) can acquire considerable importance. If the sound or voice is not tied up with a picture of its source, it may grow beyond the dimensions of the latter. Then it is no longer the voice or sound of some chance thing, but appears as a pronouncement of universal validity. . . . The surest means by which a director can convey the pathos or symbolical significance of sound or voice is precisely to use it asynchronously.

Intimacy of Sound

Acoustic close-ups make us perceive sounds which are included in the accustomed noise of day-to-day life, but which we never hear as individual sounds because they are drowned in the general din. Possibly they even have an effect on us but this effect never becomes conscious. If a close-up picks out such a sound and thereby makes us aware of its effect, then at the same time its influence on the action will have been made manifest.

On the stage such things are impossible. If a theatrical producer wanted to direct the attention of the audience to a scarcely audible sigh, because that sigh expresses a turning-point in the action, then all the other actors in the same scene would have to be very quiet, or else the actor who is to breathe the sigh would have to be brought forward to the footlights. All this, however, would cause the sigh to lose its essential character, which is that it is shy and retiring and must remain scarcely audible. As in the silent film so in the sound film, scarcely perceptible, intimate things can be conveyed with all the secrecy of the unnoticed eavesdropper. Nothing need be silenced in order to demonstrate such sounds for all to hear—and they can yet be kept intimate. The general din can go on, it may even drown completely a sound like the soft piping of a mosquito, but we can get quite close to the source of the sound with the microphone and with our ear and hear it nevertheless.

Subtle associations and interrelations of thoughts and emotions can be conveyed by means of very low, soft sound effects. Such emotional or intellectual linkages can play a decisive dramaturgical part. They may be anything—the ticking of a clock in an empty room, a slow drip from a burst pipe, or the moaning of a little child in its sleep.

Sound Cannot be Isolated

In such close-ups of sound we must be careful, however, to bear in mind the specific nature of sound which never permits sound to be isolated from its acoustic environment as a close-up shot can be isolated from its surroundings. For what is not within the film frame cannot be seen by us, even if it is immediately beside the things that are. Light or shadow can be thrown into the picture from outside and the outline of a shadow can betray to the spectator what is outside the frame but still in the same sector of space, although the picture will show only a shadow. In sound things are different. An acoustic environment inevitably encroaches on the close-up shot and what we hear in this case is not a shadow or a beam of light, but the sounds themselves, which can always be heard throughout the whole space of the picture, however small a section of that space is included in the close-up. Sounds cannot be blocked out.

Music played in a restaurant cannot be completely cut out if a special close-up of say two people softly talking together in a corner is to be shown. The band may not always be seen in the picture, but it will always be heard. Nor is there any need to silence the music altogether in order that we may hear the soft whispering of the two guests as if we were sitting in their immediate vicinity. The close-up will contain the whole acoustic atmosphere of the restaurant space. Thus we will hear not only the people talking, we will also hear in what relation their talking is to the sounds all round them. We will be able to place it in its acoustic environment.

Such sound-pictures are often used in the film for the purpose of creating an atmosphere. Just as the film can show visual landscapes, so it can show acoustic landscapes, a tonal milieu.

Educating the Ear

Our eye recognizes things even if it has seen them only once or twice. Sounds are much more difficult to recognize. We know far more visual forms than sound forms. We are used to finding our way about the world without the conscious assistance of our hearing. But without sight we are lost. Our ear, however, is not less sensitive, it is only less educated than our eye. Science tells us in fact that the ear can distinguish more delicate nuances than our eye. The number of sounds and noises a human ear can distinguish runs into many thousands—far more than the shades of color and degrees of light we can distinguish. There is however a considerable difference between perceiving a sound and identifying its source. We may be aware that we are hearing a different sound than before, without knowing to whom or what the sound belongs. We may have more difficulty in perceiving things visually, but we recognize them more easily once we have perceived them. Erdmann's experiments showed that the ear can distinguish innumerable shades and degrees in the noise of a large crowd, but at the same time it could not be stated with certainty whether the noise was that of a merry or an angry crowd.

There is a very considerable difference between our visual and acoustic education. One of the reasons for this is that we so often see without hearing. We see things from afar, through a windowpane, on pictures, on photographs. But we very rarely hear the sounds of nature and of life without seeing something. We are not accustomed therefore to draw conclusions about visual things from sounds we hear. This defective education of our hearing can be used for many surprising effects in the sound film. We hear a hiss in the darkness. A snake? A human face on the screen turns in terror toward the sound and the spectators tense in their seats. The camera, too, turns toward the sound. And behold the hiss is that of a kettle boiling on the gas-ring.

Such surprising disappointments may be tragic too. In such cases the slow approach and the slow recognition of the sound may cause a far more terrifying tension than the approach of something seen and therefore instantly recognized. The roar of an approaching flood or landslide, approaching cries of grief or terror which we discern and distinguish only gradually, impress us with the inevitability of an approaching catastrophe with almost irresistible intensity. These great possibilities of dramatic effect are due to the fact that such a slow and gradual process of recognition can symbolize the desperate resistance of the consciousness to understanding a reality which is already audible but which the consciousness is reluctant to accept.

Sounds Throw No Shadow

Auditive culture can be increased like any other and the sound film is very suitable to educate our ear. There are however definite limits to the possibilities of finding our way about the world purely by sound, without any visual impressions. The reason for this is that sounds throw no shadows—in other words that sounds cannot produce shapes in space. Things which we see we must see side by side; if we do not, one of them covers up the other so that it cannot be seen. Visual impressions do not blend with each other. Sounds are different; if several of them are present at the same time, they merge into one common composite sound. We can see the dimension of space and see a direction in it. But we cannot *hear* either dimension or direction. A quite unusual, rare sensitivity of ear, the so-called absolute—is required to distinguish the several sounds which make up a composite noise. But their place in space, the direction of their source cannot be discerned even by a perfect ear, if no visual impression is present to help.

It is one of the basic form-problems of the radio play that sound alone cannot represent space and hence cannot alone represent a stage.

Sounds Have No Sides

It is difficult to localize sound and a film director must take this fact into account. If three people are talking together in a film and they are placed so that we cannot see the movements of their mouths and if they do not accompany their words by gestures, it is almost impossible to know which of them is talking, unless the voices are very different. For sounds cannot be beamed as precisely as light can be directed by a reflector. There are no such straight and concentrated sound beams as there are rays of light.

The shapes of visible things have several sides, right side and left side, front and back. Sound has no such aspects, a sound strip will not tell us from which side the shot was made.

Sound Has a Space Coloring

Every natural sound reproduced by art on the stage or on the platform always takes on a false tone-coloring, for it always assumes the coloring of the space in which it is presented to the public and not of the space which it is supposed to reproduce. If we hear a storm, the howling of the wind, a clap of thunder, etc., on the stage we always hear in it the *timbre* proper to the stage not in the *timbre* proper to the forest, or ocean, or whatnot the scene is supposed to represent. If, say, a choir sings in a church on the stage, we cannot hear the unmistakable resonance of Gothic arches; for every sound bears the stamp of the space in which it is actually produced.

Every sound has a space-bound character of its own. The same sound sounds different in a small room, in a cellar, in a large empty hall, in a street, in a forest, or on the sea.

Every sound which is really produced somewhere must of necessity have some such space-quality and this is a very important quality indeed if use is to be made of the sensual reproducing power of sound! It is this *timbre local* of sound which is necessarily always falsified on the theatrical stage. One of the most valuable artistic faculties of the microphone is that sounds shot at the point of origin are perpetuated by it and retain their original tonal coloring. A sound recorded in a cellar remains a cellar sound even if it is played back in a picture theater, just as a film shot preserves the viewpoint of the camera, whatever the spectator's viewpoint in the cinema auditorium may be. If the picture was taken from above, the spectators will see the object from above, even if they have to look upwards to the screen and not downwards. Just as our eye is identified with the camera lens, so our ear is identified with the microphone and we hear the sounds as the microphone originally heard them, irrespective of where the sound film is being shown and the sound reproduced. In this way, in the sound film, the

fixed, immutable, permanent distance between spectator and actor is eliminated not only visually . . . but acoustically as well. Not only as spectators,
but as listeners, too, we are transferred from our seats to the space in which
the events depicted on the screen are taking place.

Dialogue and Sound
SIEGFRIED KRACAUER

The term "sound" is commonly used in two senses. Strictly speaking, it refers to sound proper—all kinds of noises, that is. And in a loose way it designates not only sound proper but the spoken word or dialogue as well. Since its meaning can always be inferred from the contexts in which it appears, there is no need for abandoning this traditional, if illogical, usage.

Introduction

Early Misgivings

When sound arrived, perceptive filmmakers and critics were full of misgivings, in particular about the addition of the spoken word, this "ancient human bondage," as one of them called it.[1] They feared, for instance, that speech might put an end to camera movement—one fear at least which soon turned out to be unfounded.[2] To Chaplin a talking Tramp was so utterly unconceivable that he satirized conventional dialogue in both *City Lights* and *Modern Times*. As far back as 1928—the Russian studios had not yet introduced sound apparatus—Eisenstein, Pudovkin, and Alexandrov issued a joint Statement on sound film in which dim apprehensions alternated with constructive suggestions. This Statement, still of the highest interest, was probably inspired and edited by Eisenstein. A student of materialistic dialectics, he acknowledged sound as a historic necessity because of its emergence at a moment when the further evolution of the medium depended on it. For with the plots becoming ever more ambitious and intricate, only the spoken word would be able to relieve the silent film from the increasing number of cumbersome captions and explanatory visual inserts needed for the exposition of the intrigue. On the other hand, Eisenstein and his co-signers were convinced that the inclusion of dialogue would stir up an overwhelming desire for stage illusion. Their Statement predicted a flood of sound films indulging in " 'highly cultured dramas' and other photographed performances of a theatrical sort."[3] Eisenstein did not seem to realize that what he considered a consequence of dialogue actually existed long before its innovation. The silent screen was crammed with "highly cultured dramas." "Misled by the fatal vogue of 'adaptations,' " said Clair in 1927, "the dramatic film is built on the model of theatrical or literary works by minds accustomed to verbal expression alone."[4] It might be added that all these filmmakers and critics accepted sound later on, though not unconditionally.

Basic Requirement

The pronounced misgivings in the period of transition to sound can be traced to the rising awareness that films with sound live up to the spirit of the medium only if the visuals take the lead in them. Film is a visual medium.[5] To cite René Clair again, he says he knows of people less familiar with the history of the movies who stubbornly believe some otherwise well-remembered silent film to have been a talkie; and he shrewdly reasons that their slip of memory should give pause to all those reluctant to endorse the supremacy of the image.[6] The legitimacy of this requirement follows straight from the irrevocable fact that it is the motion picture camera, not the sound camera, which accounts for the most specific contributions of the cinema; neither noises nor dialogue are exclusively peculiar to film. One might argue that the addition of speech would seem to justify attempts at an equilibrium between word and image, but it will be seen shortly that such attempts are doomed to failure. For sound films to be true to the basic aesthetic principle, their significant communications must originate with their pictures.

In dealing with sound, it is best to treat dialogue—or speech, for that matter—and sound proper separately. Especially in the case of speech, two kinds of relationships between sound and image should be considered. The first concerns the role they are assigned—i.e., whether the messages of a film are primarily passed on through the sound track or the imagery. The second concerns the manner in which sound and image are synchronized at any given moment. There are various possibilities of synchronization. All of them have a bearing on the adequacy of the spoken word to the medium.

Dialogue

The Role of the Spoken Word

PROBLEMATIC USES
What caused Eisenstein's gloom when he anticipated that the arrival of sound would generate a flood of "highly cultured dramas"? No doubt he feared lest the spoken word might be used as the carrier of all significant statements and thus become the major means of propelling the action. His fears were all too well-founded. At the beginning of sound the screen went "speech-mad," with many filmmakers starting from the "absurd assumption that in order to make a sound film it is only necessary to photograph a play." [7] And this was more than a passing vogue. The bulk of existing talkies continues to center on dialogue.

Dialogue in the Lead. The reliance on verbal statements increases, as a matter of course, the medium's affinity for the theater. Dialogue films either reproduce theatrical plays or convey plots in theatrical fashion. This implies that they automatically turn the spotlight on the actor, featuring him as an insoluble entity, and by the same token exile inanimate nature to the background. [8] Most important, emphasis on speech not only strengthens this tendency away from camera-life but adds something new and extremely dangerous. It opens up the region of discursive reasoning, enabling the medium to impart the turns and twists of sophisticated thought, all those rational or poetic communications which do not depend upon pictorialization to be grasped and appreciated. What even the most theatrical-minded silent film could not incorporate—pointed controversies, Shavian witticisms, Hamlet's soliloquies—has now been annexed to the screen.

But when this course is followed, it is inevitable that out of the spoken words definite patterns of meanings and images should arise. They are much in the nature of the loving memories which Proust's narrator retains of his grandmother and which prevent him from realizing her crude physique as it appears in a photograph. Evoked through language, these patterns assume a reality of their own, a self-sufficient mental reality which, once established in the film, interferes with the photographic reality to which the camera aspires. The significance of verbal argumentation, verbal poetry, threatens to drown the significance of the accompanying pictures, reducing them to shadowy illustrations. [9] . . .

Equilibrium. Those aware of the theatrical effects of dialogue film and yet adverse to reducing the role of verbal communications tend to envisage the above-mentioned possibility of an equilibrium between word and image as a workable solution. Allardyce Nicoll considers Max Reinhardt's film *A Midsummer Night's Dream* a case in point, and defends the latter's equal concern for "visual symbols" and "language" on the strength of an interesting argument. Shakespeare's dialogue, says he, addressed itself to an audience which, confronted with a growing language and still unaccustomed to acquiring knowledge through reading, was much more acutely alert to the spoken word than is the modern audience. Our grasp of spoken words is no longer what it was in Shakespeare's times. Reinhardt is therefore justified in trying to enliven the dialogue by supplementing it with an opulent imagery. This imagery, Nicoll reasons, mobilizes our visual imagination, thus benefiting the verbal communications whose stimulating power had long since subsided.[10]

The fallacy of Nicoll's argument is obvious. In fact, he himself seems to doubt its conclusiveness; before advancing it, he admits that one might as well condemn *A Midsummer Night's Dream* for assigning to the pictures on the screen a role apt to divert the audience from the appeal of Shakespeare's language. Well, exactly this is bound to happen. Because of their obtrusive presence the luxuriant images summoned by Reinhardt cannot be expected to revitalize the dialogue by stimulating the spectator's allegedly atrophied sensitivity to it; instead of transforming the spectator into a listener, they claim his attention in their own right. So the word meanings are all the more lost on him. The balance to which the film aspires turns out to be unachievable. . . .

Perhaps the most noteworthy attempt at an equilibrium between verbal and pictorial statements is Laurence Olivier's *Hamlet,* a film which breathes a disquiet that is much to the credit of its director. Olivier wants to transfer, undamaged, all the beauties of Shakespeare's dialogue to the screen. Yet endowed with a keen film sense, he also wants to avoid photographed theater and therefore plays up the role of the visuals and the significance of cinematic devices. The result is a tour de force as fascinating as it is exasperating. On the one hand, Olivier emphasizes the dialogue, inviting us to revel in its suggestive poetry; on the other, he incorporates the dialogue into a texture of meaningful shots whose impact prevents us from taking in the spoken lines.

During Hamlet's great soliloquy the camera, as if immune to its magic, explores his physique with an abandon which would be very rewarding indeed were we not at the same time requested to absorb the soliloquy itself, this unique fabric of language and thought. The spectator's capacity being limited, the photographic images and the language images inevitably neutralize each other;[11] like Buridan's ass, he does not know what to feed upon and eventually gets starved. *Hamlet* is a remarkable, if quixotic, effort to instill cinematic life into an outspoken dialogue film. But you cannot eat your cake and have it.

CINEMATIC USES

All the successful attempts at an integration of the spoken word have one characteristic in common: they play down dialogue with a view to reinstating the visuals. This may be done in various ways.

Speech De-emphasized. Practically all responsible critics agree that it heightens cinematic interest to reduce the weight and volume of the spoken word so that dialogue after the manner of the stage yields to natural, lifelike speech.[12] This postulate is in keeping with the "basic requirement"; it rests upon the conviction that the medium calls for verbal statements which grow out of the flow of pictorial communications instead of determining their course. Many filmmakers have accordingly de-emphasized speech. Cavalcanti remarked in 1939: "Film producers have learned in the course of the last ten years that use of speech must be economical, and be balanced with the other elements in the film, that the style employed by the dialogue writers must be literal, conversational, nonliterary: that the delivery must be light, rapid, and offhand, to match the quick movements of the action, and the cuts from speaker to speaker."[13]

René Clair's Paris comedies, for instance, meet these requests to the letter; the dialogue in them is casual, so casual in fact that their characters sometimes continue to converse while disappearing in a bar. For a moment you may still see them linger behind the window and move their lips with appropriate gestures—an ingenious device which repudiates drastically the goals and claims of dialogue film proper. It is as if Clair wanted to demonstrate *ad oculos* that the spoken word is most cinematic if the messages it conveys elude our grasp; if all that actually can be grasped is the sight of the speakers.

The tendency toward embedding dialogue in visual contexts is perhaps nowhere illustrated so strikingly as in that episode of *Ruggles of Red Gap* in which Charles Laughton as Ruggles recites Lincoln's Gettysburg Address. At first glance, this episode would seem to be about the opposite of a fitting example, for, in delivering the speech, Ruggles is not only fully conscious of its significance but eager to impress it upon his listeners in the bar. His recital, however, also serves another purpose, a purpose of such an immediate urgency that it outweighs the impact of Lincoln's words themselves. The fact, established by their rendering, that Ruggles knows them by heart reveals to the audience his inner metamorphosis from an English gentleman's gentleman into a self-reliant American.

In complete accordance with this major objective, the camera closes in on Ruggles's face when he, still talking to himself, mumbles the first sentences of the speech, and then shows him again as he stands up and confidently raises his voice. The camera thus anticipates our foremost desire. Indeed, concerned with the change Ruggles has undergone rather than the text he declaims, we want nothing more than to scan his every facial expression and his whole demeanor for outward signs of that change. The episode is a rare achievement in that it features a speech which so little interferes with the visuals that, on the contrary, it makes them stand out glaringly. Things are arranged in such a manner that our awareness of the speech's content kindles our interest in the meanings of the speaker's appearance. Of course, this is possible only in case of a speech which, like Lincoln's, is familiar to the audience. Since the listeners need not really pay attention to it to recall what belongs among their cherished memories, they may take in the words and yet be free to concentrate on the accompanying pictures. Imagine Ruggles advancing a dramatically important new thought instead of reciting the Gettysburg speech: then the audience would hardly be in a position to assimilate the simultaneous verbal and pictorial statements with equal intensity.

Speech Undermined from Within. When first incorporating the spoken word, Chaplin aimed at corroding it. He ridiculed speeches which, had they been normally rendered, would infallibly have conveyed patterns of language-bound meanings. The point is that he did not render them normally. In the opening sequence of *City Lights* the orators celebrating the unveiling of a statue utter inarticulate sounds with the grandiloquent intonations required by the occasion. This sequence not only makes fun of the inanity of ceremonious speeches but effectively forestalls their absorption, thus inviting the audience all the more intensely to look at the pictures. In the feeding machine episode of *Modern Times* Chaplin attains about the same ends with the aid of a gag which works like a delayed-time bomb. When the inventor [salesman] of the machine begins to explain it, his whole performance is calculated to trap us into believing that he himself does the talking; then a slight movement of the camera makes us abruptly realize that his sales talk comes from a record player. As a joke on our gullibility this belated revelation is doubly exhilarating. And naturally, now that the man whom we believed to be the speaker is exposed as a dummy, a leftover from mechanization, we no longer pay attention to what the phonograph is pouring forth but turn from naïve listeners into dedicated spectators. (In two of his more recent films, *Monsieur Verdoux* and *Limelight,* Chaplin has reverted to dialogue in theatrical fashion. From the angle of the cinema this is undeniably a retrogression. Yet Chaplin is not the only great artist to have suffered from the limitations of his medium. One grows older, and the urge to communicate pent-up insight precariously acquired sweeps away all other considerations. Perhaps Chaplin's desire to speak his mind has also something to do with his lifelong silence as a pantomime.)

Groucho Marx too undermines the spoken word from within. True, he is given to talking, but his impossible delivery, both glib like water flowing down tiles and cataclysmic like a deluge, tends to obstruct the sanctioned functions of speech. Add to this that he contributes to the running dialogue without really participating in it. Silly and shrewd, scatterbrained and subversive, his repartees are bubbling self-assertions rather than answers or injunctions. Groucho is a lusty, irresponsible extrovert out of tune with his partners. Hence the obliqueness of his utterances. They disrupt the ongoing conversation so radically that no message or opinion voiced reaches its destination. Whatever Groucho is saying disintegrates speech all around him. He is an eruptive monad in the middle of self-created anarchy. Accordingly, his verbal discharges go well with Harpo's slapstick pranks, which survive from the silent era. Like the gods of antiquity who after their downfall lived on as puppets, bugbears, and other minor ghosts, haunting centuries which no longer believed in them, Harpo is a residue of the past, an exiled comedy god condemned or permitted to act the part of a mischievous hobgoblin. Yet the world in which he appears is so crowded with dialogue that he would long since have vanished were it not for Groucho, who supports the spectre's destructive designs. As dizzying as any silent collision, Groucho's word cascades wreak havoc on language, and among the resultant debris Harpo continues to feel at ease.

Shift of Emphasis From the Meanings of Speech to its Material Qualities. Filmmakers may also turn the spotlight from speech as a means of communication to speech as a manifestation of nature. In *Pygmalion,* for instance, we are enjoined to focus on Eliza's Cockney idiom rather than the content of what she is saying. This shift of emphasis is cinematic because it alienates the words, thereby exposing their material characteristics.[14] Within the world of sound the effect thus produced parallels that of photography in the visible world. Remember the Proust passage in which the narrator looks at his grandmother with the eyes of a stranger: estranged from her, he sees her, roughly speaking, as she really is, not as he imagines her to be. Similarly, whenever dialogue is diverted from its conventional purpose of conveying some message or other, we are, like Proust's narrator, confronted with the alienated voices which, now that they have been stripped of all the connotations and meanings normally overlaying their given nature, appear to us for the first time in a relatively pure state. Words presented this way lie in the same dimension as the visible phenomena which the motion picture camera captures. They are sound phenomena which affect the moviegoer through their physical qualities. Consequently, they do not provoke him, as would obtrusive dialogue, to neglect the accompanying visuals but, conversely, stir him to keep close to the latter, which they supplement in a sense.

Examples are not infrequent. To revert to *Pygmalion,* it is the type of Eliza's speech which counts. Her manner of expressing herself, as recorded by the sound camera, represents a peculiar mode of being which claims our attention for its own sake. The same holds true of those parts of the dialogue in *Marty* which help characterize the Italian-American environment; the bass voice in the coronation episode of *Ivan the Terrible;* the echo scene in Buñuel's *Robinson Crusoe;* and the lumps of conversation tossed to and fro in *Mr. Hulot's Holiday.* When in Tati's admirable comedy, one of the most original since the days of silent slapstick, Hulot checks in at the reception desk of the resort hotel, the pipe in his mouth prevents him from pronouncing his name clearly. Upon request, he politely repeats the performance and, this time without pipe, enunciates the two syllables "Hulot" with so overwhelming a distinctness that, as in the case of his initial mutter, you are again thrust back on the physical side of his speech; the utterance "Hulot" stays with you not as a communication but as a specific configuration of sounds.

"There is something peculiarly delightful," says Ruskin, ". . . in passing through the streets of a foreign city without understanding a word that anybody says! One's ear for all sound of voices then becomes entirely impartial; one is not diverted by the meaning of syllables from recognizing the absolute guttural, liquid, or honeyed quality of them: while the gesture of the body and the expression of the face have the same value for you that they have in a pantomime; every scene becomes a melodious opera to you, or a picturesquely inarticulate Punch."[15] This is, for instance, confirmed by the song which Chaplin as a . . . waiter improvises in his *Modern Times:* a hodgepodge of melodious, if incomprehensible, word formations, it is both an attractive sound composition in its own right and an ingenious device for attuning the spectator perfectly to the pantomime which the involuntary rhapsodist is meanwhile performing.

And of course, Ruskin's observation accounts for the cinematic effect of multilingual films. A number of them, partly semi-documentaries, were produced after World War II. G. W. Pabst's *Kameradschaft* and Jean Renoir's *La Grande Illusion,* both bilingual, anticipated this trend which grew out of the tribulations of the war when millions of ordinary people, cut off from their native countries, intermingled all over Europe. In the Rossellini film *Paisan,* which reflects most impressively the ensuing confusion of mother tongues, an American G.I. tries to converse with a Sicilian peasant girl; he soon supplements unintelligible words with drastic gestures and thus arrives at an understanding of a sort. But since this primitive approach is not achieved through the dialogue itself, the sounds that compose it take on a life of their own. And along with the dumb show, their conspicuous presence as sounds challenges the spectator empathically to sense what the two characters may sense and to respond to undercurrents within them and between them which would, perhaps, be lost on him were the words just carriers of meanings. The theater which hinges on dialogue shuns foreign languages, while the cinema admits and even favors them for benefiting speechless action.

Emphasis on voices as sounds may also serve to open up the material regions of the speech world for their own sake. What is thought of here is a sort of word carpet which, woven from scraps of dialogue or other kinds of communications, impresses the audience mainly as a coherent sound pattern. Grierson coins the term "chorus" to define such patterns and mentions two instances of them: the film *Three-cornered Moon*, in which the chorus or carpet consists of bits of conversation between unemployed people queueing up in bread lines; and *Beast of the City*, a Hollywood film about the Chicago underworld, with an episode which features the monotonous wireless messages from police headquarters. "It went something like this: 'Calling Car 324 324 Calling Car 528 528 Calling Car 18 18,' etc., etc. . . ."[16] Now these "choruses" may be inserted in such a way that it is they rather than the synchronized visuals which captivate the spectator—or should one say, listener? Being all ear, he will not care much about what the pictures try to impart.

On the surface, this use of speech seems to go against the grain of the medium by disregarding the visual contributions. And yet it is cinematic by extension. The voice patterns brought into focus belong to the physical world about us no less than its visible components; and they are so elusive that they would hardly be noticed were it not for the sound camera which records them faithfully. Only in photographing them like any visible phenomenon—not to mention mechanical reproduction processes outside the cinema—are we able to lay hold on these transitory verbal conglomerates. The fact that they palpably form part of the accidental flow of life still increases their affiliations with the medium. An excellent case in point is *Jungle Patrol*, a Hollywood B picture about American combat fliers in New Guinea. This film culminates in a sequence of terrific air fights which, however, are not seen at all. What we do see instead is a loudspeaker in the opeartions hut hooked in to the planes' intercoms. As the ill-fated fights take their course, different voices which seem to come from nowhere flow out of the radio set, forming an endless sound strip.[17] To be sure, we grasp the tragic implications of their blurred messages. But this is not the whole story they are telling us. Rather, the gist of it is the constant mutter itself, the fabric woven by voice after voice. In the process of unfolding, it sensitizes us to

the influences of space and matter and their share in the individual destinies. . . .

EXISTING THEORIES
          . . . The problem is: what do the varying relationships between
image and speech imply for the latter's inadequacy or adequacy to the medium?
          It might be best to take a look at the existing theories first. Most
critics hold that, for an integration of sound into film, much, if not all, depends upon the methods of synchronization. This is not to say that they would
ignore the significance of the role assigned to speech; as has been pointed
out above, they usually repudiate the ascendancy of dialogue in favor of
films in which speech is kept subdued. But they practically never think of
establishing a meaningful connection between that role and the manner in
which words and visuals are synchronized. And their emphasis on synchronization techniques indicates that they take them to be the decisive factor.
          This bias goes hand in hand with the tendency, equally wide-
spread in theoretical writings, to follow the example of the Russians, who
not only championed counterpoint and asynchronism when sound arrived
but plainly assumed that both procedures are inseparable from each other.
In their joint Statement of 1928 Eisenstein, Pudovkin, and Alexandrov declare: "*Only a contrapuntal use* of sound in relation to the visual montage
piece will afford a new potentiality of montage development and perfection." [18] And somewhat later Pudovkin remarks: "It is not generally recognized that the principal elements in sound film are the asynchronous and not
the synchronous." [19] He and Eisenstein took it for granted that asynchronism inevitably calls for a contrapuntal handling of sound and, conversely,
the latter for asynchronism. Presumably it was their obsession with the montage principle which made them believe in the supreme virtues of this particular combination, blinding them to other, equally rewarding possibilities.
The reader need hardly be told that the Russian doctrine entails, or at least
encourages, the no less untenable identification of parallelism with "synchronism." [20]
          Even though, thanks to three decades of talkies, modern writers
in the field are more discerning than the authors of this oversimplified doctrine,[21] they continue in a measure to endorse the latters' insistence on the
cinematic merits of asynchronous sound and its contrapuntal use. And Pudovkin's main argument in support of his proposition is still fully upheld. He
defends asynchronism—or counterpoint, for that matter—on the ground that
it conforms best to real-life conditions, whereas cases of parallelism, says he,
materialize much less frequently than we are inclined to think. To prove his
thesis he constructs the example of a cry for help from the street which stays

with us as we look out of the window, drowning the noises of the moving cars and buses now before our eyes. And what about our natural behavior as listeners? Pudovkin describes some of the ways in which our eyes happen to wander while we are following a conversation. We may go on watching a man who has just finished talking and now listens to a member of the party; or we may prematurely look at a person all set to answer the actual speaker; or we may satisfy our curiosity about the effects of a speech by scanning, one by one, the faces of the listeners and studying their reactions.[22] All three alternatives . . . are drawn from everyday life; and all of them represent at least borderline cases of asynchronism, with word and image being interrelated in contrapuntal fashion. The gist of Pudovkin's argument is that this type of synchronization is cinematic because it corresponds to our habits of perception and, hence, renders reality as we actually experience it.

A NEW PROPOSITION

No doubt the theories presented here carry much weight. Yet . . . they suffer from two shortcomings. First, they attribute to the methods of synchronization independent significance, even though these methods are only techniques which may serve any purpose, cinematic or not. Second, they plead for contrapuntal asynchronism on the ground that it reflects faithfully the manner in which we perceive reality. What accounts for the cinematic quality of films, however, is not so much their truth to our experience of reality or even to reality in a general sense as their absorption in camera-reality—visible physical existence.

How dispose of these shortcomings? Let us proceed from the following observation: Any filmmaker wants to canalize audience attention and create dramatic suspense as a matter of course. Accordingly, he will in each particular case resort to such methods of synchronization as he believes to be the most fitting ones. Supposing further he is a skilled artist, his choices are certainly "good" in the sense that they establish the narrative as effectively as is possible under the given circumstances.

But are they for that reason also necessarily "good" in a cinematic sense? Their adequacy to the medium obviously depends upon the "goodness" of the narrative which they help implement. Does the narrative grow out of verbal or visual contributions?—this is the question. The decisive factor, then, is the role which speech plays within the contexts under consideration. If speech is in the lead, even the most knowing filmmaker cannot avoid synchronizing it with the images in ways which disqualify the latter as a source of communication. Conversely, if the visuals predominate, he is free to avail himself of modes of synchronization which, in keeping with the cinematic approach, advance the action through pictorial statements.

An interesting fact emerges at this point. As I have emphasized, the existing theories usually recommend a contrapuntal treatment of asynchronous sound, while cautioning against parallel synchronization. Now it can easily be shown that my new proposition corroborates these theories up to a point. In case verbal communications prevail, the odds are that the imagery will parallel them. The reverse alternative—speech being de-emphasized—greatly favors counterpoint, which stirs the visuals to become eloquent. Eisenstein and Pudovkin were of course not wrong in advocating a contrapuntal use of sound. But from the present viewpoint they did so for the wrong reasons. . . .

Sound Proper

About the Nature of Sounds

Sounds—this term meaning exclusively noises here—can be arranged along a continuum which extends from unidentifiable to recognizable noises. As for the former, think of certain noises in the night: they are, so to speak, anonymous; you have no idea where they come from.[23] At the opposite pole are sounds whose source is known to us, whether we see it or not. In everyday life, when we hear barking, we immediately realize that a dog must be around; and as a rule we do not go wrong in associating church bells with the sound of chimes.

Those puzzling noises which the night is apt to produce attune the listener primarily to his physical environment because of their origin in some ungiven region of it. But what about the many identifiable noises at the other end of the continuum? Take again chimes: no sooner does one hear them than he tends to visualize, however vaguely, the church or the clock tower from which they issue; and from there his mind may leisurely drift on until it happens upon the memory of a village square filled with churchgoers who stream to the service in their Sunday best. Generally speaking, any familiar noise calls forth inner images of its source as well as images of activities, modes of behavior, etc., which are either customarily connected with that noise or at least related to it in the listener's recollection. In other words, localizable sounds do not as a rule touch off conceptual reasoning, language-bound thought; rather, they share with unidentifiable noises the quality of bringing the material aspects of reality into focus. This comes out very clearly in scenes where they are combined with speech. It could be shown above that in the great dialogue scene of Orson Welles's *Othello* the intermittent footfalls of Iago and the Moor, far from increasing the impact of the dialogue, help shift audience attention to the protagonists' bodily presence.

In sum, as Cavalcanti once put it, "noise seems to by-pass the intelligence and speak to something very deep and inborn."[24] This explains why, in the era of transition to sound, those addicted to the silent staked their last hopes on films that would feature noises rather than words.[25] So Eisenstein in a 1930 talk at the Sorbonne: "I think the '100% all-talking film' is silly. . . . But the sound film is something more interesting. The future belongs to it."[26] According to René Clair (who, incidentally, did not share Eisenstein's illusions about the future), the connoisseurs' preference for noises then rested upon the belief that, as material phenomena, they evoke a reality less dangerous to the images on the screen than the kind of reality conveyed by the all-out talkie.[27] Nothing would seem to be more justified than this belief. Sounds whose material properties are featured belong to the same world as the visuals and, hence, will hardly interfere with the spectator's concern for the latter.

Yet is the filmmaker really obliged under all circumstances to emphasize the material characteristics of the sounds he inserts? Actually, he is free to divest certain sounds of their natural substance, so that they no longer refer to the physical universe from which they flow; disembodied entities, they then assume other functions. As a matter of course, this possibility involves exclusively localizable noises.

Reliance on Symbolic Meanings

Indeed, localizable noises often carry familiar symbolic meanings. And if the filmmaker capitalizes on these meanings in the interest of his narrative, the noises yielding them turn from material phenomena into units which, much like verbal statements, serve as components of mental processes.

René Clair playfully uses sound this way when he shows the main characters of his Le Million scrambling for the jacket which they believe to harbor the coveted lottery ticket. Instead of resorting to "synchronous" sound, he synchronizes the scramble with noises from a Rugby game. These commentative noises virtually parallel the actual fight and at the same time relate contrapuntally to it. Evidently they are intended to establish an analogy between the visible fight and an imaginary game; their purpose is to ridicule the seriousness of the scramble by making the participants look like Rugby players who toss the jacket about as if it were a ball. Assuming the asynchronous ball noises really implement Clair's intentions, they affect us not so much through their material qualities as through their function of signifying a Rugby game—any Rugby game, for that matter. It is their symbolic value which counts. In consequence, they do not induce the spectator closely to watch the pictures but invite him to enjoy an amusing analogy which has all the traits of a literary *aperçu*. In fact, what the sounds try to suggest might have been imparted by words as well. The whole scene is problematic cinematically because it culminates in a jocular comparison which, being imposed from without on the images of the scramble, inevitably obscures their inherent meanings. Add to this that the commentative noises may not even fulfill the function which Clair assigns to them; it is doubtful indeed whether they are specific enough to be necessarily associated with the idea of a ball game. Not all identifiable sounds are familiar to all the people; nor can all such sounds be localized with absolute certainty. Perhaps, many a spectator, unable to grasp the significance of the Rugby noises, will find them merely bizarre. . . .

Sometimes, especially in theatrical adaptations of stage dramas, the symbolic potentialities of familiar sounds are exploited in a crude manner palpably inspired by venerable stage traditions. As the tragic conflict approaches its climax, the surge of human passions is synchronized with the sinister noises of a storm outdoors. Raging nature, suggested by these asynchronous actual sounds, is thus made to parallel the impending catastrophe in gloomy interiors for the purpose of intensifying audience participation. Such a use of sound will hardly ingratiate itself with the sensitive moviegoer. It rests upon the premise of a closed universe in which natural events correspond to human destinies—a notion incompatible with camera-realism, which presupposes the endless continuum of physical existence. Moreover, the attention which the spectator must pay to the symbolic meaning of the storm noises preempts his concern for the meanings of their material characteristics. Because of its emphasis on mental reality the whole arrangement is not likely to benefit the pictures.

Another possibility in a similar vein is the following: the howling storm denoting an upheaval of nature may be synchronized, counterpointwise, with shots of peaceful family life in order to forewarn the audience that malevolent forces are about to invade that world of peace. Yet while in the example discussed just above, the storm noises convey a meaning which can easily be grasped, paralleling the obvious meaning of the soaring human passions, these very same noises are well-nigh unintelligible when they relate contrapuntally to pictures whose significance strongly differs from theirs. The reason is that the symbolic content of identifiable sounds is too vague to serve, by itself alone, as a basis for the construction of analogies or similes. It is highly improbable that a spectator immersed in the peaceful images on the screen will conceive of the howling storm as an ominous portent. Perhaps he will believe the discordant storm noises to be sheer coincidence—an explanation, by the way, which would at least do justice to the preferences of the medium. But be this as it may, one thing is sure: the symbolic counterpoint aspired to falls flat. Sound used contrapuntally must relate to the synchronized images in an understandable way to signify something comprehensible.

So much for sound symbolism. Filmmakers have resorted to it only sporadically. What they usually feature is not so much the symbolic meanings of recognizable noises as the material properties of sounds, identifiable or not. The subsequent analysis bears exclusively on sounds in the latter sense.

Role

Sounds in their capacity as material phenomena do not weaken the impact of the juxtaposed pictures. This all but self-evident assumption implies that the role which sounds are made to play in a film is a negligible factor. Speech and sound proper differ radically in that the former's dominance blurs the visuals, whereas the occasional dominance of noises is of little consequence. Supposing shrill screams or the blasts of an explosion are synchronized with images of their source and/or its environment: much as they will leave their imprint on the spectator's mind, it is unlikely that they will prevent him from taking in the images; rather, they may prompt him to scrutinize the latter in a mood which increases his susceptibility to their multiple meanings—are not the screams and the blasts indeterminate also?

One might even go further. Sounds share with visible phenomena two characteristics: they are recorded by a camera; and they belong to material reality in a general sense. This being so, camera explorations of the sound world itself can be said to lie, by extension, in a cinematic interest. Flaherty, who was loath to entrust the spoken word with any important message, extolled the contributions of "characteristic" sounds: "I wish I could have had sound for *Nanook*. . . . It takes the hiss of the wind in the North and the howls of the dogs to get the whole feeling of that country."[28] Now, filmmakers have at all times used close-ups and other devices to exhibit the innumerable phenomena which comprise camera-reality. So the late Jean Epstein's proposal to penetrate the universe of natural sounds in a similar manner would seem to be quite logical.

Epstein's general idea was to break down, by means of sonic slow motion, complex sound patterns into their elements. In his *Le Tempestaire* he thus details the various noises of which a violent storm consists, synchronizing them with remarkable shots of the ocean. The film, an experiment as ingenious as it is fascinating, extends the cinematic approach into the region of sound in such a way that the acoustic revelations and the pictorial communications reinforce rather than neutralize each other. Epstein himself accounts for his procedures in this film as follows: "Like the eye, the ear has only a very limited power of separation. The eye must have recourse to a slowing down. . . . Similarly, the ear needs sound to be enlarged in time, i.e., sonic slow motion, in order to discover, for instance, that the confused howling of a tempest is, in a subtler reality, a manifold of distinct noises hitherto alien to the human ear, an apocalypse of shouts, coos, gurgles, squalls, detonations, timbres and accents for the most part as yet unnamed." In analogy to slow-motion movements these unnamed noises might be called "sound reality of another dimension."[29]

Notes

1. René Clair, *Réflexion faite: Notes pour servir à l'histoire de l'art cinématographique de 1920 à 1950* (Paris: Gallimard, 1951), 141.

2. Siegfried Kracauer, *From Caligari to Hitler* (Princeton: Princeton University Press, 1947), p. 205.

3. Sergei Eisenstein, *Film Form: Essays in Film Theory*, ed. and trans. Jay Leyda (New York: Harcourt, Brace, 1949), pp. 257–59.

4. Clair, *Réflexion faite*, p. 116.

5. See, for instance, Georges Charensol, "Le cinéma parlant," in Marcel L'Herbier, ed., *Intelligence du cinématographe* (Paris: Editions Corréa, 1946), 170; Mortimer J. Adler, *Art and Prudence: A Study in Practical Philosophy* (New York: Longmans, Green, 1937), p. 541; Ernest Lindgren, *The Art of the Film* (London: Allen and Unwin, 1948), p. 106.

6. Clair, *Réflexion faite*, p. 43.

7. Alberto Cavalcanti, "Sound in Films," *Films*, 1, No. 1 (November 1939):29.

8. See Hanns Eisler, *Composing for the Films* (New York: Oxford University Press, 1947), p. 77. Clifford Leech, "Dialogue for Stage and Screen," *Penguin Film Review*, no. 6 (April 1948):100, likewise rejects stage dialogue because "the epigrams, the patterned responses, the set speeches need the ceremonial ambiance of the playhouse and the living presence of the player."

9. René Barjavel, *Cinéma total: Essai sur les formes futures du cinéma* (Paris: Les Editions Denoël 1944), p. 29, remarks that the imagination of the spectator watching a dialogue film "builds from the words showered down on him and replaces the images on the screen by those which the dialogue suggests to him." See also Clair, *Réflexion faite*, pp. 146, 150, 158, 188.

10. Allardyce Nicoll, *Film and Theatre* (New York: Thomas Y. Crowell, 1936), pp. 178–80.

11. Cf. Balazs, "Das Drehbuch oder Filmszenarium," in *Von der Filmidee zum Drehbuch* (Berlin 1949), p. 77.

12. For instance, Balazs, ibid., pp. 76–77; Rudolf Arnheim, *Film* (London: Faber and Faber, 1933), p. 213; Leech, "Dialogue for Stage and Screen," pp. 99–101.

13. Cavalcanti, "Sound in Films," p. 31.

14. Cf. Horst Meyerhoff, *Tonfilm und Wirklichkeit: Grundlagen zur Psychologie des Films* (Berlin: B. Henschel, 1949), pp. 75–76; Arnheim, *Film,* p. 213.

15. John Ruskin, *Praeterita: Outline of Scenes and Thoughts Perhaps Worthy of Memory in My Past Life* (London: R. Hart-Davis, 1949), p. 106.

16. Forsyth Hardy, ed., *Grierson on Documentary* (New York: Harcourt, Brace, 1947), pp. 115–16.

17. I am indebted to Mr. Arthur Knight for having this film brought to my attention.

18. V. I. Pudovkin, *Film Technique and Film Acting,* trans. Ivor Montagu (New York: Lear, 1949), p. 143; also Eisenstein, *Film Form,* p. 258.

19. Pudovkin, *Film Technique,* p. 157.

20. Arnheim, *Film,* p. 251, cautioned against this confusion as early as 1930.

21. For instance, K. Reisz, *The Technique of Film Editing* (London and New York: Focal Press, 1953), *passim.*

22. Pudovkin, *Film Technique,* pp. 159–60; part 2, pp. 86–87.

23. See Cavalcanti, "Sound in Films," pp. 36–37.

24. Ibid., p. 37.

25. So Clair in 1929; see his *Réflexion faite,* p. 145.

26. Quoted by Dwight Macdonald, "The Soviet Cinema: 1930–1938," *Partisan Review,* 5, no. 2 (July 1938):46.

27. Clair, *Réflexion faite,* p. 145.

28. Arthur Rosenheimer, Jr., "They Make Documentaries," *Film News,* 7, no. 6 (April 1946):10, 23. At the beginning of the sound era, Walter Ruttmann in his *Melody of the World* delighted in recording the din of traffic, the screech of a saw. These reproductions were as many discoveries.

29. Jean Epstein, "Sound in Slow Motion," in Gideon Bachmann, ed., *Jean Epstein, 1897–1953: Cinemages,* no. 2:44.

Slow-Motion Sound   JEAN EPSTEIN

In the fascination which descends from a close-up and weighs on a thousand faces knit together in the same moment of shock, on a thousand souls seized by the same emotion; in the magic which glues the eye to the slow-motion image of a runner taking flight at each stride or the fast-motion image of a seedling expanding into an oak; in images that the eye is incapable of shaping, either as large, or as near, or as enduring, or as fleeting as these, you come on the essence of the cinematographic mystery, the secret of the hypnosis-machine: a new knowledge, a new love, a new possession of the world through the eyes.

Until these last few years, and virtually until these last few months, the sound track, consecrated to the old forms of speech and music, revealed to us nothing of the acoustical universe that the ear itself had not always been accustomed to hear. Drowned in this superabundant banality, the prophetic murmur of the train-wheels that carried off Jean de la Lune had to wait a long while for someone to continue in that direction. Nevertheless, today, a number of foreign films show the results of research which has tended to improve the recording of the sound—in the direction of a true high-fidelity, both psychological and dramatic, a deeper and more precise realism than that within the means of all-purpose sound, taken as impossible to regulate.

Already, it's no longer a matter of simply hearing people speak but of hearing them think and dream.

Already the microphone has crossed the threshold of the lips, slipped into the interior world of man, moved into the hiding places of the voices of consciousness, of the refrains of memory, of the screams of nightmares and of words never spoken. Echo chambers are already translating not just the space of a set but the distances within the soul.

In this refinement of the sound film, it would clearly seem necessary to experiment and find out what the process of slow-motion, which is still enriching the visual realm with so many yet unseen aspects, might be able to add. I posed this problem, from the technical standpoint, to a sound engineer, M. Leon Vareille, who became interested in it and solved it in a simple and elegant manner, as the mathematicians say. And so, throughout *Le Tempestaire* I was able to use the noise of the sea-wind, rerecorded at variable speed, up to a ratio of 4:1.

The effect of this slow-motion sound, of this stretching of acoustical vibrations in time, is double. On the one hand, with the lowering of the frequency of the vibrations, the tone drops one octave each time the ratio is increased by one unit. Thus, the same sound can be recorded in several different registers. This permits, by editing and mixing, the creation of a true score, purely out of sound. The composer Yves Baudrier, who created this score with a great deal of intelligence, also had enough talent to introduce only an extremely restrained instrumental melodic line through this natural music, which does not detract from the sound experiment, and does not tend to warp the public's judgment on the experiment itself.

Another effect of slow-motion sound is the analysis into parts of complex sounds. Like the eye, the ear has only a very limited power of separation.

The eye must appeal to a bringing-closer and an enlargement in space, obtained by a telescope, to perceive that a fence, which appeared to be a continuous surface, is in fact made up of stakes planted at intervals. The eye must use a slowing-down; which is to say an enlargement in time, to see that a boxer's jab, which appeared a single and rectilinear movement at constant speed, is in reality a combination of multiple and infinitely varied muscular movements. In the same way, the ear needs a glass to magnify sound in time, which is to say slow-motion sound, to discover, for example, that the monotonous and blurred howling of a storm breaks up, in a more refined reality, into a crowd of very different and never before heard sounds: an apocalypse of shouts, cooings, rumblings, squealings, boomings, tones, and notes for most of which no name exists. A less rich example can just as well be chosen: the sound of a door opening and closing. Slowed down, this humble, ordinary sound reveals its complicated nature, its individual characteristics, its possibilities of dramatic, comic, poetic, or musical meaning.

Of course, this inarticulate language of things is, for our poor ear, most often nothing but a neutral or irritating noise, sometimes barely perceptible. The normal impressions on the sound track give back too little discourse in too little time: mixed, compressed, crushed into each other in an undecipherable brouhaha.

In drawing out the detail, in separating the sounds, in creating a sort of close-up of the sound, slow-motion can allow all beings, all objects to speak. And so that misunderstanding of the Latinists, which made Lucretius say that objects cry, becomes an audible reality.

We already know how to watch the grass grow, now we shall be able to hear it.

(Translated by Robert Lamberton)

Modern Sound Theory

The transition to sound posed a crisis to classical film theory: the elaborate theoretical constructs developed during the silent era to account for the fact that film was understood and thus somehow "like a language" had to be either adapted to accommodate verbal language or junked. In refusing either course, theorists compromised: they accommodated sound but not speech. Cutting themselves off from historical fact, they held the cinema accountable to theory, rejecting any cinema that failed to meet their standards. Contemporary theory, produced during the sound era, never faced the crisis of its predecessor. Though not all modern theorists agree with Bazin that the existence of the cinema precedes its essence, they nonetheless accept not only the sound film but also the talking film as givens. No longer marginalized, sound and language share with the image an equal status.

While earlier filmmaker-theorists such as Clair view asynchronous sound as a means of serving the image, their contemporary counterparts, such as Robert Bresson, endow the sound track with an independent status equal to that of the images. For Clair, the off-screen sound of a door slamming and a car driving away *complements* the image of Bessie Love's anguished face watching from a window. For Bresson, sound should *replace*, not complement, an image. For Clair, the sound "liberates" the images, eliminating the need to show the off-screen action. For Bresson, sound "dominates" the image (or, the image dominates the sound): sound laid over a bare, blackened, or darkened image becomes the primary channel of information for the viewer, virtually effacing the role of the image. Bresson's statements on sound remain somewhat enigmatic. The excerpts reprinted here from his *Notes on Cinematography* were written as working memos to himself and, for that reason, are not concerned with theoretical argumentation of the sort found in Eisenstein's, or even Vertov's, written work. Nonetheless, these notes constitute a modern-day

Declaration of Independence, as it were, for the sound track and, when read in conjunction with Bresson's films, constitute a coherent program for creative sound practice.

In "Direct Sound," Jean-Marie Straub, a former assistant to Renoir *(French Cancan, Elena et les hommes)* and Bresson *(A Man Escaped),* and his collaborator (and wife) Danièle Huillet make a case for "direct sound," that is, for the simultaneous recording of sound and image, as opposed to the postrecording practices employed by the Italian film industry. Combining a Renoiresque authenticity in their abhorrence of dubbing with a Bressonian economy in their paring down of visual and aural information to a minimum, the Straubs' films, such as *Not Reconciled* (1965), *The Chronicle of Anna Magdalena Bach* (1967), *Othon* (1970), and *Moses and Aaron* (1975), strive for the integrity and simplicity that early sound films possessed before the advent of mixing and rerecording.

Like Renoir and Bresson, the Straubs reject illusionism, but they do so out of a commitment that is ideologically as well as aesthetically informed. Dominant sound recording practices, whether American, European, or Italian, are seen as weapons of the bourgeoisie, producing stories, characters, and spaces that are inherently false. The Italian cinema, which postrecords all sound, and the American cinema, which combines direct and postrecorded sound, both violate, for the Straubs, the integrity of sound and space—the Italians by dubbing previously shot images and the Americans (presumably) by recreating spaces through the *mixture* of direct and rerecorded sound. Both practices transform space, while those of direct sound respect it. By forcing themselves to shoot in real settings with direct sound techniques that eschew manipulation, the Straubs create a documentary record of the sound of the space that has an inviolable purity. Direct sound redeems their "stories," "characters," and spaces from the artificial, Esperanto-like, manufactured world of bourgeois representation.

The Straubs' ideological project is related to a modernist concern for the role of the spectator/auditor, a concern also to be seen in the work of Metz and Doane. For the Straubs, dubbing not only betrays the image but also dupes the viewers, making them "deaf and insensitive" and thus perpetuating their passive status. Direct sound respects not only the integrity of real space but the freedom of the viewer to construct it in a nonillusionistic way.

Christian Metz's attempts, in "Aural Objects," to identify and describe sound in terms of how it is perceived derives, in large part, from the phenomenological orientation of his early theoretical work. Thus Metz, unlike classical theorists who base their discussion of sound upon analytical reflection, extensive conceptualization, and prior theorization, begins his study with a description of how we experience sound. Sound is perceived as an attribute or characteristic of an object; it is understood in terms of the object that creates the sound. Therefore, the sound of whistling is incompletely recognized until it is identified as "the whistling *of the wind in the trees.*" Yet Metz, following Roman Jakobson's argument in "Is the Cinema in Decline?," considers sound to be an auditory object in its own right; it is a perceptible signifier similar in status to the image.

What interests Metz here is that sound, though an object like other objects, is clearly understood by spectators not as an object in itself but as a characteristic of another object. In other words, our perception of it involves the implementation of processes of identification that rely on our knowledge of the world. We do not perceive sound directly. Rather our perception of it is socially constructed. Metz's discussion of sound functions as a critique of phenomenology: we experience sound and, for that matter, all other objects through a body of knowledge that is mobilized to make perception possible. For Metz, sound, as a perceptual object, is a socially constructed unity. To study sound is to recognize its place within a larger ideological structure, a relationship that Mary Ann Doane further delineates in "The Voice in the Cinema: The Articulation of Body and Space."

In contrasting silent and sound film, Doane maintains that the silent cinema provided a unity of expression. Although actors could not speak, their bodies, through facial expression and gesture, visualized dialogue. The sound film potentially threatens this unity. The cinema is now based on a "material heterogeneity" (that is, image and sound), and that heterogeneity runs the risk of exposing itself as such—as not unified—unless its duality is carefully concealed. For that reason, sound must be "married" to the image so that it can preserve a sense of unity. Lip-sync guarantees the integrity of the actor who is really only a construction of sound and image, anchoring the voice to a visible presence on the screen. Voice-off poses a distinct challenge to the body's illusory unity. Though the voice comes from behind the screen, it refers to a visual space that is unseen. Sound practice seeks to homogenize these "two" spaces. The off-screen voice is naturalized by linkage to a character depicted in the fiction, becoming part of the narrative structure (as seen in the suspenseful suppression of shots of Dr. Soberin's face—although we hear his off-screen voice—in *Kiss Me Deadly*) or conventionalized in the form of an omniscient narrator (as seen in the documentary's use of authoritative voice-over).

Similarly, the evolution of sound technology is seen as an attempt to conceal the sound's means of production, an attempt to reduce "the distance perceived between the object and its representation," thus creating an illusion of presence that preserves what Doane calls the "fantasmatic body" of the actor. At the same time, sound film operates in three different spaces—that of the diegesis or fiction, that of the screen, and that of the auditorium. But classical narratives strive to deny the last two spaces in their realization of the fiction, eliminating any potential conflict among the three spaces. Although the cinema is composed of heterogeneous materials, sound practice and technology work to deny this heterogeneity. For Doane, only by assaulting this illusory unity can the cinema break the grip of the dominant ideology that determines the cinema's repressive patriarchal politics.

Notes on Sound   ROBERT BRESSON

Sight and Hearing

To know thoroughly what business that sound (or that image) has there.

☐

What is for the eye must not duplicate what is for the ear.

☐

If the eye is entirely won, give nothing or almost nothing to the ear.* One cannot be at the same time all eye and all ear.

☐

When a sound can replace an image, cut the image or neutralize it. The ear goes more toward the within, the eye toward the outer.

☐

A sound must never come to the help of an image, nor an image to the help of a sound.

☐

If a sound is the obligatory complement of an image, give preponderance either to the sound or to the image. If equal, they damage or kill each other, as we say of colors.

☐

Image and sound must not support each other, but must work each in turn through *a sort of relay*.

☐

The eye solicited alone makes the ear impatient, the ear solicited alone makes the eye impatient. *Use these impatiences.* Power of the cinematographer who appeals to the two senses *in a governable way.*

Against the tactics of speed, of noise, set tactics of slowness, of silence.

(Translated by Jonathan Griffin)

*And *vice versa*, if the ear is entirely won, give nothing to the eye.

Direct Sound: An Interview with Jean-Marie Straub and Danièle Huillet

Question: Italy has, to the rest of the world, the reputation of being the country that dubs "the best." The Italians don't just dub the foreign films, but Italian ones as well: they are shot without sound, or with an international sound track, then they are dubbed. You are members of that group—and they are few enough—who film directly with sound, that is, who film the images and record at the same time the sounds of those images.

Straub: Dubbing is not only a technique, it's also an ideology. In a dubbed film, there is not the least rapport between what you see and what you hear. The dubbed cinema is the cinema of lies, mental laziness, and violence, because it gives no space to the viewer and makes him still more deaf and insensitive. In Italy, every day the people are becoming more deaf at a terrifying rate.

Huillet: The thing is still sadder when you think that it's in Italy that, in a certain sense, Western music, polyphony, was born.

Straub: The world of sound is much more vast than the visual world. Dubbing, as it is practiced in Italy, does not work with the sound to enrich it, to give more to the viewer. The greatest part of the waves that a film contains come from the sound, and if in relation to the images the sound is lazy, greedy, and puritan, what sense does that make? But then, it takes courage to make silent films.

Huillet: The great silent films give the viewers the freedom to imagine the sound. A dubbed film doesn't even do that.

Straub: The waves that a sound transmits are not just sound waves. The waves of ideas, movements, emotions, travel across the sound. The waves that we hear in a Pasolini film, for example, are restrictive. They do not enhance the image, they kill it.

Question: There are filmmakers like Robert Bresson or, better, Jacques Tati who use dubbing intelligently. Certain Tati films would be much less rich if they didn't have an artificial sound.

Straub: You can make a dubbed film, but it is necessary to use a hundred times more imagination and work to make a direct-sound film. In effect, the sonorous reality that you record is so rich that to erase it and replace it with another sonorous reality (to dub a film) would take three or four times the amount of time needed to shoot the film. On the contrary, the films are usually dubbed in three days, and sometimes in a day and a half: there is no work. It would make sense to shoot without sound and then make an effort with the sound, in counterpoint to the image. But filmmakers tend to paste the background noises to the silent images that give the impression of reality, the voices that don't belong to the faces we see. It's boring, vain, and a terrible parasitism.

Question: Filming with sound costs less than dubbing.

Straub: Yes, but that would kill the dubbing industry and it violates the local customs.

Huillet: Directors prefer to dub out of laziness: if you have decided to make a film with direct sound, the locations that you choose have to be right not only in terms of the images but also in terms of the sound.

Straub: And that is translated into a thorough analysis of the whole film. For example, our last film, *Moses and Aaron,* the Schoenberg opera, we shot in the Roman amphitheater of Alba Fucense, near Avezzano, in Abruzzi. But we weren't looking for an ancient theater. What we wanted was simply a high plateau, dominated, if possible, by a mountain. We started to look for this plateau four years ago, in a borrowed car, and we put 11,000 kilometers on it, driving more on back roads and country lanes than on paved roads, through all of southern Italy, down to the middle of Sicily. In the course of this research, we didn't see one high plateau, no matter how beautiful, that was good for the sound, because when we found ourselves on a plateau, everything was lost in the air and the wind. And, if there was a valley, we were assaulted by the noises from below. We were therefore obliged to reconsider our intentions and we discovered what we wanted, which was a basin or crater. And in the end, we saw that to film in a basin, in our case the amphitheater, was better for the images also, because we had a natural theatrical space in which the subject, instead of being dissolved, was concentrated. We followed the opposite course of the Taviani brothers or Pasolini, who look for pretty spots, postcards such as you see in magazines, in which the subject of the film is dissipated instead of being localized. For us, the necessity of filming with direct sound, of recording all the singers you see in the frame, of getting at the same time their songs and their bodies that sing, led us to discoveries and we arrived at an idea that we never would have had otherwise.

Question: Filming in direct sound means also editing in a certain way, rather than in another.

Straub: That's obvious. When you film in direct sound, you can't allow yourself to play with the images: you have blocks of a certain length and you can't use the scissors any way you want, for pleasure, for effect.

Huillet: It's exactly the impossibility of playing with the editing that is discouraging. You can't edit direct sound as you edit the films you are going to dub: each image has a sound and you're forced to respect it. Even when the frame is empty, when the character leaves the shot, you can't cut, because you continue to hear, off-camera, the sound of receding footsteps. In a dubbed film, you wait only for the last piece of the foot to leave the range of the camera to cut.

The Art of Illusion

Question: Many filmmakers don't believe in an empty frame with sound that continues off-camera, because they want cinema to be a frame: it should have nothing outside. They deny the existence of a world outside the frame. In your films, the off-screen space is something that exists and is materially felt.

Straub: That's another illusion of the dubbed film. Not only are the lips that move on the screen not the ones that say the words you hear, but the space itself becomes illusionary. Filming in direct sound you can't fool with the space, you have to respect it, and in doing so offer the viewer the chance to reconstruct it, because film is made up of "extracts" of time and space. It's possible to not respect the space you are filming, but then you have to give the viewer the possibility of understanding why it has not been respected and not, as is done in dubbed films, transform a real space into a confused labyrinth and put the viewer into the confusion, from which he can no longer escape. The viewer becomes a dog who can't find its young.

Question: In sum, direct sound is not merely a technical decision but a moral and ideological one: it changes the whole film and especially the rapport that is established between the film and the viewer.

Huillet: I must say this: when you arrive at the conclusion that you must do a film like that, you cut yourself off from the industry, more or less completely. If you refuse to film with just a general sound track, if you refuse to dub your film, if you refuse to use such and such an actor because he's been seen too much and it's absurd to always use the same faces, it's over. You cut yourself off completely. In fact, the main reason for dubbing is industrial: only by accepting the dictatorship of dubbing can you use two or three stars from different countries in the same film.

Straub: And the result is an international product, something stripped of words, onto which each country grafts its respective language. Languages that don't belong to the lips, words that don't belong to the faces.

But it's a product that sells well. Everything becomes illusion. There is no longer any truth. In the end, even the ideas and emotions become false. For example, in *Allonsanfan*, and I mention this film because it's not worth talking about Petri's or Lizzani's, there is not a single moment, not one instant where there is a true, human emotion. Not even by accident, by chance. It's trash. It has only the illusion of a comic book.

Question: Many filmmakers identify the international aesthetic with the popular aesthetic, and accept dubbing, stars from different countries, and the rest, because they think it's the only way to make successful films.

Straub: The international aesthetic is an invention and weapon of the bourgeoisie. The popular aesthetic is always a personal aesthetic.

Question: For the bourgeoisie, there is no art that is not universal. The international aesthetic is like Esperanto.

Straub: Exactly. Esperanto has always been the dream of the bourgeoisie.

(Translated by Bill Kavaler)

Aural Objects   CHRISTIAN METZ

How do we perceive the aural world? This problem is particularly important in the case of sound cinema (which today is simply *the* cinema), television, radio, etc. However, unless it is a question of the sounds of spoken language, sound has been studied far less than the visual, our civilization greatly privileging the latter. Caught between the two, "sound" is often left aside.[1]

How is it possible that we are capable of recognizing and isolating the sound of "lapping" on the sound track of a travelogue or among the confused rustling sounds heard when walking in a forest? How is this possible even when we don't know its source, even if we identify other quite different sounds as "lapping" at other times? It must be that "lapping" exists as an autonomous aural object, the pertinent traits of its acoustic signifier corresponding to those of a linguistic signified, to the semes of the sememe "lapping." Four of these traits appear readily, resulting from their "closest" commutations:

1) This sound is relatively weak (as opposed to "uproar," "yelling," "ruckus," etc.).

2) It is discontinuous, whereas a "clamor," a "whistling," a "background noise," isn't.

3) It is acoustically double, or at least not single, if by double one means that its occurrences break down into at least two successive sounds: /--/. . . . /--/. . . . /--/. . . . (In this respect, the first three phonemes of the linguistic signifier, *l-a-p*ping,[2] can be considered onomatopoeic.) Commutation shows that other identifiable sounds don't present this characteristic and that each of their occurrences is "single"; thus "detonation," or "blow," or "crash" when referring to sounds. It's the same opposition as between FLOP and CLACK.[3]

4) This sound is experienced as "liquid," or as if caused by a

This selection constitutes the concluding section (pp. 153–61) of "Le perçu et le nommé," first published in *Pour une esthétique sans entrave—Melanges Mikel Dufrenne* (Paris: Editions 10/18, 1975), pp. 345–77, and reprinted in *Essais sémiotiques* (Paris: Editions Klincksieck, 1977), pp. 129–61. In the earlier portions of this article, Christian Metz argues that the process of perception is inseparably entwined with that of naming, and thus with the cultural lexicon which informs the individual's segmentation of the real world. In the section reprinted here, Metz extends this argument from visual objects to sound "objects," e.g., the various identifiable segments into which we divide—according to culture-specific norms—the cinema sound track.

liquid, whereas "rubbing" and "scraping" in their aural sememe present the
trait "solid," while "hissing" and "whistling" are "gaseous."

These four traits, and all of those of the same group that I am
leaving out, are what auditory perception and language have in common.
There is no sense in asking whether they define the French word "lapping"
(clapotis) or "lapping" as a characteristic noise, since the sound and the word
exist only in relation to each other. Our four traits constitute the level of articulation where the two coincide, by virtue of the metacodic status of language.

Ideological Undermining of the Aural Dimension

There is, nonetheless, a difference between the visual and the aural in their
cultural definition. When I have recognized a "floor lamp" and can name it,
the identification is completed and all that I could add would be adjectival
in nature. But, on the contrary, if I have distinctly and consciously heard a
"lapping" or a "whistling," I only have the feeling of a first identification, of
a still incomplete recognition. This impression disappears only when I recognize that it was the lapping *of a river,* or the whistling *of the wind in the
trees:* in short, the recognition of a sound leads directly to the question: "A
sound of what?" At first glance, this seems paradoxical, since the sememe
of the initial identification ("whistling," "hissing," "rubbing," etc.) corresponds to strictly aural profiles, while those of the final identification (the wind,
the river), which have nothing of the auditory, name the source of the sound
rather than the sound itself.

In language as the metacode of sounds, the most complete identification is obviously that which simultaneously designates the sound and its
source ("rumble of thunder"). But if one of the two indicators has to be
suppressed, it is curious to note that it's the aural indicator that can most
easily be suppressed with the least loss of recognizability. If I perceive a
"rumble" without further specification, some mystery or suspense remains
(horror and mystery films depend on this effect): the identification is only
partial. However, if I perceive "thunder" without giving any attention to its
acoustic characteristics, the identification is sufficient.

One might respond by saying that the example is tendentious,
since thunder is an object consisting of nothing but sound (it can't be seen,
only lightning is seen). But the situation remains the same for objects which
are not completely defined by their sound. If I allude to the "buzzing of a
machine," my reader doesn't know exactly what I am talking about ("What

machine?"). Although my classification of the sound was precise, I was too vague concerning its source. It would suffice for me to invert my axis of precision, for me to say "It's the sound of a jet plane," in order for everyone to feel that I expressed myself clearly, and to be satisfied. As soon as the source of the sound is recognized (jet plane), the taxonomies of the sound itself (buzzing, whistling, etc.) can only provide, at least in our era and geographic location, supplementary precisions, which are felt to be dispensable, of a *basically* adjectival nature, even when linguistically they are expressed by nouns. At the discursive level, we are no longer naming, but already describing to a certain extent.

Ideologically, the aural source is an object, the sound itself a "characteristic." Like any characteristic, it is linked to the object, and that is why identification of the latter suffices to evoke the sound, whereas the inverse is not true. "To understand" a perceptual event is not to describe it exhaustively but to be able to classify and categorize it:[4] to designate the object of which it is an example. Therefore, sounds are more often classified according to the objects which transmit them than by their own characteristics.

There is nothing natural in this situation: from a logical point of view, "buzzing" *is* an object, an acoustic object in the same way that a tulip is a visual object. Language takes that into account—or at least the lexicon does, in the absence of discourse—since a great number of recognizable sounds, relegated to the rank of characteristics, still correspond to nouns—this is a sort of compromise which doesn't prevent auditory traits from participating more weakly than others in the dominant principle of object recognition. On the other hand, as soon as it becomes a question of naming the concept of aural object itself, it is necessary to add to the word "object" the epithet "aural," as I have been doing and as advocates of concrete music do, while no precision is required for that which should logically be called "visual object": we consider it self-evident that a banner is an object (with no adjective needed) but we hesitate over a hoot; it's an infra-object, an object that is only aural.

On Primitive Substantialism

There is a kind of primitive substantialism which is profoundly rooted in our culture (and without a doubt in other cultures as well, though not necessarily in all cultures) which distinguishes fairly rigidly the primary qualities that determine the list of objects (substances) and the secondary qualities which correspond to attributes applicable to these objects. This conception is reflected in the entire Western philosophic tradition beginning with notions put forth by Descartes and Spinoza. It is also clear that this "world view" has something to do with the subject-predicate structure particularly prevalent in Indo-European languages.

For us, the primary qualities are in general visual and tactile. Tactile because touch is traditionally the very criterion of materiality.[5] Visual because the identification processes necessary to present-day life and to production techniques rely on the eye above all the other senses (it is only in language that the auditory order is "rehabilitated," as if by compensation). The subject is too vast for this study. Nevertheless, it is possible to begin to discern certain qualities which seem to be "secondary": sounds (evoked above), olfactory qualities (a "scent" is barely an object), and even certain sub-dimensions of the visual order such as color.[6]

In a clothing store, if two articles of clothing have the same cut, and are only distinguishable by color, they are considered to be "the *same* sweater (or pair of pants) in two different colors." Culture depends on the permanence of the object, language reaffirms it: only the adjective has varied. But if the two articles of clothing are the same color but have different cuts, no one will say or think that the store was offering "the same color in two different articles of clothing" (an incorrect formula, and not by accident, since color is in the grammatical position of subject). One would be more likely to say that these were "two articles of clothing," this scarf and this skirt, for example, "of the same color." The utterance puts color back in its place, that of predicate: these are two distinct objects which have an attribute in common.

"Off-Screen Sound" in the Cinema

The division between primary and secondary qualities plays a large role in one of the classical problems of film theory, that of "off-screen sound." In a film a sound is considered "off" (literally off the screen) when in fact it is the sound's source that is off the screen; therefore an "off-screen voice" is defined as one which belongs to a character who does not appear (visually) on the screen. We tend to forget that a sound in itself in never "off": either it is audible or it doesn't exist. When it exists, it could not possibly be situated within the interior of the rectangle or outside of it, since the nature of sounds is to diffuse themselves more or less into the entire surrounding space:

sound is simultaneously "in" the screen, in front, behind, around, and throughout the entire movie theater.[7]

On the contrary, when a visual element is said to be "off," it really is: it can be reconstructed by inference in relation to what is visible within the rectangle, but it is not seen. A well-known example would be "the lure": the presence of a person on a side of the screen is surmised when you can only see a hand or shoulder; the rest is out of the visual field.

The situation is clear: the language used by technicians and studios, without realizing it, conceptualizes sound in a way that makes sense only for the image. We claim that we are talking about sound, but we are actually thinking of the visual image of the sound's source.

This confusion is obviously reinforced by a characteristic of sound that is physical and not social: spatial anchoring of aural events is much more vague and uncertain than that of visual events. The two sensory orders don't have the same relationship to space, sound's relationship being much less precise, restrictive, even when it indicates a general direction (but it rarely indicates a really precise site, which on the contrary is the rule for the visible). It is perfectly understandable that film technicians should have based their classification on the less elusive of the two elements. (However, it should be remembered that the phylogenetic choice of a particular acoustic material, the sound of the voice, for the signifiers of human language, is probably due to similar reasons: phonic communication is not interrupted by darkness or by night. You can speak to someone who is in back of you, or who is behind something, or whose location is unknown. The relatively weak relation to space provides multiple advantages which the human race would not have benefited from had a visual language been chosen.)

But, to get back to off-screen sound, the laws of physics do not adequately explain this persistent confusion between the aural object itself and the visual image of its source (yet even the most literal definition of off-screen sound rests on this confusion). There is something else behind it, something cultural that we have already encountered in this study: the conception of sound as an attribute, as a nonobject, and therefore the tendency to neglect its own characteristics in favor of those of its corresponding "substance," which in this case is the visible object, which has emitted the sound.

Semiology and Phenomenology

The above heading poses an epistemological question which is not new. It seems to me that the semiological project in its entirety, because of its initial

anchoring in a concern for the perceptible signifier and its perceptible transformations, etc., defines itself in a certain way as the continuation of phenomenological inspiration. I myself have "admitted" to this necessary stage
(this debt, also) in the first chapter of my first book.[8]

Of course, these "continuations" are also always reversals, reactions. The phenomenologists wanted to "describe" the spontaneous apprehension of things (and they sometimes did that with a correctness which
will become less quickly outmoded than certain semiological overstate-
ments). They were not sufficiently aware of the fact that this "apprehension" is in itself a product, that therefore it could very well be "otherwise"
in cultures not of the describer. But (and I'm not trying to create paradoxes)
it remains true that these conclusions are also beginnings. It is a great illusion
of positivistic scientism to blind itself to all that is nonscientific in science, or
in the effort toward science, without which it could not even exist. We are
all, at some time, phenomenologists, and those who declare themselves as
such at least have the merit of admitting to a certain kind of relationship to
the world, which is not the only possible relationship, nor the only desirable
one, but one which exists in everybody, even if it is hidden or unknown.

When I think about my own field of research, cinematographic
analysis, how could I hide from myself—and why would I— the fact that an
entire body of previous cultural knowledge, without which a "first viewing"
of the film would not even be a *viewing* (nor would any of the subsequent
"viewings," which become more fragmented, less descriptive, and, in another sense, more "semiological")—that an entire body of knowledge already present in my immediate perception is necessarily mobilized to make
it possible for me to work? And how could I miss the fact that this body of
knowledge is—that it is and isn't—the "perceptual *cogito*" of phenomenology? The content is the same, the status we grant it is not.

In this study, I wanted to show that the perceptual object is a
constructed unity, *socially constructed,* and also (to some extent) a linguistic
unity. We find ourselves quite far, you could say, from the "adverse spectacle" of subject and object, from the cosmological as well as existential (or
at least transcendental) "there is" in which phenomenology wanted to place
our presence in objects, and the presence of objects in us. I am not so sure,
or else this "distance" is only along certain axes, and does not imply a complete rupture of the horizon. Obviously, I spoke of semes, of pertinent optical traits, etc., that is to say, of elements whose nature is to have no lived
existence and which are on the contrary—on the contrary or for that very
reason?—the conditions of possibility of the lived, the structures of production which create the lived and are abolished in it, which simultaneously find
in it the site of their manifestation and their negation: the objective determinants of subjective feeling. To concentrate interest on this latent stratum

is to stray from the phenomenological path. But the manifest stratum, besides the fact that it has its own reality, authorizing potential or completed studies, is the only stratum available to us in the beginning, even though we soon leave it behind.

I have tried to understand why perception proceeds by means of objects. But I first felt, and felt strongly, that it does in fact proceed this way: phenomenologists have always made the same claim. In order for me to have tried to dismantle the "objects" which so strike the native (and at first, even in order for me to have had that desire), it was necessary that I be that native myself, and that I be struck by the same things as he. Every psychoanalytic project begins by a "phenomenology," according to the analyst's own terminology. This is true not only for this domain. Every time something is to be explained, it is more prudent to begin by experiencing it.

(Translated by Georgia Gurrieri)

Notes

1. A widespread opinion has it that the privileging of spoken language in our civilization results in an underdevelopment of visual richness. And that isn't false. But this is even more true of the aural richness of "sounds" which are in direct competition with language, due to the fact that language also has a signifier of the aural order.

2. [The original example given by Metz is the French word *clapotis*, in which he considers the first two phonemes, c-l-apotis, to be onomatopoeic.]

3. Onomatopoeias, which are exceptions to the "arbitrariness" of linguistic signification, represent the only case in which there is a direct connection between the signifier of the metacode (language) and the totality of the object-code (perceptual code). See the important work of Pierre Guiraud for cases of this type, where the linguistic signifier appears to be "motivated."

4. In the field of semiology, this idea has been developed in a particularly clear manner by Luis J. Prieto, notably in *Messages et signaux* (Paris: Presses Universitaires de France, collection "Le linguistique," 1966). In chapter 2, "Le mécanisme de l'indication," pp. 15–27, Prieto makes the point that every indication is an indication of a category, that a category has no meaning outside its relationship to a complementary category (or categories) in the realm of discourse which is presupposed in each case, etc.

5. I had already been led to this remark via a completely different route in my article "A propos de l'impression de réalité au cinéma" (1965), taken from pp. 13–24 of vol. 1 of *Essais sur la signification au cinéma* (Paris: Klincksieck, 1968), notably pp. 18–19.

6. There is a reason why film without color, the black-and-white film, was "possible" (culturally, in relation to demand) for many years, and still is to a large extent, that the odor-film has no past or future development, that the "sound talkie" (today's usual film) is almost always more talk than sound, the noises being so impoverished and stereotyped. In fact, the only cinematographic aspects that interest everyone, and not just some specialists, are the image and speech.

7. This relates to another characteristic fact about present-day cinema. The visual events are only "reproduced" by means of certain distortions in perspective (absence of binocular depth, the rectangular screen which distorts real vision; etc.). But auditory aspects, providing that the recording is well done, undergo no appreciable loss in relation to the corresponding sound in the real world: in principle, nothing distinguishes a gunshot heard in a film from a gunshot heard on the street. Bela Balazs, the film theoretician, used to say that "sounds have no images." Thus the sounds of a film spread into space as do sounds in life, or almost. This difference in perceptual status between what is called "reproduction" in the case of the visible, and that to which the same name has been given in the case of the audible, already seemed important to me in "Problèmes actuels de théorie du cinéma," *Essais sur la signification au cinéma*, vol. 2, pp. 57–58 and in *Langage et cinéma* (Paris: Larousse, 1971), pp. 209–10.

8. *Essais sur la signification au cinéma*, published thanks to Mikel Dufrenne, to whom we pay homage today in the diverse studies which compose this volume. [The reference is to *Mélanges Mikel Dufrenne* ("Pour une esthetique sans entrave"), where Metz's article was first published.]

The Voice in the Cinema:
The Articulation of Body and Space
MARY ANN DOANE

Synchronization

The silent film is certainly understood, at least retrospectively and even (it is arguable) in its time, as incomplete, as lacking speech. The stylized gestures of the silent cinema, its heavy pantomime, have been defined as a form of compensation for that lack. Hugo Münsterberg wrote, in 1916, "To the actor of the moving pictures . . . the temptation offers itself to overcome the deficiency [the absence of "words and the modulation of the voice"] by a heightening of the gestures and of the facial play, with the result that the emotional expression becomes exaggerated."[1] The absent voice reemerges in gestures and the contortions of the face—it is spread over the body of the actor. The uncanny effect of the silent film in the era of sound is in part linked to the separation, by means of intertitles, of an actor's speech from the image of his/her body.

Consideration of sound in the cinema (in its most historically and institutionally privileged form—that of dialogue or the use of the voice) engenders a network of metaphors whose nodal point appears to be the body. One may readily respond that this is only "natural"—who can conceive of a voice without a body?[2] However, the body reconstituted by the technology and practices of the cinema is a *fantasmatic* body, which offers a support as well as a point of identification for the subject addressed by the film. The purpose of this essay is simply to trace some of the ways in which this fantasmatic body acts as a pivot for certain cinematic practices of representation and authorizes and sustains a limited number of relationships between voice and image.

The attributes of this fantasmatic body are first and foremost unity (through the emphasis on a coherence of the senses) and presence-to-itself. The addition of sound to the cinema introduces the possibility of re-presenting a fuller (and organically unified) body, and of confirming the status of speech as an individual property right. The potential number and kinds of articulations between sound and image are reduced by the very name attached to the new heterogeneous medium—the "talkie." Histories of the cinema ascribe the stress on synchronization to a "public demand": "the public, fascinated by the novelty, wanting to be sure they were hearing what they saw, would have felt that a trick was being played on them if they were not shown the words coming from the lips of the actors."[3] In Lewis Jacobs's account, this fear on the part of the audience of being "cheated" is one of the factors which initially limits the deployment of sonorous material (as well as the mobility of the camera). From this perspective, the use of voice-off or voice-over must be a late acquisition, attempted only after a certain "breaking-in" period during which the novelty of the sound film was allowed to wear itself out. But, whatever the fascination of the new medium (or whatever meaning is attached to it by retrospective readings of its prehistory), there is no doubt that synchronization (in the form of "lip-sync") has played a major role in the dominant narrative cinema. Technology standardizes the relation through the development of the synchronizer, the Moviola, the flatbed editing table. The mixing apparatus allows a greater control over the establishment of relationships between dialogue, music, and sound effects and, in practice, the level of the dialogue generally determines the levels of sound effects and music.[4] Despite a number of experiments with other types of sound/image relationships (those of Clair, Lang, Vigo, and, more recently, Godard, Straub, and Duras), synchronous dialogue remains the dominant form of sonorous representation in the cinema.

Yet, even when asynchronous or "wild" sound is utilized, the fantasmatic body's attribute of unity is not lost. It is simply displaced—the body *in* the film becomes the body *of* the film. Its senses work in tandem, for the combination of sound and image is described in terms of "totality" and the "organic."[5] Sound carries with it the potential risk of exposing the material heterogeneity of the medium; attempts to contain that risk surface in the language of the ideology of organic unity. In the discourse of technicians, sound is "married" to the image and, as one sound engineer puts it in an article on postsynchronization, "one of the basic goals of the motion picture industry is to make the screen look alive in the eyes of the audience. . . ."[6]

Concomitant with the demand for a lifelike representation is the desire for "presence," a concept which is not specific to the cinematic sound track but which acts as a standard to measure quality in the sound recording industry as a whole. The term "presence" offers a certain legitimacy to the wish for pure reproduction and becomes a selling point in the construction of sound as a commodity. The television commercial asks whether we can "tell the difference" between the voice of Ella Fitzgerald and that of Memorex (and since our representative in the commercial—the ardent fan—cannot, the only conclusion to be drawn is that owning a Memorex tape is equivalent to having Ella in your living room). Technical advances in sound recording (such as the Dolby system) are aimed at diminishing the noise of the system, concealing the work of the apparatus, and thus reducing the distance perceived between the object and its representation. The maneuvers of the sound recording industry offer evidence which supports Walter Benjamin's thesis linking mechanical reproduction as a phenomenon with contemporary society's destruction of the "aura" (which he defines as "the unique phenomenon of a distance, however close it may be"[7]). According to Benjamin,

[the] contemporary decay of the aura . . . rests on two circumstances, both of which are related to the increasing significance of the masses in contemporary life. Namely, the desire of contemporary masses to bring things "closer" spatially and humanly, which is just as ardent as their bent toward overcoming the uniqueness of every reality by accepting its reproduction.[8]

Nevertheless, while the desire to bring things closer is certainly exploited in making sound marketable, the qualities of uniqueness and authenticity are not sacrificed—it is not any voice which the tape brings to the consumer but the voice of Ella Fitzgerald. The voice is not detachable from a body which is quite specific—that of the star. In the cinema, cult value and the "aura" resurface in the star system. In 1930 a writer feels the need to assure audiences that postsynchronization as a technique does not necessarily entail substituting an alien voice for a "real" voice, that the industry does not condone a mismatching of voices and bodies.[9] Thus, the voice serves as a support for the spectator's recognition and his/her identification of, as well as with, the star.

Just as the voice must be anchored by a given body, the body must be anchored in a given space. The fantasmatic visual space which the film constructs is supplemented by techniques designed to spatialize the voice, to localize it, give it depth, and thus lend to the characters the consistency of the real. A concern for room tone, reverberation characteristics, and sound perspective manifests a desire to recreate, as one sound editor describes it, "the bouquet that surrounds the words, the presence of the voice, the way it fits in with the physical environment."[10] The dangers of postsynchronization and looping stem from the fact that the voice is disengaged from its "proper" space (the space conveyed by the visual image) and the credibility of that voice depends upon the technician's ability to return it to the site of its origin. Failure to do so risks exposure of the fact that looping is "narration masking as dialogue."[11] Dialogue is defined, therefore, not simply in terms of the establishment of an I-you relationship but as the necessary spatializing of that relationship. Techniques of sound recording tend to confirm the cinema's function as a *mise-en-scène* of bodies.

Voice-off and Voice-over

The spatial dimension which monophonic sound is capable of simulating is that of depth—the apparent source of the sound may be moved forward or backward but the lateral dimension is lacking due to the fact that there is no sideways spread of reverberation or of ambient noise.[12] Nevertheless, sound/image relationships established in the narrative film work to suggest that sound does, indeed, issue from that other dimension. In film theory, this work to provide the effect of a lateral dimension receives recognition in the term "voice-off." "Voice-off" refers to instances in which we hear the voice of a character who is not visible within the frame. Yet the film establishes, by means of previous shots or other contextual determinants, the character's "presence" in the space of the scene, in the diegesis. He/she is "just over there," "just beyond the frameline," in a space which "exists" but which the camera does not choose to show. The traditional use of voice-off con-stitutes a denial of the frame as a limit and an affirmation of the unity and homogeneity of the depicted space.

Because it is defined in terms of what is visible within the rectan-gular space of the screen, the term "voice-off" has been subject to some dispute. Claude Bailblé, for instance, argues that a voice-off must always be a "voice-in" because the literal source of the sound in the theater is always the speaker placed behind the screen.[13] Yet, the space to which the term refers is not that of the theater but the fictional space of the diegesis. Never-theless, the use of the term is based on the requirement that the two spaces coincide, "overlap" to a certain extent. For the screen limits what *can be seen* of the diegesis (there is always "more" of the diegesis than the camera can cover at any one time). The placement of the speaker behind the screen simply confirms the fact that the cinematic apparatus is designed to promote the impression of a homogeneous space—the senses of the fantasmatic body cannot be split. The screen is the space where the image is deployed while the theater as a whole is the space of the deployment of sound. Yet, the screen is given precedence over the acoustical space of the theater—the screen is posited as the site of the spectacle's unfolding and all sounds must ema-nate from it. (Bailblé asks, "What would be, in effect, a voice-off which came from the back of the theater? Poor little screen . . . "[14]—in other words, its effect would be precisely to diminish the epistemological power of the im-age, to reveal its limitations.)

The hierarchical placement of the visible above the audible, ac-cording to Christian Metz, is not specific to the cinema but a more general cultural production.[15] And the term voice-off merely acts as a reconfirmation of that hierarchy. For it only appears to describe a sound—what it really refers to is the visibility (or lack of visibility) of the source of the sound. Metz argues that sound is never "off." While a visual element specified as "off" actually lacks visibility, a "sound-off" is always audible.

Despite the fact that Metz's argument is valid and we tend to repeat on the level of theory the industry's subordination of sound to image, the term voice-off does name a particular relationship between sound and image—a relationship which has been extremely important historically in diverse film practices. While it is true that sound is almost always discussed with reference to the image, it does not necessarily follow that this automatically makes sound subordinate. From another perspective, it is doubtful that any image (in the sound film) is uninflected by sound. This is crucially so, given the fact that in the dominant narrative cinema, sound extends from beginning to end of the film—sound is never absent (silence is, at the least, room tone). In fact, the lack of any sound whatsoever is taboo in the editing of the sound track.

The point is not that we "need" terms with which to describe, honor, and acknowledge the autonomy of a particular sensory material, but that we must attempt to think [about] the heterogeneity of the cinema. This might be done more fruitfully by means of the concept of space than through the unities of sound and image. In the cinematic situation, three types of space are put into play:

1) The space of the diegesis. This space has no physical limits, it is not contained or measurable. It is a virtual space constructed by the film and is delineated as having both audible and visible traits (as well as implications that its objects can be touched, smelled, and tasted).

2) The visible space of the screen as receptor of the image. It is measurable and "contains" the visible signifiers of the film. Strictly speaking, the screen is not audible although the placement of the speaker behind the screen constructs that illusion.

3) The acoustical space of the theater or auditorium. It might be argued that this space is also visible, but the film cannot visually activate signifiers in this space unless a second projector is used. Again, despite the fact that the speaker is behind the screen and therefore sound appears to be emanating from a focused point, sound is not "framed" in the same way as the image. In a sense, it *envelops* the spectator.

All of these are spaces *for the spectator,* but the first is the only space which the characters of the fiction film can acknowledge (for the characters there are no voices-off). Different cinematic modes—documentary, narrative, avant-garde—establish different relationships between the three spaces. The classical narrative film, for instance, works to deny the existence of the last two spaces in order to buttress the credibility (legitimacy) of the first space. If a character looks at and speaks to the spectator, this constitutes an acknowledgment that the character is seen and heard in a radically different space and is therefore generally read as transgressive.

Nothing unites the three spaces but the signifying practice of the film itself together with the institutionalization of the theater as a type of metaspace which binds together the three spaces, as the *place* where a unified cinematic discourse unfolds. The cinematic institution's stake in this process of unification is apparent. Instances of voice-off in the classical film are particularly interesting examples of the way in which the three spaces undergo an elaborate imbrication. For the phenomenon of the voice-off cannot be understood outside of a consideration of the relationships established between the diegesis, the visible space of the screen, *and* the acoustical space of the theater. The place in which the signifier manifests itself is the acoustical space of the theater, but this is the space with which it is least concerned. The voice-off deepens the diegesis, gives it an extent which exceeds that of the image, and thus supports the claim that there is a space in the fictional world which the camera does not register. In its own way, it *accounts for* lost space. The voice-off is a sound which is first and foremost in the service of the film's construction of space and only indirectly in the service of the image. It validates both what the screen reveals of the diegesis and what it conceals.

Nevertheless, the use of the voice-off always entails a risk—that of exposing the material heterogeneity of the cinema. Synchronous sound masks the problem and this at least partially explains its dominance. But the more interesting question, perhaps, is: How can the classical film allow the representation of a voice whose source is not simultaneously represented? As soon as the sound is detached from its source, no longer anchored by a represented body, its potential work as a signifier is revealed. There is always something uncanny about a voice which emanates from a source outside the frame. However, as Pascal Bonitzer points out, the narrative film exploits the marginal anxiety connected with the voice-off by incorporating its disturbing effects within the dramatic framework. Thus, the function of the voice-off (as well as that of the voice-over) becomes extremely important in *film noir*. Bonitzer takes as his example *Kiss Me Deadly*, a *film noir* in which the villain remains out of frame until the last sequences of the film. Maintaining him outside of the field of vision "gives to his sententious voice, swollen by mythological comparisons, a greater power of disturbing, the scope of an oracle—dark prophet of the end of the world. And, in spite of that, his voice is submitted to the destiny of the body . . . a shot, he falls—and with him in ridicule, his discourse with its prophetic accents." [16]

The voice-off is always "submitted to the destiny of the body" because it *belongs* to a character who is confined to the space of the diegesis, if not to the visible space of the screen. Its efficacity rests on the knowledge that the character can easily be made visible by a slight reframing which would reunite the voice and its source. The body acts as an invisible support for the use of both the voice-over during a flashback and the interior monologue as well. Although the voice-over in a flashback effects a temporal dislocation of the voice with respect to the body, the voice is frequently returned to the body as a form of narrative closure. Furthermore, the voice-over very often simply initiates the story and is subsequently superseded by synchronous dialogue, allowing the diegesis to "speak for itself." In *Sunset Boulevard* the convention is taken to its limits: the voice-over narration is, indeed, linked to a body (that of the hero), but it is the body of a dead man.

In the interior monologue, on the other hand, the voice and the body are represented simultaneously, but the voice, far from being an extension of that body, manifests its inner lining. The voice displays what is inaccessible to the image, what exceeds the visible: the "inner life" of the character. The voice here is the privileged mark of interiority, turning the body "inside-out."

The voice-over commentary in the documentary, unlike the voice-off, the voice-over during a flashback, or the interior monologue, is, in effect, a *disembodied* voice. While the latter three voices work to affirm the homogeneity and dominance of diegetic space, the voice-over commentary is necessarily presented as outside of that space. It is its radical otherness with respect to the diegesis which endows this voice with a certain authority. As a form of direct address, it speaks without mediation to the audience, bypassing the "characters" and establishing a complicity between itself and the spectator—together they understand and thus *place* the image. It is precisely because the voice is not localizable, because it cannot be yoked to a body, that it is capable of interpreting the image, producing its truth. Disembodied, lacking any specification in space or time, the voice-over is, as Bonitzer points out, beyond criticism—it censors the questions "Who is speaking?," "Where?," "In what time?," and "For whom?"

This is not, one suspects, without ideological implications. The first of these implications is that the voice-off[17] represents a power, that of disposing of the image and of what it reflects, from a space absolutely *other* with respect to that inscribed in the image-track. *Absolutely other and absolutely indeterminant.* Because it rises from the field of the Other, the voice-off is assumed to know: this is the essence of its power. . . . The power of the voice is a stolen power, a usurpation.[18]

In the history of the documentary, this voice has been for the most part that of the male, and its power resides in the possession of knowledge and in the privileged, unquestioned activity of interpretation. This function of the voice-over has been appropriated by the television documentary and television news programs, in which sound carries the burden of "information" while the impoverished image simply fills the screen. Even when the major voice is explicitly linked with a body (that of the anchorman in television news), this body, in its turn, is situated in the nonspace of the studio. In film, on the other hand, the voice-over is quite often dissociated from any specific figure. The guarantee of knowledge, in such a system, lies in its irreducibility to the spatiotemporal limitations of the body.

The Pleasure of Hearing

The means by which sound is deployed in the cinema implicate the spectator in a particular textual problematic—they establish certain conditions for understanding which obtain in the "intersubjective relation" between film and spectator. The voice-over commentary and, differently, the interior monologue and voice-over-flashback speak more or less *directly to* the spectator, constituting him/her as an empty space to be "filled" with knowledge about events, character psychology, etc. More frequently, in the fiction film, the use of synchronous dialogue and the voice-off presuppose a spectator who *overhears* and, overhearing, is unheard and unseen himself. This activity with respect to the sound track is not unlike the voyeurism often exploited by the cinematic image. In any event, the use of the voice in the cinema appeals to the spectator's desire to hear, or what Lacan refers to as the invocatory drive.

         In what does the pleasure of hearing consist? Beyond the added effect of "realism" which sound gives to the cinema, beyond its supplement of meaning anchored by intelligible dialogue, what is the specificity of the pleasure of hearing a voice with its elements escaping a strictly verbal codification—volume, rhythm, timbre, pitch? Psychoanalysis situates pleasure in the divergence between the present experience and the memory of satisfaction: "Between a (more or less inaccessible) memory and a very precise (and localizable) immediacy of perception is opened the gap where pleasure is produced." [19] Memories of the first experiences of the voice, of the hallucinatory satisfaction it offered, circumscribe the pleasure of hearing and ground its relation to the fantasmatic body. This is not simply to situate the experiences of infancy as the sole determinant in a system directly linking cause and effect but to acknowledge that the traces of archaic desires are never annihilated. According to Guy Rosolato, it is "the organization of the fantasm itself which implies a permanence, an insistence of the recall to the origin." [20]

Space, for the child, is defined initially in terms of the audible, not the visible: "It is only in a second phase that the organization of visual space insures the perception of the object as *external*" (p. 80). The first differences are traced along the axis of sound: the voice of the mother, the voice of the father. Furthermore, the voice has a greater command over space than the look—one can hear around corners, through walls. Thus, for the child the voice, even before language, is the instrument of demand. In the construction/hallucination of space and the body's relation to that space, the voice plays a major role. In comparison with sight, as Rosolato points out, the voice is reversible: sound is simultaneously emitted and heard, by the subject himself. As opposed to the situation in seeing, it is as if "an 'acoustical' mirror were always in function. Thus, the images of entry and exit relative to the body are intimately articulated. They can therefore be confounded, inverted, favored one over the other" (p. 79). Because one can hear sounds behind oneself as well as those with sources *inside* the body (sounds of digestion, circulation, respiration, etc.), two sets of terms are placed in opposition: exterior/front/sight and interior/back/hearing. And "hallucinations are determined by an imaginary structuration of the body according to these oppositions . . ." (p. 80). The voice appears to lend itself to hallucination, in particular the hallucination of power over space effected by an extension or restructuration of the body. Thus, as Lacan points out, our mass media and our technology, as mechanical extensions of the body, result in "planeterizing" or "even stratospherizing" the voice.[21]

The voice also traces the forms of unity and separation *between* bodies. The mother's soothing voice, in a particular cultural context, is a major component of the "sonorous envelope" which surrounds the child and is the first model of auditory pleasure. An image of corporeal unity is derived from the realization that the production of sound by the voice and its audition coincide. The imaginary fusion of the child with the mother is supported by the recognition of common traits characterizing the different voices and, more particularly, of their potential for harmony. According to Rosolato, the voice in music makes appeal to the nostalgia for such an imaginary cohesion, for a "veritable incantation" of bodies.

The harmonic and polyphonic unfolding in music can be understood as a succession of tensions and releases, of unifications and divergences between parts which are gradually stacked, opposed in successive chords only to be resolved ultimately into their simplest unity. It is therefore the entire dramatization of separated bodies and their reunion which harmony supports. (p. 82)

Yet, the imaginary unity associated with the earliest experience of the voice is broken by the premonition of difference, division, effected by the intervention of the father whose voice, engaging the desire of the mother, acts as the agent of separation and constitutes the voice of the mother as the irretrievably lost object of desire. The voice in this instance, far from being the narcissistic measure of harmony, is the voice of interdiction. The voice thus understood is an interface of imaginary and symbolic, pulling at once toward the signifying organization of language and its reduction of the range of vocal sounds to those it binds and codifies, and toward original and imaginary attachments, "representable in the fantasm by the body, or by the corporeal mother, the child at her breast" (p. 86).

At the cinema, the sonorous envelope provided by the theatrical space together with techniques employed in the construction of the sound track works to sustain the narcissistic pleasure derived from the image of a certain unity, cohesion, and, hence, an identity grounded by the spectator's fantasmatic relation to his/her own body. The aural illusion of position constructed by the approximation of sound perspective and by techniques which spatialize the voice and endow it with "presence" guarantees the singularity and stability of a point of audition, thus holding at bay the potential trauma of dispersal, dismemberment, difference. The subordination of the voice to the screen as the site of the spectacle's unfolding makes vision and hearing work together in manufacturing the "hallucination" of a fully sensory world. Nevertheless, the recorded voice, which presupposes a certain depth, is in contradiction with the flatness of the two-dimensional image. Eisler and Adorno note that the spectator is always aware of this divergence, of the inevitable gap between the represented body and its voice. And for Eisler and Adorno this partially explains the function of film music: first used in the exhibition of silent films to conceal the noise of the projector (to hide from the spectator the "uncanny" fact that his/her pleasure is mediated by a machine), music in the "talkie" takes on the task of closing the gap between voice and body.[22]

If this imaginary harmony is to be maintained, however, the potential aggressivity of the voice (as the instrument of interdiction and the material support of the symptom—hearing voices—in paranoia) must be attenuated. The formal perfection of sound recording in the cinema consists in reducing not only the noise of the apparatus but any "grating" noise which is not "pleasing to the ear." On another level, the aggressivity of the filmic voice can be linked to the fact that sound is directed *at* the spectator—necessitating, in the fiction film, its deflection through dialogue (which the spectator is given only obliquely, to overhear) and, in the documentary, its mediation by the content of the image. In the documentary, however, the voice-over has come to represent an authority and an aggressivity which can no longer be sustained—thus, as Bonitzer points out, the proliferation of new documentaries which reject the absolute of the voice-over and, instead, claim to establish a democratic system, "letting the event speak for itself." Yet, what this type of film actually promotes is the illusion that reality speaks and is not spoken, that the film is not a constructed discourse. In effecting an "impression of knowledge," a knowledge which is given and not produced, the film conceals its own work and posits itself as a voice without a subject.[23] The voice is even more powerful in silence. The solution, then, is not to banish the voice but to construct *another* politics.

The Politics of the Voice

The cinema presents a spectacle composed of disparate elements—images, voices, sound effects, music, writing—which the *mise-en-scène*, in its broadest sense, organizes and aims at the body of the spectator, sensory receptacle of the various stimuli. This is why Lyotard refers to classical *mise-en-scène* (in both the theater and the cinema) as a kind of somatography, or inscription on the body:

. . . the *mise-en-scène* turns written signifiers into speech, song, and movements executed by bodies capable of moving, singing, speaking; and this transcription is intended for other living bodies—the spectators—capable of being moved by these songs, movements, and words. It is this transcribing on and for bodies, considered as multi-sensory potentialities, which is the work characteristic of the *mise-en-scène*. Its elementary unity is polyesthetic like the human body: capacity to see, to hear, to touch, to move. . . . The idea of performance . . . even if it remains vague, seems linked to the idea of inscription on the body.[24]

Classical *mise-en-scène* has a stake in perpetuating the image of unity and identity sustained by this body and in staving off the fear of fragmentation. The different sensory elements work in collusion and this work denies the material heterogeneity of the "body" of the film. All of the signifying strategies for the deployment of the voice discussed earlier are linked with such homogenizing effects: synchronization binds the voice to a body in a unity whose immediacy can only be perceived as a given; the voice-off holds the spectacle to a space—extended but still coherent; and the voice-over commentary places the image by endowing it with a clear intelligibility. In all of this, what must be guarded is a certain "oneness."

This "oneness" is the mark of a mastery and a control and manifests itself most explicitly in the tendency to confine the voice-over commentary in the documentary to a single voice. For, according to Bonitzer, "when one divides that voice or, what amounts to the same thing, multiplies it, the system and its effects change. Off-screen space ceases to be that place of reserve and interiority of the voice. . . ."[25] This entails not only or not merely increasing the number of voices but radically changing their relationship to the image, effecting a disjunction between sound and meaning, emphasizing what Barthes refers to as the "grain" of the voice[26] over and against its expressivity or power of representation. In the contemporary cinema, the names which immediately come to mind are those of Godard (who, even in an early film such as *Vivre sa vie* which relies heavily upon synchronous sound, resists the homogenizing effects of the traditional use of voice-off by means of a resolute avoidance of the shot/reverse-shot structure—the camera quickly panning to keep the person talking *in frame*) and Straub (for whom the voice and sound in general become the marks of a nonprogressive duration). The image of the body thus obtained is one not of imaginary cohesion but of dispersal, division, fragmentation. Lyotard speaks of the "postmodernist" text which escapes the closure of representation by creating its own addressee, "a disconcerted body, invited to stretch its sensory capacities beyond measure."[27] Such an approach, which takes off from a different image of the body, can be understood as an attempt to forge a politics based on an erotics. Bonitzer uses the two terms interchangeably, claiming that the scission of the voice can contribute to the definition of "another politics (or erotics) of the voice-off."[28] The problem is whether such an erotics, bound to the image of an extended or fragmented body and strongly linked with a particular signifying material, can found a political theory or practice.

There are three major difficulties with the notion of a political erotics of the voice. The first is that, relying as it does on the idea of expanding the range or redefining the power of the senses, and opposing itself to meaning, a political erotics is easily recuperable as a form of romanticism or as a mysticism which effectively skirts problems of epistemology, lodging itself firmly in a mind/body dualism. Secondly, the overemphasis upon the isolated effectivity of a single signifying material—the voice—risks a crude materialism wherein the physical properties of the medium have the inherent and final power of determining its reading. As Paul Willemen points out, a concentration upon the specificities of the various "technico-sensorial unities" of the cinema often precludes a recognition that the materiality of the signifier is a "second order factor" (with respect to language understood broadly as symbolic system) and tends to reduce a complex heterogeneity to a mere combination of different materials.[29] Yet, a film is not a simple juxtaposition of sensory elements but a discourse, an enunciation. This is not to imply that the isolation and investigation of a single signifying material such as the voice is a fruitless endeavor but that the establishment of a direct connection between the voice and politics is fraught with difficulties.

Thirdly, the notion of a political erotics of the voice is particularly problematic from a feminist perspective. Over and against the theorization of the look as phallic, as the support of voyeurism and fetishism (a drive and a defense which, in Freud, are linked explicitly with the male),[30] the voice appears to lend itself readily as an alternative to the image, as a potentially viable means whereby the woman can "make herself heard." Luce Irigaray, for instance, claims that patriarchal culture has a heavier investment in seeing than in hearing.[31] Bonitzer, in the context of defining a political erotics, speaks of "returning the voice to women" as a major component. Nevertheless, it must be remembered that, while psychoanalysis delineates a preoedipal scenario in which the voice of the mother dominates, the voice, in psychoanalysis, is also the instrument of interdiction, of the patriarchal order. And to mark the voice as an isolated haven within patriarchy, or as having an essential relation to the woman, is to invoke the spectre of feminine specificity, always recuperable as another form of "otherness." A political erotics which posits a new fantasmatic, which relies on images of an "extended" sensory body, is inevitably caught in the double bind which feminism always seems to confront: on the one hand, there is a danger in grounding a politics on a conceptualization of the body because the body has always been *the* site of woman's oppression, posited as the final and undeniable guarantee of a difference and a lack; but, on the other hand, there is a potential gain as well—it is precisely because the body has been a major site of oppression that perhaps it must be the site of the battle to be waged. The supreme achievement of patriarchal ideology is that it has no outside.

In light of the three difficulties outlined above, however, it would seem unwise to base any politics of the voice *solely* on an erotics. The value of thinking the deployment of the voice in the cinema by means of its relation to the body (that of the character, that of the spectator) lies in an understanding of the cinema, from the perspective of a topology, as a series of spaces including that of the spectator—spaces which are often hierarchized or masked, one by the other, in the service of a representational illusion. Nevertheless, whatever the arrangement or interpenetration of the various spaces, they constitute a *place* where signification intrudes. The various techniques and strategies for the deployment of the voice contribute heavily to the definition of the form that "place" takes.

Notes

1. Hugo Münsterberg, *The Film: A Psychological Study* (New York: Dover, 1970; orig. 1916), p. 49.

2. Two kinds of "voices without bodies" immediately suggest themselves—one

theological, the other scientific (two poles which, it might be added, are not ideologically unrelated): 1) the voice of God incarnated in the Word and 2) the artificial voice of a computer. Neither seems to be capable of representation outside of a certain anthropomorphism, however. God is pictured, in fact, as having a quite specific body—that of a male patriarchal figure. *Star Wars* and *Battlestar Galactica* illustrate the tendencies toward anthropomorphism in the depiction of computers. In the latter, even a computer (named Cora) deprived of mobility and the simulacrum of a human form is given a voice which is designed to evoke the image of a sensual female body.

3. Lewis Jacobs, *The Rise of the American Film: A Critical History* (New York: Teachers College Press, 1968), p. 435.

4. For a more detailed discussion of this hierarchy of sounds and of other relevant techniques in the construction of the sound track see Mary Ann Doane, "Ideology and the Practice of Sound Editing and Mixing," paper delivered at Milwaukee Conference on the Cinematic Apparatus, February 1978, and reprinted in this volume.

5. Ibid.

6. W. A. Pozner, "Synchronization Techniques," *Journal of the Society of Motion Picture Engineers*, 47, no. 3 (September 1946):191.

7. Walter Benjamin, "The Work of Art in the Age of Mechanical Reproduction," in *Illuminations*, ed. Hannah Arendt, trans. Harry Zohn (New York: Schocken Books, 1969), p. 222.

8. Ibid., p. 223.

9. George Lewin, "Dubbing and Its Relation to Sound Picture Production," *Journal of the Society of Motion Picture Engineers*, 16, no. 1 (January 1931):48.

10. Walter Murch, "The Art of the Sound Editor: An Interview with Walter Murch," interview by Larry Sturhahn, *Filmmaker's Newsletter*, 8, no. 2 (December 1974):23.

11. Ibid.

12. Stereo reduces this problem but does not solve it—the range of perspective effects is still limited. Much of the discussion which follows is based on the use of monophonic sound, but also has implications for stereo. In both mono and stereo, for instance, the location of the speakers is designed to ensure that the audience hears sound "which is roughly coincident with the image." See Alec Nisbett, *The Technique of the Sound Studio* (New York: Focal Press, 1972), pp. 530, 532.

13. C. Bailblé, "Programmation de l'écoute (2)," *Cahiers du Cinéma*, no. 293 (October 1978):9.

14. Ibid. My translation.

15. C. Metz, "Le perçu et le nommé," in *Essais sémiotiques* (Paris: Editions Klincksieck, 1977), pp. 153–59.

16. Pascal Bonitzer, "Les silences de la voix," *Cahiers du Cinéma*, no. 256 (February–March 1975):25. My translation.

17. Bonitzer uses the term "voice-off" in a general sense which includes both voice-off and voice-over, but here he is referring specifically to voice-over commentary.

18. Bonitzer, "Les silences de la voix," p. 26. My translation.

19. Serge Leclaire, *Démasquer le réel*, p. 64, quoted in C. Bailblé, "Programmation de l'écoute (3)," *Cahiers du Cinéma*, no. 297 (February 1979):46. My translation.

20. Guy Rosolato, "La voix: entre corps et langage," *Revue française de psychanalyse*, 38 (January 1974):83. My translation. My discussion of the pleasure of hearing relies heavily on the work of Rosolato. Further references to this article will appear in parentheses in the text.

21. Jacques Lacan, *The Four Fundamental Concepts of Psycho-analysis*, ed. Jacques-Alain Miller, trans. Alan Sheridan (London: The Hogarth Press and the Institute of Psycho-Analysis, 1977), p. 274.

22. Hanns Eisler, *Composing for the Films* (New York: Oxford University Press, 1947), pp. 75–77.

23. Bonitzer, "Les silences de la voix," pp. 23–24.

24. Jean-François Lyotard, "The Unconscious as Mise-en-scène," in *Performance in Postmodern Culture*, ed. Michel Benamou and Charles Caramello (Madison: Coda Press, Inc., 1977), p. 88.

25. Bonitzer, "Les silences de la voix," p. 31.

26. See Roland Barthes, "The Grain of the Voice," in *Image-Music-Text*, trans. Stephen Heath (New York: Hill and Wang, 1977), pp. 179–89.

27. Lyotard, "The Unconscious as Mise-en-scène," p. 96.

28. Bonitzer, "Les silences de la voix," p. 31.

29. Paul Willemen, "Cinema Thoughts," paper delivered at Milwaukee Conference on Cinema and Language, March 1979, pp. 12 and 3.

30. See Laura Mulvey, "Visual Pleasure and Narrative Cinema," *Screen*, 16 (Autumn 1975):6–18, and Stephen Heath, "Sexual Difference and Representation," *Screen*, 19 (Autumn 1978):51–112.

31. For a fuller discussion of the relationship some feminists establish between the voice and the woman see Heath, "Sexual Difference," pp. 83–84.

PART III: PRACTICE

Practice and Methodology

Because the possible sound-image relationships are so many and so varied, writers often try to deal with sound by categorizing these relationships. Two of the most successful attempts are the chapters on sound by David Bordwell and Kristin Thompson, in their seminal textbook *Film Art: An Introduction,* and by Noël Burch, in his pioneering *Theory of Film Practice.*

Bordwell and Thompson are primarily concerned with how sound functions *perceptually,* that is, in terms of directing the attention and shaping the perceptions of the filmgoer. They outline various categories that distinguish among sounds as they are experienced. Thus sounds possess different acoustic properties: loudnesses, pitches, and timbres. Filmmakers carefully select, then combine sounds to construct a sound narrative that, as in the battle sequence of *Seven Samurai,* cues and guides the viewer through the complex action of the scene. The authors analyze the basic sound-image relationship in terms of the categories of rhythm, fidelity, temporality, and spatiality and then discuss examples of various combinations of categories.

In "On the Structural Use of Sound," Burch uses a Marxist-formalist approach to isolate the ways in which sound functions *dialectically.* The basic dialectic of sound and image is broken down into oppositional subsets, such as "live" and "dubbed" sound, and into various mismatches, such as long shots with close-up sound. Basic categories of sound such as dialogue, music, and sound effects introduce a range of possible permutations in their combination; for instance, dialogue can be rhythmic, or sound effects can be orchestrated. For Burch, the various modes of interaction among these categories have dialectical implications for the aesthetic organization of the sound track, implications that unfortunately are ignored by all but a handful of contemporary, experimental filmmakers.

Bordwell and Thompson also explore the juxtaposition

of opposed elements; but unlike Burch, their possible combinations include some that are merely *different* as well as some that are directly opposed. Whereas Burch polemically addresses the issue of how sound *should* function, Bordwell and Thompson attempt to exhaust all of its *possible* functions. The value of both approaches lies in the construction of a grammar of sorts for film sound and of categories useful for analyzing its formal structure.

Fundamental Aesthetics
of Sound in the Cinema
DAVID BORDWELL and KRISTIN THOMPSON

The Powers of Sound

Many people tend to think of sound as simply an accompaniment to the real basis of cinema, the moving images. These viewers assume that the people and things pictured on the screen just produce an appropriate noise. But in the process of film production the sound track is created separately from the images and can be manipulated independently and flexibly.

Consider some of the advantages of sound for a film. First, it engages another sense mode: our visual attention can be accompanied by an aural attention. (Even before recorded sound was introduced in 1926, the "silent" cinema recognized this by its use of accompaniment by orchestra, organ, or piano.) Second, sound can *actively shape how we interpret the image.* In one sequence of *Letter from Siberia,* Chris Marker demonstrates the power of sound to alter our perception of images. Three times Marker plays the same footage—a shot of a bus passing a car on a city street, three shots of workers paving a street. But each time the footage is accompanied by a completely different sound track. Compare the three versions tabulated alongside the sequence (Table 1). The verbal differences are emphasized by the sameness of the images; the audience will interpret the same images completely differently, depending on the sound track.

The *Letter from Siberia* sequence also demonstrates a third advantage of sound. Film sound can direct our attention quite specifically within the image. When the commentator describes the "blood-colored buses," we will look at the bus and not at the car. When Fred Astaire and Ginger Rogers are tapping out an intricate step, chances are that we watch their bodies and not the silent nightclub spectators looking on. In such ways, sound can guide us through the images, "pointing" to things to watch. This possibility becomes even more complex when you consider that the sound cue for some visual element may *anticipate* that element and relay our attention to it. Suppose we have a close-up of a man in a room and we hear the creaking of a door opening; if the next shot shows the door, now open, the viewer

Table 1 *Letter from Siberia* Footage

Images	*First commentary*
**Figure 1**	Yakutsk, capital of the Yakutsk Autonomous Soviet Socialist Republic, is a modern city in which comfortable buses made available to the population share the streets with powerful Zyms, the pride of the Soviet automobile industry. In the
**Figure 2**	joyful spirit of socialist emulation, happy Soviet workers, among them this picturesque denizen
**Figure 3**	of the Arctic reaches, apply themselves
**Figure 4**	to making Yakutsk an even better place to live. Or else:

Second commentary	Third commentary
Yakutsk is a dark city with an evil reputation. The population is crammed into blood-colored buses while the members of the privileged caste brazenly display the luxury of their Zyms, a costly and uncomfortable car at best. Bending	In Yakutsk, where modern houses are gradually replacing the dark older sections, a bus, less crowded than its London or New York equivalent at rush hour, passes a Zym, an excellent car reserved for public utilities departments on account of its scarcity.
to the task like slaves, the miserable Soviet workers, among them this sinister-looking Asiatic,	With courage and tenacity under extreme difficult conditions, Soviet workers, among them this Yakut
apply themselves to the primitive labor	afflicted with an eye disorder, apply themselves to
of grading with a drag beam.	improving the appearance of their city, which could certainly use it.

Or simply:

will likely focus his or her attention on that door, the source of the off-screen sound. In an opposite way, if the next shot shows the door still closed, the viewer will likely ponder his or her interpretation of the sound. (Maybe it wasn't a door, after all?) Thus the sound track can clarify image events, contradict them, or render them ambiguous. In all cases, the sound track can enter into an *active* relation with the image track.

Moreover, as V. F. Perkins has pointed out, sound brings with it a new sense of the value of silence. "Only with color as an available resource can we regard the use of black-and-white photography as the result of a conscious artistic decision. Only in the sound film can a director use silence for dramatic effect." [1] In the context of sound, silence takes on a new expressive function.

A final advantage: Sound bristles with as many creative possibilities as editing. Through editing, one may join shots of any two spaces to create a meaningful relation. Similarly, the filmmaker can mix any sonic phenomena into a whole. With the introduction of sound cinema, the infinity of visual possibilities was joined by the infinity of acoustic events.

Fundamentals of Film Sound

Acoustic Properties

To pursue in detail the acoustic processes that produce sound would take us on a long detour. We should, however, isolate some qualities of sound as we perceive it. These qualities are familiar to us from everyday experience.

LOUDNESS
Perceived sound results from vibrations in air; the amplitude of the vibrations produces our sense of volume. Film sound constantly manipulates volume. For example, in dozens of films a long shot of a busy street is accompanied by loud traffic noises, but when two people meet and start to speak, the loudness of the noise drops. Or, a dialogue between a soft-spoken character and a blustery one is characterized as much by the difference in volume as by the substance of the talk. Needless to say, loudness is also affected by perceived distance; often the louder the sound, the closer we take it to be. Some films exploit radical changes in volume for shock value, as when a quiet scene is interrupted by a very loud noise.

PITCH

The frequency of sound vibrations governs pitch, or the perceived "highness" or "lowness" of the sound. Pitch is the principal way we distinguish music from other sounds in the film, but it has more complex uses. When a young boy tries to speak in a man's deep voice and fails (as in *How Green Was My Valley*), the joke is based primarily on pitch. In the coronation scene of *Ivan the Terrible, Part I*, a court singer with a deep bass voice begins a song of praise to Ivan, and each phrase rises dramatically in pitch—which Eisenstein emphasizes in the editing, with successively closer shots of the singer coinciding with each change. When Bernard Herrmann obtained the effects of unnatural, birdlike shrieking in Hitchcock's *Psycho,* even many musicians could not recognize the source: violins played at extraordinarily high pitch.

TIMBRE

The harmonic components of a sound give it a certain "color" or tone quality—what musicians call timbre. When we call someone's voice nasal or a certain musical tone mellow, we are referring to timbre. Again, filmmakers manipulate timbre continually. Timbre can help articulate portions of the sound track; for instance, timbre differentiates musical instruments from one another. Timbre also "comes forward" on certain occasions, as in the clichéd use of oleaginous saxophone tones behind seduction scenes. More subtly, in the opening sequence of Rouben Mamoulian's *Love Me Tonight* people pass a musical rhythm from object to object—a broom, a carpet beater—and the humor of the number springs in part from the very different timbres of the objects.

As the fundamental components of film sound, loudness, pitch, and timbre usually interact to define the sonic texture of a film. At the most elementary level, loudness, pitch, and timbre enable us to distinguish among all of the sounds in a film; we recognize different characters' voices by these qualities, for example. But at a more complex level, all three interact to add considerably to our experience of the film. Both John Wayne and James Stewart speak slowly, but Wayne's voice tends to be deeper and gruffer than Stewart's querulous drawl. In *The Wizard of Oz* the disparity between the public image of the Wizard and the old charlatan who rigs it up is marked by the booming bass of the effigy and the old man's higher, softer, more quavering voice. *Citizen Kane* offers a wide range of sound manipulations: echo chambers alter timbre and volume, and a motif is formed by the inability of Kane's opera-singing wife to hit accurate pitch. In *Citizen Kane* shifts between times and places are covered by continuing a sound "thread" and varying the basic acoustics: a shot of Kane applauding dissolves to a shot of a crowd applauding (shift in volume and timbre); Leland beginning a sentence in the street cuts to Kane finishing the sentence in an auditorium, his voice magnified by loudspeakers (shift in volume, timbre, and pitch). Such examples suggest that the elementary properties of sound afford a rich set of possibilities for the filmmaker to explore.

Selection and Combination

Sound in the cinema takes three forms: *speech, music,* or *noise* (also called *sound effects*). Occasionally a sound may share categories—is a scream speech or noise? is electronic music also noise?—and filmmakers have freely exploited these ambiguities. (In *Psycho,* when a woman screams, we expect to hear the human voice and instead hear "screaming" violins.) Nevertheless, in most cases the distinctions hold. Now that we have an idea of the role of acoustic properties, we must consider how speech, music, and noise are selected and combined for specific functions within films.

The creation of the sound track resembles the editing of the image track. Just as the filmmaker may select from several shots the best image, he or she may choose what exact bit of sound from this or that source will best serve the purpose. And just as the filmmaker may link or superimpose images, so may he or she join any two sounds end to end or one "over" another (as with commentary "over" music). Though we aren't usually as aware of the manipulation of the sound track, it demands as much selection and control as does the visual track.

Selection of the desired sound is a necessary step in the process. Normally, our perception filters out irrelevant stimuli and retains what is most useful at a particular moment. As you read this, you are attending to words on the page and (to various degrees) ignoring certain stimuli that reach your ears. But if you close your eyes and listen attentively to the sounds around you, you will become aware of many previously unnoticed sounds—distant voices, the wind, footsteps, a radio playing. As any amateur recordist knows, if you set up a microphone and tape recorder in a "quiet" environment, all of those normally unnoticed sounds suddenly become obtrusive. The microphone is unselective; like the camera lens, it does not automatically achieve the desired result. Sound studios, camera blimps to absorb motor noise, directional and shielded microphones, sound engineering and editing, and libraries of stock sounds all exist so that a film's sound track may be carefully controlled through selection. Unless a filmmaker *wants* to record all of the ambient noise of a scene, simply holding out a microphone while filming will rarely suffice.

Because normal perception is linked to our choices, the director's selection of the sounds in a film can control the audience's choices and thus guide the audience's perception. In one scene from Jacques Tati's *Mr. Hulot's Holiday* vacationers at a resort hotel are relaxing. In the foreground guests quietly play cards; in the depth of the shot, Mr. Hulot is frantically playing ping-pong. Early in the scene, the guests in the foreground are murmuring quietly, but Hulot's ping-pong game is louder; the sound cues us to watch Hulot. Later in the scene, however, the same ping-pong game makes *no* sound at all, and our attention is drawn to the muttering card players in the foreground. The presence and absence of the sound of the ping-pong ball guides our expectations and perception. If you start to notice how such selection of sound guides our perception, you will notice that filmmakers often use sound to shift our attention.

Such examples depend not only on selection but also on the filmmaker's *combining* of various sonic elements. It is the mixing of sounds in a specific pattern that constitutes the sound track as we know it. We have already seen that mixing is a careful and deliberate production procedure. What we must now notice is what functions the particular mix can have in the total film. Obviously the mix can range from very dense (e.g., a scene containing the babble of voices, the sounds of footsteps, Muzak, and plane engines at an airport) to total silence, with most films falling in between. In addition, the filmmaker may create a mix in which each sound modulates and overlaps smoothly with the others, or one that is composed of much more abrupt and startling contrasts.

The possibilities of combining sounds are well illustrated by the final battle sequence of Akira Kurosawa's *Seven Samurai*. In a heavy rain, marauding bandits charge into a village defended by the villagers and the samurai. The torrent and wind form a constant background noise throughout the scene. Before the battle, the conversation of the waiting men, footsteps, and the sounds of swords being drawn are punctuated by long pauses in which we hear only the drumming rain. Suddenly distant horses' hoofs are heard off-screen; Kurosawa cuts to a long shot of the bandits; their horses' hoofs become abruptly louder. (This is typical of the scene: the closer the camera is to a sound source, the louder the sound.) When the bandits burst into the village, yet another sound element appears—the bandits' harsh battle cries, which increase steadily in volume as they approach. The battle begins. The muddy, storm-swept *mise-en-scène* and rhythmic cutting gain impact from the way in which the incessant rain and splashing are explosively interrupted by brief noises—the screams of the wounded, the splintering of a fence one bandit crashes through, the whinnies of horses, the twang of one samurai's bowstring, the gurgle of a speared bandit, the screams of women when the bandit chieftain breaks into their hiding place. The sudden intrusion of certain sounds marks abrupt developments in the battle. The scene climaxes after the main battle has ended: offscreen horses' hoofs are cut short by a new sound—the sharp crack of a bandit's rifle shot, which fells one samurai. A long pause, in which we hear only the driving rain, emphasizes the moment; the samurai furiously throws his sword in the direction of the shot and falls dead into the mud. Another samurai races toward the bandit chieftain, who has the rifle; another shot cracks out and he falls back, wounded; another pause, in which only the relentless rain is heard. The wounded samurai kills the chieftain. The other samurai gather. At the scene's end, the sobs of a young samurai, the distant whinnies and hoofbeats of now riderless horses, and the rain all fade slowly out. The relatively dense mix of this sound track (accomplished entirely without music) gradually introduces sounds to turn our attention to new narrative elements (hoofs, battle cries) and then goes on to modulate these sounds smoothly into a harmonious whole. This whole is then punctuated by abrupt sounds of unusual volume or pitch associated with crucial narrative actions (the archery, women's screams, the gunshots).

Dimensions of Film Sound

We have now seen what sounds consist of and how the filmmaker can take advantage of the widely different kinds of sounds available. In addition, the way in which the sounds relate to other film elements gives them several other dimensions. First, because sound occupies a duration, it has a *rhythm*. Second, sound can relate to its perceived source with greater or lesser *fidelity*. Third, the sound relates to visual events that take place in a specific time, and this relationship gives sound a *temporal* dimension. And fourth, sound conveys a sense of the *spatial* conditions in which it occurs. These categories begin to reveal that sound in film is actually a very complex thing; let's look at each category briefly.

Rhythm

For our purposes, sounds can be considered to be organized *rhythmically* when strong and weak beats form a distinct pattern and move at a distinct pace. (This definition of rhythm combines features that musicians would distinguish as "meter," "rhythm," and "tempo.") But even this simple definition is complicated by the fact that the movements in the images themselves have a rhythm as well. In addition, the editing has a rhythm; a succession of short shots creates a fast rhythm, whereas shots held longer slow down

the editing's rhythm. Moreover, all three types of sound on the sound track have their own rhythmic possibilities independent of one another. The gasping voice of a character who lies dying has a slower rhythm than the voice of a racetrack announcer. Music obviously may have different rhythms in a film. Finally, sound effects also vary in rhythm (compare the plodding hoofs of a farmhorse and a cavalry company riding at full speed).

But in most cases the rhythms of editing, of movement within the image, and of sound do not exist separately. Sound usually accompanies movements and often continues over cuts. Sound may motivate figure or camera movement. Thus there exists the potential for a considerable interplay among these three types of rhythm. No one "appropriate" combination exists.

Possibly the most common tendency is for the filmmaker to match visual and sonic rhythms to each other. An obvious example is the typical dance sequence in a musical; here the figures move about at a rhythm determined by the music. But variation is always possible. In the "Waltz in Swing Time" number in *Swing Time* the dancing of Astaire and Rogers moves quickly in time to the music. But no fast cutting accompanies this scene; indeed, there is no cutting at all within the dance, for the scene consists of a single long take from a long-shot distance. Another example of close coordination between screen movement and sound comes in the animated films of Walt Disney in the 1930s; Mickey Mouse and the other Disney characters often move in exact synchronization with the music, even when they are not dancing. (This nondance matching of movement with music in fact came to be known as "Mickey Mousing.")

The filmmaker may choose to create a disparity among the rhythms of sound, editing, and image. One way of accomplishing this is to keep the source of the sound off-screen and to show something else on-screen. Toward the end of John Ford's *She Wore a Yellow Ribbon,* the aging cavalry captain, Nathan Brittles, watches his troop ride out of the fort just after he has retired; he regrets leaving the service and desires to go with the patrol. The sound of the scene consists of the cheerful title song sung by the departing riders and the quick hoofbeats of their horses. Yet only a few of the shots show the horses and singers, who move at a rhythm matched to the sound. Instead, the scene concentrates our attention on Brittles, standing almost motionless by his own horse. (The moderate rate of cutting lies between these two rhythms.) The contrast of fast rhythm of sound with the shots of the solitary Brittles functions to emphasize his regret at having to stay behind for the first time in many years.

Several great directors have used music that might seem to have a rhythm inappropriate for the visuals. In *Four Nights of a Dreamer* Robert Bresson includes several shots of a large, floating nightclub cruising the Seine.

The boat's movement is slow and smooth, yet the sound track consists of lively Calypso music. (Not until a later scene do we discover that the music comes from the boat.) The strange combination of fast music with the slow passage of the boat creates a languorous, mysterious effect. Jacques Tati does something similar in *Playtime*. In a scene outside a Parisian hotel, tourists climb aboard a bus to go to a nightclub; as they file slowly up the steps, raucous, jazzy music begins. The music again startles our expectations because it seems inappropriate to the images; in fact, it belongs with the next scene, in which some carpenters awkwardly carrying a large plate-glass window seem to be dancing to the music. By starting the fast music over an earlier scene of slower visual rhythm, Tati creates a comic effect and prepares for a transition to a new space.

Chris Marker has carried this contrast between image and sound rhythms to what may be its logical limit, in *La Jetée*. This film is made up almost entirely of still shots; except for one tiny gesture, all movement within the images is eliminated. Yet the film has a narrator, music, and sound effects of a generally dynamic rhythm. The result is not at all "uncinematic," but rather it has great effectiveness because of the originality of the concept and the care and consistency with which this juxtaposition of rhythms is carried through the whole structure of the film.

These examples suggest some of the ways in which rhythms may be combined. But of course most films also vary their rhythms from one point to another. A change of rhythm may function to shift our expectations. In a famous sequence Sergei Eisenstein develops the sound from slow rhythms to fast and back to slow: the battle on the ice in *Alexander Nevsky*. The first twelve shots of the scene show the Russian army prepared for the attack of the German knights. The shots are of moderate, even length, and they contain very little movement. The music is comparably slow, consisting of short, distinctly separated chords. Then, as the German army rides into sight over the horizon, both the visual movement and the tempo of the music increase quickly, and the battle begins. At the end of the battle Eisenstein creates another contrast with a long passage of slow, lamenting music and little movement.

Fidelity

By fidelity we don't mean "high-fi" in the sense of the quality of recording. Here we are speaking of whether the sound is faithful to the source as we conceive it. If a film shows us a barking dog and the sound track has a barking noise, that sound is faithful to its source—the sound maintains fidelity. But if the sound of a cat meowing accompanies the picture of the barking dog, there enters a disparity between sound and image—a lack of fidelity.

Fidelity has nothing to do with what originally made the sound during filming. As we have seen, the filmmaker may manipulate sound independently of image; accompanying the image of a dog with the meow is no more difficult than accompanying the image with a bark. Note, however, that fidelity is purely a matter of our expectations. In production the bark or meow might be produced electronically or by an animal-imitator. Fidelity involves conventional expectations about sources, not knowledge of where the filmmaker actually obtained the sound.

A play with fidelity most commonly functions for comic effect. Jacques Tati is one of the directors most skillful at employing various degrees of fidelity. In *Mr. Hulot's Holiday* much comedy arises from the opening and closing of a dining-room door. Instead of simply recording a real door, Tati inserts a twanging sound like a plucked cello string each time the door swings; aside from being amusing in itself, this sound functions to emphasize the patterns in which waiters and diners pass through the door. Another master of comically unfaithful sound is René Clair. In several scenes of *Le Million* sound effects occur that are not faithful to their sources. When the hero's friend drops a plate, we hear not shattering crockery but the clash of cymbals. Later, during a chase scene, when characters collide, the impact is portrayed by a heavy bass drum beat. Similar manipulations of fidelity commonly occur in animated cartoons.

But as with low- or high-angle framings, there is no recipe that will allow us to interpret every manipulation of fidelity as comic; some nonfaithful sounds have serious functions. In Hitchcock's *The Thirty-Nine Steps* a landlady discovers a corpse in an apartment. A shot of her screaming face is accompanied by a train whistle; then the scene shifts to an actual train. Though the whistle is not a faithful sound for an image of a screaming person, it provides a striking transition.

Finally, in some special cases fidelity may be manipulated by a change in volume. A sound may seem unreasonably loud or soft in relation to the other sounds in the film. Curtis Bernhardt's *Possessed* alters volume in ways that are not faithful to the sources. The central character is gradually falling deeper into mental illness; in one scene she is alone, very distraught, in her room on a rainy night. We begin to hear things as she does; the ticking of the clock and dripping of raindrops gradually magnify in volume. Here the shift in fidelity functions to suggest a psychological state.

Space

Sound has a spatial dimension because it comes from a *source,* and that source may be characterized by the space it occupies. If the source of a sound is a character or object in the story space of the film, we call the sound *die-*

getic. The voices of the characters, sounds made by objects in the story, or music coming from instruments in the story space are all diegetic sound.

On the other hand there is *nondiegetic* sound, which does not come from a source in the story space. Familiar examples of such sound are easy to find. Much music added to enhance the film's action is nondiegetic; when a character is climbing a sheer cliff and tense music comes up, we don't expect to see an orchestra perched on the side of the mountain. Viewers understand that the movie music is a convention and doesn't issue from the space of the story. The same holds true for the so-called omniscient narrator, the disembodied voice that gives us information but does not belong to any of the characters in the film. Orson Welles speaks the nondiegetic narration in his own film *The Magnificent Ambersons,* for example. Nondiegetic sound effects are also possible. In *Le Million* various characters all pursue an old coat with a winning lottery ticket in its pocket. They converge backstage at the opera and begin racing and dodging around one another, tossing the coat to their accomplices. But instead of putting in the sounds coming from the actual space of the chase, Clair fades in the sounds of a football game; because the maneuvers of the chase do look like a football game, with the coat as ball, this enhances the comedy of the sequence. We hear a crowd cheering and a whistle's sound; yet we don't assume that the characters present are making these sounds (so this is not a manipulation of fidelity, as with the earlier examples from *Le Million*). The nondiegetic sounds create comedy by making a sort of audiovisual pun.

What are the possibilities of diegetic sound? We know that the space of the narrative action is not limited to what we can see on the screen at any given moment. If we know that several people are present in a room, we can see a shot that shows only one person without assuming that the other people have dropped out of the story. We simply have a sense that those people are off-screen. And if one of those off-screen people speaks, we still assume that the sound is coming from part of the story space. Thus diegetic sound can be either *on-screen* or *off-screen,* depending on whether its source is within the frame or outside the frame.

Simple examples will illustrate this. A shot shows a character talking, and we hear the sound of his or her voice; another shows a door closing, and we hear a slam; a person plays a fiddle, and we hear its notes. In each case the source of the sound is in the story—diegetic—and visible within the frame—on-screen. But the shot may show only a person listening to a voice without the speaker being seen; another shot might show a character running down a street and the sound of an unseen door slamming; lastly, an audience is shown listening while the sound of a fiddle is heard. In all of these instances, the sounds come from within the story—again diegetic—but are now in a space outside the frame—off-screen.

. . . Off-screen sound can suggest space extending in various directions beyond the visible action. In *American Graffiti,* a film that plays heavily on the distinction between diegetic and nondiegetic music, off-screen sounds of car radios often suggest that all of the cars on the street are tuned to the same radio station. Off-screen sound may also control when we begin to formulate expectations about off-screen space. In *His Girl Friday* Hildy goes into the press room to write her final story. As she chats with the other reporters, a loud clunk comes from an unseen source. Hildy glances off left, and immediately a new space comes to our attention, though we haven't seen it yet. She walks to the window and sees a gallows being prepared for an execution. Here off-screen sound initiates the discovery of fresh space.

A brilliant use of a similar device comes in John Ford's *Stagecoach.* The stagecoach is desperately fleeing from a band of Indians; the ammunition is running out, and all seems lost until a troop of cavalry suddenly arrives. Yet Ford does not create the situation this baldly. He shows a medium close-up of one of the men, Hatfield, who has just discovered that he is down to his last bullet; he glances off right and raises his gun. The camera pans right to a woman, Lucy, praying. During all this, orchestral music, including bugles, plays nondiegetically. Unseen by Lucy, Hatfield's gun comes into the frame from the left, ready to shoot her to prevent her from being captured by the Indians. But before he shoots, an off-screen gunshot is heard, and Hatfield's hand and gun drop down out of the frame. Then the bugle music becomes somewhat more prominent, and Lucy's face changes as she says, "Can you hear it? Can you hear it? It's a bugle. They're blowing the charge." Only then does Ford cut to the cavalry itself racing toward the coach. Rather than focusing on the mechanics of the rescue, Ford uses off-screen sound to restrict our vision to the initial despair of the passengers and their growing hope as they hear the distant sound. The sound of the bugle also emerges imperceptibly out of the nondiegetic music; only Lucy's line tells us that this is a diegetic sound which signals their rescue.

Are there other possibilities for diegetic sound? Often a filmmaker uses sound to represent what a character is thinking. We hear the character's voice speaking his or her thoughts even though that character's lips do not move; presumably other characters cannot hear these thoughts. A character may also remember words, snatches of music, or events as represented by sound effects. This device is so common that we need to distinguish between *internal* and *external* diegetic sound. External diegetic sound is that which we as spectators take to have a physical source in the scene. Internal diegetic sound is that which comes only from the mind of a character; it is subjective. (Nondiegetic and internal diegetic sounds are often called *sound over* because they do not come from the real space of the scene.)

In the Laurence Olivier version of *Hamlet,* for example, the filmmaker presents Hamlet's famous soliloquies as interior monologues. The character registers the appropriate emotion on his face, but does not move his lips while we hear his voice saying the words, "To be or not to be . . . ," and so on. Hamlet is the source of the thoughts we hear represented as speech, but the words are only in the character's mind, not in his physical space. Hence the words are simple diegetic, but internal.

To summarize: Sound may be diegetic (in the story space) or nondiegetic (outside the story space). If it is diegetic, it may be on-screen or off-screen, internal ("subjective") or external ("objective").

One characteristic of diegetic sound is the possibility of suggesting the *distance* of its source. Volume is one simple way to give an impression of distance. A loud sound tends to seem near; a soft one, more distant. The horses' hoofs in the *Seven Samurai* battle and the bugle call from *Stagecoach* exemplify this.

In addition to volume, timbre may suggest the texture and dimensions of the space within which a sound supposedly takes place. In *The Magnificent Ambersons* the conversations that take place on the baroque staircase have an echoing effect, giving the impression of huge, empty spaces around the characters. The skillful filmmaker will pay attention to the quality of the sound, taking advantage of the possibilities of variation from shot to shot.

In recent years technical developments have added the possibilities of stereo, quadraphonic, and other multichanneled systems to the filmmaker's range. This means that the sound can suggest location not only in terms of distance (volume, resonance) but also by specifying *direction*. In stereo versions of David Lean's *Lawrence of Arabia,* for example, the approach of planes to bomb a camp is first suggested through a rumble occurring only on the right side of the screen. Lawrence and an officer look off right, and their dialogue identifies the source of the sound. Then, when the scene shifts to the besieged camp itself, the stereo sound slides from channel to channel, reinforcing the visual depiction of the planes swooping overhead. Multiple channels make it possible to delineate space precisely.

In general, the spatial relations of sounds in films are clearly diegetic or nondiegetic. But because film is such a complex art form, involving the combination of so many elements, some films blur the distinctions between diegetic and nondiegetic sound. Since we are used to placing the source of a sound easily, a film may cheat our expectations.

There is a moment in *The Magnificent Ambersons* when Welles creates an unusual interplay between the diegetic and nondiegetic sounds. A prologue to the film outlines the background of the Amberson family and the birth of the son, George. We see a group of townswomen gossiping about the marriage of Isabel Amberson, and one predicts that she will have "the worst spoiled lot of children this town will ever see." This scene has involved diegetic dialogue. After the last line, the nondiegetic narrator resumes his description of the family history. Over a shot of the empty street, he says: "The prophetess proved to be mistaken in a single detail merely; Wilbur and Isabel did not have *children*. They had only one." But at this point, still over the shot of the street, we hear the gossiper's voice again: "Only one. But I'd like to know if he isn't spoiled enough for a whole carload." After her line, a pony cart comes up the street, and we see George for the first time. In this exchange the woman seems to reply to the narrator, even though we must assume that she cannot hear what he says; after all, she is a character in the story and he is not. Here Welles playfully departs from conventional usage to emphasize the arrival of the story's main character.

This example from *The Magnificent Ambersons* juxtaposes diegetic and nondiegetic sounds in an ambiguous way. In other films a single sound may be ambiguous because it seems to fall with equal logic into either category. This is often true in the films of Jean-Luc Godard. He narrates some of his films, but sometimes he seems also to be present in the story space just off-screen. Godard does not claim to be a character in the action, yet the characters on the screen sometimes seem to hear him. In an early scene in *Two or Three Things I Know About Her* Godard's voice introduces the actress Marina Vlady and describes her, then does the same with the character that Vlady plays, Juliette Janson. He speaks in a whisper, and we are not sure whether she can hear him or not. Later in the scene she gives answers to questions seemingly asked by someone off-screen. Yet we do not hear the questions themselves and don't know if Godard is asking them from his position behind the camera as director. We are never sure whether Godard is nondiegetic narrator or diegetic character; in the latter case, his role would have to be something like "director/narrator of *Two or Three Things I Know About Her.*" This uncertainty is important for Godard, since in some of his films an uncertainty as to diegetic or nondiegetic sound sources enables him to stress the conventionality of traditional sound usage.

The distinction between diegetic and nondiegetic sound is important not as an end in itself but as a tool for understanding particular films.

Time

Sound relates temporally to filmic images in two ways: viewing time and story time. By *viewing time* we mean the physical length of the film—the time it takes the film to be projected. This usually differs from *story time*, that is, the time assumed to pass in the film's action. Events may cover a number of years in the characters' lives (story time), but most films we see in theaters take only about two hours to watch (viewing time). Viewing time becomes an instrument of the plot's manipulation of story time.

A sound may be juxtaposed in any temporal relationship with an image. The matching of sound with image in terms of our viewing time is called *synchronization*. When a sound is synchronized with the image, we hear it at the same time as we see the source produce the sound on the screen. Most dialogue between characters is matched so that the lips of the actors move at the same time that we hear the appropriate words.

When the sound does go out of synchronization during a viewing (e.g., through an error in projection), the result is quite distracting. But some imaginative filmmakers have obtained good effects by using out-of-sync, or *asynchronous*, sound. One such example occurs in a scene in the musical by Gene Kelly and Stanley Donen, *Singin' in the Rain*. The story is set in the early days of sound in Hollywood; a famous pair of silent screen actors have just made their first talking picture, *The Dueling Cavalier*. Their film company previews the film for an audience at a theater. In the earliest days of "talkies," sound was often recorded on a phonograph record to be played along with the film; hence the chances of the sound's getting out of synchronization with the picture were much greater than they are today. This is what happens in the preview of *The Dueling Cavalier*. As the film is projected, it slows down momentarily, but the record keeps running; from this point all the sounds come several seconds before their source is seen in the image. A line of dialogue begins, *then* the actor's lips move. A woman's voice is heard when a man moves his lips, and vice versa. The humor of this disastrous preview in *Singin' in the Rain* depends on our realization that the sound and image are supposed to be matched, but actually occur separately.

A lengthier example of a play with our expectations about synchronization comes in Woody Allen's film *What's Up Tiger Lily?* Allen has taken an Oriental spy film and dubbed a new sound track on, but the English-language dialogue is not a translation of the original; rather, it creates a new story in comic juxtaposition with the original images. Much of the humor results from our constant awareness that the words are not perfectly synchronized with the actors' lips. Allen has turned the usual problems of the dubbing of foreign films into the basis of his comedy.

Synchronization relates to *viewing* time. But what of *story* time? If the sound takes place at the same time as the image in terms of the story events, it is *simultaneous* sound; if the sound occurs earlier or later than the story events of the image, the sound is *nonsimultaneous*.

Most of the time a film's sound is simultaneous, with image and sound both in the present. We are familiar with this from countless dialogue scenes, musical numbers, chase scenes, and so forth. We shall call this simultaneous diegetic sound *simple diegetic*.

Table 2 Temporal Relationships of Sound in Cinema

	Space of source	
	Diegetic (story space)	Nondiegetic (nonstory space)
Temporal relation: 1. Sound earlier than image	Displaced diegetic: External: sound flashback; image flashforward Internal: Memories of character heard	Sound marked as past put over images (e.g., sound of a Winston Churchill speech put over images of Britain today)
2. Sound simultaneous with image	Simple diegetic: External: dialogue, effects music Internal: thoughts of character heard	Sound, marked as simultaneous with images, put over images
3. Sound later than image	Displaced diegetic: External: Sound flashforward; image flashback with sound continuing in the present; character narrates earlier events Internal: Character's vision of future heard	Narrator in present speaks of events shown as being in past; sound marked as later put over images (e.g., reminiscing narrator of The Magnificent Ambersons)

But scenes with nonsimultaneous sound are relatively familiar as well. Diegetic sound can occur in a time either earlier or later than the time of the image. In either case we shall call it *displaced diegetic* sound. As we saw earlier, both types of diegetic sound can have either an external or an internal source.

As these categories suggest, temporal relationships in the cinema are complex. To help distinguish them, Table 2 sums up the possible temporal and spatial relationships which may exist between image and sound.

Diegetic Sound

We have already discussed simple diegetic sound, both external and internal. This is the commonest kind of sound in films. Some concrete examples may help clarify the distinctions among the other categories.

1. *Sound earlier than image.* Displaced diegetic sound may recall an earlier scene through the repetition of sound from that scene while the images on the screen remain in the present. In a scene in Hitchcock's *Psycho* the repeated sounds are memories recalled by the central character, Marion Crane. In a previous scene Marion's boss has told her to deposit a large sum of money in the bank. Instead, she steals the money, and we see her driving away. The images show Marion in a medium close-up behind the wheel of her car. On the sound track, however, we hear an exact repetition of the lines spoken earlier by her boss; this sound is her memory of the earlier scene.

Less common but still possible is external sound that forms a sound flashback. Joseph Losey's *Accident* ends with a shot of a driveway gate. We hear a car crash, but the sound represents the crash that occurred at the *beginning* of the film. Since no one is remembering the scene and since the sound is from an earlier time than the image, we have an external sound flashback.

2. *Sound later than image.* Displaced diegetic sound may also occur at a later time than that of the images. Probably the most familiar use of this category is the narrator who tells a story that has occurred in the past. In Ford's *How Green Was My Valley* the man Huw narrates the story of his boyhood in Wales. Aside from a glimpse at the beginning, we do not see him as a man, only as a boy; the words of the narration are spoken by a man's voice in a period long after that of the events we see on the screen.

An internal use of sound that is later than the images is rare, but there are a few cases. Later in the scene from *Psycho* described above, Marion begins to imagine what her boss *will* say on Monday when he discovers the theft. While the image of her driving the car remains on the screen, we hear internal displaced diegetic sound representing a *later* time: a character's premonition on the sound track.

Sound may belong to a later time than the image in another way. In some cases, particularly in films of the 1960s and 1970s, the sound from the next scene begins while the images of the last one are still on the screen. This is called a *sound bridge*. Sound bridges create transitions, since we see one image, say, of a person's face, but hear what seems an inappropriate sound, perhaps of a band playing. Then a cut reveals a new locale and time, and we see the band which was the source of the music. Since the sound belongs to the later scene, the moment before the cut uses nonsimultaneous sound.

Examples of sound flashforwards (external displaced diegetic) are rare, perhaps nonexistent, but such a use is logically possible in the cinema.

Nondiegetic Sound

Most nondiegetic sound has no relevant temporal relationship to the story. When "mood" music comes up over a tense scene, it would be irrelevant for us to ask if it is happening at the same time as the images, since the music has no relation to the space of the story. But occasionally the film-maker may use a type of nondiegetic sound that does have a defined temporal relationship to the story. For example, Orson Welles's narration in *The Magnificent Ambersons* speaks of the action as having happened long ago, in a different era of American history.

Summary

All of these temporal categories offer us ways of making important distinctions in analyzing films. Fritz Lang's *Secret Beyond the Door,* for example, has an unusual combination of internal displaced diegetic and internal simple diegetic sound. In the first third of the film, the heroine's wedding is about to take place; her voice is heard recalling the circumstances that led to her marriage. This interior monologue is in the present tense. Over the scenes from the past, the monologue is internal displaced diegetic, but over the framing scenes of the wedding, her voice continues as internal simple diegetic. As a whole, the film depends on the contrast of two types of internal speech: the character's mind reacts to immediate situations (simple diegetic), and her mind reflects on past events (displaced diegetic). In such cases the various categories of sound help sharpen our awareness of the ways in which sound can combine with images. . . .

Note

1. V. F. Perkins, *Film as Film* (Harmondsworth, Middlesex: Penguin, 1972), p. 54.

On the Structural
Use of Sound NOËL BURCH

The fundamental dialectic in film, the one that at least empirically seems to contain every other, is that contrasting and joining sound with image. The *necessary* interrelationship of sound and image today appears to be definitely established fact, as even the most doubting critic must concede once he has examined the history of film. From the very beginnings of our art, starting with Méliès's showings of his films in the basement of a Paris café, audiences and filmmakers alike felt the need for some sort of sound (that is, musical) background for these images whose *silence* was unbearable,[1] despite the fact that it was this very silence that was the source of a great dramatic art now unfortunately lost.[2]

Robert Bresson, commenting on his own film practice, has made some rather revealing and pertinent remarks on the dichotomy of sound and image.[3] According to this filmmaker, sound, because of its greater realism, is infinitely more evocative than an image, which is essentially only a stylization of visual reality. "A sound always evokes an image; an image never evokes a sound," Bresson contends, and he then goes on to state, with just a touch of false naïveté, that he replaces an image with a sound whenever possible, thus remaining completely faithful to the principle of maximum bareness and spareness underlying his creative method.

But is this the real essence of the problem of the relationship between sound and image? Aside from the fact that Bresson's second tenet does not really seem to follow from the first, I am not entirely certain that sound is as realistic as all that, although it certainly can be. Gregory Markopoulos's film *Twice a Man,* for instance, is preceded by some five minutes of sound effects that half the audience is apt to describe as falling rain and the other half as a crowd applauding. Obviously the image could help us decide, but as it happens the screen is blacked out, so that the sound in effect occurs off-screen and is therefore precisely the sort of sound Bresson maintains can replace an image. As this example indicates, the ease with which a sound can be "deciphered" can vary as much as the ease with which the image can be "read." An extreme auditory "close-up" of a drop of water dripping into a sink is as difficult to recognize for what it really is as an extreme visual close-up of the joint of a woman's thumb (see *Geography of the Body* by Willard Maas). Any sound engineer can tell us how difficult it is to make certain sounds seem "natural," particularly if they occur off-screen—that is to say, without the explanatory support furnished by the image. Bresson himself always uses easily identifiable off-screen sounds such as footsteps and creaking doors, thereby considerably limiting his sound palette. And Bresson's contention notwithstanding, a face or landscape filmed without extraneous "effects," although always a stylization of reality, as we are aware *after the fact*, will seem just as "realistic" as a door we merely hear creaking on the sound track. The evocatory effect of sound seems to me to relate more to the powers of suggestion inherent in off-screen space in everything relating to it: an off-screen glance is just as evocative. There does not seem to me to be anything *inherently* evocative in the nature of sound, even if off-screen space is obviously frequently brought to life through the sound track.

It seems that the essential nature of the relationship between sound and image is due not to the difference between them but rather to the similarity between them. [It can be argued that] a camera's nonselectivity contrasts with the natural process of selection of the human eye [and that as a consequence each composition must be considered] as a totality. There is a similar difference between the way the human ear hears and the way a microphone records. As an example, we might use a conversation taking place inside a moving car. In a real-life situation such as this, it is usually quite easy to ignore any sounds that might interfere with our comprehension (the noise of the motor, the wind, the radio, and so on) and grasp what our fellow passengers are saying *despite* such sounds. A microphone recording the same conversation under the same conditions could not distinguish between the different sounds, however, and would jumble them all together;[4] and the sounds emerging from the single source of the loudspeaker in the theater would all be equally "present," much as a camera reduces the three-dimensionality of real space to the two-dimensionality of screen space.

Just as a game in progress on a pinball machine cannot be filmed in a comprehensible manner without somehow toning down the surface reflections on the glass above, so too the possibilities of recording a comprehensible conversation in a car are rather slight. For such a conversation to be understandable, background noises and dialogue must be recorded separately and their relative levels determined during the sound mix.[5]

Because of the "equal presence" of all the sound components of a film as they are channeled through the "funnel" of the loudspeaker in the theater, an overall "musical" orchestration of all the distinct elements of the sound track seems to be imperative, in somewhat the same manner that the way in which a visual image is perceived demands that constant attention be paid to the total visual composition.

There are certain dialectical possibilities inherent in the very nature of the sound track. . . . I shall now attempt to draw up a list of these.

The example of the car presupposes the existence of at least two
different kinds of *auditory material,* "live" or "synchronous" sound on the
one hand and recomposed sound produced by a mix—two types of sound
that unquestionably provide the two poles of a dialectic. . . . This sound
dialectic would normally occur in conjunction with the dialectical alternation
of "live" and "staged" shots and reinforce it. In actual practice, however,
"improvised" shots are often completely postsynchronized ("dubbed") in a
sound studio, whereas carefully staged shots are often accompanied by
background sounds recorded live. Generally, it is a question of mere con-
venience: the director simply chooses the handiest means available to make
the scenes being filmed as "lifelike" and as comprehensible as possible.
Nonetheless, a complex interaction among these four poles is quite conceivable, and it might well become an essential underlying pattern for a new
kind of film. . . . Even now, alternations between live and reconstituted sound
occurring in conjunction with the corresponding visual alternations provide
certain television programs with a very simple yet very effective structural
framework. A transition from the noiseless environment of a sound stage or
sound studio to the chaotic bustle of life in a shot taken in the street enormously enhances the viewer's awareness of the sudden break implicit in such
a transition. This break, moreover, is experienced in an infinitely more *physical* manner than would have been the case had one carefully controlled shot
been followed by one only a little less carefully controlled, if only because
of the sudden tremendous increase in both the area and the indeterminacy
of the off-screen space. The ambient silence a studio provides is one of the
principles underlying studio recording, in fact; sounds are then introduced
into it in such a way as to make our awareness of off-screen space as clear
and simple as possible; and the greater or lesser differentiation of off-screen
space provides another possible way of interrelating the various dialectics.

Another essential sound parameter results from the *apparent microphone distance.* A number of very complex auditory phenomena, the most
important being resonance or "echo," are what determine the apparent distance between the recording microphone and the sound source (or more
accurately, between this source and the theater loudspeaker, usually located
just behind the screen). Structural interactions between auditory and visual
space can be created rather easily through the use of this parameter, and
significant but isolated attempts to do so exist in the contemporary film. (The
very fact that such attempts are relatively rare provides yet another proof of
my contention that sound experimentation is at least ten years behind other
areas of investigation of the formal possibilities of film; the reasons for this
will be examined at the end of this [essay].)

The long shots of a couple walking on the beach and talking to each other in a sound close-up in Agnès Varda's *La Pointe courte* provide perhaps a rather rudimentary example of the manner in which a sound "presence" can counterpoint a visual one. Orson Welles in his *Othello,* however, by emphasizing and even exaggerating the congruency of auditory presence and visual presence, has creatively demonstrated the dynamic possibilities inherent in juxtapositions of extreme close-ups and long shots. Extreme close-ups are associated with an extremely intimate sound "presence," the long shots with an exaggerated booming echo, and the sharp contrast between them serves as one of the elements of the deliberately jerky *découpage* of this film. . . .

Another form of interaction between visual space and sound presence perhaps even richer in potential can be found in Mizoguchi's *The Crucified Lovers,* a film that even today remains at the very forefront of experimentation in the relations of sound and image. Toward the end of the film, prior to the lovers' final capture, when Sessame's brother steals off to get the police, the silence that attends his slipping away into the distance is suddenly interrupted by a musical motif played fortissimo, percussively, on the zitherlike *samisen* in extreme sound close-up. The contrast between the remoteness of the visual "subject" and the close proximity of the sound "subject" produces an extremely startling effect; it is almost as if a new character had suddenly appeared in the shot in an extreme visual close-up, although it is precisely the absence of any new visual presence in the area close to the camera and the resulting *surprise*[6] that makes this moment such a dramatically tense one.

It will be noticed that, concerning the modes of interaction between the various sound materials as well as those between auditory and visual space, I make no distinction between music, dialogue, and sound effects. These two types of dialectical interaction can in fact involve any sort of sound. Shared as it is by a small but growing minority of filmmakers these days, this attitude brings the ultimate aim of contemporary experiments in the use of sound a step closer to realization: the creation, that is, of a coherent, organically structured sound track in which the forms of interaction between sound and images will be closely tied to other interactions between the three basic types of film sounds: dialogue; music; and sound effects, whether identifiable or not. Mizoguchi's *The Crucified Lovers* is a pioneer effort in this direction as well.[7] The particular quality of Japanese music (to be discussed further below) with its predominance of abrupt percussive sounds and its eminently "graphic" structures obviously made it easier to create some form of interaction between sound effects and music. Yet, even granting the advantage Japanese music confers, Mizoguchi's sound track is a unique achievement in the history of cinema. In a scene in which the hero hides in an attic, a succession of sounds with a distinct rhythm of their own created by the wooden bowls from which the hero has been eating, then by a ladder banging against the wall, provide the first notes (of somewhat indeterminate pitch) in a musically orchestrated structure that goes on to incorporate instruments with tone qualities similar to those of these "natural" sound effects. Another musical passage ends on a "note" that in fact is the sound of a door closing in frame. Aside from the organic, dialectical link established in this way between "functional" sound effects and music, the very fact that the sound effects are synchronous with a visual image results in other interactions, this time between the images and the entire sound tissue of the film, which at times shifts without a break from an off-screen to an on-screen "presence."

Another possible relationship between sound, particularly music, and image (a dialectical relationship insofar as it periodically draws sound and image together) involves the creation of an *analogy* between them. A scene of struggle in a bamboo thicket is accompanied by a brief flurry of sounds made on instruments similar to wood blocks that are strongly suggestive of the sounds that might result were one to tap on the bamboo stalks filling the screen. It is difficult to conceive of this approach ever leading to any very substantial developments, yet Eisenstein considered this a very important form of interaction (as exemplified in the coronation scene in *Ivan the Terrible,* where the close-up of the imperial globe is accompanied by an extremely low and resonant bass note), just as he attributed great importance to all other forms of analogy between sound and image, as his analysis of Prokofiev's score of *Alexander Nevsky* indicates.

Let us now return to a possibility suggested above, that of integrating sound effects and music into a single sound texture. Obviously dialogue, the third form of sound, can also play a role in creating such a relationship. Once again, there is no doubt that Japanese theatrical diction, with its shrieking, panting, rumbling sounds constituting a tonal range similar to that of Schoenbergian *Sprachgesang,* is particularly capable of organically interacting with other forms of sound so as to create a single complex sound texture. Mizoguchi (in *The Crucified Lovers* and other films) and Kurosawa (notably in *The Lower Depths* and *The Hidden Fortress*) have explored some of the possibilities of "musically" orchestrating dialogue, if not specifically incorporating them into the overall sound complex. Yet it is Josef von Sternberg, approaching the Japanese language "from the outside" (the dialogue in *The Saga of Anatahan* is not supposed to be comprehensible to the audience), who most consciously exploited the resources of that language, sometimes closely coupled with stylized sound effects, to create purely auditory patterns.

Nonetheless, the most interesting attempt to treat dialogue as both the vehicle for the dramatic action and musically organized sound is Abraham Polonsky's "film maudit," *Force of Evil.* Here the entire dialogue takes the form of alliterations, dissonant rhymes, and rhythmical effects of every sort, even at times serving as a sort of "relay" for the sound effects, as when knocks on a door repeat the rhythm and timbre of the preceding line of dialogue.

In the examples thus far cited, sound effects, even when treated in close dialectical association with music or dialogue, have in each case been related in some manner either to an event seen on-screen or to an off-screen event linked in some way to the action and playing some role in it (as the sea-shell curtains in *Anatahan* or the knocks on the door in *Force of Evil* do). Certain sound technicians, however, have explored the possibility of treating sound effects much more freely, giving them the role the musical score purportedly plays in most films that have one. The person in France to have most systematically experimented with this approach is Michel Fano, a composer turned sound engineer and then filmmaker, but whose attention is primarily directed toward what his Brazilian counterparts refer to as "audioplastics"—that is, with the conception and technical execution of the entire sound complex, during not only the editing but also the actual shooting as well, insofar as preconceived sound structures can determine certain visual components. Michel Fano's most interesting work has been in collaboration with Alain Robbe-Grillet, whose films represent the most exhaustive and thoroughgoing attempts I know of to organize musically off-screen sound. Mizoguchi, as we have seen, created a sound texture in which visually identifiable on-screen sounds synchronous with the image were intimately associated with musical elements (occurring, by definition, off-screen), these two sound parameters being linked through similarities in tone quality as well. Although among the first to realize the importance of the use of sound in *The Crucified Lovers,* Michel Fano nonetheless proceeds in an altogether different manner. He often starts with a visual element (the garage or the harbor in *L'Immortelle,* for instance) and then progressively incorporates off-screen sounds into the sound track, organizing them into "musical" structures—hammer blows supposedly coming from the garage, a concert of sirens from the ships in the harbor—thereby contrasting a highly articulated and "graphic" off-screen auditory space with the plastic and dynamic organization of the images.

This extreme stylization of off-screen sound (in which synchronous elements can function as rhythmical punctuation—the pneumatic train doors and the hardware store chimes in *Trans-Europ-Express* are two notable examples) is achieved through the organization of real-life sounds (usually left just as they are or tinkered with only a little bit) into structures that, if not exactly serial (the sounds involved often being of indeterminate pitch and in any case untempered), nevertheless are quite similar to the strategies of contemporary music.

Fano thus far has not included all three types of sound (sound effects, music, and dialogue) as components, nor has he established the constant "relays" with the image that are needed if the full *dialectical* implications of this type of organization of sound are ever to be realized. This would obviously require the total collaboration of filmmaker and sound engineer throughout every stage of the conception and execution of a film.[8] A first step has nonetheless been taken, and there is no reason why a filmmaker should not some day be able to create a vast dialectical interaction between sound and image by applying, among others, the principles of serial organization to his *découpage*, exploiting, on the one hand, the various temporal and spatial dialectics we have outlined, and, on the other, the possible forms of combining the three types of sound and integrating the resulting auditory configurations with the film's overall plastic conception.

Fano is not altogether alone in his research in this direction. When Jacques Rivette asked Jean-Claude Eloy to create the sound effects and music for *The Nun,* he indicated his interest in this kind of experimentation. And a group of young Brazilians, working notably with Pereira dos Santos on his *Vidas secas,* have shown talent and sensitivity to the plastic organization of sounds motivated by the image (as particularly demonstrated by the incredible beauty of the prolonged creaking of a cartwheel that serves as a "musical" accompaniment to the credit sequence in this film).

The accomplishments of these young Brazilians, however, also reflect the desire on the part of a large number of filmmakers to eliminate entirely any sort of traditional music score, believing as they do that more or less structured sound effects,[9] possibly combined with musical themes drawn from our classical musical heritage (as, for example, the use of fragments from *La Traviata* in *Trans-Europ-Express* or motifs from Beethoven's quartets in *Une Femme mariée*) can and should replace what in their eyes is a totally discredited convention. In view of the very bad uses to which musical scores have been put in the sound film, this attitude can easily be defended. Nevertheless, to reject categorically the possibility of complete auditory stylization that music provides is to deprive oneself somewhat arbitrarily of a raw material that, when properly approached, can lead to an undeniable enrichment of a film. Without its musical score, *The Crucified Lovers,* for instance, would be a rather minor work. For, no matter how moving Chikamatsu's story is, the film is far from the plastic equal of *Sansho the Bailiff* or *The Life of O'Haru;* it is the score and the sound effects that make the film into a near masterpiece.

Films about which the same can be said are few in number, as there are few works of cinema in which music is an organic and integral part of the overall formal texture. As I have already indicated, Japanese classical music seems particularly amenable to this sort of integration.[10] It would appear that this is due to the extremely flexible, supple, "open" quality of this music (which is not subject to the "tyranny of the bar-line" as Western music is and above all is not restricted to tonal structures) that makes it infinitely more adaptable to the eminently nonmeasurable rhythms of film "action" and film editing. Japanese music, however hieratic, seems to have a freer flow, an empirical quality closer to that of the film image. Moreover, as was mentioned in the discussion of *The Crucified Lovers,* a large number of the timbres found in Japanese music are similar to everyday sounds, thus making the organic interaction of sound effects and music suggested here easier to achieve.

What might a Western filmmaker conclude from these observations? The generalized use of Japanese music in its pure state is obviously not possible in Western cinema. One revealing fact, however, might be pointed out here: Japanese music was not really accessible to the Western ear until after the introduction of atonal music; young serial composers see profound affinities between their work and classical Japanese music, as would not have been the case with any Western musician before Debussy.

Serial music, then, the most "open" form in the history of Western music, with its unprecedented rhythmical freedom and its use of timbres that classical musicians considered vulgar noises, seems uniquely suited to organic, dialectical integration of music with sound effects, as well as with the filmed image, whereas traditional tonal music with its predetermined forms, its strong tonal polarities, and its range of relatively homogeneous tone colors can provide only an autonomous continuity existing *alongside* that of the images, merely running parallel to the dialogue and sound effects or accompanying the images with a musical synchronicity of the sort found in animated cartoons.[11] Serial music, on the other hand, provides the most open form conceivable. In its interstices, every form of sound has a natural place, and it can provide an ideal complement to the "irrational" quality of the concrete image as such as well as to the more rational structures created by the *découpage.* Serial composers starting with Webern were, moreover, the first to consider silence as an essential musical component. After a long period during which the talking picture with a musical score seems to have been haunted by the terror, or perhaps the memory, of silence, young filmmakers have at last begun to be aware of the dialectical role silence can play relative to sound. These filmmakers have even succeeded in making a subtle yet basic distinction between the different "colors" of silence (a complete dead space on the sound track, studio silence, silence in the country, and so forth), thus glimpsing some of the structural roles such silences can play (as is particularly evident in *Deux ou trois choses que je sais d'elle*).

The reader will rightly feel that this [essay is somewhat sketchy]. This is largely because it was written ten years too early, for, as has already been said, the evolution of film sound lags far behind that of the film image. Even in the most "advanced" contemporary films (*Une Simple histoire, Last Year at Marienbad, Nicht Versöhnt, Persona,* and others), sound plays the role of a "poor relation" of the image: from the standpoint of its inherent possibilities, it participates in the experimental search for new forms only in the most minimal sort of way. The few experimenters who could remedy this situation have thus far not been given the means with which to do so. To organize successfully and totally a sound track both internally and relative to the image, to create a total sound texture and bring every one of its components under control (by manufacturing street sounds from discrete real sounds, for instance), the amount of money budgeted for sound in an ordinary film project would have to be doubled. That subtleties of this sort should seem rather pointless to those who finance films is more or less to be expected, and thus the immediate future looks bleak. But one can always hope that the qualified experimenters will some day find the means with which to carry out successfully the formal research that is crucial if cinema is ever to realize fully its inherent potential in this area.

(Translated by Helen R. Lane)

Notes

1. It is usually maintained that this silence was unbearable only because it allowed the noise of the projector to be heard. This silence, however, is no less painful in situations where the projector noise cannot be heard, as is the case at the Cinémathèque Française. Fritz Lang's *Mabuse* made a much greater impression on all of us when we were finally able to see it with a musical accompaniment like that provided in the days of silent film. Admittedly the music in this case is little more than sound background; nevertheless, it provides a time scale against which the "rhythms" of the *découpage* became far more concrete.

2. Garrel's completely silent film *Le Révélateur,* as well as many "new American" films, seem to indicate that this is not entirely true.

3. In a program in the *Cinéastes de notre temps* series, directed by François Weyergans.

4. Under certain conditions directional—that is, selective—microphones can remedy this, but this fact does not invalidate the present argument, at least insofar as human perception is concerned; especially when the peculiar and rather bad quality of the sound thus obtained results in merely another stylization, a phenomenon comparable to what happens to a voice heard over the telephone.

5. Godard, who is quite interested in sound interference of this sort, often records similar scenes in synchronous sound (or recreates the same effect in a studio), doubtless to make us aware of the effort our ear must make to understand whatever message is being transmitted.

6. See Chapter 8 of Noël Burch, *Praxis du cinéma* (Paris: Gallimard, 1969); English translation by Helen R. Lane published as *Theory of Film Practice* (New York: Praeger, 1973).

7. A certain amount of similar experimentation can be found, although in far less systematic form, in some of Mizoguchi's other films, notably in *Story of the Late Chrysanthemums, The Life of O'Haru,* and *Sansho the Bailiff.*

8. Just before the French edition [of *Praxis du cinéma*] went to press, I saw *L'Homme qui ment (The Man Who Lies),* the admirable outcome of all the experiments Fano had undertaken previously, a film in which the three types of sound are integrated in an almost flawless manner, although their integration with the image and the film's *découpage* is perhaps a bit too episodic. And of course we must now add Fano's own film on animals, *Le Territoire des autres,* his most important experiment to date.

9. The opposite procedure, in which musical and paramusical elements replace certain sound effects, resulting in a form of dialectics of materials, often explored when sound was first introduced (notably in Boris Barnet's *Okraina,* the first feature film to have a sound track based on artificial sounds, obtained by filming geometrical patterns directly on the optical track) and by Sternberg in his *Saga of Anatahan,* has apparently been temporarily abandoned, except for its use in purely experimental films. This dialectic nevertheless is rich in possibilities, and it will surely soon be explored again.

10. Aside from the Mizoguchu films already mentioned, other films in which this integration is partially achieved are Kon Ichikawa's *Enjo* and Ishida's *Fallen Flowers* (1939).

11. The exceptions to this seemingly general rule are few and far between. One of the most noteworthy is Giovanni Fuco's score for *Cronaca di un amore,* where the use of two instruments with strongly contrasting tone qualities (a saxophone and a piano, usually used separately), of a musical style closely associated with the film's *découpage* and even with the dialogue, and of a quite subtle musical development in which the themes consist of little more than recurring musical intervals creates a "graphic" relationship between music and film; the score in fact is one of the principal elements contributing to the film's unity.

Pioneers

Just as most of the discussion about sound aesthetics was generated during the period between 1927 and 1932, so, too, most of the film history texts have concentrated on that period of transition. Historians focus on the technological developments that led to the viability of feature-length sound films, on the subsequent technological advances that freed filmmakers from the restrictions of sound shooting, and, finally, on those few films of the period that are now considered masterpieces. The approach of highlighting glorious exceptions makes sense in that the best films of the period were usually those whose creativity stemmed from a frontal attack on the restrictions of sound recording. These films are for the most part musicals. And even the nonmusicals are so stylized as to flout realistic conventions.

In this anthology, the above approach is represented by the excerpt from Arthur Knight's famous history, *The Liveliest Art,* which surveys key early sound films by Lubitsch, Vidor, Clair, Walsh, and Mamoulian. Knight explains the limitations of early sound shooting and then shows how these directors nevertheless achieved camera freedom, whether by shooting in silent style and adding sound later or by refusing to accept technological restrictions.

Ron Mottram's essay may be seen as complementary to Knight's. Whereas Knight discusses films considered to be the enduring classics of the period, Mottram looks in detail at films less often revived. He concentrates on the first American sound films by directors who were previously either major silent film directors or stage directors. Some of these films work in their entirety; others are less successful as a whole but have noteworthy moments of inventive sound. As a group, they reveal that much more was technically feasible at the time than is usually acknowledged. By demonstrating that efforts to overcome the severe restrictions of sound recording came earlier and more frequently than is commonly assumed, Mottram goes a long way in demystifying the myths that have been perpetuated about the early sound period.

If Mottram's approach shows that the classics should not be isolated from the context of other films of the period, Lucy Fischer's essay on *Applause* demonstrates that famous virtuoso achievements should not be isolated from the larger aesthetic context of a given film. *Applause* is the film most frequently cited in essays on early sound. References are made to such technical accomplishments as its innovative use of two-channel recording and its use of tracking shots (at a time when the camera was usually immobilized in a soundproof booth). Fischer's close analysis shows that the entire film contains innovative experiments with the possibilities of dialogue, music, and sound effects. She argues that the sense of reality, density, and depth achieved through sound in *Applause* functions in tandem with a visual establishment of depth to create a sense of "palpable" space.

Whereas Mamoulian creates a habitable space in *Applause,* Vertov does everything he can to *break* the illusion of real space in *Enthusiasm.* Fischer's essay on Vertov's film, one of the earliest Russian sound films, considers *Enthusiasm* as it relates both to available sound technology in Russia and to sound theories contemporary with the film. As in her essay on *Applause,* Fischer finds that the film's use of sound is integral to its aesthetic aims and demonstrates how "the very techniques that Vertov utilizes to break the spatial illusion serve simultaneously to advance the film's political and thematic content."

Noël Carroll also considers sound as integral to the directors' aesthetic in his article on Lang and Pabst. However, his approach is to establish the two films as paradigms for the alternative directions film would take in response to the availability of sound, not only in 1931 Germany, but in general. Carroll sees Lang's *M* as a paradigm of the "silent sound film": the type of film that uses sound as a manipulative montage element. By contrast, Pabst's *Kameradschaft* is seen as a forerunner of films observing Bazin's realist aesthetic: sound, like camera movement, is used by realists to record rather than to reconstitute reality.

The last film dealt with in this section is John Stahl's *Back Street.* This 1932 Hollywood melodrama is quite different from the films discussed above; while those films exert a forceful, obtrusive style, *Back Street* would seem to operate within the Hollywood invisible tradition described by Mary Ann Doane in "Ideology and the Practice of Sound Editing and Mixing." Yet Martin Rubin holds that, by "pushing" sound conventions to an extreme, Stahl creates a distinctive tonal quality that can ultimately be seen as an expression of the director's attitude about the role of sound in relation to image. Rubin's approach to sound suggests that there is still much work to be done on sound in films with sound tracks that have hitherto been neglected because they don't assert their importance.

The Movies Learn to Talk:
Ernst Lubitsch, René Clair,
and Rouben Mamoulian ARTHUR KNIGHT

Liberating the Camera: Ernst Lubitsch

It is to the eternal credit of genuinely creative and courageous men like Ernst Lubitsch, Rouben Mamoulian, Lewis Milestone, King Vidor, and Raoul Walsh that they had the ingenuity and vitality to circumvent the experts and lift the new medium out of the rut of dully photographed plays and vaudeville routines into which it had fallen [at the advent of sound]. They had no rules to go on, no precedents to quote. They had the opposition of the sound men to contend with, and the indisputable fact that at the box offices across the nation almost any film was making money as long as it talked. But these men sensed that talk alone was not enough, and that the public would soon tire of the novelty of sound for sound's sake and demand again to see a *movie*. It was their pioneer work that brought forth the techniques to make the movies move again.

Ernst Lubitsch, by 1929 the top director at Paramount, made the important discovery that a talking picture did not have to be *all* talking, nor did the sound track have to reproduce faithfully each sound on the set. In his first talkies, *The Love Parade* (1929) and *Monte Carlo* (1930), he included many passages that were shot without dialogue or any other synchronized sound. For these, he was able to bring the camera out of its soundproofed box and proceed in the old silent techniques, moving his camera freely, changing its position frequently. Music or effects were put in later. One of the high points of *The Love Parade* was a running gag with Maurice Chevalier telling a risqué joke to members of the court. Each time he approaches the tag line, his voice sinks to a confidential whisper, a door closes, or the camera leaps outside to view the effect of his story through a window. Audiences of 1929 were delighted to find a new element in the talkies—silence!

Working mainly on the Maurice Chevalier–Jeanette MacDonald musicals, Lubitsch quickly established himself as one of the most inventive directors of the period. With his strong feeling for the relationship between music and visuals, he brought back some of the rhythm that had been present in the silent films. In *Monte Carlo,* for example, Lubitsch cuts together the sounds of a train getting under way. As it picks up speed, the characteristic tempo of the wheels is translated into the music of the theme song, "Beyond the Blue Horizon." The impressive wedding ceremony in *The Smiling Lieutenant* (1931) was staged without the confining microphone, but each opening door, every step down the great flight of marble stairs, every gesture of the players was timed to the beat of a score that was dubbed in later. He was the first to be concerned with the "natural" introduction of songs into the development of a musical-comedy plot, the first to find a cinematic way to handle verbal humor in the new medium.

But Lubitsch also knew how to use the sound camera to serious purpose. In *Broken Lullaby* (1932), his one dramatic film of this period, he emphasized its antiwar theme in many brilliantly conceived shots. The sights and sounds of an Armistice Day parade are glimpsed between the crutches of a one-legged soldier. Early in the film, while a minister is praying for peace, the camera in ironic counterpoint moves slowly down the center aisle of the cathedral, past row on row of kneeling officers, their spurs gleaming, their swords stiff by their sides. By shooting such sequences silent and adding the sound later, Lubitsch obtained not only greater freedom for his camera but the kind of control of the elements in his scene essential to artistic creation. The "Lubitsch touch," that sparkling combination of wit and irony already famous in the silent film, reached its fullest expression in his early talkies.

Meanwhile, King Vidor in his first talking picture, *Hallelujah!* (1929), explored the possibilities of the sound track to evoke mood and atmosphere. It was an all-Negro picture made, for the most part, in Memphis, Tennessee, and the swamps of Arkansas. The fact that the film was done largely on location, away from rigid studio supervision, gave Vidor an enviable amount of freedom for that time. Much of it he shot silent, later creating an impressionistic sound track for all but the direct dialogue passages. The rhythmic swell of Negro spirituals, a woman's scream or a barking dog heard in the distance, the sounds of the swamp and the river supplied the dominant mood or emotional tone for many of the scenes. The whole final sequence, a frenzied pursuit through the swamps, was shot silent with beautiful, long traveling shots of pursued and pursuer. Only later, back in the studio, did Vidor add the magnified sounds of breaking branches, the screech of birds, agonized breathing, and the suck of footsteps stumbling through the mire. Without the present-day equipment for reading sound, without synchronizers or multiple-channel sound mixers Vidor performed a tremendous feat. He showed that the source of a sound is less important than its quality, that sound can create an emotional aura about a scene quite independent of the words and faces of the actors. In *The Cock-Eyed World* (1929), Raoul

Walsh ingeniously intercut brief silent shots with the camera in motion into static shots while his characters spoke. Lewis Milestone worked in much the same way in making his *All Quiet on the Western Front* (1930), photographing his scenes of troops on the march and in the trenches with a silent camera and adding in later the whine and crash of bombs, the clatter of small-arms fire, and the shrieks and moans of the wounded and dying.

This process of adding sound later to scenes shot with silent cameras, known as postsynchronization or dubbing, played an important role in freeing directors from the early notion that everything seen must be heard or that everything heard must be seen. Once postsynchronization had been achieved, such a literal use of sound was clearly no longer necessary. We might see an ordinary street scene, but the dialogue has been postsynchronized to eliminate the irrelevant honks and screeches that would blur the words. Or a director might let us hear the crash of an automobile while showing us only the horrified faces of the onlookers. The experience of postsynchronizing such scenes in the recording studio helped directors to realize that, essentially, the sound track is a composite of many sounds—voices, music, and all sorts of noises and effects—and that all of these were completely under his control. Each sound could be independently distorted, muffled, exaggerated, or eliminated at will. The director could shoot his scene with a silent camera and dub in the sound for it later. He could reinforce dialogue passages with music, combine them with noises, or bury them under other, postsynchronized sounds. And as the technicians provided more and better equipment to facilitate the handling of sound, these manipulative possibilities within the sound track assumed an ever greater importance. Postsynchronization became the first point of departure in the development of the new art.

The other was an improvement in the camera itself. During the first years of sound, the camera had been forced into a small soundproofed booth to keep the whir of its mechanism from reaching the sensitive, cranky microphone. As long as it remained confined, most directors were willing to work in long, static "takes." Often, three cameras simultaneously photographed the same scene from different angles, very much as in television today. This technique vastly simplified the problems of cutting and matching the sound to its proper visual, but it also produced a slow, draggy effect upon the screen. The choice of camera positions was too limited and too arbitrary to produce a truly cinematic effect. During 1930, however, the cameras began to emerge from these boxes, enclosed now in soundproofed "blimps" which, while still cumbersome, permitted a far greater freedom of movement. It then became the director's problem to force the reluctant sound experts to give that new mobility full rein, to demand from them more flexible microphone setups. In shooting his first film, *Applause* (1929), Rouben

Mamoulian demanded two microphones on a single set, one to record the voice of Helen Morgan as she sang a lullaby to her daughter, the other to record the girl's whispered prayer in bed. The experts argued that this would necessitate the use of two separate channels, a thing unheard of at the time. "Unheard of but not impossible," Mamoulian insisted—and proved his point. Today nine channels are not unusual for a single shot, while on stereo-phonic epics the number may rise to as many as fifty.

Not only was the number of microphones increased, but their quality improved. They became more "directional," able to hear only in one area so that the director could manipulate other sounds in other portions of his scene. Before long, the stationary microphones were being replaced by mikes suspended on long booms that could be swung to follow the players anywhere. Thus, slowly, the sound experts of Hollywood were defeated by directors with fresh ideas about the nature of the new art—and the prestige and stamina to fight them through.

Mastering the Sound Track: René Clair

Perhaps the first director to appreciate fully the implications of sound was the Frenchman René Clair. Originally opposed to the whole idea, he insisted on the predominant importance of the visual element, declaring that the sound film need not and should not be, to use his own term, "canned theater." This opinion, almost revolutionary among filmmakers at the time, was bril-liantly confirmed in a trio of sparkling comedies that quickly made Clair the most admired and imitated director in the world. In *Sous les toits de Paris* (1929), *Le Million* (1931), and *A nous la liberté* (1931), he worked with a minimum of dialogue, using music, choruses, and sound effects to counter-point and comment upon his visuals. In this principle of asynchronous sound, sound used against rather than with the images, Clair discovered a new free-dom and fluidity for the sound medium. Why show a door closing when it is enough merely to hear it slam? Or why listen to a clock's ticking just be-cause it is shown? In *Le Million* there is a brief glimpse of a clock on a man-tel shelf, a clock elaborately overdecorated with porcelain cupids blowing trumpets. Clair's sound track at that point carries a blast of trumpets. In *Sous les toits* a fight takes place at night near a railway embankment. The fight is almost obscured by the shadows, but its force and fury are conveyed in the roar of the passing trains heard on the sound track. In *A nous la liberté*, Clair goes so far as to kid the whole notion of synchronous sound by show-ing his heroine singing away at her window while the hero admires from afar. Suddenly something goes wrong with the voice—it whines and whirs, then fades away. A moment later, while the young fellow is still looking up at the window, the girl appears in the street, the song begins again and we discover that what we have been listening to all along is a phonograph record from another apartment.

Because Clair's early sound films were both musicals and comedies, he could permit himself an impish audacity denied practitioners of the more serious forms, whose dramatic themes forced them to use more straightforward techniques. Their efforts at realism made it difficult for them to break with the conventional practices that quickly surrounded the microphone soon after it had made its appearance in the studios. Clair, on the other hand, could ignore conventional sound, omitting the characteristic noises of a street, a factory, or an opera house altogether unless they served his purpose. It was *his* world, and he did with it as he wished.

And because above all he liked music and the dance, his pictures flash along like ballets. The incessant chases, the scramble after the flying bank notes in *A nous la liberté,* the mad party that opens and closes *Le Million*—all are set to gay, infectious tunes. Choruses sing a witty commentary upon the action as it unfolds. Whole sequences are bound together by music alone. In the opening reel of *Sous les toits de Paris* a street singer is vending the title song of the film. While the camera wanders up and down the street, peering into the apartments and shops, one by one the people of the neighborhood join in the song. In this way Clair quickly introduces the principal characters in his story and gaily sets the mood of the entire film. Throughout his pictures, music functions in dozens of bright and unexpected ways, playing an integral part in the development of his diverting stories.

What Clair had done, what creative directors everywhere were trying to do at the same time, was to discover how to control all the elements that went into the making of a sound film as completely as, in the simpler days of silence, one could control everything that went before the camera. He demonstrated to everyone's satisfaction that much of silent technique was still valid, that it was the image and not the word that kept the screen alive. Sound, and especially asynchronous sound, could add its own grace notes, its deeper perceptions, its enrichment of mood and atmosphere—but not independently of the visual.

Because René Clair had instinctively grasped this principle in his first three films, and turned them out with a flair and finish unmatched anywhere at the time, his pictures had a profound effect upon other directors. He had achieved what they were groping toward. He had brought back into films spontaneity, movement, rhythm. The extent of his influence is immediately revealed by a comparison of the opening reel of his *Sous les toits* with the first sequences of Geza von Bolvary's *Zwei Herzen im Dreiviertel*

Takt (1930) or the "Blue Horizon" number in Lubitsch's *Monte Carlo* (1930). But more important than imitation are the innumerable films of the early thirties that suggest his liberating spirit. In Germany Eric Charrell's *Congress Dances* (1931), in England Victor Saville's *Sunshine Susie* (1932), and in Hollywood films like Frank Tuttle's *This Is the Night* (1932), Gregory La Cava's *Half-Naked Truth* (1932), and Lewis Milestone's *Hallelujah, I'm a Bum* (1933), all reveal not only a new freedom in the use of sound but also—as in the Clair films—a rhythmic structure imparted by the sound track.

Clair's work was especially valuable to those men in the American studios who were themselves seeking to liberate the talking film from the confines of "canned theater." More daring than they dared to be, the fact that such pictures had found considerable popular as well as critical success was helpful in encouraging them to go ahead—quite apart from any technical lessons they might have learned. In this respect the early sound period was very much like the first decade or so of the silent era. The medium itself was still in a highly experimental stage, and directors looked to the box office to tell them how successful they were with the new techniques, and to the works of one another for useful hints that they could incorporate into their own efforts. In this period of search and confusion, Clair's pictures appeared as beacons to the future. And if Clair had a tendency to overstress the silent techniques in his early films, they provided a healthy counterinfluence to the overaccenting of the sound track in the films made by almost everyone else.

Exploring the New Medium: Rouben Mamoulian

Perhaps the leading director of dramatic films in this country to rebel against "canned theater" movies during the early years of sound was Rouben Mamoulian—ironically, one of the many Broadway directors brought to the studios in 1929 specifically to make "canned theater." Despite his theater background, Mamoulian sensed at once the differences between the two forms. He felt that the camera could and should move, appreciated the importance of the close-up for dramatic emphasis, fought against the prevalent notion that the source for every sound must be seen. For him, the camera was far more than a passive observer looking on while actors recited their lines—and the function of the director was more than merely helping the actors to say their lines better. He had to help the audience find what was dramatically significant in a scene, picking out what was important with his camera, making it seem fresh and illuminating through the imagination and inventiveness of his visuals.

In his first two talking pictures, *Applause* (1929) and *City Streets* (1931), Mamoulian gave repeated evidence of his desire to move away from stereotyped techniques. A particularly effective moment in *Applause* began with a close-up of Helen Morgan, the aging burlesque queen, reminiscing about her youth; as she speaks, the camera leaves her tired, dissipated face and wanders across the room to a photograph of her as a lovely young girl. At another point, a long tracking shot shows only the feet of the heroine as she leaves the theater, and the feet of the men she encounters as she walks home. The nature of each encounter is revealed as fully in the footsteps as in the fragments of conversation accompanying the scene. In *City Streets* a montage of china figurines is used symbolically over the clash of voices in one of the film's key dramatic scenes. Dialogue spoken earlier in the picture is heard again over a huge, tear-stained close-up of Sylvia Sidney as she recalls the past. Even as in Griffith's day, the producers protested that the public would never understand what was going on, that hearing a sound without seeing its source would only confuse the audience. Mamoulian stuck to his point, however; audiences did understand—and the sound "flashback" has become a standard technique in talkies ever since.

By the time he made *Dr. Jekyll and Mr. Hyde* (1932), Mamoulian had full control of his new medium. From start to finish, it was a virtuoso work; almost every scene revealed the director's desire to break away from a literal use of the camera and a conventional use of sound. The entire first reel was shot in the first-person technique, the camera assuming the identity of Dr. Jekyll. From that position we see his hands as he plays the organ, the shadow of his head upon the music rack. When Jekyll is ready to go out, the butler hands hat, cloak, and cane directly to the camera. After a carriage ride through the streets of London, it enters the doors of a medical school and passes on into the operating theater. Here a complete 360° turn around the hall brings the camera to rest for the first time upon the face of Dr. Jekyll (Fredric March). Quite apart from its indisputable pictorial effectiveness, this use of the subjective camera built a growing suspense, a curiosity about the appearance of the man we know will turn into the monstrous Hyde. The transformations themselves were ingeniously achieved upon the screen (Mamoulian has steadfastly refused to divulge the secret of his technique), accompanied by a vivid, synthetically created sound track built from exaggerated heartbeats mingled with the reverberations of gongs played backwards, bells heard through echo chambers, and completely artificial sounds created by photographing light frequencies directly onto the sound track. The recordists referred to it as "Mamoulian's stew," but it was probably the screen's first experiment with purely synthetic sound.

Outstanding for its understatement both of sound and visual was Mamoulian's handling of the scene in which Hyde murders "Champagne Ivy" (Miriam Hopkins). Hyde forces the thoroughly frightened girl to sing her pathetic music hall song. Suddenly he bends over her, passing completely out of the frame. For a long moment the shot reveals only the bedpost, a highly ornamental carving of the Goddess of Love. Then the singing stops abruptly, and Hyde's triumphant face rises once more into view. We need be shown no more.

The impact of René Clair's films upon men who, like Mamoulian, were themselves concerned with the creative use of sound is perhaps most clearly revealed in Mamoulian's next picture, *Love Me Tonight* (1932). Although in the tradition of the Jeanette MacDonald–Maurice Chevalier musicals that Ernst Lubitsch had been making so successfully, suddenly the form is freer, lighter, more imaginative than ever before. Greater liberties are taken with reality, and less effort is made to explain or excuse the obviously absurd to the audience. In the midst of a hunt, deer bound across the screen in dreamy waltz time; or characters march about a French château gleefully caroling, "The son of a gun is nothing but a tailor." Through this kind of fantasy, in which trick sound is combined with trick camera to create a world of gay illusion, the literal techniques of the realistic dramas were jolted loose, stirred about. The experience of making such musicals provided directors with new insights into their craft that inevitably carried over into the more serious forms. There was a pronounced tendency toward more vivid imagery, a more imaginative use of sound, even in stories still written mainly in the theatrical tradition. . . .

American Sound Films, 1926–1930   RON MOTTRAM

Early Sound Films by Silent Directors

It is clear how the coming of sound changed the economic and industrial structure of the American cinema. Less clear, however, is how sound changed the aesthetics of the medium. The great generalization, that the earliest sound films, 1926–30, were static, dull, and anchored to the spoken word, has begun to give way to a new appraisal based on a wider selection of the films made in these years. What is emerging is a cinema much more varied and imaginative than the conventional wisdom has claimed, especially as seen in the work of the great directors from the silent period. Consequently, Warner Bros.' *The Lights of New York* no longer can be accepted as exemplary of the condition of American filmmaking during the transitional period. There were, of course, films that fit this model, but there also were many that successfully overcame the interconnected technical and aesthetic problems posed by early sound production. How these problems were solved and the specific strategies used by the different studios in making the changeover still need to be researched with the kind of thoroughness that has recently been applied to the pre-Griffith cinema and that has undermined most of what the film history texts tell us. Some general points can be made about the transition, however, that, when combined with discussion of specific films and directors, will indicate the potential richness of the early American sound film.

The first feature-length sound films were really silent films with synchronized musical accompaniment and some sound effects. Warner Bros.' *Don Juan* (1926) and Fox's *Seventh Heaven* (1927) and *Sunrise* (1927) are notable examples. All three were made by experienced silent film directors: Alan Crosland *(Don Juan)*, Frank Borzage *(Seventh Heaven)*, and F. W. Murnau *(Sunrise)*. In these films, and others like them, sound as musical accompaniment was seen to be a useful device to increase the box-office attraction of the more prestigious productions. While these silent films with musical scores were being released, however, the same studios were venturing into part-talking and all-talking films that were being given to either lesser directors or newer, untried directors from the stage. In addition to a naïve belief that stage-directing experience would result in successful talking films, there were other commercial and aesthetic reasons for this procedure. Studio heads were interested in protecting the drawing power of their best directors, while the best directors were concerned that they protect their reputations by first learning the workings of sound and by becoming sure that sound was an artistically viable element of filmmaking before making their own sound films. Thus, in many cases, the lesser directors were used in working out some of the problems of sound while the better directors prepared themselves to tackle sound should sound prove to be more than a passing fad. Even when the leading directors did get their first sound films, they were often assigned dialogue directors to assist in the production and to ensure that the dialogue scenes were handled "correctly."

A good example of this practice is John Ford's first sound film, *The Black Watch* (1929),[1] which illustrates the use of music and song to comment on and to develop the narrative. Working against Ford's creative contribution, however, are some awkwardly staged dialogue scenes added by the studio and directed by Lumsden Hare, an English actor who played the major in the film and who received production credit as Dialogue Director. Ford discussed Hare's role in an interview with Peter Bogdanovich:

That was another picture they changed after I'd gone. Winfield Sheehan was in charge of production then, and he said there weren't enough love scenes in it. He thought Lumsden Hare was a great British actor—he wasn't, but he impressed Sheehan—so he got Hare to direct some love scenes between Victor McLaglen and Myrna Loy. And they were really horrible—long, talky things, had nothing to do with the story—and completely screwed it up. I wanted to vomit when I saw them.[2]

The Black Watch is a highly stylized production, and it is this stylization that justifies, or rather is completely integrated with, the film's use of music and song. The film employs artificial sets, numerous military formalities and rituals, a "thou shalt" style of speaking on the part of the Indians, echoes in the sound, and a great deal of marching with bagpipes and singing, more so than can be justified by the narrative action. The music is, in fact, a kind of exteriorization of the soul of the Black Watch. Although the early scenes that take place in England introduce the stylization, they are far more natural than the scenes that take place in India. The Indian scenes are worked out as if they were a child's fantasy. They utilize extensive back lighting, bizarre sets and costuming, and a nonnatural acting style.

Through this stylization and the use of music to portray an idealization of military traditions and a romantic fantasy of military exploits, Ford escapes one of the traps of so many early sound films—the utilization of sound merely to record dialogue, to put emphasis on talk for its own sake. Instead, music is part of the whole fabric of expression, more expressive than words alone, and far more than merely a background for the dramatic action. It actually becomes a second level on which the narrative develops meaning, on which the ideas of tradition, duty, war, and romantic fantasy, which make up the film's content, are explored.

The Black Watch, as well as the first sound films of other important directors from the silent period, reveals that an understanding of film form was more significant to the rapid development of sound-film technique than was experience with the theater and spoken dialogue. The films these directors made during and shortly after the transitional period prove that the introduction of sound did not fundamentally change the nature of cinema but provided cinema with an additional expressive element that the best directors quickly mastered.

Another example, though more problematic than The Black Watch, is Raoul Walsh and Irving Cummings's In Old Arizona, made in the later part of 1928 and released in January 1929. Like Ford, both Walsh and Cummings were directors with considerable experience; Walsh especially had established his credentials with such notable productions as The Thief of Bagdad (1924) and What Price Glory? (1926). Noted for its early use of outdoor sound recording, In Old Arizona occupies an important, if somewhat overrated, place in the changeover to sound. For the most part it restricts itself to direct synchronous sound recording within an essentially realistic style and, because of this, tends to bog down in its numerous slowly paced and drawn-out dialogue sequences. These sequences suffer from many of the typical problems of the period. Not quite sure how dialogue can be handled, the actors tend to speak too carefully, emphasizing individual words and phrases so that the microphone and recording apparatus will pick up clearly what they are saying.

Unlike other early talkies, however, In Old Arizona has strengths that are attributable to the directors' silent film experience. The most important is a freer use of the camera, which is manifest not in the elaborate moving shots characteristic of Applause but in a greater concern with expressive camera placement. Rather than just recording a scene from multiple camera setups, as was typical at the time, the directors seem to have shot many of the scenes from angles that are organically connected to the action. This quality is particularly noticeable in the outdoor scenes, in which long shots play the role that they traditionally do in the western film—of placing the characters and action in a specific relation to the landscape—and in which close shots often relate to the viewpoints of the characters, as, for example, in the stage holdup when high angles of the Cisco Kid and low angles of the stage drivers establish the relationship of the participants. In interiors, also, the camera often crosses the 180° line when intercutting between characters, giving views not normally attained by using multiple camera setups. In outdoor scenes the camera often pans to follow an action, such as the arrival and departure of the stagecoach, the progress of the stage across the landscape, and the Cisco Kid on his horse. In one scene the camera begins to pan with an action, the stagecoach leaving town, and continues the pan after the coach disappears from view, finally ending on a group of Mexicans playing music and singing. The scene then fades out on this bit of local color that has helped to establish the Mexican border location of the film.

Although most of the sound in the film is used synchronously, as evinced in the dialogue scenes and in the often-remarked-upon fact that the sound gets softer or louder as characters and objects move away from or toward the camera (a realistic effect produced by the direct recording of sound in the outdoor scenes), there are several cases of effective use of asynchronous sound as well.

In one instance, after the sergeant (Edmund Lowe) has unknowingly met the Cisco Kid (Warner Baxter) for whom he has been searching, the blacksmith tells the sergeant who the friendly stranger was. To show quite literally that the laugh is on the sergeant, the sound track contains a donkey's heehaw that comes from off-screen. A donkey sound is used later in the same manner, again to comment on the sergeant.

At other places in the film a phonograph record is associated with the Cisco Kid and his romance with Tonia Maria. Toward the end of the film, when Tonia Maria has taken the sergeant for her lover, the Kid returns unexpectedly to catch the sergeant and Maria together. Their being together, however, is represented, at first, only in terms of the sound. As the Kid approaches Maria's house, he hears the record that up until then he thought was reserved for him, and so understands that Maria is unfaithful. During this same sequence the full effect of Cisco's heartbreak is registered by showing his reaction to Maria telling the sergeant that she never loved Cisco. We are never shown Maria making this confession. We hear only the lines as we see a close shot of Cisco reacting to them.

Of lesser stature than either Ford or Walsh, but nevertheless directors with considerable silent film experience, were Alan Crosland and Victor Fleming. Both brought a knowledge of visual storytelling to their early sound films that helped place their work above the average 1929 production.

In addition to *Don Juan,* Crosland made *The Jazz Singer* (1927), a silent film with several synchronous music sequences, and one other part-talkie, *Glorious Betsy,* in 1928. His first all-talking picture, *On With the Show,* came in May 1929, followed by a second talking film, *General Crack,* In December 1929. *On With the Show,* though below the standard of his silent films and of his later sound films, shows a veteran director straining against the limitations of early sound.

The film opens with a quite surprising dolly shot that crosses a street, enters a theater lobby, and tracks with two people who are talking. A shot like this clearly shows that by the spring of 1929 a high degree of fluidity was possible in the treatment of sound. As the film progresses, and especially in the backstage scenes, Crosland frequently has his camera adopt angles that the typical static talkie would never have sought out, such as high-angle shots down upon the backstage area.

Victor Fleming's first talking film was *The Virginian*, released in November 1929. That same year he made two other sound films, *Abie's Irish Rose*, released in January, having some talking sequences, and *Wolf Song*, released in March, containing some singing sequences. *The Virginian* has many of the faults associated with early talkies, such as poor dialogue delivered in an awkward, stilted manner, even by Gary Cooper and Walter Huston, who the very next year in *Morocco* (Cooper) and *Abraham Lincoln* (Huston) showed themselves to be quite at ease with spoken dialogue. Also, the use of sound is largely restricted to synchronous reproduction. But Fleming does attempt to use natural and environmental sounds to create a feeling for the outdoor locations where much of the film was shot. As does *In Old Arizona*, *The Virginian* makes use of outdoor sound recording, and the sounds of typical western elements, such as cattle, trains, and wagons, to expand the world of the action, to give a feeling of openness, of an ongoing world that the film is revealing, the quality that Siegfried Kracauer called "endlessness."

Fleming manages to endow the film with a fair degree of fluidity, especially by employing tracking shots, which are extensive in the opening scenes and which sometimes record sync dialogue. The film is also paced much more according to the unfolding action of the narrative rather than according to dialogue. The action is terse, avoids melodramatic situations, and draws reality and strength from the outdoor locations.

Late in 1929 and early in 1930 Lewis Milestone, another veteran silent director, made his first two all-talking films, *New York Nights*, released in December 1929, and *All Quiet on the Western Front*, released in April 1930. *All Quiet on the Western Front* was, of course, the film that brought Milestone recognition and was noteworthy for its emphasis on visual treatment, which was given an added sense of reality through the direct use of the sounds of war. Although the film contains many sync dialogue sequences, Milestone tried to apply sound so that it wouldn't interfere with what was essentially a visual conception. This led to the asynchronous use of sounds, such as: gunfire over shots of soldiers being killed and over the young soldier reaching out for the butterfly, only his hand and arm visible on the screen; and the conversation between Lew Ayres and the French girl over a shot of their clothing hanging on the end of the bed. Once again a silent film director tried to use sound without sacrificing the basic elements of silent film style.

The most successful and most important example of a silent film director treating sound creatively in the earliest period was Josef von Sternberg's *Thunderbolt*, released in June 1929, which showed that sound could be treated as creatively as the images, even at this early period. Along with his other 1929 film, *The Blue Angel*, and the 1930 *Morocco*, Sternberg achieved a transition to sound that was freer from difficulties than that of any other American director.

Most impressive in *Thunderbolt* is the use of sound to create off-screen space, so that the world of the film is almost always greater than that represented on the screen. We hear conversations, singing, gunshots, sirens, a baby crying, without seeing the sources of the sounds. This kind of asynchronous use of sound is the very opposite of the idea of the dull, static, endlessly talking early sound film.

The best uses of sound occur in the nightclub sequence at the beginning and throughout the prison sequences that make up the second half of the film. In the nightclub, Thunderbolt (George Bancroft) and Ritzy (Fay Wray) have a confrontation in which she tells him that she wants to start a new life. As they go to a back room in order to talk things over in private, the nightclub singer begins a torch song, which is about the breakup of a love affair. At first, Sternberg just uses the song as part of the entertainment background that has been going on throughout the scene, but as Bancroft and Wray walk toward the private room, Sternberg begins to cut between Bancroft and the singer, showing that Thunderbolt is listening to the song. This clearly establishes the song itself as a narrative tool. On one level the song functions as a realistic part of the action of the nightclub, while on another, and more important, level as a commentary on the main narrative line. At the end of the nightclub sequence, the police raid the nightclub in an attempt to catch Thunderbolt, but when the lights are turned off, he makes his escape. The police give chase, but Sternberg never stages this action. Instead, he "shows" it to us by concerning himself with Ritzy's ambiguous reaction to the chase: her desire to be free from Thunderbolt and her hope that he gets caught versus her old love for him and her hope that he escapes. Sternberg does this by keeping the camera on Ritzy and using the off-screen sound (mostly gunfire) of the chase. The scene fades out, and a double ambiguity is created that leaves the viewer wondering about both Ritzy's feelings and Thunderbolt's escape or capture.

The prison scenes are much too complex to describe in detail but work essentially by establishing a tension between discrete spatial units, the individual cells in which the prisoners are kept, and the unified world of the prison as a whole, which is separated from the outside world. Throughout the prison part of the film, we either see the prisoners in their individual cells, or we hear them talking from the cells off-screen. The prisoners are almost constantly talking to each other, even though in most cases they cannot see each other. The sound creates the unity of a group of men waiting on death row, as well as their antagonisms, especially those that exist between Thunderbolt and Bad Al Frieberg and, more important, between Thunderbolt and Bob Morgan (Richard Arlen). At times, Sternberg uses music—the singing of a black inmate and the playing of the prison orchestra—to comment ironically on the state of character relationships and on the actions taking place in this closed world.

As he does in his later films, Sternberg completely eliminates irrelevant sounds, such as footsteps, so that only meaningful sounds are heard. And like his other experienced colleagues, Sternberg brings to this early sound film the freedom of camera movement and placement that was one of the basic means of visual expressiveness of the silent film. *Thunderbolt* employs a considerable number of panning and tracking camera movements, as well as carefully chosen camera positions, which indicate that Sternberg avoided the use of multiple camera setups and placed the camera according to the meaning of the action.

Since silent films were already in production as sound was arriving, another type of talking film made its appearance: the film that was released as a talkie but in fact was started as a silent and then converted into a talkie. By this I don't mean what is usually referred to as part-talkie or one containing talking sequences, for these were unmistakably silent films into which a few talking sequences had been inserted, the silent sequences still utilizing titles and a musical accompaniment. The film I am talking about eliminates titles by dubbing in dialogue and sounds that appear to be synchronous, but in fact are not, and then adds actual synchronous dialogue sequences. The overall effect is that of a generally fluid visual treatment in most of the film interrupted by short scenes of conversation that are static in nature. The scenes shot silent are likely to run at a different speed from those shot in sync.

A good example is William Wellman's *Chinatown Nights* (1929). The story is told largely by means of the camera and the cutting. There is a great deal of camera movement, considerable intercutting between characters, and a strong emphasis on composition and lighting—all the earmarks of a late silent film. At the same time, dialogue is used to help explain and develop the action. Much of the relationship between Chuck Riley (Wallace Beery) and Joan Fry (Florence Vidor) is developed in terms of what they say to each other, as it would be in any talkie of the period, but there are moments in which it is obvious that dialogue has been dubbed in order to enrich the meaning and effect of a sequence that had been originally developed silently. Often these two types of scenes are meshed together into a whole sequence. An example is a scene in which Chuck throws Joan out of his apartment after she has betrayed him to the police. The betrayal scene itself and the confrontation with the police were shot with sync sound and are basically static in conception and execution. The confrontation between Chuck and Joan after the police have left, however, is much more dynamic, with the camera moving in response to the characters' actions. Wellman does not abandon sound in this scene, but he dubs it in and uses it asynchronously. Joan is out in the hallway, and Chuck slams the door closed. As she pleads with him from off-screen, the camera stays on Chuck in his apartment. In this way Chuck's hurt at Joan's action, his anger at having to throw her out, and Joan's pleading for him to understand her actions and not to cast her off can all be portrayed without intercutting between the two or resorting to the use of titles. This illustrates the kind of flexibility that sound brought to the cinema to enrich its expressive means and how sound could be used by a director who understood the basic techniques of cinematic storytelling. With the possibility of postdubbing, it was demonstrated that the talkie director did not have to be a slave to simple synchronization of sound and image.

Films by Stage Directors Imported by Hollywood

As mentioned earlier, Hollywood studios, in the confusion of the transition to sound, thought it advisable to import stage directors from New York since they were experienced in handling dialogue. This practice, though it did little to advance the sound cinema, introduced the notion of the filmed play or canned theater. Perhaps I should say reintroduced, since that notion goes back to the pre-World War I cinema of Film d'Art and Famous Players in Famous Plays. But with sound the possibility of a meaningful canned theater emerged. As André Bazin has pointed out, in the theater the text is the thing, and the introduction of the talkie for the first time made it possible for the cinema to be faithful to the text of a play. Many of the imported stage directors brought with them taste and talent in the staging of dramatic action and the handling of actors that should not be denigrated; they helped create a type of film different from that developed in the silent days under the direction of Ford, Sternberg, Griffith, Chaplin, and others. The work of these silent masters and of some of the directors that followed them reinstated whatever had been sacrificed to the microphone, but even their work was enriched by a growing sophistication in the handling and writing of dialogue that was strengthened by the best stage directors.

The stage imports can be divided into two groups, those who either had a definite flair for cinema, or at least aspired to use the film medium as an instrument essentially different from the stage, and those who had little feeling about cinema and endeavored to use the medium primarily for its capacity to reproduce theater for a large audience. To the first group, for example, belong George Cukor, Rouben Mamoulian, and James Whale, and to the latter John Cromwell, Russell Mack, and George Abbott. Hamilton McFadden, a minor stage import, is an example of someone who falls somewhere between these two categories.

Cukor did not really get started until after the period under consideration, so that his work with sound began in a time that had already solved most of the technical problems and had made significant aesthetic advances. Mamoulian is somewhat of an exception, even from the first group, because of his highly self-conscious use of cinematic technique and his specific effort to shatter the limitations that sound had imposed on cinema in 1928–29. He did not want his films to look like stage productions, and he set about to move the camera, use sound asynchronously, and establish narrative and character relationships in a primarily visual manner.

James Whale (*Journey's End,* 1930; *Frankenstein,* 1931; *Waterloo Bridge,* 1931) disguised his theatrical manner in a consciously expressionist style drawn from the German films of the 1920s. Despite cinematic flourishes, such as odd camera angles, *Frankenstein*'s scenic manipulations and settings and the treatment of interior spaces, especially Frankenstein's castle, are highly artificial and constantly smack of the theater and its conventions. John Baxter argues that Whale's horror films are not especially typical of him and that his "elegant British-influenced melodramas" even more clearly define his career.[3] Certainly, the subject matter of *Journey's End,* its setting in the confines of a dugout in World War I, and its theatrical origin lend themselves more directly to a theatrical presentation.

John Cromwell began directing in 1929. At first his stage talents were used in association with veteran director Eddie Sutherland in two stage-oriented musical comedies, *Close Harmony* and *The Dance of Life* (based on George Walters and Arthur Hopkins's *Burlesque*). He then went on to direct two more films that same year, *The Mighty* (an action melodrama) and *The Dummy* (a comedy based on Harvey O'Higgins and Harriet Ford's play *The Dummy*). Of the five films he directed in 1930, two were based on plays, *For the Defense* (Elmer Rice's *For the Defense*) and *Seven Days Leave* (co-directed with Richard Wallace and based on James Barrie's *The Old Lady Shows Her Medals*). In addition, he directed a rather straightforward and generally faithful adaptation of *Tom Sawyer.*

Russell Mack came to the cinema in 1930 and directed three films, *Big Money, Night Work,* and *Second Wife. Second Wife,* based on Charles Fulton Oursler's play *All the King's Men,* is a typical stage-oriented talkie of the period. It is confined almost entirely to one set, with the outside world referred to in the dialogue rather than shown. For the most part, the camera does not cross the 180° line, and it maintains a medium distance from the actors, although it sometimes pans to follow their movements back and forth across the room. The action, character relationships, and themes are established almost entirely through the dialogue. Despite this, the film is far from being dull. It is well acted, well staged, and a good representation of a theatrical experience that benefits from the intimacy possible through the camera.

Hamilton McFadden came to the cinema in 1929 and made four films in 1930, two of which were based on plays: *Are You There?, Crazy That Way* (Vincent Lawrence's *In Love with Love,* 1927), *Harmony at Home* (Harry Delf's *The Family Upstairs,* 1926), and *Oh, for a Man!* Although generally theatrical in style and material, McFadden's films show some concern with the possibilities of the cinema, giving the camera a role beyond that of mere recorder and transforming the theatrical basis of his scripts.

His *Are You There?* is a musical comedy that stars stage import Beatrice Lillie as a lady detective hired by a duke to expose a gold digger who is after his father. It has some of the anarchic spirit of the Marx Brothers, manifest in a lack of structure that undercuts much of its staginess and its plodding pace, and in several scenes McFadden moves his camera in such a way as to call into play a notion of space that is alien to the stage. The best example occurs in the opening scene, which begins on a close shot of a door and dollies back as people enter and exit frame past the door until the main characters enter. Off-screen space comes into play in such a way that the limited setting takes on a sense of reality that many of the other settings in the film, photographed from static camera positions, do not have.

More imaginative is *Oh, for a Man!* An opera singer (Jeanette MacDonald) falls in love with a burglar (Reginald Denny), and despite the clash of their two worlds, the characters eventually get together. As with *Are You There?* the sound is primarily the synchronous recording of dialogue and music, but McFadden makes some attempt to adapt cinematic points of view through placing his camera in active relation to the action. For example, in the opening scene MacDonald is singing an aria from *Tristan and Isolde.* The camera cuts to a high-angle shot looking down on the stage past some electricians standing high above on a platform. In the course of a coin-flipping game they are playing, they turn the spotlight away from MacDonald. Through this simple action and the camera placement used to give it meaning, the film makes an ironic comment on the main character.

When the best of the silent film directors, such as Ford, Walsh, and Sternberg, made their first sound films, they encountered not only technical problems and limitations but a definite aesthetic challenge as well, and they obviously felt a need to incorporate the element of sound into their overall artistic methods. The imported stage directors, on the other hand, with few exceptions, came to the cinema without a highly developed sense of cinematic form and expressiveness and were content with using the medium for a variation of theatrical *mise-en-scène.*

In doing so they did no disservice to the cinema but merely used its technical, and some of its artistic, means according to their own theatrical talents, and the best of them contributed to the rapid maturing of the talkie. In one sense they provided a phase of talkie development that was probably necessary, and, once passed through, helped the talkie again to merge into the mainstream of cinematic development. Together, the first sound efforts of the established silent film directors and the best work of the stage-trained directors give the lie to the great generalization that sound, in its earliest uses, brought forth only static, dull movies anchored to the spoken word. There were, of course, films that fit this description, but there were also many that prove that the problems of a film like *The Lights of New York* were overcome rapidly and often with great imagination.

Notes

1. Only Warner Bros. made an all-talking feature in 1928. All the other major studios came out with their first all-talking features in 1929, beginning with the Fox Company's release of *In Old Arizona* in January. Thus 1929 is the key year by which to test the results of the changeover to sound.

2. Peter Bogdanovich, *John Ford* (Berkeley: University of California Press, 1968), p. 50.

3. John Baxter, *Hollywood in the Thirties* (New York: Paperback Library, 1970), p. 71.

Applause: The Visual and Acoustic Landscape
LUCY FISCHER

Observation has proved that the combination of word and picture aroused two kinds of reactions in audiences. Some were quite incapable of getting a united impression from picture and sound. The people on the screen suddenly appeared startingly incorporeal, flat, shadowy and inanimate, while from somewhere outside the picture and quite disconnected with it came the voices. Or else the voice came from the mouths of these screen figures and these, as though animated by the sounds, suddenly seemed more vivid, plastic and real than in silent film.[1]

These words were written by Rudolf Arnheim in 1933 as part of a chapter on the sound cinema in his book *Film.* Although Arnheim's ultimate purpose in the text was to warn us of the dangers of the sound track—its tendency to bolster the realistic film illusion—he nonetheless managed to point out something quite important about the sound-film medium. For Arnheim's observation contains two crucial insights: that *both* sound and image have particular spatial attributes, and that the successful fusion of visual and auditory tracks is not as *automatic* as is commonly supposed.

More deeply submerged in Arnheim's remarks is yet another assumption, one that may at first glance seem surprising. According to Arnheim it is *sound,* and not image, that carries the most emphatic sense of spatiality. As he writes in another passage, "Sound arouses an illusion of actual space, while a picture has practically no depth."[2]

While one might reject Arnheim's final conclusion regarding the incompatibility of sound and image, and question his assertion of there being a qualified sense of depth contained within the image, his remarks prove, nonetheless, extremely useful. For while other critics of the period[3] seemed insensitive to the spatial quality of sound, Arnheim immediately recognized its primacy. ("Sound," he said, "is very strongly indicative of space."[4]) And while other critics seemed to believe that the fusion of sound and image was a quite automatic phenomenon (some sanctioning, while others condemning that formal merger), Arnheim sensed that the creation of a sound/image illusion was a highly tenuous process, and one whose success revolved around the parameter of *space.*

It is from this theoretical perspective that the extraordinary power of Rouben Mamoulian's early sound film *Applause* (1929) becomes comprehensible. In watching and listening to *Applause* we are immediately struck by the difference between it and the standard sound-film fare of the period. Whereas other films seem "incorporeal" and "inanimate" (to use Arnheim's words from the opening quotation), in *Applause* sound seems to function to make the image "more vivid, plastic and real." Yet while we immediately sense the singularity of *Applause,* the reasons for its perceived superiority are not so instantly clear. And it will be the purpose of this paper to articulate and render them lucid.

Applause falls within the genre of backstage musical drama, and is based on a novel by Beth Brown. It tells the story of an aging burlesque stripper named Kitty Darling (Helen Morgan) and her loving attempts to raise her daughter, April (Joan Peers). On the level of the plot, *Applause* is pure formula and convention, transcended only by the poignant and sublime performance of Helen Morgan. But plot is clearly not what interests Mamoulian. Rather it is the depiction of *atmosphere,* the rendering of the crass and seedy half-world of burlesque. As Mamoulian states in a 1971 interview, "As a preliminary education [for the film] I went to all the burlesque houses . . . what interested me [was] . . . burlesque with its tawdriness, vulgarity and sadness.[5]

Thus, in talking about the film, Mamoulian focuses not upon the issue of dramatic structure, or characterization. Instead, he emphasizes the aspect of *setting,* of the material locale in which the narrative action unfolds. Significant, in this respect, is the fact that the very first shot of *Applause* is that of an uninhabited space—an empty street down which blow handbills for the arrival of burlesque queen Kitty Darling.

It is this sense of a physical, corporeal universe that is everywhere apparent in the aural and visual *mise-en-scène* of *Applause.* Rather than simply employing a particular place of action, Mamoulian seeks to "build a world"—one that his characters and audience seem to inhabit. And that world is "habitable" because Mamoulian vests it with a strong sense of space. Unlike other directors of the period,[6] he recognizes the inherent spatial capacities of sound and, furthermore, understands the means by which they can lend an aspect of depth to the image.

On the visual level, Mamoulian employs a variety of techniques to create a world of palpable space; and the film can be seen as a virtual tour de force articulation of the parameters of length, height, and depth. A sense of *length* (or of the horizontal axis) is created largely through camera movements, of both panning and tracking varieties. In a remarkable shot toward the opening of the film we see the stage and orchestra pit of a burlesque theater. The camera begins focused upon a drum, then pans right-to-left across the musicians' faces. It then moves up to the stage and executes a track in the opposite direction. Finally it rests upon the women's faces, and reverses the direction of its movement once more. In this highly intricate and peripatetic shot (worthy of Jean Renoir) the horizontal plane has been emphatically introduced, only to be underscored again in later sequences.

Height is established in a somewhat more complex fashion. There are, first of all, a series of vertical pans. To move from the feet to the faces of the aforementioned chorus girls, the camera executes a vertical pan. On the other occasions in the film the camera pans dramatically from a character's feet to his or her face. One instance occurs when Kitty's womanizing lover, Hitch (Fuller Mellish, Jr.), is seen standing over Kitty, who is sprawled out on her living room floor. The camera moves down from his head to his feet and then up again, stressing not only the spatial aspect of height but the psychological fact of his dominance over her. Later in the film the parameter of height is again strongly invoked by a dramatic camera pan up the side of the Empire State Building, to find April and her boyfriend, Tony (Henry Wadsworth), courting at the top.

But more subtle means of creating awareness of the vertical plane are also utilized, although they are achieved without the aid of camera movement. Mamoulian continually makes us aware of the various levels on the vertical scale. Most often we view things from what may be called normal eye level, but sometimes we view things from almost ground level. The best example of this latter technique comes in a scene in which Hitch bends down to tie his shoelace and peers voyeuristically at April's legs. At other times (as in the shots of the stage from runway level) we view things from a middle height.

Mamoulian also takes advantage of both extreme high- and low-angle shots to reinforce this dimension. One thinks of the high-angle shot above Kitty on the dressing room sofa, as the chorus girls file around her to admire her newborn baby; or of the high-angle shot of Kitty sitting on the living room floor singing "What Wouldn't I Do for That Man?" Perhaps the most dramatic, however, is the extreme high-angle shot of the stage, as seen from the viewpoint of two men in the balcony. The film also contains a series of assertive low-angle shots: for example, the one (from Kitty's point of view) of the chorus girls circling around her; or the Eisensteinian low-angle shot of the vulgar, burlesque manager whom Kitty calls on the telephone.

Various techniques are also employed to created the sense of *depth*. The camera continually moves toward or away from objects, thus articulating the space in between. The camera, for example, tracks into the room in which Kitty is teaching the young April how to dance, or later tracks in toward April and a nun at the convent school. The camera also follows characters as they maneuver through space. In many scenes the camera tracks behind someone as he or she advances through the dense backstage area, or through a city crowd.

But there are also depth-creating effects that do not rely on camera movement. Even in shots in which the camera is stationary, there is often a tremendous amount of background and foreground movement, all of which makes us aware of the depth of the space. Whenever two characters are talking backstage, there is a constant flow of movement on other planes within the frame. In the background there may be a few girls exercising; or on the diagonal a woman may be walking, fixing her garter.

Mamoulian also employs the technique of rack-focus to create the sense of depth. One thinks, for example, of the shot in which April and Hitch are watching the outline of Kitty as she performs behind the stage curtain, or of the shot in which Hitch peers lasciviously at April's legs. Although not technically a camera movement, this device achieves much the same effect, for through rack-focus it is as though we were being pulled toward or away from an object, and thus made conscious of the spatial distance that intervenes.

Often Mamoulian accomplishes a sense of depth by placing the camera in such a way that it must look *through* things in order to focus upon its subject. In the convent scenes we often look at things through trees or gates. In the backstage scenes we often peer through ropes, flimsy curtains, or groups of people. At one point we see the burlesque audience through the legs of the chorus girls; and at another, we see the stage with our sight line obstructed by a pole. All of these are, of course, not accidental. Rather, they are reminders of the density of space that exists within the depicted environment.

In a manner similar to that of Josef von Sternberg, Mamoulian manages to use decor itself as a means of evoking the tactile-spatial world. We notice the depth of space in the frame partly because it is so cluttered. Kitty's room, for instance, is not experienced as a studio "set," because it is redeemed from the flatness and artificiality so prevalent in film decor of the time. Chairs are strewn with clothes; walls hung haphazardly with photographs; mantels filled with knicknacks; windows draped with curtains. It is not so much that these touches are realistic. It is that, as used by Mamoulian, they give us the profound sense of objects *taking up space,* existing within space. And the sheer number of objects that appear in the Mamoulian frame tends to dynamize space itself. Even the costumes worn in the film (though dictated by burlesque fashions) seem to be making a spatial-tactile statement, with their layers of feathers and organza.

Shadows in the film serve a similar function. In the scenes in which they are used (Hitch's shadow on the wall, looming over April and Kitty; Kitty's shadow on the backstage curtain) they serve not only as tools of expressionism but as constant reminders of the three-dimensionality of space.

This delineation of visual space in *Applause* would be noteworthy in and of itself, if just for its extraordinary sense of palpable physicality. But it is all the more remarkable when once considers that it was done in 1929, a year in which severe restraints were placed upon camera technique as a result of the coming of sound. As mentioned earlier, much of the sense of depth created in *Applause* can be credited to its virtuoso camera movement. Yet it is common knowledge that in the first years of sound, camera movement was considered all but impossible. Since the standard camera of 1929 had been designed in the silent era, without consideration of its mechanical noise, it had to be soundproofed for sync-sound filming. Until small "blimps" were developed around 1931, cameras were encased in huge cabinets in which the director and technicians were housed while shooting. Known ironically as "iceboxes" because of the degree of heat in their interior, these cabinets were heavy and bulky, and made camera movement incredibly cumbersome.

Mamoulian, however, refused to accept this technological limitation and forced an unwilling crew to wheel the icebox around the set. As Mamoulian recalls, in his discussion of one particular sequence,

I wanted to do the whole scene in one shot by keeping the camera moving. They had little wheels on the bungalow and you had to have ten men to move it and stop it. So I had the floor marked, the focus set to change, the lights ready, and . . . everybody going mad . . . we made a take. I went home and was miserable. I thought this could be the end of me in films.[7]

When one thinks of the awkwardness of the filming process, one is even more impressed by such tracking shots in *Applause* as the one that takes place during April's leave-taking from the convent school. The shot begins with the camera looking down a deep corridor. April and a nun walk away from the camera toward a window at the end of the hall, and the camera follows behind them. They then turn right and walk out of view, but the camera pauses at the stained-glass window. It then turns right and looks down another deep corridor which terminates in a chapel. It then tracks down the corridor, hesitates once more, and moves off to the left following the nun.

Clearly Mamoulian's use of camera movement dynamizes the viewer's sense of visual space. And it makes one consider that perhaps Arnheim's experience of the images of early sound films as "incorporeal" resulted not from any inherent flatness of the image but rather from the historical fact that so many works of the period were devoid of this depth-creating camera strategy.

But the creation of a sense of spatiality in *Applause* is not merely a product of camera movement and visual *mise-en-scène*. Rather, it is, to a great extent, generated by Mamoulian's use of *sound*. For as another theorist of the era, Bela Balazs, once noted in *Theory of Film,* our very perception of optical space is intimately tied to our experience of sound:

A completely soundless space . . . never appears quite concrete, and quite real to our perception; we feel it to be *weightless* and *unsubstantial,* for what we merely see is only a vision. *We accept seen space as real only when it contains sounds as well, for these give it the dimension of depth.* [Italics mine][8]

It is this association of visual and auditory factors in the creation of depth that Mamoulian intuitively grasped and articulated so adeptly in the formal structure of *Applause.*

Applause was, of course, Mamoulian's first film. He was one of a host of stage directors imported to the film industry during the first panic of the coming of sound. Though Paramount was primarily interested in him for the direction of dialogue,[9] Mamoulian's interest in cinema was oriented toward more abstract modalities of sound. As he remarked to Andrew Sarris in a 1966 interview:

I was convinced that sound on the screen should not be constantly shackled by naturalism. The magic of sound recording enabled one to achieve effects that would be impossible and unnatural on the stage or in real life, yet meaningful and eloquent on the screen.[10]

If one examines Mamoulian's previous theatrical experience, however, one realizes that he was no newcomer to the notion of experimentation with sound. As well as having directed stage plays, Mamoulian had directed many operas, and in his 1927 production of *Porgy & Bess* he had used the following effect as an opening.[11] Mamoulian called it the Symphony of Noises and described it as follows:

The curtain rose on Catfish Row in the early morning. All silent. Then you hear the Boum! of a street gang repairing the road. That is the first beat: then beat 2 is silent; beat 3 is a snore—zzzz!—from a Negro who's asleep; beat 4 silent again. Then a woman starts sweeping the steps—whish—and she takes up beats 2 and 4, so you have: Boum!—whish!—zzzz!—whish!—and so on. A knife sharpener, a shoemaker, a woman beating rugs, and so on, all joining in. Then the rhythm changes: 4:4 to 2:4, then to 6:8 and syncopated and Charleston rhythms. It all had to be conducted like an orchestra.

Many things are revealed by Mamoulian's description of his Symphony of Noises. Clearly it shows that he was ripe for the new sound-film medium and that he viewed sound as a formal element to be manipulated according to its unique aesthetic principles. It also demonstrates that for Mamoulian sounds were an essential element in creating an environment, and that dialogue was by no means the sole conveyor of meaning. Rather, concrete noise, as well, could be expressive.

But how exactly does Mamoulian handle sound in *Applause*, and how is its articulation related to the creation of a sense of visual space? First of all, when one compares the sound of the film *Applause* to that of other products of the era, what most distinguishes it is the *density* of its acoustic track. Many of the early talkies have an auditory as well as visual flatness. If characters are talking that is all we hear (except, perhaps, for some background "musak"). The sound atmosphere is thin and rarefied, lacking in perceptual truth.

Mamoulian's "sound space," however, is always filled and it offers an auditory counterpart for the visual "clutter" we experience. Some scenes that come to mind as exemplary of this technique are: the theater bar scene in which Joe King (Jack Cameron) shouts above the general din in order to find a doctor to deliver Kitty's baby; the scene in which April arrives at her mother's hotel and speaks to someone in the noisy lobby; or the scene in which April and escort go to the raucous Harlem theater to see Kitty perform. All of these sequences are characterized by what we might term several *layers* of sound: there is usually one layer of dialogue as well as many additional layers of noise (talking, music, street sounds, etc.). This sound density lends the frame an aura of truth, for it seems to replicate our real-life perception of auditory stimuli. In a text entitled *Explorations in Communication*, Marshall McLuhan and Edmund Carpenter write of auditory experience:

The universe is the potential map of auditory space. We are not Argus-eyed but we are Argus-eared. We hear instantly anything from any direction and at any distance within very wide limits. . . . Whereas the eyes are bounded, directed, and limited to considerably less than half the visible world at any given moment, the ears are all-encompassing, constantly alert to any sound originating in their boundless sphere.[12]

It is precisely this notion that Mamoulian seems to have grasped about the nature of sound. He understands that in life we are continually hit with a barrage of noise, a cacophony whose component parts are not always discrete or distinguishable to our ear. As Siegfried Kracauer explains in his *Theory of Film*: "In general one hears a *row*, that is—to use a mechanical analogy—a sort of resultant of all the noisy forces within earshot."[13]

In addition to conforming to our real-life perception of sound, this density of the auditory track functions to emphasize our sense of the spatial *world* depicted in the film. For as Carpenter and McLuhan remark in the previously quoted essay: "The essential feature of sound . . . is . . . that it *fills space*. We say 'the night shall be filled with music' just as air is filled with fragrance. . . ." [Italics mine] [14]

Another aspect of aural perception that Mamoulian seems to have understood is that in life we can never turn off the melange of sound, for there is no way to "shut" our ears. Thus in *Applause* even though characters change their position (leave rooms, go backstage, etc.), sounds from other locations aggressively pursue them. When April and escort approach the Harlem burlesque theater, low-level noises from within are heard before they enter. As Kitty sits in her hotel room, having taken an overdose of drugs, a conversation between two lovers in the hallway wafts into her chamber. When clapping begins as a character is on the stage, it continues to be heard, in muted form, when he or she goes backstage.

This modulation of sound, due to the location of the perceiver, has obvious spatial implications. Since sounds are modified as we shift our position (from onstage to backstage, etc.), they make us aware that they *pass through space*. And since sounds continue to be heard when their sources are no longer present, they remind us of locales beyond our view.

This comprehension of the omnipresent quality of sound was by no means automatic in the early sound era. Even very skillful directors like von Sternberg used sound with less auditory sensitivity. Thus in *Thunderbolt* (1929) or *The Blue Angel* (1930) sounds virtually seemed to shut off when characters moved from one space to another.

Aside from replicating our real-life aural perception, Mamoulian's use of a densely layered sound track in *Applause* functions to create a sense of *spatial ambience*. The undecipherable background dialogue, the vaudeville music, the street noises, all construct for us a sense of the material world which the characters inhabit. They are "characteristic" of the burlesque environment, and form a kind of "tonal milieu." Balazs writes most insightfully about this particular aspect of sound:

It is the business of the sound film to reveal to us our acoustic environment, *the acoustic environment in which we live* . . . . all that has speech beyond human speech, and speaks to us with the vast conversational power of life and incessantly influences and directs our thoughts and emotions, from the muttering of the sea, to the din of a great city. [15]

By creating a highly textured and layered acoustic atmosphere Mamoulian was again violating the contemporary rules of sound-film practice. For it was the aim of most dialogue engineers to eliminate all ambient noise in order to foreground the spoken text. Thus technicians sought to counter the omnidirectional quality of early microphones, which tended to pick up all background sounds within their range. But for Mamoulian, ironically, these noises were crucial, and were to be accorded equal status to speech.

The density of the "acoustic landscape" achieved in *Applause* seems all the more remarkable when one considers yet another prevalent practice of the early sound era: that of extreme soundproofing of the set to assure a "perfect" but sterile recording. As a Mr. Joe Coffman remarked in a 1930 issue of the *Transactions of the Society of Motion Picture Engineers:* "Unfortunately most 'deadening' materials do what the term signifies . . . ; on a dead stage, with absorbing materials used for set construction, the recording inevitably lacks life and brilliance." [16]

Yet on the sound stages of Paramount's Astoria studios (presumably the very same stages that were to produce in that year the comic, but acoustically lifeless, *The Cocoanuts*) Mamoulian managed to create an aurally dynamic sound-film. Part of Mamoulian's success, however, was due to the fact that he stubbornly refused to stay within the confines of a studio situation. Thus one of the more interesting sequences in the film seems to have been shot in sync-sound, on location, in the New York city subways.

Another aspect of the new sound medium that Mamoulian intuitively appreciated was its capacity to reveal *silence*. As Balazs observes, the effect of silence can only be rendered when sounds are present, for.there is never an absolute auditory void. What we mean by silence is that things are so quiet we can hear certain noises, distant or close, that we do not usually perceive: "if we can hear the crack of a whip a mile away—then we are hearing the silence around us. We feel the silence when we can hear the most distant sound or the slightest rustle near us." [17] Thus Balazs's main point is that silence (revealed through the sounds of objects in the environment) is basically a *spatial experience*.

In Kitty's suicide scene, Mamoulian provides us with an example of this use of silence. In a prior sequence, Hitch has come home and told Kitty that she is no longer wanted for lead roles in burlesque; that she is an old, fat blonde who is past her theatrical and sexual prime. Kitty, panic-stricken, has called several agents in an attempt to prove herself a desirable property, but has been given the brush-off in each case. Hitch tells her that her "meal ticket" from now on is April, but Kitty knows that her daughter wants to leave show business to marry Tony. Hitch walks out on her and April goes off to meet her sailor. Kitty is left alone in the hotel room.

The scene, rendered in a virtuoso single shot, begins with Kitty standing in the center of the room. The camera pans away from her to a picture of Hitch on the mantel, and back again to her in the middle of the room. The camera pans in a similar manner two more times: first to a picture of Hitch on the wall, and then to a picture on a table of April in convent dress. Kitty, with a look of despair on her face, then turns her back to the camera, walks through the living room and bedroom, and enters the bathroom. The camera tracks behind.

Up until this point there has been an almost absolute silence—one that is quite unreal, as in a silent film. But as Kitty opens the medicine cabinet and begins rifling around for sleeping pills the noise of her breathing and the clinking of bottles becomes almost deafening. The scene ends on a sound dissolve—the jangling water glass in Kitty's room is transformed into the sound of a cymbal, played in the restaurant where Tony and April are eating.

This rendering of silence through sound is even more apparent in the following sequence in which we observe Kitty after she has taken the fatal overdose. She is sitting in a chair near the window, her face illuminated by an off-screen blinking neon sign. She says nothing. What we hear is a highly contrived collage of city noises: train whistles, bells, horns, and sirens. We are aware of a clock ticking in the room and a couple speaking in the hallway. Through these "acoustic close-ups" we are made profoundly aware of the physical silence that surrounds her: a void that permits the intrusion of sounds from the abrasive world outside.

What Mamoulian has, of course, done in this sequence is not to render *absolute* silence but silence *perceived*. Though the scene is narratively situated in Kitty's point of view, we in the audience participate in her perceptual experience vicariously.

It is interesting to note that the creative use of silence was not new to Mamoulian, but rather issued from his background on the stage. A year before making *Applause* he had directed a play on Broadway entitled *Wings Over Europe*. In one particularly suspenseful scene Mamoulian had employed the following theatrical technique:

There was a clock on the mantel of the set. You never heard it of course. But during this silence I had the stage manager carry a metronome from way backstage down to the front. So the ticking of the clock becomes louder, until the whole audience could hear it."[18]

The parallels to Kitty's suicide scene are clear.

It is also significant that the suicide sequence is characterized by an *asynchronous*[19] use of sound: that is, the image of the object causing the sound is not present simultaneously on the screen. A controversy concerning the proper use of sound had, of course, been going on ever since its technological birth. Theorists had warned against a simplistically synchronous use of sound and called for experimentation in contrapuntal technique.

Eisenstein, for example, had in 1928 bemoaned what he feared would be an era in which sound recording would "proceed on a naturalistic level, exactly corresponding with the movement on the screen and providing a certain 'illusion' of talking people, of audible objects."[20] His prophecy, as we know, proved correct and most early sound films evidence a decidedly banal, causal relationship between sound and image (e.g., the phone rings and we see it).

Mamoulian somehow avoids the trap and even makes asynchronous sound one of his primary techniques. Examples abound. The city throughout the film, although an important character, is revealed largely through sound effects unaccompanied by images. (As April arrives in New York it is mainly the sounds of the city that affect us; we never really see their source.) One thinks as well of the scene in which we hear Kitty and Hitch arguing off-screen, while the camera focuses upon a photograph of Kitty as a young woman.

But Mamoulian experiments with sound in still other ways in *Applause*. At one point he tries to create a kind of sound montage. After her first night away from the convent, April dreams. On the screen we see a montage of grotesque close-ups of burlesque girls, musicians, and ogling men, juxtaposed with serene images of convent life. The sound track parallels this montage with an aural mix of burlesque tunes and the "Ave Maria." In one of Mamoulian's later films, *Dr. Jekyll and Mr. Hyde* (1932), he was to carry this innovative technique a step further. As described by Arthur Knight, the transitions from the character of Jekyll to Hyde were

accompanied by a vivid, synthetically created sound track built from exaggerated heartbeats mingled with the reverberations of gongs played backwards, bells heard through echo chambers, and completely artificial sounds created by photographing light frequencies directly onto the sound track. The recordists referred to it as "Mamoulian's stew," but it was probably the screen's first experiment with purely synthetic sound.[21]

Still two other areas of Mamoulian's use of sound bear examination—those of dialogue and music. As stated previously, one of the greatest problems with early sound films was their concentration on dialogue. Not only was there too much talking, but the nature of the language used was often stagey and artificial. In theater where the visual parameter is generally less emphatic, words can carry a great deal more weight than they can in film. When theatrical dialogue is transferred to the cinema, it most often seems stifled and tends to impede the narrative flow.[22]

To make matters worse, the filming of dialogue scenes in most early sound films was highly unimaginative. The camera almost invariably showed the person speaking, and while the conversation was going on most background noise was eliminated (except, perhaps, for some conventional theme music).

In *Applause,* however, Mamoulian avoids these pitfalls. The dialogue itself is conversational, colloquial, offhand, and seems to embody Balazs's notion of "weightless words."[23] One is also peculiarly affected by the poignant quality of Helen Morgan's voice, and is reminded of Balazs's statement about the sound film's potential for revealing acoustic coloring: "the spoken word is not merely the reflection of a concept—its intonation, its *timbre,* at the same time make it an irrational expression of emotion."[24] For precisely this reason the *sound* of Ms. Morgan's voice stays with us and haunts us, independent of the content of what she has said.

But what seems most noteworthy about Mamoulian's dialogue is the manner in which it is embedded within the general aural texture of the film. In many scenes (e.g., when Joe King and Kitty are speaking while performing onstage) one can hardly hear the dialogue because of all the other acoustic activity in the frame. In another scene (one which evidences the first use of two-track sound mixing) Kitty sings while April says her prayers. Almost never is a single thing happening acoustically at any one time. Almost never (except, perhaps, in the scenes with Tony and April) do we experience a flattening out of the acoustic environment in order to facilitate the foregrounding of characters' speech.

Mamoulian's use of music in *Applause* is also worthy of note. It seems both surprising and logical that *Applause* is often classified as a musical.[25] It is surprising because *Applause* lacks the artificial and contrived use of production numbers so common in the movie musical; but fitting in that music plays such an integral part in the creation of the physical environment of the film.

But how exactly is music used? First of all, the film contains only two brief instances of background or filler music—one being the theme of "Alexander's Ragtime Band" played over the opening titles, and the other being a few seconds of band music played over a scene transition.[26] Secondly, the film contains only one instance of symbolic "theme" music: the use of organ music and the "Ave Maria" for the convent scenes. The rest of the film is suffused with music, but it all issues from a causal source; it is all motivated by the events of the narrative (e.g., burlesque routines, marching band music, Kitty's singing).

Aside from having the music arise more naturally than in most musical films Mamoulian even downplays the musical numbers themselves. They seem to embody the same offhand, colloquial quality as his dialogue. Mamoulian resists making his burlesque numbers glamorous productions and keeps them as sleazy and down-to-earth as possible. He even restrains from building musical numbers around his star, Helen Morgan, a woman who was, of course, known for her voice. The times she sings ("What Wouldn't I Do for That Man" and "Give Your Baby Lots Of Lovin' ") she utters fragments of tunes and sings them *a cappella*. No disembodied orchestra, no temporary halt in the narrative, no soft-focus close-up of the star. Yet the beauty that arises from Mamoulian's sparse treatment is haunting and undeniable.

This use of causally related music is important because it forms one of the central aspects of the acoustic landscape rendered in the film. The music is not so much important in itself as it is in giving us the sound and resonance of the burlesque world. For as Kracauer observes, ambient music "resembles natural sounds in its strong affiliation with the *environment*. . . . [A] hurdy-gurdy melody enlivens the street in which it lingers. It is the *location* of the melody, not its content which counts." [Italics mine][27]

Mamoulian does, of course, use music for certain dramaturgical purposes. When Tony and April are in the restaurant, at the moment that Kitty is taking a drug overdose, the orchestra just happens to be playing the two songs that she has sung, thus reminding us of her back in her room. But music never serves that function alone; it is always integrally related to the environment from which it issues.

A final aspect of Mamoulian's use of sound in *Applause* remains to be explicated, an aspect that is of crucial importance to the creation of audiovisual spatiality in the film. Throughout *Applause* Mamoulian seems acutely aware of the fact that sounds are modified according to their distance from the perceiver. Although this seems an obvious perceptual point, the need for soundmen to follow the dictates of acoustic perception was not at all an accepted tenet of the early sound era. Rather than thinking sound theory through within a conceptual framework, most technicians simply did what they knew best how to do. Since most sound engineers had been recruited from radio, they often followed broadcast technique, a strategy that proved less successful in the sound-film medium. As Joe Coffman remarked,

In some ways it is unfortunate that the radio industry supplied most of the sound experts of the film industry. In radio broadcasting it usually is desirable to present all sounds as coming from approximately the same plane—that of the microphone. And so levels are raised and lowered to bring all sounds out at approximately the same volume. . . . But in talking picture presentations it is very desirable to achieve space effects and dramatic variation of volume level.[28]

Applause does achieve such "space effects" through the subtle manipulation of acoustic perspective. When the distance between camera and subject shifts, the sound level changes accordingly. One thinks, for example, of the scene in which there is a change in voice level as the camera shifts from a close-up of chorus girls singing onstage to a long shot of them from the audience's point of view; or of the scene in which a change in sound level and quality accompanies the camera shift from an on-stage view of a girl singing "Everybody's Doin' It" to a backstage one.

What this reference to acoustic perspective makes clear is an issue that has underlain our entire previous discussion: the question of *auditory perception*. For not only does Mamoulian create a palpable spatial world in *Applause;* he creates a world that seems visually and auditorially *perceived*. When coupled with the highly material sense of visual space portrayed in the film, the effect upon the audience is not only one of witnessing characters inhabiting a space but rather of inhabiting that space *themselves*, of "being there."

It is this sense of a spatial world delineated and *perceived* that explains the sensual power of *Applause*. For as Bela Balazs has so aptly stated:

Just as our eye is identified with the camera lens, so our ear is identified with the microphone. . . . In this way, in the sound film, the fixed, immutable, permanent distance between spectator and actor is eliminated not only visually . . . but acoustically as well. Not only as spectators, but as listeners, too, we are transferred from our seats to the space in which the events depicted on the screen are taking place.[29]

Strangely, even the title, *Applause*, seems to "bridge" the perceptual gap of which Balazs speaks. For it can be read as referring simultaneously to the burlesque audience within the cinematic diegesis, and to us, the audience, who experience Mamoulian's monumental film.

Notes

1. Rudolf Arnheim, *Film* (London: Faber and Faber, 1933), p. 235. Although this text was published in 1933, it is an English translation of essays written earlier in German. It was impossible to locate the original date of each essay.

2. Ibid.

3. An exception to this generalization is Bela Balazs, whose writing on sound will be discussed later in this essay.

4. Arnheim, *Film*, p. 224.

5. James R. Silke, ed., *Rouben Mamoulian: "Style Is the Man"* (Washington, D.C.: The American Film Institute, 1971), p. 7.

6. I am thinking of such directors of the early sound era as Roland West, Josef von Sternberg, Howard Hawks, Harry Beaumont, etc., who made competent sound films, but did not demonstrate a particular sensitivity to the spatial aspects of the aural medium. Bryan Foy, of course, would be a prime example.

7. Silke, *Rouben Mamoulian*, p. 11.

8. Bela Balazs, *Theory of Film* (New York: Dover, 1970), pp. 206–7.

9. Silke, *Rouben Mamoulian*, p. 6. Mamoulian is quoted as saying, "They wanted me to go in and direct dialogue for two years."

10. Andrew Sarris, *Interviews with Film Directors* (New York: Avon Books, 1967), pp. 346–47.

11. The Symphony of Noises was later used in *Love Me Tonight* (1932).

12. Edmund Carpenter and Marshall McLuhan, eds., *Explorations in Communication* (Boston: Beacon Press, 1960), p. 68.

13. Siegfried Kracauer, *Theory of Film: The Redemption of Physical Reality* (London: Oxford University Press, 1960), p. 67.

14. Carpenter and McLuhan, *Explorations in Communication*, p. 67.

15. Balazs, *Theory of Film*, p. 197. The term "tonal milieu" used above is a phrase Balazs uses on p. 211 of his text.

16. Joe Coffman, "Art and Science in Sound Film Production," *Transactions of the Society of Motion Picture Engineers*, 14 (February 1930): 176.

17. Balazs, *Theory of Film*, p. 206.

18. Silke, *Rouben Mamoulian*, p. 19.

19. Although I object to the term "asynchronous" as imprecise and confusing, and would prefer the term "acausal" sound, I am using it because it is conventionally associated with the technique I am discussing.

20. Sergei Eisenstein, *Film Form: Essays in Film Theory*, ed. and trans. Jay Leyda (New York: Harcourt, Brace, 1949), p. 258.

21. Arthur Knight, *The Liveliest Art* (New York: New American Library, 1957), p. 158.

22. I mean to except from this generalization such films as Dreyer's *Gertrud* which *purposefully* use theatrical technique as part of the work's overall formal and thematic structure.

23. Balazs, *Theory of Film*, p. 229.

24. Ibid., p. 230.

25. The Theater 80 St. Marks, in New York City, has included it in its repertoire of the movie musical.

26. The scene transition referred to is that which occurs between the scene of Kitty and Joe King in her room, and April in the convent.

27. Kracauer, *Theory of Film*, p. 144.

28. Coffman, "Art and Science in Sound Film Production," pp. 173–74.

29. Balazs, *Theory of Film*, p. 215.

Enthusiasm:
From Kino-Eye to Radio-Eye[1]
LUCY FISCHER

. . . Listen!
The locomotives groan,
and a draft blows through crannies and floor;
Give us coal from the Don!
Metal workers
and mechanics for the depot!
At each river's outlet, steamers
with an aching hole in their side,
howl through the docks:
"Give us oil from Baku!"
While we dawdle and quarrel
in search of fundamental answers,
all things yell:
"Give us new forms!"

There are no fools today
to crowd, open-mouthed, round a "maestro"
and await his pronouncement
Comrades,
Give us a new form of art—
an art
that will pull the republic out of the mud.
Vladimir Mayakovsky
From: "Order No. 2 to the Army of Arts" (1921)[2]

The year 1930 would not seem to have been a very pleasant one for Dziga Vertov. On the political front it was a year that saw a hardening of the Stalinist regime and with it the aesthetic of Socialist Realism. (Vertov was radically opposed to this aesthetic.) On the technical front, it was a year that found Soviet cinema disoriented by the advent of sound and its filmmakers conflicted as to its proper use. (Vertov was in the vanguard of this conflict.) On the personal front, it was a year that saw Vertov's dismissal from VUFKU, the Pan-Ukrainian Committee of Cinema and Photography. (Vertov, of course, had been charged with the sin of formalism.) But 1930 was also the year in which Vertov made *Enthusiasm,* a film that it may be useful to see as the object upon which these other lines converge.

Earlier in 1930 Vertov had written a plan for the film, giving it the dual titles of *Symphony of the Donbas* or *Enthusiasm.* This plan described mainly the visual shots to be included in the film. But it is more interesting to note that during 1929[3] he had written another treatment for the film, one that was conceived almost totally in terms of sound. *Enthusiasm* was to be Vertov's (and one of Russia's) first sound films, and his fascination with the new medium is apparent in his writing:

A clock ticks. Quietly at first. Gradually louder. Still louder. Unbearably loud (almost like the blows of a hammer). Gradually softer, to a neutral, clearly audible level. As if the beating of a heart, only considerably louder.[4]

The fact that he could conceive of and describe in advance an independent sound track for the film is, in itself, extraordinary; but less so, when one considers the concerns of Vertov's youth. His academic background seems to have been quite broad. He studied music at a conservatory in Bialystok and then attended medical school. While there he pursued an interest that had been his since childhood—that of creative writing. After completing several novels, Vertov explains in his *Notebooks:*

all was transformed into a fascination with a montage of stenographic notes and sound recording—in particular a fascination with the possibilities of documenting sounds in writing, in attempts to depict in words and letters the sound of a waterfall, the noise of a sawmill, in musical-thematic creations of word montage.[5]

As historian Georges Sadoul makes clear in his work on Vertov, in such pursuits the latter was no doubt influenced by the Italian Futurist art movement, then concerned with the use of sound in general and industrial noise in particular. In 1911, Bailla Pratella had written a "Manifesto to Futurist Musicians" in which he had called for the expression of "the musical soul of the masses, of great industrial timber yards, of trains, of trans-atlantic ships, of . . . the glorification of electricity."[6] In 1912, Marinetti had said that writers should "give the word" to objects and machines and introduce noise into literature. In 1913, painter Luigi Russolo had written: "Let us travel together across a great modern capital, ears more attentive than eyes, and we will vary the pleasure of our sensibility in distinguishing the gurgling of water, of air, of gas in the metal pipes."[7]

As Sadoul points out,[8] the phrase "ears more attentive than eyes" seems certainly to have been a key one for Vertov. For in 1916 he set up a Laboratory of Hearing in which to conduct such Futurist-influenced sound experiments. Thus we find, strangely, that the filmmaker most known for his concern with the *eye* was really, at first, most concerned with the *ear*. And one can see *Enthusiasm,* which Vertov himself referred to as "a symphony of noises," as an almost postponed event—one that he was somehow ready for in the twenties, but which was not, technologically speaking, ready for him.

But let us return to Vertov's sound scenario of 1929. Examining this along with the 1930 treatment of the visuals, we realize that we have what amounts to separate sound track and visual track conceptions for the film. One might read into this fact the notion that the sound track is primary. (After all, its plan did come first and seems to have been written with more care and detail.) But this may be unfair. What can certainly be inferred, however, is that Vertov intended to treat the sound and visual elements in the film as separate and *equal.* This general attitude toward sound had, of course, been called for by Eisenstein (and Pudovkin and Alexandrov) in 1928. Eisenstein feared that most of the first sound films would be those in which sound recording would "proceed on a naturalistic level, exactly correspond-ing with the movement on the screen . . . providing a certain *illusion* of talking people, of audible objects, etc."[9] This, he felt, would destroy mon-tage, and thus he called for sound to be treated as "a new montage element (as a factor divorced from the visual image)." As a means of accomplishing the divorce of sound from picture, he proposed "its distinct nonsynchroni-zation with the visual images."

In 1930, Vertov made his own statement on the sound film, partly in reaction to that of Eisenstein:

Declarations about the need to keep visual moments from coinciding with audible moments, just like declarations about the need to have only sound films or only talkies aren't worth a bean. In sound film, as in silent film, we distinguish only two kinds of films: documentary (with real conversations and sounds) and play-films (with artificially prepared conversations and sounds). Neither documentaries nor play-films are obligated to have visible moments coincide [or not coincide] with audible mo-ments. Sound shots and silent shots are edited alike; they can coincide [or not co-incide] in montage or they can mix with each other in various combinations.[10]

Clearly Vertov, like Eisenstein, is concerned with the integrity of the sound track, the creation of sound as well as visual montage. But his conception of this is perhaps more radical. He rejects Eisenstein's notion of achieving aural independence through a mere nonsynchronization of visual and audi-tory material, and, as we shall see in examining *Enthusiasm,* achieves it through concepts of editing and synchronization of a more subtle nature. But, more importantly, Vertov is also, like Eisenstein, wary of the sound film's potential for naturalistic illusion. However, he proceeds to interpret and sub-vert that illusionism in a fundamentally different manner.

Enthusiasm is, first of all, a documentary, which, on one level, is about the efforts of the Don Basin region to accomplish certain industrial-agricultural tasks of the First Five-Year Plan. These tasks consist mainly of the mining of coal, the production of steel, and the harvesting of wheat (in that order). It is an ode to the cooperative enthusiasm of Soviet workers and a lesson concerning the interrelatedness of their various tasks in achieving State Socialism. What occurs in the Don Basin is a synecdoche for what is occurring in Russia at large. But *Enthusiasm* is obviously more than this. And perhaps an examination of the first section of the film (the only section which is, significantly, *not* about the Five-Year Plan) will help to make the film's deeper meaning clear. For what is important about the first part of *Enthusiasm* is that, examined microcosmically, it can reveal to us the essential structures of the film in its entirety. It can reveal Vertov's theory of sound and how it relates to his conception of film in general.

What one is most struck by in the first section of *Enthusiasm* is the sense of incredible tension that exists between the sound and visuals. The sound physically pushes itself away from the screen; and the two seem related in the manner of magnets with poles aligned—physically separate, but interacting through lines of force. Because of this dynamism, we are continually made aware of the sound track and visual track as separate entities. This, of course, arises from Vertov's highly experimental use of sound in the film. He studiously avoids the conventions already developed for the sound film in Britain and the United States (like synchronous dialogue, naturalistically related sound and image, and background "musak"), and instead employs the abstract and dissociative technique of audiovisual collage.

But before confronting the precise nature of that collage, it is useful to answer two questions: (1) *Why* does Vertov create this radical audiovisual disjunction; and (2) *How* does he accomplish it? One might conjecture, for example, that it is merely a virtuoso attempt to edit sound shots as flexibly as visual shots, and ascribe its disorienting use of sound montage to Vertov's earlier experience with Futurist experimentation. But this would be looking at the aesthetics of the film without regard to its political content.

The crucial thing to remember is that *Enthusiasm* is a documentary, a film whose sound as well as visuals are documentary in nature. And if one examines briefly Vertov's theory of documentary (best known in the form of Kino- or Cinema-Eye) some puzzling aspects of the film fall into place. For Vertov's conception of Cinema-Eye applies exactly to his notion of Radio-Eye; what holds for his theory of cinematic visuals applies to his theory of cinematic sound as well.

To summarize, Vertov's first assumption politically is that the masses must be educated and conscious of the social, economic, and political workings of the Soviet state: "We need conscious men, not an unconscious mass. Submissive to any passing suggestion." [11]

His second assumption is that the average human being, with the normal human perceptual apparatus and limitations of time and space, is severely handicapped in his ability to be cognizant of these factors. The world is "a whirlpool of contacts, blows, embraces, games, accidents, athletics, dances, taxes, spectacles, robberies, and incoming and outgoing papers, against a background of seething human labor. How is the ordinary unarmed eye to make sense of this visual chaos." [12]

His third assumption is that machines (for example, the camera and the sound recorder) have the capability that humans do not, to perceive life and, furthermore, to organize its chaos into a meaningful whole. This is due largely to their more perfect recording mechanisms and their powers of mobility: "Slicing into the seeming chaos of life Kino-Eye attempts to find answers in life itself. To find the resultant force among the millions of phenomena related to any given subject." [13]

His use of the term "resultant force" gives us another clue, which is that Vertov regards the process of filmmaking as a *scientific* endeavor. His task is "to combine science with cinematic depiction in the struggle to reveal truth . . . to decipher reality." [14] This is important because just as the scientist's depiction of the world has nothing to do with the average man's *perception* of the world (e.g., I see the sun "rise" and "set" and do not see the turning of the earth on its axis), so Vertov's depiction of the world in cinematic terms, though documentary, will be far from isomorphic with our perception of it. His model is life as it exists independent of the human perceptor, not life as experienced by Man.

And finally, as Annette Michelson has stated in her seminal work on *The Man with the Movie Camera*,[15] Vertov in his radical concern with mass consciousness wants the viewer of his documentary films to be continually aware that he is watching a film. He wants to break the mesmeric spell of the cinema to ensure its didactic powers. If the masses watch a play-film with even approved socialist content, they may be swayed by the powers of the medium, and its actors, and not persuaded, intellectually, by the truth of its arguments.[16] For Vertov the people must have knowledge and not belief; and to ensure this, one must subvert the power of the cinematic illusion: "For the Kinok demystification is equally important on the screen and in life." [17]

Thus, the use of sound in *Enthusiasm* is not just a virtuoso attempt at sound collage, art for art's sake. It is a radical attempt to break the naturalistic illusion of the sound medium.

"Long live the class consciousness of healthy men with eyes and ears to see and hear with." [18]

This is borne out by a close reading of the first section of the film in terms of both technique and content. For what is the subject of the first section of *Enthusiasm* if not the process of demystification itself? On the level of content, the film begins with images of Russia in the grips of hypnosis by Tsarism and religion. We are flooded with images that reconstruct the period: the Tsarist monogram, church bells, statues of Christ, genuflecting worshippers, crucifixes, etc. Counterpointed with these images are sounds of liturgical choirs singing, people intoning the mass, sacred music, cuckoos, and ticking clocks. Most sound-image relations fall under the category of asynchronicity, with the exception of the church bells, which are simultaneously seen and heard.

Intercut with these images of religious and monarchal worship are images of staggering drunks. It is not difficult to interpret Vertov's statement; religion is, after all, the opiate of the people.

In the next sequence, Vertov centers on the process of demystification. The act of coming out of the political-religious trance is accomplished, symbolically, through the destruction of a church and its subsequent conversion into a public social club. In this very spectacular sequence, we see multiple prismatic images of the church spire appear on the screen and jump around. A split-screen image of the crucifix is seen with each cross bending toward the other as though falling. Other images of crucifixes vibrate and go round in a circle. The impact of the visuals is underscored and accentuated by the sound track, which consists of drum rolls that are carefully matched to the rhythm of the images.[19] Finally, we see the castrated church spire fall to the ground, accompanied by a large crash on the sound track. This is repeated several times in a dramatic climax to the sequence.

Ultimately, in a series of reverse shots accompanied by band music, we see socialist flags fly onto the front of the defrocked church and the inverse religious conversion is accomplished. Religion is seen and heard for what it is and eliminated. "The perfumed veil of kisses, murders, doves and prestidigitation is lifted."[20] The people are finally conscious. The red star flies up and magically the church is transformed; and magic is, perhaps, the point. For only the Cinema Eye/Ear can see and hear in this extraordinary way—can straddle time and space, uniting visually and aurally events that to the average person are unrelated ("freed from time and space, I coordinate any and all points of the universe wherever I may plot them"[21]). And it is also the point in that Vertov continually makes sound and image so "tricky" that one is aware of the trick. He is like a magician who performs tricks only to reveal to us how they are done; only to instruct us against falling for tricks in the first place.[22]

The content of the first section of the film reveals something else as well. The very first visual shot is an ambiguous image of a young woman, who puts on headphones and sits in front of some kind of switchboard: (likely, the "radio-telegraph" mentioned in Vertov's sound scenario). It is an image that will continue to reappear and punctuate the section as a leitmotif. The woman is usually seen in the posture of listening; hence, the preponderance of close-up shots of her ears and earphones. It soon becomes clear that this woman serves the function of standing for the film *listener*. At one point, in fact, as she puts on her earphones, the sound track carries the voice of a man shouting: "Attention. Attention. Leningrad speaking . . . RV3 . . . at a wavelength of 1,000 meters. We now broadcast the march, "The Final Sunday," from the film, *Symphony of the Donbas.*"[23] This is immediately followed by the image of a conductor leading an orchestra which is presumably playing the very music that she is listening to.

The woman serves essentially two functions. Within the context of the film she seems to play the role of sound "monitor," a member of the film production crew who audits the sound recording process.[24] On another level, however, she seems to stand outside the film, and in this capacity is identified with the film audience itself.

Clearly, the iconography of this preface to *Enthusiasm* reveals Vertov's commitment to cinematic reflexivity, to sabotaging all filmic illusions—in this case, those pertaining to the medium of sound. Just as in *Man with the Movie Camera* we are made aware of the Cinema-Eye, so in *Enthusiasm* (or, "Woman with the Earphones") we are forced to be conscious of the Cinema-Ear.

The last time the radio-telegraph woman appears is during the final shots of this section, when demystification of religion is accomplished. Significantly, she is seen without earphones, sculpting a bust of Lenin.

There is also another aurally reflexive element in this introductory section: the orchestra conductor. Early on in the film we hear orchestral music accompanying certain images. But it is not until many shots *later* that Vertov shows us this very music in the process of being conducted. It seems both an instance of audiovisual time reversal and an example of Vertov's desire to reveal the filmmaking process. It may also be an apologia for what is probably the only studio-recorded sound shot within the film.

Vertov had very rigid notions of the need for pure documentary footage. As an earlier quote reveals, for him the important distinction in the sound film was not between asynchronization and synchronization but between real and artificial conversations and sounds. One might ask, however, *why* the distinction is so important, why the bell sound used in the film could not have been recorded on a sound stage or created in a sound effects machine. But one need only examine Vertov's statement about the apple: "If a fake apple and a real apple are filmed so that one cannot be distinguished from another on the screen, this is not ability, but incompetence—inability to photograph."[25]

And so it is with sound. But it is also important to remember that Vertov considered himself a scientist and was concerned with using sound as *evidence*.[26] We can learn, for example, about the human body by seeing a plastic model of the skeletal system. But then we are only taking on faith that it corresponds to what is actually beneath the skin. However, if we dissect a cadaver and observe a real skeletal system we have evidence. And it is the same with film.

But how, specifically, on the level of sound technique, does Vertov help to break the aural cinematic illusion, the illusion that we are "there" listening, and remind us we are listening to a film? On the most general level he causes the viewer to feel profoundly disoriented in the sound space of the film. His means of achieving this are numerous and can be found in an examination of the first section of the film:

1. *Disembodied Sound:* During the shots of the radio-telegraph woman we intermittently hear on the sound track a clock ticking and a mechanical cuckoo. These sounds remain, however, disembodied and are never identified with anything depicted on the screen.

2. *Sound Superimposition (from various sound spaces):* At points in the first section of the film the clock ticking is heard "over" the church bells. Clearly the clock and bells are spatially unrelated.

3. *Sound/Visual Time Reversal:* The example of the orchestra conductor has already been cited.

4. *Abrupt Sound Breaks:* During the title sequence the Komsomol band music abruptly changes to cuckoo calls; and later a woodwind march is abruptly cut off by the loud tolling of a bell. The most extreme example of this occurs during a march sequence when the music is actually broken off three times for moments of silence, as though someone had lifted a needle off a record and placed it down again.

5. *Abrupt Tonal Contrasts:* This technique is similar to the one above. However, instead of involving sound "breaks" it involves stark tonal contrasts (e.g., the cut from the light sound of a woodwind march to the heavy tolling of a church bell).

6. *Sound Edited to Create an Effect of Inappropriate Physical Connection to the Image:* The best example of this occurs before the destruction of the church. We see on the screen a succession of static images: a church spire, a madonna, a statue of Christ, a Tsarist monogram. Each one is accompanied on the sound track by the tolling of a bell. The feeling that arises from this particular coupling of sound and image is that the very same impact of the bell clapper that causes it to toll also "causes" the image to appear on the screen. It is as though the bell could toll not only sounds but pictures.

7. *Synthetic Sound Collage:* At points in the film, the sound mixing becomes so synthetic that one is reminded of its artificiality, of its status as pure film sound. An example occurs during the section in which

religion is exposed. Accompanying the images of icons and genuflecting worshippers are sounds of bleating horns, organ music, church bells, etc.

8. *Inappropriate Sounds:* The spire "crash," when listened to closely, seems to be the sound of an explosion.

9. *Mismatchings of Sound/Visual Distance:* Often the visuals are in medium shot or long shot while the sound is in close-up. For instance, when the spire falls we are much farther away visually than we are aurally.

10. *Mismatchings of Sound/Visual Location:* At points it is clear that while a visual has been shot in exteriors, the sound to which it is linked has been shot in interiors. This pertains to the shot in which drunks seen out of doors are accompanied by liturgical music clearly recorded indoors.

11. *Metaphorical Use of Sound:* The cuckoo is used in an openly semantic way. Its superimposition over church bells "says" that religion is insane, or, perhaps, "for the birds." The ticking clock (which is not realistically cued) becomes, metaphorically, the mechanical pulse of the nation, its "heartbeat," as Vertov puts it in the sound scenario.

12. *Sound Distortion:* Vertov openly employs sound distortion in certain sections of church bell tolling. This, of course, has semantic implications as well, in alluding to the warped teachings of the church. As we hear the distorted chiming, however, we see on the screen the normal movement of the bell. Thus a further sound/image disjunction is established.

13. *Technological Reflexivity:* In the first section we have two shots of loudspeakers hung in the corners of the rooms. We also have the commentator on the sound track mention the film, *The Symphony of the Donbas.* Furthermore, we have the presence of the radio-telegraph woman.

14. *Association of One Sound with Various Images:* Over the course of the film a single sound will be synchronized to a variety of images. This breaks the illusion that any particular image is the source of that sound; or that the sound and image synchronized were recorded at the same time or in the same space. An example of this technique is the sound of a strange, high-pitched whistle which at one point accompanies shots of the mines, and at another, shots of the steel foundry.

15. *Simple Asynchronism of Sound and Image:* Examples of this are the church choir sounds versus images of drunks; Komsomol march versus the image of a train; the tolling bell versus the image of Christ's statue.

Accompanying these techniques of aural reflexivity Vertov, of course, employs deconstructive visual strategies to reinforce our consciousness of film *qua* film. Perhaps his most general method involves a total liberation from a "realistic" mode of spatial presentation. The spaces of consecutive shots are almost never contiguous; and it is impossible ever to reconstruct the geography of the settings we are in. Vertov's framing of shots contributes to this disorientation. Almost all the images in this section are shot at any angle. The surfaces upon which people, buildings, and machines stand are framed so as to be almost never parallel to the horizontal axis of the screen. Since things are not positioned this way in our real-life experience we are constantly reminded of the mediation of the Camera-Eye. A second related technique Vertov employs is to misframe a shot and then "correct" it. In one shot, for example, the image of a church appears askew. The camera then rotates until the image straightens out and is perpendicular to the bottom of the screen.

Superimpositions, prism shots, split-screen effects, reverse shots, and decelerations are used quite lavishly. The last shot of the section contains an acceleration that makes clear Vertov's concern. We have on the screen a static image—that of the church which has been converted into a social club. Instead of shooting it at normal speed, however, Vertov has shot it so that it appears in accelerated motion. The church of course remains "still"; but clouds rush past it in fantastic pixilation. On a semantic level, Vertov is most likely aiming at a sense of the socialist state "rushing into the future." But on a formal level, by taking what is essentially a static shot and giving it synthetic acceleration, Vertov underscores the fact that the church exists within the space of a film. The introductory section also contains such visually reflexive elements as: a shot of the movie theater; an image of a drunk who visibly "shoos" away the cameraman; and exaggerated camera movements that remind us of its mechanical presence (its "drunken" movement in following an inebriated man; its swinging movement in paralleling the ringing of a bell).

But to return to the issue of sound, in the industrial and agricultural sections of the film which follow, we find an extension of Vertov's technique of audiovisual editing. In our discussion of the opening sequence of the film we had noted how Vertov's use of a distorted church bell and cuckoo sounds, in addition to being aurally reflexive, had thematic relevance to his critique of Tsarist Russia. In the agricultural and industrial sections, Vertov elaborates on this *semantic* use of sound. In these sections, however, the major thematic emphasis has shifted from a critique of the Russia of the past, to a celebration of the Soviet state of the present. Specifically, Vertov wishes to delineate the *interrelatedness* of the various Donbas tasks which conjoin to fulfill the directives of the first Five-Year Plan. Thus Vertov will employ a single sound (like that of the "Internationale" being sung) to unify such diverse images as a workers' meeting, a coal miner, and a train leaving for the Donbas. Furthermore, Vertov cuts fluidly, without transition, between sounds of one kind of Donbas activity and another: from the sound of a train bringing coal workers, to that of farmers singing in the field. This technique asserts the fundamental unity and connection between the various labor tasks. A similar semantic function can be ascribed to many of the asynchronous sound/image relations in the film. For example, the disembodied shouts of

"Hurrah" which accompany the images of the coal miners are clearly meant to stand for the massive support of other Donbas workers. Thus throughout *Enthusiasm* the very techniques that Vertov utilizes to break the sound illusion serve simultaneously to advance the film's political and thematic content.

In addition to entailing the elaboration of these semantic strategies, the agricultural and industrial sections do, of course, involve an extension of Vertov's reflexive aural techniques as well:

1. *Sound Acceleration:* At one point in the film the Komsomol music becomes accelerated in a manner possible only through varying the speed of the recorded sound track.

2. *Sound Reversal:* In the agricultural section involving a peasant dance, a man plays an accordion. The second time a musical theme is heard it has a strange quality and *seems* to have been mechanically reversed.

3. *Images of Soundmen:* In several shots of the film a soundman can literally be seen on the screen, recording. One such shot occurs in the agricultural section as the women are stacking hay. Clearly, this reminds the viewer of the sound recording process and parallels the presence of the cinematographer in *Man with a Movie Camera.*

But what is *most* astonishing when one considers the complexity of audiovisual editing in *Enthusiasm* are the production circumstances under which it was made. For as Vertov himself suggested, we must not merely judge *Enthusiasm* in an absolute or general sense ("outside of time and space") but rather appreciate it "in relation to the given state of the development of the sound cinema."[27]

The Soviets were, or course, late in obtaining sound technology because it was not a crucial aspect of the first Five-Year Plan.[28] Also, it was legislated that all materials for sound equipment should be made in Russia's own workshops and foundries, rather than imported from capitalist countries. Thus it was not until 1928–29 that Shorin and Tager's sound systems were demonstrated.

The development of portable and open-air equipment presented additional problems; and it was not until August 1929 that Tager and Obolensky tested an open-air system in the streets of Moscow.[29] Since Vertov's concern in *Enthusism* was with documentary, rather than studio, sound, such equipment was mandatory for on-location shooting, and he had to await its development. In an article written by Vertov in 1931, after the film's completion, he recounts the difficult process involved in producing the apparatus for his project:

The urgent manufacture of a mobile sound-recording installation was made the main question of the day. Comrades Timartsev, Tchibissov, Kharitonov, and Moltchanov, collaborators in the laboratory of Professor Shorin, worked day and night to assemble the installation. During the course of April we proceeded with the first attempts at shooting. Next we filmed May Day, then the port of Leningrad, and finally, after the apparatus had undergone some modifications, we left for Kharkov to film the Eleventh Congress of the Ukrainian Party. After filming the Congress, the apparatus was again modified and we left for the Donbas.[30]

Thus, *Enthusiasm* was a pioneer work in the development of on-location sound technique (Vertov called it an "icebreaker . . . of sound-film documentaries"[31]). As such it provided concrete evidence for the possibility of documentary sound and countered a then prevailing theory, advanced by sound engineer Ippolit Sokolov, that all film sound required studio postsynchronization.[32] *Enthusiasm*, however, proved otherwise and realized Vertov's desire to "move over from the velvet coffin of the soundless studio and plunge into the terrible thunder and iron clanging of the Donbas."[33]

In addition to pioneering the use of mobile recording equipment, Vertov and his crew experimented with other aspects of audiovisual registration. According to Vertov's "Report to the First Conference of the Workers on Sound Film"[34] his collaborators tested three modes of recording. First they took the picture and sound at different times on different negatives; second, they took the picture and sound synchronously on different negatives; third, they took both picture and sound synchronously on the same negative. From these tests they concluded that the final method provided the highest quality visual and aural material.

But the optimal procedure for recording sound and image led to difficulties and challenges in the editing process. For Vertov was severely hampered by the lack of sophisticated sound-editing machinery. As he explains it:

We had at our disposal neither a sound-editing table nor the least apparatus for organizing sound and visual cine-material . . . nevertheless we did not follow the line of least resistance, we did not exploit the favorable fact that we were provided in the Donbas with a mobile installation and that consequently the majority of sounds were recorded on the same strip as the image. We were not content to simply have the sound and image coincide and we followed the line which, in our situation, was that of maximum resistance, that of the complex interactions of sound and image.[35]

Curiously, the few instances in which sound and image do simply coincide in *Enthusiasm* (e.g., the workers' speeches) are experienced by the audience as a kind of unexpected shock. Which reminds us that what Vertov has created in *Enthusiasm* is a work in which sound almost never seems to issue from the screen. Most sound films create for us a certain illusion: we see on the screen the image of a man starting a car, and hear, simultaneously, on the sound track, a noise that is appropriate to it in terms of content and aural quality. The two merge, overlap perfectly, and seem united. This unity in a sense places the spectator perceptually within the space of the film; he experiences the scene as though he were "there." By breaking this unity (by having sound and image to some degree "repel" each other) Vertov leaves him forever within the space of the theater. It seems probable that this disjunction was what Vertov hoped to ensure in his operation of the sound system during the London screening of the film:

When Vertov attended the presentation of his first sound film, *Enthusiasm*, to the Film Society of London on November 15, 1931, he insisted on controlling the sound projection. During the rehearsal he kept it at normal level, but at the performance, flanked on either side by the sound manager of the Tivoli Theatre and an officer of the Society, he raised the volume at climaxes to an ear-splitting level. Begged to desist he refused and finished the performance fighting for possession of the instrument of control.[36]

Vertov intended for us not to be referred to the space of the film, but rather to the space of the outside world. This statement may seem confusing and paradoxical in that *Enthusiasm* in no way seems to replicate our impression of reality. In its radical disruption of the cinematic illusion, in its insistence on documentary evidence, it seems to us less real, less documentary than even most fiction films.

But this is not paradoxical if one recalls that for Vertov the notion of documentary in no way implied a document of the human experience of the world, one confined by an imperfect biological perceptual apparatus and bodily limitations of time and space. For Vertov, his films were a document of a world unmediated by normal human perception. "My road," he said, "is to a fresh perception of the world."[37]

The purpose of this liberation from human experience (and thus the rationale for a complexity of technique) was to afford the viewer a conceptual knowledge unavailable to him in his normal perceptual stance, to allow him to "decipher in a new way the world unknown to him."[38]

Vertov said: "Truth is our object. All our devices, modes and genres are means. The ways are various but the end must be one—truth."[39] But his critics misunderstood. Ignoring his intent, they chastised his means. His artistic virtuosity was gratuitous, his technique, formalistic. Vertov was forced to leave VUFKU. But all this was not happening in a vacuum. It was occurring against the backdrop of certain political and artistic developments. A new aesthetic policy was taking over. According to Dickinson and de la Roche: "The new policy, known as socialist realism, aimed at a *simple* naturalism and adventures in individual virtuosity were considered unnecessary *if the subject could explain itself in plain statement.*" (Italics mine)[40]

But for Vertov the subject could never explain itself in plain statement. And a simple naturalism could mystify, entice, and entertain the viewer, but could never provide him with evidence for knowledge about the real world. Finally, for Vertov the paradox lay not within the structure of his films but within the fact that although truth itself be simple, "it is far from simple to show the truth."[41]

Notes

1. Vertov seems alternately to have used the term "Radio-Ear" and "Radio-Eye" in relation to his conception of the sound film. In a statement of 1925, for example, he uses "Radio-Ear" to describe, specifically, the *sound track* of a film and talks of establishing "a visual class bond (Kino-Eye) and an auditory bond (Radio-Ear) between the proletariat of all nations." *Articles, Journaux, Projets,* trans. Sylvanie Mossé and Andrée Robel (Paris: Cahiers du Cinéma, 1972), p. 74. (My translation.) In a statement of 1929 (ibid., p. 133) Vertov seems to use the term "Radio-Eye" to mean *sound film* (i.e., sound plus image). Thus he talks of the Kinoks Radioks having moved from Kino-Eye to Radio-Eye, "that is to say, to the audible, radio-diffused Kino-Eye." It is because the term "Radio-Eye" seems to be more inclusive and appears in the later writings that it is used in this paper.

2. Vladimir Mayakovsky, "Order No. 2 to the Army of Arts" (trans. Max Hayward and George Reavy) in Patricia Blake, ed., *The Bedbug and Selected Poetry* (London: Weidenfeld and Nicolson, 1960), pp. 147–48.

3. The dates for the sound and visual scenarios for *Enthusiasm* come from the German edition of Vertov's writings: *Dsiga Wertow: Aufsätze, Tagebucher, Skizzen,* ed. Herman Herlinghaus with the collaboration of Rolf Liebmann (Berlin: Institute für Filmwissenschaft and der Deutschen Hochschule für Filmkunst, 1967), pp. 314 ff.

4. P. 282 of Vertov's collected works in Russian. Included in *Kino-Eye: The Writings of Dziga Vertov,* ed. Annette Michelson and trans. Kevin O'Brien (Berkeley: University of California Press, 1984).

5. Dziga Vertov, "The Writings of Dziga Vertov," trans. S. Brody, in P. Adams Sitney, ed., *Film Culture Reader* (New York: Praeger, 1970), pp. 361–62.

6. Georges Sadoul, "Dziga Vertov," *Cahiers du Cinéma* (May-June 1970):19. (My translation.) The material in this article is also contained in Sadoul's book on Vertov: *Dziga Vertov* (Paris: Editions Champs Libre, 1971).

7. Ibid., p. 21.

8. Ibid.

9. Sergei Eisenstein, *Film Form: Essays in Film Theory,* ed. and trans. Jay Leyda (New York: Harcourt, Brace, 1949), p. 258. (Italics mine.) The next two quotes by Eisenstein are taken from the same text, pp. 258–59.

10. Dziga Vertov, "The Vertov Papers," trans. Marco Carynnyk, *Film Comment* (Spring 1972):50. The material within the brackets is my own additional translation of material taken from "Responses à des Questions" in *Cahiers du Cinéma* (May-June 1970):16.

11. Dziga Vertov quoted in Annette Michelson, *"The Man with the Movie Camera:* From Magician to Epistemologist," *Artforum* (March 1972):66.

12. Dziga Vertov, "The Vertov Papers," p. 46.

13. Ibid., p. 48.

14. Dziga Vertov, "The Writings of Dziga Vertov," p. 362.

15. This concept of subverting the cinematic illusion is a central point in Michelson's article.

16. It would be interesting here to contrast the didactic means of a play-film (like Eisenstein's *The Old and the New*) with those of *Enthusiasm*.

17. Dziga Vertov, "From the Notebooks of Dziga Vertov," trans. Marco Carynnyk, *Artforum* (March 1972):75.

18. Dziga Vertov quoted in Michelson, *"The Man with the Movie Camera,"* p. 66.

19. My description of these sequences is taken from a print of *Enthusiasm* that has been restored by Peter Kubelka and is shown in repertory at Anthology Film Archives in New York City. The Museum of Modern Art has the Gosfilmofond version that formed the starting point for Kubelka's restoration.

20. Dziga Vertov, quoted in Michelson, *"The Man with the Movie Camera,"* p. 66.

21. Dziga Vertov, "The Writings of Dziga Vertov," p. 359.

22. Michelson's notion of Vertov's movement "from magician to epistemologist" is central here.

23. From the translation of the film's titles by Kevin O'Brien for Anthology Film Archives.

24. There may be some support for seeing the radio-telegraph woman as standing for a sound monitor in that, according to Jay Leyda in *Kino* (London: Allen and Unwin, 1960, p. 282), part of *Enthusiasm* was recorded on a nonportable sound system that was hooked up to a Radio-Center.

25. Dziga Vertov, "The Writings of Dziga Vertov," pp. 368–69.

26. See Annette Michelson's use of the term, *"The Man with the Movie Camera,"* p. 64.

27. Dziga Vertov, *Articles, Journaux, Projets*, p. 152. (My translation.)

28. Leyda, *Kino*, Chapter 13.

29. Ibid., p. 279.

30. Dziga Vertov, *Articles, Journaux, Projets*, p. 152. (My translation.)

31. Ibid., p. 153. (My translation from the French.)

32. Ibid., p. 156. (My translation from the French.)

33. Dziga Vertov, "Report to the 1st Conference of the Works of Sound Film" (delivered in the summer of 1931). According to Vlada Petric, the manuscript of this Report is kept in the Herbert Marshall Archive, Center for Soviet and East European Studies, Southern Illinois University, Carbondale. I wish to thank Vlada Petric for bringing this Report to my attention and for his translations of passages from it.

34. Ibid. (My description of Vertov's methodology is based on Petric's paraphrase of portions of the Report.)

35. Dziga Vertov, *Articles, Journaux, Projets*, pp. 154–55. (My translation.)

36. Leyda, *Kino*, p. 282.

37. Dziga Vertov, "The Writings of Dziga Vertov," p. 359.

38. Ibid.

39. Dziga Vertov, "From the Notebooks of Dziga Vertov," p. 81.

40. Thorold Dickinson and Catherine de la Roche, *Soviet Cinema* (London: Falcon Press, 1948), p. 27.

41. Dziga Vertov, "The Writings of Dziga Vertov," p. 365.

Restoring *Enthusiasm:*
Excerpts from an Interview with Peter Kubelka

Lucy Fischer: I wanted to ask you some questions about your reediting of *Enthusiasm.* Can you tell me when you first saw the film?

Peter Kubelka: First I want to say that you used the word "reediting"; but it's not really reediting; it's just a restoration. I only corrected the relation between sound track and image so as to bring it back to the original state. I have already noticed that some people speak of a Peter Kubelka "version," but I don't want that. I only tried to come as close to the original as possible. I first saw *Enthusiasm* at the Yugoslavian Film Archive. Mr Achimowitz, who is one of the curators there, and likes Vertov very much, told me that I should see it. He said that I should only see the first reel of the film because the rest was not so good. That, interestingly enough, corresponds to the fact that the rest of the film was more out of sync than the first reel. This was in 1965 or 1966; and, of course, I was very impressed by the film.

LF: Were you immediately aware of the fact that the film needed restoration and interested in undertaking such a project? Or was there a time lapse?

PK: There was a big time lapse. I only saw the first reel at this time; I saw the rest of *Enthusiasm* in 1967 when the Austrian Film Museum had its first Vertov retrospective.

I realized then that the rest of the film was out of sync. Also, there were whole passages where I always fell asleep, which is a strange thing to do in a Vertov film. When I restored the film I found out that these sequences had real articulations which come out only by the sync events.

LF: To which sections are you referring?

PK: There is a sequence when the Plan comes into the film and you have this display model going around and around. Then also, the industrial sequence where there are many lorries going. But this is now one of the most exciting sequences because here Vertov worked in an absolute sync event articulation. He especially worked in this sequence with the specific sound of certain machines and the sound appears exactly when the machine appears. When the camera changes the visual field, the sound changes also.

This sequence is now completely in sync. It was, however, most difficult to find because previously it was completely out of sync. In the original version you saw this huge sledge-hammer (moved by three people) come down in close-up. Knowing the grammar of Vertov it was impossible that there was no sound with that image. It could have been a purposeful silence; but the sledge-hammer could not have just come down without any relation to the sound track. This sequence was very difficult to work on because here the sound was out of sync by more than 300 frames and visually there were more hits of the hammer than I had sound.

LF: Did Vertov synchronize silence with one of the sledge-hammer hits?

PK: Not silence, words. And this is one of the finest grammatical achievements of Vertov in film. He starts by introducing a strong rhythmic accent; when the hammer comes down . . . BOOM! You hear a strong sound, so that you get used to this accent. After some time the hammer comes down and when the hammer hits the object you don't hear natural sound anymore, you hear a word, a passionate call.

This brings us to how I did the restoration. I did it without any written or other references. I did it only on the basis that I was a filmmaker who understood Vertov's way of composing.

LF: On a technical level, how did you proceed?

PK: What we began with was a normal positive, composite print with sound from Gosfilmofond's negative in Moscow. We separated it, which means we made an image negative and a sound negative. We also made a sound track on magnetic perforated tape. But then I did not work with the tape. The optical sound permits you also to see the sound writing and you can see if the original flow of sound signals is maintained or if there has been a cut. You see every cut. Then when I analyzed the sound track I found out how the cuts that Vertov himself had made looked. And then I found out how later restoration cuts looked, or how cuts that projectionists who had ruined the print looked. Which means that the print on which I worked was not made from the original negative; but, apparently, was made from a negative which had been made from a print.

Of course, Gosfilmofond had searched for the best print available but the print had gone through several stages of destruction and restoration—at least one stage of very bad restoration, namely a cosmetic restoration where the people who had restored it had cut away edges of the sound or the image in order to make it fit.

And there was a restoration phase where black leader had already been put in to make up for missing elements in the image. Anyway, in spite of the black leader, all the places where there was lip sync were out of sync in the old versions. So this was the state in which I found the film. When I started to work with the separated image and sound I only realized how the film was gaining in brilliance and precision and it really changed completely. In the first reel, for example, it was out of sync only by a few frames and you still got, more or less, what was meant. But the *start* of the sync was always ruined. But when it's really in sync, it comes "Bang!" and immediately works and that's very different. You remember in the first reel, there are images of bells and then crosses which are faded out, one-two-three. In the restored version you have rhythmic accents on everything and in the other version you did not.

LF: How did you correct for the lack of precise synchronization?

PK: The working process was that I had the image work print and then the optical sound, and I tried to find the right place and went forward and backward and adjusted it until I found the right place. Again, to defend myself, I do not want people to view this as *my* version. What I did was really just to find out how it originally was and I did not cut one single frame, either from the sound or from the image. When the image was too long, I put silent leader in the sound to make it match again. When the sound was too long I put black leader in the image. So nothing is lost. I must point out very strongly that this is not a restoration like those of the nineteenth century, when they restored paintings by painting things in to make it look like the original. This is not what I did. I did not make a cosmetic restoration. It can be undone anytime and it will be in the state in which I found it.

LF: How close to the original do you believe that your restored version comes?

PK: There remain some places in the film where I am still not sure if it's in the right sync. And they occur near the Plan sequence. There are some moments which are not up to the level with which I would credit Vertov; and I was not able to find a more convincing relation between sound and image than the one that was there. But I would say that the film is now 90 percent in sync and there were differences in sync from between two or three frames to more than 300 frames.

You know, Vertov had to change the title of the film from *Enthusiasm* to *Symphony of the Donbas.* But the real title is *Enthusiasm.* This is what he wanted. Now that the film is restored this is what you really feel. You can feel this drive, this enthusiasm. You can feel that and you did not feel that before.

Lang and Pabst: Paradigms
for Early Sound Practice   NOËL CARROLL

The coming of sound caused a crisis in film aesthetics. Some theoreticians, notably Arnheim, refused to endorse the shift at all. Sound, for them, was a return to canned theater, a regression to the pre-Griffith era before film had weaned itself from the stage.

More adventurous thinkers, however, embraced the new device and attempted to incorporate it into the aesthetic system of silent film. Eisenstein, Pudovkin, and Alexandrov, in their famous 1928 statement on sound, and Roman Jakobson, in a rarely discussed 1933 article entitled "Is the Cinema in Decline?," proposed that sound be understood as a montage element: aural units should be juxtaposed against the visuals, just as shots should be juxtaposed against shots. Jakobson, ironically, answers someone like Arnheim in the same manner that Arnheim would have answered someone like Clive Bell. Jakobson tells the opponent of sound that his opposition is not based on a thoughtful look at the possibilities of the new medium. Jakobson argues that the sound element in a scene can be asynchronous and contrapuntal, thereby diverging from mere reproduction. This possibility enriches cinema, for added to all the conceivable visual juxtapositions of the silent film are inestimably large reservoirs of sound counterpoints.

The Eisenstein-Jakobson reaction to sound was conservative in one sense. It was an attempt to extrapolate the basic concepts of a silent film aesthetic to a new development, recommending montage as the basic paradigm for dealing with sound. By the forties, another kind of recommendation was evolved by Bazin, one diametrically opposed to the general silent film predisposition toward stylization and manipulation.

In Bazin, the recording/reproductive aspect of film, that nemesis of silent film artists and theoreticians alike, became the center of a theory that made recommendations about the types of composition and camera movement that would best enable the filmmaker to re-present reality in opposition to the silent film urge to reconstitute it. The formation of Bazin's theory was closely related to the emergence of sound. In the thirties, a filmmaker like Renoir responded to the introduction of sound as an augmentation of film's recording capabilities, and he evolved a realist style that roughly correlated with the notion of film as recording. Bazin described and sought foundations for Renoir's practice, and in so doing defined the predominating ethos of the sound film until the sixties.

The contrast between the reconstitutive response to sound, and the realist's, is much discussed and should not be belabored. But it is important to emphasize that this debate is not merely abstract speculation. Both positions are also artistic dispositions, embodied in the actual practice of important filmmakers. The debate is not only so many words but also many films. Consequently, apart from its dubious theoretical interest, the debate can be historically informative not only about the general directions and transitions in film history but also about the place of individual films within that evolution.

Two films, Fritz Lang's M and G. W. Pabst's Kameradschaft, are especially interesting in this regard. There are many coincidental similarities between them: both are German; both are by major Weimar directors; both date from 1931; both were produced under the auspices of Nero Films; and both share the same cameraman, Fritz Arno Wagner. Yet, stylistically they diverge greatly. M seems to look to the past, to silent film, for its style while Kameradschaft presages the future. Nineteen-thirty was the key year in Germany's transition to sound. In September 1929, only 3 percent of German production was in sound. By September 1930, the total jumped to 84 percent. Thus, the 1930–31 period was one of crisis, one where major German filmmakers had to reorient themselves to their medium. Lang and Pabst both did, but each in highly distinctive ways, ways which in fact represent in a nutshell the major themes in the dialectic about the appropriate direction of sound film.

M is what might be called a silent sound film. Other examples would include Dreyer's Vampyr, Lang's own Testament of Dr. Mabuse, Vertov's Enthusiasm as well as Three Songs of Lenin, parts of Pudovkin's Deserter, Buñuel's L'Age d'Or, and Clair's early sound films, especially A nous la liberté. Calling these silent sound films is not meant disparagingly. Each of these represents a major achievement. Yet that achievement in each case derives from a penchant for asynchronous sound based on a paradigm of montage juxtaposition as a means to manipulate, to interpret, and to reconstitute pro-filmic events.

The importance of montage for M can be demonstrated by a brief look at one of its key scenes, the parallel development of the gangster and government strategy sessions concerning the pursuit of the child-killer. This sequence is not only a matter of parallel, temporal editing; it also involves the articulation of a comparative montage that ultimately equates the police and the gangsters. The two meetings correspond to each other along many dimensions. Both record the same type of event—a search. Both involve similar actions—characters standing and speaking. At this simple visual level, there is a striking resemblance between the behavior of the two groups. Indeed, there is even a similarity in the positions taken in the separate groups, e.g., there are both official and criminal hardliners. At times, the editing almost elides the two meetings; a criminal could be seen as addressing an official and vice versa.

Visual details of the two meetings strongly correspond. Smoke is emphasized in both places. Indeed, cigarettes and cigars lit in the criminal meeting are followed by shots of the smoke-filled police session as if the fumes had transmigrated across the cut. Perhaps this is not only montage but overtonal montage. The elision of the two events is also supported by at least one lightning mix: a gesture begun in one shot by the gangster leader is completed by the Minister of the Interior. This multidimensional comparative montage, of course, is grounded by a thematic point—namely, the identification of the two groups. Lang, here, is critical of the police. Like the criminals, their major concern is self-interest—their "operation" is also being disrupted by the child-killer. They want to catch him in order to get the public "off their backs" and return to "business as usual." Stylistically, in the best Soviet tradition, this pejorative equivalence is emphasized through an elaborate set of comparative juxtapositions.

The commitment to montage shapes Lang's attitude to the sound track. Elsie's death is a good example of this. She is late. Her mother asks people if they have seen the child. Excited, the mother begins calling out her kitchen window. Her voice carries over several shots, including a plate set for dinner, the apartment stairwell, and a yard, presumably in the neighborhood. These are all places where, given the time of day, we might expect to find Elsie. But we don't see her. The mother's poignant voice, audibly dropping as the camera cuts further and further away, plus these shots, communicates the idea of danger. This is montage of the most basic sort—a visual idea plus an aural one engenders a new concept. Editing is, in short, the model for sound.

The use of montage in both the visual and the sound editing in M does not appear to be a casual technical decision about the best way to solve this or that local problem concerning the most efficient means to represent this or that scene. The montage style of M seems consistent. More than that, it seems organic, to use a concept of Eisenstein's.

The most sophisticated versions of the montage aesthetic involved a coordination of style and content. For Eisenstein, the dialectical structure of montage corresponded with the revolutionary subject matter of his films; for Vertov, editing mirrored the modes of thinking of the new socialist society that he celebrated; for Buñuel, montage juxtaposition manifested the irrational by literalizing the primary processes. In each case, the relationship between form and content converged into an organic, functional whole. Similarly, Lang's use of montage in *M* seems of a piece with his theme.

To understand the relation of montage to Lang's thematic preoccupations, we should describe the film's subject. *M* is above all a film of investigation. Extended sequences of the film lovingly dote on the process of gathering evidence. We hear Lohmann's telephone discussion with the Minister of the Interior as we watch the police collecting and examining fingerprints, candy wrappers, cigarette packages, etc. We hear that they have fifteen hundred clues. Throughout the film, Lang returns to the theme of physical evidence. After the raid on the cabaret, not only does Lohmann nab a handful of criminals by careful attention to telltale clues, but his assistants pile up a magnificent assemblage of guns, knives, drills, chisels, hammers, etc. More clues for more crimes. And, toward the end of the film, when Lohmann reads the report about the gang's entry into the warehouse, Lang dissolves from the written words to the pieces of evidence they enumerate. Lang seems visually obsessed with evidence, showing us much more than the narrative requires.

Of course, this visual concern with evidence is integrally related to the plot. The police's interest in evidence is projected onto the audience. In a limited way, we are simultaneously immersed in these clues along with the police. This is especially important at the beginning of the film, where for almost the first third we, like the police, have not identified the killer. He has been kept off-screen, or with his back to the camera, or in a dark place, or with his hat covering his face. Here, our position is strictly analogous to the authorities'. We have clues, for instance his whistle, but we haven't gotten our man. The framing of shots and the narrative conspire to make the spectator's relation to the screen that of a sleuth. Like the police, we base our knowledge of the killer on his traces, e.g., his shadow, his voice, his whistle.

The editing throughout *M* can be seen in light of this first section. Lang often edits actions in such a way that first we see or hear a trace, or a part, or an effect of an off-screen character before we see that character. We see the child-killer's reaction to the blind man at the trial before we can identify the blind man. At the very end we see the criminals raise their hands above their heads before we know the police have arrived. In some cases, we never see the off-screen action, as with Elsie's death; here our knowledge is wholly reliant on traces.

Lang's editing seems predicated on provoking the audience to infer unseen, off-screen presences and actions. Even after the audience knows who the child-killer is, it does not leave off its investigatory role, because by consistently presenting scenes where the audience must infer off-screen agents from their traces Lang continues to make the spectator's relation to the events in the film analogous to a detective's relation to his clues. That is, an investigation involves reasoning from traces and effects to their causes—their agents. Lang's framing and his editing engender the same sort of reasoning—from trace to agent—in many scenes, including even scenes that don't involve off-screen criminals. It is as if Lang's preoccupation with the process of investigation were so intense that he used the process as a general model for framing and editing throughout. A similar point might be made about the large number of overhead shots in the film. These shots mime the posture of investigation, that of the detective bending over a city map or a discarded package of cigarettes.

M is an exemplary case of an organic film. The narrative structure, the framing, the use of sound to present off-screen traces, the overhead angulation, and the order of editing, all seem coordinated to induce an investigatory attitude on the part of the audience—thereby simulating, to a limited extent, the fictional experience of the characters in the viewing experience of the spectators. Montage is the key here. And in the tradition of Eisenstein, Vertov, and Buñuel, it is montage based on imitating modes of thought.

Whereas *M* is a film based on editing, *Kameradschaft* relies far more on camera movement. Since the two films share the same cameraman, Wagner, this difference seems attributable to the divergent conceptions of the sound film held by Pabst and Lang. Pabst and Wagner had begun to use camera movement extensively in the silent period, notably in *The Love of Jeanne Ney*. As the industry changed to sound, Wagner was one of the first Germans to blimp the camera. The mobility this gave him was unleashed effectively in Pabst's *Westfront 1918*, especially in the sequence where the troops crawl along the trenches to mount an attack. *Kameradschaft* marks the high point of Pabst's and Wagner's experimentation with camera movement, not only because the camera movement is interesting in and of itself, but because it is integrated into a complex system of composition that presages the development of sound realism culminating with directors like Rossellini, DeSica, and Ray.

The subject of *Kameradschaft* is a French mine disaster circa 1919. Its theme is blatantly socialist; German miners race across the border to rescue their brother workers. The recent war casts a dark shadow on the action, but the heroic self-sacrifice of the Germans, in the name of working-class unity, dispels French distrust and results in a celebration of proletarian cooperation. This theme is not only stated in the film but is also reinforced by the narrative structure, which, in the Soviet tradition, employs a mass hero, thereby democratizing the drama. Instead of a single protagonist or a single set of protagonists knit together by one story, there are several central stories occurring concomitantly.

Kameradschaft is perhaps most interesting in terms of its composition. Like *Battle of Algiers*, but thirty years earlier, *Kameradschaft* builds images that often evoke the illusion of documentary footage. Pabst achieves this by intermittently acting as if his camera were restrained in relation to the disaster as a documentary camera would be. For instance, there is a scene of the German rescue crew being given instructions before it enters the French mine. Pabst shoots this from behind the German team. The camera tracks past their backs, as they listen, until there is a break in the line of men. At that point, the camera turns and moves into this space in the crowd so that the audience can see the French official who is speaking. But the camera doesn't dolly in; it remains about ten yards away. What is the significance of this distance? I submit that it is to identify the camera as an observer. It reminds the viewer of a documentary because the camera stays outside the action. In a period before zooms, to move into the action for a close shot of the speaker would interfere with and interrupt the rescue. These men don't have time to pose for pictures. The camera has to stay out of their way. Throughout *Kameradschaft*, documentary distances of this sort are evoked, abetting an illusion of a spontaneous recording of the event. This is not to say that all or even most of the shooting respects the "documentary distance." Still, as in Rossellini's *Paisan*, it happens often enough to induce a heightened sense of realism.

The camera's relation to the physical environment is especially interesting. It is important to emphasize that the mines are sets, brilliantly executed by Erno Metzner and Karl Vollbrecht. Yet in a way these are curious sets; often they deny the camera a clear view of the action. In one of the opening shots of the French mine, the camera begins following a character who is pushing a heavy coal bin down a tunnel. Then the camera elevates somewhat and tracks along the ceiling of the tunnel where a diagonal vein has been cut out of the earth and propped up with a veritable forest of short, thick wooden pillars. There are miners digging in this narrow space. You can see them hacking away behind and between the wooden props. The camera then swoops down, picking up the character with the coal bin again. He has stopped at a chute that runs up to the vein where the miners are working. Coal pours into the empty bin.

One thing to note about this shot is that it exemplifies a realist's concern with making the process by which coal is removed and transported inside a mine visibly intelligible—i.e., it enables the audience to see how a mine operates. But more importantly, the shot also demonstrates another realist preoccupation, crucial to Pabst's composition throughout. That is, our view of the miners is obscured by those wooden props; the human element in the scene is blocked by the physical structure of the set. The physical details of the environment restrict the human interest we may have in the characters in favor of details of the environment.

Of course, in a documentary, you must deal predominantly with preexisting environments, which will not always allow you to get clear shots of the action. Pabst and Metzner have built that factor into their sets. Recurrently throughout the film, a tangle of pipes, wires, broken posts, and all manner of debris inhabits the foreground of shots, preventing a clear view of the human action. It is as if Pabst imagined what the problems of a documentary cameraman would be in such a situation, and then had Metzner build a set where Wagner could imitate some of those limitations. In turn, this evocation of documentary elements heightens the viewer's sense of verisimilitude.

Physical elements of the set literally obstruct our view of the drama. When the grandfather drags his grandson into an underground stable, he sets the boy down in an empty stall. This is a charged scene, dominated by the grandfather's emotion. But we cannot see the grandfather's face. A wide board, part of the side of the stall, is in front of the old man, denying a clear view of him at this dramatically important moment.

The significance of this shot should be understood in terms of realism, specifically in terms of the archaeological temperament of many realists. Whether a Stroheim or a Zola, the realist packs his work with details in an effort to reproduce the particular environment of the event depicted. Pabst does this when he introduces and elucidates the German miners' surprising overhead "locker" system. But Pabst differs from a realist like Stroheim in that he packs not only the background with details but also the foreground. This is an extension of the means at the disposal of the realist. The archaeological realist seeks to increase the weight of environmental detail relative to the dominant human action of the story. This does not mean that the archaeological realist overwhelms the main story, or even that detail has equal weight with the story, but only that the role of detail, as a focus of audience attention, be appreciably greater than one finds in the sparse decors of typical narrative films of the period. Stroheim weighted the background of *Greed* with details, and then used the deep-focus long take to prompt the audience to explore the environment. Pabst does this as well, amplifying Stroheim's practice by often filling the foreground with details, thereby compositionally displacing characters from their privileged position as the first object of audience attention.

Pabst also uses the beginnings or the ends of shots to emphasize physical detail. A shot may open on an object and be held for a second before a character enters. Or, a shot may be held on a detail after a character exits.

Related to Pabst's concern with physical detail is his handling of actors. People often walk in front of the camera. Also, important characters, involved in major actions in the story, are sometimes in the background of the shot behind groups of extras. When the grandfather sneaks into the mine, the camera tracks with him, but between the old man and the lens stands the French rescue crew as well as several imposing steel columns. For brief intervals, the old man disappears from view. What is involved here is a complex compositional acknowledgment of the situation being represented. Standard narrative composition designs its environment and blocks actors so that important characters are at the center of visual attention. The realist deviates from this practice, giving the details of the event and the place portrayed more prominence. The realist acknowledges more complexity in the world, but the realist does not recreate the world. Realism, like standard narrative composition, is a style of representation, not reproduction, of actual reality. But as a style it acknowledges the complexity of situations by giving detail more compositional attention than does the solely drama-centered narrative.

The realists Bazin endorsed were involved in what could be thought of as a kind of cinematic land reclamation. They repossessed areas of cinematic space, unused in standard narrative composition. Specifically, they resettled the back of the shot and the sides of the shot. They were concerned with depth of field and what Bazin calls "lateral depth of field." Both these preoccupations are central to *Kameradschaft.*

The saga of depth of field is well known. Standard narrative composition, according to Bazin, pays scant attention to background. It either obliterates it by close shots or masks it by soft focus. The background may also be downplayed via abstraction. The background of the standard narrative shot is not so abstract as to call attention to itself, but there is so little visual detail that there is no reason for the eye to dwell there. A table, a chair, a telephone, and a picture are enough. And don't have Mother enter the background to answer the phone while Dad and Junior are having a crucial dramatic conversation in the foreground, because that will divert attention.

Renoir, Wyler, Welles, and the neorealists rebelled against this. The background became an arena of activity; in *Rules of the Game,* sometimes as many as three separate stories are contesting the action in the foreground. *Kameradschaft* similarly upholds this principle of overall composition. Of course, *Kameradschaft* differs from *Rules of the Game.* Primarily, Renoir places interrelated dramatic actions on different compositional planes— Schumacher searches for his wife in the foreground, while the poacher sneaks off with her in the background. Pabst, instead, implodes the frame with the physical and social facts of the situation. Whereas Renoir concentrates on the personal, psychological economy of the drama, Pabst is an anthropologist and an archaeologist. Both rely on depth of field, but they are realists with different types of interests. Pabst is concerned with enriching the environment, wheras Renoir primarily enriches the drama.

Disaster lurks throughout *Kameradschaft*. Explosions, cave-ins, floods, and fires mercilessly erupt. The depth-of-field technique is especially powerful in these scenes. A man will run down a tunnel that is collapsing behind him. Metzner's engineering ingenuity with these catastrophes is overwhelming. Tons of stones are falling within a few feet of the actors playing the trapped miners. Everything is captured in one shot, engendering an awesome feeling of authenticity. Bazin claimed a heightened sense of verisimilitude for depth-of-field shots involving danger. Pabst exploits that effect more than a decade before Bazin conceptualizes it as a central factor in realism.

Of all the ways in which *Kameradschaft* corresponds to Bazin's characterization of film realism, camera movement is the most significant. To elucidate this, I should start with a brief review of Bazin's interest in camera movement. He applauds Renoir's tendency toward incessant lateral panning and tracking. Renoir follows his characters, rather than preblocking the scene in such a way that the camera remains stationary throughout. Bazin appreciates this use of camera movement for two reasons. First, it imbues the scene with a sense of spontaneity. And second, it treats the relation between on-screen space and off-screen space cinematically.

This second reason is somewhat obscure and requires comment. Bazin believes that the stationary, preblocked scene treats the film frame like the border of a stage or a painting. That is, the picture and the play are presented as boxes that are spatially discontinuous with their surroundings. The preblocked, stationary scene treats on-screen space on the box model. In distinction, repeated lateral panning and tracking subvert one's sense of the frame as a self-contained box and affirm the continuity of on-screen space and off-screen space. The frame is not analogous to the proscenium arch, which lifts the action out of a spatial continuum with the wings of the theater, setting it in some virtual realm. Rather, the film frame is only the viewfinder of the camera as it moves over a spatially continuous world; lateral panning and tracking acknowledge the presence of that real world and make the on-screen image's continuity with it a matter of the audience's felt attention.

It is this aspect of realism Bazin dubs "lateral depth of field." Like ordinary depth of field, this style is realistic relative to a more standard type of composition. That is, standard practice treats the frame as a theatrical box; the realist repudiates this, thereby acknowledging spatial continuity by subverting the artifice imposed on the image by standard practice.

Pabst constantly emphasizes lateral depth of field in *Kamerad-*

schaft. As in Renoir, there are many slight axial pans in the film. When the crowds run to the exploding French mines, Pabst includes several shots that begin with a group of people running in one direction across the frame. Then the camera pans slightly to the point where two streets intersect. At that corner, the first group of people turn and join an even larger group which is running away from the camera. Through the use of these slight axial pans, Pabst emphasizes the spatial contiguity of all of the people who are converging on the mine. Throughout the film, this type of panning recurs in order to articulate the spatial contiguity of converging action. Pabst often uses panning to represent a character's point of view. Here, the synthetic space of editing is repudiated, resulting in the felt sense of a spatially continuous environment.

Of course, the large camera movements of the film enhance the sense of a spatial continuum as well. Where possible, Pabst knits the different areas of action together with long, snaking tracking shots. I am not denying that there is a great deal of editing in the film. However, there is also a great deal of camera movement, especially for the period. Moreover, much of this camera movement is used in situations where the normal practice of the period would be to fall back on the analytic editing procedures of silent film. Again, to understand what is realist about *Kameradschaft*, it is necessary to consider it as a deviation from standard practice. Much of the film corresponds to the editing bias of the period. But there are also other tendencies, found in the camera movement, which, given the film-historical context, can be interpreted as an acknowledgment of spatial continuity that affirms the role of film as the recorder of a spatially continuous world.

The theme of off-screen space is also inherent in many of Pabst's stationary compositions. When the French rescue crew receives its instructions, the body of one of the miners is cut off by the side of the frame. This type of framing recalls a strategy found in nineteenth-century realist paintings like Manet's *At the Cafe*. The point is to emphasize the continuity of the depicted environment beyond the border of the frame. The innumerable pipes, wires, and tunnels in *Kameradschaft* serve an analogous function; they are the kinds of objects that by their very nature remind the audience that they are part of a larger off-screen spatial network.

Since off-screen space is also important in *M*, it is instructive to consider the different ways Pabst and Lang use it. Lang keeps very specific things off-screen. Examples include: the child-killer, the murder, the gangsters as they break down the attic door, and the police as they raid the kangaroo court. I have already argued that the reason Lang does this is to mobilize an investigatory attitude that corresponds to the theme of detection. But another point can also be made. The agents and events kept off-screen are generally associated with danger. This is especially true of the off-screen agents. They constitute threats to what is on-screen. In my examples, for instance, the gangsters threaten the child-killer, and later the police threaten the gangsters. This is a formal articulation of Lang's theme of paranoia. The off-screen threats are a pictorial means of expressing the paranoid obsession with unseen and invisible enemies. Lang's *films noirs,* like *The Big Heat,* will employ similar strategies. His *1000 Eyes of Dr. Mabuse* takes the theme of invisible danger as its major subject. For Lang, in other words, off-screen space has a symbolic function within his paranoid vision. It has dire connotations as an invisible, menacing empire. In Pabst, off-screen space is just off-screen space, emphasized for its own sake. Of course, in Lang off-screen space is literally contiguous with on-screen space. But that is not its aesthetic point. Lang is interested in developing a subjective world-view, while Pabst is striving for an objective view of the world.

For Bazin, camera movement is also associated with spontaneity. The connection here, I think, must be understood historically. That is, it must be understood in the context of a dominant style based on preblocked stationary compositions that suggested theatrical artifice. The preblocked stationary composition gives the impression that the action is preordained and circumscribed. Thus, a style that allows the character to lurch off-screen, forcing the camera to follow him, may have the connotations of freedom and spontaneity. Such camera movement is realist in contrast to a preexisting style that is artificial. It is spontaneous in contrast to a style that gives the action the impression of being controlled.

For Pabst, this sense of spontaneity is central to his attempt to promote the illusion that the film is a documentary recording. In some scenes, like the German visit to the French bar, almost three-quarters of the shots contain camera movement. The feeling engendered is that the cameraman is pursuing an unstaged action, shifting his point of view as the event develops. This sensation is induced especially when the German and French rescue teams meet underground. The leaders of the two groups shake hands; the camera dollies in. First, it heads for the Frenchman. But then it turns and moves into a close-up shot of the handshake. This slight change in camera direction is significant. It is as if, mid-movement, the cameraman changed his mind about what was the important element in the scene. I am not denying that all the shots in *Kameradschaft* are preplanned. Yet they often feel unplanned. The shot of the handshake has the look of involving a spontaneous decision on the part of the cameraman. Throughout the film, camera movement has the look of following the action rather than delimiting it. The camera seems to be an observer, with the result that the film projects the illusion of a spontaneous recording of an event.

Surprisingly, Bazin does not appreciate *Kameradschaft.* He compares it with *Grand Illusion* since both films employ more than one language. But, he remarks, Renoir gets more thematic mileage out of his polyglot format. Why doesn't Bazin notice the camera movement aesthetic implicit in *Kameradschaft?* One reason might be that there are still vestiges of the silent sound film in Pabst. For instance, there is a fantasy sequence where the sound of a hammer tapping a pipe metaphorically becomes the rattle of a machine gun. Nevertheless, the dominant tendency of the film is toward the sound film style Bazin advocates. Indeed, Pabst not only claims the background and the sides of the frame for realism; he takes over the foreground as well.

The transition from silent film to sound not only involved a question about how sound would be used. It also prompted a reevaluation of the nature of the medium. For Pabst, sound was associated with the recording capacity of film. This led him to a reassessment of the image. He sought and found compositional strategies, including camera movement, which amplified the idea of film as a recording. A whole style evolved in the process of coordinating composition with the commitment to recording. The stylistic system Pabst developed was not the only one available. *M* presents another alternative. But that alternative is based on a very different response to the significance of sound. Steeped in the methods of the silent film, Lang attempts to turn sound into a montage element. The underlying presupposition of Lang's system is that the nature of film is to reconstitute reality, not to record it. In Lang, sound is modeled on preexisting technique whereas in Pabst technique must be remodeled to accommodate sound, specifically to accommodate sound conceived of as entailing a commitment to recording.

Sound caused a major theoretical crisis in the film world. By using the term "theoretical," I do not mean simply that it was a crisis for theoreticians. More importantly, it was a crisis for artists. A framework was needed to understand the aesthetic significance of this new element. Two major ones presented themselves. Sound could function as an element of manipulation as it does in *M.* This is to interpret sound in terms of a silent film paradigm. Or a new paradigm could be embraced, one that responded to sound as increasing film's commitment to recording. In *Kameradschaft,* Pabst accepts this option. It prompts him to develop a highly original camera style, one that presages Renoir. As such, *Kameradschaft* is one of the watershed films in cinema history. I do not mean to use *Kameradschaft* to disparage *M. M* is surely one of the greatest films ever made. My point is that *Kameradschaft,* a generally neglected film, is *M*'s peer insofar as it proposes a fully consistent stylistic alternative. In the dialectic between manipulation and recording, both films speak eloquently at a time of crisis and uncertainty.

The Voice of Silence: Sound Style in John Stahl's *Back Street*
MARTIN RUBIN

A good place to start in analyzing the sound track of *Back Street* is with *how* it sounds—with that distinctive tonal quality that marks all of John M. Stahl's major melodramas of the early 1930s, from *Back Street* (1932) through *Magnificent Obsession* (1935). Do you know what sound is like in a museum or on a street very early in the morning? Footsteps crunching through a crust of snow in an empty field, water lapping against a pier at night? Then you have an idea of what Stahl's early thirties melodramas sound like: in back of every sound, there is silence.

This tonal quality is an important part of the characteristic austerity of Stahl's style. The baroque crescendos of Douglas Sirk (Stahl's successor and frequent remaker at Universal), underscored by Frank Skinner's florid musical scores, stand at the opposite pole to Stahl's sober handling of the same material. In Stahl's films, background noise—the steady shuffle of pedestrians, the hum of traffic, the murmur of the crowd—can be orchestrated as a drone note, a *ground* that discharges the melodramatic lightning of the plot and keeps returning it to an even keel, a steady hum of sobriety.

Another quality of the sounds in *Back Street* is their distinctness, their separation, their extremely clear definition. The sharp clip-clop of horses' hoofs, the crisp report of doors opening and closing, the clean tread of footsteps—these are just a few examples of "incidental" sounds as clear and selective as a tap on a crystal glass. A passage in which the heroine Ray Schmidt (Irene Dunne) empties out her purse and then carefully replaces the items, one by one, seems motivated mainly as an aural tour de force in differentiating the distinctive sound each object makes—lipstick tube, compact, comb, coin, etc.—as it falls back into the purse.

In part, Stahl's proclivity for selective and highly accentuated elements in the sound track is dictated by the conventionally literal sound style and simplified mixing technology of early sound films. But Stahl takes the convention and *pushes* it, determines it excessively, and so forges it into a style. An example occurs during Walter (John Boles) and Ray's first streetcorner rendezvous in *Back Street*. In a long take, the two characters walk toward the foreground, talking as the camera falls back before them; their conversation is continually punctuated by horse-drawn carriages that clip-clop across the background in a direction perpendicular to that of the couple's walk. The sound of the carriages is *too* loud, *too* distinct; it begins to contradict the visual position of the carriages (in the background, in soft focus) to the point where the sound is almost lifted out of the image. The sound of the carriages becomes not just background accompaniment to the visually foregrounded conversation but a competing element with it. In general, Stahl's sounds tend to separate out rather than merge into a general mélange, both in the way they separate from other sounds (a type of sound mixing that verges on antimixing) and in the way they can become separate, to a certain extent, from the images that contain them.

Stahl's tendency to keep the elements of a shot discrete and distinct *almost* to the point of separation—sound from sound, sound from image, character from character, character from space—is an indication of his analytical temperament. However, Stahl's mode of analysis is not the one typically assigned in classical film theory[1]—that is, of aggressively breaking down the elements of the shot via cutting, camera movement, asynchronous sound, expressionistic lighting and composition, etc. Instead, Stahl prefers to stand back and observe, to show the integral whole but also to accentuate our awareness of its discrete component parts. From this derives the quietness and surprising expressiveness that typify Stahl's camerawork, and his ability to see through his characters to their other sides (e.g., the calm awareness of Walter's selfishness and Ray's excessive deference in *Back Street*, the sexual timidity conveniently served by Bea's exaggerated attachment to her daughter in *Imitation of Life,* the almost voluptuous death-wish underlying Bobby Merrick's playboy recklessness in *Magnificent Obsession*—insights either absent or not as clearly observed in the various remakes of these films). It is a clumsy hunter who charges his prey; Stahl prefers to stand back quietly and let his targets reveal themselves.

In relation to this analytical mode in *Back Street*, not only are different sound elements in the same shot kept unusually distinct from each other, both in a paradigmatic (i.e., conversation and background noise in the walking scene) and a syntagmatic (i.e., the sounds of the various objects in the purse scene) direction, but Stahl also emphasizes the distinctness of different *discourses* in the sound track and uses each of them for specific thematic purposes. In *Back Street*, each of four major discourses has its distinct presence and function—the discourse of dialogue, the discourse of background noise, the discourse of music, and, last and most crucially, the most austere of all sound-track elements: the discourse of silence.

The opening shots of *Back Street* present us with a mixture, a mélange. After an initial title placing the action in "the good old days before the 18th Amendment," the camera pulls back from a detail-shot of two brimming beer-mugs to show Ray Schmidt and her date seated at a table, then (after a semi-invisible cut to a slightly longer shot from the same angle) sweeps laterally across the beer-garden to show festive diners hoisting beer mugs, couples dancing, the band playing and finally pulls back to show the entire ensemble framed by tree branches in the foreground. The sounds heard off-screen in the opening image (conversation, shuffling feet, music) are all united with their sources in the course of a single movement. Three of the sound track's four discourses—dialogue, background noise, and music—are fused together. (The fourth—silence—will gradually assert itself until it dominates the final shot of the film.) The opening scene presents an image of harmony and integration, which the film will almost immediately begin . . . "breaking down" is perhaps too strong a term . . . *resolving* into its discrete parts.

One of the first methods Stahl uses is the articulation of sound (especially background noise) and silence, the pointing up of the distinction between them. It isn't just a case of sound tapering off into silence, but of sharply accentuated alternations of sound and silence. The fanfare of the first scene dissolves into the momentary silence of Ray's family seated on their front porch. These types of alternations are used throughout the film, culminating in an exaggerated variation on the technique, amounting virtually to a baring of the device, when a deafeningly loud drill outside Ray's New York apartment suddenly stops (leaving a chatterbox neighbor still in mid-shout), then starts up again, then stops dead. Less pronounced but scarcely less noticeable is the way in which conversations continually lapse into long silences—for example, during the scene in which Ray's sister reveals her pregnancy, or the scene where Walter tells Ray he isn't taking her to Europe.

Silence is distinguished from background noise by alternation, and from conversation by interruption. Through the selectivity and precise exaggeration of the sound mixing, conversation is distinguished from background noise, as in the example of Ray and Walter's walking scene cited above. It would probably be possible to find examples in which each of the four sound-track discourses is distinguished from the others in nearly every possible permutation. However, it should be noted that silence is the privileged discourse in these permutations; it is distinguished the *most*—if only because it is generically distinguished from the other three to begin with: they are all sounds, while it is silence, nonsound.

Each of the four sound-track discourses is distinguished from the others not only physically but also thematically. Each accumulates different functions and associations; each constitutes a distinct and clearly defined "voice."

(1) Background noise is the voice of the outer world, of progress, of time. In the second scene of the film, the front-porch conversation of Ray's family (her mother scoffs at the notion of automobiles and advises the automotive inventor Kurt to put his money in horses) is counterpointed by the off-screen clip-clop of horses and the creaking of carriage frames; then Kurt seats Ray in his newly built auto and runs the motor while he proposes to her. Ray is initially associated with the horse-and-buggy era: she enters the scene by stepping off a horse-drawn trolley.

The sounds of horses and buggies in the background accompany Ray and Walter's first streetcorner rendezvous. In a similarly shot scene in which, after a two-year separation, they meet again in New York, a shift occurs: the background is now crossed by horse-drawn vehicles *and* automobiles in about equal proportion. But, because it is snowing, the previously dominant sound of horses' hoofs is muffled, while the chugging of automobile motors is unaffected, and so the motor noise "takes over" the background.

From this point on, sounds of motor traffic, together with the construction-site noises of drilling and riveting, become a constant background accompaniment to the New York scenes, and the familiar sound of horses disappears. This development is capped at the end of the scene in which Ray chooses to stay with Walter once and for all, although she knows she can never marry him. "I love you, Ray," he declares; the film cuts directly to a shot taken from the front of a moving train. The off-screen engine chugs loudly down the tracks, while a superimposed title announces that the date has advanced approximately twenty years to 1932: it is the sound of passing time.

(2) Music is the voice of the past, of memory, of an idealized state, of a lost moment frozen in time and left behind by its inexorable advancement. The association is planted in the first scene, where the establishment of "the good old days before the 18th Amendment" is accompanied by turn-of-the-century band music. The film's crucial lost moment—Ray's missed appointment with Walter and his mother—occurs during a band concert in the park.

When Walter begins to tell his son the story of his liaison with Ray, his voice dies out on the sound track, and an image is superimposed of the park band playing "Let Me Call You Sweetheart." After several seconds, the sound and image of the band fade away, and Walter is heard finishing the story. Here music is explicitly associated with memory and substitutes for Walter's recounting of the past.

The most spectacular instance of this musical association occurs in the final scene when, just before her death, Ray reimagines the lost moment ("I wonder, Walter, what would have happened if I'd met your mother that day in Eden Park . . ."). The scene dissolves to the band playing "Let Me Call You Sweetheart," which rings out loudly and joyously on the sound track as Ray arrives on time and completely charms her prospective mother-in-law. Here the film has gone beyond the real past into the ideal past. The conditional past tense (I would have arrived on time, he would have introduced me, she would have liked me) usurps the simple past tense (I was late, they left, he got married); the lost moment is recaptured and transformed.

(3) Dialogue—the voice of the characters—is a bit more slippery to deal with. It is probably the least distinguished (in both senses of the word) of the four voices. Although virtually every conversation in the film occurs in the foreground plane, the privileged position of the words themselves is frequently undermined by the presence of background noise (the stylized balance of the mixing "foregrounds" the background noise). Hence, the two lovers are privileged more by their position in the image (which is not as strongly challenged by background information) than by their position on the sound track.

Even when the dialogue is not being undermined by background noise, it frequently undermines itself. To put it bluntly, this is not a screenplay distinguished by its deathless prose, its witty dialogue, its poetic declarations of love. This does not mean, however, that the dialogue's very ordinariness does not have its function and logic within the scheme of the film. The two main characters are not—and are not meant to be—especially remarkable people, neither in terms of charisma (compare the more glamorous star-power of Charles Boyer and Margaret Sullavan in the 1941 remake) nor in terms of position (compare the 1961 remake, where John Gavin is a dynamic department store magnate and Susan Hayward a fabulously successful fashion designer). They are generally least remarkable when they are talking, especially Walter, who is capable of saying things that are quite fatuous (when Ray complains about how empty her life is in the back-street flat, Walter exclaims incredulously, "Empty? When you have *me?*").

A remarkable proportion of *Back Street*'s dialogue is devoted to prattle, banalities, and small talk. Dialogue is the least privileged of the four voices in the film, just as silence is the most privileged. Dialogue is easily usurped by the other three voices—by background noise (the loud drilling from the construction site), by music (the band concert that supplants Walter's spoken flashback), and by silence (conversations that lapse into silence).

Language itself becomes suspect, unreliable, misleading, harmful—an instrument of maliciousness (the gossips who malign Ray's reputation); of evasion ("No, I don't mind," Ray lies glumly when Walter installs her in the apartment as his mistress); of misunderstanding ("We're going to Europe!" Walter says; "Wonderful!" Ray exclaims, not realizing that she is not included in his "we"); of callousness ("You should have been with me!" Walter enthuses as he describes the delights of his European trip to the neglected Ray); and of delusion ("We're going to have tomorrow all to ourselves," Ray tells Walter on the day before his death).

Perhaps most importantly, language carries with it the power of *naming*, which threatens the tenuous transcendence in the central love relationship. "Is this your husband?" the nosy neighbor asks, holding up a picture of Walter; Ray doesn't reply. When Walter comes in unexpectedly on Ray and her neighbor, Ray says in confusion, "This is . . . is Walter." When Kurt renews his proposal to Ray later in the film, she attempts to confess, "You know what I am? . . ."; "Ray Schmidt! Finest girl I ever knew!" he cuts in before she can finish. It is Walter, in an especially thoughtless moment, who comes closest to naming the name: when Ray asks to have his child, he blurts, "You're not my wife!," then immediately apologizes.

To name would be to say, "No, that's not my husband, that's the man who keeps me," "This is my lover," "You know what I am? I'm a kept woman," "You're not my wife—you're my paid mistress." In other words, name it—use language to describe it—and the whole relationship threatens to become sordid, tawdry, common. This is certainly not the intention of the film, which ultimately sees it as exalted, moving, special. But any transcendence achieved by the lovers must come through on the levels of image and music (the two "purest" voices) rather than those of language and noise. Small talk, big image.

In this configuration, the telephone functions as a privileged signifier, encapsulating the inadequacy of dialogue, of language, of verbal communication. As a modern-age invention, similar in importance to the automobile, the telephone links up thematically with the first voice, that of progress and passing time. The essence of the telephone in *Back Street* is separation—separation of person and person, voice and body, sound and image, image and image. The telephone makes its first appearance in the limbo of Ray's back-street apartment and is consistently associated with her isolation, whether in New York or Paris. The telephone is the central device around which the powerful scene of Walter's death is structured. The integration of the film's opening scene comes full circle here to fully articulated separation: close-ups of the helpless Ray shrieking hysterically into the phone ("Walter! Don't leave me!") are intercut with impassive close-ups of Walter's phone, still off the hook, while off-screen are heard the distraught voices of his family and physician ("Doctor, doctor!" "He's passed on . . .").

(4) The telephone signifies pure "sound track"—that is, sound

divorced from image—which is revealed to be inadequate. The direction of the film's resolution, of its final transcendence, is that of image divorced from sound—that is, of pure image, of silence.

The film ends in silence. At the end of the "flashback" to Eden Park, Walter, in close shot, asks Ray, "Shall we go?" The sound of the band concert abruptly dies out; a quick dissolve matches the close shot of Walter with a silent shot of Walter's framed photo on the table beside Ray (the close shot of Walter is emptied of sound and frozen in time). Close-up of Ray, who says, "I'm coming, Walter. I'm coming. I'm . . ." Her voice trails off. Her head slowly sinks to the table and lies beside Walter's photo. Long hold; absolute silence; a clear, bright light slowly bathes Ray's face. Except for a quiet reprise of "Let Me Call You Sweetheart" on the fade-out, this final scene is dominated by silence. Silence is the voice of the image.

The key movement in the 1932 version of Back Street is the central couple's separation from history, their countermovement to the flow of time. At the beginning of the film, Ray rejects Kurt, an inventor of the twentieth-century paradigm, the automobile. Ray sits perched in Kurt's auto while the motor idles; then the motor is switched off—in a sense, she never really gets into the twentieth century. (In contrast, the 1941 version begins with Ray leading a parade in an automobile while the crowd waves placards announcing, "The Machine Age Is Here.") The scenes of Ray and Walter walking perpendicularly away from the flow of traffic in the background have the effect of turning them onto a new axis, another dimension, away from the flow of the world, perhaps even outside of the real past (the horse-drawn carriages in the background) and of time itself (at the end of the film, Ray and Walter do not go back to the real past, but to an ideal, recreated past—a past that never was).

In the final shots of Ray curled up in an armchair and buried in sorrow, she seems cut off from the world altogether. The conditional "flashback" is the crowning stroke of this movement to stop time and enter again into the past. When Ray says, "I'm coming, Walter," she means that she is coming back to that day of the band concert, to retrieve the lost promise of Eden Park. The presentation of the flashback seems so simple and right, and yet the same device is bungled in the two later versions, partly because it is unsupported by the thematic and stylistic articulation of the past that the 1932 version so painstakingly develops. The plush 1941 version settles for nothing more than conventional Gay Nineties nostalgia, while the bland 1961 version has no sense of the past at all, the ten or fifteen years of the action all seeming to take place around 1960. In these films, the final "flashback" seems an extraneous gimmick, while in the 1932 version it is the inevitable climax of the film, of its movement against the grain of progress, of the destiny of two people left behind by a changing era, isolated in the back streets of time where the traffic of history rarely if ever passes by.

The general thematic movement of the 1932 *Back Street* is against the flow of history. The film stigmatizes the apparatus of technological progress (not only the automobile but also the telephone, thereby evoking another form of mechanical voice transmission: the microphone)[2] and it valorizes an idealized romantic past represented by image and music. All of this can be interpreted as a reflexive subtextual reference to the industry-wide trauma occasioned by the recently accomplished transition to the talking film—an anxiety noted by Stahl himself in a 1932 *Hollywood Reporter* article entitled "Oh, the Good Old Days/Gone Are the Days When Directing Was a Cinch":[3]

Anyone who doesn't think this business is getting tougher and tougher for the director, as well as a lot of other people I could mention, simply doesn't know his footage. . . . In the good old days it used to be a cinch. . . . But not any more. . . . In the dear, dead days of silent pictures we could fix up anything with a printed title. . . . The advent of the talking picture within the past four years has ushered in an entirely new phase of this bewildering and fast-growing industry, and what the future may bring forth no man can tell.

Stahl perhaps had reason to be especially sensitive to the ideas of obsolescence, divorcement from progress, and a lingering identification with the silent cinema. After several years as a top silent director, Stahl did not receive a directorial credit from 1927 to 1930—a period coinciding almost exactly with the film industry's conversion to sound. After selling out his interest in Tiffany-Stahl, where he had served as production chief, he found himself out of work in 1930.[4] Stahl's position in an industry that almost passed him by was not secured until after the successful preview of *A Lady Surrenders* in September 1930, at which point Universal rewarded him with a three-picture contract.[5]

The transcendence for the characters at the end of Stahl's *Back Street* occurs on the level of the image—or, to be a little more precise, of image and music (i.e., the music during the conditional "flashback," the music under the final fade-out). In other words, the film is ultimately dominated by the two purest of the sound track's four voices—pure sound (music) and pure image (silence). Music and image are, of course, precisely the elements of the silent film.

The ending of *Back Street* confirms a hierarchy of the four voices in the film. Music is established as the most privileged of the three audible voices (music, background noise, dialogue), a position prepared by closely preceding scenes in which music supplants background noise (Ray and Walter's stroll around the ship's deck—for the first time in the film, crowd noises, etc., are conspicuously excluded) and music supplants dialogue (the superimposed band concert during Walter's explanation to his son). In the conditional "flashback," all three of these voices are present (music of the band, sound of the crowd, dialogue of the characters), but the music, in its loudness, forcefulness, and emotional resonance, dominates the scene.

Then the three audible voices, dominated by music, are in their turn dominated by the image, as expressed in the final transition when the sound of the "flashback" abruptly dies out and the scene quickly dissolves into the framed photograph of Walter—the audible discourses are swallowed up by the discourse of the image. The visual separation of Walter's death scene (a scene based on dialogue and its apparatus: the telephone) gives way to the visual concentration of Ray's death scene—an unbroken close shot composed mainly of Ray's face, Walter's photograph (signifier of the discourse of the image), and silence (voice of the image).

Back Street reflects an anxiety over the role of the sound track typical of the early sound period. However, this film's particular response to the problem is more idiosyncratic than typical. Rather than expressing its anxiety over sound through an avoidance of dialogue (*à la* Chaplin), a minimization of dialogue (*à la* the so-called shy talkies derided even by such conservative theorists as Arnheim and Balazs), or a separating-off of sound via asynchronization and montage strategies (*à la* Clair and Eisenstein), *Back Street* privileges the discourse of the image through its interplay within a *mise-en-scène* containing the other discourses of sound in film. It is Stahl's particular talent for observing distinctions-within-wholeness that enables him to send a last valentine to the lost Eden of the silent film, while at the same time taking the main road of the fully articulated talking picture.

Notes

1. For example, Bazin's description of analytical editing; Eisenstein's theories of montage; Balazs's valorization of the close-up; Clair's and Eisenstein's notions of asynchronous, contrapuntal sound.

2. As is well known, the Vitaphone system for talking pictures was a direct outgrowth of technology developed by AT&T for improved telephone transmission.

3. John M. Stahl, "Oh, the Good Old Days/Gone Are the Days When Directing Was a Cinch," *The Hollywood Reporter*, May 16, 1932, p. 23.

4. "Film Magnate Takes Vacation," Los Angeles *Times*, January 12, 1930.

5. "Stahl Signed by Universal," New York *Telegraph*, September 14, 1930.

Stylists

It is revealing that most of the directors of the sound classics of the early thirties—Mamoulian, Lubitsch, and Clair, for example—did not continue to make films with particularly interesting sound tracks. Perhaps this is because their early sound films represent not an accommodation with but a direct attack on sound. As soon as sound recording and mixing techniques no longer obstructed their visions, these directors seem to have lost interest in using sound creatively.

By contrast, a handful of directors in the history of the narrative cinema almost always used sound expressively. In each case these directors have a distinctive sound style that is inseparable from their visual and thematic concerns. And when their visual style shifts, their aural style undergoes a corresponding change. The sound stylists represented in this section of the anthology are Orson Welles, Alfred Hitchcock, Jean Renoir, Robert Bresson, and Jean-Luc Godard. These filmmakers have completely different approaches toward sound; they have in common only an appreciation and realization of its potential.

To some extent these stylists extend the usages of sound pioneered by the early directors. Each of the essays in this section, for example, contains examples of sound dislocated from or substituting for the original source. Thus the titular protagonists of Hitchcock's *Birds* are sometimes heard but not seen, the spiritual entrapment of the leading character in Bresson's *Mouchette* is suggested by the sound of crackling originally associated with the trapper and his prey, and the Marquis in Renoir's *Rules of the Game* is represented by the sound of his musical toys. But perhaps more significant is the way these directors developed the use of synchronized sound (including speech) without resorting to the redundant "talking heads" or static "canned theater" that had been feared at first.

Directors who exploit sound in this way depend on the

conventions of inconspicuous sound recording and editing at the same time that they play with them. For example, Penny Mintz explains how Orson Welles disorients the viewer by mismatching visual and aural cues: voices may sound a little too close to match the apparent distance of the speakers, or characters may sound closed in when they appear to be speaking outdoors. But these slight "errors" in perspective are not consciously noticed. Mintz traces a progression toward fragmentation and disorientation created by such sound manipulation in four films (*Citizen Kane, The Magnificent Ambersons, The Lady from Shanghai,* and *Touch of Evil*) and suggests that the resulting sense of dislocation is central to the experience of Welles's art.

Hitchcock, too, exploits expectations established by synchronized sound. In *The Birds* the manipulation is less of sound perspective than of sound quality, a manipulation possible because of the stylized nature of the partially electronic sound track. Elisabeth Weis, after analyzing Hitchcock's sound style in general, ends with an analysis of *The Birds* in which she argues that distinctions originally set up among human, mechanical, and avian noises eventually break down. By the end of the film, birds sound like machines, people sound like birds, and machines sound like birds or people, a series of aural exchanges matched by the thematic and visual concerns of the film.

Weis's essay also provides a model for analyzing the evolution of a director's sound style. She argues that though Hitchcock pioneered expressionistic sound with his "knife sequence" in *Blackmail* (1929), he gradually became more realistic during his career. One could trace a reverse shift in Renoir's career. Renoir's first sound feature, *La Chienne* (1931), was also the first French film to be shot and recorded on location. But in the fifties, when the rest of the film world began to shoot outdoors more and more, Renoir chose to move indoors to film several very stylized movies on theatrical subjects. The two-dimensional, static, and highly histrionic use of sound in such films as *The Golden Coach* (1952) and *French CanCan* (1954), however, is appropriate to the emphasis on artifice in these works. The theatrical films aside, one tends to characterize Renoir's style as it is represented by *Rules of the Game* (1939), with its deep-focus, long-take, long-shot aesthetic. Michael Litle demonstrates in his detailed analysis of *Rules of the Game* that there is indeed a realistic sound style in the film that is analogous to the director's visual style. Sound equivalents of deep focus can be found in Renoir's use of off-screen sound and multilayered foreground and background sound. However, drawing on semiological methodology, Litle argues that Renoir uses sound on levels that go well beyond the apparent realism so carefully established.

Despite their different styles, Welles, Hitchcock, and Renoir can actually be yoked together insofar as all three directors, regardless of their strategies for manipulating or distorting sound, developed aural styles that on some level do not distract the audience from the narrative flow of the film. By contrast, filmmakers Bresson and Godard have little interest in traditional storytelling or three-dimensional character; hence, neither makes any pretense of observing normal sound conventions whereby noises remain subservient to dialogue and dialogue remains subservient to image. In other words, neither Bresson nor Godard relegates sound to a secondary position. Lindley Hanlon discusses below how in Bresson's *Mouchette,* a film with typically sparse dialogue, sound functions as an independent element of composition and meaning. Sound effects and silence emphasize the hostility of the heroine's environment, and music suggests the possibility of spiritual redemption.

Like Bresson, Godard does not favor dialogue over other sounds. In his essay on Godard's use of sound, Alan Williams discusses several uses of language other than conversation. Williams goes on to discuss how Godard's films upset the usual hierarchy whereby manipulation of sound is relatively "transparent." He suggests that Godard's aversion to directional microphones and postproduction refining of individual sound tracks results in a sound track somewhat analogous to the Bazinian ideal of "long takes with great depth of field." For Williams, Godard's sound tracks demonstrate the ways in which sounds can act independently not only of the image but of one another. In short, Godard's work represents a veritable compendium of the possibilities of sound.

Orson Welles's Use of Sound
PENNY MINTZ

Sound and space are immutably related whether they complement one another or, as is often the case in the movies of Orson Welles, they conflict.
Welles's early films, especially *Citizen Kane*, were remarkable for the way in
which sound was used to elongate space. The screen was forced to give up
part of the flatness of its nature. In later films sound is put to a variety of
uses, not the least of which is a negation of reality. What we hear no longer
works in conjunction with what we see. Eisenstein might have called it har-
monized counterpoint. The sound is temporally synchronized with its source,
but at the same time mismatched in terms of space (that is, apparent distance and surroundings). As a result there is a tension created between the
space and the sound; between our aural and visual perceptions. If this tension remains unresolved, a partial fragmenting of our senses takes place.
Sound becomes disembodied and takes on a force and presence of its own.

Every time a movie is projected on that screen in front of us we
relinquish part of the power we have over our psyches. The narrative film
invites us to participate in a fantasy, and to a certain extent we always do.
The creative artist is able to take advantage of the vulnerable position in which
the moving-picture medium places its audience, in order to present a previously unavailable experience. Orson Welles is such an artist. He gains control over our ability to organize the barrage of stimuli that is constantly assaulting us. A careful study of *Citizen Kane, The Magnificent Ambersons,
The Lady from Shanghai,* and *Touch of Evil* reveals a progression toward
manipulation of the viewer's powers of concentration, his visual and aural
perception, and disorientation of his spatial and temporal organization.

If there is a progression toward fragmentation and disorientation
in these four films of Welles it is not to be found within the narratives. In
these four movies the narratives move away from fragmentation toward
consolidation in terms of time, place, and structure. *Kane* moves forward
and backward through time and space; it covers perhaps three generations
(Kane's lifetime). While *The Magnificent Ambersons* is composed of a number of glimpses of moments just before and during Georgie Amberson's life,
with an intensive examination of one experience (his reaction to the Mor-
gans), the narrative is limited to a forward movement in time, and the action

takes place within the perimeters of one small city. The geographic area covered in *The Lady from Shanghai* is quite extensive, but in a dramatic sense the narrative movement is more limited than it would be if it took place within the confines of a small town. The drama's settings are forced upon the hero, first as an employee, then as a prisoner. He doesn't have the freedom that Georgie and Kane are allowed. In addition, temporal and structural elements are incontestably consolidated. There is a beginning, a middle, and an end, with a climax and a denouement—all of which takes place within one year. Finally, *Touch of Evil* is the most compact of all. Its narrative is so tightly interconnected it unravels rather than unfolds. It is wholly contained within a twenty-four-hour period, and all the action takes place around one point on the Mexican-American border.

Disorientation is accomplished not within the narrative structures of the films but by fragmentation of our perceptions and manipulation of our responses. In order to understand how this comes about, it is necessary to have a clear conception of the role that sound has played in the history of film, and particularly of the processes of aural perception.

There are three basic modes of cinematic sound: spatial sound, ideational sound, and music. Everything we hear either falls into one of these categories or is a combination of two or more of them.

Spatial sounds obey the laws of real sound. Our ears place the source of the sound within space. We are not limited, aurally, as we are visually, by the flat screen. If the sound track of a movie accurately conforms to the behavior of natural sound in space, we receive aural cues which determine distance, direction, and, to a certain extent, the surroundings of the source. The result is a definition of space—a substantially less illusionary sense of depth.

Surroundings are determined by volume and quality of sound. For example, a sound emitting from a closet full of clothing will be appreciably different in quality from the identical sound emitting from a cave. Compare the quality of Kane's voice in the halls of Xanadu to that of his voice in the car on the way to the picnic. The reason for this difference is that various objects absorb and reflect different amounts and frequencies of sound. It follows, then, that noise heard from inside a room will not sound exactly like the same noise heard from the other side of a glass partition, or a closed door—a variation Welles carefully manipulates when Quinlin enters the hotel room to strangle Joe Grandi in *Touch of Evil.*

The reason I have concerned myself with something that seems so obvious is that when this factor is ignored, or purposely used to distort the duplication of real sound, the mismatch makes us vaguely uncomfortable, slightly dislocated, usually without our knowing why. The reaction is very subtle. A sort of floating tension is created that can be used, by the filmmaker, in directing audience response. Welles uses this device, in *The Lady from Shanghai* and *Touch of Evil*, but leaves the tension unresolved. The voices in the postexplosion confusion in *Evil*, for example, sound as if they were being emitted within a confined area, but the scene takes place in the open air. The disembodied quality that the voices have as a result sets a pattern that is reinforced throughout the movie. It has the effect of partially disorganizing our perceptions: the visuals and aurals don't fit.

Direction is understood biaurally. Our ears are incredibly sensitive: we can detect a time difference between the two ears, if the onset of the sound is sharp, of 0.65 milliseconds. This, coupled with an appreciation of the minute difference in volume due to the sound shadow the head casts, and one ear catching the sound wave at a different point in its compression-rarefaction phases, accounts for the accuracy with which we determine direction. Unfortunately, the closest we can come to experiencing it in the (monaural) cinema is by interpreting visual cues. We know where a voice is coming from because we see the speaker's lips moving. If the source of sound is outside our visual field we follow the gaze or reaction of a character on the screen.

Distancing is the one aural space-defining factor of which all filmmakers are aware. That's not to say that they use it properly. Amplitude increases as the source of sound moves toward us, but because there are so many variables in sound production, and because of our poor aural storage and/or retrieval systems, we aren't able to make any more than a crude approximation of absolute distance. That's why movies, which have all their dialogue varying from close-up to medium shot, do not expend much effort modulating the volume as the camera or characters move.

Sound, then, opens up and makes us aware of space. The accurate and the creative uses of volume alone have the effect of giving depth to the flat screen image. Using sound in this way was one of the most impressive innovations of *Kane* and is also prominent in *Ambersons*. There may be no scene in the history of film that is more two-dimensional than the good-bye at the train station between Georgie Amberson and his uncle. Visually, we perceive depth on a flat surface by certain cues such as lines diminishing to a vanishing point, objects in the distance getting smaller, objects cut off by others in front of them, etc. In this scene, with the two men surrounded by a mist, there are no visual cues—so there is really no feeling for depth until the older man turns and walks diagonally across the screen. Even then, it is only the sound of his receding footsteps that gives us a sense of space.

Welles was not satisfied with merely defining space. In *Shanghai* and *Evil* he deliberately undermines space perception by mismatching the sound and its source. The roar of the jalopies is heard in close-up long before they approach the motel in *Evil*. In the middle of an intimate scene between Mike and Elsa in *Shanghai*, Grisby's voice intrudes in close-up while the sound of the launch he is in is distanced correctly. Grisby is nowhere near the couple. In fact, his voice always seems a little too loud, a little too close. The sound takes on a presence of its own.

Welles goes beyond undermining aural reality. By substituting and confusing sound with its reproduction and objects with their reflections, silhouettes, and shadows, Welles manages to separate sound from its source, and from space. By the end of *Shanghai* we have no idea from what direction the sound is coming. By the end of *Evil* we have not only lost all sense of distance and direction, we are also confused about the source itself. Quinlan's and Menzies's voices physically separate from their bodies, as the sound track is taken, in part, from a small receiver/tape recorder that is picking up transmissions from a concealed microphone carried by Menzies. We hear the voices in tinny close-up, off the radio receiver, at the same time we see the two men moving in the distance.

At one point, as they are crossing the bridge into Mexico, sound becomes directly involved in its own dissociation from its source. Quinlan hears the echo of the recording of his voice, a sound which is twice removed from the filmic reality, but which has a central place within the narrative. It leads directly to Menzies's death. We don't see the actual shooting—we only experience it secondhand, through sound. We don't even hear it directly. We see a close-up of the tape as it records and plays the events that are going on above, on the bridge. Moments later, we hear the playback, with the camera again focused on the recorder. This repeat is no different from our first experience, and no more closely related to real filmic space, time, or character.

The fragmentation of the relationship between a sound and its source is such a dominating feature throughout *Evil* that we don't even notice all sorts of anomalies in sound, space, and narrative. We don't find it peculiar for Vargas to turn his back on the blind lady so that she won't hear him telephoning his wife; nor are we disturbed by the fact that he doesn't hear Suzy's shouts from the hotel fire escape, even though we hear her voice booming across the crowd that has gathered below her, and through which he drives in search of her. His visual and aural dislocations aren't questioned because our own are so pronounced.

Most of the time the kinds of sounds that define space are sound effects and background noise. Straight dialogue usually draws and holds our attention away from the spatial dimension: we are more concerned with what is being said than the relationship between the source and space. Dialogue has the effect of taking us out of space and placing us in the realm of ideas. The transition is completed by the sound editor's toning done of background noise. Normally, we have the ability to disregard distracting stimuli and focus our attention on whatever we choose. Cinema usurps that power. It may be the speed at which images are presented, or the rapidity with which we are shifted about in time and space, but whatever the cause there is a pronounced impairment of our ability to tune out surrounding stimuli and the sound editor has to do it for us. Reintroducing or increasing the level of these effects takes us back to the spatial dimension. Our attention is caught by the aural change and the switch is made.

This gives us a whole new perspective for appreciating the courtroom sequence in *Shanghai*. Welles has no intention of allowing us to focus on the trial proceedings. Thus, he makes escape to the ideational difficult by constantly reintroducing spatial elements. Coughing and whispering in the jury box are typical of this effort, as are the cutaways to audience reactions. The first few times Welles cuts away, he synchronizes the cut with sound. The later cutaways have no track but they have a noisy effect. We can almost hear the rustling. When Elsa finally admits to having kissed O'Hara in the aquarium, the camera does not cut away, but we hear the silence and feel the weight of the courtroom bearing down on her.

If conversation takes us out of space, what is the effect of narration? The narrator is twice removed from spatial reality. Not only are his words ideational, consequently flattening the screen image, but his intrusion upon the story reminds us of the unreality of the whole filmic experience. The result is a reflexivity that is increased by Welles's deliberate flouting of narrative convention. The narrator is supposed to set the scene, and perhaps fill in some background, but it is clearly against the "rules" for his words to be synchronized to the character's lips. " 'Fine weather we're having,' I said to break the ice," says O'Hara, *as narrator*, over a medium close-up of O'Hara walking and talking beside Elsa's carriage. Convention dictates that we already be within the scene. The character can, and should, speak his own lines. Anything that goes against a convention (and our expectation) calls attention to itself and reflects on the medium that has promulgated that convention. We end up, momentarily, conscious of the film as a vehicle of fantasy.

There are a number of forms narration can take. Welles apparently prefers to fade the narrator out during the first quarter of the film and then in again toward the end. He uses this method in both *Ambersons* and *Shanghai*. This would ordinarily leave a large center portion virtually without moments of reflexivity. Welles lets this happen in *Ambersons*, but in *Shanghai* and *Evil*, where there is no narrator at all, Welles regularly forces us to become aware of the film as a medium by manipulating our expectations of musical convention.

Background music in a Hollywood movie sometimes has its source within the ongoing scene; usually it is just mood music added in the sound mix. It is never supposed to compete for our attention. Such is not the case in *Shanghai* or *Evil*. Typically, the music and the visuals start out simultaneously, with the music belonging in the background. All of a sudden we are made to realize that the music is *real* music within the film's narrative. It eventually slips back into the background. The first shot after Elsa's singing scene in *Shanghai* is of Elsa sunning herself on the ship's deck. O'Hara is at the wheel. On the sound track is brassy popular music of the forties. It is brought to our attention because it is loud and incongruous with the rather idyllic visual. Suddenly the music stops, and a disc jockey starts to talk. It is only Elsa's radio. The disc jockey goes off, and soft music comes on. This becomes background music that is toned down when Elsa and O'Hara begin to talk.

In an earlier scene in the same film, a jukebox and its music is brought to our attention when the record ends. Goldy turns to a waiter and says, "Would you put these in crank number four? That's all we want to listen to." After this, the music returns to its place in the background until it is again referred to in the conversation. By constantly surprising us with new methods of presenting this pattern—from background to foreground—the effect remains fresh. The music has been brought to our attention and has served the movie reflexively.

In *Evil* our awareness of music is so intense that it takes on an ideational quality. We respond to it directly rather than to the mood it creates. The volume and persistence of the irritating music in the motel scenes invades our consciousness much as it does Suzy's. It is a pervasive force in her presence and seeps into Vargas's as well by way of his car radio, but it belongs by association to the teenage hoodlums. This isn't the only association of character and music that exists in the film. Mexican nightclub music belongs to Joe Grandi and player-piano to Tanya, the Marlene Dietrich character. Most of the time, although not always, these sounds also conform to spatial limitations. There are times when what had been real music swells to reinforce a climax in the narrative, and other times, especially with the player-piano music, when the sound is toned down under conversation that is put into aural foreground.

Music, dialogue, effects, or any other type of aural signal can also be used ideationally, as a transitional element when the narrative is moving through time and/or space. When *Shanghai*'s Elsa leaves the nightclub in Acapulco, the orchestra music follows her and continues, reduced to a single guitar, when she meets O'Hara. In *Kane* Susan's singing in the parlor is heard, without a lapse, over the dissolve which moves us to the parlor at a later date. Then Kane's applause turns into light clapping heard behind Leland's campaign speech. Leland's voice in turn becomes Kane's heard over the microphone in a large auditorium.

The transitions between scenes become tighter across the four movies. In *Evil* almost every scene has some element to bridge the gap to the next. Grandi's nephew decides to call his uncle for instructions, and we cut away from him at the phone to Quinlan and Grandi in a bar. A few seconds later the telephone in the background rings. We leave these two men when Grandi puts a coin in the jukebox, a machine whose music is associated with the Grandi boys, who are at the motel, where rock and roll is being piped into Suzy's room.

The transitions in *Shanghai* are not as tight as they are in *Evil*, and in *Ambersons* they are rarely anything but straight cuts. In *Kane* the aural equivalents of match dissolves are used in conjunction with visual dissolves to move us across spatial-temporal coordinates, but the process is different in the later films. In *Kane* the sound is a device used to make the transition smoothly. In *Evil* an element integral to one scene is present in, and brings us to, the next.

Spatial definition is one of two perceptual contributions to the aural experience. The other is an attention-focusing mechanism. We are perpetually surrounded by noise, but we are only aware of part of it. The rest is toned down by our mental processes and remains on a lower level of consciousness. Generally, our attention is drawn to an object that is producing sound, especially if it is moving or given visual prominence in some other way. There is an interesting maneuver in *Shanghai* that manipulates and moves our attention by changing only what we hear. As Elsa enters the courtoom, we follow her movement down the aisle. On the sound track we hear the noise that surrounds her. The camera stops as she finds a row with a seat, but the sound continues forward, carrying our attention with it, away from Elsa to the courtroom proceedings at the far end of the room. These are sounds that were previously unheard.

Loud or unremitting sounds force themselves on our attention, as in the motel scenes in *Evil*. Any change in volume or quality also attracts our attention, so we could be diverted by a new sound, especially if it is coming from outside our visual field. This probably stems from a survival instinct: anything that makes a noise within hearing distance is a possible threat, especially if we were previously unaware of its presence, and we respond involuntarily to such a stimulus. This reaction is used in *Ambersons* as a means of splitting our attention. We watch the grandfather, in close-up, contemplating death while we listen to a discussion of the estate Isabel has left. In another scene, we are paying attention to Fanny and Georgie arguing when, from off-screen, comes the voice of the Ray Collins character complaining about noise and finally saying, "I'm going to move to a hotel."

Welles is extremely conscious of the mechanisms of attention. Early in *Kane* there is a scene of Thompson, the reporter, after his unsuccessful attempt to interview Susan. Just before he leaves, he makes a call from a telephone booth in the extreme foreground. He should be the center of attention, as we usually attend to that which is producing a sound. Furthermore, he is close to us and heard in aural close-up. The nightclub music is in the background, partially shut out when he closes the door. Nevertheless, a substantial portion of our attention is drawn away from the sound, through the left window of the phone-booth door, and across the room to Susan where she slumps in a pool of light. If sound attracts our attention, so does light. The result is that we are unable to focus completely on either one of the stimuli presented to us. In this case the two are compatible: the telephone call concerns Susan. Furthermore, one is completely visual and the other is completely aural, as Thompson stands in a shadow. There isn't too much competition between them. In *Shanghai* and especially in *Evil*, there is often so much confusion and competition among the elements within the frame that the audience finds itself unable to organize and process all the information. Consider the scene immediately after the explosion in *Evil*. There are a great many people, all being introduced to one another and to us, talking and milling about. Characters critical to the narrative pop onto the scene and, just as quickly, disappear. Welles doesn't give us any indication as to what we should pay attention to. The result is a diffusion of our faculties—and a feeling of relief when we finally leave with Vargas's wife.

In a later scene the fragmenting is done somewhat more delicately. In the scene where Vargas is talking on the blind woman's telephone, his turning away does bring sound to our attention. We think about what an unnecessary movement he has made. By calling attention to itself, it works reflexively. At the same time, another part of our attention is drawn out the window, where we see Menzies and Grandi. These two characters are seen in long shot, fussing and arguing with one another. The elements in this example, and in the previous one, work against each other to split our focusing abilities.

When Welles does give us something to concentrate on in *Shanghai* and *Evil*, it is often something that seems peripheral to the narrative. The water glass and pills in *Shanghai* are forced on us well before they play any part in the narrative. Similarly, in *Evil*, the camera is on Vargas while Quinlan interrogates his suspect after having "found" the dynamite. It's a critical moment until we realize that it's Vargas's reaction to the shoebox that's important. We are continually left mildly disconcerted and dislocated by the conflicting demands on our attention.

Welles doesn't limit himself to physiological means when it comes to playing with our perceptions. He takes advantage of other, more complex social responses. We can't help but attend to Bannister as he laboriously leaves the witness stand in *Shanghai*. How often are we allowed to stare unabashedly at someone who is crippled? We are hardly aware of the summoning of his wife to the stand, even though the prosecuting attorney, who requests permission to call Elsa from the audience, is standing in the extreme foreground. There's also the ringing telephone in the judge's chambers as O'Hara fights to get away. That's a sound to which we have a conditioned response, and Welles uses that response to ensure our diversion— and to prompt a certain building up of tension, which is turned to comic relief when the judge reacts for us and answers the phone.

Persons suffering from schizophrenia complain of being bombarded by sensations, and a lack of control over their consciousness. Paranoid types often believe that outside forces have taken over their thought processes. Such claims would not be totally irrational for the moviegoer— especially if he's watching a movie by Welles. In such a situation his perception of reality is torn apart. Sound no longer defines space. Unable to focus his attention, he becomes dislocated within the narrative. If art is a reexperiencing of our mental and emotional conditions within a new context, Orson Welles is one of the world's supreme artists.

The Evolution of Hitchcock's Aural Style and Sound in *The Birds*

ELISABETH WEIS

In a famous attack on Hitchcock's work, Penelope Houston complained that in *The Birds* "most of the menace [comes] from the electronic sound track to cover the fact that the birds are not really doing their stuff." [1] In the second half of this essay I shall argue that the great reliance on sound effects in *The Birds* is not only an aesthetic strength but a logical outgrowth of Hitchcock's creative development at that point in his career. But I cite Miss Houston's comment here for its representative implication that Hitchcock's use of film sound is a "poor relation" to his manipulation of the image. The belief that aural techniques are a means of expression inferior to visual ones is shared by most film scholars, and, indeed, by many filmmakers. Insofar as most directors do not realize the potential of the sound track, sound is indeed a secondary component. But there are enough glorious exceptions— Hitchcock's films among them— to prove that sound can be an equal partner to the image.

Hitchcock himself appears to have accepted the bias against sound in defining "pure film" as film that expresses its meaning visually—specifically through montage. [2] But a close examination of his statements reveals that he is objecting not to sound but to an excessive reliance on dialogue. He told Truffaut, for example, "In many of the films now being made, there is very little cinema: they are mostly what I call 'photographs of people talking.' When we tell a story in cinema, we should resort to dialogue only when it's impossible to do otherwise." [3] Hitchcock's condemnation of static dialogue sequences does not include sound effects or music. His often-stated goal is to hold the audience's fullest attention, and to this end he will apply whatever techniques seem most effective for his purposes. In his desire to maintain close control over his audience's reactions he never overlooked the possibilities inherent in the sound track.

From the time of his first sound films, Hitchcock treats sound as a new dimension of cinematic expression. He hardly ever uses it redundantly but rather as an additional resource. Indeed, he was actually very proud of his control over the sound track. As he told Truffaut, "After a picture is cut, I dictate what amounts to a real sound script to a secretary. We run every reel off and I indicate all the places where sounds should be heard."⁴ Such attention to sound is rare in commercial filmmaking. Most American directors leave all but a few important decisions to their editors and sound editors.⁵ Of course, the proof of Hitchcock's claim about control of the sound track does not lie in his words but in his films. Close analysis of his work reveals a consistent aural style, one that is inseparable from his visual style and ultimately inseparable from his meaning.

To appreciate Hitchcock's attitude toward sound it is necessary to understand the conventional way sound is handled. In the Hollywood studio tradition the film sound track is divided among three categories: dialogue, sound effects, and music. These categories reflect a literal separation of the sound elements on discrete tapes or tracks that is maintained until the three sets of tracks are combined at the final mix, where each of three specialists controls one type of track.

Despite the studio tradition of separating the three sound tracks, Hitchcock does not conceive of them as separate entities. One distinctive element of his aural style is a continuity in his use of language, music, and sound effects that reflects his ability to conceive of their combined impact before he actually hears them together. Nor does Hitchcock take for granted the conventional functions of a given track; there is an intermingling of their functions in many instances. In three films where Hitchcock eliminates scoring, for example, he uses sound effects to much the same atmospheric effect: wind in *Jamaica Inn*, waves in *Lifeboat*, bird caws in *The Birds*. As I explain below, if in *The Birds* avian noises imitate the functions of music (instead of musical cues, bird cries maintain the tension), in *Psycho* music (screeching violins) imitates birds at various points.

This intersection of effects extends to Hitchcock's use of the dialogue track. Although Hitchcock played a large part in the creation of the screenplay, his films show less creative interest in the dialogue per se than in such noncognitive forms of human expression as screaming and laughter. Their value as sound effects is usually as important as their significance as human utterances. With typical perversity Hitchcock can find something healthy in a scream and something sinister in laughter. For example, in both versions of *The Man Who Knew Too Much* a scream saves a life; in *Rear Window*, James Stewart's scream for help finally acknowledges a previously resisted dependence on others. By contrast, laughter, the last sound in *Blackmail*, is associated with the heroine's feelings of guilt.

Similarly, Hitchcock often pays less attention to what a character says than to how he says it. A person's actual words are less significant than his definition as glib or taciturn, voluble or quiet. One central motif is silence, which confers (negative) moral values on a character associated with it. A character's avoidance of speech may be a symptom of ruthless efficiency, emotional immaturity, or moral paralysis. Thus, villains who murder noiselessly, heroes afraid to express their love, and heroines who conceal evidence of a crime are all related in the Hitchcockian scheme.[6]

If human utterances sometimes function more like sound effects, conversely, Hitchcockian sound effects may function more like language. Hitchcock often ascribed very precise meanings to his effects. He told one interviewer: "To describe a sound effect accurately, one has to imagine its equivalent in dialogue."[7]

Hitchcockian music, too, is interesting less as a separate entity than for its connections with other aspects of the film. Film music is traditionally divided between source music (music that supposedly originates from a sound source on the screen) and scoring (background music unacknowledged by characters within the film itself but accepted as a movie convention). Hitchcock's filming inspired a number of brilliant scores. However, it is both problematic and misleading to analyze scoring as an integral part of Hitchcock's aural style. For Hitchcock, as for other directors, the composition of the music is the aspect of filmmaking over which he had least control.

Much more valid in an analysis of Hitchcock's aural style than a study of the scoring for his films is a study of his attitude toward source music. Like such other masters of sound as Renoir and Godard, Hitchcock had an abiding interest in finding ways to incorporate music into the very heart of his plot. Indeed, music is an essential component of the story in over half of his sound films, and eight of his protagonists are musicians. He can thus manipulate the audience's familiarity with and expectations about popular music as a way of defining character and controlling our responses without having to introduce any extraneous element. Hitchcock turns a piece of music into a motif that he handles like his other recurring aural or visual images. He loves to yoke music with murder. Think of the Albert Hall climax of *The Man Who Knew Too Much* or the association of villains with innocent tunes in *Shadow of a Doubt* ("The Merry Widow Waltz") and *Strangers on a Train* ("The Band Played On"). By using source music Hitchcock had control over the music because it was available before production, unlike scoring, which is normally written only after the composer has seen a rough cut of the film.

If one distinctive attribute of Hitchcock's sound track is the frequent intersection of the functions of the sound effects, music, and dialogue tracks, his sound track is also distinctively contrapuntal to the visuals. That is to say, the sounds and images rarely duplicate and often contrast with each other. During a Hitchcock film we are typically looking at one thing or person while listening to another. By separating sound and image Hitchcock can thus achieve variety, denseness, tension, and, on occasion, irony.

It is possible to generalize about Hitchcock's overall aural style because many elements of it remain relatively constant and distinctive. It is also possible to distinguish several different aural styles within his oeuvre. To some extent, these various styles correspond with chronological periods in Hitchcock's career, and they also correspond roughly with his visual styles during those periods.

The most important shift of style in Hitchcock's films involves a move from expressionism toward greater realism. From the beginning of his career until about 1966 Hitchcock became more and more interested in audience involvement. He moved toward realism in an attempt to increase audience identification through his protagonists, an emotional identification that depended to an extent on a relative invisibility of technique. Not surprisingly, the biggest shift in his career came in his move in 1939 from England to Hollywood, where the American predilection for stylistic realism matched his own interests. (In subject matter the American films are in many ways less realistic than the finely observed films about English behavior, but that is another matter.) The bigger budgets and technical expertise available to Hitchcock in American studios enabled him to switch to a style less dependent on such techniques as miniatures and editing that are more distracting even to the untrained eye than are full-scale sets and lengthy tracking shots. In his British films Hitchcock often resorts to both aural and visual expressionistic effects in moments when he wants to reveal the feelings of his characters. In his American films Hitchcock uses sound as a way out of visual expressionism. His distortions of sound draw less attention to his style than would their visual equivalents because audiences are less likely to notice aural than visual distortions.

In his American films Hitchcock generally works harder to establish connections between the audience and his characters. Whereas his British villains are likely to be overtly insane or criminal characters, in the American films the audience is forced to identify with the evil impulses in relatively attractive and normal people. Hitchcock in America is interested in the malevolence of so-called normality and in destroying audience complacency by making the viewer complicitous with evildoers. In order to force the identification between character and viewer he has to move the audience inside the minds of his characters without resorting to distracting techniques. Thus Hitchcock paradoxically gives up expressionism, a film style originally developed to penetrate a character's mind, when he is most seriously interested in exploring the psyche.

Tom Gunning has referred to the shift from the British to the American films as "a shift from melodrama to psychodrama"—a shift in focus from external events to a character's mind.[8] Gunning's distinction implies a lessening in distancing devices in the American films. In the American psychodramas events may be just as melodramatic, but the exaggerations of technique or plot are motivated within the context of the films because they are presented as the perceptions of one or another character. It is the character whose perceptions are melodramatic, not Hitchcock, and thus he can present the most outrageous situations or characters without worrying about their verisimilitude. The most exaggerated techniques function as a realistic re-presentation of a character's perception.

The manipulations of sound in Hitchcock's earliest sound films, by contrast, are quite openly experimental. In *Blackmail* and *Murder* Hitchcock can be observed trying both to overcome the technical obstacles of early sound shooting and to establish his personal attitudes toward the relation between sound and picture. Most of the experiments are in the expressionistic mode, the two most famous examples being the subjective distortion of the word "knife" in *Blackmail* and the interior monologue in *Murder*. Both experiments are attempts to convey a character's thoughts and feelings. Yet at the same time both techniques draw attention to themselves as tricks and leave the audience emotionally outside the characters. In the British films that followed, Hitchcock continues to experiment with expressionistic sound techniques, but with one exception the techniques tend to be bravura effects in films that are otherwise less interested in penetrating the psyches of their main characters. The exception is *Secret Agent,* the film in which Hitchcock most consistently sought to use expressionistic techniques to convey the feelings of his protagonists. *Secret Agent* is the British film in which aural techniques clearly predominated over most other considerations when Hitchcock was planning the film. (In order to convey his heroine's sense of guilt here, Hitchcock used everything from distorted sound, to sound collages, to sound that bleeds into different scenes, to subliminal sound.)

At about the point when Hitchcock settled down to make a series of widely acclaimed films at the Gaumont studios, he consolidated his treatment into what might be called his classical style—a term chosen because it implies an apparent simplicity of form, an art that conceals art. Starting with *The Man Who Knew Too Much* (1934) Hitchcock found ways of building less obtrusive aural ideas into the very conception of his screenplay. In both versions of that film, for example, the heroine's need to scream during a concert represents a concrete embodiment of a central tension running through many of his films: the problem of how to reconcile the need for personal expression with the need for social order.

Whereas the Gaumont films combine a relatively invisible, classical style with occasional outbursts of expressionism, by contrast, the American films operate in a more fluid, consistent style. Most of the American films of the 1940s and 1950s can be called subjective films because in them Hitchcock is concerned with presenting characters and events through the distorted interpretation of one character. In a subjective film Hitchcock may never bother to provide an objective alternative to the way things are presented. The quintessential subjective films are *Rebecca, Suspicion,* and *Rear Window.* When Mrs. Danvers has no footfall in *Rebecca,* that is because the heroine perceives her as somewhat less or more than human.

Hitchcock takes subjectivity one step further in four American films made between 1943 and 1954 in which he experiments with highly restricted space. In *Lifeboat, Rope, Dial M for Murder,* and *Rear Window,* Hitchcock limits himself to a single set. Having established such stringent visual limitations, Hitchcock uses sound in a highly creative way, often depending on it to establish tension. In other films Hitchcock often creates tension between what is in frame and what is out of frame. In the single-set films he creates tension between on-set and off-set space. People outside the room (or, in one case, boat) are a source of either menace or salvation. And in all of the single-set films but *Lifeboat,* Hitchcock suggests that on-set space may be subjective while noises from off-set space represent reality. The use of what might be called "aural intrusion" as a metaphor for the penetration of the psyche by this reality is a distinctive component of Hitchcock's style.

It is possible to argue that *The Birds* continues the subjective tradition in which aural intrusion plays an essential role. But I find that in *The Birds* Hitchcock moves beyond audience identification with any character. And just as there is no sole victim whose perceptions we share, there is no single source of fear that can be attributed to a mere misrepresentation of reality. In *The Birds* Hitchcock deals abstractly with fear itself, rather than with any particular manifestation of it. He does give shape to these fears in the form of birds, but the birds are less important for what they are than for the reactions they elicit. And *The Birds* is especially dependent on sound because of the nonspecific quality of sound effects.

Indeed, *The Birds,* together with *Secret Agent* and *Rear Window,* is one of the three most important Hitchcock films for sound. Its sound track deserves some extended analysis because it is the film in which Hitchcock combines the greatest interest in controlling sound with the greatest technical capacity to do so. Hitchcock's emphasis on sound effects is indicated by the fact that he forgoes background music in *The Birds* for the first time since *Lifeboat* twenty years earlier.[9] (In both cases, the starkness of the scoreless sound track emphasizes the vulnerability of a human community in a hostile natural environment.) *The Birds* is also Hitchcock's most stylized sound track—it is composed from a constant interplay of natural sounds and computer-generated bird noises. The particular emphasis on the sound track at this point in Hitchcock's career would seem to have resulted from two converging developments, one technical, one artistic.

The technical development was the new sophistication of electronic sound. According to Donald Spoto, "All the bird noises were devised by Bernard Herrmann, Remi Gassman, and Oskar Sala on an electronic instrument called the Trautonium . . . with which every noise and effect was orchestrated, every sound filtered and altered to support the feeling Hitchcock wanted in each scene."[10] "Until now," Hitchcock told Truffaut, "we've worked with natural sounds, but now, thanks to electronic sound, I'm not only going to indicate the sound we want but also the style and the nature of each sound."[11] Such an interest in new technical challenges was, of course, characteristic of the director who experimented with synchronized sound, elaborate camera movement, and 3-D as soon as each became available to him. Indeed, the challenge of mastering a new technology provided a major creative stimulus for Hitchcock.

The personal artistic development involves Hitchcock's interest from about 1958 to 1963 in going *beyond* point-of-view shots identified with a given character, an interest begun in *Vertigo,* developed in *Psycho,* and culminating in *The Birds.* In these three films, the director seeks most seriously to touch directly the fears of the audience.[12] They are his least detached, most unsettling and haunting films. These films introduce terror through the experience of a character with whom we identify, but then Hitchcock removes the surrogate and we experience the sensation more directly. At the end of *The Birds* the characters may or may not have escaped their assailants, but the audience is left behind, in a world where the birds—which represent any terrifying, uncontrollable forces—have prevailed.

When Hitchcock aims toward direct audience involvement, he often shifts from a dependence on the visuals to a greater dependence on aural techniques. In *Vertigo* the emphasis is still visual; the sensation of vertigo is created most specifically through computer-generated designs for the titles and later through shots that combine tracking out with zooming forward. To be sure, Herrmann's score, with its hypnotic arpeggios, is important, but it is part of an overall effect and not dominant during Hitchcock's vertigo-producing sequences. In *Psycho* the scoring generally maintains the tension in moments of relative tranquillity. But during the killings the music picks up the visual motif of birds as predators; violins are scraped during the three attacks to sound like shrieking birds. Sound and visual effects work together to provide three of Hitchcock's most terrifying sequences. (That the scoring alone is not so terrifying is indicated by the fact that on the fourth occasion when the violins shriek—during Norman's run down from the house after Marion's murder—the audience does not cringe in terror.)

A crucial aspect of the *Psycho* scoring is that the shrieking not only associates Norman with his stuffed birds of prey but also associates the viewers with the on-screen victims. That is to say, the cries of the victims, the screeches of the violins, and the screams of the audience merge indistinguishably during violent sequences. The distinction between screen victim and audience is broken down. By contrast, in the subjective films the violent sequences (such as the cornfield attack in *North by Northwest* or the struggle on the carousel in *Strangers on a Train*) rarely elicit screams. But the attacks in *Psycho* almost always incite the audience, and Hitchcock has guaranteed these screams by inserting them into the sound track to prime the viewer's response. During Norman's attack on Lila there are screams added to the violin shrieks that may or may not be attributed to Norman or Lila. It does not matter who makes them. The moment is one of abject terror for attacker, victim, and viewer alike.

If each attack in *Psycho* evokes such strong identification between victim and viewer, how then does Hitchcock move beyond identification with the characters to more direct audience involvement? The impact derives from the severity of the attacks plus the interchangeability of the victims. The viewer suffers more intensely and more often in *Psycho* than he has in past Hitchcock films. But because the viewer survives the attacks of each character with whom he had identified, he begins to feel a generalized terror dissociated from any specific victim.

By the time of *The Birds*, screeches are even more important than the visuals for terrorizing the audience during attacks. Indeed, bird sounds sometimes replace visuals altogether. Moreover, Hitchcock carefully manipulates the sound track so that the birds can convey terror even when they are silent or just making an occasional caw or flutter. As Truffaut points out, "The bird sounds are worked out like a real musical score."[13] Instead of orchestrated instruments there are orchestrated sound effects. Thus in *Psycho* music sounds like birds, while in *The Birds* bird sounds function like music. Hitchcock even eliminates music under the opening titles in favor of bird sounds. And once Hitchcock has established the birds as a menace, he controls suspense simply by manipulating the sounds of flapping and bird cries that recur quite systematically for the rest of the film. At any point in the film a bird noise can be introduced naturally, so Hitchcock has a means of controlling tension that is effective and unobtrusive—even less noticeable than music would be. Of course, he also introduces birds visually, but the audience is much more conscious of their appearances than of their sounds. To introduce a bird visually without an attack is to tease the audience with a red herring, and so Hitchcock cannot manipulate the visuals as freely for suspense as he does the sound track.

One reason the sound effects in *The Birds* directly touch the fears of the audience is that they are relatively abstract—especially the bird cries. It is probably the abstract stridency of bird cries that accounts for their appeal to Hitchcock in *Blackmail* (Alice's chirping canary), *Sabotage* (a saboteur's bird shop), *Young and Innocent* (the sound and sight of shrieking seagulls that precede the disclosure of the corpse), and *Psycho* (the violin shrieks).

(I do not include some mewing seagulls heard in *Under Capricorn* or *Jamaica Inn* because Hitchcock uses the sound there not for emotional resonance but simply for atmosphere, as any director might.) Since the bird cries are partly computer-generated in *The Birds,* that sound is particularly non-specific, as is the electronic flutter that indicates the flapping of wings. The bird sounds are often so stylized that if the visual source were not provided, the sounds could not be identified. The effect of the resulting ambiguity is to universalize the noises.

The bird sounds are all the more abstract and terrifying when they come from unseen sources. As in many a horror film, the enemy is most threatening when invisible. Perhaps the film's most frightening attack is the sixth, in which only a bird or two is seen. Mitch has boarded up the windows of his house. (Ironically, his hammering, which is heard before it is seen, sounds like the tapping of beaks, a dominant noise during the attack.) The situation is claustrophobic: as the human victims listen to and fight off the assault, they realize that the home is as much a trap as a protection. The attack's end is signaled by the receding of bird noises. Meanwhile the audience has felt as threatened as the characters. By keeping the menace aural rather than visual Hitchcock has once more broken down the barrier between audience and screen. The theater and the living room have seemed one continuous space—one continuous trap. If this were the only attack, *The Birds* would be a subjective film (from Melanie's perspective). But the attacks are not restricted to any character's private space.

There is a second scene in which the bird noises clearly are more menacing than the sight of them alone. William Pechter describes the shift in mood: "In one of the most amazing images of the film, we suddenly see the town, now burning in destruction, in a view from great aerial elevation; from this perspective, one sees everything as part of a vast design, and the scene of chaos appears almost peaceful, even beautiful; then, gradually the silence gives way to the flapping of wings and the birds' awful shrieking, and the image, without losing its beauty, is filled with terror as well." [14] We can distinguish the added effect of the sound because it is introduced later than the visuals and changes the mood of the shot. It is significant to the viewer's response that the sequence begins from Melanie's point of view but shifts with the overhead shot to the apparently safe persepctive of the birds themselves. At first we feel relief at our emotional removal from the holocaust below, but with the introduction of the terrifying screams we soon feel that even this space is threatening; there is no place where we can feel secure.

Another reason *The Birds* is so unsettling is that there is no apparent logic or predictability to the birds' attack. (Hitchcock said, "I made sure that the public would not be able to anticipate from one scene to another.") [15] Hitchcock promotes that unpredictability by carefully shifting between whether we first see or hear the birds. The choice depends on whether he wants suspense or surprise for the attack. The first attack is made by one gull on Melanie as she drives a motorboat. The gull enters the frame well before Hitchcock adds the sound of wings or the bird's screech. He has now established suspense; after having been surprised the first time, we now know that the birds can strike without warning. Any bird caw can make us nervous. Hence one little noise can keep us alert even during the seemingly peaceful interludes.

There are seven attacks in all, and Hitchcock clearly was challenged by a desire to differentiate them. There are two sets of variables that he seems to be manipulating in relation to the sound effects: whether the birds are introduced first aurally or visually and whether the birds are ominously noisy or ominously silent.

For the silence of the birds can be even more frightening than their shrieks. Before the attack on the schoolchildren, Hitchcock shows the birds silently increasing in number, unnoticed at first, as they gather in the playground. In counterpoint to their ominous silence we hear the innocent voices of children singing. (The preparation for the scene is considerably more terrifying than its realization. The attack itself is so ambitious as a special effects project that the more sophisticated viewer tends to speculate about how Hitchcock created the effects rather than to identify with the victims.)

Hitchcock himself described how for the seventh and last attack he no longer needed to have the birds scream:

When Melanie is locked up in the attic with the murderous birds we inserted the natural sounds of wings. Of course, I took the dramatic licence of not having the birds scream at all. To describe a sound accurately, one has to imagine its equivalent in dialogue. What I wanted to get in that attack is as if the birds were telling Melanie, "Now we've got you where we want you. Here we come. We don't have to scream in triumph or in anger. This is going to be a silent murder." That's what the birds were saying, and we got the technicians to achieve that effect through electronic sound.[16]

Thus Hitchcock has characterized his birds in the same way that he characterized many of his murderers; their silence is a sign of their control. (This central Hitchcockian motif of the villain who keeps control by keeping silent is seen as late as in *Family Plot*, which juxtaposes a pair of kidnappers who operate in mute efficiency with a pair of bumbling, inefficiently garrulous heroes.) Having established this connection between silence and supremacy, Hitchcock maintains it for the rest of the film. In his words:

For the final scene, in which Rod Taylor opens the door of the house for the first time and finds the birds assembled there, as far as the eye can see, I asked for a silence, but not just any kind of silence. I wanted an electronic silence, a sort of monotonous low hum that might suggest the sound of the sea in the distance. It was a strange, artificial sound, which in the language of the birds might be saying, "We're not ready to attack you yet, but we're getting ready. We're like an engine that's purring and we may start off at any moment." All of this was suggested by a sound that's so low that you can't be sure whether you're actually hearing it or only imagining it.[17]

The shift in terror in *The Birds* from noise to silence is essential to its aims. The film eventually makes us feel just as vulnerable in moments of relative tranquillity as in chaos. It is one thing to feel threatened when under attack; it is another to be frightened at all times, to feel that life is a permanent state of siege. Thus Hitchcock has achieved his career-long aim of making us wary, not so much of blatant evils, but of our precarious daily condition.

Another aspect of the film's sound track that is so insidiously frightening is the cross-identification of noises human, mechanical, and avian. Although the major antagonists in the film are the natural order (birds) and the human order, the distinctions become blurred when we consider that both worlds are associated at times on the sound track with mechanical sounds. The associations can be made precisely because Hitchcock has established a norm of abstracted, stylized sounds. The birds, when screeching and flapping their wings, sound at times like an engine screeching and crackling.

Hitchcock describes the low hum of their menacing silence as "like an engine that's purring," and throughout the film motor noises seem to link bird and human noises. Under the opening titles the electronic flapping sounds of wings are intermingled with the almost imperceptible sound of a truck motor. Although we see birds during the titles (the titles, as abstracted as the sound track, are presented as fragments that converge and then disintegrate), we do not see a truck till their close, when a van roars by shortly after a trolley car, on a busy San Francisco street where Melanie is walking. She enters a bird shop where she will meet Mitch and attempt to talk to him over the loud sounds of bird chatter. The sequence ends with Melanie rushing into the street to watch Mitch's car take off noisily. The bird store has no doors, and the sounds of chirping cross-fade into the sounds of traffic. Thus Hitchcock has shifted by the end of the first sequence from bird sounds with an undercurrent of truck noise, to obvious truck noise crossfading to bird noise, to bird noise plus human speech, to bird noise crossfading to truck noise.

A few minutes later Melanie is herself driving a sports car. During this sequence (in which Melanie takes two birds to Mitch's sister) Melanie shifts noisily and often. In one shot a hill hides the car at first, and we know of her impending approach only by the engine noise. In another, a close-up of the lovebirds swaying on their perches as she rounds the corners too fast is accompanied by the sound of screeching tires and shifting gears. It may be that Hitchcock wants us to identify Melanie with mechanical noises because at this point we are to perceive her behavior as cold and mechanical. He stresses her intrusion into the peaceful hamlet of Bodega Bay by contrasting the noisy sports car with the quiet streets. He then associates Melanie with the noise of a motorboat she rents to deliver Mitch's birds. It is possible to interpret the film as implying that Melanie does indeed bring the bird attacks with her to the town.[18] This interpretation is supported by the emphasis Hitchcock puts on Melanie's noisy approach by car to the town and by her noisy departure in the last shot of the film (an extremely long take of the car in which she and Mitch's family are escaping), the motor sound gradually dying out as they disappear into the distance.

Motor noise is associated with a second woman in the film, Mitch's mother, who resembles Melanie in appearance and apparent coldness. Hitchcock has described his use of motor noise as an extension of the mother's feelings just after she discovers a neighbor who has been killed by the birds:

The screech of the truck engine starting off conveys her anguish. We were really experimenting there by taking real sounds and then stylizing them so that we derived more drama from them than we normally would. . . . In the previous scene we had shown that the woman was going through a violent emotion, and when she gets into the truck, we showed that this was an emotional truck. Not only by the image, but also through the sound that sustains the emotion. It's not only the sound of the engine you hear, but something that's like a cry. It's as though the truck were shrieking.[19]

Insofar as the women are doubles, there has been an aural reversal. Earlier, when Melanie was still untouched by a deeply felt experience, she was identified as something less than human by being associated with her car motor. Now the mother is indeed suffering, and the motor is taking on human qualities. As first a person sounds like a machine; now a machine sounds like a person.

But the machine also sounds like a bird. Hitchcock uses the word "shrieking" to imply that he was anthropomorphizing the truck, but the word he has chosen also describes bird noises. In other words, there are aural cross-references of all sorts: the birds sound like machines because of the electronic origins of their sounds, the human beings sound like birds (especially when the children shriek during attacks), and in the above example the machines sound like birds and/or people. The aural exchanges in the film match its overall visual exchanges. It starts in a bird shop where hundreds of birds are caged. By the end of the film it is the human beings who are caged by birds, in phone booths, homes, and vehicles. All in all, the film offers a bleak picture of humanity as trapped by forces beyond its control; the world depicted seems all the more impersonal and hostile because of the mechanical nature of the sound track.

There is one more issue raised by the aural continuities of things human, avian, and mechanical, and that is the nature of filmmaking itself. Any film requires a certain subordination of human subjects to mechanical and technical necessities. Hitchcock's closed style has always emphasized that technical control, and *The Birds* is the most mechanical of all his films. Not only does the sound track incorporate computer-generated noises, but the visuals include 371 trick shots combining drawn and model animation and elaborate matting techniques.[20] The birds, then, are the mechanical creation of a director who fully exploits the mechanical resources of his medium.

But Hitchcock further emphasizes his connections with the birds. The shift from Melanie's point of view at the start of the gas station sequence to the final aerial shot is quite literally a shift to a bird's-eye view. But it is also a shift to the omniscience of the director himself. Hitchcock is fond of overhead shots that reveal his characters to be trapped by a destiny that they cannot control. Within the world of film, however, it is not fate but the director who is in control. Hitchcock's avian and human attackers are simply the agents of a malevolent fate imposed by the director on his characters.

The birds are in control, but so is the director. His last shot is a composite of thirty-two pieces of film[21] and dozens of artificial and natural bird sounds. In previous shots the predominant sound has been that low, artificial hum of menace. This "electronic silence" is so important to the tension that when Mitch tenuously starts up and drives Melanie's sports car out of the garage there is absolutely no motor sound—from the same car that Hitchcock has previously shown to be particularly noisy. Thus, the silence that Hitchcock ascribes to the birds is ultimately a sign of the director's control over his characters, his viewers, and his art.

Notes

1. "The Figure in the Carpet," *Sight and Sound*, 32 (Autumn 1963):164.

2. See, e.g., his interview with Peter Bogdanovich in *The Cinema of Alfred Hitchcock* (New York: Museum of Modern Art, 1963), p. 4.

3. François Truffaut, *Hitchcock* (New York: Simon & Schuster, 1967), pp. 42–43.

4. Ibid., p. 224.

5. Interview in 1975 with Rudi Fehr, editing supervisor, Warner Bros.; editor of *Dial M for Murder* and *I Confess*.

6. I have tried to make this essay self-sufficient. But readers who want further elaboration or substantiation are referred to my book, *The Silent Scream: Alfred Hitchcock's Sound Track* (East Brunswick, N.J.: Fairleigh Dickinson University Press, 1982).

7. Truffaut, *Hitchcock,* p. 224.

8. Oral communication.

9. *Rope* also has no score, but there is a considerable amount of source music from the on-screen piano and a radio that is left on.

10. *The Dark Side of Genius* (New York: Hopkinson and Blake, 1983), p. 460.

11. Truffaut, *Hitchcock,* p. 224.

12. Donald Spoto, in his *The Art of Alfred Hitchcock* (New York: Hopkinson and Blake, 1976), makes a similar point about *Psycho.*

13. Truffaut, *Hitchcock,* p. 223.

14. "The Director Vanishes," *Moviegoer,* 2 (Summer/Autumn 1964):48.

15. Truffaut, *Hitchcock,* 217.

16. Ibid. p. 224.

17. Ibid. p. 225.

18. See, e.g., John Belton, "Hitchcock: The Mechanics of Perception," *Cinema Stylists* (Metuchen, N.J.: Scarecrow, 1983). Belton argues that *The Birds* is a subjective film in which the whole world is a reflection of Melanie's state of mind.

19. Truffaut, *Hitchcock,* p. 224.

20. Peter Bogdanovich, *The Cinema of Alfred Hitchcock* (New York: Museum of Modern Art, 1963), p. 45.

21. Ibid.

The Sound Track
of *The Rules of the Game*   MICHAEL LITLE

Renoir alone in his searchings as a director prior to *La Règle du Jeu* had forced himself to look back beyond the resources provided by montage and so uncovered the secret of a film form that would permit everything to be said without chopping the world up into little fragments, that would reveal the hidden meanings in people and things without disturbing the unity natural to them.

"Evolution of the Language of Cinema"—André Bazin

Pasternak: Did you find the transition from silent to sound difficult for you?
Renoir: No, not at all. As a matter of fact, the sound helped me.
P: In what way?
R: I found a certain pleasure in using the sounds. I started to be interested, not so much in words, but in sounds. In the expressions of the human being helped by the emission of sounds. The sounds may be a cry, a whisper, perhaps not a word, perhaps not a sentence. To explain myself, I must quote a conversation I had often with the wonderful fellow who played the part of the actor in my picture *The Lower Depths*. His name was LeVigan. We used to say we should make sound films, but not talking films. We should invent an international language which would be no language at all. The actors would never explain things, but would emit sounds. You know, like a bird has sounds, or a dog: quee-euee, qua-qua, pa-pa, kee-kee, woo-woo, wee-wee. That would be the dialog. But not at all logically built words and sentences. Of course, that cannot be done. But that was a way to express what we were feeling about sound. . . .

From interview by James D. Pasternak conducted June 1954 and printed in *The Image Maker,* ed. Ron Henderson

Following the lead of Alain Resnais, who first commented on the coherence of the sound track of *La Règle du Jeu,* I recorded and replayed the track repeatedly. I was interested in André Bazin's observation that Renoir's films before the coming of sound had an "inachieved character," an observation one could certainly disagree with in light of the magnificent silence of *Nana.* But after experiencing the wedding of sound and picture in *La Nuit de carrefour* (1932) and *La Chienne* (1931), I felt Bazin had a point: sound permitted Renoir a great leap forward. Why?

I wanted to accept Bazin's premise about cinematic realism—recorded sounds ought to add to the ontological power of recorded images—

but Renoir's own statement implied a desire to use sound *expressionistically,*
metaphorically. In working out this contradiction, I felt I might gain insight
into the structure of *The Rules of the Game,* a film which has repeatedly
struck me as highly metaphorical, despite the tightly woven realism of its
surfaces.

Noël Burch, in *Theory of Film Practice,* sets down some useful
parameters for the analysis of sound tracks: live or dubbed, off-screen or on-
screen, apparent mike distance (close or far away). In addition, I would add
volume, ambient context (in a hallway, outdoors, or over a telephone), and
the interaction of several sound sources at once. Here Bazin's comments on
depth of field of the image in "Evolution of the Language of Cinema" can
be transposed to apply to the sound track: foreground we hear a dialogue,
in the background or off-screen we hear other sounds, music, for example.

In *La Chienne,* a scene occurs which consists of a single take.
Michel Simon shaves by the window in front of which he often paints. Mixed
with the sounds of the courtyard, we hear a piano. In the background, across
the courtyard, a woman works in her kitchen. As Simon goes to get a fresh
towel the camera tracks with him, then returns to a slightly different position
in front of the window. Now we can see another window across the courtyard. In it there is a little girl playing the keyboard. Halting and lyric, the
music underscores the feeling of the scene, without subtracting from its synchronous unity. Since the sound and picture occur in the same frame, we
could call it metonymic, a side-by-side linguistic relation.

Burch states in his book that "there are few works of cinema in
which music is an organic and integral part of the over-all formal texture."
If at one pole of our definition of "organic use of music" we place the above
scene, we might place at the other pole, say, the battle sequence of *Alexander Nevsky.* In the former case, the music fits into the structure of the
image (just off-frame) and into the structure of the narrative (the character
hears music as he shaves). In the case of *Nevsky,* the music functions in
neither of these ways; rather it works as commentary and counterpoint to
the composition, movement, and montage of the battle scenes. Were Bazin
to argue a case about the ontology of sound comparable to his famous
"Ontology of the Photographic Image," he might say that the difference between Renoir's use of sound in *La Chienne* and Eisenstein's in *Nevsky* is
the difference between an immediately apprehended illusion and an illusion
created out of a synesthetic dualism. Technically, it is the difference between
live and postrecorded sound. More to the point of a structural critique, it is
the difference between the metonymic and the metaphoric mode. The piano
and the man shaving are side by side, in contiguity, whereas Prokofiev's orchestra stands for its object, the battle sequence, in the manner of a metaphor.

This is not to say that equating "realism" with metonomy and "expressionism" with metaphor will get us any farther toward an understanding of art and communication than the traditional form–content dichotomy did. Though metonomy has more to do with style and texture, and metaphor has more to do with meaning and association, the operation of the two modes is interwoven, as Barthes notes, like the two sides of a sheet of paper.

Toni, famous as the precursor of neorealism (Visconti apprenticed on the film), full of naturalistic dialogue and rigorously naturalistic in its use of music (a guitarist within the film provides the music), contains a sound which, for all its realism, is powerfully metaphorical. Three men are seated on a hillside above a quarry talking: Toni, his older friend Fernand, and a fellow worker. They are joking about what they would do if they had a million dollars. Toni has just been in a fight with his boss, who also rivals him for the affections of Marie. A dynamite blast goes off and Fernand shouts, "Oh malheur!" Perfectly *in context,* simply one link in a metonymic chain, the explosion and Fernand's response nonetheless stand for the danger inherent in the triangle; the event both echoes and foreshadows other events in the film; it sets in motion a ripple of associations. Active on the metonymic plane (within the setting, a live sound), yet our attention travels along metaphorical paths.

Analysis of the Beginning and End of *La Règle du Jeu*

The proper exposition of this essay would be oral—a commentary that parallels the playing of the track. For that I shall substitute a written description of the sounds alongside an *explication de texte.* I have enclosed in parentheses information from the visuals necessary to understand the track. Included in the sound track is the content of the speech.

TEXT	ANALYSIS
A Mozart's "Danse Allemande" introduces the track. Suddenly we are engulfed in the shapeless noise of a crowd. (Picture tracks along mike cable from sound booth to lollipop mike and female announcer.) We hear the buzz of an airplane. The excited voice	An antinomy is laid out in the first two sound units: dubbed Mozart versus the crowd noise. The carefully ordered pattern of the music stands in direct opposition to the shapeless noise of the crowd. In addition the associations that follow from recog-

of the female says, "This is Radio-City speaking," and explains that a transatlantic aviator has just landed. We hear the name "André Jurieux" shouted, above the crowd's roar, then in official tones a congratulatory phrase, and a different response. The latter voice exclaims "Octave!" and in intimate tones two men exchange greetings. They laugh. The female voice of the announcer insinuates itself into the dialogue, imploring for a speech from the aviator. Loudly (into the mike) he accuses a woman of betrayal. (Picture cuts to a boudoir where a woman listens to the radio. Cut back to field.) In the monotones of a technician a man lists the equipment on the airplane. Octave and Jurieux exchange phrases.

nition of those sounds as cultural indices point to meanings that flex between eighteenth- and twentieth-century modes, between mechanical codes and spontaneous feelings, between a privileged musician spectator class and a homogenous mass. At this point we have an interface—a cut quite simply—joining the two elements metonymically. The foreground figure of the announcer's voice emerges from the background roar. It is clear from the content of her speech that she stands for the crowd ("Speak to *us*, Jurieux"). Soon she becomes a middle-ground figure as we listen to Octave and Jurieux. In this cross section of the track we can find the paradigmatic metaphor of the film: the rules of the game. In this case it is a game of speaking to the masses. When Jurieux accuses Christine of betrayal and it goes over the air, he has broken the first rule, one of decorum. Although the theme of the individual out of joint with his amorous context was borrowed from Musset's *Les Caprices de Marianne,* Renoir casts the net of its implications into the twentieth century: the hero who flew the Atlantic can't handle his communications. The radio stands metaphorically for the spilling over of personal desire into social decorum: it is a device which brings the private voice to the public ear.

B   The acoustic presence of the track changes from the outdoor noise of the crowd to the indoor quiet of a room and we hear a dialogue between two women, introduced as Lisette and Madame. Lisette's voice is flat and

From their dialects and the very sound of the women's voices, we associate dualisms like: upper and lower class, sensitive and comic, foreign and French. Quite obviously the film will be about classes, the bourgeois and

informal. Madame's is deep and cadenced. Dialects are, respectively, provincial and Parisian with a foreign accent. The room's presence changes to that of a corridor and we hear feet walking, a brief question from the mistress, a response from a man. Over a radio receiver we hear the voice of a male announcer against distant crowd noise. The radio cuts off in the middle of a phrase. In marked contrast to the staccato speech of the announcer, the calm and suave voice of a new character speaks, the Marquis de la Cheyniest.

C   In a rhetorical tone, he asks her if she thinks he is a liar. Upon her negative response he walks away and dials a telephone. Another music box begins to play as he speaks. We do not hear the voice at the other end. (Picture cuts to Geneviève's apartment.) Now we do not hear the Marquis, neither do we hear the music box. Geneviève's voice is cool and her speech rhythms Parisian. In the background a radio announcer tells us that the concert will continue and a tinny accordion waltz begins to play. Several male voices continue a discussion of Christine, Jurieux, and la Cheyniest apparently touched off by the radio bulletin about Jurieux's landing. Christine's foreign birth is confirmed. Geneviève makes a cynical remark about the nature of love. The men laugh and then all utter "hmm, hmm." (9½ minutes.)

the servant. Following the thread of their meaning we discover what will be a prime subject of one-to-one conversations in the film—what is natural in love and friendship. The recurrent theme of one-to-one discussions is sexual love, curiously, always in a nonamorous context: Octave and Jurieux, Christine and Lisette, Geneviève and the Marquis. Given the *form* of dialogue (two-way conversation), we can expect discourse on the subject of love. Thus, over and again we will hear the reverberation of that original intrusion of desire on decorum at the airport— that spilling of the private into public.

When the Marquis switches off the radio and plays a mechanical bird, the other pole of the fundamental audio metaphor is replayed. Two kinds of sound—preconceived, formal, and self-contained versus spontaneous, undisciplined, and self-revealing. The bird is played *at the same time* as the Marquis makes his ambivalent speech to Christine about Jurieux's infatuation, providing a whimsical and mechanical counterpoint to an earnest but dishonest expression of trust. When la Cheyniest returns to the phone and calls Geneviève he plays a different tune (amorous game), but the same quality prevails—a sense of order, enclosure, a tight mechanical game—in dialectical opposition to the channel-jumping effect of the telephone and the radio. The two auditory devices are mixed into one metaphor, a metaphor which will achieve its nemesis at the playing of the giant mechanical organ, the background music which will dominate the gropings of the characters toward communication outside the rules of the game.

Following the opening reel of the film, the relationships are laid out: two intersecting triangles (Jurieux-Christine-the Marquis and Geneviève-the Marquis-Christine) with Octave acting as confidant and go-between. Octave persuades the Marquis to invite Jurieux to his estate. The Marquis has lost the key to his new musical bird and reluctantly consents. Octave dances to a wind-up record player with the maid, who will be at the center of a third triangle, Marceau-Lisette-Schumacher. The guests assemble at the chateau, Christine makes a speech in an attempt to clear the air, and the two worlds of the servant to the aristocrat are elaborated. The hunt begins. Through binoculars, Christine sights her husband embracing Geneviève.* At that instant a hunting horn sounds. The second part of the analysis begins with the party in reels 8 and 9.

A (Start of eighth reel.) Piano music and finale. (Close-up shot of score and track downwards to Charlotte's hands.) Applause. Actors discuss doing an encore. Christine leaves. Audience clamors for "author, author." Piano starts again. Singing. Robert and Jurieux ask where Christine went. Octave asks them to pull his bear suit off.

Opening the sequence, music formalizes our attention—this is theater. Camera makes it clear, however, that the music is within immediate context. Alternation between collective and individual signals, like chorus and response, is violated by Christine. Openly now both husband and suitor seek her.

B Reprise of piano, this time "danse macabre" (camera shows keys playing themselves). Screams. Christine says she's had too much to drink. Schumacher calls Lisette. Octave asks Christine: "Aren't we acting anymore?" She: "I've had enough of the drama." Robert asks Jurieux if he's seen Christine. Octave asks for help with his bear suit. Charlotte suggests game of cards to the homosexual:

Repetition of mechanical musical device, this time in a form which emphasizes its paradoxical nature—that which Charlotte played, she is horrified to see playing itself. Christine confirms: she's out of control too. Off-screen music accompanies antic dance of triangles: Robert-Christine-Jurieux and Schumacher-Lisette-Marceau. Dialogue about card game echoes problem of three's. Parallel ironies in

---

*Just as the radio is a metaphor of the ability of the cinema to transcend spatial limitations, so the binoculars are a metaphor of the ability of the close-up to act as voyeur.

"With two people?" "Go and get the General." "Danse macabre" ends. (Faint cheers and trumpets—from off-screen.) Geneviève asks Robert to take her away. "Where to? This is my home. First I must talk to Christine." Octave shouts, "Pull, pull!"

that what both mistress and wife demand from their men—to be taken away from it all—the men refuse them, on the grounds of property in the case of Robert, and propriety in the case of Jurieux.

C   A polka starts (off-screen). In intimate tones poacher and aristocrat discuss "this notorious question of relations between men and women." Each gives his idea. Polka ends and Robert snaps his fingers to signal for Marceau to escape the gun of Schumacher. (End of eighth reel: 8 minutes.)

Classless music underlines crossing of class lines. Marceau, in danger of his life, whispers that the important thing is to have fun. Fingersnap a simple aural device to punctuate a change in tone.

The scene just above of Marceau and the Marquis is, structurally, the reversal of the scene at the opening of the film between Lisette and Christine: two men and two women talking about love and friendship between the sexes. The level of meaning articulated by the scenes in isolation can be read from the lines. The women agree that nothing seems natural these days, that the more you give men the more they want, that of "friendship with a man . . . you might as well talk of the moon in broad daylight." The men conclude that the Moslems have a good idea in their harems, that it's a shame to hurt a woman, that "when a woman is having a lark she's off her guard, you can do what you like with her." But the level of meaning articulated by the parallelism of the scenes—by their repetitive structure—arises from the variations between them, and from the context as defined by what happens in the film around them. Similarly, the gamekeeper Schumacher is compared, by his placement in context, to the Marquis—both jilted husbands, both keepers of the game. (The Marquis restores order at the end of the film, reestablishing the social game in his epitaph for Jurieux.)

A   Applause fades out. Horn fanfare. Haltingly, Robert introduces the "culmination of [his] career as a collector of instruments *musicaux* and *méchanique.*" Scattered laughs. Robert laughs nervously and shouts, "One!" Oohs and aahs. "Two!" Louder response and applause. Robert screams, "Musique!" A giant me-

Robert's counterpart in Musset's *Les Caprices de Marianne,* a judge, is described by one of the characters as "more concerned with the form than the facts of justice." The mechanical organ is equivalent to the law—impersonal, mechanical, a thing which functions by rules. Organ plays off-screen counterpoint to the ballet

chanical organ plays a fast circus tune. (Medium close-up of Robert, proud of his machine's success.) Music becomes distant and we hear Marceau, mouth full, bragging how he will put Schumacher in his place. His words echo in the kitchen as boots descend the creaking stairs. In familiar but suspicious tones, Schumacher orders Lisette to get him a glass of wine. In broadly humoring tones she consents. (In background Marceau sneaks away.) Schumacher brags what he'd do to Marceau: "a gunshot!" He hits the table for emphasis and Marceau jumps. Music upstairs fades out. Lisette praises Alsace. A deafening crash occurs as Marceau knocks some plates over. Shouts of pursuit as Schumacher tries to catch Marceau. Voices recede from the mike as actors move upstage from camera (cut to upstairs foyer). Distant applause, as Marceau and pursuer burst out of kitchen. Robert orders a stop, soon shouting hysterically.

Christine's voice cuts through the noise, close to mike, angry at Jurieux. Marceau crosses, begging their pardon. Robert and Jurieux scuffle. Octave takes Christine outside. She complains to him about Jurieux, while shouts continue off. Octave soothes her. Schumacher and Marceau enter again. A gunshot punctuates a sudden silence.

B "Hesitation Waltz." Robert: "Christine has disappeared." Geneviève begins screaming. More screams. Laughter between Christine and Octave. Outside, Octave pre-

in the kitchen, reminding us of the parallel events upstairs. Foregrounding Schumacher's utopian speech about Alsace plays ironic counterpart to the poacher who sneaks away in the background. Parallel irony of the Marquis's situation: at the height of his glory, his wife is with Jurieux. In each of the chambers of the chateau a disruption in the social order occurs: the poacher fails to make his escape, the aristocrat fails to control his servant, the idealistic lover fails to sweep his lady off her feet. The din of the organ penetrates everywhere. Social gamekeeper fails to keep the rules in order as his lower-class mirror (the other husband) goes after the poacher. The noise and energy of one event interrupt another, which, in its turn, becomes discordant. Musical changes come often in this section which functions, in terms of rise and fall of noise levels, as the last upheaval before the climax.

Waltz reinforces that expectancy. The silence of Octave's symphony functions rhythmically as a rest, thematically as just another failure of humans to create their own aural des-

tends to conduct a symphony. Waltz off reaches end of phrase. He gives up and, sad, asks Christine to leave him alone. Waltz terminates. Applause. (Pan of ballroom.)

C Organ starts again. Women laugh. Gunshot. The general comments: "Another act!" Shouts off. Gunshots off. Geneviève gets hysterical again. Robert orders Corneille to "get this comedy stopped." "Which one?" is his deadpan reply. Another shot, and the volume of the organ tells us we're back in the ballroom. Continual screaming. The organ jams and emits a loud cacophony. Men shout and women scream. Organ and shouting stop. (The gun has been knocked out of Schumacher's hand.) Marceau, out of breath, gives profuse thanks to the lesbian (for blocking Schumacher's shot). Repulsed by his embrace, she says: "It was nothing, nothing."

tiny, to invent a music of pure spirit rather than to submit to a mechanical ballet.

The last of a series of syntagms to begin with music: the whole party scene is constructed on a musical model—repetition of rhythmic phrases, cycling higher and higher to a climax ABA'_1, ABA'_2, ABA'_3, where A is initial statement of complex theme, involving a number of people, B a simplified statement usually with two, and A' a restatement involving both elements. Organ functions as continuo. Complete breakdown of the rules of the game—a cacophonous hysteria initiated by Christine's attempt to withdraw from her part in the play, to redefine her sexual role.

The killing which follows is an inverted echo to the cacophony of the scene just analyzed. It takes place outdoors in silence (we hear only the crickets) and is the result of both Schumacher and Marceau mistaking the identity of the lovers in the greenhouse, whose voices they cannot hear. Like Christine with the binoculars, it's a case of seeing without understanding, of a visual divorced from its sound. The archetypal resolution of cinematic drama, the gunshot, pronounces its verdict: love outside the rules of the game backfires. A long decrescendo follows.

The sound track of *La Règle du Jeu* may be viewed at one level as a system of signifiers made up of sounds which by virtue of their indexical significance point to the voices of their owners, the actors. The voices, the presence of the rooms, the music of the instruments in the frame—by virtue of the recording process—share an existential bond with the objects of which the sound is *index*. At this first level of signification it seems to me important to note that our perceptions are oriented in the direction of the "real." One could disturb this orientation by, for example, throwing the sound track out of sync with the picture, by playing it backwards, etc. Immediately the illusion of a *direct* recording is gone. By carefully retaining this first level of significance (not dubbing, not laying music over) Renoir has captured our belief in the *representations*.

Add next the iconic qualities of the sounds, their denotative level of meaning. As soon as we understand that Christine's accent *denotes* the dialect of a foreigner, and that further, Lisette's dialect sounds like that of a servant, we add a level of signification: the women's voices portray two social classes. The actresses may exaggerate the tonal qualities of their voices to reinforce this impression. To the extent that there is conscious and repeated manipulation, there is iconic significance. The voice is stylized.

A third level of signification overlapping the other two operates when, for example, we interpret the music of the mechanical bird as a pattern based on a preexistent code, the codes of nineteenth-century song, the method of mechanical reproduction of musical patterns, etc. Add next what Christine says about the mechanical bird, that she prefers it to the radio. In order to decode its significance at this symbolic level, we must hold several bits of meaning in our heads, some of which spring from the elaborated code of the film—we have just heard Christine's suitor's indiscretion over the radio—some of which may come from the restricted definitions we already carry with us concerning the two media—radio as twentieth-century device, music box as nineteenth. The danger of this last stage of meaning is that we will misread the text, adding an interpretation which may mislead us. So we must look for evidence within the context to corroborate our readings. Since Octave speaks three times of Jurieux as a clumsy twentieth-century hero, and the general speaks often of the aristocratic *savoir faire* of the Marquis as a quality which is "rare in our times," it seems reasonable to let the connotations stand. Further connotations may accumulate through the elaboration of the metaphors: privacy, order, wealth attach to the Marquis and his birds; indiscretion, confusion, heroics attach to the aviator.

The process of signification does not stop at a single symbol or at a pair of symbols, though it must begin there. Early in the film, Lisette and Christine discuss the difference between love and friendship. Lisette implies it is impossible to be friends with a man. The group of cardplayers at Geneviève's continue the articulation of this theme, implying that Christine's foreignness to the rules of the Parisian game of love has made her relationship with Jurieux indiscreet. That is, friendship has a code of behavior, as does marriage or sexual love, that is defined by certain implicit rules of communication. Jurieux's public disclosure violated the rule of decorum. In contradistinction, we see the Marquis obeying the rules when he telephones his mistress in secret (he closes the door). That is, an affair is within the code of behavior so long as it is kept from one's mate. That the prime mover of the plot is an *avowal* of love, and not any sexual act, sharpens the ironies considerably—even Jurieux's death is based on an error of interpretation (Schumacher thinks it is Lisette's lover). At this level of signification the film as a whole spreads a net of meanings as broad as its title implies—the rules of the game: game of love, game of triangles, game of upper and lower classes, game of social communication, game of friendships (male to male, female to female, male to female). As the slaughter of the rabbits makes brutally clear, the game is for keeps, a game of love and death. The consummate irony of Jurieux's death, an error of interpretation on the jealous Schumacher's part, reveals the danger which underlies violation of the rules of amorous conduct. In the battle for Christine's affection, for a place in the world, and for the respect of one's fellows, who survives? The man of whom the chef said:

La Cheyniest may be a foreigner, but he had me summoned the other day to give me a telling-off about a potato salad. You know, or maybe you don't know (music begins) that in order that this salad be edible, one must pour the white wine on the potatoes when they are still boiling hot, which Celestin didn't do because he doesn't like burning his fingers. Well, the master sniffed that straight away (music continues). You say what you like, but that, that's a man of the world!

The plot of *La Règle du Jeu* is built on a semiological-question—the relation of sound to meaning. Renoir provides us with specific metaphors in the first scenes: the microphone and radio, devices for separating sound from visual information which reach across the boundaries of privacy and break down the games of property and propriety. Jurieux's broadcast avowal of love and betrayal sets in motion the action which will culminate in his death. The telephone and music box, devices which affirm privacy and one-to-one connections, are symbols of the counterforce, the established order of the Marquis. The breakdown of the mechanical organ parallels the breakdown of the social order. Sound-over-parallel montage (from the airport to Christine's boudoir and Geneviève's card salon) and off-screen sound (hearing music from upstairs in the servant's kitchen) are cinematic techniques which underscore this dialectic. Christine's binoculars and Schumacher's dim vision through the greenhouse are metaphors on communication of a visual nature: they see but misunderstand. The alienation of sound and picture is equivalent to the division of desire and decorum, of eros and order. When the Marquis restores decorum on the front steps of the chateau, he makes a formal speech (the typically nineteenth-century mode of public address and an echo of Christine's earlier explanation of her relation to Jurieux) in which he says it was simply an error of interpretation which caused Jurieux's death. The paradigmatic game, it seems finally, has more to do with communication than with savoring either potato salad or triangular affairs.

Sound in Bresson's *Mouchette*
LINDLEY HANLON

> The sound track invented silence.
> Robert Bresson, *Notes on Cinematography*

Robert Bresson's greatest achievement has been the redemption of sound in the cinema from the obscurity of the secondary role it has traditionally played. Sound and the absence of sound play a fundamental role in Bresson's films, in the structuring and intensification of visual images and as an independent element of composition and signification. Sound is Bresson's most important source of narrative economy, never duplicating an image's message. Sound may even be substituted for that image. The exchange of sound for image relieves Bresson's films of the redundancy of conventional sound realism and frees sound for use as an emblem. Sound functions consistently throughout *Mouchette* as a structural and symbolic medium.

Mouchette lives in a threatening, enclosed environment, a personal, social, and metaphorical "prison," guarded by the strict, silent, and brutal members of a rural French community. The estranged outsider, Mouchette will watch and listen to the world around her just as Mathieu, the gamekeeper, does in the first shots of the film. Sounds register the threat of that world and her defiance toward it. Sounds register the ritual actions of the life of the community, and music suggests the solace of religious belief and the possibility of another life.

The theme of entrapment is brilliantly evoked on the level of both sound and image in the first major scene of the film, after the titles. The structural possibilities of sound are introduced in these first shots as well. After a long shot of Mathieu, the game-warden, running through the woods, very close shots of him next to a tree emphasize the confining aspect of the frame, as he watches Arsène, the poacher, setting his traps. Mathieu's eyes move back and forth furtively like those of a bird, his head still. The rustle of dry leaves and the crunch of footsteps represent what he is watching off-screen. The sound is very distinct and loud, as if heard by someone with sharply heightened attention to the sounds as such. These close, flat shots of an as yet unidentified character and intensified sounds are a typically oblique beginning to a Bresson film. There is no establishment of a space, time, or narrative connection between this scene and the previous shot of a woman in church. The situation and actions of these people are introduced almost abstractly, abruptly, piece by piece, with no narrative interrelationships and explanations provided. Only gradually do we infer the identity of characters from conversations and confrontations between them. From this moment on, the crackling sound of leaves crushed under foot will signify by itself the presence of someone in the woods. Sound will systematically represent action in off-screen space that we may see only later if at all.

Bresson then proceeds to intercut shots of Mathieu spying and Arsène setting traps and making the rustling noise we have previously heard. The sound carries over the cut, bridging the shot change. Dogs bark in the distance, suggesting a world beyond the cramped space to which we have been introduced. A very marked silence ensues as they wait in their separate spaces in separate shots for the game to arrive. Bresson continues cutting back and forth between Mathieu, Arsène, and the partridge. As a partridge is caught in one of the rings of thread Arsène has constructed, loud and long sounds of thrashing in leaves and wings beating break this silence and amplify the horror of the act of capture. The rustling of leaves continues as Mathieu, the gamekeeper, closes in on Arsène, the poacher. Mathieu approaches the bird, which is struggling to free itself from the collar around its neck. As he lets the bird loose, it flies upward and into the distance with a loud flapping of wings.

The sequence introduces a sound trope that recurs throughout the film, along with other strategies, to suggest the similarities between Mouchette and the game stalked throughout the film. Throughout the film the same sharp, crisp crackling of leaves and branches is heard as Mouchette hides like an animal in the forest and grass for shelter and listens for threatening sounds around her that signify the presence of Arsène and Mathieu or anyone else who might discover her whereabouts and enforce their will on her. Once as Mouchette waits and watches in the forest, a partridge flies up making the same flapping sound and reminding us of the first scene of capture. The symbolic force of the sound builds through these repetitions and cross-references. The sound of wind and rain close in and assault her as she crouches beside a tree. Later in the film the crackling of the fire that Arsène builds before the rape scene reminds us of the sound of crackling leaves and adds to our sense of Mouchette as a trapped animal. Arsène pursues her around the room, and she hides under the table on all fours. Although initially an encounter where Mouchette exhibits her warmth and compassion for Arsène, nursing and singing to him during his epileptic seizure, the communion between them is turned into terror as Arsène forces her back against the fire that, like him, threatens to consume her.

Still other sounds convey the sense of her entrapment in spatial terms clarified by the precise directionality of the sounds as she glances left, right, and forward to assess their location and danger. Her father returns drunk one evening as she is caring for the baby and her mother. On one side of her (off-screen right) the baby cries shrilly. To her off-screen left, her father is stretched out on a mattress imitating the acceleration and shifting of a motor. Sound seems to close in on her from all sides in a situation of oppression and hopelessness. Often the putt-putt sound of her father's truck, used to transport contraband liquor, is heard off-screen to signal his approach, which brings habitual reprimands for using his liquor to soothe her mother's pain. In response to the sound of the truck and the flash of headlights, she quickly refills the gin bottle to its previous level with water from the faucet.

The loudness of these sounds sets off and calls attention to the excruciating silence that pervades the relationships of these people who seem to have known each other so long that verbal communication is infrequent and terse. Physical sounds become one of the few indicators or transmitters of interpersonal communication or its lack. The repeated sound of footsteps as the men enter the bar, the mechanical sound of the habitual placement of glasses on the bar, and the slurping of liquor being poured show the almost identical approaches of Arsène and Mathieu to Louisa, the barmaid. While unifying the shots, the sounds intensify their competition for her attention. Drinking becomes a continuous ritual in the film, the rhythm of which is recorded in the alternation of the sound of bottles and glasses clanking with the slurp of gin. For her work in the café Mouchette receives a few coins that she hands over to her father in exchange for a drink, a system of exchange that serves as her initiation into a lifetime habit.

Just as the sound of the truck indicates her father's presence, so does the sound of Mouchette's clogs become an emblem for her disposition. The defiant clunk-clunk-clunk of these wooden shoes as she walks across the pavement and hard floors registers her rebellious inclinations and heroic defiance. She clunks conspicuously into her classroom where the other girls are much more genteel and obedient. She clunks across the road away from them as they huddle together to gossip, presumably about the boys who ride away on motorbikes. She turns haughtily away from these boys, who call her names and mock her with obscene gestures, and clatters alone down the road. The clogs send mud spattering up around her as she stamps in a puddle in the churchyard in front of her father who shoves her ahead into the church. Finally she has the courage to snap back "Merde!" to her father as she leaves the house. Her shoes make a squirting, gushy sound as she plods through the mud in the woods on her way to Arsène's cabin. When she visits the old lady, who speaks to her of the attractions of death, Mouchette scornfully rubs mud into the woman's carpet. Her clogs are her one weapon against the hostile world around her.

Mouchette's repeated acts of defiance, to which she seems in-stinctively drawn, are memorable because of their accentuated sound di-mension. In the row of girls singing the song about "hopeful horizons open to those without hope," Mouchette is conspicuously silent. Her silence seems a refusal on her part to sing the words that she, and we, sense in no way describe the dismal life she leads. For her refusal to sing, she is yanked over to the piano where she is forced to sing by the schoolmistress. The wrong note sounds out painfully each time as the schoolmistress sounds out the correct notes on the piano and barks "Chante! Chante! "["Sing! Sing!"] at Mouchette. She sings the song correctly, only when it expresses her real emotions, to Arsène, whom she cares for in the cabin. When she returns to the line of girls to sing, we hear the wrong note again, and tears fall down Mouchette's cheeks, the sign of her total humiliation.

Action upon action, sound upon sound accumulate as the film progresses; they hint at the character of Mouchette, who, like most of Bres-son's characters, is highly enigmatic. After this ordeal, she leaves the school and crosses the street to crouch down behind the shoulder of the road. She hurls mud balls across at the girls that land with a dull thud on their crisp, clean clothing. At home she efficiently makes coffee in a skillful, carefree way, humming, turning the coffee mill around and around, enjoying the ratchety noise, and clanking the coffeepot and waterpot on the stove. She pours the coffee continuously into the four bowls lined up next to each other for that purpose. She repeats the slurping ritual with the warm milk. The actions in-dicate her amazing spirit amidst such hardship. These actions and the sounds associated with them define the range of Mouchette's power to influence those around her. These sounds ring out as the only traces of her existence reg-istered in the world around her, the continuity and impressions of which are preserved in the film.

The role of sound is very closely allied with the role of objects that produce them in the film. Bresson places great importance on the re-velatory nature of automatic actions and gestures, in particular the way we handle objects in our everyday activities, which may indicate the deeper lev-els of our unconscious more accurately than the words we utter or the dra-matic actions we engage in. Physical reality, which cinema had supposedly redeemed, has never had a more articulate spokesman than Bresson, through the medium of sound. The accentuation of physical sounds gives the world around the characters in Mouchette a hollow, empty, hard, cold feeling, as if these objects and people existed in a hollow box filled with sound vibra-tions and echoes. Bresson's stress on the physicality of these objects and on the materiality of the world (given almost excruciating representation in his 1983 film L'Argent) suggests the lack of any spiritual warmth or energy to protect the characters and comfort them in what we might imagine as a sort of existential buffer zone. The harsh, naked quality of the sounds, accentuated by their startling loudness and by the lack of intermediate, background noise as filler, intensifies the hostility of the characters toward each other, exhibited as well in their actions. Bresson suggests that neither the natural physical world nor the physical world man has created is benevolent. Mouchette is pelted by rain and wind that we hear; the moon, in contrast, is silent, dark, and menacing. The crackle of leaves underfoot is as pronounced and unforgiving as the sound of Mouchette's clogs on the paved road or stone floor.

There are special moments when a human being may interact with physical objects and thereby transform them into signs of an interior state, as when Mouchette expresses a certain lightheartedness as she makes coffee in the morning. Yet ultimately, except in those special moments of grace, and except for innocents like Mouchette, the world and the people who populate it in Bresson's films are unenlightened and hostile. Moment after moment of suffering are set end to end in *Mouchette,* like so many empty gin bottles lined up under the bar. Yet the harsh arena through which these characters walk serves all the better to highlight those very rare moments of great warmth and beauty that mark for Bresson the possible spiritual quality of man. Through the paradoxically violent sound of the crash of bumper cars, Mouchette's smile radiates for a special moment as her glance meets that of a young man who crashes into her in play. That moment of happiness is brutally ended when her father slaps her violently as she approaches the boy at the next concession. In a similarly paradoxical and tragic situation, Mouchette's song seems all the more tender when juxtaposed against the violence of Arsène's fit. Bresson's gentle creatures seem all the gentler and more vulnerable by contrast with the severity of the world around them.

Mouchette's suicide is clearly an escape from this existence. She wraps herself in an organdy dress as a buffer against the ground; the dress rips as she begins her roll down a hill to death. The sound of a motor off-screen holds out the one chance Mouchette has of resisting the temptation of death. She looks up as the bushes stop her at the water's edge, rises, and walks up the hill raising her arm. A farmer drives up the road away from her. She waves and opens her mouth, but the sound of the tractor motor drowns out her voice. In the distance the farmer waves back as if saying hello. She rolls down the hill again and into the water, which envelops her as the screen fades to black, and the solemn strains of Monteverdi are heard. We are left to ponder her motivation, but the chain of harsh sounds adds to the chain of other materials from which we can infer connections in Bresson's highly fragmented narrative. Death seems to define Mouchette's horizon of hope better than physical and social reality.

While sound in Bresson films is always related to the narrative situation and the characters, sound has also provided Bresson with a means of unifying shots in a sequence whose temporal, spatial, and narrative identity may at first appear unclear. As the aural representation of off-screen space within the context of a shot, sound provides a natural bridge to that shot. A typical aural trope in *Mouchette* consists of a shot that focuses on an empty architectural space with the sound of footsteps heard off-screen. A person enters the field of the shot, moves through the space of the shot, with the sound of his footsteps continuing over the cut to the next space, perhaps an interior, which the character enters in countershot. There are many examples of the use of sound to unify images structurally, a hallmark of Bresson's style: Mouchette's entrance into the classroom and her house, Mathieu's entrance with Arsène's traps, and the continuous sound of her father's truck and traffic outside the house.

This unusual focus on an empty space tends to make us wonder where the character is, asserting his absence, causing us to await his presence. Like the hollow sounds that come to symbolize the void in which they are produced, images of empty spaces begin to represent that void as well. The entrance of a character into an empty space underlines the loneliness of the character, his isolation from those around. Further, what lurks beyond the frame is unknown and possibly threatening. Twice Mouchette's father enters the frame and shoves her forward. The schoolmistress moves into the frame and pulls Mouchette over to the piano, holding on to her neck with her fingers, as the collar of Arsène's trap encircles the neck of the bird or rabbit caught in it. Arsène enters her space to violate her. The shot's space then represents the character's private zone where others trespass. In contrast to this aural and spatial void is the bumper-car sequence, the most active and "filled-up" sequence in the film. Music, cars crashing, smiles, and lots of people surround Mouchette and convey a momentary "fullness" in her life. Her father shoves her out of the one situation in which she is about to make human contact with another, and thereby enforces the isolation and emptiness of her life. In the last shot of the film she has literally dropped out of sight, leaving an empty, uninhabited space that music enters to fill with a sense of spiritual presence.

Once the identity of the sound and its associated source have been visually established, the sound can then stand alone without recourse to an image of its source. The sound produced by an action off-screen may replace a change of shot to that off-screen space. It is this ability of sound to signify independently that contributes to the density, intensity, and economy of Bresson's style.

One other sound is very important in Bresson's narrative composition, the sound of the human voice. In *Mouchette* the characters speak to each other infrequently, but when they do speak, the quality and rhythm of their voices add to the aural texture of the film and convey aspects of their character: the short, choppy, hard sentences exchanged between Louisa and Mathieu, punctuated by the clank of glasses on the bar; the snapped command of the schoolmistress, "Chante! Chante!," accompanied by pounding on the piano keys; the low, soft, fading voice of the mother; the sparse phrases of Mouchette and her pretty singing voice; the crude verbosity of Arsène. Traditional dramatic articulation and artifice are absent. It is the human voice that stretches across the emptiness of the world and seeks a response. It is the silence of that voice that indicates the unspeakable humiliation and suffering of the characters. When Mouchette smiles, sings, or swears, her voice conveys the reserve of passion beneath the inscrutable surface of her face. The sound of the voice contributes to the rich rhythmic modulations of the sound track that are echoed at the beginning and end of the film in the strains of the Monteverdi *Magnificat*.

Like the warm, human glances that penetrate the world's void, music in Bresson's films suggests the possible solace of another, future world. The first shot of *Mouchette* shows the girl's mother anguished and desolate as she leaves a church. She asks what will happen to her family and says that her chest feels as if there were stone there. Her loud footsteps on the stone floor reiterate the cold, hard reality that pervades the film. Then, in marked contrast, the solemn, rich tones of the *Magnificat* intervene and continue over the titles. The music suggests in its text that her question will be answered mercifully and in its sound that there exists a transcendent beauty to which this image of suffering must be related. The *stile concertante* (concerto style) of the excerpts from the *Magnificat* places one set of instruments against another as an echo, with organ *continuo*. The runs of sixteenth notes played by the strings contrast with the solemn, sustained notes of the voices in a slow, choralelike setting. This echo effect suggests a certain spatial hollowness and a question-and-answer structure that might represent the humble below (the voices), in this case the woman, beseeching the Lord above (the instruments). The rising lines of sixteenth notes seem to mimic and promise the "exaltation of the humble" stated in the text: "et exultavit humiles" ["and (He) hath exalted the humble"]. For these reasons, the Monteverdi music can suggest a final redemption, a horizon of hope for Mouchette and her mother, "the humble," whose sufferings are recorded in the film. The film "exalts the humble."

Occurring at the beginning of the film and again after Mouchette's death, the music accompanies much less footage than similar scores in *Un condamné à mort s'est échappé* or *Pickpocket*, where musical phrases would occasionally coincide with special moments in these films as a rich *continuo* for the image phrases and as a similar evocation of another spiritual world. From *Mouchette* on, Bresson uses music only at the beginning or the end of a film unless the source of the music can emanate from the space and situation of the film narrative. Bresson considers his use of music in the earlier films a mistake, a deviation from his firm economy built on concrete, realistic detail. In the later films, the music is more directly and literally allied with characters and their actions within the fiction of the film. It is a more subtle, less intrusive means on Bresson's part of authorial commentary on the action of the film. Yet, as an indefinite correlative of unspoken thoughts and feeling, and as commentary, its narrative function is the same.

Recurring after Mouchette's death, the Monteverdi music seems to function as Bresson's requiem for the girl, who has wrapped herself in shroudlike vestments. The death of Mouchette is such a surprise that the music helps us reassess the events of her life and ponder the sum total of their meaning for her. Even as she is rolling down the hill we assume she is playing a rather odd game, although she has come from the old woman who has spoken to her of her own affinity with the dead. The words of the *Magnificat* affirm the possibility of another life after death and sanctify Mouchette's decision to escape from the despair of her own life: "deposuit potentes de sede" ["He hath put down the mighty from their seat"]. Perhaps Mouchette has asked herself the question her mother poses at the beginning of the film: "Sans moi, que deviendront-ils?" ["Without me, what will become of them?"]. She seems to have decided that her life holds out no hope of a bearable answer to that question from the evidence Bresson has set before us in shot after shot of her misery. But we may infer that she believes in the words of the *Magnificat* that the humble will be exalted and redeemed.

Other phrases of music are as organized and meaningful, although less obvious as commentary, emanating as they do from within the fictional situation. For example, in the bumper-car montage sequence, the carnival music consists of carefully orchestrated phrases, each associated with a particular person and situation, although the music appears to emanate at random from sources on location. The music reflects Mouchette's emotional states and underscores conflicts among Louisa, Mathieu, and Arsène, registered in the dissonance of the phrases of music associated with each. Rather lively rock music bridges the forty-six shots of the bumper cars, creating a smooth, continuous flow in space and time, and reflecting Mouchette's amusement. The swiftly changing angles and speeds of the cars are punctuated by the sound of collisions. The scene is a typically perverse and complicated mixture of violence and gentleness on Bresson's part. This carnival scene and the music associated with it occur at the exact center of the film, framed at the beginning and end of the film by highly structured classical music. Between these instances of music, the continuity of highly organized and audible sounds throughout the film works as a rhythmic *continuo* essential to the structure of the film.

In subsequent films Bresson continues to exploit and refine the emblematic and structural possibilities of sound. In *Une Femme douce* the husband's footsteps echo over the cuts between past and present and call attention to the deathlike silence that pervades their rooms, whether the young woman is dead or alive. The sound of closing doors accents their arrivals and their departures from one another, as well as his searches for her and for some reason to account for her death. In *Quatre Nuits d'un rêveur*, the tape recorder registers Jacques's fantasy life in a disembodied fashion, a chant that he plays back to himself for solace and inspiration. Both films use contemporary popular source music as a correlative of the characters' moods.

The juncture of sound and music, meaning and sign, word and phrase in *Lancelot du Lac* is perfect and sums up Bresson's remarkable achievements as a sound composer. Each sound is set off clearly from each other and reappears throughout the film as a haunting reminder of earlier scenes and its symbolic function there. The sound track is a set of sound themes and variations: the panting and neighing of horses and pounding of racing hoofs; the clatter and crash of armor; the groans and gagging on blood as a knight is engorged and falls to the ground; the haunting warning of crows and the bird outside Guenièvre's window; the march of drums and flourish of bagpipes heralding the events of the tournament; the horn that signals the time of day; the church bell and singing of a *Benedictus;* and the scrape and echo of footsteps passing through stone corridors. In *Lancelot du Lac* sound conveys the epic emptiness of a past age, just as the zip and click of a cash machine signifies the cash nexus of our own age in his recent film *L'Argent.* The creak and strain of armor reminds us at every moment of the barriers that men have constructed between themselves as part of their eternal warfare. The hollow rituals of combat in which they engage are conveyed by the repetition of motions and the sounds associated with them: mounting horses, taking the lance, closing the helmet, riding off through the dark woods. The final shot of a creaking pyre of haunted suits of armor is Bresson's supreme metaphor for the emptiness of these physical shells of men for whom the spiritual quest is lost. The neighing of horses and the gnawing squawk of crows warn these men of the destruction and defeat in store, like messengers from a heavenly realm. The darting eyes of the horses, like Balthazar's, survey and shy away from the repeated follies of men. Sound in all of Bresson's films alerts us to an unheard world of threat and sorrow to which we have previously remained willfully deaf.

Godard's Use of Sound ALAN WILLIAMS

The following notes are intended to provoke discussion of Godard's sound tracks, their relations to his image tracks, and the range of options and interests that these display. The selection of examples is relatively arbitrary, and there is no attempt at discussion of the development of the director's sound practices. Godard is one of the most able and original manipulators of recorded sound in the history of cinema, and merely to detail the broad outlines of his use of sound is a task that can only be begun here.

I. "Raw Materials"

What sorts of sounds does Godard seek out with or arrange for his microphones? (By analogy with "pro-filmic" events, we would call these "pro-microphonic" sounds.) As with so much of world cinema throughout its history, Godard's cinema privileges spoken language. Unlike most other bodies of work, however, Godard's films do not privilege *dialogue,* in the accepted sense of the word, within this domain. "Conversation" is only one possible type of language use in a Godard film. There are also, most notably, *reading aloud, composing aloud for transcription, interviewing, giving a prepared speech or lecture, free association,* and *translation.* Of these, I will discuss only the two that seem most extensively employed: reading aloud and interviewing.

Reading a text aloud is a particularly frequent activity in Godard films. One senses this happening even when the voices are unknown, off-screen, or when (quite frequently) a voice begins off-screen and the speaker is afterwards revealed visually to be reading. Intonation patterns, pronunciation, and most other characteristics of spoken language are audibly different in reading aloud as opposed to "spontaneous" speech. Poetry, which in French shows the most marked of such differences (mute *e*'s are spoken, close to equal weight is given to each syllable), is merely the most audible instance of this. Pornography, journalistic exposés, advertising copy, doggerel: the sheer variety of recited texts is remarkable. Their significance is difficult to specify in general, but seems, rather, context-bound—for example, the pornographic texts in *Masculin féminin* that seem to emphasize the major characters' sexual insensitivity. Still, the choice of means is significant. Perhaps what is at stake is that language is thus shown to be *separable* from the people who speak it. It does not merely "express" them but also works through them. "One's own" voice is shown to be simply a particular variety of language use.

Another important function Godard allots to spoken language is the *interview*. There are two principal variants: either the interviewer is unseen and unheard, the interviewee responding to an unheard voice; or two diegetic characters are involved, in which case the interviewer, though audible and—typically—visually placed beforehand, is off-screen during the interview proper. One immediate implication of this device is easy enough to decipher; in exploiting the interview, Godard has hit upon a suitable format for exploring power relations as expressed through and enforced by language use. The power to ask questions is the power to be off-screen, a director-figure, as with the police in *Vivre sa vie* and *Masculin féminin,* or the young people in the latter film who trade dominance linguistically and cinematically in scenes that are really a series of interviews posing as casual conversation. (The subject: what else but sexual preference . . .)

Frequently, however, interviews seem to take place simply as an efficient means of exposition that also marks off an authorial intervention—as with the numbered dialogues with the camera in *La Chinoise* or the less rigidly structured interventions in *Tout va bien.* When "the film" interviews a character, the issue is less the power of the director vis-à-vis the characters (though this is clearly a factor) than it is the possibility that the characters may have *this* particular relation to filmic narration. The films do not merely "observe" their characters; through an unheard but obviously powerful language function they prod the characters into verbal action. This, in fact, seems to be the most general point to be drawn from the variety of language uses in Godard's work: that any one mode of functioning is merely what is being done *now* with language—replaceable by something else at almost any moment. Thus, the numerous possible linguistic options become elements in a large-scale *montage* that operates in the sphere of language.

This phenomenon of montage-within-an-information-channel can be seen even more clearly in the case of *sociopolitical markers* of language use. One of the most simple and striking ways to emphasize, within a fiction film, that language conveys the historical position of a character/actor (geographical origins, class position, etc.) is to employ actors with marked accents. Godard has had a strong predilection for this tactic, with a marked but by no means absolute preference for American accents—from Jean Seberg in *Breathless* through Jane Fonda in *Tout va bien.* It's possible to argue that the director simply likes the sounds so obtained, but it is also reasonable to point out that this device brings out, by extension, the variety of accents present in most collections of "native speakers" of French. Another way to obtain the same effect is to introduce "real" people among the fictional characters. In *Vivre sa vie* Godard has Nana, the central character, converse with a philosopher (Brice Parrain). The contrast between the two in accent, diction, and so on is almost as great as between Belmondo and Jean Seberg in *Breathless*. It's not that Parrain speaks pedantically; in fact, he is refreshingly informal (he slurs words, uses some genteel slang), as is political writer Francis Jeanson in a comparable juxtaposition in *La Chinoise*. But in both cases the differences in orientation of the two speakers emerge clearly in accent, use of subordinate clauses, forms of posing a question, etc. (In *La Chinoise*, Veronique's fragmented language confronts the measured linearity and regular cadences of Jeanson—the cool guerrilla versus the seasoned ideologue and establishment member.) It's possible to speak of such appearances as revealing Godard's respect for "reality," but it seems more precise to say that such figures are valued—as are linguistically marked Americans, Italians, Russians, Germans—for their status as perpetually evident *social artifacts*. (With regard to the image track, such characters have a similar function of underlining the sociohistorical functioning of gesture, as witness the elaborately "foreign" movements of the Italian boss in *Tout va bien*, the posture and hand motions of the francophone black in *La Chinoise*, etc.)

The moment one compares Godard's use of language with that of almost any other director—say, François Truffaut or Howard Hawks—one notices how much wider is the range of accents (sociopolitical markers) and language uses (modes of linguistic action, types of power relations)—even in the case of "normal dialogue" between two relatively neutral voices. (In fact, Godard's fondness for odd voices in unusual linguistic modalities makes relatively conventional film dialogue seem strange when it occurs in one of his films.) There is what one might call both a Bazinian and an Eisensteinian aspect to this work on language. The accents and language uses are of great interest in and of themselves, and Godard may be said to be fascinated by the broad spectrum of linguistic reality. This is the Bazinian side of his aural sensibility. But these varying types and uses of language confront one another, appear as elements of a combinatory set (a *combinatoire*). This is what might be called an Eisensteinian, or perhaps a Vertovian, heritage. These are not in conflict; rather, they require one another.

Although this sketch of Godard's treatment of language is accurate in its broad outlines, it is important to note that there are quite different mixtures of language phenomena in various films. What remains constant is the activation of a noticeable range of options. *Masculin féminin*, for example, makes only slight use of foreign accents—enough to raise the issue, but hardly the wild diversity displayed in *Tout va bien* or *Contempt*. On the other hand, *Masculin féminin* makes remarkably extensive use of the diegetic, generally informal interview (a major character, Paul, does interviews for a living for most of the film), while *Tout va bien* uses both diegetic and directorial (silent interviewer) ones, and *Contempt* virtually abandons this technique in favor of the activity of *translation.*

A similar situation of diversity within a consistent strategy of "montage within the (sound) frame" holds for Godard's use of music. If anything, his treatment of music is even broader ranging than that of language. Each film, again, has its own particular recipe of distinct ingredients. Narrative films employ three categories of music: diegetic performance (whether sync or postsync—a distinction normally inoperative, but which Godard frequently activates); quotation of recorded artifacts (whether the quotation is diegetic or not); and so-called soundtrack music (taken to be part of the film's narrational apparatus). Most typically, commercially viable films create a musical continuum in which these distinctions are operative logically but not immediately evident in terms of musical materials. In a Fellini film, the same sort of Nino Rota tunes—often the same tunes—play from jukeboxes, are sung by characters, and get manipulated as narrational background. Godard does nothing of the sort. He typically employs completely distinct sorts of materials for each category: contemporary French pop for the performances, tunes by Brassens and perhaps a Mozart quartet for the recorded quotations, and neoromantic scores by Delerue or Legrand for the "movie" music—to cite an imaginary but typical distribution. (Godard can move very far from these loose norms—as far as Stockhausen's percussion ensemble in *La Chinoise* is from Legrand or Delerue.) A relatively constant trope in all the films is the mixing of elite culture (Bach, Mozart) with particularly crude pop tunes by the likes of Françoise Hardy or Chantal Goya. The sound track scores then occupy an intermediate position between these "high" and "low" musical cultures. Although generalizations are always dangerous, it could be said that one immediate result of Godard's musical eclecticism is that the social positions of the various musical styles are in this way emphasized. Another probable result, also emphasized by strictly narrative means, is to underline the fact that music in Western society is a consumer item (Nana sells records in *Vivre sa vie;* Madeleine is a pop singer in *Masculin féminin*).

Turning finally to what is broadly termed "sound effects," we encounter a field where Godard is somewhat more single-minded than in language or music. The sounds that interest him are, almost without exception, mechanical in origin: car horns *(Weekend)*, construction noises *(Two or Three Things I Know About Her)*, traffic noises penetrating cafés or apartments (everywhere), gunfire *(Vivre sa vie)*, pinball machines (one of the director's favorite sounds). Two noteworthy aspects of this preference are: (1)

the sounds are recorded at remarkably high levels; and (2) the characters seem peculiarly unresponsive to them—it's as if they are unaware of their sonic environment except to the extent that it assumes culturally rationalized forms. Where, as is typical in Godard's "location" recordings, the spectator strains to decipher dialogue (subtitling tends to make this seem easier than it actually is), the characters seem better adapted to urban noise than the film audience is made to feel. The sheer weight of this "natural" sound is made all the more evident by what is, in such a context, perhaps the ultimate sound effect: *silence*, which when it arrives—abruptly, as do most of Godard's sounds—is eerily soothing.

II. Sound Recording, Sound Editing

Of the various *nouvelle vague* directors, Godard seems one of those most influenced in his filmmaking by the thought of André Bazin (the spiritual mentor to all the young critics of *Cahiers du cinéma* in the early 1950s). One sees this in his fondness for sequence shots, for location shooting, his frequent use of nonactors and improvised stories, even his taste for the overtly theatrical (recall Bazin's comments on "Theatre and Cinema").[1]

Consider a Godard scene set in a Parisian café. Ambient noise is prominent, the actors' voices compete with it. Perhaps a jukebox plays, and its sound is subject to dual distortion, of the initial recording and the rerecording in a new acoustic environment.[2] Or a pinball machine makes disconcertingly loud thumps and boings. The overall sound tone (hear, for example, *Vivre sa vie* or *Two or Three Things*) emphasizes the treble, and the bass has the thump characteristic of nonstudio work. What is strange and vaguely shocking about Godard's use of sound in these and other equivalent scenes may best be suggested by comparing what he does with a Hollywood rendering of the same basic acoustic situation: any Warners film of the late thirties through the early fifties will do as a model (to cite merely the specific reference I have in mind—most TV movies will do for a present-day approximation). Where Godard's pro-microphone sounds compete for dominance, the American studio style has a startlingly precise ebb and flow of background noises as they relate to foreground: car horns "just happen" to occur in conversational pauses; the entire sense of sonic ambience recedes when narratively significant information appears. In such a recording practice, pinball machines are well mannered, their frequencies equalized so as not to impinge on the tonal range of human voices. There is, in sum, a clear and reassuring *hierarchy* of sonic importance, and this is reinforced by a kind of step-system of sonic presence, sounds being made to seem either very close (important) or distant ("atmosphere").

This Hollywood sound track, despite relaying the same diegetic information about events in the café, would convey quite a different message about what kind of a film is giving us access to this information. The two renderings of pro-microphonic events conjure up quite different processes of assimilating knowledge; they represent, with little metaphor intended, two distinct means of *writing* film sound—or, to avoid the figure entirely, two *recording practices*. (Writing is one of the oldest and still the most socially significant means of recording, but it remains both conceptually and historically a member of the larger class of recording systems, which presumably also includes all so-called iconic signs.)[3] I will not argue, however, that in eschewing Hollywood sound practices Godard somehow "deconstructs" classical narrative; if the death of Hollywood were his purpose, he would be using far too much ammunition and aiming it too haphazardly. I will try to suggest below what I think his purposes are; for the moment, the comparison with "transparent" sound recording practices will help to suggest what they are not.

Godard's ambient sounds, when present, refuse to go away when "more important" information appears. In other words, at least in his location sound recording, he refuses to do the spectator's work. (We will see shortly that he is not above making choices on the spectator's behalf, but when this happens it is, to understate the matter, obvious and unconventional.) Classical narrative sound recording is "transparent"—or *inaudible* as recording—in the same way that classical visual practices are. It follows the assumed demands of an ideal listening spectator. The ambient noise that recedes during dialogue in a Hollywood film is the sonic equivalent of the visual background that disappears during a close-up (or is de-emphasized by lighting, character movement, and so forth). As in the case of the visual close-up this type of editing goes unnoticed by seeming to answer to the requirements of the fiction.[4] We are so accustomed to "inaudible" sound manipulation that Godard's café seems acoustically strange while Hollywood's does not. Commercial narrative sound recording practices employ literally hundreds of edits and changes of level per sequence and yet these are quite difficult to hear without practice. Godard's (generally) omnidirectional microphones and his refusal to mix and edit sound within a track once recorded[5] result in a sonic texture that is *continuously audible,* both by the fact of implicit comparisons with "normal" sound and by the work required in listening.

It can be argued that all this makes Godard a sonic "realist," and certainly his location recording techniques are strong evidence for a possible Bazinian influence. Whether "realistic" or not (the problem is that the result sounds highly stylized), Godard's refusal to edit and mix transpar-

ently results in a close aural equivalent of long takes with great depth of field.
Bazin called Wyler's deep-focus technique "democratic," as opposed to the
hierarchical nature of classical editing; Godard's location sound is similarly
egalitarian in that it does not pick and choose for the auditor. Godard, of
course, does not leave the matter there. A significant result of his ambient
noise levels and continuous sense of acoustic environment is that it is impossible to slip in and out of a sound take imperceptibly. Where sound begins, one knows it. (A contemporary television equivalent may be found in
the highly layered sound—artifically produced, of course—in *Hill Street Blues*,
where fades to and from black are accompanied by sound fades. There are
few other ways to negotiate such transitions in an orderly way. Most Robert
Altman films, acoustically related to Godard's practices though means and
final effects are quite different, use the same tactic.) Far from concealing the
sonic transitions to his location scenes, Godard emphasizes them. A typical
tactic is to begin a scene silent and bring in sound abruptly, coinciding with
a mechanical event such as a door closing or a car horn. Where this does
not happen, silence accompanying an introductory title card or the end of a
preceding quiet sequence serves the same purpose. The dense *mise-en-scène*
of Godard's location sound enables him, in other words, to use sound recordings as large-scale montage units. A café or street scene that follows a
tranquil idyll in an apartment produces an audible confrontation of different
sound spaces. (Robert Altman and the makers of *Hill Street Blues* not only
mitigate their thick sound textures by synchronous fades and by frequent
music overlaps, but they maintain a relatively constant sound tone, avoiding
precisely the juxtapositions of loud noise and relative quiet that Godard makes
so much of. One might call their sound aesthetics pseudo-Bazinian.)[6]

But not all of Godard's films emphasize this sort of location sound
work. As might be expected (presumably due both to producer pressure and
to extended technical resources), the higher the budget, the more studiolike
Godard's sound, as witness *Tout va bien* and *Contempt*, for example. When
Godard records in a studio or in an isolated location (sonic isolation equals
extensive capital and/or labor, in film even more than in life), he does not
produce an ersatz of his Parisian cafés. In *Tout va bien*, in particular, the
acoustic feel of a studio set becomes an important component of that film's
repertoire of sonic elements. In one striking case, a cut to a long horizontal
tracking shot of the factory set is accompanied by what seems to be a nondiegetic silence—but is shortly revealed to be, instead, a simultaneous cut to
a set of microphones whose location is (initially) off-screen right. The moving camera eventually reveals both the source of subsequent sounds and the
fact that the initial silence was the expression of an acoustic environment
and not an electronic suppression of noise.

Godard seems to compensate for the relatively quiet background of "good" sound work by an increased interest in sound montage within (rather than between) particular sequences. In one revealing example, from *Contempt*, a filmmaking team visits a sleazy, almost empty theater to observe a singer they are considering for a film role. The sequence begins conventionally enough, with music brought up at the end of previous shots (the characters in a car) and the end of the song's introduction coinciding with the observers taking their seats. Cut to an archetypal Godardian lateral tracking shot (completely butchered in 16mm reductions currently available) of the seated filmmakers. This type of shot alternates, more or less, with shots of the stage show, singer and dancers. During the latter shots, the sound track carries the singer's song, in obvious and cavernous playback. During the lateral tracks, the sound cuts back and forth between the song in playback and recorded sync dialogue with no music whatever. What is instructive about this example is that one shot is accompanied by two alternate and incompatible renderings of the acoustic environment. Precisely where norms of commercial film sound would dictate an up-and-down play of dialogue and music levels (abetted by reduced or no echo in the music track, to lessen its obtrusiveness), Godard provides a particularly obvious and paradoxical sonic montage.

But it is in *Tout va bien* that sound montage within sequences is most pervasive. Of the wealth of work on sound in that film, one example must suffice. In the last narrative sequence, Jane Fonda observes a demonstration in a supermarket. Visually, this scene employs one of Godard's most successful and intricate lateral tracks. Sonically, there are three elements: sync sound recording of the chaotic scene, supposed internal monologues of the Fonda character, and, always introducing the latter (and recorded separately, not part of the market sounds), those annoying French public address chimes. (Americans will be most familiar with these from airports, though they are also used in large stores for promotional announcements.) Without the chimes, and with at least one initial closer shot of Fonda coinciding with the first monologue, the sequence would be logically unproblematic in its use of sound. But Godard introduces "private thoughts" as public announcements (which, for the purposes of the film itself, they are), and by so doing emphasizes the disparateness of the materials he is working with.

Other sound montages in *Tout va bien* range from the striking (presence/absence of location sound in the worker narratives) to the acceptable if noticeable (Jane Fonda in English overdubbed into French) to the semantically obscure (the three distinct sound quotations that accompany the film's last shot).[7] For all of this formal experimentation, the film remains, to me at least, the least sonically jarring of Godard's because of its "quality" sound recording, and to that extent the least typical. The principal point to be drawn, however, is that even in a big-budget star production Godard did not abandon formal work on sound but merely shifted it slightly in register.

III. Bazin. Eisenstein or Vertov? "Permutational Formalism."

That there is a Bazinian inspiration in Godard's image and sound recording practices seems indisputable, both on biographical and on cinemato-graphic/aesthetic grounds. But the contemporary tendency to dismiss Ba-zin's writings as idealist and to reject completely his notion of "realism" threatens to lead Godard criticism astray. Consider the following citation, from the celebrated "Ontology of the Photographic Image":

The objective nature of photography confers on it a quality of credibility absent from all other picture-making. *In spite of any objections* our critical spirit may offer, *we are forced to accept as real* the existence of the object reproduced, actually re-presented, set before us, that is to say, in time and space. (*What Is Cinema?* pp. 13–14, emphasis added)

I would argue that the italicized phrases are not incidental to this passage, and that we should take seriously the implied metaphor of *domination* by the image. "We are *forced* to accept" things, despite our "objections." What we are forced to do, in fact, is to rediscover, via the power of the image (there is always a passive-masochistic subtext in Bazin's language) what we ordinarily ignore. Bazin's "realism" frequently coincides, in fact, with the Russian formalist notion of "defamiliarization," reality *made strange:*[8]

It is not [possible or habitual—A. W.] for me to separate off, in the complex fabric of the objective world, here a reflection on a damp sidewalk, there the gesture of a child. Only the impassive lens, *stripping its object of all those ways of seeing it, those piled-up preconceptions,* that spiritual dust and grime with which my eyes have covered it, is able to present it in all its virginal purity to my attention and consequently to my love. (p. 15, emphasis added)

Where Godard would most obviously disagree with Bazin, in these passages, is in the choice of examples. The reality Bazin wishes revealed reeks with connotations of primal Nature à la Rousseau (the child, the sun, and elsewhere mountains, etc.). Godard's preferred reality, and most particularly his sonic reality, is pinball machines, the roar of the métro, the *mechanical.* (Both of these are limit-cases: where critic and filmmaker can presumably agree is on the real-izing of the *cultural fact.*) Godard's sounds assault the spectator, force him/her to listen, to be astonished at their power—which is so easily obscured by the perceptual "dust and grime" of everyday life. Hollywood sound practices are wholly unsuitable to this sort of endeavor, imitating as they do the everyday preconceptions and habits of attention that obscure the real.

If Bazin had written a critique of Hollywood sound practices, it seems likely that it would have been argued along lines similar to his analysis of "classical editing" of the image. Like classical editing, "inaudible" sound practices aim for verisimilitude (analogy with everyday experience) and not realism (which is, at least potentially, *strange*). Classical editing, both of image and sound, "presupposes, of its very nature, the unity of meaning of the dramatic event" (p. 36—where this is said of montage in general). But unity of meaning is synonymous, in Bazin's thought, with "spiritual dust and grime," since reality is held to exceed perpetually any attempt at unifying it. Unity of meaning is always unity *for someone* (Bazin's phenomenological heritage)—or for an implied spectator surrogate. It is, like classical editing, "mental and abstract" (p. 39) and offers the *"illusion* of objective presentation" (ibid., emphasis added) rather than the irreducibility of objects and events themselves.

It takes very little rearranging of these views to make them, not merely Godardian, but Eisensteinian. Of course, Eisenstein himself turned stylistically into something of a Bazinian before the fact (or perhaps a Wellesian) in his sound films—though not for wholly theoretical reasons. He certainly anticipated Bazin's view of long takes, action arranged within the frame, and so on, as preferable to analytical and dramatic editing *à la* Hollywood. But Eisenstein, as Bazin was wont to point out, viewed montage as a means to an end of "unity" beyond but related to that produced in classical practices. In "The Cinematographic Principle and the Ideogram,"[9] Eisenstein proposed that cinema images were manipulable in the same manner as hieroglyphs: "bird" plus "mouth" equals "to sing," and so forth. Conflict on one level produces unity on a higher (conceptual) level. This was precisely Bazin's objection to Eisenstein—that the world was, as in classical editing, submitted to an analysis and subsequently reconstituted as a unity.

When one examines Godard's approach to montage, it becomes possible to argue that he would have, generally, the same objection. There are moments where montage fragments do seem to coalesce into a sort of unity, but these are the exception. The most spectacular example, at least as regards sound-image (vertical) relations—which is where one finds most of the Eisenstein-inspired montage in Godard—is unquestionably to be found in *Two or Three Things I Know About Her*. In that film, one of Godard's sonically typical café scenes incorporates enormous close-ups, larger with each appearance, of the surface of a cup of espresso coffee in which cubes of sugar are being dissolved. (One cube drops in at the beginning of one of the shots; bubbles constantly appear and spiral, galaxylike.) The effect, which will be recalled by anyone who has seen the film, is both strong and extremely difficult to describe. It is, first of all, a montage of *scale:* sound takes in the entire dramatic space, while visuals become increasingly restricted. The coffee cup becomes a kind of meditation object that all conversation and sound seems to be "about." The verbal concerns of the sound track seem trivial compared to the visual patterns that become, increasingly, minimal and abstract.

But although this example is arguably similar to Eisenstein's sound-image manipulation in, for example, *Alexander Nevsky,* it is not really typical in Godard's work. (Rather, it is a kind of privileged moment in the film, whose impact seems to depend largely on context and on, precisely, its relative uniqueness in the work.) It seems likely that the more typical instances *(Contempt, Tout va bien)* would be taken in Eisenstein's view as evidence of the sin of "formalism." "Formalist jackstraws" was Eisenstein's catch-phrase denunciation of Dziga Vertov's work, and by this he seems to have meant any manipulations of filmic materials utilized apparently for their own sake and not as part of an overall (unified) generation of meaning. Where Eisenstein saw conflict as a way of producing (higher) unity, Vertov seems to have valued conflict on all levels both in itself and as a metaphor for physical and social processes. Godard and J.-P. Gorin, in adopting for a time the name "Dziga Vertov Group" for their work, may have been proclaiming their allegiance to the latter viewpoint. This is, however, a difficult argument to pursue, given current limited knowledge of Vertov's films and theoretical writings. (I have attempted elsewhere to analyze one sequence from *Man with a Movie Camera* in terms that implicitly foreground the differences between that film and Eisenstein's work.)[10] It helps, nonetheless, to emphasize that most of Godard's "montage" effects serve not to unify but to *keep separate* their constituent elements.

If Vertov is a difficult figure to invoke for an approach to Godard's textual structuring practices, a less historically remote parallel may be found in Noël Burch's *Praxis du cinéma* (first published in 1969, and thus coinciding nicely enough with the period of Godard's major researches).[11] Burch argued for a conception of cinema analogous to the organizational tactics of serial music. Cinematic textuality could be viewed as the organization of a known, restricted set of parameters: spatiotemporal characteristics of edits, relations between screen space and off-screen space, "live" versus "recomposed" sound, and so on. These "dialectics" could interact and intersect, and Burch seems to have valued (he now rejects most of the book's argument) films to the extent that they exploited such organizational possibilities. Hanoun's *Une Simple histoire,* for example, had "the most elaborate, most rigorously controlled formal structure of any feature film thus far made" and was (as a result?) "one of the few genuine masterpieces in the entire history of cinema" (p. 81).

There are, indeed, many sequences in Godard's films that seem ready-made for Burch's analytic vocabulary and theoretical concepts. The theater sequence from *Contempt*, the examples cited from *Tout va bien*, the "structural" intrusions of silence in *Vivre sa vie* all seem to follow formal parameters at the expense of narrative logic. The use of music throughout *Vivre sa vie*, which has been subjected to a close and useful analysis by Royal S. Brown,[12] seems particularly formalized: musical segments end one shot, intrude early in a subsequent shot at an analogous point with regard to camera movement, later bridge a similar pair of shots, and so on. Brown summarizes his argument, in terms that strongly recall Burch, that the film was conceived "as a quasi-musical structure" (p. 320).

Particularly with reference to sound and to sound-image relations, such arguments can be made about Godard's work, but one wonders if they don't stop short of a full account of cinematic means and ends. It's worth noting that in *Praxis du cinéma* Noël Burch found Godard less consistent and formally interesting than Marcel Hanoun or Alain Resnais. There does seem to be a "musical"/formal aspect to Godard's work, but it's not clear that this is an end in itself. Imagine a semicircular track clockwise around two characters in conversation, accompanied by sound X, then a similar track counterclockwise with sound Y, followed by a stationary shot from above with both sounds X and Y, perhaps mixed and played simultaneously. (Nothing quite so rigid occurs in Godard's work, but there are passages that approach this degree of formal organization—for example, the credits of *Vivre sa vie*.) The best label I can provide for this sort of organizational work is "permutational formalism": a set of mutually exclusive formal options are combined and recombined according to an implicit "truth table" of their possible relations. This is the kind of structuration called for in *Praxis du cinéma*, and Godard does seem frequently enough to follow such a program, albeit not as consistently as the Noël Burch of 1969 would have liked. It seems, in fact, that Godard is enough of a permutational formalist to provide the *sense* of an underlying set of categories (Burch's "dialectics")—sound-track music versus source music, interviewing versus reading aloud, sync sound versus silence versus vertical montage—without necessarily exploiting the categories as thoroughly as one might expect. I would argue that the division of filmic elements into relatively discrete sets is in fact Godard's primary stylistic goal, and that the formal play of discrete categories only occurs to the extent necessary to establish and maintain them. In this sense, Godard is a *minimal* permutational formalist, and it is not an accident that the hypothetical example invoked above does not exist in any of his films.[13]

It seems most probable that sound plays a crucial role in Godard's minimal permutational formalism precisely because sound elements are, generally, subject to clearer and simpler differentiation than visual ones—at least this is the situation in Western, representational cinema as we know it. There is a greater range of relatively discrete uses of verbal language as opposed to gesture, for example, and the image track is commonly held to convey two information channels (moving images, writing) as opposed to three for sound (speech, music, sound effects). Godard does, of course, employ such differentiations as are possible with image recording—types of camera movement, editing, or color, images versus writing, images that contain writing versus titles, etc. But by its sheer quantity of possible "dialectics," and in their possible relations to the image track, recorded sound plays an essential and decisive role in the structuration of his films.

However, if formal play is a means and not the end, then what is achieved in Godard's intricate, dense film structures? First of all, the impact of the "raw materials" is preserved. The Bazinian quest for a strange and aggressive visual and sonic reality may go on because premature abstraction (unification of elements in the film) is prevented. The physical existence of recorded sounds and images is maintained as psychological fact. "Formalism" and the documentary quest for "reality" are, in Godard's work, not mutually exclusive but mutually necessary. One result of the sheer impact of Godard's pro-filmic materials is the deep sensual pleasure that looking at and listening to a Godard film can produce, a kind of awed attention to the texture of visual and sonic facts. (The coffee cup in *Two or Three Things* has a kind of oppressive but fascinating power, and it serves for me as an emblem of Godard's refined but very real *sensualism*.)

But if the sensory impact of recorded sounds and images is maintained by their textual differentiation and organization, so are the sociohistoric associations of the objects and events represented. Although subject to internal, formal differentiation, Godard's images and sounds are not random selections of recorded physical occurrences. In maintaining what Brecht called the "separation of elements,"[14] Godard's films pose questions, provoke thought. But this separation must be perpetually renewed, in the cinema above all, where the search for "unity" is a spectatorial habit reinforced by whole lifetimes of passive consumption. Godard's use of sound is at the heart of what can be labeled a postwar modernist version of Brecht's epic theater:

When the epic theatre's methods begin to penetrate the opera the first result is a radical *separation of the elements*. . . . So long as the expression "Gesamtkunstwerk" (or "integrated work of art") means that the integration is a muddle, so long as the arts are supposed to be "fused" together, the various elements will all be equally degraded, and each will act as a mere "feed" to the rest. The process of fusion extends to the spectator, who gets thrown into the melting pot too and becomes a passive (suffering) part of the total work of art. Witchcraft of this sort must of course be fought against. Whatever is intended to produce hypnosis, is likely to induce sordid intoxication, or creates fog, has got to be given up.

Words, music, and setting must become more independent of one another. (Brecht on Theatre, pp. 37–38)

Notes

1. All references to Bazin are to *What Is Cinema?* (Berkeley: University of California Press, 1971).

2. For a description of how one "realistic" (which is to say, reconstituted, ersatz) playback effect is obtained via conventional sound editing practices, see Larry Sturhahn, "The Art of the Sound Editor: An Interview with Walter Murch," *Filmmakers Newsletter,* 8, no. 2 (December 1974):22–25. This entire text can quite profitably be compared with Jean Collet, "An Audacious Experiment: The Soundtrack of *Vivre sa vie,"* in Royal S. Brown, ed., *Focus on Godard* (Englewood Cliffs, N.J.: Prentice-Hall, 1972), pp. 160–62.

3. This is not an argument that I can pursue here, but the interested reader is referred to the tantalizing hints and references in Chapter 11 of Christian Metz's *Langage et cinéma* (Paris: Larousse, 1971).

4. See my "Is Sound Recording Like a Language?" *Yale French Studies,* no. 60 (1980):51–66.

5. See Jean Collet, "An Audacious Experiment."

6. "What I really want is for sound to be texturally uniform. If a picture sounds looped, it would be odd to have 5 lines in it recorded live. I would loop those lines to get uniform texture." Walter Murch, in Larry Sturhahn, "The Art of the Sound Editor."

7. According to Godard, these represent the three political forces of the film: dominant bourgeois attitudes, conformist communism, and radical leftism. The effect is noteworthy as one of the few certifiable attempts at "intellectual montage" *à la* Eisenstein in Godard's work.

8. "After we see an object several times, we begin to recognize it. The object is in front of us and we know about it, but we do not see it—hence we cannot say anything significant about it. Art removes objects from the automatism of perception in several ways." Victor Shklovsky, "Art as Technique," in L. T. Lemon and M. J. Reis, eds., *Russian Formalist Criticism* (Lincoln: University of Nebraska Press, 1965), p. 13.

9. In *Film Form: Essays in Film Theory,* ed. and trans. Jay Leyda (New York: Harcourt, Brace, 1949).

10. "The Camera Eye and the Film: Notes on Vertov's 'Formalism,' " *Wide Angle,* 3, no. 3 (1979):12–17.

11. Paris: Gallimard; English translation by H. R. Lane as *Theory of Film Practice* (New York: Praeger, 1973). All page references are to the translation.

12. "Music and *Vivre sa vie,"* *Quarterly Review of Film Studies,* 5, no. 3 (Summer 1980):319–33.

13. Nor do many of Burch's examples exist anywhere but in his book, as witness the notorious set of footnotes on page 31.

14. See John Willet, ed. and trans., *Brecht on Theatre* (New York: Hill and Wang, 1964).

Contemporary Innovators

Robert Altman could easily be numbered among the greatest sound stylists; like the directors covered in Section 3, he uses sound creatively in virtually all of his films. However, Altman is included in this section because his style is closely linked with new trends in sound technology, some of which he himself developed. Charles Schreger's article "Altman, Dolby and the Second Sound Revolution" here discusses Altman not only as a distinctive stylist but also in the context of such technologies as eight-track recording and the Dolby system. Schreger also cites major films of the seventies in which sound plays a crucial role "either as the subject or the technique."

A common denominator of several films mentioned by Schreger is the contribution of sound specialist Walter Murch, who is often a full collaborator on the films of George Lucas and Francis Ford Coppola. Murch's credits include the sound for Lucas's *THX-1138* and *American Graffiti* and Coppola's *Godfather* films, the editing of Coppola's *The Conversation,* and the sound design of *Apocalypse Now.* In the interview included below, Murch discusses how he approaches a new assignment and how he works. He prefers the British "horizontal" system (wherein each sound editor works on a given type of sound effect throughout the film) to the traditional Hollywood "vertical" system of editing sound effects (wherein each sound editor is assigned all of a given reel). Throughout the discussion Murch provides examples from his work on *Apocalypse Now,* for which he won an Academy Award.

In fact, the emergence of sound technicians like Murch may be the greatest change in sound practices in the last decade. While there are still directors, notably Terrence Malick and Martin Scorsese, who maintain distinctive personal aural styles, the creative impetus today may come not from a director but from a sound specialist whose participation is more central than was that of the old sound editors. Marc Mancini's essay describes the art and technique of these specialists, who are often called "sound designers."

The drawback to the ascendancy of sound designers is that on occasion their sound tracks are either better than the film as a whole or not organic to it. At the other extreme from the collaborative Hollywood system is the world of independent filmmaking. Indeed, the most original and coherent uses of sound today can often be found in the work of the avant-garde, who do not feel beholden to Hollywood conventions of "invisible" narrative recording and mixing. Fred Camper discusses the achievements of several avant-garde filmmakers with particularly dense sound tracks. But he also points out the importance of silence in recent films: inasmuch as pretalkie silents were actually accompanied in most cases by music or other sounds, it is only the emergence of sync sound that made silence a true choice and a deliberate aesthetic statement. Camper ends by distinguishing various types of silence in the work of such avant-gardists as Ernie Gehr and Stan Brakhage.

Altman, Dolby,
and the Second Sound Revolution
CHARLES SCHREGER

It was the early autumn of 1927. F. W. Murnau's masterpiece, *Sunrise*, had just been released; Buster Keaton's masterpiece, *The General*, was playing the nabes; Josef von Sternberg was making the *Underworld* look like a beautiful place; Garbo was making *Love* with John Gilbert. . . .

The time was right for the introduction of sound films. By the mid-twenties, talking machines—radio, the telephone, Victrolas—were no longer considered the playthings of the rich; now they were necessities for the nation's huge middle class. It was, perhaps, the first generation of literates who got more information and entertainment by listening than by reading. America was suddenly sound-conscious.

In 1978, America seems sound-obsessed. You can feel the full impact of a symphony or a rock concert in your living room; you can take it with you in your car or in a pocket-sized radio; you can—must—hear it in a dentist's office or an elevator. You can be transported or anaesthetized by it at the local disco; you can hear a mixed-media simulcast, one track on TV, the other on FM. And you can, of course, buy it on records and tapes. In 1977, the music industry grossed almost $3.5 *billion*—$1 billion more than the 15,000 U.S. theaters took in at the box office.

Grosses are persuasive to moguls. So are demographics. The same age group that buys albums, car radios, and expensive stereo equipment— the eighteen- to thirty-year-olds—supports the film industry. When this audience goes to the theater, they want to hear the movie as well as see it— and hear it as well as they would at home or at a live concert. In 1927, the quality of the sound that seemed to be coming from Al Jolson was superior to that from radios and records. Today's moviegoers demand parity, and they're a lot more sophisticated. So are today's moguls—especially those, like Robert Stigwood, Jerry Weintraub, Neil Bogart, Berry Gordy, and Irving Azoff, who made their first millions in the music business. And, most important, so are the filmmakers, who are eager to experiment and innovate. In dozens of recent and forthcoming movies, you can see—or, rather, hear—it coming: the second Sound Revolution.

Two small clues: crickets and Crickets. In Terrence Malick's *Days of Heaven*, the nights on a Panhandle farm are filled with the sound of crickets. In *The Buddy Holly Story*, Gary Busey's voice, as he sings "That'll Be the Day" in a roller rink, is in perfect synchronization with his lip movement—because it was recorded live (as were the songs in *At Long Last Love* and *Nashville*). The specific effects here are less important than implied principles. One is technical: movies now have superior sound fidelity. The other is aesthetic: moviemakers are pledging fidelity to superior sound. And both principles indicate that the Hollywood film is today, more than ever, in the service of a heightened realism. Sound works with image to put the audience *on* that farm, or *in* that rink.

With sound as with image, of course, it takes a collaborative art to convince us that a movie is life; and it takes modern technology to make the art possible. Was it the availability of complex sound equipment that sparked Hollywood's fascination with high-quality sound on film? Or did a few daring directors have a vision (or hear voices) and then seek out the hardware and soundmen to help them realize it? Whatever the answer, the short list of sound-conscious directors comprises a baker's dozen of some of the industry's most successful, esteemed, and adventurous talents. In alphabetical order: Robert Altman, Michael Cimino, Francis Coppola, Milos Forman, Philip Kaufman, Stanley Kubrick, George Lucas, Terry Malick, Alan J. Pakula, Ken Russell, Martin Scorsese, Jerzy Skolimowski, Steven Spielberg.

A is for Altman, the filmmaker most closely associated with sound experimentation. In his case, at least, the idea preceded the technology. As early as *Countdown* (made in 1967), he has been developing the practice of overlapping dialogue—or, as he calls it, "live sound effects." It's a tradition that goes back through the fast-talking films of Howard Hawks, Frank Capra, and Preston Sturges, to the 1928 Broadway production of Hecht and MacArthur's *The Front Page* (directed by George S. Kaufman), to the double monologue delivered by Higgins and Pickering in Shaw's *Pygmalion* (1913), and even to the stychomythia of classical Greek drama.

Altman concentrated, though, not on the rapid alternating of short lines of dialogue but on dialogue simultaneously spoken by two or more characters: a wall of sound, a Tower of Babel, a film of bit players trying to get their two cents' worth in. It was another way of making movies like life—where a conversation is carried on in bursts of words and grunts, where people interrupt each other's sentences, where the participants are straining to be heard above the noise of the subway, the TV, or other people's voices. *California Split* was Altman's sound breakthrough. He had found the technology—the eight-track recording system—and, as he's said, made the film as an *étude*, as a test of the equipment and techniques he was planning to deploy even further in *Nashville*.

The key difference in the eight-track system is that each actor, instead of speaking into an overhead boom microphone (which picks up all the sound in a scene: the noise of the location as well as the voices of the performers), is equipped with a tiny radio mike, and speaks into *it*. There are no wires or cables; the sound is broadcast from the mike to a receiving unit. Each performer gets one channel, and the sound is individually controlled. For technical reasons, one channel must be eliminated; so, under the eight-track system, seven actors can speak at once. A separate recording unit picks up the background noise. On *A Wedding*, Altman had *two* eight-track units operating simultaneously: during many scenes, fourteen different people were "miked" and can be heard on the sound track.

Besides distinguishing individual sounds more clearly in a crowded scene, the system allows for improvisation. The actor isn't tied down; he can move outside the normal confines. One actor can interrupt another—just as in real life—without the director working out complicated cues with the boom operator. And the director can use long shots more freely; he needn't worry about the sight, or the shadow, of cables and overhead microphones. By now, Altman has worked the bugs (the scratching sounds from the mike rubbing against the actor's clothing, the occasional interference of CB calls over the radio equipment) out of the system, to the extent that he's been able to eliminate boom mikes on his films.

Altman's interest in sound extends beyond overlapping dialogue and the eight-track system. He has recorded live all the music in his films since *Nashville*. Telephone calls are also done live in his films. When Keith Carradine interrupts his tryst with Lily Tomlin to dial a girlfriend in New York, he's actually speaking with someone on the other end. It's a technique subsequently employed in other films, notably Pakula's *All the President's Men*— for which Jim Webb, Altman's longtime sound location mixer, handled the sound chores.

The dauntingly elaborate job of mixing (rerecording) *A Wedding* was performed by Richard Portman on a computer-controlled board at the Samuel Goldwyn Studios. When Altman recently moved his Lion's Gate studios from Westwood to a larger place in West Los Angeles, it was "mainly to have our own dubbing and rerecording stage. We were lucky to get Dick Portman, who's considered one of the very best recording mixers, to run it. If this proves a success—and we believe it will be, because we're pretty sophisticated about sound—then the business of doing sound on other people's films will support the rest of our organization." Two rerecording stages will be built; one room will be equipped with a computer that allows a single mixing technician to do the work of three or four.

In his search for the perfect sound system, Altman found a vital ally in Ray Dolby—the Englishman who invented the Dolby noise-reduction system. For years, Dolby (which hereafter will refer to the system and not the man) had been taking the hiss out of stereo tapes, FM radios, and records. Almost every record company has used Dolby equipment during some phase of production, because it reduces background noise and improves frequency response, allowing for sharper highs and lows.

"Frequency response" is an obscure concept to many. It may help some if we say that Dolby adds two-and-a-half octaves to the range. The rest can try a little experiment. Listen to any music, on a good stereo system, with the treble and the bass turned all the way down. At first it will sound confined, but after a few minutes your ear will grow accustomed to the flatness. Now turn up the bass and treble to their normal levels—and suddenly there will be a brightness, a fullness, to the sound. It will sound real; it will be there with you. That's the difference Dolby makes.

The earliest use of Dolby on film was, naturally enough, for rock documentaries *(The Grateful Dead)* and fantasies (Ken Russell's *Tommy*). But sound-conscious filmmakers soon recognized its potential, and not just to take out the hiss. "What Dolby does," says writer-director Michael Cimino, "is to give you the ability to create a *density of detail* of sound—a richness so you can demolish the wall separating the viewer from the film. You can come close to demolishing the screen."

With *The Deer Hunter,* his first Dolby film, Cimino toiled mightily to ensure that very effect. He spent six month's shooting the film and *five* months mixing the sound track. One short battle sequence—200 feet of film in the final cut—took five days to dub. Another sequence recreated the 1975 American evacuation of Saigon; Cimino brought the film's composer, Stanley Myers, out to the location to listen to the auto, tank, and jeep horns as the sequence was being photographed. The result, according to Cimino: Myers composed the music for that scene in the same key as the horn sounds, so the music and the sound effects would blend with the images to create one jarring, desolate experience.

If *Nashville* (Altman's first Dolby film) could not have been made without Dolby, then *The Shout,* Jerzy Skolimowski's new film, surely *would* not have been made without it. The movie's two dramatic climaxes take place when holy madman Alan Bates lets loose a bloodcurdling shout—and the audience is suddenly inundated with a multitrack, all-enveloping, hurricane-force sound. Perhaps this "shout" will do for Dolby what the rollercoaster ride in *This Is Cinerama* did for an earlier movie audience: provide a frisson that is remembered as an effective gimmick. The shout may not demolish the screen, but it comes close to demolishing the eardrums.

But there are other advantages to Dolby, besides making the moviegoer think he has a typhoon between his ears. The system allows for increased power: Scorsese's *The Last Waltz* is superior as a sound experience to, say, The T.A.M.I. Show and Monterey Pop—the first great rock concert films—because what you hear is what the performers played. The system also allows for increased clarity: the heavy Chicago accent of Linda Manz in Days of Heaven would be otherwise unintelligible. And for increased subtlety: the low rumbling of the mother ship in Spielberg's Close Encounters of the Third Kind comes to our ears sooner and, because we hear it almost before we're aware of it, sounds more ominous. Imagine how much more dramatic the quiet moments in 2001 would have been if Dolby had been available to Kubrick in 1967. Silence, as well as sound, is clearer with Dolby.

However elaborate the system allows filmmakers to be, there's still room for improvement. When the Crickets sing in The Buddy Holly Story, the movie sounds great; but the rest of the film was recorded in mono, and you can almost hear the extra speakers click on when the songs start, and off when they're finished. A wedding-reception sequence in The Deer Hunter features a lot of Ukrainian folk music; but when there's a cut from one character to another, the direction of the sound changes, too, and it's needlessly disorienting. There's no more intelligent use of sound than in Days of Heaven—the insects' chirp blending with the machine's whirr, the subtler sounds of breathing and heartbeats—but, with all that care, voices and lip movements are occasionally out of sync; and, when a plane flies overhead, you can hear the shift in sound between speakers on either side behind the screen.

[As of 1978,] fewer than a dozen film-mixing studios in the United States, and another three or four in England, are Dolby-equipped. It costs about $40,000 to modify an existing facility—plus the expense of retraining personnel who have been working under the older system. To get a good Dolby mix, it's generally necessary to consider the sound track during the shooting—and even script—stages. That happens infrequently; most filmmakers don't begin thinking about Dolby until they're dubbing.

So far, there have been only a few Dolby-encoded sound tracks. In a sense, Star Wars—the first wide-release Dolby stereo-optical film—was Dolby's Jazz Singer. Ben Burtt, the film's sound editor, was hired by producer Gary Kurtz a full six months before a single foot of film was exposed. For more than a year he collected sounds at factories, zoos, airports, anywhere—sounds that would eventually be integrated into the final mix to represent the lasers and the voices of R2-D2, C3PO, and the aliens.

The care paid off. When the box-office receipts of George Lucas's space fantasy went into the stratosphere, the interest in Dolby zoomed, too. The interest of moviegoers as well as moviemakers: informal surveys by Twentieth Century–Fox indicate that Dolby-equipped theaters significantly outgrossed non-Dolby theaters playing the film. Indeed, in most of the [1977–78] hit movies—*Star Wars, Smokey and the Bandit* (CB's), *Saturday Night Fever* (discos), *Close Encounters, Grease*—sound has played a crucial role, either as the subject or the technique.

It was Lucas's mentor, Francis (Ford) Coppola, who predicted, back in 1971, that sound would be the next major preoccupation among American filmmakers. When he set up his American Zoetrope studios in San Francisco, Coppola devoted much of the facility's space—and his own money and ingenuity—to sound equipment. And he hired a sound technician, Walter Murch, who quickly became a full collaborator on Coppola's and Lucas's films. Murch not only orchestrated the eerie, metallic sounds in Lucas's first feature, *THX-1138,* he co-authored the screenplay. He supervised the rock-and-roll songs of Lucas's *American Graffiti,* which popularized the practice of rock oldies commenting on the action of a film. He created the beautifully intricate "sounds track" of *The Conversation;* and while Coppola was on location shooting *The Godfather: Part II,* Murch edited—and subtly restructured—this landmark film in seventies sound.

Speaking with the quiet assurance of a pioneer. Murch contends that the *technical* potential of film sound has been reached. He adds: "The challenges of putting together a sound track are not totally on the technical level. That's a very important part, but 80 percent is in finding the right and appropriate combination of sounds—and putting them in the right place." Robert Altman agrees: "I think we've used up the technology—it all came with the Space Age—and now, I think it's pretty safe to say, there won't be many big advances in the next fifteen years, other than technique." The scientists have done their job; now it's up to the artists.

That hope must be tempered with a warning. As Steve Katz, a Dolby consultant says: "Sound is a chain. As soon as you get one bad link, you're dead." Today, the weak link is the last one: the sound systems in many theaters. It shouldn't be a problem. The Disney studio exhibited *Fantasia* with stereophonic sound back in 1940; Fox attached the process to its CinemaScope films, starting in 1953; *Woodstock* brought the Space Age to the multitrack Age of Rock.

But, until Dolby, stereo was confined to magnetic prints. Most theaters in the United States and Europe are equipped only to play optical prints—where the sound track is printed on a small strip to the left of the picture, and read by a photoelectric cell that picks up the variation in the amount of light transmitted through the track. Magnetic prints, which offer the best possible sound quality, also cost about 50 percent more than optical prints ($1,200 each vs. $800). Theaters must convert projection equipment to play magnetic prints—an expensive process—and distributors must make two sets of prints. And whereas optical tracks wear at about the same rate as the print's image, magnetic prints tend to disintegrate faster than optical prints.

Dolby would seem the solution to this dilemma, because it makes stereo possible for relatively little money. It costs more to dub a film in Dolby stereo than in standard mono—about $25,000 more—but the addition is almost insignificant, given that the average cost of a major-studio movie today is about $5 million. And for a theater to convert to Dolby, the cost is modest: about $5,000, if the theater is already equipped for stereo.

But one should never underestimate the stinginess of an exhibitor. Robert Altman puts it bluntly: "Most of the problems with sound in film today are in the reproduction. Sound in theaters—the overwhelming majority of theaters—is just terrible. The acoustics, the speakers, everything. You just cannot police the exhibitors. They won't spend the money. To them it's a joke." So Altman must act as his own policeman. Like a few other concerned filmmakers, he stays with his pictures at least through the initial distribution, handpicking first-run theaters with the proper sound and projection equipment.

But what are sound enthusiasts like Cimino and Phil Kaufman to do? *The Deer Hunter* and Kaufman's *Invasion of the Body Snatchers* are scheduled for saturation openings later this year [1978]; it's tough to police several hundred theaters at once. Cimino and Kaufman may be waking up these nights from nightmares as strong as those their films mean to induce; they fear that all the effort they've put into their movies' sound will be lost once the pictures reach their audience. Even the Dolby theaters (there are some 700, and the rate is growing at a healthy 500 a month) are often poorly maintained. The result can be dreadful sound from quality equipment.

But even the exhibitors may be becoming sophisticated, and for the same reason as the moguls: money. Theater owners aren't installing— and promoting—this equipment out of a disinterested respect for the Dolby technicians. They aren't putting Dolby on their marquees because there are no more movie stars; they're doing it because Dolby *is* a new star. They're finally realizing that quality sound can mean better business. *Star Wars* started it; *The Last Waltz* helped; *Grease* put it over. (*Grease*, like *Days of Heaven* and Milos Forman's *Hair*, was shown in 70mm primarily because of the improved sound quality the format makes possible.)

And now drive-ins are taking tentative steps into the Sound Age. A technique known as Cine-Fi was introduced [in 1977], and has been installed in a couple of dozen outdoor theaters. Cine-Fi makes it possible to throw away the single-speaker squawk boxes and transmit the sound track through the patron's car radio. It costs the average 400-car drive-in about

$10,000 to install the system. But the possibilities are intriguing: dual-language films, and even drive-in stereo.

These breakthroughs in sound don't mean that filmmakers will suddenly ignore the image—that movies will become an elaborate form of radio for a new generation in the dark. But we can be forgiven for feeling the sense of excitement audiences must have experienced a half-century ago. Today, though, the sound is clean and clear—and more provocative developments are imminent. Perhaps we are entering a period in film history that will someday be labeled the Second Coming of Sound. But, for now, we can hear an older sound in our ears: the voice of Al Jolson promising that "you ain't heard nothin' yet."

Sound Mixing and *Apocalypse Now:*
An Interview with Walter Murch
FRANK PAINE

Image and sound are linked together in a dance. And like some kinds of dance, they do not always have to be clasping each other around the waist: they can go off and dance on their own, in a kind of ballet. There are times when they must touch, there must be moments when they make some sort of contact, but then they can be off again. There are some films where the contact is unbroken: the image leads and the sound follows—it never deviates from what you actually *see*, what is directly indicated. Other films are way out there—what you are hearing has only the smallest physical relationship to the image. Yet there is—there has to be—some kind of connection being made, a mental connection, Out of the juxtaposition of what the sound is telling you and what the picture is telling you, you (the audience) come up with a third idea which is composed of *both* picture and sound and resolves their superficial differences. The more dissimilar you can get between picture and sound, and yet still retain a link of some sort, the more powerful the effect.

The relationship is always shifting, though, in any film. Sometimes it is very close and then it will open way up and the sound will do something completely off the wall, and then zoom back in again. But that's where it starts to be like a dance. I mean, they're dancing together and then they go off, and then they come back, and cross, and go in different directions again.

An example of this is something we tried to do in *Apocalypse Now.* At the very beginning of the film, Captain Willard (Martin Sheen) is in a hotel room in Saigon. He wakes up and looks out of the window, and what you hear are the off-screen policeman's traffic whistle, the car horns, motorbikes, the little fly buzzing in the windowpane, etc. Then he sits down on the bed and starts talking, in narration, about how his heart is really in the jungle and he can't stand being cooped up in this hotel room. Gradually, what happens is that all of those street sounds turn into jungle sounds: the whistle of the policeman turns into a cricket; the car horns turn into different kinds of birds; and the fly turns into a mosquito. You are watching

Willard sitting in his hotel room, but what you are hearing is a very strong jungle background. One reality is exchanged for another. The thread that links them is the fact that although his body is in Saigon, his mind is in the jungle. That's what Willard really wants to get back to. By gradually making that shift you've presented the audience with a dual reality which—on the face of it—is absurd, but one which nevertheless gets at the dilemma of this particular character.

The first thing in approaching a new project is to make a list of sounds which you think might be necessary or effective, but which were not in the film when it was shot. Think as deeply as you can about the characters in the film and the environment in which they move. Find moments at which you can, gracefully, add to the character, or his motives, or the story, or whatever, and not interfere or detract. There are times when too much texture would simply get in the way. There are other times when you can, deftly, put little things in there that don't seem like you put them there but which, nonetheless, add up: somebody closes the refrigerator door and there is a little tinkle of glass from inside—that means the refrigerator is full. The function of sound at this level is very close to art direction. Where does this guy live? Is it close to a freeway? Add some traffic. What kind of doors does he have in his apartment? Hollow core with Schlage locks? Put them in. Etc.

The other thing is to think of the sound in layers, break it down in your mind into different planes. The character lives near the freeway, so you've got this generalized swash of traffic sound, but then occasionally a plane flies over: these are the long, atmospheric sounds. On top of these you then start to list the more specific elements: the door closes, the gunshots, the bats that live in the attic—who knows? Isolated moments. Once you've done that, once you can separate out the backgrounds from the foregrounds, and the foregrounds from the mid-grounds, then you go out and record those specific things on your list separate from everything else. You record the freeway without the planes; then just the planes. You record the bats squeaking without any other kind of background noise. And then you build it up, one sound track superimposed on another, like one of those little Easter eggs which has different planes of stuff in it—little ducks in the foreground, then the bunnies, the grass, and the sky. And hopefully it will all go together, and it will look like a coherent whole that not only seems to exist on its own, but which connects with certain things in the story, certain things in the character. Since each of those layers is separate, you can still control them, and you can emphasize certain elements, and de-emphasize others the way an orchestrator might emphasize the strings versus the trombones, or the tympani versus the woodwinds.

There's a difference in approach between the traditional Hollywood way of putting a sound track together and the way that it is done in

England. On *Apocalypse,* we worked pretty much with the English system. The fact is: if you have to do a certain amount of work in a certain limited amount of time, you have to employ more than one person. You can't do it all yourself. So, how do you allocate the jobs? The way in Hollywood has been to hire one person as sound supervisor, and that person selects all the sound: where the sound will go, what kind of sound it is, and records it if necessary. And then he says, "Joe, come in here." And Joe comes in, and he says, "Here's reel 8," and he gives Joe the picture and then this stack of sounds. "I've marked on the picture where all of these sounds should go. Cut 'em in." And Joe says, "Right." Joe goes away, and a week later, he comes back with all of those sounds cut in. Joe is reduced in his responsibility. It's more of an assembly line procedure. He has certain bolts that he has to screw on to the frame at certain points. There is a certain amount of initiative that he has, but it's contained. He also doesn't see the whole film, or rather he doesn't work on the whole film. He works on Reels 2 and 8 and 12. And so he doesn't really get into what all of the intermediate reels are all about. That's Fred and Mack and Peter's responsibility.

The English system is to swing around and look at the problem horizontally, rather than vertically. Which is to say, each sound editor will weave one thread of sound through the fabric of the entire film. One sound editor will take all helicopters in the film, another sound editor will take all the gunshots in the film, another all of the boat sounds, and another all of the jungle sounds. That way each of the editors, within his own domain, is able to think of and work with the film as a whole. He is able to research, say, all of the available helicopter sounds that there are and make sure that they have a tonal and textural variation throughout the course of the film, the way red threads in a rug would. So it's not just the same stupid red thread, but here is a little crimson, here is pink, depending on what's lying next to it. And inevitably in a film, you might have recorded maybe one really great sound—a helicopter, for instance. There's just something about the way it was recorded that's great. If one person is doing it, he will say, "It really should be here. This is where the greatest helicopter sound in the film should be, right here." And he'll put that there. If it's all being done by different people, they all want that same helicopter sound, and they all try to cut it in. Theoretically, the sound supervisor is supposed to supersede all of that and say, no, it should go here, but it's better, I think, for one person to be in charge of that thread. It's like having concertmeisters in an orchestra. The lead violinist, who thinks only about the violins. And when the conductor wants to talk about the violins, he talks to the concertmeister. And so each of the sound editors is a concertmeister of his own string section, which may happen to be the helicopters. He will develop that as a coherent whole within itself over the course of the film. Also, just for their own well-being

and sanity, as individuals who work on a film with a great deal of commitment for a long time, it's better that they work on the whole film than that
they feel like they're punching in and punching out each day, just being given
the bolts to be put on the film. After a while, I think people become brutal-
ized by that kind of treatment, and they lose any kind of interest or contact,
which is something that begins to reinforce itself within the traditional Hollywood system, where you have only so much time; there isn't that much
commitment to the film. The way the thing is geared, the sound editors don't
have the total vision of what the sound is all about. They can certainly see
the film as a whole, maybe, once or twice, but they are not working on all
of it all the time.

There are disadvantages to both systems, nonetheless. The dis-
advantage of the English system is that you may get moments where the left
hand doesn't know what the right hand is doing. And the person who's doing
the helicopters has constructed this elaborate thing, but so has the guy that's
done the jungle, and they're going to be competing. You still need, in the
English system, some one person who has the overall thing, who says, "I
know there's a lot of helicopter action here visually, but I don't want a lot
of heavy helicopter sound there. So let's just cut in what is minimally necessary. Because although we see helicopters there, I want the jungle to be
really dominant." And so you have to have somebody who can step back
and look at the total effect of the sound over each of these individual departments. Otherwise, you'll have conflicts.

We talked about the layers of sound for the editing of a film. But
I think it's generally misleading to say, "Well, that sequence had eighty tracks,
it must be great." Ideally, for me, the perfect sound film has zero tracks. You
try to get the audience to a point, somehow, where they can *imagine* the
sound. They hear the sound in their minds, and it really isn't on the track at
all. That's the ideal sound, the one that exists totally in the mind, because
it's the most intimate. It deals with each person's experience, and it's obviously of the highest fidelity imaginable, because it's not being translated
through any kind of medium. So, at a certain point, there were 160 tracks
for *Apocalypse*. That is an awful lot, but on the other hand, if somehow I
could have achieved the same effect with no tracks, I would have been more
impressed. Or one track. If there had been one sound that did all of that, so
mysteriously, I would be more impressed. But what that means is: thinking
very, very deeply, and being very, very lucky in getting exactly the right thing.
And if you can do that, then the number of tracks is meaningless. But, generally speaking, it doesn't happen very often, if ever, to get that one thing.
That's just an abstract ideal that I always strive for.

I believe that there have always been sound films, since the invention of films, and there will always be silent films. You can look at tele-

vision shows today, or even some features, and there really is no "sound" in them. There is talking, and there's music, maybe, but the part of the brain that is interested in sound and texture and the meaning of sound as music is totally uninvolved. The sound in those films is conveying little pellets of information—the door closed, the person said this—and there's no duality, no stretching. So there are silent films today: they've got sound tracks, of course, but emotionally, they're silent. Whereas you can look at Chaplin's silent comedies and certain other films and they depend tremendously on the sound: the sound that the wardrobe made when it fell on him. You can "hear" all of the dishes break. Those films are using sound. They're asking you to imagine the sound of things. So they are sound films, even though they are completely silent. You try to track yourself along the boundaries between those two things—that's where you swing between zero tracks and 160 tracks.

The Sound Designer   MARC MANCINI

As the technological underpinnings of film have grown increasingly complex, so too has the number of credits that roll by at a movie's end. From amidst this dense, democratic latticework of names, however, one credit has begun to emerge prominently: the sound designer.

Sound designers—a term used familiarly only since the mid-1970s—are what cinematographers are to lighting and visual composition, what production designers are to set construction and prop display. They guide the sound of a motion picture from beginning to end, interpreting the director's expectations, "hearing" the script and storyboards, coordinating with the composer and sound editor, contributing to the mixing process, even ensuring that what is heard in the theater is of optimum quality. Decades ago, they might have been called supervising sound editors (they often still are), but that title has a craftsy connotation that downplays the true nature of their job: they are aural artists.

A multiplicity of factors has led filmmakers toward more careful sound design. Bombarded by ever-deepening visual information, audiences must have heightened sound effects, if only to perceive them at all. Improved theater speaker systems make further demands on filmmakers who must stretch their sonic creativity to compensate. "Action" movies, whose dialogue is often trivialized, especially depend on music and sound effects to carry their emotive levels. The accretion within the fantasy/science fiction genres that began in the late 1970s also abets the work of sound designers: there is no better way to authenticate chimeric worlds than through familiar noises.

Above all, sound designers are rising above some old prejudices. From ancient times to the McLuhanist present, creativity has usually been yoked most tightly to seeing: to imagine is to visualize. Terms like motion pictures, cinema, and television trace their etymological roots to visual concepts, not to audio ones. It is not surprising, then, that so many silent movie directors and theoreticians—most notably Rudolf Arnheim—viewed the arrival of sound to motion pictures as a nearly apocalyptic event.

For half a century, then, the residue of this phonophobia has muffled ambition, with only a *Citizen Kane*, *Lumière d'Eté*, or *The Conversation* to evince any kind of aural ambition. But it would seem that René Clair's 1929 prediction that "the interpretation [rather than the mere imitation] of noises may have more of a future" has finally borne fruit, and it is the modern sound designer who has taken charge of the harvest.

Frank Serafine sits at his keyboard. He hits middle C, and one hears a middle C motorcycle. He can also play a B-flat motorcycle or a D-sharp one, and at these pitches the original sound may mutate into that of a buzzsaw or some gargling creature.

It seems disorientingly strange to hear sound effects emanating from what looks like an electric organ, but the device that Serafine has played is an Emulator, a powerful synthesizer that has become an important tool for sound design.

The use of computers and synthesizers for movie sound effects production dates back to *Forbidden Planet* (1956), for which Louis and Bebe Barron composed a disquieting effects and music track through purely electronic means. Because of the limited, primitive state of the art, however, synthesizers did not come into widespread cinematic use until the 1970s. During this period, several farsighted individuals began to realize that certain capabilities that early synthesizers possessed (for example, the "barnyard" and "wind" keys of the old Melotron unit) might be used for purposes beyond novelty.

Frank Serafine was one of these. A student of classical and Eastern music, Serafine was also fully comfortable with the growing interdependence of music and electronics. In 1975, he began using synthesizers to score planetarium light shows and in 1977 designed the sound effects for the opening of Disneyland's Space Mountain ride. It was a natural career step from this to his admirable sound effects for *Star Trek: The Motion Picture*. Since then, Serafine has become a pacesetter in the race to perfect synthetic sound.

For his work, Serafine relies on three principal devices: a Prophet 5 analogue synthesizer, which generates sound through purely electronic means; the Emulator digital synthesizer, which samples and then reshapes real sounds; and an Atari 800 computer, which can store, categorize, and index any effect on a floppy disc and retrieve it in 1.5 seconds.

At first, Serafine structured his effects with purely electronic sounds, but experience soon taught him that sounds work best when they retain a residue of living energy and emotion, even if they have been processed beyond the recognizable.

When conceiving a sound effect, Serafine will first analyze the physical nature of its source: is it delicate, is it awkward, does it fly? Next, he will attempt to pinpoint its affects: can it frighten, is it calming, must it astonish you?

Serafine's work for *Tron*, the first feature film to be entirely computer-animated, is illustrative. Every nonliving thing seen in *Tron*'s artificial world has no direct counterpart in the real world. Serafine was therefore obliged to anchor the film's alternate reality to our everyday experience through his blended sound effects. A bulky vehicle drones with the propeller noises of an old aircraft bomber (for menace) and the Goodyear blimp (for bulk). The whoosh of a disc-weapon combines the scream of an angry monkey with the crack of a whip, creating a device that sounds aerodynamically swift and distressingly aggressive.

Serafine's attention to the emotive content of sound effects extends beyond a film's images all the way into the audience itself. His dream is to discover specific, repeatable ways of manipulating a viewer-listener's response to a movie. On a very basic level, he often matches pitch to camera angle, a practice used frequently by Orson Welles's soundmen, Bailey Fesler and James Stewart: high angles often suggest weak, strident sounds, low angles rumbly, hulking ones. Likewise, a distant sound source must be not only weak but diffused, in much the same way as landscape painters haze out faraway details. More subtly, Serafine—like some high-tech version of Rimbaud—applies various synesthetic theories of color-sound coordination. He is convinced that yellows evoke high-register notes, reds connote hot, shimmering resonances, and greens summon more bass tones.

Serafine, at the moment, is augmenting his sound tracks through an EXR Exciter, a device that television commercials deploy (along with sound compression) to magnify their salespitches. By smoothing out unnatural build-ups in sound waves, the Exciter conforms sound to make it optimally agreeable and insistent. (It is this that allows commercials to seem louder without *being* louder.) Serafine has adapted the Exciter in order to make certain sounds or voices seize the movie audience's attention, a procedure conventionally done by sudden brute loudness, by the lowering of nonessential noises on the sound track, or through stereophonic directioning in the theater.

Yet to see Serafine at work is not to watch someone calibrating or tooling sound effects; it is to watch someone who composes and performs them. He will often completely run through a sequence, accompanying with swooshes and bangs the action on the screen. It was in an almost musical manner that he buttressed *Tron*'s light-cycle sequence, leaving the finer synchronization to his sound editor. As such, Frank Serafine, master of the silicon chip, is also a familiarly comforting figure, a throwback to those bygone virtuosos who, with their mighty Wurlitzers, syncopated America's silent movie dreams.

The Wurlitzer would have been a natural instrument for Jimmy MacDonald to play, since as a young man he found himself whiling away some of his best hours in the grand silent movie palaces of the 1920s. Instead, he chose to perform as a drummer in tent shows and on steamships, all the while hedging his bets by pursuing an engineering degree. Though he did serve as a surveyor for the City of Burbank, this never displaced his musical activities. In one of those serendipitous strokes for which fate is well known, MacDonald's band was brought in to record for a Mickey Mouse short in 1934. The band left; Jimmy stayed. Now semiretired, MacDonald remains the dean emeritus of sound designers.

To create effects quickly and cleanly was what MacDonald was hired to do; so with few helpers and the limited technology of the day, he located shortcuts that still dumbfound today's sound experts. First, he would score his effects on a music staff, each note denoting the duration of a sound and each note annotated to indicate its identity or source. Though he was not above mixing and editing prerecorded sounds, he more often than not would work just like a radio soundman, ingeniously performing his effects directly to the projected image.

There is a congruence between MacDonald's performancelike approach and that of Serafine, but the major difference is that MacDonald's most reliable tools were his hands, feet, and, above all, his vocal chords. If a film needed a bear growl—and bears are notoriously uncooperative at growling—then MacDonald would roar through the top of a hurricane lamp. If a snake hiss was sought, then MacDonald would flutter his tongue to produce the best hisses ever heard. And when Walt Disney tired of doing Mickey Mouse's voice, as he did in the mid-1940s, then MacDonald took that over as well.

MacDonald's springy vocalizations would have been enough to make him a legend, but the musician-turned-engineer-turned-sound designer had an additional, more elegant skill. MacDonald is probably the greatest fashioner of sound effects props who ever lived. To walk onto the Burbank stage where his gadgets are stored is to enter a sorcerer's den. There are many traditional devices, such as gongs, mallets, and small-hinged doors, which trace their ancestry to radio, burlesque, legitimate theater, and, most likely, campfire raconteuring. Others, though, are one-of-a-kind relics: a giant round vat used to create the cauldron bubbles in Snow White; a rotating valve device that produced the chugs of Dumbo's locomotive; a series of truck brake drums that, when struck, produced the sounds of giant bells in countless Disney films.

How MacDonald thought up these contraptions is a mystery even to him. There seem to be three ways to conceptualize a sound effect. One is quite direct: one simply goes to the original source itself. However, as any sound person will explain, what one hears does not necessarily correspond to what a microphone will hear: an ocean roar, for example, when recorded, might take on a mushy, hissy homogeneity. Paradoxically, certain old, badly recorded sounds have become the industry standard, so much so that people often fail to recognize a real gunshot simply because it doesn't resemble a movie gunshot.

There is a second cognitive route, and it often involves some kind of analogous visualization: to simulate shore breakers one might record the sound of water spouting from a huge hose onto a gravel surface. This kind of visual association is recurrent in sound effects design. For example, the standard for duplicating the crunch of footsteps in fresh snow is to stroll one's fingers on cornstarch, an ingenious procedure, yet one in which the image of walking on a white, powdery substance logically connects the two and probably suggested the effect in the first place. Of course, such metaphorical thinking can lead to absurdity. On *The Black Hole,* an effects editor once tried to conceive what sound the title's swirling phenomenon might make. His recording of a flushing toilet was hardly a towering moment in sonic creativity.

The third path toward sound effects is the most subtle, and it is the one that Jimmy MacDonald has traveled over and again: it consists of sounds that have no visual congruence. To conceive of such an effect requires a protean leap of imagination, for shortly after birth humans become strongly visual creatures for whom time and television further diminish the audible world's conscious impact. Yet sound designers, to a degree that only the blind can understand, *can* compare sounds in their mind's ear, for want of a better term, free of the sometimes misleading interference that visualizations can conjure. Psychologists label such people "audiles," and certainly it was one such individual who realized that crumpled cellophane evokes crackling fire, or that a bending sheet of metal can duplicate thunder, or, for Fred Astaire in *The Pleasure of His Company,* that San Francisco foghorns sound like rhinoceri in labor.

Jimmy MacDonald's greatest gift is to make equally improbable, leaping connections. At times, of course, his discoveries are the result of trial and error or of happenstance. While recording the well-advertised sounds of Rice Crispies for a breakfast scene, MacDonald noticed that they could also substitute for a rainstorm. But many of his custom devices remain totally mysterious until operated. Disney once passed by and, seeing a cylinder filled with peas and nails, questioned MacDonald about its function. MacDonald turned it slowly, and out came the sound of rain; cranked faster, it reproduced fully believable surf. Two weeks later, MacDonald found that his weekly paycheck had been more than doubled.

Being trusted by Disney, and being assigned most often to animated features, MacDonald had uncommon leeway in creating his effects. A character's footsteps might become musical notes, a practice still quite symbolic when compared to the more analogous tire skids or dopplered jet whooshes of Warner Bros.' Road Runner. Yet the wide latitude that cartoons gave MacDonald enabled him to fill Disney's library with nearly 28,000 sound effects, a legacy that MacDonald and his apprentice, Wayne Allwine, transferred in 1983 to pure and stable digital recordings.

And what does Jimmy MacDonald think of that new category, the sound designer? "I'm sorry, but what's a sound designer?"

The term "sound designer" seems to have first been used by Walter Murch, yet it is to one of Murch's Lucasfilm colleagues, Ben Burtt, that the title is most frequently associated. Ben Burtt, a three-time Academy Award winner, is, like many others, skilled at inductively building or analogizing sound effects. Yet unlike many, he can work in a deductive, historical fashion as well. Given a sound effect, Burtt can probably identify the film from which it first emerged, the studio where it was created, and the person who may have contrived it in the first place. Burtt can recognize a sound artist by his footsteps.

This kind of archaeological reasoning leads to the sort of reverential reconstructions for which Burtt is well known. Typical is Burtt's admiration for the arrow sounds contained in Warners' effects library, which he traced to the 1938 *Adventures of Robin Hood*. After nearly half a century, however, the recording had lost its quality and fell short of the fidelity required by contemporary systems. Attempts at recreating the *Robin Hood* sounds proved fruitless, since modern arrows are nearly silent. So Burtt tracked down the individual who had designed the original acoustically dramatic arrows and, with his assistance, reproduced the singing quality with which *Raiders of the Lost Ark*'s darts fly.

Burtt's ascent is a well-documented one. A film buff who as a child would record and replay the sound tracks of his favorite movies, he enrolled at the University of Southern California's film school with the intention of becoming a director. His aural skills still latent, he received a student job cataloguing the Columbia sound library, which had been donated to the University. A call by *Star Wars* producer Gary Kurtz to U.S.C. led to a successful interview for Burtt. He was given carte blanche to work out of his apartment near the U.S.C. campus for a year, in order to collect at a leisurely pace those sounds that might be useful. Several proved to be just that. Burtt blended the sounds of his TV set and an old 35mm projector to create the hum of a light saber. He tapped the wires of a radio tower to obtain the snap of laser bolts. And he conjured the whoosh of Luke Skywalker's landspeeder by recording the roar of the Los Angeles Harbor Freeway through a vacuum-cleaner pipe.

Clearly, Burtt has a keen ear for compelling sounds, but what makes his work special is how his effects vault to a film's foreground. Normally, one only perceives a sound effect on a subconscious level. The final War Room pyrotechnics in *War Games*, for example, are easily recallable, yet their accompanying sound effects are not. (Each missile track line that traces its way across the display map is accompanied by a whoosh, and each entry on the TicTacToe board by a ping.) Had audience members been aware of these effects—and they weren't supposed to be—they would have realized the foolishness of arcade game noises on a Norad display. Imbedded in the onslaught of visual information, however, these evocative sounds subliminally worked their not-so-quiet magic.

Ben Burtt also professes the classical dictum that a successful sound track commands little conscious attention, but his own effects prove otherwise. Few effects are more recallable than the screech of an X-wing fighter, the hum of a light saber, or the beeps of R2-D2. There are clear reasons for this. Thus far, Burtt has composed for comic-book films, with sounds necessarily etched out in jagged lines. He coordinates carefully with the film's composer, placing his sounds between notes and at contrasting pitches. Like Serafine, he prods one's attention by alluding to vaguely familiar, organic sounds (the screech of a Star Wars T-Fighter is a drastically altered elephant bellow). In addition, his insistence on completely original or refurbished classic sounds counters the numbness listeners have to recordings heard a thousand times: his gunshots in *Raiders* become fresh events.

Most of all, Burtt has an enviable ken of motion picture dialectics. He engineers sound montages in which noises are either layered or linear; that is, overlapping (as in E.T.'s voice, which is a mix of sounds made by eighteen different animals and people, including dogs, raccoons, an old lady, and actress Debra Winger), or arranged sequentially in a brief, concentrated unit. The Millennium Falcon's door, for instance, first clunks, then hisses, and finally squeaks—all in less than a second. Irvin Kershner so trusted this effect that in *The Empire Strikes Back* he sometimes photographed the opening of a spaceship door by stopping the camera, taking the door out completely, and resuming the action. Burtt's whoosing sounds convinced audiences that the doors had rapidly slid aside, when they had, in fact, suddenly disappeared from the screen.

Burtt also has a remarkable ability, through sound, to build offscreen space. A good sound person remembers that a movie screen is not simply a self-contained frame but a window on a much broader reality. Burtt's skills, however, go far beyond environmental stretching: his sounds often literally tell the story.

It has often been said that the auditory world of a George Lucas film is as alive as its visual one, and this may be due in part to the thoughtful quality control that Lucasfilm offers to its exhibitors. But most of all, it is because Burtt's sounds bring pleasure in themselves, and when carrying a film's intent, achieve euphony in the word's classic sense. In his deployment of sounds *as* meaning and sounds *with* meaning, Ben Burtt is an effects designer worth listening to.

Frank Serafine and his synthesizers, Jimmy MacDonald with his props and vocalizations, Ben Burtt, the refabricating archaeologist—each has arrived at a singular yet effective style; each is an aural auteur. Notwithstanding, all three clearly share a certain common ground. That they each have training in music seems significant but not surprising, considering the new emphasis on percussion that Stravinsky, Prokofiev, and Varèse introduced to twentieth-century composition. More curiously, most sound designers have been drummers (MacDonald, Burtt, and Murray Spivack, another legendary sound mixer at RKO and Fox, all played the drums). Early in life, then, sound designers seem drawn to, or trained by, audile, timing-oriented thinking. That thinking is also frequently a very private experience, an aesthetic deed only sparingly shared. Burtt designed his facility to be operable by only one person. Serafine hires assistants only when necessary. And MacDonald confesses that at first he was very inhibited in performing at foley sessions. No doubt his years as Disney's only sound effects director were not due solely to economic constraints.

Pragmatically, all three have few techno-fears. Though Serafine is clearly the most adventurous in this area, both Burtt and MacDonald applaud any scientific advance that can help their cause.

The embryonic science of psychoacoustics holds a special interest for them. MacDonald points out that he was ever on the lookout for curious psychophysical effects. To his bemusement, his blending of a cymbal sound, a soldering iron tone, and the hum of a degausser device once caused a group of sound mixers to become so ill that they fled the mixing room. Burtt has reported similar phenomena, as has Serafine. All three dream of forging sounds that could predictably and efficiently set off more felicitous sensations.

Indeed, sound designers, by fashioning a coherent, aesthetically pleasing substructure for a film's images, abet directors in their efforts to strike the proper chords of an audience's emotions. Technologically based but humanistically conceived, their work combines the best available from both man and machine.

It seems mischievously appropriate, then, that George Lucas, an enthusiastic patron of sound design, placed at the heart of his *Return of the Jedi* the image of a yarn-spinning, anthropomorphic robot, C3PO, enchanting an audience of alien creatures through the universal language of sound effects. In both the archetypal world of *Star Wars* and the real world of its creators, a sound designer shares grandly in the elegant, rousing act of storytelling.

Sound and Silence in Narrative and Nonnarrative Cinema
FRED CAMPER

A film may be either a sound film or a silent film. A silent film is intended to be projected in silence. A sound film is intended to be projected with accompanying sounds. Conventional wisdom is that these are only two categories of film, but the situation is in fact more complex. For one thing, the classical "silent" film was usually intended to be shown with sound. A great variety of sound accompaniments were used, from live music, to music on record, to sound effects, to live spoken commentary. But as the sound was not determined rigidly in advance by placing it directly on the film strip, as was done after 1929, the sound could vary from performance to performance or be absent entirely. Today, many of these pre-1929 films are shown without sound.

Additional varieties of sound accompaniment, intended and otherwise, have been cited by independent filmmakers in recent years. Andy Warhol once remarked that for his silent films (which often had very little action and very long takes), he had assumed that the audience would provide the sound track. In fact, they often did. How serious Warhol was in this remark, and how strongly this expressed assumption figured in the actual making of his films, we cannot know. Stan Brakhage, the maker of numerous silent films, has lamented that his films are often shown with the projector in the auditorium, its machine-sound all too audible, and wondered if he hadn't miscalculated in the making of some of his films by assuming that they would be shown in a more complete silence.

Thus there are really three major categories: those films that are intended to be accompanied by a sound track not on the film strip itself, whether live music, spoken commentary, sound-on-tape, a record player, or intended audience sounds; films with a predetermined sound track placed on the film strip; and films that are intended to be projected in silence. The first, hybrid category, which we might call silent-with-sound, was dominant in cinema until about 1929; the "sound" film took over soon after. As has happened with other media as a result of technological change, the emergence of a new technology has created a renewed sense of opposite possibilities: so that the invention of the "true" sound film allowed, some years later, for the emergence of our final category, the "true" silent film. While surely some very early films were first projected in silence, as were some avant-garde films of the 1920s, it is only with the invention of sound that silence becomes a true choice for film. The act of making a silent film in the 1950s, by the filmmaker Stan Brakhage, whose previous films had had sound, was dictated not by a lack of means or by a lack of technology. It was an aesthetic choice, and the silence that resulted therefrom was, as we shall see, a new kind of environment for film projection.

2

Now that we have established that there are three, rather than two, types of cinema, we shall ask if any generalizations can be made about each, apart from the specifics of individual films. For the silent-with-sound film made before 1930, a great variety of sound accompaniments was used. The one we are most familiar with today is live musical accompaniment, whether performed by a full orchestra or on a keyboard, as is often done in revivals of "old" films. In these cases, the sound does not come directly from the screen but rather from off to one side, or from below, and the audience is always aware of the presence of live performers, a presence that is often acknowledged by applause. Thus the audience is always made aware of sound-as-artifice, of the sound as an addition to the image, rather than as an integral part of it. Sound and image occupy somewhat separate spaces in the viewer's consciousness, and their combination is not a strictly additive one. One assumes that this would be even more strongly true for films accompanied by live commentary.

Some independently made films of recent decades are accompanied by sounds other than those that may or may not be on the film strip. Often the filmmaker will provide a separate tape or play records. Even when such sounds come directly from speakers behind the screen, the synchronization is inexact, and slightly different on each projection, so that an element of performance is interjected that prevents the sound and image from being precisely wedded. In Ken Jacobs' film *Blonde Cobra*, the sound on the film is added to by a live radio playing in the audience, making the notion of sound-track-as-performance powerfully explicit. The result of such techniques has one curious similarity to live music accompanying a silent film, in that a certain separateness between sound and image is maintained in both cases.

The true sound film, by contrast, can marry sound and image as precisely as it wishes, by placing the sound track directly on the film strip in the form of encoded light patterns or magnetic signals that are read by the projector. In the Hollywood sound film, the dominant form of sound is lip-sync and synced background effects (whether recorded live or added later). Music is also present, but it is usually of subsidiary importance to the "live" sound.

Sync-sound has been attacked by filmmakers virtually since its inception.[1] The objection raised is that one adds little to cinema by combining an object with its natural sound; this simply and naïvely attempts to return the film image to the status of an object in nature. Arguments are presented instead for introducing a disparity between sound and image for expressive ends, or for not using sound at all. That there is much to be said for such arguments I will try to demonstrate subsequently; for now I wish to investigate what the actual effect of sync-sound is on the viewer. One sits in one's chair, in the theater, and sees a character speaking on the screen, while at the same time hearing his voice coming from the same location. Object and sound are united into a single unit. But the nature of the sound is very different from the nature of the film image. Sound fills the space of the theater, while the image (at least in the literal sense) remains confined to the rectangle of the screen. Two effects ensue. The sound gives the action that it accompanies a spatial presence; the image gains the illusion of filling the air around one, as the sound itself does. At the same time, the viewer is always aware of the disparity between the limited space of the image and the "unlimited" space of the sound. The first effect is a great aid to a narrative film trying to work an illusionary spell on its viewers; the second has allowed for subtle and creative manipulation of sound in the most conventional films. Off-screen sound, for instance, helps point out the difference between sound and image, as well as calling attention to the limits of the frame and to what lies beyond. Thus a filmmaker can make an "illusionistic" film without literally collapsing that film into the objects it depicts; the subtleties of image and sound combination can be used toward creative ends. In general, then, synchronous sound, emanating from right beside or behind the screen, has the effect of spatializing the film image, both by lifting it into the space of the screening room and by calling attention to its limited boundaries.

The ability to synchronize sound directly with image need not be used to unite object with the sound that produced it. Films from Vertov's *Enthusiasm* to Kubelka's *Unsere Afrikareise,* from Maclaine's *The End* to Baillie's *Quick Billy,* do much of their work with the difference created between sound and image. It often seems a well-concealed fact of film history that numerous filmmakers have used sound-on-film for other than the sync effect and that these usages, by helping to redefine the limits of possibility for sound in film, have redrawn the limits of cinema itself. Any investigation of the varieties of sound film must turn much of its attention to avant-garde cinema, and while a full investigation along these lines is beyond the scope of any single article, some specific examples will be offered.

Our third category of cinema, the "true" silent film, would seem at first glance to be the simplest category of all. But to make and show a silent film in recent decades has a particular meaning that derives in part from the dominance of sound film, even in independent filmmaking. The viewer enters a screening room and is shown a work unaccompanied by sound but obviously made during a period when sound was available. What is the point? Viewers often find this experience disconcerting, especially at first; our culture, after all, is saturated with sound (and *noise*) of one kind or another, and it increasingly seems we lack opportunity to experience silence. But silence is alive with its own possibilities. A silence "filled" with film images is different from any other type of silence, and in the realm of silent film there exist many varieties of silence.

It seems clear that when silence is the filmmaker's choice the viewer is being asked to look at the film image in a new isolation and with a new attentiveness. The space of the room is rendered less relevant; all attention must be focused on the screen. Without sound to spatialize it directly, the image, whatever its content, hovers before the viewer in a kind of mysterious and slendid isolation, like a fragile chimera. Freed from either an accompanying orchestra or an accompanying sound-track-on-film, the work can now operate solely for the eyes and, through them, address the mind.

Now that some general comments on each of our three categories have been offered, we can investigate some of the varieties of sound and silence that exist within each category.

3

In the case of the silent-with-sound film, the effects of live music and spoken commentary have already been noted. The commentator, who would often "explain" the action of early narrative films, serving the function that the extensive subtitles of later silent-with-sound narratives fulfilled, must have had an effect very different from anything we experience today. Films shown in such a manner may have appeared as mere illustrations of a spoken narrative, or as extensions of an earlier tradition, that of the lantern show. We still have insufficient historical information about the use of sound in early films to come to any firm conclusions, but what is clear is that sound, the sound-image relation, and the function of film itself were all extremely fluid, as narrative cinema emerged from the vast array of nineteenth-century arts and entertainments that helped spawn it.

The silent-with-sound film often had another form of sound accompaniment, which is closer to the use of sound in the "true" sound film. Sound effects were often produced on machines situated behind the screen in near-perfect synchronization with the action. Recorded music was played on records. Actors located behind the screen would attempt to speak or sing in lip-sync. Whether or not these efforts succeeded, it is clear that the impulse to make sync-sound films was with the cinema from its beginning.

In addition to the audible sounds that accompanied the silent-with-sound film, there is another stratum of sound possibilities inherent in such works: that of the sounds suggested by the imagery, movement within the frame, or editing rhythm. In an early text on this subject,[2] Stan Brakhage connects sounds that are literally suggested by things seen with the "sound sense" appealed to through movement and editing, and he goes on to discuss how the invention of the sound film helped reduce the use of this possibility.

Recent decades of independent filmmaking have seen a return to the sound-as-performance tradition of the silent-with-sound film. Of course, this tradition never died completely, as anyone who has ever attended a screening of home movies accompanied by the maker's narration knows all too well. Independent filmmakers have often tried to make use of the imprecision of sound that is not on the film; of, for instance, the fact that a record or sound-on-tape will never synchronize with the film the same way on each projection. This injects an element of indeterminacy into the sound-image relation that is not inconsistent with development in other fields of art.

4

The varieties of the "true" sound film are many. The use of sound in the Hollywood film is a good deal more various than is usually assumed. In particular, however directly "fundamental" the effect of the dialogue may be in pointing to the important action, a film's overall sound track can have a distinctive quality that does much to affect the film's tone and meaning. Thus, in Hawks's screwball comedies, such as *Twentieth Century,* the use of rapid-fire, overlapping dialogue gives the films a frenetic pace that is not otherwise present—that is not, for instance, inherent in the editing.[3] The sound tracks of Orson Welles's films often seem to take on a life of their own, the presence of his characters' voices being as vivid in sound (even when the words are hard to decipher) as their bodies are in the images, a heritage, perhaps, of his work in theater and radio. These sound tracks tend to project the characters' voices into the theater with intense physical force. Welles makes great use of the spatial qualities of sound mentioned earlier; his sound has a palpable, physical presence that is a perfect extension of the extreme physicality of his shooting style. Just as the figure of Quinlan dominates the frame in *Touch of Evil*, so his voice's gutteral aggressiveness dominates the sound track. *Touch of Evil*'s ending takes the form of a spatial labyrinth to express the themes of deception and corruption; similarly, the sound in this final scene is a mixture of live and tape-recorded voices, and the spatial perspective of these voices alters from shot to shot, as the perspective of the imagery also shifts. Or, one might consider Aldrich's *Kiss Me Deadly*, whose sound track is a veritable masterpiece of loudness, of machine drone, of multiple sounds aggressively layering themselves on top of the action in a manner analogous to the multileveled imagery, but with the greater visceral impact that sound can produce. Loud radios, the sounds of a boxing gym, and above all the roar of auto engines all lead to the sound of the film's ultimate "machine," the Bomb, which is revealed at the end.

Robert Bresson makes a very different use of synchronous sound. Sounds that appear to derive from the image or its environs help give each shot a presence that goes far beyond its physical details. The sound has intensely spatial qualities; sounds that ought to be merely realistic sound effects attain a larger-than-life presence throughout the films. These sounds are combined with foreshortened, powerfully static, even ascetic images to help suggest that each image represents far more than it shows. Shots finally are made into vehicles that unite characters and objects in a natural order of things that sees each object as a part of a larger and not-fully-representable whole. Throughout these films, sound suggests dimensions to the image beyond what can be seen: both on a literal level, when the sound comes from off-screen, and metaphorically, as the sound adds a mysterious level of spatiality to images that are themselves curiously despatialized. This effect results largely from Bresson's mysterious and brilliant use of sound presence, realized through subtleties in recording and sound editing, which in turn depends on the more general fact, already noted, that sound accompanied by image can extend that image beyond the screen surface, and out from it, along the lines of the sound waves coming out from the screen across the room toward the viewer. While a Hollywood film may make use of this to make the actor's presence more lifelike, Bresson, with his emphasis on background and off-screen sounds, and through the peculiar presence he invests in his on-screen sounds, makes use of this effect to create sound tracks that evoke a sense of an unseen, mystical reality. This reality, while rooted in the visible world (from which the sounds we hear derive), is in no sense limited to, or even literally visible, in it.

5

For as many varieties as may exist of synchronous sound in film, there are at least as many varieties of asynchronous sound. The great maker of asynchronous sound films is Peter Kubelka, an Austrian "avant-garde" filmmaker who has at times lived and taught in the United States. His *Unsere Afrikareise (Our Trip to Africa)*, which began as a documentary of a group of Europeans on a hunting trip, is perhaps the densest and most ecstatic compendium of the possibilities of asynchronous sound in the cinema. Kubelka's technique is to marry precisely—rhythmically and thematically—an image with a sound that derives from elsewhere. Thus a popular tune recorded off of the radio seems perfectly matched to the writhings of a dying animal; a gunshot is heard at the very moment a man's hat is blown off his head. Kubelka, at least at early showings of his films, was adamant about wanting the speaker as close to the screen as possible. His "asynchronous" sound is in fact synchronous, in that sound and image are clearly matched. At times they seem to unite rhythmically as closely as lips and sound do in lip-sync. The difference, of course, is that one is very aware that the sound married to an image in no way comes from the natural object, but that Kubelka has made a new entity, which has some of the qualities of an object in the natural world and yet also is a comment on that world.[4]

By contrast, Kenneth Anger in *Invocation of My Demon Brother* concentrates on another aspect of sound, its visceral quality. The sound track of this film is aggressively loud, repetitious music (performed by Mick Jagger on a Moog synthesizer). The screening room is literally filled with the sound track's drone. The film's images are densely packed, saturated with brilliant patches of light, and often symbolically suggestive; together with the "invocation" of the title there is a suggestion that the images are attempts to call up powerful spirits or demons. This sense is aided by a sound track that by virtue of its rhythmic repetitiveness and loudness seems to leap off of the screen and invade the viewer's body and nervous system. Sound, in other words, is used to suggest that the images are more than merely images, but are meant to have the power to effect literal changes in physical reality.

An even more extreme use of sound can be found in Christopher Maclaine's *The End*. In this rarely screened masterpiece, a narrator tells a series of barely coherent stories of people who are living the last day of their lives. The film elevates disjunction and discontinuity to an essential way of understanding a world threatened with nuclear annihilation. At crucial points in the film, the narrator directly addresses the audience ("The person next to you is a leper"), often asking the viewers to find themselves up on the screen, or even to supply the narrative. This form of address breaks the two conventions that generally determine all film sound: that sound either comes from the image (sync) and thus is wedded to it, by a kind of simple addition, or that it does not come from the image, and is meant to alter it, to combine with it to form a new entity ("multiplication"). The sound in *The End* is at the points of audience-address neither additive nor multiplicative; by breaking the image-sound illusion, Maclaine uses sound to alter fundamentally the function of the image. He attacks our complacent belief that the film we are viewing is an entity separate from us, and in the shattering of that separateness the film is brought out from the screen, and out of the air around us, and into the very context of our lives: we are asked to *participate*. The film has been made into an event, almost like a performance, or an improvisational recitation. For this film, that is precisely Maclaine's purpose: to make the viewer aware that the characters' suicides may also be his own; to place the viewer amidst the stories depicted on the screen; to establish the viewer as a partial cause of and potential victim of the "grand suicide of the human race."

Finally, we should consider Joseph Cornell's *Rose Hobart* (1939). This is, strictly speaking, a silent-with-sound film, as the sound track, a piece of music, was always played on record when Cornell showed the work. Even today, one can rent a sound-on-tape version of the film, which is truer to Cornell's projection of it than the sound-on-film version.

Rose Hobart consists of reedited fragments of a 1931 Hollywood film, *East of Borneo*. Cornell reedits to remove narrative causality, and the film is shown with a color tint, which has the effect of distancing the image from the viewer. By reediting and tinting an early sound film and projecting it with music rather than with its own sound, Cornell seems to have been making an homage to the silent film. The imagery attains a magical separateness, a kind of enchantment, that is characteristic of many silent films but seems to have been lost as a possibility for narrative film with the introduction of sync-sound, which tends to render the presence of the actors as more directly physical. The viewer reads the images in *Rose Hobart* as windows on some wonderfully separate and other world.

While Cornell's film is in part a comment on the difference between sound and silent filmmaking, the effect of his own use of sound is itself extraordinary. Rather than adding any sense of "life" to the film, the music has the effect, as Annette Michelson has pointed out,[5] of making the film seem more silent. The footage Cornell uses is strongly suggestive of sound—not only do characters speak, but volcanoes erupt. Yet his quiet, continuous music suppresses these suggestions and places the film in a kind of ethereal and imaginary space for the viewer. The representational images that would suggest sound are instead *themselves* silenced by Cornell's treatment of them, and this film, originally a silent-with-sound, and now often shown in a sound-on-film version, is in a deeper and nonliteral sense a purely silent film. Cornell's silence is that of the removal of the images from the life they ostensibly embody, and as well the removal of the images from the viewer's immediate space and time. The otherness that the images attain is a separateness no sound, and no sound-provoking image, could describe.

6

Now we come to the last of our categories, the "true" silent film, which, despite some predecessors, was made fully possible only by the invention of sound. Many of the first American avant-garde films were silent—Maya Deren's *Meshes of the Afternoon* and the *Early Abstractions* of Harry Smith were originally shown without sound. But the most consistent master of the silent film is Stan Brakhage. Yet an examination of only a few of his films will show that just as a sound filmmaker may use different kinds of sound tracks for different films, so a silent filmmaker may use different kinds of silence.

       One of Brakhage's first silent films, and his first masterpiece, is *Anticipation of the Night*. This film is structured as the subjective journey of a protagonist, whose shadow and hands we see in occasional shots, toward suicide. The camera careens violently across space, tracing the arc of that journey. In an amusement park scene, children hurtle rapidly toward the camera, analogously to the camera's movement. The subject matter mostly does not suggest sound emanating from it, as Brakhage has identified the silent film as doing, and the movements rarely suggest audible sound. In this sense, *Anticipation of the Night* is a "truer" silent film than many others— not only does it have no sound, but its images do not usually evoke sounds. At the same time, the distinctively rhythmic qualities in the camera movement and editing stimulate the viewer's senses, rhythmically, as sound might; the film produces distinct effects on the viewer's physiology that are analogous to those of sound. It is no accident that Brakhage has consistently claimed music as a deep source of inspiration to him as a filmmaker. His frequent statement that he makes silent films because sound tends to dominate image is important in this regard: the absence of sound gives the images, and all their subtleties, a new priority in the viewer's consciousness, and allows them to speak with their own unique, musiclike rhythms.

Fourteen years after *Anticipation of the Night*, Brakhage completed *The Riddle of Lumen*. Also a "true" silent film, this can be described most simply as an inventory of different varieties of light that exist in the world. The editing avoids developing any obvious rhythmic continuities from shot to shot, and the movements within shots are generally smaller and subtler than those of *Anticipation of the Night*. One might call it "chamber music" rather than "symphonic," but the differences go deeper. The film's editing functions partly to separate images from each other; the links at cuts are made on the subtlest details of movement or shape, while the differences between adjacent images are much more apparent. The viewer is given to understand that each image represents a unique and miraculous form of light; that since no two lights are the same, each image must remain apart. While the viewer's sense of rhythm is appealed to, subtly, his body is in no sense stimulated as in *Anticipation of the Night*. Instead, he sees the images as apparitions, hovering about the screen, separate from him. Whereas the movements of *Anticipation* projected themselves into the screening room, into the viewer's space, in a manner analogous to the way sound projects, the images of *The Riddle of Lumen* remain in their own space. Thus we have a deeper kind of silence, a silence of imagery that does not broadly stimulate the viewer's body, a silence that speaks to his inner eye.

This newer and more "silent" silence is carried to further extremes in some of the Brakhage films that followed. *The Text of Light* consists almost entirely of images of light patterns in a crystal ashtray, though the source is never made visible in the film. Each image is full of vast internal complexities of shape, depth, and shifting light patterns. The light movements sometimes do suggest things that are visible in the world—appearing to make metaphors, for instance, for the movement of light across a natural landscape—but those sights that are suggested are generally events that are themselves without known sounds. Two recent series of "abstract" films, the *Romans* and *Arabics*, carry such filmmaking to its limits. These films consist of images, and movements, that are suggestive of nothing in the external known world. Their silence is thus absolute and total. By placing the viewer in a void without easily recognizable coordinates, the filmmaker plunges his viewer into an unknown realm of inwardness in which sight, thought, and consciousness are finally separated from anything external.

7

A survey such as this cannot hope to deal with all the various categories of sound and silent film, to say nothing of all the important uses of sound and silence in particular films. The use of live lip-sync in *cinéma vérité* and "direct cinema" documentaries, for instance, has gone unmentioned, though the effect of their sound tracks is rather different from that of a Hollywood film's sound track. Some of the independent filmmakers mentioned have made very different uses of sound in other of their films, and many independent filmmakers who have used sound brilliantly have gone unnamed (one thinks of Breer, Frampton, Gehr, Landow, Markopoulos, and Peterson, to name only six).

Similarly, other independent filmmakers have created different kinds of silence than Brakhage has. Ernie Gehr's *Table* is a film consisting of rapid, frame-by-frame color changes. The film acts quite powerfully, even violently, on one's perception; every nerve ending, it seems, is touched by its continual pulsing. The film's effect is to engage all of the viewer's perceptual apparatus and nervous system so totally that the question of sound cannot even arise; it is as if all sensory inputs have been filled by what one sees on the screen.

By contrast, Bruce Baillie's *Tung* offers a totally other form of silence. Images of delicacy and fragility pass by with ghostlike elusiveness, an elusiveness emphasized by the superimposed text of a short poem. In Gehr's *Table* the viewer's awareness of every detail of his present existence is heightened by the engagement of his physiology;[6] in *Tung* the viewer is lifted out of the time and space of his own presence, and the silence of the latter film is one of removal rather than engagement.

8

One major use of sound has been to implant the existence of objects depicted on the screen more firmly in the physical world. Lip-sync unites body and voice, giving us an object with some resemblance to a natural being. Elements of cinematic expression (camera movement, framing, lighting) can then modify this depicted natural world to comment on the lives the characters lead. In the melodramas of Douglas Sirk, for instance, framing devices entrap characters to express more truly the nature of their fate.[7] The asynchronous sound of Kubelka's *Unsere Afrikareise* unites object with unexpected sound, forming an entity unlike any in the natural world, but with its own almost naturelike physical presence. Sound, which by its nature tends to appeal more to the body than does image, can be used to render images more palpable.

One of the many uses of silence is to remove an image from its attachment to the natural world. The rhythmic qualities of *Tung,* or Gehr's *Serene Velocity,* or of Brakhage's *Arabics* may appeal to one's inner sense of rhythm and thus to elements of the viewer's body. But any such appeal is far different from that of a sound film: the physical is at most suggested by image, rather than presented, as by sound. Silent film has the potential, realized in different ways in some of the films mentioned, to place the viewer in a new state of isolation. Presented with images drained of the "life" that sound can impart, the viewer is thrust more deeply into a contemplation of their inner mysteries, and of his own state of being as well. The silence of such films is not merely the silence that comes from the absence of sound: it is a deeper silence, in which the noise of the external world has been stilled, in order to allow the contemplation of other sounds—as from the body, the nervous system, the mind, in a revelatory purity.

When one considers the vast difference between perceiving the rectangle of light called the film image and listening to film sound, one is hardly surprised that the aesthetics of sound have been so violently battled over since the inception of the sound film. Our aim has been not to effect any resolution of these issues, as a "solution" would likely limit rather than expand the possibilities of cinema, but rather to enumerate varieties of past achievements, in the hope that they may lead the way into an even more varied future.

Notes

1. See, for example, "A Statement," by Eisenstein, Pudovkin, and Alexandrov, in Sergei Eisenstein, *Film Form: Essays in Film Theory,* ed. and trans. Jay Leyda (New York: Harcourt, Brace, 1949); "The Silent Sound Sense," by Stanley Brakhage, *Film Culture,* 21 (Summer 1960): 65–67; and Jonas Mekas, "Interview with Peter Kubelka," *Film Culture,* 44 (Spring 1967):42–47.

2. Brakhage, "The Silent Sound Sense."

3. Peter Bogdanovich, "Interview with Howard Hawks," *Movie,* 5 (December 1962):10.

4. It is interesting to note that after considerable polemicizing against sync-sound, Kubelka made his most recent film, *Pause!,* with sync-sound *only,* demonstrating once again the limitations of any proscriptive theory of cinema.

5. "The effect of this very dominant, highly rhythmic score, generally played with a volume in excess of Cornell's stated intentions is, curiously, an intensification of the film's silence. It is as if the rhythm, pitch, and intensity dispel the subliminally sensed voice issuing from Rose Hobart's moving lips. We cannot hear the words we speak for her. Rose Hobart moves with the splendor of *Gradiva*, enveloped in a silence, intensified by music, through a landscape decomposed, a space distilled, into a blue inane." Annette Michelson, "Rose Hobart and Monsieur Phot: Early Films from Utopia Parkway," *Artforum* (June 1972):57.

6. ". . . a desire less to express myself and more of making something out of the film material itself relevant to film for spiritual purposes. The intention is to be able to savor and examine the composition. . . . What I mean by 'spiritual' is sensitizing the mind to its own consciousness by allowing the mind simply to observe and digest the material, film phenomena presented, rather than manipulating it to evoke moods and sentiments." Ernie Gehr, in "Ernie Gehr Interviewed by Jonas Mekas, March 24, 1971," *Film Culture*, 53–54–55 (Spring 1972):26–27.

7. See, for example, my *"The Tarnished Angels,"* *Screen*, 12, no. 2 (Summer 1971).

Appendix: A Narrative Glossary
of Film Sound Technology
STEPHEN HANDZO

All technical terms indicated in boldface type in this appendix can also be found in the index.

This glossary is organized into the following four sections:

I. Evolution of the Recording Medium
II. Microphone Placement: A Sound Strategy
III. Postproduction
IV. Presentation in the Theater

Although the sound track contributes mightily to the screen's illusion of reality, film sound itself is the product of artifice. Dialogue, sound effects, and music may all come out at the same time, but they do not go in at the same time. Normally only the dialogue—and not necessarily all of that—is recorded while the image is being photographed (a process variously known as sync-sound, lip-sync, production, or "live" sound, direct or original recording). For technical, aesthetic, or commercial reasons, dialogue may be postsynced or "dubbed" in whole or in part. Most of the dramatic uses of sound, such as those achieved through music, sound effects, or narration, are added after filming in the postproduction phase.

It has been repeatedly demonstrated, first in the early "talkie" era and again in the 1960s (when *cinéma vérité* documentary created a vogue for "direct" sound), that merely recording the sound environment in which shooting takes place is seldom satisfying realistically or aesthetically. Why this is so can be seen and heard in early sound films. In one of John Gilbert's disasters, *The Way of a Sailor* (1930), Gilbert and Leila Hyams are seen talking on the beach at Santa Monica. Not only does the surf overwhelm the dialogue with a hiss that sounds like bacon frying, it varies from the two-shot to his close-up to her close-up, suggesting that a recording engineer, oblivious to the background, was trying to raise the woman's voice. While sound made film acting more realistic, the difficulties of location recording forced many scenes into the studio in front of process screens or painted backdrops either in entirety or as a "cover set" intended to be preceded and/or followed by long shots filmed without sound in actual places. Ten years later, the scene might well have been played on a sound stage in front of a rear-projected ocean in order to get a "clean" dialogue track while stock library effects of ocean sounds and perhaps a "love theme" played on the high strings would be added later.

Today, the demand for visual realism would move that scene outdoors again. Although there have been great advances in microphone technology, merely pointing a microphone at actors amid a noisy location would still not be very satisfactory. One possible solution to the problem of filming our beach scene—the use of small microphones concealed in the player's chest area, clipped or taped just below the mouth and connected either by a radio link to the main recorder or by wire to a tiny recorder carried on the actor's person—would be precluded here by the costuming or lack of it.

The most practical solution would be to take the original noisy production sound and use it as a **cue track** ("guide track") for the actors to redo their lines postsynchronously in a recording studio, through a process known as **looping** or **dialogue replacement.** Yet the **ambient** (background) noise, although intrusive, is essential to convey reality. While at the location, a recordist would likely tape several minutes of **wild sound** (sound not synchronized to any particular shot) of breaking waves, gulls, beach noises, etc., to be cut into effects tracks. In the mix, some music filtered to sound like a distant portable radio could be added.

The end product would not just be better technically than the 1930 track but, surprisingly, more realistic, since many subtle sounds that were not formerly picked up would combine to create a sound portrait of a beach.

Also, a microphone—within the limits of its design and pick-up pattern—responds to sound objectively, while human beings experience the sound environment subjectively through attention mechanisms. In order to indicate the couple's growing interest in each other, the director might wish to have the background sounds fade down gradually as the dialogue unfolds. Suppose a later scene reveals the man at the beach to be unhappily married; he might "tune out" his wife's nagging to hear the voice of the girl at the beach as an aural flashback. These effects—achieved easily today when sound tracks can be copied, kept separate, or recombined—represented considerable victories in the early days.

Sound films existed as a technological and commercial reality first and as a dramatic medium second. Early sound technicians came from the telephone, broadcasting, or record industries, where previous experience was not extensive (electrically recorded phonograph records went on sale in 1925, network radio broadcasting began in 1926, and the "talkies" appeared in 1927) or even relevant. Knowing how to record in a studio or broadcasting station helped little when taking sound on film locations. In the memoirs of veteran directors, a legend has been perpetuated of the early sound era as a collective nightmare when soundmen sacrificed visual quality and pacing to attain sound that was itself far from ideal. There was, of course, no precedent for dealing with the most crucial question of all: the relationship of sound to picture in terms of space ("perspective") or time ("contrapuntal sound"). The 1928 manifesto in which three leading Soviet directors proposed "asynchronous" sound envisioned effects that could not be executed satisfactorily for several years to come. Sound came in with a clubfoot; yet before long the much maligned technicians solved the problems and created a medium that could be manipulated by the director as readily as picture alone had been.

I. Evolution of the Recording Medium

Some aspects of sound filmmaking have changed very little: reproduction in the theater is not so different from what it was in 1927. The media for making original recordings have changed drastically, with advances at each stage spurred by the technical and aesthetic limitations of the previous process. Because vestiges of earlier systems are found at appropriate stages of current practice, the best way to grasp the basics of sync-sound filming and editing is through a chronological survey of its evolution.

Sound-on-Disc (Vitaphone) ca. 1926–29

Most early attempts at "talking pictures" used phonograph records; these systems invariably failed because of the mechanical problems of maintaining synchronization and because the old acoustical records in conjunction with a mechanical, air-filled amplifier gave a "tinny" sound. With the advent of the electron tube amplifier, Warner Bros. introduced the first commercially successful sound pictures in 1926.

By today's standards, or even by those of the time, a disc system seems a foredoomed anachronism, but recall that Warners launched the "talkie" revolution with *The Jazz Singer* almost inadvertently. The system was adequate for their initial purpose—best inferred from the Vitaphone premiere of a year earlier. The feature presentation *Don Juan*, exhibited with symphonic score and rudimentary sound effects, was entirely conceived and produced as a silent picture (obviously photographed with hand-cranked cameras). Vitaphone was fully intended to be compatible with the expected continued production of silent pictures. Even the so-called sound speed standard of 24 frames per second or 90 feet per minute was established by Western Electric engineers who had put tachometers in first-run theaters in Chicago to determine the average projection speed of silent films.

Filmed specifically for the premiere (at 24 f.p.s.) were one-reel shorts designed to show off the system's capacity for precise sync (Will Hays spoke, guitarist Roy Smeck plucked his instrument). The shorts served in lieu of the costly "presentation" shows, just as the recorded score was intended to provide a standardized musical accompaniment to replace the highly variable efforts of piano players, organists, and pit orchestras.

Sound-on-disc offered better reproduction than early sound-on-film. But the limitations of the process became increasingly obvious as Warners edged into talking features. Vitaphone employed 12- or 16-inch discs grooved similarly to 78 r.p.m. records but rotating at the LP speed of 33⅓ r.p.m. for a maximum playing time of seven or nine minutes (somewhat less than the eleven minutes of the full one thousand feet of the then standard projection reel). Aside from the problem of discs arriving at the theater cracked or broken, it was harder to maintain sync through the changeovers required for a talking feature than in a one-reel film or a silent film with a loosely synchronized score. Sync could be lost simply by the projectionist bumping into the turntable (this was very easy to do as it was located at the rear of the projector and was connected by a shaft to the same drive motor). Sync would then be restored by working a lever to speed up or slow down the disc. If the film broke, an equivalent number of frames of black leader would have to be spliced in to replace the damaged footage.

The film was threaded with the "Picture Start" frame in the aperture of the projector, and the disc was cued by placing the stylus next to an arrow by the innermost groove of the record, which played from the center out. Apart from the danger of putting the wrong disc with the film, each thread-up required several minutes so that the tendency in shooting was to use the maximum playing time of the disc. Dramatic action was expressed through lengthy chunks of dialogue, a practice that prompted complaints of "staginess." Many of the early Vitaphone productions were in fact stage plays (even unproduced plays) or musicals. If an actor flubbed a line, the entire disc was scrapped. Because it was not possible to edit a disc, the sound governed the picture. Warners developed a system of interlocked turntables that made it possible to "dub" as many as eight discs onto one. This allowed the use of shorter takes by putting the sound for several short scenes onto one disc without losing sync. From the beginning, picture editing was possible because Vitaphone filmed with multiple cameras as in 1950s live television, although this editing was more mechanical than creative. The "master camera" filmed the principals; angles such as close-ups were cut in simply by replacing an equivalent number of feet and frames. During the period when silent films were being converted to "part-talkies," a master scene would be filmed with sound but the close-ups from the silent version might be retained for the cutaway reactions.

Disc recording survived for certain "in house" uses: to prerecord musical numbers for "playback" on the set (Grace Moore's songs in the 1934 *One Night of Love* used the new "hill-and-dale" system of disc cutting to achieve the highest fidelity music recording possible); to make "acetate" reference checks to monitor quality before the film was developed; and to provide music departments with a record of their work.

Sound-on-Film, Single System (Movietone) ca. 1927–29

At the time of the Vitaphone premiere a system for recording and reproducing sound-on-film was in all essential respects complete. De Forest Phonofilm of 1923–24, although a financial (and artistic) failure, was a technical milestone in that for the first time in commercial exhibition electronic amplification was applied to reproduce sound intelligence inscribed directly on film by electrical energy converted into a fluctuating beam of light. In projection a steady beam of light from the exciter bulb passed through modulations of light and dark on the sound track and was converted by a photoelectric cell into electrical impulses.

Sound-on-film is based on the simple principle that one form of energy can be converted to another with suitable devices. A microphone converts sound waves into electrical impulses; putting the speech current through a narrow loop of wire in a magnetic field will cause the wire to vibrate closer or farther away from itself according to the applied electrical waveform ("electromagnetic vocal chords"); a light beam shining through the fluctuating gap between the wires would be modulated in intensity, thus "writing" sound information on unexposed film in motion. This was the Western Electric light valve.

The developed negative would show the sound information as black lines against a clear background. In Western Electric's **variable density** system (used by all major producers except the RCA-affiliated RKO Radio initially), the sound track looks much like the Universal Product Code on supermarket items; lines closer together indicate higher frequencies—literally more frequent—while the degree of blackness-to-transparency (density) indicates the **amplitude** or volume.

In the RCA Photophone **variable area** system, a galvanometer activates a rotating mirror, which produces a squiggly line on the sound track much like the waveform pattern on an oscilloscope. Sound output is governed by size—a fatter line indicating a greater amplitude—and frequency by the closeness of the waves. A low, loud sound would resemble the teeth of a ripsaw and a soft, high-pitched tone would look like a hacksaw blade.

Both density and area tracks are compatible in projection. Initially, density tracks offered better speech intelligibility chiefly because plosive consonants were limited by the inherent design of the system, whereas variable area tracks went quite easily into overload. After limiters were developed, variable area became the preferred format. It was less affected by variations in processing, e.g., amplitude loss due to underdevelopment. All modern tracks are variable area, including Dolby SVA (stereo variable area).

In reproducing optical sound, the light reaching the film is constant from the so-called **exciter bulb** but is modified by the changing ratio of light to dark in the sound track. The sound pick-up is a **photoelectric cell** (resembling the "electric eye" that keeps an elevator door open) and moves the needle on a built-in exposure meter. Photosensitive materials struck by light will emit enough electrons in proportion to the amplitude and wavelength of the light to produce a small DC current, which is then preamplified to provide an adequate input level to the theater sound system.

Theodore W. Case, whose system had been taken over by De Forest, realized that sound-on-film had a better chance of being adopted if it were made compatible with industry practice. Case modified the standard Bell & Howell 35mm camera used by all major producers, placing his "Aeolight" (light valve) twenty frames down the film path from the aperture and protruding at an angle from the rear of the camera. (Because film is really a series of still pictures exposed intermittently in the camera gate while sound recording requires continuous movement, there must be some distance between the two to cushion the different types of movement.) This necessitated relocation of the **soundhead** containing the optical reproducer from the top of the projector in the De Forest system to below it, establishing a 20-frame **displacement** between sound and picture. All of this was accomplished by the time William Fox bought the rights to the system, which was renamed Movietone.

Movietone's greatest early successes came in the newsreel field where speed counted for more than quality; contact printing from the edited camera negative yielded a release print in perfect sync that could be shipped to the theaters. Audiences were astounded in May 1927 to see Lindbergh's take-off for Paris and hear the engine of the "Spirit of St. Louis." So deeply ingrained is the myth that *The Jazz Singer* was the first sound film that it is in some ways astonishing today to hear the flat Yankee voice of President Calvin Coolidge honoring Lindbergh on his return to America in an era known today only from silent archival footage (cf. *Zelig*). The Movietone News instituted regularly in October 1927 did not have (and would not have had) the melodramatic commentary, music, and sound effects that newsreels later acquired. The segments were introduced by titles and used the direct production sound.

According to Earl Sponable, co-inventor of the Fox-Case system, Fox was so anxious to get into the market for talking pictures that Movietone News equipment was diverted into entertainment shorts. John Ford in Peter Bogdanovich's interview book claims that he was the first director to take the sound system outdoors (for *Napoleon's Barber*, released November 1928), but this is absurd given a full year of Movietone News by then. Ford's half-hour film may have been the first entertainment film made outdoors with sound, but even that is doubtful.

Even in 1928 critics were complaining that Vitaphone never went outside. (Exterior shots were shot silent.) Movietone tweaked Vitaphone by filming its first all-talking feature *(In Old Arizona)* outdoors. Vitaphone responded by finally putting its equipment on a truck. Movietone then did what a disc-based system could never do—it filmed sync-sound from a moving vehicle. In *Sunny Side Up* an actor riding a motorcycle exchanged dialogue with the passenger in a sidecar. It was direct sound with, as William K. Everson has noted, the microphone boom shadow on the road to prove it. (Soon all such scenes would be made with rear projection.)

Sound-on-film's greatest advantage was its ability to be spliced so that a sound take could be very long or very brief and constructed from several takes or angles. This facility was not immediately exploited. De Forest filmed all Phonofilms with head-to-toe shots in the manner of a vaudeville sketch; even the most primitive Vitaphone shorts had a minimum of three angles. Splices were initially annoying because breaks on the sound track were read by the photocell as output and produced audible thumps. Case solved this drawback as early as 1926 by **blooping** the splice with a dot of heavy black ink (still marketed years later as "Movietone Ink"). Blooping was later performed on the negative with a hole punch or on the positive with a diamond-shaped **blooping patch** of black celluloid.

Less manageable was the problem of the 20-frame displacement between sound and image. (On a splicey print, splices are not followed by garbled sound until about a second later.) In editing single system, the editor had to make the cut 20 frames ahead of the action in order not to lose words. This meant that after each cut there was a lag of five-sixths seconds, during which the sound ambience was that of the previous shot—before anyone spoke. Fades and dissolves, then still made in the camera, became difficult or nearly impossible to execute. Development of the negative was an unsatisfactory compromise between the pleasing gray scale desired for the picture and the high contrast required by the sound track. The graininess of the emulsion degraded the upper frequencies and read on the reproducer as noise. Single system shooting was soon relegated to the news field. (Not all newsreels were single system; RCA Photophone claimed that a separate sound film gave Pathe News superior quality to Movietone. Cameras modified for single system shooting were also used in inaccessible locations.) Some sources have claimed that Fox was editing with the 20-frame displacement as late as 1931, but this is unlikely except possibly for second-unit (location) work.*

Double System Sound-on-Film ca. 1929–51

Whereas Warners and Fox entered talkies through the back door with equipment designed for other purposes, studios that went "all-talking" in the middle of 1929 worked from the beginning with a sound track on a second strip of film that could be cut separately from the picture yet in sync with it. The sound recorder, like the film camera, had a capacity of 1000 feet and was driven in sync to it either by "selsyn" (interlock) motors or AC synchronous motors operated from the same power source so that fluctuations in speed due to voltage drops would be the same for both devices. The introduction of special fine-grain emulsions for the sound recording negative shifted noise to the higher frequencies above the voice range; preflashing the film with light of a certain wavelength would further reduce noise ("noiseless" recording).

Instead of working in "projection sync" with the sound in advance of the picture, editors worked in "editorial sync" ("bench sync"), and were thus able to match picture and sound splices to the frame. Using the visual image of the clapper and the "spike" made in the optical track by the stick, the editor could line up sound and picture in a **synchronizer,** a manually operated set of interlocked sprocketed wheels that could hold two or more strips of film in sync sprocket-hole-for-sprocket-hole. The Moviola Company developed motorized editing machines with a viewing glass for the silent picture footage and a separate optical soundhead for the track. The new editing ability it made possible was flaunted in the 1933 State Fair: four barkers, each speaking a few words, divide the announcement: "This is/ the last/ night of/ the State Fair."

Once sound had been separated from picture, the next logical step was to keep separating tracks so that music and sound effects instead of being recorded live on the set could be lined up to the picture after being

---

*Several of Fox's early-talkie musicals had sequences in Multicolor that would seem to have dictated separate sound.

recorded separately. Three—and even four—soundhead Moviolas were built once advances in rerecording made possible **mixing,** whereby several sound tracks could be combined into one.

This development unleashed the potential of musical films. In 1929–30 the filming of musicals was chained essentially to a live stage performance. But by 1933 production numbers such as those staged by Busby Berkeley could be built up from segments filmed to a prerecorded vocal or piano-rhythm accompaniment and edited together employing fades, dissolves, wipes, and other novelty effects of the then new optical printer. The edited film was then rescored for full orchestra and sound effects were added. The 1933 *King Kong* was a showcase not just for special effects photography but for the possibilities of sound rerecording, with Murray Spivack's noises and Max Steiner's music bringing the little animated figures to life much as the space wars in the George Lucas pictures or Clint Eastwood's car chases today derive their force from music and/or sound effects. Having separate tracks for music and effects also did away with the practice of shooting films in several languages with different casts because only the voice track would have to be replaced for foreign release.

Double System Sound with Magnetic Film ca. 1951–60

Magnetic recording offers better fidelity than optical sound, can be copied with less quality loss, and can be played back immediately without development. Magnetic recording was used as early as 1945 for nonsynchronous recording, i.e., music, and spread rapidly. Loren Ryder won a 1950 technical Oscar for converting Paramount entirely to magnetic sprocketed film for recording, editing, and mixing; within a year magnetic film was being used for 75 percent of Hollywood feature production and postproduction.

The recording apparatus was still quite bulky, although Ryder and Paramount, among others, used a 17.5 mm rather than 35 mm format operating at half-speed to reduce cost and weight for original production sound. A suitcase-sized version of this equipment was used on location in Egypt in 1955 for *The Ten Commandments.*

Editing was essentially the same with magnetic heads replacing the optical reproducers on the Moviola. A magnetic head was added to the synchronizer to locate the sync-mark (made by the sound of the clapper or electronic beep) that would then be punched with a hole.

Some editors had become so good at reading optical sound that they were slowed down by having to play tracks back through a "squawk box"; for several years, studios continued to provide an optical track alongside the magnetic stripe on the "work track."

Contemporary monaural sound components are recorded on a .200" oxide stripe inboard of the sprocket holes on otherwise clear sprocketed 35mm film except for a balance stripe containing no information but ensuring even contact with the recording head and preventing a lopsided wind. Before conversion to the optical track on the release prints, the multiple monaural dubbing units are mixed down to three .200" stripes (music/dialogue/effects) on **full-coat magnetic** stock, i.e., oxide across the full width of the film. This format was also used to record music multitrack and to provide stereo recording for early CinemaScope films.

Because of the many generations film sound goes through from original recording to the release print, the shift to magnetic sound reduced quality losses from photographic development. But although sound technicians had hoped for a general shift to magnetic release prints, the higher costs daunted producers and exhibitors. Most films continued to be released with monaural optical tracks only.

Double System Sound with ¼" Tape and Sync-Pulse ca. 1960 to Date

With ¼" tape widely used in broadcasting, the record industry, and even in the home, its adaptation to film was inevitable but haphazard. Under such names as Rangertone and Pilot-tone, various companies offered recorders employing "electronic sprocket holes" in the form of a sync-pulse recorded on the tape. A 60 Hz (cycle) sync-pulse generated in the camera-drive motor serves as a record of the film speed. Each frame of the film is indicated by 2.5 cycles per frame (60 cycles per sec. ÷ 24 frames per sec. = 2.5 cycles per frame). This relation is fixed even if camera, recorder, or both are running off-speed (23 f.p.s. = 57.5 c.p.s., etc.). For the purposes of editing, a **transfer** is made from the ¼" tape to sprocketed magnetic film, which is matched to picture in the usual manner. Through a device called a **resolver,** each 2.5 cycles of the sync-pulse on the tape causes one frame of magnetic film to be pulled through a recorder.

The first ¼" tape machine to achieve wide popularity was the Nagra invented in 1959 by Stefan Kudelski. The Nagra used either 7" open-reel tape when operated from a stationary position or 5" tape when carried from a shoulder strap with the lid closed. A monaural full-track (one direction) recording could be made at one of three speeds—of these, 7.5 i.p.s. is the standard for production work. Although the Nagra offered cost savings because it used regular tape for original recordings rather than the expensive magnetic film, it was not immediately adopted by the studios. On the sound stage where sync between a camera and a recorder was maintained by plugging both into the same power source, the Nagra, albeit smaller and lighter, did not function that differently from the old film equipment. But documentary filmmakers immediately seized on the potential of the Nagra; in conjunction with innovations and modifications from the filmmakers themselves it became the staple of the *cinéma vérité* movement of the 1960s.

Lightweight cameras with motors driven by battery belts were coming into being. As the Nagra, too, could be battery operated, it was possible to film in actual places with the participants speaking for themselves without being interpreted by a commentator. Initially the sync-pulse was produced by a small AC generator connected to the camera motor and conducted by a cable to the recorder **(cable-sync)**. The Maysles brothers found even this confining and began shooting with Kudelski's crystal-controlled motor, which keeps the camera running at precisely 24 f.p.s. while the recorder has its own oscillator to put a 60-cycle pulse on the tape with no direct physical connection. This system is called **crystal-sync**.

The documentary film advanced the technology of feature production. Today with crystal-sync it is possible to run several cameras in sync to one recorder or even several recorders in sync to the camera(s). In the early 1970s the briefcase-sized transistorized recorders were joined by tiny recorders like the Stellavox or Nagra SN (about the size of a paperback book) that can be worn in a jacket pocket or carried in a handbag, allowing each player in a scene to be individually "wired for sound."

II. Microphone Placement: A Sound Strategy

The earliest sound films were made with omnidirectional microphones—like those supplied with or built into cheap home tape recorders today—that picked up sound in a nondirectional 360° pattern, recording too much random sound relative to the voices.

A promising development of the early 1930s was the bi-directional microphone developed for radio interview programs that picked up sound in a figure-eight pattern. Resembling a giant electric shaver, this microphone was eagerly adopted for long shots and music recording although omnidirectional mikes were still used for medium and close-up shots. In 1936, RCA found that combining the two types produced a **cardioid** (heart-shaped) pick-up pattern fanning outward from the tip that was especially sensitive to sounds coming from the front and relatively dead to sounds at the rear and sides. In this form it was called a **unidirectional** (later just "directional") mike, although the first version, that familiar capsule-shape used by the NBC radio network, had a switch that enabled it to be used as omni-, bi-, or unidirectional. These mikes were used experimentally in Hollywood in the late 1930s, notably in Frank Capra's *You Can't Take It with You*. Directional mikes designed primarily for film work were introduced by Western Electric in 1939 and 1940 and won RCA a technical Oscar in 1941.

Modern directional mikes are of a **condenser** (electrostatic) type looking like a slim flashlight and picking up sound at a 150° radius. They have excellent frequency response and sensitivity but are delicate, susceptible to damage from moisture, shock, and—even when not connected—from loud noises. (When not in use, they are kept in a velvet-lined wooden case.)

There are also **highly directional** ("shotgun") mikes, recognizable by their length, where the angle of acceptance resembles an elongated "heart" **(super-cardioid).** Contrary to widespread belief, the pick-up is not as concentrated as the beam of a flashlight, but merely narrower than a directional mike. "Shotguns" are used when intrusive ambient noise requires more precise miking. For sync-sound shooting with the actors, only the voices are wanted. Ambient sound needed to give reality to the scene is recorded wild (nonsynchronously) and added in postproduction. Because the "shotgun" is especially sensitive to sound at its front, it may be placed up to twelve feet from the speaker, making it useful for wide-angle shots.

In general, the best position for a directional mike is at arm's length in front of the player and just above the head. **Sibilance,** the high-frequency whistling or "essy" sound, can be minimized by pointing the microphone slightly to the left or right or toward the speaker's knees, though pointing the mike at the floor produces **boominess** or bass accentuation. When two players converse in a shot, the mike must be rotated between them or one player will be "off mike."

Because of increasing specialization in microphone design and because scenes formerly made in the controlled environment of the sound stage are now often filmed on location, a sound strategy (in both senses) is needed for mike selection and placement. Uniform quality is maintained when the same type of microphone and even the same actual microphone is used for the entire production; each scene, however, presents its own acoustical problems. It is necessary to understand not only the capabilities of different microphones but the three types of sound present in the acoustical environment.

Direct sound issues from the source itself, such as those frequencies coming from an actor's mouth. (Unfortunately, "direct" sound is also a synonym for the original production sound, a meaning not relevant here.) When a person is close to us, we hear essentially **direct** sound including low-frequency chest tones. As the person moves farther away, we hear more of the **reflected** sound. Reflected sound is produced by the direct sound bouncing off the walls, floor, etc. Reflected sound is much more complex in character than direct sound because the surfaces are at different distances from the source and have widely varying reflective properties. Interiors that contain a lot of hard surfaces—glass, stone, metal, etc.—are said to be "live" because of their high reflectivity. Soft or porous materials, like carpeting, draperies, and upholstered furniture, are sound deadening. As furniture is moved into an empty room, the acoustics become "dead." The reflected sound or harmonics include higher frequencies than the direct or fundamental sound. The materials such as rough plaster or acoustic tile that are used to soundproof studios from outside noises also effectively destroy the reflected sound (unless panels are put in to provide some reflected sound or liveness). Aside from mismatched lip movements, postsynchronized dialogue is betrayed by the fact that the dubbing studio does not sound like any place but a dubbing studio, i.e., it is acoustically "dead."

The third kind of sound is ambient sound, consisting of noises present in the filming environment. Broadly, in making dialogue recordings the direct sound is *always* wanted, ambient sound *never* wanted, and reflected sound wanted in relation to the acoustics implied by the camera position.

The ambient sound itself has direct and reflected frequencies, but these become important only when recording sound effects and the noise itself becomes a source. Despite *every* attempt to control background noise (even in indoor filming), there is always some ambient sound from fluorescent lighting, elevators, air conditioners, etc. In controlled filming these can be silenced, but each room has a distinct **presence** of subtle sounds created by the movement of air particles in that particular volume. A microphone placed in two different empty rooms will produce a different **room tone** for each. One of the oddest sights in filmmaking is that of a microphone being aimed seemingly at nothing. This is because there may be some shots that can be filmed **M.O.S.**—an archaic term dating from the German-speaking colony of directors in early-talkie Hollywood who expedited shots not requiring sync-sound dialogue by calling for shooting "mit out sound." Room tone is needed for M.O.S. interiors because there is never *no* sound even when nothing is happening on the screen (except possibly when indicating death, memory, a Godardian "alienation effect," etc.). The sound track "going dead" would be perceived by the audience not as silence but as a failure of the sound system. Room tone is also needed to restore the ambience destroyed by dialogue replacement.

Until the 1960s, the dominant convention in sync-sound filming was to treat the microphone as the "ear" of an imaginary participant-observer whose "eye" was the camera. This is the principle of **perspective,** analogous to the discovery by painters during the Renaissance that an illusion of spatial depth could be created by having the background recede toward a vanishing point relative to the foreground. In sound, an aural sense of space is created by varying the ratio of direct to reflected and ambient sound in accord with the image; unlike a painting, a film has many points of view, including those produced by wide-angle and telephoto lenses that do not correspond to "normal" vision.

The principle of perspective was discovered inadvertently during the early sound era when the prevailing practice was to shoot with as many as eight cameras interlocked to a single sound channel. Microphone placement was dictated by the framing of the longest shot, with the result that the close-up was miked too distantly, producing a "faraway" sound (too much reflected sound). Decoupling the close-ups from the long shot became possible once sound-on-disc became obsolete and more skill was acquired in editing sound-on-film. A master shot would be filmed containing all the characters, who would speak the dialogue all the way through as in a stage play. Then the close-ups or other angles would be filmed and the sound recorded by microphones just above the frame.

The difference in microphone placement between close-up and long shot need not be great and indeed cannot be. A modern directional microphone is intended for use at a distance of at least two feet from the speaker's mouth even in "choker" close-ups; a directional microphone picks up considerable echo and ambient noise and cannot be moved quite as far as the shot might seem to dictate. A reverberent sound that makes the actor seem to be coming from the bottom of a well is invariably a sign of too distant placement. Unlike a lens, which can be focused at a great distance, a microphone has a limited pick-up pattern and the actors' voices quickly drop off relative to the ambient and reflected sound. The difference in microphone placement between close-up and long shot may be as little as eighteen inches and not much more than four feet even when the change of camera distance is fairly great.

Microphone placement is governed by the *perceived* space, not the actual distance from camera to subject. A close-up filmed with a long focal-length lens would be miked intimately.

Orson Welles in *Citizen Kane* adapted radio's technique of creating aural depth by placing actors at different distances from the microphone and using wide-angle lenses to make them seem further apart than they really were. In some cases perspective might be achieved by using more than one microphone, e.g., one microphone on characters grouped in the foreground and a high microphone over someone in the rear of the shot.

The microphones used during the early sound era, manufactured by Western Electric or RCA, derived from telephone or broadcasting applications where reflected and ambient sound would be masked by the direct sound issuing from a speaker's mouth in close proximity.

In the earliest all-talking feature, *The Lights of New York*, the microphone actually is the mouthpiece of a candlestick phone on the desk of a gangster barking orders to his henchmen ("Take him for a ride"). It was quite common in the earliest talkies for the mike to be concealed in flower-pots, fruit bowls, shrubbery, overhead light fixtures, or anything that would bring it close to the actors. Because the microphone was essentially nondirectional, the exact position did not matter very much (unlike directional mikes, which must be pointed at the actors) so long as the actors remained grouped near the mike.

In 1929s *The Desert Song*, the principals and chorus performed stiffly under suspended but immobile microphones. Floor stands were also employed behind draperies or at the side of the set.

Later, booms were developed so that an actor could traverse the set while speaking without having to be cross-faded from one microphone to another. In addition to following action, the boom could move to match the height of the person speaking.

The old, heavy studio boom with rubber tires and even a steering wheel has largely been replaced with the hand-held **fishpole.** For moving shots, such as those made with the hand-held Steadicam, a pistol grip is often employed.

The tendency of the omnidirectional microphone to pick up excessive reflected sound created certain problems. Natural sounds such as footsteps, door slams, etc., were often too loud relative to dialogue.

A form of ambient sound that gave a great deal of trouble in the early days came from the camera itself. The 1920s industry standard Bell & Howell camera is invariably described by old-timers as sounding like a "threshing machine." The camera was contained in a wooden booth with a glass window called an "icebox"—really an unventilated sweatbox for the camera operator—that in its later stages was put on wheels to accommodate moving camera shots. Around 1929 the camera itself was contained in an acoustical housing called a **blimp,** initially a homemade contraption that was later designed to fit the outlines of the camera. For outdoor shots where the camera noise would be obscured by other ambient sounds, it was sufficient to have the camera in a quilted cover called a **barney;** this may explain the proclivity in early sound films for locations with a lot of noise—a motorcycle in *Sunny Side Up*, a printing press in *The Front Page*, a train in *Love Me Tonight*.

The Bell & Howell gave way to the Mitchell NC (New Camera), in its later version **self-blimped** (BNC = Blimped New Camera). In modern cameras the moving parts are silenced. Panavision claims its camera to be silenced to within two feet of the microphone. This is quite sufficient for normal purposes because the directional microphones in use are so sensitive to sound from the front that they are intended to be used at some distance from the actor. Indeed, at less than two feet from the speaker's mouth, a cardioid microphone produces a degraded high-frequency response called a **proximity effect.**

The omnidirectional mike, as we know from watching pop singers and TV reporters, can be held very close to the mouth. While the need for proximity has made the omnidirectional microphone obsolete for boom placement, it has a very important role in modern film-making. Small omnidirectional microphones of the tie-clip sort seen on TV discussion programs or lavaliers taped to a shirt front are so close to the speaker's mouth that setting a recording level for the direct sound effectively excludes most of the ambient and reflected sound.

These microphones are also widely used for shots made out-of-doors where the space around the actors precludes overhead placement or when the film equipment would attract attention from passers-by. A camera with a long focal-length lens concealed in a van or positioned on top of a building could follow actors through Central Park or crowded city streets. Shots in cars formerly done with process (rear projection) are now made in actual vehicles. A cable concealed in the player's clothing connects the microphone to a small recorder or to a tiny radio transmitter picked up at the main recorder. In the latter usage, the lavalier is called a **radio mike** ("wireless" or "RF" mike) but is more likely to be found at an FBI "sting" operation than a broadcasting studio.

An innovation from the *cinéma vérité* team of Richard Leacock and Robert Drew, who used it as early as 1960, the radio mike is expedient but objectionable. Clicks and pops may result from electrical interference in the radio link. The microphone itself is intentionally deficient in low-frequency response to compensate for its placement against the speaker's chest; voice quality, unless carefully equalized in rerecording, may sound audibly different when intercut with footage filmed with an overhead mike. Because the microphone must be concealed in the costume, the sound-collecting area is masked by fabric that muffles high frequencies and may rustle as the actor moves. The actor may also go slightly "off mike" when directing a line to another actor by turning the head and not the entire upper body. Because the microphone is in a fixed relationship to the actor's mouth, a "close-up" sound is produced regardless of camera angle. Where early multicamera sound films suffered from "long shot" sound in close-ups or had Al Jolson's voice at the same level whether he was on-screen or off, today's films violate perspective by having big voices come from little people. The TV series *I Spy* popularized this; the leads were filmed with radio mikes on the streets of Hong Kong and other such exotic locales. Woody Allen does so routinely. Unfortunately, this practice undermines the expressive power of the long shot and undercuts the illusion of reality without creating a new stylistic convention along the contrapuntal lines envisioned by Eisenstein.

Actually, perspective in outdoor filming is easy to achieve. Except in a canyon or its urban equivalent of a playground surrounded by tenements, outdoor sound typically contains little or no reflected sound. As long as the sound effects track is sufficiently detailed to provide a convincing ambience, the voices need only be raised or lowered in the mix to match the visual space.

Although the news or documentary filmmaker would hotly contest this, outdoor scenes in general are easy to film. (Fox got a lot of publicity by shooting *In Old Arizona* out-of-doors; actually the Western desert setting reduced potential problems with reflected or ambient sound.) Whether the dialogue is recorded with an overhead mike, a chest mike, or looped in the studio, the voices will consist essentially of direct frequencies. In a fictional film, production sound flawed by excessive ambient sound or **wind noise** (the "whoosh" that requires microphones out-of-doors to be encapsulated in a mesh windscreen or "wind sock") would be relegated to a cue track and later looped. Shots made outdoors usually have the actors far enough from the camera that looping is not immediately detectable.

The greatest problem in recording out-of-doors is that background noise is not just excessive but uneven. A master shot filmed on a city sidewalk may contain the sound of an airplane that drops out on a close-up made a few minutes later. Even when engine noise or electrical interference from the car's ignition does not render unusable the production sound of a scene made in a moving vehicle, a large truck may be heard in one shot but not another. Sometimes the production sound when otherwise intelligible can be salvaged by judicious placement of sound effects. A stock or "wild" track of an airplane engine or truck could be faded up to cover the ambient noise in the first shot and faded down after the cut. Otherwise, the entire scene would be looped and a new ambience reconstructed synthetically.

The most difficult sound problems are posed by shooting in real interiors. Because the whole point of shooting in actual locations is to show the actors in relation to the background, framing may require the microphone to be so far away as to cause an excessive amount of reverberation. Chest mikes or looping produce an airless "dead" sound at odds with the visual information, although to some extent reverberation can be added electronically in the mix. Natural sounds such as footsteps that would be picked up by an overhead mike are lost and must be added postsynchronously.

In early Hollywood sound films there is a surprising amount of exterior shooting with "live" sound; later 1930s and 1940s exteriors not faked in the studio but made in actual places are more apt to be looped. What one virtually never finds are scenes made in real interiors. The major exception to this is the extraordinary group of "semidocumentary" features made by Louis De Rochemont expanding his *March of Time* technique of recreating events in actual places, e.g., *The House on 92nd Street, 13 Rue Madeleine, Boomerang.* Although usually cited for their newsreel-like photography and then unusual employment of real locations, these films are also landmarks in sound practice representing the most extensive use of "direct" sound between the early 1930s and the Nagra/"New Wave"/*cinéma vérité* era. In *Boomerang* (1947), except for the voice-over narration and some looping on exteriors, production sound accompanies scenes made in courtrooms, cell blocks, lawyers' offices, and police stations. Using the directional microphone introduced in the early 1940s, the recordings contain more reverberation than heard on the sound stage-bound films of the era. Natural sounds—e.g., the dialing of a telephone—are too prominent, but this "liveness" was apparently accepted by the audience along with the commentary and quasi-martial music as a "documentary-signifier." De Rochemont's style does not seem to have been emulated outside of pseudodocumentary productions, although Joseph H. Lewis's *Gun Crazy* (1949) uses "live" sound for both the meat-packing plant robbery and the famous single-take bank robbery (filmed with the camera and sound recording equipment mounted in the back of the getaway car).

How sound is actually taken is governed by economic as well as aesthetic considerations. The greatest expense of a film normally occurs during shooting. Each film has a shooting schedule based on its budget, and progress is gauged in the number of pages of script shot. Although almost everyone subscribes to the proposition that "live" sound from an overhead boom placement is much preferable to either postsynchronization or chest mikes, the reality is that sound quality is the first thing to be sacrificed once the production falls behind schedule and all that matters is to get the shot. Chest mikes are particularly used in the cost-constrained environment of series television where the home receiver's tiny speaker goes far to disguise shortcomings. The chest mike is particularly well suited to the shooting style of television, where it is common to cover a scene with a single take, often using a zoom lens that varies the space above the actor, as opposed to the more deliberate architecture of camera placement found in better features. The chest mike is thus an expedient compromise between the laborious craftsmanship of an acoustically correct microphone placement for each shot, as in old-fashioned Hollywood studio productions, and the total disregard of sound that obtains when it is a foregone conclusion that the production sound is merely a guide for total postsynchronization, e.g., the mixed-nationality "action-adventure" co-productions in which the Italians specialize where the production sound in four or five languages is replaced in dubbing for the various territorial "pre-sales."

Even with the best of intentions, the sound crew is generally not hired until a few days before the start of shooting; rarely, if ever, does the "location scout" evaluate sound problems along with visual appeal. Traffic or other noise may make postsynchronization inevitable. It is also quite common to forget to record crowd noises with the assembled extras during shooting; phony-sounding stock effects or underpopulated looping jobs must suffice.

The inefficiencies of early Hollywood talkies seem staggering in retrospect. Until rerecording improved, separate French-, German-, and Spanish-speaking versions were made. Musical accompaniment required having an orchestra present on the set; early-talkie musicals were essentially produced as "live" Broadway shows with endless man-hours consumed in cast and crew rehearsals and sundry takes; the simultaneous recording of principals, orchestra, and chorus employed up to all four of the microphone inputs on the broadcast-type rack amplifiers then in use.

In those days, the sound "mixer" turned his dials to balance male and female voices, contemptuously classifying actors anxious about their careers as "bloopers" (boomy voices), "essers" (sibilant voices), etc. A **mixer** can be a device or a person. In New York, with a history of small-crew independent and documentary production, the person who sets levels, determines microphone placement, and operates the mixing panel is called the soundman (a term as imprecise as it is sexist), a figure known in England as the recordist. The traditional Hollywood term is production sound mixer—as distinguished from the rerecording mixer who is only involved in postproduction. There are also scoring mixers and sound effects mixers whose functions are self-explanatory. Since 1969, the Academy Award for sound recording has named both the production mixer and the rerecording mixer(s).

Despite the term, relatively little mixing is done in shooting today. Instead, the mixer aims to get good original recordings at full levels free from distortion and background noise and, it is hoped, to match microphone placement to the camera position. Major technical and aesthetic reshaping is left for the postproduction phase where the overhead is lower, the facilities are more sophisticated, and the possibility of alternative versions exists. Sound levels, once set, are seldom touched during shooting, in contrast to the early practice of "riding the gain" (constantly altering levels to follow high or low voices).

The VU meter on the recording equipment is calibrated showing percentage of modulation in decibel levels; 0 db equals 100 percent modulation. Each increase or decrease of 6 db halves or doubles the percentage of modulation. Even the loudest passages must not exceed 100 percent modulation (the red line on the meter). Some studios record so that the needle stays at an average level of −14 db (only 20 percent of modulation).

The worst form of distortion is **overrecording** (recording at too high a level). As long-time MGM sound director Douglas Shearer once put it, "You can only pour so much milk into a quart bottle, and then it spills over." The degraded waveform produces a raspy sound that cannot be corrected. Distortion is prevented by moving the microphone, lowering the level, or both. **Underrecording** (recording at too low a level) is far less serious and can be compensated for in rerecording, although this results in lowering the **signal-to-noise** ratio. Professional equipment has a high signal-to-noise ratio—noise meaning **ground noise** such as the hiss inherent in recording tape oxides or **system noise** from electronic circuits—not background noises, which, however unwelcome, are considered part of the signal.

Continuous frequency noises such as 60 Hz AC hum or camera noise can be minimized in the final mix through the use of dip filters that remove a narrow part of the frequency spectrum. Unfortunately, such filtering may also impinge on the voice range.

Each additional "open mike" will contribute additional ambient noise. It is the preferred practice to film scenes as much as possible with a single microphone. When the nature of the shot requires that a second microphone be used on someone away from the main grouping of actors, the mikes are fed through a microphone mixing panel and cross-faded so that the total level of ambient sound is not increased: one "pot" (potentiometer) is brought up as the other is turned down. Before booms were invented the mixer might have to cross-fade as many as four microphones. Having two booms on a set proved adequate to cover virtually any combination of actors. Using two microphones in close proximity to record the same sound creates the possibility of a **cancellation effect** or out-of-phase condition unless one knows for certain that the microphones and connectors are wired identically; this situation is positively indicated when the sound level from two microphones is less than either individually.

When multiple microphones are used, instead of mixing into a single channel, better control can be obtained by using multitrack recording equipment that gives each microphone a discrete track. Rouben Mamoulian claims to have initiated multitrack recording (two strips of 35mm film in interlock) as early as 1929 for a scene in *Applause* where he wanted a young girl saying her prayers and her burlesque-queen mother singing a pop-tune lullaby both to be at equal volume and each to be intimately miked. This was not entirely successful owing to the fidelity loss in early rerecording. By

1934, in *The Gay Divorcee*, the voices and orchestra were being recorded on separate sound-track films to keep the lyrics from being obscured by the orchestra (still on the set).

Cinerama co-founder Hazard E. Reeves used a six-track 35mm magnetic recorder and six to eight omnidirectional microphones to create *This Is Cinerama*'s widely admired 360° sound effects. With three-track 35mm equipment in wide use for recording music in the early 1950s, the three-track format was used for production sound on Twentieth Century–Fox CinemaScope productions. (Even before CinemaScope, Fox had been experimenting with multiple microphones, recording on three optical tracks.) Three microphones were used in true stereo perspective. A person at screen left would be heard in the theater from the left-hand speaker, one from the right microphone on the right-hand speaker, and an actor could traverse all three speakers when crossing the screen without affecting the voice levels of other characters in the shot or off-screen voices. Studios other than Fox argued that essentially the same thing could be accomplished with a "directional" mix without the increase in ambient sound from multiple "open" mikes. Cameramen never liked it; lighting was difficult enough without creating a shadow from one microphone, let alone three. Even Fox apparently stopped shooting with multiple microphones at some point in the late 1950s or early 1960s. Although Russia's Mosfilm Studios remained committed to true stereo on the set, using as many as five microphones on a boom, stereo faded in America as sprocketed sound-recording film gave way to ¼" tape. Nagra has long offered an accessory mixer with multiple microphone inputs, but only recently has it made a two-track version of the industry-standard Nagra IV.

In recent years Robert Altman's Lion's Gate Studios has attracted attention by using multitrack equipment derived from the pop music industry for films *(Nashville, A Wedding)*, with a large number of characters speaking simultaneously. Most multitrack recording today really consists of multiple monaural tracks. Stereophony requires at least *two* microphones on a sound source far enough away that direct and reflected sound are picked up in three-dimensional perspective. Chest mikes are so close to the actor's mouth that giving each actor a small recorder or connecting the actors by cable or radio to multitrack equipment eliminates the reflected sound. The real advantage is that tracks in the mix can be balanced to achieve clarity, even when many people are speaking at the same time.

Actors, especially "method" actors, find film work confining. From the standpoint of the production mixer and the editor, a good actor is one who can read a line at the same pace and volume every time. Some inexperienced actors will get excited and speak louder and faster during the take than in rehearsals. Rehearsals are needed by the mixer to set levels and by the boom person to follow movement of the actors and to rotate the microphone to the player speaking.

During a take, the procedure is to start the recording machine first, then the camera. The assistant director enters the frame with the **clapper** (or "clapstick"), universal symbol of the film set; the clacking sound made as the stick is brought into contact with the slate enables the editor to line up sound and picture. Actually, automatic slating devices that fog a "blowout" frame on the film and place a 1000 Hz "beep" on the tape now perform this function, but the manual slate also marks the shot by scene and take number. Early crystal-sync systems in severing the umbilical cable between camera and recorder also wiped out the automatic slating feature, but this was reestablished with a VHF radio link devised by documentarists Leacock-Drew Associates. The new MacMarker has a two-inch-high Liquid Crystal Display indicating scene and take number and "speaks" silently to the tape via a voice synthesizer and a radio link. In a documentary film, the "slate" may be nothing more than someone tapping the microphone or clapping his hands on-camera.

III. Postproduction

The first step in the editing of dialogue and picture is "syncing up the dailies" (a.k.a. rushes). Because the recorder is started first, the sound is matched to the work print made from selected takes of the original camera negative. Ideally, the sound film is synchronized to the original before work-printing so that the original, the work print, and the sound track all can be coded with the same **edge numbers.** Edge numbers consist of a letter and four or five numerals that advance one digit per foot of film, e.g., A5037, A5038, printed in yellow ink between the sprocket holes and the edge of the film. In this way sound and picture can be kept in sync even after the slates have been cut off by referring to the numbers and using the frame counter on the synchronizer.

The director, editor, cinematographer, and others involved in the production view the dailies in a screening room equipped with double-system or **interlock** projection equipment. The editor and the lab doing the processing will have prepared matched numbered rolls for both sound and picture, e.g., Reel #109, Sound #109. At this stage the slates are left in so that the director may evaluate different takes for facial expression, line reading, etc. There may also be some rolls of M.O.S. footage containing establishing shots, inserts, etc. Generally picture editing takes precedence over sound editing. If the action requires going from a closer to a longer shot during a line of dialogue, rather than waiting for the end of the line the editor will cut on action and "lay under" the rest of the line from the closer shot rather than try to cut between words. It's possible to do this because lip-sync is most noticeable in close-up; the reverse, laying sound from a medium shot under a close-up, would not work very well because of the lip movements.

Dialogue Replacement (Looping)

Because of drastic changes in microphone placement from one shot to another, or excessively "live" acoustics, or background noise, or the need to excise profanity for television release, part or all of the dialogue in a scene may be postsynced. **Looping** involves cutting loops out of identical lengths of picture, sound track, and blank magnetic film. The actor listens to the cue track while watching the scene over and over. He rehearses his line so that it matches the wording and lip movements and then a recording is made, which can be done over if needed. The cutting of loops has largely been replaced by **automatic dialogue replacement** (ADR). Picture and sound are interlocked on machines that can run forward-backward. If the actor flubs, the machine is reversed, the line spoken again, and so onto the next one. This can be tedious, even grueling, work for the actors. If there is a better way, it is probably the new system trademarked as Wordfit that digitalizes the phonemes in the cue track and by imperceptible changes in pitch stretches or shrinks the replacement dialogue to match the waveforms in the original for perfect lip-sync. All of these systems assume an original track, however flawed, to work from. In some fringe productions such as porno films or the later European films of Orson Welles the postsync is so dreadful that the original sound was presumably lost or never even taken. Those filmgoers who demand subtitled prints are objecting more to foreign players dubbed into American English than to dubbing per se; the *titled* versions of many foreign films have mostly or entirely postsynchronized dialogue often replacing production sound in several languages.

A good looping job requires a stage large enough to accommodate panels simulating hard or porous wall surfaces and large enough to allow varied microphone placement so that the perspective implied in the shot can be matched and "recording booth acoustics" avoided. The old radio drama practice of grouping actors so that background characters are further from the mike also helps.

Dubbing in the sense of voice replacement was originally called **vocal doubling.** Just as there were stunt doubles for fight scenes—or body doubles today for nude scenes—voice doubles turned nonsinging actors into vocalists by performing just outside of camera range. There were many situations in which doubling could not be done during shooting—as when Louise Brooks refused to return for the retakes needed to turn the silent *Canary Murder Case* into a talking picture—so "doubling" became conjoined with "dubbing," a term already in use in the record industry for copying discs, to mean sound added after filming. (Margaret Livingston spoke Brooks's lines, thus salvaging silent footage that remained in the film.)

In England the final mix is called dubbing, a term rarely used in America anymore, although the interlocked film recorders that perform the actual rerecording are called "dubbers" and the mixing studio in Hollywood is often called the dubbing stage or dubbing theater. In its narrower meaning dubbing survived as the term for "ghost" voices even though after 1933 virtually all musical numbers were in fact **prerecorded** whether by the billed performer or such specialists as Marni Nixon, who "dubbed " Deborah Kerr *(The King and I)* and Audrey Hepburn *(My Fair Lady)*. Rosalind Russell's songs in *Gypsy* consisted of her own voice augmented by Lisa Kirk's, making it arguable who dubbed whom.

Voice-overs

Nonsynchronous speech applied to a previously filmed scene is called **voice-over.** Alexander Scourby, Burgess Meredith, David Wayne, Gary Merrill, and the late Hugh Marlowe have had profitable second careers as TV commercial voice-overs, a term also used for the narration in documentary films or even features. **Voice-under,** which is essentially the same thing, is sometimes used to describe speech that begins lip-sync as in a "talking head" shot of an interviewee and continues "under" archival footage of war, political campaigns, etc.

Often used as a crutch to bridge continuity gaps, particularly when drastic reediting has taken place, verbal narration has many other uses in fiction films: as introduction to a flashback whether over a point-of-view shot or the face of the player; as "thinking out loud" to replace the archaic theatrical devices of the aside or soliloquy, especially in Shakespearean films; as interior monologue à la Joycean stream-of-consciousness for a character with an active fantasy life *(The Seven Year Itch, Taxi Driver);* as letters spoken by their authors in lieu of photographic inserts; as an aural flashback recalling advice, warnings, "famous last words," etc.

Narration is always on a separate track from the dialogue. Any great variations in speech—such as in volume or microphone placement—

require making separate dialogue tracks so that the mixer can anticipate changes rather than trying frantically to adjust the "pot" or filters.

Sound Effects

Dialogue editing occupies most of the interest of the director and the editor; on major films, sound effects and music editing are the work of specialists who work from the cut film. Consequently, the most important editing decisions are made at the beginning. Usually, a change in scene produces a new sound ambience, although sometimes the dialogue from the previous shot continues under the new scene, thus creating a kind of parallel action between sound and picture. Anticipation may be created by bringing the sound of the next scene in a little early. A cut to a jarring noise—a favorite device of Orson Welles—can be relied on to wake up the audience.

All sounds other than speech, music, and the natural sounds generated by the actors in synchronous filming are considered sound effects, whether intended to be noticed by the audience or not. The big studios and large independent services maintain vast libraries of effects ranging from unsurpassed stand-bys to others too outdated or general to be appropriate. Wild sound is also taken on location for a specific production when the crew and other distractions can be silenced long enough to allow it. There are "sound designers" who specialize in electronic or mechanical effects that often serve the illusion better than the actual thing. The helicopters in *Apocalypse Now* were created by Walter Murch using no real aircraft but speeded-up and processed versions of the sound of a chain twirled against a paper bag.

An expedient way of generating mundane effects is the **foley** technique (named after an Ed Foley of Universal), which consists of matching live sound effects "to picture," well illustrated in *Modern Romance*. Albert Brooks, playing a sound editor, runs in place on a foley stage in time to the projected image of a character in a science-fiction TV series after selecting a plausible surface to represent a "space floor" from pits of asphalt, linoleum, gravel, etc.

In the optical sound era, effects editors would actually frame cut footsteps matched visually to M.O.S. scenes. Magnetic sound mandated foley, as did the widespread use of lavalier and radio mikes that do not pick up footsteps or other natural sounds that overhead mikes record. Replacement dialogue, of course, requires foley; foley is the effects equivalent of looping and is often done on the same stage. The foley stage at Glen Glenn in Hollywood has numerous props including a water tank.

War films, science-fiction films, and disaster films may use numerous effects tracks, gunshots on one, explosions on another, sirens on a third. Complex sounds may be built up from several tracks, the actual sound augmented or **sweetened** with a library effect. In traditional Hollywood practice, sound effects editing is performed "horizontally" rather than "vertically," i.e., instead of an assistant or assistants being responsible for the same types of sound effects all the way through the picture, each is given a 1000-foot reel to "shape up" so that several reels can be worked on simultaneously. Instead of mixing down, the modern practice is toward keeping sound effects tracks separate so that individual sounds can be "featured" or de-emphasized selectively, something that cannot be done when all the effects are "married." If there is any single trend that can be observed in sound effects practice, it is toward a much more detailed background sound ambience. This is largely the result of 1960s *cinéma vérité* and features, such as Godard's *My Life to Live,* influenced by it in which parts of the dialogue are obscured by the (direct) sound of such objects as cups, saucers, and dishes. Today these "realistic" sounds are carefully built up track-by-track. Oddly, it was a pre-New Wave Hollywood film, Robert Wise's 1954 *Executive Suite,* that set the trend; a sound effects track filled with street noises evoked the harsh reality of the business world, fades and dissolves were replaced by direct cuts, and underscoring was replaced by natural sounds, even under the **main title** (opening credits). On the whole, sound effects have gained at the expense of underscoring.

Film Music

Underscoring is music motivated by dramatic considerations (the "invisible orchestra") while **source music** is realistically part of the scene whether visually performed (a marching band, street musicians, etc.) or from a real source (radio, TV set, etc.) on- or off-screen. The term underscoring is also used to refer to the music that was considered good only when not noticed. Underscoring is now mainly found in television where **tracking** (assembling a score by editing music tracks from earlier episodes) is commonplace. The musician's union long ago ended this practice in features and even the cheapest productions now have original scores.

One reason why the relationship of music to image is often so gratuitous is that the composer normally does not come onto the project until the rough cut or later. Scoring is the last step before the final mix and thus the last opportunity for nervous filmmakers to alter the tone and style of the film in a major way.

Because actions may have to be performed in shooting in time to music that has not yet been written let alone recorded, a **temporary mu-**

sic track may be played back on the set. Obviously when scenes involving music are a major part of the dramatic action, the after-the-fact approach of most film music is unworkable. For example, the waltz in MGM's *Madame Bovary* was composed before shooting, staged on the set to a temporary piano track, and postsynched with the orchestra as in a musical.

In the heyday of the Hollywood studio system, it was the practice to preview with a temporary music track; MGM's Rudy Kopp was the master of this practice, splicing this piece by Stothart to that piece by Kaper so skillfully that the eventual score sometimes came as a letdown. In working with stock music for television, industrial films, or trailers (which usually do not have their own music but are tracked from the feature), the music editor must locate a point at which the instrumentation, key, and tempo are close enough to permit a **segue** (transition without pause) from one piece of music to another. In dramatic radio this was done by cross-fading two turntables; in films it was done with two tracks or simply a splice—with luck, on the beat. Library music will intentionally include some repetitious phrases to facilitate editing. The composer of an original score may prepare such repetitions if additional editing is expected after scoring.

Because many films are deadly when viewed without music, pictures even today are often **pretracked** for "in house" screenings to executives or to aid in editing. It is an old editor's trick to cut M.O.S. scenes to classical or stock music so that the tempo and phrasing lend structure to the footage. The composer must then write music that is similar yet different.

The first step in scoring is **spotting,** or deciding which scenes shall have music, where it is to begin, and where it will end. This is done in a screening room where the director will no doubt voice strong opinions. The "spotting run," in addition to allowing the composer to make intuitive decisions—the composer is usually the first person not connected with the production to see it objectively in quasi-finished form—lets the composer and music editor time each **cue** (each distinct piece of music needed whether source or underscoring) with a stopwatch. Veteran composer Miklos Rozsa has stated that writing to a stopwatch is the first and most difficult skill to master; eminent composers often never grasped it and left the film field in disgust.

On a Moviola, the music editor creates a **breakdown** or timing sheet, converting feet of film into seconds (even tenths or hundredths of seconds) minutely detailing all of the action in a cue so that the composer can write to any variation desired. The close synchronization of music to action is called **mickey-mousing,** a term coined by David O. Selznick to describe an early score by Max Steiner that evidently reminded him of the sort of music in Disney cartoons where dancing skeletons play their rib cages accompanied by xylophones, etc. A notorious example of Steiner's "catching" action musically was the two-note "crippled" motif for Leslie Howard's limp in *Of Human Bondage.* "Mickey-mousing" triumphantly suited the animated protagonist of *King Kong* with descending chords "catching" the massive tread of the approaching ape. It was possible to "catch" not only physical action but facial expressions, dialogue (Steiner claimed that his model for scoring under dialogue was the recitative in Wagner's operas), and even sound effects. Steiner blended music into airplane engines *(King Kong),* a rock drill *(The Fountainhead),* prison shop machinery *(White Heat),* a ticking bomb *(The FBI Story),* and even used human voices as wind *(The Lost Patrol, The Garden of Allah).*

Steiner's music was based heavily on his invention of the **click track,** a record of the tempo of visual action converted into a beat. Click tracks also are used to "chase" an *a capella* vocal with a postsynchronized orchestration or to "catch" cuts where the editor has cut M.O.S. footage to a quasi-musical rhythm. Originally click tracks were made by having the music editor punch holes at equidistant intervals—e.g., a "twelve-frame click"—into black leader that would be read as sound by an optical reproducer. (Because this was so tedious, lengthy scenes would employ loops of clicks.) Now there are digital metronomes that can produce clicks electronically on magnetic film. While some action, such as marching or calisthenics, has a uniform cadence, much does not and therefore requires a **variable click track,** e.g., the jagged rhythms accompanying the clank of swords in an Errol Flynn dueling scene.*

The modern trend is away from "catching" action to illuminating the implicit values in a scene. Jerry Goldsmith has been quoted as having decided, on the basis of watching old pictures on television, that films should have music less often but more strategically placed, i.e., fewer but longer cues. **Long cues** accompanying lengthy visual passages allow a composer to emulate classical form: Goldsmith's *The Blue Max* features a passacaglia for an air battle; Victor Young developed a fugue from an Irish folk theme for *The Quiet Man*'s turnabout.

Short cues are a few bars of music that serve as punctuation. **Stingers** are the sustained high-pitched chords (i.e., musical italics) that accompany knives aimed at the heart or the bass chords that follow fainting wives as they drop the telegram from the War Department. Georges Delerue, no less, "stings" Karen Silkwood's discovery of her contamination. **Quotations** are snatches of familiar themes, e.g., "Rule, Britannia!" under a shot of the door of No. 10 Downing St.

Largely passé in features, short cues survive in television as a

---

*Because frequent and rapid changes in tempo may be too difficult for the musicians—who face the conductor rather than the image—to execute, a compromise meter may be found that will "catch" most of the action and let the audience's imagination synchronize the rest.

carry-over from radio where little fanfares or harp glissandos served as "intro" or "outtro," distinguishing the program from the commercial break, and as aural fades and dissolves indicating a change of time or place. They are particularly used in sit-coms or soap operas with so few sets that transitions may not be self-evident.

On the recording stage, the conductor is alerted by a **streamer,** a three-foot scratch in the film at the end of which is a punched hole producing a flash of light on the screen that acts as the start cue. There may also be additional streamers within the cue to "catch" a particular action with a musical phrase in the Steiner manner. The conductor has headphones and can listen to the dialogue or possibly a click track under visual scenes.

In 1930 underscoring (where it had not been eliminated altogether in a general reaction against unmotivated music caused by the overproduction of musicals) was no longer performed during dialogue scenes but on the scoring stage.* Originally this was a small padded stage. In their preoccupation with elimination of echo, the engineers wanted "damped" or "dry" acoustics. The music directors pleaded for larger stages with "live" acoustics. In the late 1930s and 1940s, the recording session resembled a symphony concert with four or five overhead mikes. Because film music exists only to be recorded, the conductor's function of balancing the players was gradually taken over by the scoring mixer, thus saving time in rehearsals but diminishing any connection with a live performance. First, sections of the orchestra, and then even individual instruments, were separated from each other by acoustical partitions called **flats;** directional microphones are used—sometimes one microphone for every two musicians. Unusual instrumentation is possible, e.g., clarinet solo against brass. As the older generation of concert and theater musicians has given way to those raised in the multitrack environment of pop music and television commercials, electronic instruments and synthesizers abound.

For prerecording of musical numbers, the technique since the late 1930s has been to record the orchestra first. The vocalist in a recording booth then listens over headphones to the playback of the orchestra and his or her own performance with the added vocal kept on a separate track or stripe. The number is then mimed during shooting.

Rerecording (Mixing)

In preparation for the final mix, the various sound effects editors, music editors, and the foley and ADR specialists work under the direction of a

*The end of multicamera shooting made it impossible to edit scenes that had music under dialogue.

supervising sound editor. (The person billed as "film editor" typically deals with the picture film and the one or two tracks of production dialogue.) Because of the high degree of specialization inherited fron the big studio assembly-line era and the jurisdictional lines among union locals, it is easy for the postproduction sound team to work at cross-purposes: the foley editor may continue to build up effects tracks for a scene that the director has decided instead to cover with music. The supervising sound editor will also listen to the production sound with the rerecording mixer to decide whether noise between the lines can be "cleaned out" electronically or whether the scene must be looped.

The supervising sound editor schedules the mix. Certain studios (or rather the personnel associated with them) are in such demand that the facility must be booked months in advance; this exerts great pressure at the postproduction stage, particularly if shooting has exceeded the schedule. At present the cost of studio time in Hollywood is about $700 per hour—or about $5,000 to $6,000 per day for the use of the facility and the services of three mixers at the console. (In New York, the going rate is $450 per hour with one mixer. The Hollywood philosophy is that when three elements—dialogue, sound effects, and music—are controlled by only two hands, one element is bound to suffer. Apart from ideologically pro-East Coast directors—Woody Allen, Sidney Lumet, Elia Kazan—major features filmed in New York City are typically mixed in Hollywood.) Delays due to missing or poorly prepared tracks or indecision by the director are thus quite costly. In the absence of strong involvement by the director, the supervising sound editor may take creative control of the mixing process.

Mixing originated in the postsynchronization of music and sound effects in the dying days of the silent film. Early talkies typically contained M.O.S. scenes that required the addition of effects or music; as soon as noise reduction made rerecording possible without audible quality loss, the same methods were used to augment sync-sound scenes. Mixing is now a subtle and complex craft with its own minor cult figures such as Richard Vorisek in New York or Robert "Buzz" Knudson and Richard Portman in Hollywood.

Although some of the new digital processes employ the record industry technique of "overdubbing" or building up track-by-track on a single tape, most mixing in films is still performed by the traditional practice of threading multiple "dubbing units" of sprocketed magnetic film containing separate music, dialogue, and sound effects elements on banks of interlocked dubbers. The playback dubbers are connected by selsyn motors to each other and to the rerecorders that produce the "master" or parallel M/D/E (music/dialogue/effects) on full-coat magnetic stock. Also in interlock are a footage counter and a projector that allows the mixer(s) to work from the actual image.

The footage counter is needed because the mixer works from **cue sheets** or logs. At the top are column headings such as Dialogue 1,2,3,4; Music 1,2,3,4; FX (effects) 1,2,3,4; at the left are numbers starting at the top with zero indicating feet of 35mm film. This system alerts the mixers to be ready for a gunshot at 10 feet, a car crash at 25 feet, or a musical cue at 40 feet.

The dubbing stage resembles in its wall surfaces and carpeting a small-to-medium-sized threater auditorium without seats; its dimensions give the mixers some idea of the reverberation time in an actual theater. The mixing console is located at the rear of the dubbing stage, its position representing the rear half of the auditorium where most patrons sit, although in practice even television films may be mixed on the same large stage as feature films rather than in smaller dubbing theaters, depending on the availability of facilities.

The primary purpose of mixing is usually to strike the right dramatic balance among dialogue, music, and effects and to avoid monotony. Contrast is more important than actual loudness; in battles or chases with a lot of sound tracks either sound effects or music may be variously featured. The mixing console also includes equalizers to perform corrective work. High-pass and low-pass filters cut bass and treble respectively.

Dip filters remove part of the spectrum such as camera noise. Other filters can reproduce a telephone or radio speaker effect. Artificial reverberation can be introduced (for instance, when the sound from a close-up has been "laid-under" a medium shot).

The traditional Hollywood practice of mixing is to have three mixers at the console for dialogue, music, and effects under a supervising rerecording mixer who is also present during the mix and has overall responsibility. Actual practice varies somewhat from studio to studio. At Universal one mixer is responsible for dialogue and music while there are *two* mixers for sound effects (a division of labor that is well suited to the increased importance of sound effects relative to music). The traditional practice at MGM was to mix dialogue and sound effects together and add music on a second pass-through. (Music at MGM was usually dubbed much lower than, say, at Warner Bros., where music was more likely to be featured.)

In the days of optical recording it was necessary for the mixer to do an entire reel at a time; a mistake required going back and starting again. Automatic limiting devices were invented to fade down music and sound effects whenever dialogue came in. This resulted in what mixers who take pride in their dramatic sense disdain as a "newsreel mix." In the early days of magnetic recording, stopping the machine produced a "click" on the track, so the tendency as in optical recording was to reduce the possibility of error by **mixing down** the dubbing units into only three tracks for music, dialogue, and effects. With the advent of **back-up recording** ("rock 'n' roll") the gap that previously betrayed recording over was eliminated and it became possible to work in shorter segments or to try an alternate style by putting picture and sound into reverse and changing only that part actually needing to be done over.

In the late 1930s, the mixing console was a larger version of the wheeled microphone mixers used on the set. There were only four input channels: one for dialogue, one or two for music, one or two for sound effects, as the nature of the film dictated. The final mix required only one re-recording mixer. By the late 1940s, practice had changed so that eight sound inputs were average, with ten or twelve common. In certain reels (films are mixed in 1000-foot, 35mm reels) there might be twenty-five tracks requiring three men on a console (dialogue/music/sound effects) and numerous rehearsals. With the advent of magnetic recording and its ability to sustain quality through several generations, the tendency was to precombine and work with fewer tracks. "Back-up" made it possible again to work with more tracks, as has the recent adoption of automation.

When magnetic film came in, the mixing consoles were rewired. Previously a single negative combining music, dialogue, and effects was made for release printing. With magnetic film, three outputs were used to put separate M/D/E stripes on one strip of full-coat magnetic film. Mixing practice varies in accordance with the budget and style of each film. In a news documentary or commercial the mix might involve only a few tracks: original sound, voice-over, a few sound effects or music cues. A made-for-TV movie or series might have sound effects built up essentially from library material containing some loops for traffic and crowd noises, and music "tracked" from stock. Series television is always mixed monaurally.* In a major feature, the sound ambience may be meticulously created with separate tracks for each type of gunfire, aircraft, animal noise, monster, car engine, etc. An hour-long TV show might be mixed in five hours, a feature in ten days, a war, science-fiction, or disaster movie in three to six weeks. The complex directional mixes in the 70mm six-track versions of George Lucas's or Steven Spielberg's films have taken up to three months to execute.

Mixing may intentionally omit some elements. Features and television programs are sent abroad with separate "M&E" (music and effects) tracks so local actors can loop the dialogue. Commercials may also be sent out with M&E to permit voice-overs with regional accents or local promotional information.

In feature films, the term "final mix" has almost no meaning. Approximately one-quarter to one-third of major release films are now of-

*In the fall of 1984, NBC's *Miami Vice* became the first stereo filmed series.

fered in four-track stereo, some of them also in six-track 70mm versions, in addition to monaural versions. Each format requires its own mix, not only because of directionality but also because of different recording curves.

The various mixes are made from three four-track "submasters" mixed down from the numerous dubbing units. Dialogue is premixed so that loop dialogue is on a separate "stripe" for electronic "reverb." The dialogue premix also enables corrective work to be performed; the tracks are "cleaned up," i.e., filtered and equalized to eliminate camera noise, adjusted for different microphones, etc. There are also four-track music and sound effects submasters. Submasters for sound effects may be mixed down from numerous tracks.

At Universal's state-of-the-art Alfred Hitchcock Theater, the mixing console has 42 inputs that can be tied in with 34 sound reproducers controlled from the console in the adjacent Dubbing Theater #3 for a total of 76 inputs and 15-channel output. Each theater has three 35mm magnetic film rerecorders capable of recording three-, four-, or six-track formats. Computerization is employed to permit concentration on aesthetic aspects of mixing: elements of an earlier mix can be retained on a "floppy disc" when only certain parts need to be done over, thus eliminating the need to control several "pots" manually; tracks not needed between cues are shut off to eliminate accidental "open" tracks.

For stereo release, sound may be put into the left, center, right, or "surround" channels as required by action, or even "panned" across channels to follow movement on the screen by a mixer using **pan-pots** or "joysticks."

A monaural production or the mono version of a stereo release requires a different approach to mixing and not just because the directionality of the sound is lost. Monaural release prints do not employ the Dolby noise reduction that enables stereo prints to contain the high-frequency range (up to 12 Khz) that is well within the capacity of a modern theater sound system to reproduce. They are still mixed in accordance with the so-called Academy curve established in 1938, rendering much of the frequency spectrum simply inaudible. Actually there were *two* Academy curves—a "mix curve" for equalization during mixing and an "end curve" for reproduction of the release print in theaters.

When optical film was used for recording and mixing, each additional generation contributed to the noise level on the release print. The amplifiers and speaker systems then in use produced a "frying" or crackling sound. Because most of this noise was concentrated in the upper frequencies, the solution was the elimination of virtually all of the "high end."

In accordance with the Academy "curve," the theaters were adjusted with an extreme "treble cut" by a technician using test films. The

Academy characteristic called for a drastic "roll off" so that sounds at 8 Khz would have a level of −15 db, and 9 Khz a level of −20 db. Filtering was also applied to the frequencies to prevent a "muddy" sound from occurring owing to the tendency of large theater speakers to favor the "low end." Frequencies were "rolled off" below 125 Hz. (The characteristic can be emulated on home equipment by turning down the treble control and also reducing the bass.)

The characteristic was established to standardize reproduction to the practices employed in mixing the sound track. Like the 24 frames per second of "sound speed" it was less a matter of setting a new standard than of codifying what already existed. In fact, the Academy standard merely adjusted theaters to the "curve" already being used by the then dominant producer, MGM.

Although not formally part of the Academy characteristic, another peculiarity of motion picture sound is the artificial boost introduced in mixing to brighten the voice track, improving speech intelligibility to compensate for such losses as the masking of upper frequencies through the speaker's location behind the perforated motion picture screen. This dialogue "preemphasis" occurs in the 2 Khz–5 Khz range.

In addition to the constricted frequency response, motion picture sound tracks have a very compressed dynamic range. Because noise is most noticeable during the quieter passages, raising the level of the theater amplifier to improve audibility of the softest sounds would also raise the system noise objectionably. Thus, the spread between pianissimo and fortissimo is change in degree rather than in kind.

Dolby noise reduction used on encoded stereo optical tracks has enabled use of a greater dynamic range and wider frequency response. Instead of eliminating the upper frequencies, Dolby encoding selectively *increases* amplification of the quiet passages in recording, making the soft sounds so loud as to mask the system noise by increasing the signal-to-noise ratio. In reproduction, the Dolby "decoder" selectively reduces amplification and restores the sound "curve" to its original shape.

Contrary to widespread belief, optical sound is not an inherently inferior medium. The sound film speed of 90 feet per minute equates to 18 inches per second, comparing quite favorably with the professional tape recording speeds of 15 or 7½ i.p.s.; the one one-thousandths of an inch light slit that scans the track should thus be theoretically capable of reproducing frequencies up to 18 Khz. Dolby noise-reduced optical tracks now employ enough of that spectrum (up to 12 Khz) that experts can not always distinguish between the magnetic master and the release print.

Because photographic sound is still greatly affected by variations in processing and printing, it takes careful control to achieve this degree of quality. In the past, the quality loss from magnetic to optical was so extreme that the film might actually have to be remixed. Electronic devices now allow the mixer to hear in advance how the release print will actually sound by using filters that emulate the quality loss in the optical recorder.

For mono release, a composite music/dialogue/effects master on 35 mm full-coat magnetic film is converted to an optical sound negative; for stereo, four-track submasters for M/D/E are mixed down to a two-track magnetic master matrix encoded (as in the quadrophonic recordings of a decade ago) to contain four channels of sound information to be derived through a processor. Monaural or stereo optical sound negatives are copied from the magnetic master, then composited with the picture internegative to produce a release print that is put back into **projection-sync** by making a **pull-down** putting the sound 20 frames in advance of the picture. (On 16mm prints the sound is 26 frames in advance of the picture.)

IV. Presentation in the Theater

Actually the current American National Standard for release prints specifies that the sound shall be printed 21 frames in advance of the picture. Using the 20-frame displacement between the "Picture Start" frame and the diamond-shaped sound start mark on the Academy ("countdown") leader or the "35mm Sound Start" on the SMPTE ("watch dial") leader produces synchronization between sound and picture at a distance of about 46 feet from the screen, i.e., the center of a typical theater. Because sound travels slower than picture, "sync" is a relative concept. In a drive-in where the sound source is next to the patron, the projectionist would have to thread with 21 frames to produce **dead sync** between the screen surface and the speaker cone. In the old-style movie palace where the audience was half a city block from the screen the lower loop would have been 19 frames. The out-of-sync condition is almost always due to misthreading by the operator, although sometimes the lab may err in making the pull-down.

It is an open secret that the theater is the weakest link in the sound chain. Some theaters play all pictures at a constant fader setting. As a result the sound is much too loud in the daytime or on weekday evenings when there are fewer patrons. People are sound absorbing; in the winter the sound should be raised to compensate for heavier clothing. Movies like *Superman* that attract popcorn-munching and voluble children must be boosted to let dialogue be heard. Trailers are mixed at as much as twice the volume of features and may have to be lowered to keep from blasting the audience's eardrums. By contrast, rock concert films are expected to be deafening, limited only by the threshold of pain.*

The nonphilosophical answer to the old conundrum about whether a tree falling in a forest would make a sound if no one were there to hear it is yes. Sound is pressure and can be measured objectively in decibels with a sound-pressure-level meter. A good theater sound system should have enough wattage to produce a "Dolby level" of 85 dbs sound pressure in the center of the auditorium for normal dialogue and a peak of 106 dbs per channel. Theater amplifiers do not have the bass and treble controls of consumer equipment. A theater sound system cannot be tuned by ear. The acoustics of each auditorium require equalization by a service technician using test films, a real-time spectrum analyzer, and microphones. (Acoustically, the "best seat in the house" is located two-thirds of the way between the screen and the rear of the auditorium, off the center line but at least 17 feet from the side wall; that is the point at which acoustic measurements are taken.) The optical reproducer has a lens to focus the light slit that, like any other lens, can be out of focus and must be reset using test films and an oscilloscope.

Early theater speakers were either a metal horn type from Western Electric that produced superior speech intelligibility or a paper cone radio-phonograph type made by RCA that afforded better music reproduction. The two were logically combined in the late 1930s using a shallow but large-diameter woofer to radiate low-frequency information (chiefly music) in a pleasing nondirectional way around the auditorium while projecting dialogue from the center of the screen. To keep dialogue from "spitting out" down the middle aisle, the "Shearer horn" (after Douglas Shearer, though at least partly the work of John K. Hilliard) used a flared multicellular horn to disperse dialogue at a wider angle including up to the balcony. Further refinements by Hilliard and James B. Lansing produced the Altec Lansing A-4 "Voice of the Theater" that is the industry standard.

Stereophonic Sound: From Disney to Dolby

For his animated concert film *Fantasia* (1940), Walt Disney used an RCA-designed system he called Fantasound to emphasize the directional character of a symphony orchestra, e.g., brass clearly separated from strings. Three oversized (.200") optical tracks (left, right, center, plus a "control" track) on

---

*Some directors take an active interest in the presentation of their films. George Lucas's TAP (Theater Alignment Program) furnishes a detailed checklist. Orson Welles specified that *Citizen Kane* and *The Magnificent Ambersons* be played at twice normal volume, with instructions on the projection leader to raise 6 db (one fader setting) above the normal RKO level.

one separate strip of 35mm film were run in interlock. For the Los Angeles premiere, Disney added a primitive "surround" channel of 96 small speakers to pick up sound from one or more of the main channels, e.g., the choir singing "Ave Maria" was heard throughout the theater. Except in six cities with Fantasound installations, *Fantasia* was not seen as Disney intended until it was reissued (in magnetic sound) in 1956.

Warner Bros. Vitasound of 1940–41 used a single optical track with a control pattern to spread the sound effects and music of *Santa Fe Trail* to left and right speakers and to boost the volume of all three at certain points; this was even less successful. With interest shifting to magnetic sound, neither system was followed up after World War II, perhaps also because the near-square screen could not put directional sound to advantage.

This situation changed with a vengeance in 1952 when *This Is Cinerama* had a galvanic effect, impossible to overstate, on a movie industry apparently dying. Much of the impact came from "point-source" sound: a source traveling across the screen, such as the famous roller coaster, would be heard across all five of the speakers behind the screen; the sound of something occurring in the left panel would issue from the left speaker, at right from the right speaker, etc.; off-screen sound came from "surround" speakers on the left, right, and rear that enveloped the audience. This was the first true stereo in accordance with the famous demonstrations of "auditory perspective" by Bell Telephone in the 1930s. (Fantasound was synthetic; nine monaural tracks were combined and given a "directional" mix without regard to original sources.) The five speakers behind the screen corresponded to five microphones placed in accordance with the visual image. One to three additional microphones recorded off-screen sound. In interlock with the three projectors, a separate strip of 35mm magnetic film contained six audio tracks and a seventh "control" track. Five of the channels were dedicated to the speakers behind the screen; the sixth "surround" channel was switched to the left or right electronically and the rear speaker was cued manually to pick up sound as needed from the other tracks.

Cinerama itself was too cumbersome, expensive, and ill-suited to dramatic storytelling to have general application, but its sound system could be copied—and was. Mike Todd (one of the original Cinerama investors) closely emulated it for the first Todd-AO production, *Oklahoma!* (1955); six tracks drove five speakers behind the screen plus "surrounds" (nineteen in New York's Rivoli theater) on 35mm magnetic film run in interlock with the 70mm picture. In later Todd-AO productions, the sound was transferred to stripes of magnetic oxide on the 70mm release print. Because of a lack of 70mm post-production facilities, actual editing and mixing was—and is—done in the 35mm gauge.

In Todd-AO, only music was recorded in six-channel stereo; dialogue and effects were recorded monophonically and "panned." In the Todd-AO system, it was possible to go from production sound to the final mix to the release print in only three generations as compared to the six or seven generations involved in premixing tracks and converting an optical release print.

A synthetic, simplified version of Cinerama's sound was employed in 1952–54 in connection with the 3-D craze. For *House of Wax*, WarnerPhonic sound consisted of three stripes on a separate magnetic film for left, right, and center stage speakers, while part of the optical track on the release print carried the shrieks and other surround sound for the auditorium speakers, a sort of three-and-a-half track system.

Twentieth Century–Fox's CinemaScope, developed as the rational alternative to 3-D and Cinerama, used four-track magnetic sound recorded on oxide stripes embossed on either side of the sprocket holes on the picture film (a process that won Reeves Soundcraft a technical Oscar). Earl Sponable, co-inventor of the original Movietone and still the technical head at Fox, taught the industry a second time to put the sound onto the picture film. A magnetic reproducer (popularly called a "penthouse") was placed on top of the projector as the optical soundhead had been in the old De Forest Phonofilm.*

Magnetic sound never really fulfilled its potential. The fourth (surround) channel was on a thinner oxide stripe than the others and produced a noticeable hiss unfortunately emphasized by the use of cheap, utility speakers lacking in bass response. (This problem was solved by use of a 12 Khz tone that switched off the channel when there was no sound information.) Someone seated at the rear of the auditorium would hear the surround sound *before* the sound from the main speakers behind the screen. This was rectified by delaying the surround track five sprocket holes (1¼ frames or 1/20 second) so that the sound from all sources would "arrive" at the same time. Studios other than Fox never bothered mixing anything into the surround channel at all; thus the four tracks were essentially three tracks (left, right, center). At first the sheer width of the CinemaScope image seemed to demand multiple sources for the sound, but the novelty soon wore off particularly when small- and medium-sized theaters squeezed CinemaScope onto smaller screens. Cost-conscious exhibitors never invested in new sound systems and installed "mixers" to combine the four magnetic tracks into one. In 1954, Fox CinemaScope films could be ordered in four-track magnetic, single-track magnetic, or conventional optical versions. Although a number of studios released major films in four-track stereo, e.g., Warners' *A Star Is Born* and Goldwyn's *Guys and Dolls*, Fox

*On a magnetic print the sound is displaced 28 frames *behind* the picture.

was the only studio releasing the bulk of its product in that format and the only one normally recording in stereo. Perspecta Sound, a pseudo-stereo system developed by Fairchild Camera and used mainly by MGM and Loew's Theaters, employed a "directional" mix encoded onto a single optical track; using subaudible signals in the track, an "integrator" in the theater split the sound into the left, right, or center speakers. In 1956, Fox partially conceded defeat, introducing a MagOptical print with the magnetic stripes and an optical track. (The aspect ratio of CinemaScope thus standardized at 2.35; this ratio had been used for the optical version but the magnetic version used the full 2.55 width.) The picture alone cost as much to process as a print with a photographic track; the cost of striping and then recording the sound magnetically raised the total cost to as much as seven times that of a normal print. The alloys used in early magnetic heads were soft and wore out under the grind of regular operation.

For much of its history, the motion picture theater offered sound equal or superior to that heard anywhere. The Vitaphone disc of the 1920s was a precursor of the LP in that it used the modern record speed of 33⅓ and lacked the abrasive that produced surface noise in phonograph records of the day. In the early 1930s, the first general use of the term "high fidelity" was in reference to RCA's improved optical sound system. The two-way woofer/tweeter arrangement of theater speakers set the standard for the hi-fi revolution of the 1950s. Cinerama, CinemaScope, and Todd-AO inspired stereo LP's, many of which at first were sound tracks, e.g., *Around the World in 80 Days.*

For a variety of reasons, theater sound declined in quality. The 1948 antitrust decision divorcing the producing companies from theater ownership reduced the former's ability to impose technological changes upon the latter, as they did in 1927–30. The replacement of motion pictures by television as the principal entertainment medium closed many theaters and left others so marginal that they economized where it would not immediately be noticed by the public—in their equipment. Eventually, speaker cones became cracked, amplifier tubes grew weak, and exciter lamps dimmed. The corporate giants that had initiated the "talkie" revolution, RCA and Western Electric, had long since departed the field, leaving behind essentially a cottage industry. The bulk of pictures were released only in optical sound and even magnetic titles were widely exhibited in optical versions. By the early 1970s there was a better sound system in the average American teen-ager's bedroom than in the neighborhood theater. Worst of all, from the exhibitor's point of view, this active moviegoing age group was also the most audio-conscious; they had learned to recognize that the underpowered theater amplifiers "clipped" the highs and that the old-fashioned speakers had inadequate bass.

Over the years, the rationale for the Academy standard became less and less valid; magnetic film replaced optical tracks for shooting, editing, and mixing; amplifiers improved as tubes ultimately gave way to solid state electronics. Yet the characteristic persisted, letting the most backward theaters set the standard for the industry as a whole.

The third major sound revolution after the "talkies" (1927–30) and magnetic stereo (1952–55) began in 1975 with the advent of optical stereophonic sound-on-film pioneered by Dolby Laboratories. Dolby noise reduction, introduced in 1966 for compact cassettes, which then suffered from severe noise levels owing to the narrow gauge and slow recording speed, burst the straitjacket of the Academy characteristic.

For the first time it was possible to have four-channel stereo sound within the lower print costs afforded by the tried-and-true method of photographic printing. The possibility of stereo had always existed; monaural variable-area tracks are bilateral, i.e., two tracks carrying the same information exist side-by-side to compensate for misalignment in projection. Having different information on the tracks could produce two-channel stereo, but Dolby employs techniques similar to "matrix" quadrophonic recording to derive four channels from two. Sound at screen left comes from the left track, at screen right from the right track. Information on both tracks is played through the center channel. The "surround" sound is also recorded on both tracks but in reverse polarity for decoding.

Because many first-run theaters still had 1950s vintage four-track magnetic stereo systems, Dolby wisely designed its system to be compatible with the bulk of existing components. Old soundheads were readily converted to stereo by replacing the photocell with a "narrow gap" solar cell having two sets of wires for stereo pick-up. Existing power amplifiers and speakers could be retained. The occasional four-track magnetic print that came along could still be played merely by pushing a button on the front of the Dolby processor that took the place of the existing preamplifier. Monaural prints (which normally do not contain Dolby noise reduction) are played by pushing a button that engages filtering to replicate the old Academy characteristic.*

The "Dolby Stereo" logotype on the screen or in advertising is always qualified with the words "in selected theaters." In some cases a separate monaural "Academy" print is made up; often a stereo print is used for both mono and stereo theaters.

Theoretically, even in a mono theater, the stereo print should give the better sound. The exaggeration of the high frequencies in a Dolby

---

* As of this writing it is likely that the Academy standard will be revised to reflect contemporary capabilities.

mix would be countered by the Academy "roll-off" in the theater amplifier, producing essentially a flat response to 9 or 10 Khz and a brighter "high end" than when using a mono print in which the sound track itself contains a "treble cut." In practice, misalignment of the film path becomes much more critical; when the azimuth—an imaginary line between the two tracks—is off-center, unequal output produces distortion. Because a mono print has the same information on two tracks, doubling the output, the stereo print must be played at twice the volume, thus also increasing hum and noise.

Although a number of Dolby Stereo releases attracted attention in 1976 (*Lisztomania,* the Streisand *A Star Is Born*), Dolby's huge success came with *Star Wars* in 1977 and was consolidated by *Close Encounters of the Third Kind.* In addition to the four-channel stereo optical versions, a number of films employed a Dolbyized six-track 70mm format differing somewhat from that used by Todd-AO. Instead of five full-range channels driving five speakers behind the screen plus a sixth "surround" channel, Dolby uses "comb" filters to separate additional channels from six discrete tracks on the print. Tracks one, three, and five drive the extreme left, center, and extreme right stage speakers as before; tracks two and four put low-frequency sound (below 250 Hz) into the "left extra" (left-center) and "right extra" (right-center) speakers to produce what Dolby amusingly called "baby boom." Because only low-frequency information is needed for the stage speakers, tracks two and four do double-duty; frequencies above 500 Hz are electronically diverted to the left or right wall "surround" speakers, spatially extending the stereo effect even including dialogue, e.g., crowd noises, off-screen shouts. The sixth "surround" channel contains frequencies below 500 Hz that are played on all the speakers at the left, rear, and right walls. "Sub-woofers" with their own power amplifiers may be connected to the "bass enhancement module" in the Dolby processor, to augment the stage speakers' extreme bass deficiencies.

It is no wonder that rock music films have been prime users of Dolby stereo. In some stereo films only the music is mixed stereophonically, with dialogue and sound effects still coming from the center channel alone. Only a few very expensive films can afford to tie up a dubbing theater for the time needed to produce a fully directional "panned" or "point-source" mix; among the most notable: *Star Wars, Close Encounters,* and the first *Superman.* In 1979 Dolby six-track added stereo surround somewhat reminiscent of the original Cinerama and used it for *Apocalypse Now, The Empire Strikes Back,* and *Raiders of the Lost Ark.*

The success of *Star Wars* and its followers, the preference of knowledgeable audiences for such theaters as Hollywood's Chinese or New York's Ziegfeld even when the same film was widely exhibited elsewhere, and the three successive sound Oscars won by the Dolby-encoded *Star Wars,*

The Deer Hunter, and *Apocalypse Now* made it clear even to the exhibitors that the old attitude that the existing sound was "good enough" or "nobody notices" could not be sustained.

Although less than half of all major release films are released in stereo and three-quarters of all theaters are not yet equipped for it, the stereo titles and the theaters that play stereo versions count for a disproportionately large share of the box-office revenue. Even some porno theaters are equipped with Dolby stereo though mercifully few films are ever exhibited in that form.

The advent of Dolby stereo coincided with a building boom creating new "multiplex" theaters (or dividing up old ones), which in turn created a market for new sound systems. Some of the new auditoriums were so tiny that there was no significant stereo effect and so poorly constructed that the sound from one theater could be heard in another.

Some manufacturers have offered simplified two-channel systems (front-back) for small theaters as well as devices that synthesize monaural tracks into pseudo-stereo.

George Lucas was so dissatisfied with many presentations of his pictures that Lucasfilm established an equipment division, Sprocket Systems, which offers the "THX" system featuring a veritable "wall of sound" from advanced-design speakers. Also in the offing for the near future are: microchip processors to identify sound formats automatically; optical stereo from four discrete channels; industry-wide standards for six-track sound (at present each engagement of a 70mm film requires that the theater be set up by a technician to accommodate different levels and different frequency responses employed by the studios, different oxides, and the introduction of Dolby-encoding); and widespread use of digital recording and mixing (recording not an analog of the sound wave but information about it so that noise can be electronically filtered without affecting dialogue, "perspective" restored electronically, etc.).

A more distant possibility from a renascent Disney studio is digital sound recorded on a fluorescent layer across the entire width of the film and then decoded by an optical "penthouse" reproducer instead of being squeezed into a narrow magnetic or optical track.

Lucas, a decade ago, prophetically complained that postproduction technology was backward and cumbersome. A safe prediction is that there will be rapid progress toward combining the sophistication and flexibility of traditional editing and mixing with computer and video-based technology. Kodak's Datakode—a sort of electronic edge number—is a magnetic control surface in a thin transparent layer across the entire back (not emulsion) of the film. Capable of recording 100 binary bits of information for each frame of picture, this code serves as a link between motion picture film and the highly automated postproduction facilities using the SMPTE "time code" developed for videotape editing; Universal is using it already. Kodak predicts that by 1990 there will be no scissors or splicing tape in any editing room.

Some believe that film will disappear altogether to be replaced by high-definition videotape with sound on a separate multitrack recorder in place of the poor audio that videotape has traditionally suffered from. It is even predicted that the projection of sprocketed film will be replaced by satellite transmission to theaters. Kodak, of course, disputes this and points out that it is selling more negative film than ever while improving both camera and print stocks beyond the capability of any electronic medium.

It would be tempting to close by quoting Al Jolson to the effect that "You ain't heard nothin' yet." But technological feasibility is one thing, economic viability another. The "third wave" of technological innovation may have crested already, just as the backlash to a surfeit of "glorious Technicolor, breath-taking CinemaScope, and stereophonic sound" resulted in *Marty* winning the 1955 Oscar as Best Picture. History gives as much reason for caution as optimism. The innovations that succeed will probably be in response to competition from home entertainment; perhaps an adaptation of some device previously ignored or tried without success, an innovation will have a better chance of being adopted if it is largely compatible with existing practices and equipment.

Sources

For the early sound era, I have relied on a series of articles published in 1947 by Earl Sponable in the *Society of Motion Picture (and Television) Engineers Journal* that is the principal source (acknowledged or unacknowledged) for most of what has been written about the transitional period. Sound-on-disc is best discussed by Art Shifrin (*SMPTE Journal*, July 1983). The flavor of the *Once in a Lifetime/Singin' in the Rain* era is best captured in *The Movie Musical: From Vitaphone to 42nd St.*, edited by Miles Kreuger (whose introduction is a succinct and accurate summary of the technological and commercial preconditions leading to the ultimate success of the sound film); in a long anonymous article in the *1929 Film Daily Year Book*; and in the last chapter of Ben M. Hall's *The Best Remaining Seats* (despite some minor inaccuracies such as misdating the premiere of *Don Juan*). The concluding chapter of William K. Everson's *American Silent Film* challenges prevailing myths about the early talkie era through the author's familiarity with the recently rediscovered films from Fox (long believed lost in a studio fire) that had been ignored in favor of the much cruder productions from Warners.

Much of the material on production sound recording came from articles by Loren L. Ryder and Ronald Cogswell in the *American Cinematographers' Manual* (3d edition). *Into Film*, by Laurence Goldstein and Jay Kaufman, has a more complete discussion of sound—particularly microphone placement—than the better-known books by Lipton or Pincus that reflect the visual bias of independent filmmaking. The achievements and aspirations of the *cinéma vérité* movement at its confident peak are best conveyed in the British magazine *Movie*, no. 8 (April 1963) through interviews with Leacock, the Maysles brothers, Jean Rouch, et al.

The section on film music derives chiefly from Ernest Gold's discussion of the mechanics of film scoring in Tony Thomas's *Music for the Movies* and Miklos Rozsa's *A Double Life*.

Raymond Spottiswoode's *Film and Its Techniques* is quite thorough on editing and mixing equipment during the optical film era though curiously ignoring the magnetic revolution then (1950) under way. The Technical and Scientific Academy Awards constitute a loose chronology of progress.

Interviews conducted by Elisabeth Weis in 1975 with Gordon Sawyer and Murray Spivack were an important source for early studio practice. John Bonner, Chief Engineer, Warner Hollywood Studio (formerly Goldwyn sound facility), and the Sound Department of Universal City Studios furnished information concerning current facilities and practices.

The technical columns in the trade magazine *Boxoffice* written by John Allen, Harley Lond, and Tony Francis deal in detail with current theater audio practice. Technical standards for the motion picture industry set by the Engineering Committee of the Society of Motion Picture and Television Engineers are published by the American National Standards Institute (Index number PH 22).

David Shepard of the Directors Guild of America generously furnished the transcript of "Film Sound in the Eighties," a two-day program presented in Hollywood on April 12–13, 1984.

Hazard E. Reeves, co-founder and former president of Cinerama, Inc., and chairman of the board of Reeves Telecom, furnished information concerning the Cinerama process and early stereophonic sound.

Technological history not otherwise credited is based on Edward Kellogg's landmark articles in *SMPTE Journal* (June, July, August, 1955) reprinted in Raymond A. Fielding's *A Technological History of Motion Pictures*, abstracting many of the earlier articles in this indispensable publication concerning sound. Over 400 references, chiefly from *SMPTE Journal* (many of which were consulted in the preparation of the present article), cover numerous aspects of equipment up to 1955.

Annotated Bibliography
on Film Sound (Excluding Music)
CLAUDIA GORBMAN

The bibliography consists primarily of books and articles published in English and French. It is organized in four sections:

    I. General Theory and Aesthetics
    II. Analyses and Case Studies
    III. General Technology
    IV. History: Style and Technology

Although these categories are by no means mutually exclusive, I hope they will provide readers the clearest access to information.

    Mixed-category essays that place film sound practice in theoretical contexts—such as the exchange between Ranald MacDougall and Arch Oboler in *Screen Writer* (1945) or Jean-Louis Comolli's and Mary Ann Doane's work in the 1970s and 1980s—are located in the *General Theory and Aesthetics* section; essays whose emphasis on the technical or pragmatic outweigh their theoretical interest are in section III. Articles written during the early sound period are listed not under *History* but under *Aesthetics* (I) or *Technology* (III), depending on emphasis. I have generally placed interviews with directors on particular films in section II, and interviews with technicians, such a sound engineers, in section III.

    The reader will find sections III and IV of the bibliography more selective, of necessity, than sections I and II. Likewise, I have aimed at giving only a sample of typical and/or theoretically interesting articles from the early sound period. The bibliography has excluded articles that draw analogies between film visuals and sound in order to examine ideas such as visual rhythm, "overtones" (Eisenstein and Sharits), and the like. Nor have I generally included (with the exception of Brakhage) essays primarily concerned with allusions to sound in silent films.

I. General Theory and Aesthetics

Altman, Charles F. "Introduction," *Yale French Studies,* no. 60 (1980):3–15. Capsule summary of technological developments (e.g., magnetic recording, multiple-channel, Dolby) in film sound subsequent to 1927, to stress the separation of production of sound and image tracks, and the constructed nature of film sound. Explores fallacies in criticism that have perpetuated devalorization of sound track.

—— "Moving Lips: Cinema as Ventriloquism," *Yale French Studies*, no. 60 (1980):67–79. Examines notion of sound-image "redundancy." Proposes model of cinema as ventriloquism—sound track as ventriloquist, image as dummy—to invert sound-image balance in criticism. Stresses complementary relationship whereby sound "uses" the image to mask its own action.

Arnheim, Rudolf. "The Complete Film" (1933), in *Film as Art*, pp. 154–60. Berkeley: University of California Press, 1957. "The complete film" (what Bazin calls the "total cinema"), toward which sound, color, wide-screen, and 3-D strive, runs counter to film's formative (artistic) tendency.

—— "A New Laocoön: Artistic Composites and the Talking Film" (1938), in *Film as Art*, pp. 199–230. "Theoretical study of the aesthetic laws whose violation made the talking film so unsatisfactory."

Asquith, Anthony. "Rhythm in Sound-Films," *Cinema Quarterly*, 1, no. 3 (Spring 1933):144–47. Sound's introduction has changed the concept of film rhythm. Emphasis on relationship between sound rhythm and visual cutting. "Dialogue is not alien to sound films . . . as long as the visual image and the dialogue have a relation beyond the merely theatrical one of synchronization."

Avron, Dominique. "Remarques sur le travail du son dans la production cinématographique standardisée," *Revue d'Esthétique*, special issue *Cinéma: Théorie, Lectures* (Paris: Editions Klincksieck, 1973), pp. 207–18. Progressive stages in filmmaking (writing, shooting, editing, mixing, optical sound track) demonstrate the tyranny of the visual: less creative attention is paid to latter phases than to former. Detailed analysis of practices at each phase, with psychoanalytically oriented approach to sound track's secondary elaboration.

Bailblé, Claude. "Pour une nouvelle approche de l'enseignement de la technique du cinéma: Programmation de l'écoute." 4-part article in *Cahiers du Cinéma*, no. 292 (September 1978):52–59; no. 293 (October 1978):4–12. Part of a general introduction to film, whose purpose is to draw together technology, psychology and physiology of perception, and psychoanalytic film theory. Begins with theory of formation of listening/speaking subject. Aural perception. In sound reproduction, that which the technological process takes away (hearer's position in real space, choice of attending to different sounds) must be carefully "given back" via practices of the sound studio. No. 297 (February 1979):45–54. Lacanian aspects of the subject in language. Summary of history of sound recording. Semiotic and psychological functions of sound track. Theoretical consideration of the microphone: since the recording apparatus is reductive, manipulation is necessary to restore/ensure impression of reality. No. 299 (April 1979):16–27. Physiology and psychology of hearing; flexibility and adapatibility of ear, as opposed to technology. Standard practices of creating temporal and spatial dimensions of auditory field in film. Monophonic film sound lacks lateral breadth and has depth, complementing image, which has inverse properties.

Bakshy, Alexander. "The Movie Scene: Notes on Sound and Silence," *Theater Arts Monthly*, 13, no. 2 (February 1929):97–107. The emergence of the talkies might complicate the situation of "Princess Art" and "King Bilge" (95 percent of film production). Praises cinema's freedom from spatial, temporal, and other limitations of the theater. Aesthetic specificity of the sound film.

Balazs, Bela. "Sound," "Dialogue," and "Problem of the Sound Comedy," in *Theory of the Film: Character and Growth of a New Art*, pp. 194–241. New York: Dover, 1970. (Original English ed., London: Dobson, 1952.) "The art of the silent film is dead, but its place was taken by the mere technique of the sound film." Advocates foregrounding and isolating details from the acoustic landscape, and collating them again in "purposeful order by sound-montage."

Baronnet, Jean. "Eloge de la phonie," *Cahiers du Cinéma*, no. 152 (February 1964):37–41. Questions standard practice of formulaic mediocrity for music, and leveling of volumes and timbres for dialogue and sound effects. Praises idiosyncrasies of the voice. Point is not to imitate codified techniques but to find the unique sound appropriate to the cinematic moment. Analogy: spontaneous "on the spot" drawings vs. official, academic paintings.

Baudrier, Yves. "Le Monde sonore," in *Les Signes du visible et de l'audible*. Paris: IDHEC, 1964.

Bonitzer, Pascal. "Les Silences de la voix," *Cahiers du Cinéma*, no. 256 (February-March 1975):22–33. The voice-over and off-screen voice: "impression of knowledge," power, point of view. Tendency to eliminate voice-over in recent political documentary—the new "silence"—is distressing since the film thereby conceals its own work and posits itself as a voice without a subject.

Bordwell, David, and Kristin Thompson. "Sound in the Cinema," in *Film Art: An Introduction*, pp. 189–219. Reading, Mass: Addison-Wesley, 1979. Well-formulated outline of the dimensions of film sound: physical, spatial, temporal. Appropriate examples and analyses—notably, Bresson's *A Man Escaped*. A key reference.

Borneman, Ernest. "Sound Rhythm and the Film," *Sight and Sound*, 3, no. 10 (Summer 1934):65–67.

Brakhage, Stan. "The Silent Sound Sense," *Film Culture*, no. 21 (Summer 1960): 65–67. "The creation of a musical or sound sense in a silent film demanded an inventiveness which has never been equalled in the history of the development of the sound film. . . . The sound sense which visual images always evoke . . . often makes actual sound superfluous."

Bresson, Robert. *Notes on Cinematography*. New York: Urizen Books, 1977. Many terse "notes" on sound interspersed throughout. Rhythmic qualities, relations to image and to narration, perception. E.g.: "A sound must never come to the help of an image, nor an image to the help of a sound."

Burch, Noël. "On the Structural Use of Sound," in *Theory of Film Practice*, pp. 90–101. New York: Praeger, 1973. Delineates parameters of structural interactions between auditory and visual space. Advocates integrating music, sound effects, speech into a single sound texture for organic film structure; cf. A. Polonsky's and M. Fano's sound tracks. Work on the sound track "lags ten years behind" that on film image.

Callenbach, Ernest. "Cinema/Sound," *Film Quarterly*, 34, no. 4 (Summer 1981):32–33. Reviews *Yale French Studies*, no. 60 (1980), special issue on film sound (cf. entry below).

Cameron, Ken. *Sound and the Documentary Film*. London: Pitman, 1947.

Cavalcanti, Alberto. "Sound in Films," *Films*, 1, no. 1 (November 1939):25–39.

Chaplin (Stockholm) 4, no. 139 (1975):180–206; 6, no. 141 (1975):312–18. Two-part inquiry on sound film (thirty-five directors respond).

Chateau, Dominique. "Projet pour une sémiologie des relations audio-visuelles dans le film," *Musique en jeu*, no. 23 (April 1976):82–98. Following Metz's lead, proposes fundamentals of semiology of sound film. Establishing that there are no grammatical criteria systematically governing audiovisual syntax (therefore giving equal status to Eisensteinian and Bazinian aesthetics), outlines new syntactic categories for sound-image relations in cinema. Uses Robbe-Grillet's *L'Homme qui ment* as a "semiological laboratory."

Chevassu, Francois. *L'Expression cinématographique: Les Eléments du film et leurs fonctions.* Paris: Pierre Lherminier, 1977. Sections on sound, noise, dialogue, off-screen voice, etc.

Chion, Michel. "Chronique du son: Direct or not direct," *Cahiers du Cinéma*, no. 331 (January 1982):p. XI (insert between 34 and 35). Postsynchronization in the hands of Fellini and others is colorful and imaginative, unlike recent French production.

—— *La Voix au cinéma.* Paris: Cahiers du Cinéma/Editions de l'Etoile, 1982. Outlines a theory of the truly "talking" cinema. Psychoanalytic theory (Lacan, Denis Vasse) influences this essay on compelling emplacements of the voice in films. Privileges "voix acousmatiques" that are neither completely within, nor clearly outside, the screen. Cinematic uses of telephone and other speaking machines, women's screams, mute characters; relates to structures of male fantasies of authority and control. Remarkable chapter on mother's voice in *Sansho the Bailiff*; other films discussed extensively include *Psycho, Testament of Dr. Mabuse, India Song, Citizen Kane.*

Close Up (London), 1927–33. Includes much criticism related to the coming of sound, by such writers as S. M. Eisenstein, H. A. Potamkin, A. Bakshy, K. MacPherson, O. Blakeston.

Comolli, Jean-Louis. "Technique et idéologie." Six-part article in *Cahiers du Cinéma*. Part 5: "Effacement de la profondeur/Avènement de la parole," *Cahiers du Cinéma*, nos. 234–35 (December 1971–February 1972):94–100. Overall project to refute Bazin's account of evolution to deep space and "realism" in favor of a materialist history emphasizing cinema as ideological apparatus. Rejects "technicist" explanation of coming of sound and related technological changes, stressing changes in production/consumption of the reality-effect. Sound brought depth to the image, which (temporarily) obviated ideological demand for deep space. Part 6: "Quelle parole?" *Cahiers du Cinéma*, no. 241 (September–October 1972):20–24. What factors determined the specific forms of the talking film? Interrelationships of economic and ideological determinations (e.g., Hollywood's response to the crash with escapist musicals, and social-problem films whose bourgeois humanist ideology recuperates "problems"). Speech in film ensures and reinforces idea of individual as hero of the fiction. The space of continuity editing is the space of dialogue.

Comuzio, Ermanno. *Colonna sonora. Dialoghi, musiche, rumori dietro lo schermo.* Rome, 1979.

Doane, Mary Ann. "Ideology and the Practice of Sound Editing and Mixing," in Stephen Heath and Theresa De Lauretis, eds., *The Cinematic Apparatus.* pp. 47–56. London: Macmillan, 1980. Responses by J-L. Comolli, P. Wollen, and D. Gomery, pp. 57–60. Ideological study of dominant sound practices examined in relation to "a certain structure of oppositions which split 'knowledge' within bourgeois ideology—oppositions between intellect and emotion, the intelligible and the sensible, reason and intuition."

—— "The Voice in the Cinema: The Articulation of Body and Space." *Yale French Studies,* no. 60 (1980):33–50. How the cinema's fantasmatic body (point of identification for the subject it addresses) "acts as a pivot for certain cinematic processes of representation and authorizes and sustains a limited number of relationships between voice and image." Psychoanalytic approach draws from Leclaire, Rosolato, Lacan, Bonitzer, Bailblé.

Eisenstein, Sergei M. "Synchronization of Senses," in *The Film Sense,* pp. 69–109. New York: Harcourt, Brace, and World, 1975. Carries montage theory over into sound film, beginning necessary "analysis of the nature of audio-visual phenomena," including the concept of vertical montage.

Eisenstein, Sergei M., Vsevolod Pudovkin, and G. V. Alexandrov. "Statement on the Sound Film," in Sergei M. Eisenstein, *Film Form,* pp. 257–60. New York: Harcourt, Brace, 1949. Manifesto on the necessity for asynchronism and counterpoint in sound film, in accord with montage theory.

Fano, Michel. "Vers une dialectique du film sonore." *Cahiers du Cinéma,* no. 152 (February 1964):30–36. Advocates musical structuration of entire sound track. Dialogue and effects will share both informational and poetic functions. Examines "morphological, syntactic, and dialectic" possibilities cinema offers to the composer.

Filmcritica, 28 (December 1977). Issue on film sound.

Fondane, Benjamin. "Du Muet au parlant: Grandeur et décadence du cinéma," in Marcel L'Herbier, ed. *Intelligence du cinématographe.* Paris: Editions Corréa, 1946 (originally in *Bifur,* no. 5 [April 1930]). The silent film had universal interest because of its appeal to the imagination, fostering a sort of creative "misapprehension." How can the sound film and the talking film retain the poetry and success of the silents? Suggests a sound aesthetics, claiming that the sound cartoon, among others, embodies it.

Gorbman, Claudia. "Bibliography on Sound in Film," *Yale French Studies,* no. 60 (1980):269–86. Includes 160-entry section on music as well as general sound theory, history, criticism, and technology, to 1978.

—— "Teaching the Soundtrack," *Quarterly Review of Film Studies,* 1, no. 4 (1976):446–52. Argues for closer and more precise attention to sound track in film analysis. Provides criteria and terminology.

Grierson, John. "Introduction to a New Art," *Sight and Sound,* 3, no. 11 (Autumn 1934):101–4.

—— "Pudovkin on Sound," *Cinema Quarterly,* 2, no. 2 (Winter 1933–34):106–8. Agrees with Pudovkin that sound should complement, not duplicate images, but P's writing fails to account for rich complexities in good sound films: "The trouble with Pudovkin is that he performs like a poet and theorizes like an elementary school teacher."

Grundy, Dr. J. B. C. "Language and Film," *Sight and Sound*, 2, no. 6 (Summer 1933); 2, no. 7 (Autumn 1933).

Gryzik, Antoni. *Introduction à la mise-en-scène du son dans le cinéma*. Thèse pour le doctorat de 3e cycle, Université de Paris I, 1981. Beginning with functions of sound in ancient theater and functions of sound-allusions in silent film, outlines a dramaturgy of "sound mise-en-scène" in cinema.

Guillot de Rhode, Francois. "La Dimension sonore," in Etienne Souriau, ed., *L'Univers filmique*, pp. 119–35. Paris; Flammarion, 1953. Demonstrates via historical and phenomenological arguments that sound is necessary to film, an integral part of the image. Philosophical commentary on audiovisual representation.

Helman, Alicja. "On the Fundamental Interactions of Sound Subcodes in Films," *Studies in Art History*, pp. 201–13. Ossolineum, 1980. Understanding the particular code in which a sound-track element participates (the English language, Romantic orchestral music, etc.) is not what semiotic studies of film sound need to do; rather, codes governing interactions of sound and image need to be described.

Higson, Andrew. "Sound Cinema," *Screen*, 25, no. 1 (January–February 1984):74–78. Summarizes presentations at Fall 1983 conference in Birmingham on Sound Cinema, focusing on semiotics of film sound and the positioning of auditor/spectator.

Howard, Clifford. "Cabbages and Kings," *Close Up*, 4, no. 6 (June 1929):45–51. The sound revolution is here to stay. "And once the creak is eliminated from the machinery, its various cogs smoothly meshed, and its many intricate parts perfectly co-ordinated, skill and energy can be focussed undistractedly upon the development of art."

Image et Son. Special issue: "Le son au cinéma," 215 (March 1968). Articles by F. Chevassu, G. Gauthier, R. Lefèvre.

Jacobs, Lewis. "Sound as Speech, Noise, Music," in Lewis Jacobs, ed., *The Movies as Medium*, pp. 243–60. New York: Farrar, Straus, and Giroux, 1970. Historical and technological overview. Then, use of sound "expands the medium's capability to heighten the impact of its subject matter and deepen the viewer's experience." Voice-over, off-screen sound, aural flashback, interior monologue, expressive use of sound effects, silence, etc.

Kracauer, Siegfried. "Dialogue and Sound," in *Theory of Film: The Redemption of Physical Reality*, pp. 102–32. New York: Oxford University Press, 1960. Truly "cinematic" dialogue: lifelike and natural speech, used sparingly so as to ensure the primacy of the visuals. Synchronism/asynchronism, parallel/counterpoint, and their permutations defined. Treatment of nondialogue sounds.

Laffay, Albert. "Bruits et langage au cinéma," *Les Temps modernes*, 2, no. 14 (November 1946):371–75.

Lambert, Gavin. "Sight and Sound," *Sequence*, no. 11 (Summer 1950):3–7.

Leacock, Richard. "For an Uncontrolled Cinema," *Film Culture*, nos. 22/23 (Summer 1961):23–25. Montage, as visual substitute for speech in silent cinema, was no longer necessary with the coming of sound. Film's realist project demonstrated.

Lefèvre, Raymond. "La Dictature de la bande-son," *Image et Son*, no. 352 (July–

August 1980):65–74. Bemoans the abuse and lack of subtlety of modern sound tracks—"imperialism of spoken discourse" and automatism of conventional scoring. Praises the creative variety of discriminating uses of sound in such masterpieces as *Blackmail.*

Levin, Tom. "The Acoustic Dimension: Notes on Cinema Sound," *Screen,* 25, no. 3 (May–June 1984):55–68. Critiques phenomenological views, such as Metz's, that recorded sound is identical to original sound. Recorded sound is "a representation already interpreted, selected, and ideologically 'framed' by its very technology." Mediation of sound through the technology of recording and reproduction involves its essential transformation.

MacDougall, Ranald. "Sound—and Fury," *Screen Writer,* no. 1 (September 1945):1–7.

Manvell, Roger. "Essentials of Film Art: Sound," in *Film,* pp. 58–76. London: Penguin, rev. ed., 1950. Early use of sound for canned theater; Arnheim's sound aesthetics; Spottiswoode's categories. Brief examples from films (e.g., *Great Expectations*) describing creative uses of sound. Concluding section on music.

Marie, Michel. "Le Film, la parole et la langue," *Cahiers du 20e siècle,* 9 (1978):67–75. Stresses the primacy of speech in the sound-film revolution; it is the dramaturgy of voices that largely determined the evolution of classical cutting in the 1930s and other aspects of filmic narrative and style through the 1950s. Three levels or "zones or articulation" where cinematic and verbal language intersect: perception/identification, film as discourse, and speech in films.

—— "Son," in J. Collet, M. Marie, D. Percheron, J-P. Simon, and M. Vernet, *Lectures du film,* pp. 198–210. Paris: Albatros, 1976. Brief outline of history of sound technology, and description of recording and mixing. The multiple sound codes in cinema; codes of sound-track composition, codes governing audiovisual relations (spatial, semantic, etc.), filmic coding of voice with respect to narration. Codification of verisimilitude and intelligibility, and alternatives. Concludes: "The sound film has only begun."

Marie, Michel, and Francis Vanoye. "Comment parler la bouche pleine?" *Communications,* no. 38 ("Enonciation et cinéma," ed. J-P. Simon and M. Vernet) (Fall 1983):51–77. Theoretical and methodological propositions for analysis of dialogue in film. Considers sound recording, positioning of auditor, degree of "naturalism," degree of improvisation, and sound-image relations. Compares meal scenes from *Le Schpountz, Adieu Philippine, Ma Nuit chez Maud.*

Martin, Marcel. "Les Phénomènes sonores," in *Le Langage cinématographique,* pp. 100–124. Paris: 7e Art, Les Editions du Cerf, 1955. Sound is not "accessory" to cinema, but is necessarily part of cinema's specificity. Demonstrates with historical and aesthetic arguments.

Mast, Gerald. "(Recorded) Sound," in *Film/Cinema/Movie: A Theory of Experience,* pp. 206–37. New York: Harper and Row, 1977. The voice: speech's value as physical sound (rhythm, tonality, etc., as well as effects of recording and reproduction) and as language. Quarrels with those who undermine semiotic importance of dialogue. Discusses nondialogue sounds.

Metz, Christian. "Aural Objects," *Yale French Studies,* 60 (1980):24–32. (Originally from "Le Perçu et le nommé," 1975.) Aural and visual perception are culture-determined, being inextricable from the process of naming (i.e., language). Status of sound perception: "Ideologically, the aural source is an object, the sound itself a 'characteristic.' " Sound is an attribute, not an object itself; hence the privileging of image-oriented nomenclature in film study.

Mitry, Jean. "La Parole et le son," in *Esthétique et psychologie du cinéma,* vol. 2, pp. 87–176. Paris: Eds. Universitaires, 1965. I: Dialogue. Examines early sound films to outline aesthetic of montage. Quantity of dialogue determines not a film's merit but rather its role in film's structure. Many films mentioned including *Broadway Melody, La Strada, Hiroshima mon amour.* Discussion of perceived differences among literary, real-life, and cinematic dialogue. Functions of voices-off. II: Music.

Morin, Edgar. *Le Cinéma ou l'homme imaginaire.* Paris: Editions de Minuit, 1956. Postwar "filmologue" Morin's "sociological anthropology" of cinema examines psychological phenomenon of film experience, including identification and pleasure. Mentions sound throughout, especially music and speech.

Nagorka, R. "Sound in Cinema: Some Observations Toward a Theory," *Cinema Papers* (Australia) (April 1974):157–59.

Oboler, Arch. "Look—Then Listen!" *Screen Writer,* 1 (December 1945):26–30.

Odin, Roger. "A Propos d'un couple de concepts: 'son in' vs. 'son off'," *Linguistique et sémiologie* no. 6. Lyon: Presses Universitaires de Lyon, 1979.

Percheron, Daniel. "Sound in Cinema and Its Relationship to Image and Diegesis," *Yale French Studies,* no. 60 (1980):16–23. (Originally in *Ça/Cinema,* 1973.) Intelligent definitions and treatment: sound on/off, diegetic/extradiegetic, synchronous/asynchronous. Charts possibilities of voice-off according to diegesis, synchronism, and address. Since music and effects tend to be "semantically impoverished types of sound," ". . . only the spoken word can constitute a highly significant system."

Petric, Vlada. "Sight and Sound: Counterpoint or Entity?" *Filmmakers Newsletter,* 6, no. 7 (May 1973):27–31. Suggests new relationships of sound to image.

Pudovkin, Vsevolod. "Asynchronism as a Principle of Sound Film," "Dialogue," and "Dual Rhythm of Sound and Image," in *Film Technique and Film Acting.* New York: Grove Press, 1960. (Originally *Pudovkin on Film Technique,* 1929, and *Film Acting,* 1937.) "Asynchronism": uses arguments about audiovisual perception to champion asynchronism principle. "Dialogue" and "Dual Rhythm": The actor and director should coordinate in dialogue editing. Principles of dialogue, editing, and problems of rhythm in *Deserter.*

—— "The Global Film," *Hollywood Quarterly,* 2, no. 4 (July 1947):327–32. Can films still be international after the coming of sound?

Read, Herbert. "Experiments in Counterpoint," *Cinema Quarterly,* 3, no. 1 (Autumn 1934):17–21. Agrees with Arnheim on aesthetic potential of asynchronism; discusses films by Grierson and Cavalcanti.

Rosen, Claude-Emile. "Le Bruit," *Revue d'esthétique,* 8, no. 2 (April–June 1955):157–70. Perceptual and aesthetic considerations of sounds (sound effects) in cinema. Detailed and complex predecessor to Metz's essay (cf. above). Also discusses notable experiments in sound films, *e.g.,* Disney.

Rosenbaum, Jonathan. "Sound Thinking," *Film Comment,* 14, no. 5 (September–

October 1978):38–41. Errata & addenda: 14, no. 6 (November–December 1978):79. An attempt to expose the "bias against sound thinking" by enumerating levels on which this bias operates (ideological, perceptual, textual, terminological, film-historical), and overviewing 1970s critical and theoretical writing on film sound. Includes bibliography.

Schaeffer, Pierre. "Le Contrepoint du son et de l'image," *Cahiers du Cinéma*, no. 108 (June 1960):7–22. Scientific essay by pioneer of concrete music in films, describing results of research on perception time for sound and images, problems of duration, rhythm, etc. Discusses several short films with "structured" sound and image tracks.

—— "L'Elément non visuel au cinéma," *Revue du cinéma*, 1 (October–November–December 1946). In three parts: 1, no. 1:45–48; 1, no. 2:62–65; 1, no. 3:51–54. Part I: Analysis of the sound track. II: Music. III: Psychology of the seeing-hearing relationship. In sound track's trichotomy, speech predominates in conventional films. But for Schaeffer, noises are primary; images "can only show things, while noises are the language of things."

Schmalenbach, Werner. "Dialogue et bruitage dans le film," *Cinéma d'aujourd'hui*, Congrès international du cinéma a Bâle. Basel: Ed. Trois Collines, 1946.

Schreger, Charles. "The Second Coming of Sound," *Film Comment*, 14, no. 5 (September–October 1978):34–37. Fifty years after Warners' first "sound revolution," the industry is undergoing a second one. Altman's sonic textures couple stylistic and technological innovations (eight-track system of individual miking, live recording of musical numbers, Dolby equipment). Economic and aesthetic aspects of Dolby in recent films.

Sharples, Win, Jr. "The Aesthetics of Film Sound," *Filmmakers Newsletter*, 8, no. 5 (March 1975):27–32.

Spottiswoode, Raymond. *A Grammar of the Film: An Analysis of Film Technique*. Berkeley: University of California Press, 1950. (Original ed., London, 1935.) Definitions and categories of film sound: speech/music/noise; realistic (diegetic)/nonrealistic; subjective/objective; parallel/contrastive. Examples.

Stephenson, Ralph, and J. R. Debrix. "The Fifth Dimension: Sound," in *The Cinema as Art*, pp. 174–200. Baltimore: Penguin, 1965. Aesthetic considerations and catalogues of examples (of sound montage, subjective sound, etc.) described with varying accuracy. The authors' aesthetic principles: "economy, restraint, appropriateness, variety, variation from reality."

Ungari, Enzo. "Sur le son: Entretien avec J-M. Straub et D. Huillet," *Cahiers du Cinéma*, nos. 260–61 (October–November 1975):48–53. Dubbing is a lie, an ideology. (S. & H. shoot films with sync-sound.) Sync-sound is not only a technique but an ideological and moral choice—which the commercial industry doesn't tolerate.

Warshow, Paul. "More Is Less: Comedy and Sound," *Film Quarterly*, 31, no. 1 (Fall 1977):38–45. Bemoans a sonorized release of Keaton's *The General* because "the absence of realistic sound is silent comedy's defining element." General aesthetic considerations follow.

Weinberg, Herman G. "The Language Barrier," *Hollywood Quarterly*, 2, no. 4 (July 1947):333–37. Reaction to Pudovkin's essay in the same issue.

Williams, Alan. "Is Sound Recording Like a Language?" *Yale French Studies*, no. 60 (1980):51–66. Argues for considering film sound as representation, not reproduction of pro-filmic sound. Undertakes examination of specific effects of sound recording as a signifying practice, drawing from Baudry's/Münsterberg's models of cinema's "pseudo-perceptions." Considers Godard's alternative sound practices.

Wood, Nancy. "Towards a Semiotics of the Transition to Sound: Spatial and Temporal Codes," *Screen*, 25, no. 3 (May–June 1984):16–24. Explores the development of spatial and temporal codes prompted by the transition from silence to sound. Essay focuses on the relation of the elimination of intertitles to the codification of temporal transitions such as dissolves, the use of dialogue overlap and nondiegetic music to create temporal continuity, the deployment of shot/reverse shot or camera movement to create a realistic sense of space, and the development of perspective to establish a coherent position of audition and thus create an auditory impression of reality.

Yale French Studies, no. 60 (1980). Special issue, ed. Charles F. Altman, *Cinema/Sound*. Theory, history, music, case studies, bibliography. Cf. Percheron, Metz, Doane, Williams, Altman, Marie, Browne, Ropars-Wuilleumier, Gorbman.

II. Analyses and Case Studies

Beylie, Claude. "Jean Renoir face au cinéma parlant," *Avant-Scène du cinéma*, nos. 251/252 (July 1980):5–19. Even in his silent films, Renoir's work was full of aural suggestion, especially in *Tire au flanc*. Then, astonishing variety of uses of sound in his sound films. Beylie sees almost Brechtian (ironic) function of songs and music in Renoir's dramaturgy. Also discusses decor.

Browne, Nick. "Film Form / Voice-over: Bresson's *The Diary of a Country Priest*," *Yale French Studies*, no. 60 (1980):233–40. *Diary*'s underlying formal issue concerns linkage and control of types of point of view. Analysis of authority of tense, voice-over, images; relationships among the film's dramatic "I," narrative "I," and camera.

Burt, W. "On the Relation of Sound and Image in *Moods*," *Cantrill's Filmnotes*, nos. 35–36 (April 1981):56–64.

Cameron, Evan William. "*Citzen Kane:* The Influence of Radio Drama on Cinematic Design," in E. W. Cameron, ed., *Sound and the Cinema*, pp. 202–16. Pleasantville, N.Y.: Redgrave, 1980. Outlines the film's "tactical innovations," with both positive and negative influences on subsequent films, and their relationships to the traditions of radio drama. Valuable discussion of principles of construction of acoustic space as developed in radio drama.

Carey, Gary. "The Music of Sound," *Seventh Art*, 1, no. 2 (Spring 1963):6–7. On Antonioni's use of music and sound.

Carroll, Noël. "Lang, Pabst, and Sound," *Ciné-Tracts*, 2, no. 1 (Fall 1978):15–23.

Analysis of *M* (1931) as a "silent sound film," rooted in formative paradigm of montage and asynchronism, and *Kameradschaft* (1931), which, on the other hand, "presages the development of sound realism."

Collet, Jean. "An Audacious Experiment: The Soundtrack of *Vivre sa vie*," in Royal S. Brown, ed., *Focus on Godard*, pp. 160–62. Englewood Cliffs, N.J.: Prentice-Hall, 1972. Direct recording on location, on a single track, with no editing, and little mixing beyond music: revolutionary approach to film sound.

Cornwell, Regina. "Study of Michael Snow's *Rameau's Nephew*," *Afterimage*, no. 7 (1978).

Daney, Serge. "L'Orgue et l'aspirateur," *Cahiers du Cinéma*, nos. 279–80 (August–September 1977):19–27. Psychaoanlytic approach to the voice in Bresson's *Le Diable probablement*.

Erens, Patricia. "Patterns of Sound *(Citizen Kane),*" *Film Reader*, no. 1 (1975):40–49. Describes three kinds of overarching sound codes at play in *Kane*: (1) qualities of the voice track (texture, rhythm, intonation, etc.); (2) semantics and syntax of spoken language; (3) sound-image (spatial) relations.

Fischer, Lucy. "*Applause*: The Visual and Acoustic Landscape," in E. W. Cameron, ed., *Sound and the Cinema*, pp. 182–201. Pleasantville, N.Y.: Redgrave, 1980. Invoking Arnheim's and Balazs's comments about sound and spatial depth, Fischer's analysis of *Applause* (1929) notes the sound track's density, its creation of spatial continuity, "spatial ambience," asynchronism, and use of silence.

—— "*Enthusiasm:* From Kino-Eye to Radio-Eye," *Film Quarterly*, 31, no. 2 (Winter 1977–78):25–34. Vertov's plans for *Enthusiasm* (1930) reveal a concept of audiovisual montage more radical and subtle than Eisenstein's. To break the spell of illusionism he invokes the "Radio-Ear" as well as the "Kino-Eye." Fischer analyzes the film's reflexive aural techniques and audiovisual editing. (For a companion piece written in 1929, see Jean Lenauer, "Vertoff, His Work and the Future," *Close Up*, 5, no. 6 [December 1929]:464–68.)

—— "René Clair, *Le Million*, and the Coming of Sound," *Cinema Journal*, 16, no. 2 (Spring 1977):34–50. Clair took an approach to sound diametrically opposite to that of American directors: subvert cinematic illusion with sound in order to restore film's poetic powers. In *Le Million*, avoids sync dialogue, uses songs and chorus, rhythmic speech and sound effects; musical continuity provides narrative continuity. Musical form as film's subject.

Gardiès, René. "Récit et matériau filmique," in *Robbe-Grillet*, Colloque de Cerisy, pp. 85–110. Paris: Union Générale d'Editions, 10/18, 1976.

Goldfarb, Phyllis. "Orson Welles's Use of Sound," *Take One*, 3, no. 6 (July–August 1971):10–14. Consequences of dissociating sound from space in *Citizen Kane*, *The Magnificent Ambersons*, *The Lady from Shanghai*, *Touch of Evil*.

Gorbman, Claudia. "Clair's Sound Hierarchy and the Creation of Auditory Space," *Purdue Film Studies Annual 1976* (West Lafayette: Purdue, 1976), pp. 113–23. *Sous les toits de Paris* has unusual sound hierarchy—music, speech, noise—which is upset only during climax in the narrative. Critical terminology for sound space needs to include "off-track sound" to parallel off-screen visual space. Analysis of Clair's use of spatial dimensions of sound and speech.

Graham, Mark. *"Padre Padrone* and the Dialectics of Sound," *Film Criticism* (Edin-
boro, Pa.), 6, no. 1 (1981):21–30. How speech, noise, music make connections between the narrative and thematic concerns. "Musical structure."

Henry, Jean-Jacques. "Claquez vos portes sur un silence d'or: Notes sur le son chez
Tati," *Cahiers du Cinéma,* no. 303 (September 1979):25–27. Entirely constructed nature of Tati's sound tracks for *Les Vacances de M. Hulot* and *Playtime.* Disregard of sync, fidelity, other aspects of auditory realism. Tati's sound
does not connect but fractures the very image.

King, Norman. "The Sound of Silents," *Screen,* 25, no. 3 (May–June 1984):2–15.
The role of musical accompaniment and speech in shaping editing rhythms in
the work of Abel Gance.

Lang, Robert. "Carnal Stereophony: A Reading of *Diva,"* *Screen,* 25, no. 3 (May–
June 1984):70–77. *Diva* progresses from a pre-Symbolic enjoyment of the innocent pleasure of the voice as pure sound to a kind of aural mirror phase, "a
metaphorical re-enactment of the entry into the Symbolic." At the end, its heroine experiences jubilation (hearing her voice for the first time) and loss (identifying with her own voice, which is now possessed by another). *Diva* traces "a
trajectory that corresponds in psychoanalysis to the child's transition from auto-
eroticism to narcissistic identification with an other."

Laurens, C. "L'Armature sonore de *L'Ange bleu* de Sternberg," *Revue du Cin-
éma/Image et son,* no. 367 (December 1981):126–29. Sternberg's use of sound
in *The Blue Angel* is "truly structural," or "dialectical" in Noël Burch's terms.

Levine, Steven Z. "Structures of Sound and Image in *The Rules of the Game,"
Quarterly Review of Film Studies,* 7, no. 3 (Summer 1982):211–24. Partly in
response to current film study's models of self-effacing discourse in diegetic films,
analyzes *Rules*'s enunciation of sound and image with respect to diegesis. Places
the film in figurative tradition of Impressionism.

Litle, M. "Sound Track: The Rules of the Game," *Cinema Journal,* 13, no. 1 (Fall
1973):35–44.

Marie, Michel. "Muriel, un film sonore, un film musical, un film parlant," in Claude
Bailblé, M. Marie, and M-C. Ropars, *Muriel: Histoire d'une recherche,* pp. 61–
122. Paris: Ed. Galilée, 1974.

—— "The Poacher's Aged Mother: On Speech in *La Chienne* by Jean Renoir,"
Yale French Studies, no. 60 (1980):219–32. Renoir's use of accents as thematic material: in *La Chienne* the voice plays crucial role in social individuation
of each character. Renoir's "commitment to treating sound as a subject and not
just as a simply illustrative and realistic atmosphere" results in density and variety of sound effects and songs as well as speech.

Pudovkin, Vsevolod. "Rhythmic Problems in My First Sound Film," in *Film Technique and Film Acting,* pp. 194–202. New York: Grove Press, 1960. Sound
film practice has slowed film rhythm; camera and editing imprisoned by speech.
Discusses problems encountered and solved in *Deserter.*

Rodakiewicz, Henwar. "Treatment of Sound in *The City,"* in Lewis Jacobs, ed. *The
Movies as Medium,* pp. 278–88. New York: Farrar, Straus, and Giroux, 1970.
Examination of aural and visual continuity, sound transitions in *The City.*

Ropars-Wuilleumier, Marie-Claire. "The Disembodied Voice *(India Song),"* *Yale French*

Studies, no. 60 (1980):241–68. "The film work of Duras offers the paradox of making the voice the means of writing, thus reintroducing, according to the Derridean project, writing into speech." Detailed analysis of opening of *India Song,* whose disjunctions and resistances "organize the film into a 'scene of writing' particularly suited to provoking an investigation which returns to theory itself."

—— "La Mort des miroirs: *India Song, Son nom de Venise dans Calcutta desert,"* *L'Avant-Scène du cinéma,* no. 225 (April 1979):4–12. Duras has given *Son nom de Venise* the same sound track as *India Song,* a sound which is never onscreen. Music, sounds, voices, and silences structure the sonic material.

Rosenbaum, Jonathan. "Bresson's *Lancelot du Lac,"* *Sight and Sound,* 43, no. 3 (Summer 1974):128–30. Emphasizes the film's clarity and simplicity, every sound's irreducible concreteness and efficacy.

Snow, Michael. "Notes for *Rameau's Nephew,"* *October,* no. 4 (1977):43–57. "To me it's a true 'talking picture.' It delves into the implications of that description and derives structures that can generate contrasts that are proper to the mode." Notes follow introductory remarks.

Straub, Jean-Marie, and Danièle Huillet. "Entretien avec Jean-Marie Straub et Danièle Huillet," *Cahiers du Cinéma,* no. 223 (August 1970):48–57. Continued in No. 224 (October 1970):40–42. Comment on theory and practice in their work, during filming of *Othon.* Politics, language, representation, direct sound.

Tati, Jacques (Serge Daney, J-J. Henry, S. Le Péron). "Entretiens avec Jacques Tati: 1. Le Son," *Cahiers du Cinema,* no. 303 (September 1979):8–13. Functions of sound in Tati's films.

Thompson, Kristin. "Early Sound Counterpoint," *Yale French Studies,* no. 60 (1980):115–40. Analysis of eleven Soviet films, 1930–34, in light of the 1928 "Statement" on sound film (cf. Eisenstein, section I). To clarify the Soviet notion of sound counterpoint in theory and practice, surveys nonnaturalistic sound-image devices and their functions in these films.

Van Wert, William. "Cinema of Marguerite Duras: Sound and Voice in a Closed Room," *Film Quarterly,* 33 no. 1 (Fall 1979):22–29. Traces dialectical relationships between sound track and image in Duras's work to *Le Camion.*

Walsh, Martin. *"Moses and Aaron:* Straub and Huillet's Schoenberg," and other sections of *The Brechtian Aspect of Radical Cinema.* London: BFI, 1981. The film "presents the opera in materialist terms through . . . elaboration of a Brechtian mise-en-scene." Close analysis of sound-image relationships to clarify and demonstrate Straub and Huillet's project.

Weis, Elisabeth. *The Silent Scream: Alfred Hitchcock's Sound Track.* Rutherford, N.J.: Fairleigh Dickinson University Press, 1982. Study of A.H.'s aural style throughout his sound period contributes both to understanding thematic preoccupations and development and to field of film sound. Narrative functions of screams, silence, diegetic tunes, spatial dimensions of sound (e.g., off-screen sound as "aural intrusion"), etc., in progressive phases of A.H.'s oeuvre.

—— "The Sound of One Wing Flapping," *Film Comment,* 14, no. 5 (September–October 1978):42–48. Hitchcock's sound style: variety, density, irony, "closed" (as opposed to Renoir and Altman's open style), sound-image counterpoint. Traces shift from expressionism toward greater realism during A.H.'s career. Extended analysis of *The Birds*'s orchestration of sound effects, which moves from terror-by-noise to terror-by-silence. Natural, mechanical, and electronic sound.

Williams, Alan. "Godard's Use of Sound," *Camera Obscura*, nos. 8-9-10 (Fall 1982):193–210. Identifies Bazinian characteristics of Godard's sound recording and mixing; also Eisensteinian idea of sound montage within a scene. Concludes by suggesting that G. is a "permutational formalist" (Noël Burch), but minimally so, not as systematic as Resnais or Hanoun, but enough to establish heterogeneity of sounds with respect to image and other sounds, with reference to Brecht's appeal for "separation of elements."

Williams, Martin T. "The Audible Image," *Films in Review*, 5 (August–September 1954):371–73. Comments on *A Place in the Sun*.

III. General Technology

Alkin, E. G. *Sound with Vision: Sound Techniques for Television and Film.* New York: Crane-Russak, 1972.

Amarasingham, Indiram. "Film-sound-space: The OSS (Optical Sound Synthesizer)," *Filmmakers Newsletter*, 4, no. 6 (April 1971):35–38.

Beatty, J. "Norma Shearer's Noisy Brother," *American*, no. 123 (May 1937):26ff. On sound engineer Douglas Shearer, techniques and problems of the job.

Bernhart, José. *Traité de prise de son.* Paris: Eyrolles, 1949.

Bigbee, Lynn. "Basic Elements of Sound Recording," *Filmmakers Newsletter*, 3, no. 12 (October 1970):36–42.

Bobrow, A. C. "The Art of the Soundman: An Interview with Christopher Newman," *Filmmakers Newsletter*, 7, no. 7 (May 1974):24–28.

Cameron, James R. *Sound Motion Pictures.* Coral Gables: Cameron Publishing Co., 1959.

Cavazutti, Enrico. "Problemi della registrazione sonora e del messaggio," *Bianco e nero*, 11, nos. 5/6 (May–June 1950):105–14.

Cowan, Lester, ed. *Recording Sound for Motion Pictures.* New York: McGraw-Hill, 1931. Reprinted lectures on sound recording technology, ca. 1930–31, originally presented at the Academy of Motion Picture Arts and Sciences School in Sound Fundamentals. Engineers and technicians speak about sound recording equipment (Vitaphone, Photophone, Movietone systems), studio acoustics and recording techniques, and sound reproduction in the theater.

Dreher, Carl. "Recording, Re-recording and Editing of Sound," *SMPE Journal*, 14, no. 6 (June 1931):756–65.

Frater, Charles B. *Sound Recording for Motion Pictures.* New York: A. S. Barnes, 1979. Standard instructional textbook for 16mm and 35mm filmmakers describing contemporary (English) sound recording, editing, and mixing equipment and techniques.

Honoré, Paul M. *A Handbook of Sound Recording.* South Brunswick, N.J.: A. S. Barnes, 1980. Clear, basic, up-to-date handbook of recording, editing, and mixing. Necessary information on acoustics, technology of microphones, tape recorders, and recording. Includes chapter on "creative sound."

Kellogg, Edward W. "The ABC of Photographic Sound Recording," *SMPE Journal*, 44, no. 3 (March 1945).

Lewin, Frank. "The Soundtrack in Nontheatrical Motion Pictures," *SMPTE Journal*, 68, no. 3 (March 1959):113–18; 68, no. 6 (June 1959):407–12; 68, no. 7 (July 1959):482–88. 1. Functions of the three components of the sound track—voice, music, sound effects. 2. Editing of the sound track as it relates to the overall production of the film. 3. Preparation of the work print and sound tracks for rerecording. 4. Rerecording.

McLaren, Norman. "Notes on Animated Sound," *Quarterly of Film, Radio and Television*, 7, no. 3 (Spring 1953):223–29. Describes each step of his animated sound technique. "A small library of several dozen cards, each containing black and white areas representing sound waves, replaced traditional musical instruments and noisemaking devices." Cards are arranged and photographed for synthetic sound track.

Marie, J. "Notes et soupirs d'un directeur du son," *Cinéma pratique*, no. 143 (February–March 1976):12–16; no. 144 (April–May 1976):56–58.

Musgrave, Peter. "The Dubbing of Sound," *American Cinematographer*, 43, no. 3 (March 1962):168–69ff.

Nisbett, Alec. *The Technique of the Sound Studio: For Radio, Television, and Film*. 4th ed. London and New York: Focal Press, 1979. Sound and microphone characteristics, sound balance for speech and music, film sound editing, etc., in relatively nontechnical approach for radio, TV, and film. Includes glossary.

—— *The Use of Microphones*. 2d ed. London and New York: Focal Press, 1983. Selection, positioning, balancing microphones for recording for film, radio, and TV.

Olson, H. F., and F. Massa. "On the Realistic Reproduction of Sound With Particular Reference to Sound Motion Pictures," *SMPE Journal*, 23 no. 2 (August 1934):63–81.

Paine, F. "Sound Design: Walter Murch," *University Film Association Journal*, 33, no. 4 (1981):15–20. Interview with sound editor Walter Murch.

Popper, Paul. "Synthetic Sound: How Sound Is Produced on the Drawing Board," *Sight and Sound*, 2, no. 7 (Autumn 1933):82–84.

Prince, David. "The Aesthetics and Practice of Sound: An Interview with Thomas Peterson," *Wide Angle*, 2, no. 3 (1978):68–72. Independent sound engineer Peterson opines on constructed and conventional nature of film sound, stressing technical quality and techniques of "invisible" sound editing.

Reisz, Karel, and Gavin Millar. *The Technique of Film Editing*. 2d ed. London and New York: Focal Press, 1968. Historical perspective, editing, theory, and practical technique. Film classics examined in terms of continuity, timing, selection of shots, sound editing.

Schaeffer, Pierre. "Les Nouvelles techniques sonores et le cinéma," *Cahiers du Cinéma*, no. 37 (July 1954):54–56. How Schaeffer began making music out of concrete sounds (musique concrète) and its natural place in cinema. New possibilities opened up by magnetic recording and editing.

Society of Motion Picture and Television Engineers. Journal (SMPTE Journal).
1950– . *Society of Motion Picture Engineers. Journal (SMPE Journal).* January 1930–December 1949.

Shearer, Douglas. "Hollywood's Tin Ear: An ABC of Sound," *Cinema Arts*, 1, no. 3 (September 1937):32–35.

Sturhahn, Larry. "The Art of the Sound Editor: An Interview with Walter Murch," *Filmmakers Newsletter*, 8, no. 2 (December 1974):22–25.

Villchur, Edgar. *Reproduction of Sound.* New York: Dover, 1965.

Walter, Ernest. *The Technique of the Cutting Room.* 2d ed. London and New York: Focal Press, 1982. Walter, visual coordinator for *Superman* I & II, details operations of editing, including sound editing, synchronizing, dubbing, etc.

Wheeler, Leslie J. *Principles of Cinematography: A Handbook of Motion Picture Technology.* Hastings-on-Hudson, N.Y.: Morgan and Morgan, 1953.

Wygotsky, Michael Z. *Wide-Screen Cinema and Stereophonic Sound.* New York: Hastings House, 1971.

IV. History: Style and Technology

Andrew, Dudley. "Sound in France: The Origins of a Native School," *Yale French Studies*, no. 60 (1980):94–114. Following a historical section on the technological and economic domination by the United States (Paramount) and Germany (Tobis) of early French sound film production, analyzes the seminal influences of Renoir's naturalism *(La Chienne)* and Grémillon's poetic realism *(La Petite Lise).*

Arnoux, Alexandre. *Du Muet au parlant: Mémoires d'un témoin.* Paris: La Nouvelle Edition, 1946. Essays written over thirty years. Silent era; reactions (disappointed at first) to the coming of sound; Renoir, Chaplin, others.

Buscombe, Edward. "Sound and Color," *Jump Cut*, no. 17 (1978):23–25. Debates with Gomery on relations between economics, technology, and ideology in cinema; here, the historiographical concern is to account for technological innovation.

Cahiers de la cinémathèque (Perpignan), 13–15 (1975). Special issue: "La Révolution du parlant."

Cameron, Evan William, ed. *Sound and the Cinema: The Coming of Sound to American Film.* Pleasantville, N.Y.: Redgrave, 1980. Historical essays (Fielding, Gomery, Noxon), testimonials (Capra, Mamoulian, Herrmann, Stewart), analytical essays (Fischer, Cameron).

Clair, René. *Cinema Yesterday and Today.* Ed. R. C. Dale. New York: Dover, 1972. "This is not a history of cinema." Yet, in editing together reflections on cinema which he wrote from the 1920s to 1970, Clair gives historical perspective to changing technology and aesthetics. Abundant material on sound.

Fielding, Raymond, comp. *A Technological History of Motion Pictures and Television: An Anthology from the Pages of the Journal of the Society of Motion*

Picture and Television Engineers. Berkeley: University of California Press, 1967. Articles from *SMPE Journal* and *SMPTE Journal* on early film technology of sound motion pictures (as well as TV). Includes E. Kellogg's "History of Sound Motion Pictures" (1955) and J. McCullough's and J. E. Aiken's papers on Tykociner (both 1958).

Fox, Julian. "Casualties of Sound," *Films and Filming:* "Part 1: King Mike," 19, no. 1 (October 1972):34–40; "Part 2;" 19, no. 2 (November 1972):33–40.

Frayne, John G., A. C. Blaney, G. R. Groves, and H. F. Olson. "A Short History of Motion-Picture Sound Recording in the United States," *SMPTE Journal,* 85, no. 7 (July 1976):515–28. Technological developments, in pursuit of ever-higher quality of sound, from 1918 (German Tri-Ergon group) to the Dolby Noise-Reduction System (1973) and the hue-modulated color photographic sound track.

Geduld, Harry M. *The Birth of the Talkies: From Edison to Jolson.* Bloomington: Indiana University Press, 1975. Copiously documented technological, economic, and critical history from invention of the phonograph, and its application to cinematograph, to sound-on-film development, to Vitaphone and *The Jazz Singer,* proliferation of sound systems and adoption by studios, to 1929.

Gomery, Douglas. "The Coming of Sound to the German Cinema," *Purdue Film Studies Annual 1976* (West Lafayette: Purdue, 1976), pp. 136–43. Applies economic models of technological invention and innovation to tracing Tri-Ergon's development and Tobis-Klangfilm's European expansion.

—— "The Coming of Sound to Hollywood," in Stephen Heath and Teresa de Lauretis, eds., *The Cinematic Apparatus: Technology as Historical and Ideological Form,* pp. 38–46. London: Macmillan, 1980.

—— "The Coming of the Talkies: Invention, Innovation, and Diffusion," in Tino Balio, ed., *The American Film Industry: An Historical Anthology,* pp. 193–211. Madison: University of Wisconsin Press, 1976.

—— "Failure and Success: Vocafilm and RCA Innovate Sound," *Film Reader,* no. 2 (1977):213–21. Of the many sound systems developed during the 1920s, what accounts for success or failure? Not only technology, but system's marketability, strategies of financing, management.

—— "Problems in Film History: How Fox Innovated Sound," *Quarterly Review of Film Studies,* 1, no. 3 (August 1976):315–30. Using much varied documentation, and economic theory of technological innovation, traces Movietone's history from Case's inventions to 1929, the apex of Fox's power.

—— "Tri-Ergon, Tobis-Klangfilm, and the Coming of Sound," *Cinema Journal,* 16, no. 1 (Fall 1976):51–61. How Tri-Ergon system was developed, and how the technology entered commercial motion picture production and exhibition. Stages of invention, innovation, and diffusion.

—— "The 'Warner Vitaphone Peril': The American Film Industry Reacts to the Innovation of Sound," *University Film Association: Journal,* 28, no. 1 (1976):11–19.

—— "Writing the History of the American Film Industry: Warner Brothers and Sound," *Screen,* 17, no. 1 (Spring 1976):40–53. Rejects standard account of Warners as verging on bankruptcy before miraculously rising to success with Vitaphone.

Green, Fitzhugh. *The Film Finds Its Tongue.* New York: G. P. Putnam, 1929.

Greenwald, William I. "'The Impact of Sound Upon the Film Industry: A Case Study of Innovation," *Explorations in Entrepreneurial History,* 4 (May 1952):178–92.

Grierson, John. "The GPO Gets Sound," *Cinema Quarterly,* 2, no. 4 (Summer 1934):215–21. How the GPO, in acquiring film sound technology, has eliminated "economic and ideologic overheads."

Hampton, Benjamin J. *History of the American Film Industry from Its Beginnings to 1931.* Ed. Richard Griffith. New York: Dover, 1970. (Originally *A History of the Movies,* 1931.) Final chapter of this business history treats the coming of sound.

Icart, Roger. "L'Avènement du parlant," *Cahiers de la Cinémathèque* (Perpignan), 13–15 (1975).

Jacobs, Lewis. *The Rise of the American Film.* New York: Harcourt, Brace, 1939. Durable social, economic, and critical history of American film from beginnings through 1930s has section on the coming of sound.

Kellogg, Edward W. "History of Sound Motion Pictures," three-part article in *SMPTE Journal.* Supplements Sponable, 1947. Contains exhaustive technological bibliography. Reprinted in Fielding (1967), pp. 174–220. I: 64, no. 6 (June 1955):291–302. Technological history from Edison, Gaumont et al.; basic inventions necessary to the sound film (selenium cells, audion tube, etc.); De Forest, Tri-Ergon, Movietone; disk and sound-on-film; the various U.S. sound systems as of the late 1920s. II: 64, no. 7 (July 1955):356–74. How the industry adopted sound in late 1920s; economic, social, legal aspects as well as technological. Discusses many early accommodations for sound, including blooping, blimps, printers, sound stages, theater equipment, processing. Early 1930s improvements (mikes, speakers, lamps). III: 64, no. 8 (August 1955):422–37. Since coming of sound, developments to improve quality. E.g., extended frequency range; optical printer; reduced distortion via uniform film development, fine-grain film stocks, compressors; multiple-speaker systems (e.g., stereo); magnetic recording.

McCullough, John B. "Joseph T. Tykociner: Pioneer in Sound Recording," *SMPTE Journal,* 67, no. 8 (August 1958):520–21. Reprinted in Fielding, pp. 221ff.

Noxon, Gerald F. "The European Influence on the Coming of Sound to the American Film, 1925–1940: A Survey," in Evan W. Cameron, ed., *Sound and the Cinema,* pp. 136–80. Pleasantville, N. Y.: Redgrave, 1980. Individual sketches of European-born directors and technicians in United States or Europe during the cinema's transition to sound, who had immediate or subsequent influence on U.S. production. German expressionism and Kammerspiel, French realism and naturalism. Uneven focus on sound per se.

Ogle, Patrick. "Development of Sound Systems: The Commercial Era," *Film Reader,* no. 2 (1977):198–212. Account of the various sound systems available to the studios in the late 1920s.

Rogoff, R. "Edison's Dream: A Brief History of the Kinetophone," *Cinema Journal* 15, no. 2 (Spring 1976):56–68.

Ryder, Loren L. "Magnetic Sound Recording in the Motion Picture and Television Industries," *SMPTE Journal,* 85, no. 7 (July 1976):528–30. First tape recorders seen in United States were captured from Germans by U.S. Army during World

War II; one was shown to author. Account of postwar developments in magnetic sound recording.

Salt, Barry. "Film Style and Technology in the Thirties," *Film Quarterly*, 30 (Fall 1976):19–32. Sections on sound clearly and simply tell which stylistic choices were facilitated by developments in technology at which historical moments. Essential starting point for any analyses of sound style in 1930s.

Sponable, Earl. "Historical Development of Sound Films," seven-part article in *SMPE Journal*, in two installments: 48, no. 4 (April 1947):275–303; 48, no 5 (May 1947):402–22.

Staiger, Janet, and Douglas Gomery. "The History of World Cinema: Models for Economic Analysis," *Film Reader*, no. 4 (1979):35–44. The Marxist model is best suited "to sort out the activities of multinational monopoly capitalists"; essay accounts for European cinema's headway into international market after 1926.

Stewart, James G. "The Evolution of Cinematic Sound: A Personal Report," in Evan W. Cameron, ed., *Sound in the Cinema*, pp. 38–67. Pleasantville, N.Y.: Redgrave, 1980. Valuable reminiscences by Hollywood soundman on evolution of sound technologies and techniques, directors he worked with, and pragmatic and aesthetic reflections gathered from experience.

Thrasher, Frederick. *Okay for Sound: How the Screen Found Its Voice.* New York: Duell, Sloan, and Pearce, 1946.

Walker, Alexander. *The Shattered Silents: How the Talkies Came to Stay.* New York: William Morrow & Co., 1979. Lively, well-documented history of Hollywood's transition to sound, mid-1926 to 1929. Retooling of the industry; changes in personnel, economics, and technology; evolution of techniques, genres, audience tastes during the period. Complements Geduld.

Wohlrab, Hans C. "Highlights of the History of Sound Recording on Film in Europe," *SMPTE Journal*, 85, no. 7 (July 1976):531–33. Presents important steps in the development of film sound-recording techniques in Europe, primarily Germany. Notes parallels with developments in the United States, but also the hot-cathode microphone and the Kerr cell. Up to magnetic recording.

Notes on Contributors

Rick Altman teaches French, comparative literature, and film at the University of Iowa. He is a former director of the Inter-University Center for Film and Critical Studies in Paris and editor of *Genre: The Musical.*

Rudolf Arnheim, professor emeritus of the psychology of art, Harvard University, is the author of *Art and Visual Perception, Visual Thinking,* and other books. The excerpts here reproduced are the final sections of an essay "A New Laocoön: Artistic Composites and the Talking Film." This essay was written in 1938 and republished in the 1957 American edition of *Film as Art,* first published in German in 1932.

Bela Balazs taught film at the State Film Institute in Moscow and is the author of *Der sichtbare Mensch, Der Geist des Films,* and *Theory of the Film.*

David Bordwell teaches film at the University of Wisconsin–Madison and is the author of *The Films of Carl-Th. Dreyer* and (with Kristin Thompson) *Film Art: An Introduction.*

Noël Burch teaches filmmaking and film theory in Paris and is the author of *Theory of Film Practice* and *To the Distant Observer: Form and Meaning in the Japanese Cinema.*

Fred Camper writes on film and has taught filmmaking and film history. He is also an independent filmmaker and lives in Chicago.

Noël Carroll teaches philosophy at Wesleyan University. He is co-editor of *Millennium Film Journal* and a regular contributor to *Dance Magazine* and *October.*

Mary Ann Doane teaches film and semiotics at Brown University and has written for *Film Reader, October, Screen,* and *Camera Obscura.*

Lucy Fischer is Director of the Film Studies Program at the University of Pittsburgh and author of *Jacques Tati: A Guide to References and Resources.*

Douglas Gomery teaches broadcasting and film courses at the University of Maryland. He is author of *The Studio System* and (with Robert C. Allen) *Film History: Theory and Practice.* He is presently at work on an economic history of the U.S. television industry.

Claudia Gorbman teaches in the comparative literature department at Indiana University and is a former director of the Inter-University Center for Film and Critical Studies in Paris.

Stephen Handzo has taught film history at Columbia University and is an Associate Member of S.M.P.T.E. and a member of the New York City projectionists' local 306 of I.A.T.S.E.

Lindley Hanlon is chairperson of film at Brooklyn College and is the author of a forthcoming book entitled *Fragments: Bresson's Film Style,* published by Fairleigh Dickinson University Press.

Arthur Knight is Professor of Film in the Division of Cinema at the University of Southern California and writes for *The Hollywood Reporter.*

Michael Litle is a film and videotape editor in San Francisco with a special interest in sound.

Marc Mancini heads the film program at West Los Angeles College and is an adjunct professor at the University of Southern California.

Christian Metz lectures on film at the Ecole Pratique des Hautes Etudes in Paris and is the author of *Film Language: A Semiotics of the Cinema, Language and Cinema,* and *The Imaginary Signifier.*

Penny Mintz previously wrote under the name of Phyllis Goldfarb.

Ron Mottram teaches cinema studies in the Department of Theater at Illinois State Univeristy.

Frank Paine was Director of Film Production and is Associate Professor Emeritus in the Department of Cinema and Photography at Southern Illinois University at Carbondale. He is now working as a writer and photographer.

Martin Rubin has taught film at Columbia University and at the New School for Social Research and has contributed articles to the *Village Voice, Movie, Film Comment,* and other publications.

Barry Salt is a lecturer in film at the Slade Film Department, University College, London, and the author of *Film Style & Technology: History & Analysis.*

Charles Schreger is the president of Triumph Films.

Kristin Thompson has taught film at the University of Wisconsin and the University of Iowa. She is the author of *Eisenstein's Ivan the Terrible: A Neoformalist Analysis* and (with David Bordwell) *Film Art: An Introduction.*

Alan Williams teaches film in the French Department at Rutgers. He is the author of *Max Ophuls and the Cinema of Desire* and has published articles in *Film Quarterly, Yale French Studies,* and other magazines.

Index

Abbott, George, 229
Abie's Irish Rose, 225
Abraham Lincoln, 225
Academy curve, 415-16
Academy of Motion Picture Arts and Sciences, 22
Accents, *see* Dialects
Accident, 198
Acoustics, *see* Sound and space
Actors' Equity, 22
Adorno, Theodor, 171
Adventures of Robin Hood, The, 366
Aeolight, 388; *see also* Light valve
Age d'Or, L', 266
Aldrich, Robert, 374
Alexander, James S., 10
Alexander Nevsky, 190, 204, 313, 342
Alexandrov, G. V., 76, 126, 135, 249, 265
Allen, Woody, 196, 399, 412
Allonsanfan, 153
All Quiet on the Western Front, 215, 225
All the President's Men, 350
Allwine, Wayne, 366
Altman, Rick, 4, 63
Altman, Robert, 49-50, 69, 338, 346, 349-50, 351, 353, 354, 403
Ambient sound, 239, 336-37, 384, 394, 395, 397, 398, 402
American Federation of Musicians, 22
American Graffiti, 193, 346, 353
American Telephone & Telegraph Corp. (AT&T), 5, 8-10, 12; *see also* Electrical Research Products, Inc.; Western Electric
Amplitude, 387
Anger, Kenneth, 375
Another Man, Another Chance, 67
A nous la liberté, 77, 216, 266
Anticipation of the Night, 377, 378
Apocalypse Now, 346, 356-60, 407, 423, 424
Applause, 211, 215-16, 219, 223, 232-46, 402
Arabics, 378, 380
Are You There?, 230
Argent, L', 69, 331

Arnheim, Rudolf, 52, 78-79, 82, 232, 236, 265, 285, 361
Around the World in 80 Days, 421
Astaire, Fred, 104, 181, 189
Astoria studios, 240
Asynchronous sound, 76-78, 83-85, 86-91, 94-95, 96-97, 108, 110-11, 120, 135-37, 138-39, 145, 163, 192, 196, 216-17, 224, 225, 241-42, 249, 255, 265, 266-67, 285, 300, 375, 385
At Long Last Love, 349
Audion, 9
Audion amplifier tube, 8, 45
Aural intrusion, 303
Automatic dialogue replacement, 405; *see also* Wordfit
Automatic slating devices, 404; *see also* Clapstick
Avant-garde, 347, 370-73, 375-80
Average shot length, 40-42
Azoff, Irving, 348

Bach, J. S., 97, 335
Background noise, *see* Ambient sound
Back Street, 211-12, 277-85
Back-up recording ("rock 'n' roll"), 414
Bailblé, Claude, 165
Baillie, Bruce, 371, 379
Balazs, Bela, 80-81, 161n, 237, 240, 243, 245, 285
Barnet, Boris, 209n
Barney, 397; *see also* Blimping
Barron, Bebe, 362
Barron, Louis, 362
Barthes, Roland, 55, 173, 314
Battle of Algiers, The, 270
Battlestar Galactica, 175
Baudrier, Yves, 144
Baudry, Jean-Louis, 45, 63, 71
Baxter, John, 229
Bazin, André, 44, 63, 69, 145, 228, 265, 272-76, 288, 312-13, 334, 336-38, 340-41
Beast of the City, 134
Beaumont, Harry, 93, 245n

Beck, Martin, 7
Beethoven, Ludwig van, 206
Bell, Clive, 265
Bellour, Raymond, 38
Belmondo, Jean-Paul, 334
Belton, John, 4, 311
Benjamin, Walter, 164
Berkeley, Busby, 391
Berlin, Irving, 13
Bernhardt, Curtis, 191
Better 'Ole, The, 13
Bettetini, Gianfranco, 52
Biased recording, 67
"Big Five Agreement," 13, 20
Big Heat, The, 275
Big Money, 230
Big Sleep, The, 38
Birds, The, 286, 287, 298, 299, 303-11
Black Hole, The, 365
Blackmail, 287, 299, 302, 305
Black Watch, The, 222-23
Blimping, 39, 47, 66, 215, 269, 397
Blonde Cobra, 370
Bloom, Edgar S., 12
Blooping patch, 389
Blooping, 47, 57, 389
Blossom Time, 18
Blue Angel, The, 226, 239
Blue Max, The, 410
Bogart, Neil, 348
Bolvary, Geza von, 217
Bonitzer, Pascal, 167, 168, 171, 172, 173, 174
Bonner, John, 426
Boomerang, 400
Boominess, 394
Booms, 389, 397, 402; *see also* Fishpole
Bordwell, David, 179-80
Borzage, Frank, 221
Bound for Glory, 67
Brakhage, Stan, 347, 369, 370, 373, 377-78, 380
Braun, B. Vivian, 77-78
Breathless, 333, 334
Brecht, Bertolt, 344-45
Breer, Robert, 379
Bresson, Robert, 69, 145-46, 150, 189, 200, 201, 286, 288, 323-31, 374
Bridge, *see* Sound bridge
Broadway Melody, 93-94
Broken Lullaby, 214

Brooks, Louise, 406
Brown, Royal, 343
Buddy Holly Story, The, 349, 352
Buñuel, Luis, 133, 266, 267, 269
Burch, Noël, 179-80, 313, 342-43
Burning the Candle, 99
Burtt, Ben, 352, 366-68

Cable-sync, 393; *see also* Crystal sync
Cagney, James, 103
California Split, 349
Camera blimps, *see* Blimping
Camera mobility, 38-39, 213, 215, 219, 223-24, 225, 227, 230, 233-34, 236, 269, 270, 273-75; *see also* Sound cameras
Cameraphone, 6-7
Cameras, *see* Mitchell BNC; Mitchell NC; Sound cameras
Camper, Fred, 347
Canary Murder Case, The, 406
Cancellation effect, 402
Capra, Frank, 38, 349, 394
Carné, Marcel, 41
Carpenter, Edmund, 238, 239
Carroll, Noël, 211
Case, Anna, 12
Case, Theodore, 15-16, 45, 388
Cass, John, 60
"Catching," 410; *see also* Mickey-mousing
Catchings, Waddill, 10-15, 23
Cavalcanti, Alberto, 78, 130, 138
Chaplin, Charles, 75, 81, 94, 99, 126, 131-32, 133, 285, 360
Chaplin, Sydney, 13
Charge of the Light Brigade, The, 41, 103
Charrell, Eric, 218
Chienne, La, 67, 287, 312, 313
Chinatown Nights, 227-28
Chinoise, La, 333, 334, 335
Chronicle of Anna Magdalena Bach, The, 146
Chronophone, 6
Cimino, Michael, 50, 349, 351, 354
Cine-Fi, 354-55
CinemaScope, 68, 403, 420, 421
Cinéma vérité, 49, 379, 383, 393, 398
Cinerama, 403, 419, 420, 421
Citizen Kane, 185-86, 287, 289, 290, 291, 294, 295-96, 361, 396, 418n
City Lights, 126, 131
City Streets, 219

Clair, René, 77, 127, 130, 138-39, 145, 163, 191, 192, 210, 216-18, 220, 266, 285, 286, 361
Clapper, see Clapstick
Clapstick, 404
Click track, 410
Close Encounters of the Third Kind, 352, 353, 423
Close Harmony, 229
Coalface, 78
Cock-Eyed World, The, 214
Cocoanuts, The, 240
Coffman, Joe, 60, 240, 244
Cogswell, Roger, 426
Comolli, Jean-Louis, 45, 55, 58, 69
Condamné à mort s'est échappé, Un, 329
Confessions of a Nazi Spy, 111
Congress Dances, 218
Contempt, 334, 335, 338, 339, 342, 343
Contrapuntal sound, see Asynchronous sound
Conversation, The, 346, 353, 361
Conversion to sound, see Studios: conversion to sound; Theaters: conversion of, to sound
Coolidge, Calvin, 19, 388
Cooper, Gary, 103, 225
Coppola, Francis Ford, 346, 349, 353
Cornell, Joseph, 376
Countdown, 349
Cowan, Lester, 38
Craft, Edward, 9, 16
Crazy That Way, 230
Cromwell, John, 229
Cronaca di un amore, 209n
Crosland, Alan, 221, 224-25
Cross-fading, 402, 409
Crucified Lovers, The, 203-4, 205, 206, 207
Crystal-sync, 393, 404; see also Cable-sync
Cues, see Long cues; Music cues; Short cues
Cue track, 384
Cukor, George, 41, 229
Cummings, Irving, 223
Curtiz, Michael, 40, 41

Datakode, 424; see also Edge numbering
Days of Heaven, 349, 352, 354
Dead sync, 417
Deer Hunter, The, 50, 351, 352, 354, 424
De Forest, Lee, 8, 9, 16, 17, 19, 22, 45, 388
de la Roche, Catherine, 259
Delerue, Georges, 335, 410

Demarest, William, 14
Deren, Maya, 377
De Rochemont, Louis, 400
Deserter, 89-91, 266
DeSica, Vittorio, 269
Deux ou trois choses que je sais d'elle, see Two or Three Things I Know About Her
Dialects, 316, 321, 332, 333-34
Dial M for Murder, 303
Dialogue, 75-82, 88-89, 101-4, 112-15, 128-35, 162-74, 204-5, 221-31 passim, 242-43, 279, 281-82, 285, 292, 299-300, 315, 328-29, 332-35, 349, 373-74, 383, 384, 386, 399, 403, 404, 416; see also Dialects; Interior monologue; Voice
Dialogue cutting point, 37-38, 57
Dialogue recording, 46, 58, 59
Dialogue replacement, 384, 395, 405; see also Automatic dialogue replacement; Dubbing; Looping; Postproduction; Postsynchronization; Sound mixing; Wordfit
Dichter, Mark, 67
Dickinson, Thorold, 259
Diegetic sound, 191-92, 193, 194-95, 197-98; see also Displaced diegetic sound; External diegetic sound; Internal diegetic sound; Simple diegetic sound
Dinner at Eight, 41
Dip filter, 402, 413; see also Filtering
Directing attention, see Sound and attention
Direct sound, 394-95; as a style, 49, 146, 150-53, 383, 400; see also Production sound; Reflected sound; Sync-sound
Disney, Walt, 46, 189, 364, 365, 418-19
Displaced diegetic sound, 197-98, 199
Displacement of sound and image, 388, 389, 390, 417
Doane, Mary Ann, 4, 63, 66, 146-48, 212
Dr. Jekyll and Mr. Hyde, 219, 242
Dr. Mabuse, 208n
Dodge City, 41
Dolby, Ray, 350
Dolby noise reduction, 50, 67, 70, 350-52, 416, 422
Dolby stereo, 353-54, 388, 422-24; see also Stereo
Dolby SVA (stereo variable area), 388
Donen, Stanley, 196
Don Juan, 13, 45, 221, 223, 385
dos Santos, Pereira, 206

Double system sound-on-film, 390-91
Drew, Robert, 398
Dreyer, Carl, 246n, 266
Dubbing, 65, 146, 150-51, 152, 202, 215, 227-28, 383, 386, 405-6, 412; of foreign languages, 27-28, 150; see also Automatic dialogue replacement; Looping; Postproduction; Postsynchronization; Sound mixing; Wordfit
Duras, Marguerite, 163
Durbin, Deanna, 105

Early Abstractions, 377
East of Borneo, 376
Eastwood, Clint, 391
Economics, see Sound and economics
Edge numbering, 37, 40, 404; see also Datakode
Edison, Thomas, 6-7, 16, 45
Editing, see Dialogue cutting point; Sound editing
Editorial sync, 390; see also Projection sync
Effects, see Sound effects
Eisenstein, Sergei, 44, 51, 76-77, 79, 126, 128, 135, 137, 138, 145, 190, 204, 242, 249, 265, 267, 269, 285, 313, 334, 340, 341-42, 399
Eisler, Hanns, 171
Electrical Research Products, Inc. (ERPI), 13, 14, 22
Electron tube amplifier, 385
Elman, Mischa, 12
Eloy, Jean-Claude, 206
Emmett, E. V. H., 98, 102
Empire Strikes Back, The, 367, 423
Emulator digital synthesizer, 362
End, The, 371, 376
Enjo, 209n
Enthusiasm, 76, 211, 247-64, 266, 371
Epstein, Jean, 81-82, 140-1
Everson, William K., 389, 425
Evolution of the recording medium, 383; see also Sound recording
Exciter bulb, 387, 388
Executive Suite, 408
EXR Exciter, 363
External diegetic sound, 193, 197

Fallen Flowers, 209n
Family Plot, 307

Fano, Michel, 205-6, 209n
Fantasia, 353, 418-19
Fantasound, 418
Fassbinder, R. W., 69
FBI Story, The, 410
Fellini, Federico, 335
Feminism, 174
Femme douce, Une, 331
Femme mariée, Une, 206
Fesler, Bailey, 363
Fidelity, 190-91, 349
Fielding, Raymond, 426
Film Booking Office, 21
Film stock, 47-48, 67
Filtering, 402, 413, 416
Final mix, 414-15; see also Sound mixing
Fischer, Lucy, 76, 211
Fishpole, 397
Fitzgerald, Ella, 163-64
Flaherty, Robert, 140
Flats: for music recording, 411
Fleming, Victor, 224-25
Flesh and the Devil, 20
Flynn, Errol, 410
Foley, Ed, 407
Foley technique, 407
Fonda, Jane, 333, 339
Forbidden Planet, 362
Force of Evil, 205
Ford, John, 189, 193, 198, 222-23, 224, 230, 389
Forman, Milos, 349, 354
For the Defense, 229
Fountainhead, The, 410
Four Nights of a Dreamer, 189
Fox, William, 15-18, 23, 388
Fox-Case Corporation, 16, 17
Fox Film Corp.: role of, in innovating sound, 15-18, 23, 45, 387-90
Foy, Bryan, 14-15, 245n
Frampton, Hollis, 379
Frankenstein, 229
French CanCan, 287
Frequency characteristics, 67
Frequency response, 351
Freud, Sigmund, 174
Front Page, The, 349, 397
Fuco, Giovanni, 209n
Full-coat magnetic stock, 392
Futurism, 248

Garden of Allah, The, 410
Garland, Judy, 105
Gassman, Remi, 304
Gaumont, Leon, 6
Gay Divorcee, The, 403
Gehr, Ernie, 347, 379, 380
General Crack, 224
General Electric, 18, 19, 20, 23, 29
Geography of the Body, 200
Gertrud, 246n
Glorious Betsy, 224
Godard, Jean-Luc, 49, 163, 173, 195, 208n,
     286, 288, 300, 332-45, 395, 408
Godfather, The, 346, 353
Godless Girl, The, 21
Goebbels, Joseph, 25, 32
Gold, Ernest, 426
Golden Coach, The, 287
Goldsmith, Jerry, 410
Goldstein, Laurence, 426
Gomery, Douglas, 3
Gordy, Berry, 348
Gorin, J.-P., 342
Graduate, The, 69
Grand Illusion, La, 133, 275
Grateful Dead, The, 351
Grease, 353, 354
Great Ziegfeld, The, 104
Greed, 271
Grieg, Edvard, 108
Grierson, John, 78, 134
Griffith, D. W., 69, 219
Ground noise, 50, 67, 402
Guback, Thomas, 25, 33
Guide track, 384
Guiraud, Pierre, 160n
Gun Crazy, 400
Gunning, Tom, 301
Guys and Dolls, 420
Gypsy, 406

Hadley, Henry, 12
Hair, 354
Half-Naked Truth, The, 218
Hall, Ben, 425
Hallelujah!, 214
Hallelujah, I'm a Bum, 218
Hamlet, 193
Handel, G. F., 111
Hanlon, Lindley, 288

Hanoun, Marcel, 342, 343
Hardy, Oliver, 42
Hare, Lumsden, 222
Harmony at Home, 230
Haunting, The, 65
Hawks, Howard, 41, 42, 245n, 334, 349, 373
Hawthorne, 9
Hays, Will, 12, 28, 386
Hecht, Ben, 349
Herrmann, Bernard, 185, 304
Hidden Fortress, The, 204
Hilliard, John K., 418
Hill Street Blues, 338
His Girl Friday, 193
Hitchcock, Alfred, 185, 191, 198, 286-88, 298-
     311
Holiday, 41
Homme qui ment, L', 209
Hopkins, Miriam, 220
House of Wax, 420
House on 92nd Street, The, 400
Houston, Penelope, 298
Howard, Leslie, 410
How Green Was My Valley, 185, 198
Hoxie, Charles, 19
Huillet, Danièle, 146
Huston, Walter, 225

"Icebox," 397
Ichikawa, Kon, 209n
Ideology, *see* Sound and ideology
Ideology of the visible, 44-45, 51-52, 54-55,
     56, 158, 165-66; *see also* Sound and ide-
     ology; Sound: traditional subservience to
     image
Imitation of Life, 41, 278
Immortelle, L', 205
In Old Arizona, 223-24, 231n, 389, 399
Interior monologue, 169, 193-94, 199, 302,
     339
Interlock projection, 404
Internal diegetic sound, 193, 197
Intertitles, 99-100
Invasion of the Body Snatchers, 354
Invocation of My Demon Brother, 375
Irigaray, Luce, 174
Ivan the Terrible, 133, 185, 204
Ivens, Joris, 102

Jacobs, Ken, 370
Jacobs, Lewis, 163
Jagger, Mick, 375
Jakobson, Roman, 147, 265
Jamaica Inn, 299, 306
Janis, Elsie, 13
Jaws, 69
Jazz Singer, The, 3, 14, 15, 45, 93, 224, 352, 385, 388
Jeanson, Francis, 334
Jessel, George, 13
Jettée, La, 190
Jewett, Frank, 8, 9, 16
Jolson, Al, 13, 14, 348, 398, 425
Journey's End, 229
Jungle Patrol, 134

Kameradschaft, 133, 211, 266, 269-76
Kaper, Bronislau, 409
Katz, Steve, 353
Kaufman, Jay, 426
Kaufman, Philip, 349, 354
Kazan, Elia, 412
Keith-Albee, 21
Kellogg, Edward, 3, 19, 426
Kelly, Gene, 196
Kennedy, Joseph P., 21
Kinetophone, 6, 7
King and I, The, 406
King Kong, 391, 410
King of Kings, 21
Kirk, Lisa, 406
Kiss Me Deadly, 148, 167, 374
Knight, Arthur, 210, 242
Knudson, Robert, 412
Kopp, Rudy, 409
Koster, Henry, 43
Kracauer, Siegfried, 52, 81, 225, 238, 244
Kreuger, Miles, 425
Kubelka, Peter, 262-64, 371, 375, 380
Kubrick, Stanley, 349
Kudelski, Stefan, 392
Kurosawa, Akira, 187, 204
Kurtz, Gary, 352, 366

Lacan, Jacques, 45, 169, 170
La Cava, Gregory, 218
Lady from Shanghai, The, 287, 289-97
Lancelot du Lac, 331
Landow, George, 379

Lang, Fritz, 108, 163, 199, 208n, 211, 266-69, 274-76
Language, *see* Dialects; Dialogue; Voice
Lansing, James B., 418
Last Waltz, The, 351, 354
Last Year at Marienbad, 208
Laughton, Charles, 103, 130-31
Laurel, Stan, 42
Lawrence of Arabia, 194
Leacock, Richard, 398, 426
Leacock-Drew Associates, 404
Lean, David, 194
Lelouch, Claude, 67
LeRoy, Mervyn, 40
Letter from Siberia, 181-83
Levinson, Nathan, 11
Lewis, Joseph H., 400
Lifeboat, 299, 303
Life of O'Haru, The, 206, 209n
Lights of New York, The, 45, 68, 221, 231, 397
Light valve, 387; *see also* Aeolight
Lillie, Beatrice, 230
Limelight, 13
Lindbergh, Charles, 18, 388
Lindsay, Vachel, 51
Lion's Gate studios, 350, 403
Lip sync, 383
Lisztomania, 67, 423
Litle, Michael, 287-88
Live sound, 202, 383, 400
Livingston, Margaret, 406
Lizzani, Carlo, 153
Location recording, 46-47, 223-24, 225, 240, 257-58, 383, 399, 400
Loew, Marcus, 23
Loew's, 23
Loneliness of the Long Distance Runner, The, 69
Long cues, 410
Looping, 384, 400, 401, 405; *see also* Automatic dialogue replacement; Dialogue replacement; Dubbing; Postsynchronization; Sound mixing; Wordfit
Lorentz, Pare, 102
Losey, Joseph, 198
Lost Patrol, The, 410
Loudness, 184, 374, 375
Love Me Tonight, 185, 220, 397
Love of Jeanne Ney, The, 269

Love Parade, The, 213
Lower Depths, The, 204, 312
Lubitsch, Ernst, 46, 210, 213-14, 218, 220, 286
Lucas, George, 346, 349, 352, 353, 367, 368, 391, 414, 418n, 424
Lumet, Sidney, 412
Lumière d'Eté, 361
Lyotard, Jean-François, 172, 173

M, 108, 211, 266-69, 274-76
Maas, Willard, 201
MacArthur, Charles, 349
MacDonald, Jimmy, 363-66, 368
Mack, Russell, 229, 230
Maclaine, Christopher, 371, 376
MacMarker, 404
Madame Bovary, 409
Magnetic mixing, 413-14
Magnetic prints, 353, 391, 392, 419-21
Magnetic recording, 48, 391-93, 403
Magnetic sound, *see* Magnetic mixing; Magnetic prints; Magnetic recording; Magnetic striping; One-quarter inch tape; Stereo; Sync-pulse magnetic recording
Magnetic striping, 391, 392
Magnificent Ambersons, The, 192, 194-95, 197, 199, 287, 289, 291, 293, 295, 418n
Magnificent Obsession, 41, 277, 278
Malick, Terrence, 346, 349
Mamoulian, Rouben, 46, 185, 210, 211, 216, 218-20, 229, 233-45, 286, 402
Mancini, Mark, 346
Man Who Knew Too Much, The, 299, 300, 302
Man with the Movie Camera, The, 251, 253, 257, 342
Manz, Linda, 352
Marathon Man, 67
March of Time, The, 400
Marie, Michel, 55
Marker, Chris, 181, 190
Markopoulos, Gregory, 200, 379
Marlowe, Hugh, 406
Martinelli, Giovanni, 12
Marty, 133, 425
Marx Brothers, The, 81, 132, 230
Marxism, 26, 63, 179
Masculin féminin, 333, 334, 335
M.A.S.H., 49

Mayakovsky, V., 247
Maysles brothers (Albert and David), 393, 426
McFadden, Hamilton, 229, 230
McLuhan, Marshall, 238, 239
Méliès, Georges, 200
Meller, Raquel, 17
Melody of the World, 111
Meredith, Burgess, 406
Merrill, Gary, 406
Meshes of the Afternoon, 377
Metro-Goldwyn-Mayer, 27
Metropolitan Opera Co., 12
Metz, Christian, 45, 64, 82, 146-47, 165-66
Metzner, Erno, 270, 271, 273
Miami Vice, 414n
Michelson, Annette, 251, 377
Mickey-mousing, 189, 409-10
Microphone booms, *see* Booms
Microphone placement, 383, 393-404
Microphones, 384, 387; bi-directional, 393; cardioid, 393; chest, 400, 403; condenser, 42, 46, 66, 394; directional, 46, 393, 394, 396, 400; highly directional, 394; lavalier, 398; moving-coil, 60; omnidirectional, 42, 46, 337, 393, 397, 398; radio, 49, 69, 70, 350, 398; ribbon, 46; shotgun, 394; supercardioid, 394; ultradirectional, 42; unidirectional, 66, 216, 393; velocity, 46, 60
Midsummer Night's Dream, A, 129
Milestone, Lewis, 215, 218, 225
Million, Le, 77, 138-39, 191, 192, 216, 217
Min and Bill, 28
Mintz, Penny, 287
Mr. Deeds Goes to Town, 103
Mr. Hulot's Holiday, 133, 187, 191
Mitchell, William D., 23
Mitchell BNC, 39, 397; *see also* Sound cameras
Mitchell NC, 38, 397; *see also* Sound cameras
Mixing, *see* Sound mixing
Mixing down, 413; *see also* Sound mixing
Mizoguchi, Kenji, 203-4, 205, 209n
Modern Romance, 407
Modern Times, 126, 131, 133
Modulation, 401-2
Monsieur Verdoux, 131
Montagu, Ivor, 77
Monte Carlo, 213, 214, 218
Monterey Pop, 352

Monteverdi, Claudio, 327, 329, 330
Moore, Grace, 387
Morgan, Helen, 216, 219, 233, 243, 244
Morocco, 225, 226
M.O.S., 395, 404; see also Wild sound
Moses and Aaron, 146, 151
Motion Picture Patents Company, 6
Mottram, Ron, 210-11
Mouchette, 286, 288, 323-31
Movietone, 17-18, 387-90; see also Sound-on-film
Movietone Ink, 389
Movietone News, 18, 45, 388-89
Moviola, 163; see also Sound moviola
Mozart, Wolfgang Amadeus, 314, 335
Multi-channel mixing, 49, 359; see also Sound mixing
Multi-channel recording, 43, 49, 211, 215-16, 349-50, 402-3; see also Applause; California Split; Sound recording
Muni, Paul, 103
Münsterberg, Hugo, 50, 162
Murch, Walter, 67, 346, 353, 356-60, 366, 407
Murder, 302
Murdock, John J., 7, 16
Murnau, F. W., 221
Music, ix, 43, 46, 89-91, 97, 100-1, 104-7, 122, 171, 204, 206-7, 217, 221, 222, 243-44, 279, 280-81, 284-85, 293-94, 300, 304-5, 313, 314-15, 317, 318, 319-20, 329-31, 335, 343, 351, 369, 376, 383, 384, 386, 387, 391, 408-11; see also Click track; Long cues; Music cues; Music recording; Short cues; Source music; Spotting; Streamers; Temporary music track; Underscoring
Music cues, 409, 410-11; see also Long cues; Short cues
Music recording, 46
Musset, Alfred de, 315, 318
Mussolini, Benito, 18
Myers, Stanley, 351
My Fair Lady, 406
My Life to Live, see Vivre sa vie
My Wife's Gone Away, 14

Nagra, 392-93, 403
Nagra SN, 393
Nana, 312
Nanook of the North, 140
Napoleon's Barber, 389

Narration, see Voice-over narration
Nashville, 49, 50, 349, 350, 351, 403
Neorealism, 272
New License Agreement, 14
Newsreels, 388; see also March of Time, The; Movietone News; Pathe News
New York Nights, 225
New York Philharmonic, 12
Nicht Versöhnt, 208
Nicoll, Allardyce, 129
Night Mail, 102
Night Work, 230
Nixon, Marni, 406
Noise, see Ambient sound; Ground noise; System noise
Noiseless recording, 390
Nondiegetic sound, 192, 194-95, 197, 199
Nonsynchronous sound, 394; see also Wild Sound
Nonsync sound, see Asynchronous sound
Nordisk, 29-30
North by Northwest, 305
North Sea, 109
Norton, E. E., 6
Not Reconciled, 146
Nuit de carrefour, La, 312
Nun, The, 206

Obolensky, L., 257
Odd Man Out, 61
Off-screen sound/space, 65, 139, 145, 148, 157-58, 165-69, 189, 193, 201, 202, 205, 226, 267, 268-69, 274-75, 288, 303, 322, 323-24, 325, 367, 371
Of Human Bondage, 410
Oh, for a Man!, 230
Oklahoma!, 419
Okraina, 209n
Olivier, Laurence, 129, 193
One Hundred Men and a Girl, 43
One Night of Love, 387
One-quarter inch tape, 392-93
1000 Eyes of Dr. Mabuse, 275
Only Yesterday, 40
On With the Show, 224-25
Optical sound, see Dolby SVA; Movietone; Phonofilm; Photophone; Sound-on-film
Original recording, see Sync-sound
Orpheum, 21
Othello, 137, 203

Otterson, John, 11-14, 20
Overdubbing, 412
Overrecording, 402

Pabst, G. W., 133, 211, 266, 269-76
Paisan, 133, 270
Pakula, Alan J., 349, 350
Pallo-Photophone, 19
Paramount, 22, 23, 27, 28
Paris Agreement, 29, 30
Parrain, Brice, 334
Pasolini, Pier Paolo, 150, 151
Pathe News, 390
Pause!, 380n
Pechter, William, 306
Perception, *see* Sound and attention; Sound
    and perception
Perfect Crime, The, 21
Perkins, V. F., 184
Permutational formalism, 343-44
Persona, 208
Perspecta Sound, 421
Peterson, Sidney, 379
Peterson-Poulson system, 29, 30
Petri, Elio, 153
Pett and Pott, 78
Phonofilm, 8, 16, 387, 389; *see also* De For-
    est, Lee; Movietone; Sound-on-film
Photoelectric cell, 387, 388
Photophone, 19-22, 387, 390; *see also* Radio
    Corporation of America (RCA); Sound-on-
    film
Pick, Lupu, 100
Pickpocket, 329
Pilgrim, The, 99
Pilot-tone, 392
Pitch, 185
Playtime, 190
Pleasure of His Company, The, 365
Pointe, La, 203
Polonsky, Abraham, 205
Porgy & Bess, 237
Portman, Richard, 350, 412
Possessed, 191
Postproduction, 383, 404-17; *see also* Sound
    editing; Sound mixing
Postsynchronization, 42, 215, 383, 384, 401,
    405, 412; *see also* Dubbing; Sound mixing
Powell, Eleanor, 104
Pratella, Bailla, 248
Prerecording, 387, 406, 411

Presence, 395
Prieto, Luis, 160n
Production sound, 58, 71, 383, 384, 400; *see
    also* Direct sound; Guide track; Live sound
Projection sync, 390; *see also* Editorial sync
Prokofiev, S., 204, 313

Prophet 5 analogue synthesizer, 362
Proust, Marcel, 128, 132
Proximity effect, 398
Psycho, 65, 185, 186, 198, 299, 304-5
Psychoanalysis, 45, 63, 169-74
Public Enemy, The, 40
Pudovkin, V. I., 76-77, 78, 126, 135-36, 137,
    249, 265, 266
Push-pull recording, 67
Pygmalion, 132, 133, 349

Quatre Nuits d'un rêveur, 331
Quick Billy, 371
Quiet Man, The, 410
Quota restrictions in Europe, 31-32
Quotations, 410

Radio Corporation of America (RCA), 5, 9, 23,
    27, 29; role of, in innovating sound, 18-22
Raiders of the Lost Ark, 67, 366, 367, 423
Rangertone, 392
Ray, Satyajit, 269
Realism, *see* Sound and realism
Rear Window, 65, 299, 303
Rebecca, 303
Recorder, 384
Recording, *see* Sound recording
Recordist, 401; *see also* Sound mixer
Reeves, Hazard, 403, 426
Reflected sound, 394-95; *see also* Direct sound
Reinhardt, Max, 129
Reisz, Karel, 61
Renoir, Jean, 41, 65, 133, 146, 234, 265-66,
    272-74, 276, 286-88, 300, 312-22
Reproduction, *see* Theaters: sound reproduc-
    tion in
Rerecording, *see* Sound mixing
Rerecording mixer, 401
Resnais, Alain, 312
Resolver, 392
Return of the Jedi, 368
Rhythm, 188, 217-18, 263
Rich, Walter, 10, 11-12, 13
Riddle of Lumen, The, 378

Rise, Chester, 19
River, The, 102
Rivette, Jacques, 206
RKO (Radio-Keith-Orpheum), 21, 29
Robbe-Grillet, Alain, 205
Robinson Crusoe, 133
Rock 'n'- roll (Back-up recording), 414
Rocky, 67
Rogers, Ginger, 104, 181, 189
Romans, 378
Romeo and Juliet, 107
Room tone, 395
Rope, 303, 311
Rose Hobart, 376
Rosolato, Guy, 169-70
Rossellini, Roberto, 133, 269, 270
Rota, Nino, 335
Rouch, Jean, 426
Rozsa, Miklos, 409, 426
Rubin, Martin, 212
Ruggles of Red Gap, 81, 130-31
Rules of the Game, The, 272, 286, 287-88, 312-22
Ruskin, John, 133
Russell, Ken, 349, 351
Russolo, Luigi, 248
Ruttmann, Walter, 111
Ryder, Loren, 391, 426

Sabotage, 305
Sadoul, Georges, 248
Saga of Anatahan, The, 204, 205, 209n
Sala, Oskar, 304
Salt, Barry, 3
Sansho the Bailiff, 206, 209n
Santa Fe Trail, 419
Sarnoff, David, 19-21, 23
Saturday Night Fever, 353
Saville, Victor, 218
Sawyer, Gordon, 426
Schenck, Nicholas, 23
Schoenberg, Arnold, 204
Schreger, Charles, 346
Scoring, see Music
Scorsese, Martin, 346, 349, 351
Scourby, Alexander, 406
Seberg, Jean, 333, 334
Second Wife, 230
Secret Agent, 302, 303
Secret Beyond the Door, 199

Segue, 409
Selznick, David, 409
Serafine, Frank, 362-63, 367, 368
Serene Velocity, 380
Seven Samurai, 179, 187-88, 194
Seventh Heaven, 18, 221
Seven Year Itch, The, 406
Shadow of a Doubt, 300
Shakespeare, William, 107, 129, 406
Shaw, George Bernard, 349
Shearer, Douglas, 402, 418
Shepard, David, 426
She Wore a Yellow Ribbon, 189
Shifrin, Art, 425
Shorin, A., 257
Short cues, 410
Shout, The, 351
Sibilance, 394
Signal-to-noise ratio, 66, 402
Silence, 117-19, 149, 184, 240-41, 277, 279, 282-83, 299-300, 307-8, 323, 338, 369-70, 372, 377-80, 395
Simple diegetic sound, 196, 197
Simple histoire, Une, 208, 342
Singing Fool, The, 28
Singin' in the Rain, 196
Single system sound-on-film, 387-90
Sirk, Douglas, 277, 379
Skinner, Frank, 277
Sklar, Robert, 25, 31, 33
Skolimowski, Jerzy, 349, 351
Smeck, Roy, 12, 386
Smiling Lieutenant, The, 214
Smith, Alfred, 18
Smith, Courtland, 16-18
Smith, Harry, 377
Smith, Pete, 98, 102
Smokey and the Bandit, 353
Snow White and the Seven Dwarfs, 364
Sokolov, I., 258
Somebody Up There Likes Me, 69
Song of Ceylon, 77
Sound: traditional subservience to image, 44-45, 51-52, 75-82, 158, 208, 299, 361; see also Ideology of the visible; Sound and ideology
——transition to: history of, in U.S., 3, 5-24, 210, 213-31, 284; history of, in Europe, 25-33; history of, in Germany, 266; pre-history, 6-10, 98-101

Sound and attention, 186-88, 295-97
—— and economics, 3, 5-36, 45
—— and ideology, 3, 4, 44-52, 54-61, 63, 146, 147-48, 150, 152-53, 156, 165-66; see also Ideology of the visible
—— and image, see Dialogue cutting point; Sound: traditional subservience to image; Sound editing; Sound mixing; Sound perspective
—— and perception, 63-66, 116-25, 137, 154-58, 178, 181, 184, 186-87, 201, 237, 239, 241, 244-45, 291, 295-97, 371, 380
—— and realism, 265-66, 269-76, 301, 312-13, 314, 337-38, 340-41, 349
—— and space, 67-68, 118, 121-22, 123-25, 152, 157-58, 164, 165-67, 170, 191-95, 211, 226, 232-45, 254-55, 289-95, 371, 372, 374, 380; see also Sound perspective
—— and technology, 37-43, 45-50, 63-71, 383-425, 440-45
—— and television, see Television sound
—— and time, 195-97; see also Displaced diegetic sound
Sound bridge, 198, 295, 324, 328
Sound cameras, 38-39; see also Mitchell BNC; Mitchell NC
Sound designers, 346-47, 352, 353, 356-68, 407; see also Postproduction; Sound editing; Sound effects; Sound mixing
Sound editing, 4, 39-42, 54-61, 64, 69, 88-90, 182-83, 258, 299, 336-40, 385, 386, 389, 391, 396, 404, 408; see also Dialogue cutting point; Edge numbering
Sound effects, 65, 87, 92-93, 94, 107-9, 117, 137-41, 144, 187-88, 200-1, 203-4, 205, 206, 219, 237-40, 242, 277-78, 279, 280, 285, 292, 298, 299, 300, 305-10, 323, 324-27, 331, 335-36, 356-57, 358, 364-66, 366-67, 373, 383, 384, 385, 391, 407-8
Soundhead, 388
Sound mixer: in New York, England, Hollywood, 401; see also Recordist
Sound mixing, 42, 43, 46, 49, 56, 64, 70, 187-88, 341, 350, 356-60, 384, 391, 411, 413-15; in England, 358-59; in Hollywood, 357-58, 413; see also Multi-channel mixing
Sound moviola, 39-40, 390-91; see also Moviola
Sound off, see Off-screen sound/space
Sound-on-disc, 6, 7, 9, 12-13, 16, 42, 385-

87; see also Cameraphone; Chronophone; Kinetophone; Vitaphone
Sound-on-film, 15-21, 28, 42-43, 386, 387-91; see also Double system sound-on-film; Movietone; Phonofilm; Photophone; Tri-Ergon
Sound perspective, 58-59, 60, 61, 68, 69, 202-3, 244-45, 287, 385, 395-96, 399
Sound recorder, 390
Sound recording, 4, 42-43, 46, 58, 59, 64, 70, 258, 336-40, 383, 385-93, 399, 400, 403; see also Dialogue recording; Location recording; Multi-channel recording; Music recording
—— in exteriors, see Location recording
Sound technicians, 384
Sound tracks, see Dolby SVA; Magnetic prints; Sound-on-disc; Sound-on-film; Stereo; Variable area track; Variable density track
Source music, 300, 335, 408; see also Music
Sous les toits de Paris, 77, 216, 217
Space, see Sound and space
Spanish Earth, The, 102
Speakers, 418
Speech, see Dialogue
Spielberg, Steven, 67, 349, 352, 414
Spivack, Murray, 368, 391, 426
Splicing early sound tracks, 389; see also Blooping
Sponable, Earl, 3, 15, 45, 389, 420, 425
Spoto, Donald, 303
Spotting, 409
Spottiswoode, Raymond, 426
Sprocket Systems (of George Lucas), 424
Squawk box, 391
Stagecoach, 193, 194
Stahl, John, 40, 41, 211-12, 277-85
Star Is Born, A (1954), 420
Star Is Born, A (1976), 423
Star Trek, 362
Star Wars, 50, 175n, 352, 353, 354, 366, 368, 423
State Fair, 390
Steiner, Max, 391, 409, 410, 411
Stellavox, 393
Stereo, 68, 194, 352, 403, 415, 418-21, 422-24; see also Cine-Fi; CinemaScope; Cinerama; Dolby stereo; Fantasound; Perspecta Sound; Todd-AO; Vitasound; Warner-Phonic sound

Sternberg, Josef von, 204, 209n, 226-27, 231, 235, 239, 245n
Stewart, James, 185
Stewart, James G., 363
Stigwood, Robert, 348
Stingers, 410
Stockhausen, Karlheinz, 335
Story of the Late Chrysanthemums, 209n
Stothart, Herbert, 409
Strangers on a Train, 300, 305
Straub, Jean-Marie, 146, 163, 173
Streamers, 411
Stroheim, Erich von, 271
Stuart, Harold, 17
Studios: conversion to sound, 22-24; see also Fox Film Corp.; Warner Bros.
Sturges, Preston, 349
Sunny Side Up, 389, 397
Sunrise, 18, 221
Sunset Boulevard, 168
Sunshine Susie, 218
Superman, 417, 423
Supervising sound editor, 411-12
Suspicion, 303
Sutherland, Eddie, 229
Swing Time, 189
Sylvia Scarlett, 41
Symphony of the Donbas, see Enthusiasm
Synchronization, 196, 249, 262-64, 371, 373, 385, 386, 388; see also Editorial sync; Lip sync; Projection sync
Synchronizer, 390
Sync-pulse magnetic recording, 392-93
Sync-sound: as a style, 286, 289, 339, 371, 374, 375, 379; see also Direct sound
—— as a technique, 383, 385, 389, 394; see also Direct sound; Lip sync; Live sound
Synthetic sound, 219, 242, 254-55, 303-4, 306, 362-63; see also Sound designers
System noise, 67, 402
Sweetening, 408

Table, 379
Tager, P., 257
T.A.M.I. Show, The, 352
Tati, Jacques, 133, 150, 187, 190, 191
Taviani brothers (Paolo and Vittorio), 151
Taxi Driver, 406

Television sound, 68, 338, 400, 408, 410-11, 414
Tempestaire, Le, 81, 140, 143-44
Temple, Shirley, 105
Temporal dimensions of sound, see Sound and time
Temporary music track, 408-9
Ten Commandments, The, 391
Tenderloin, 15
Territoire des autres, Le, 209n
Testament of Dr. Mabuse, The, 266
Text of Light, The, 378
Thalofide cell, 15, 16
Theaters: conversion of, to sound, in U.S., 13, 17, 21, 22; in Europe, 26-27; sound reproduction in, 354, 383, 385, 417-25
Thief of Bagdad, The, 223
13 Rue Madeleine, 400
Thirty-Nine Steps, The, 191
This Is Cinerama, 351, 403, 419
This Is the Night, 218
Thomas, Tony, 426
Thompson, Kristin, 179-80
Thorpe, Richard, 42
Three-cornered Moon, 134
Three Smart Girls, 105
Three Songs of Lenin, 266
Thunderbolt, 226-27, 239
THX-1138, 346
Timbre, 185
Tobis-Klangfilm, 28-29
Todd, Mike, 419
Todd-AO, 419, 421
Toland, Gregg, 39
Tommy, 67, 351
Tom Sawyer, 229
Toni, 314
Touch of Evil, 287, 289-96, 374
Tout va bien, 333, 334, 335, 338, 339, 342, 343
Tracking: of music scores, 408
Tracy, Spencer, 103
Trader Horn, 28
Trans-Europ-Express, 205, 206
Transfer: in preparation for editing, 392
Transition to sound, see Sound, transition to
Tri-Ergon, 17, 28, 45
Tron, 362-63
Truffaut, François, 305, 334

Tschaikovsky, P. I., 106, 107
Tung, 379, 380
Tuttle, Frank, 218
Twentieth Century, 373
Twice a Man, 200
Two or Three Things I Know About Her (Deux
  ou trois choses que je sais d'elle), 195, 207,
  335, 336, 341, 344

Under Capricorn, 306
Underrecording, 402
Underscoring, 408, 411
Unsere Afrikareise, 371, 375, 380

Vampyr, 266
Van Dongen, Helen, 56
Varda, Agnès, 203
Vareille, Leon, 143
Variable area track, 387, 388
Variable click track, 410
Variable density track, 387, 388
Vertigo, 304
Vertov, Dziga, 76, 145, 211, 247-64, 266, 267,
  269, 334, 340, 342, 371
Victor Talking Machine Co., 12, 23
Vidas secas, 206
Vidor, King, 46, 210, 214
Vigo, Jean, 163
Virginian, The, 96, 225
Vitagraph, 10, 11
Vitaphone, 12-15, 20, 385-87, 389; see also
  Warner Bros.
Vitasound, 419
Vivre sa vie, 173, 333, 334, 335, 336, 343,
  408
Vlady, Marina, 195
Voice, 162-74, 185, 374, 379; see also Dia-
  lects
Voice-off, see Off-screen sound/space
Voice-over narration, 102, 165, 168, 171, 172,
  181-83, 192, 293, 356, 376, 383, 400, 406
Vollbrecht, Karl, 270
Vorisek, Richard, 412

Wagner, Fritz Arno, 266, 269, 271
Wagner, Richard, 410
Wallace, Richard, 229

Walsh, Raoul, 210, 215, 223-24, 230
Walter, Ernest, 55, 57
Walton, William, 107
War Games, 367
Warhol, Andy, 369
Warner, Harry, 10-16, 23
Warner, Sam, 11, 12, 14
Warner Bros., 29; role of, in innovating sound,
  10-15, 45, 385-87
WarnerPhonic sound, 420
Waterloo Bridge, 229
Watt, Harry, 102
Wayne, David, 406
Wayne, John, 185
Way of a Sailor, The, 383
Webb, Jim, 350
Webern, Anton von, 207
Wedding, A, 350, 403
Weekend, 335
Weintraub, Jerry, 348
Weis, Elisabeth, 287, 426
Welles, Orson, 137, 192, 194-95, 199, 203,
  272, 286-88, 289-97, 341, 363, 374, 396,
  405, 407, 418
Wellman, William, 40, 227-28
West, Mae, 97
West, Roland, 245n
Western Electric, 8-10, 11, 12, 16, 18, 20, 22,
  23, 28, 29; see also Electrical Research
  Products, Inc. (ERPI)
Westfront 1918, 269
Westinghouse, 18, 23
Whale, James, 229
What Price Glory?, 18, 223
What's Up Tiger Lily?, 196
When Tomorrow Comes, 41
White Heat, 410
Wild Boys of the Road, 40
Wild sound, 384, 394, 407; see also M.O.S.;
  Nonsynchronous sound
Willemen, Paul, 173
Williams, Alan, 288
Willis, Whitney, 19
Wind noise, 399
Winger, Debra, 367
Wings Over Europe, 241
Winterset, 104
Wise, Robert, 408
Wizard of Oz, The, 65, 185

Wolfflin, Heinrich, 69, 70
Wolf Song, 225
Women, The, 41
Woodstock, 353
Wordfit, 405; *see also* Automatic dialogue
   replacement
Wright, Basil, 77-78
Wyler, William, 41, 42, 338

Yale French Studies, 4
You Can't Take It with You, 394
Young, Victor, 410
Young and Innocent, 305

Zola, Emile, 271
Zukor, Adolph, 23
Zwei Herzen im Dreiviertel Takt, 217

For the right to reprint copyrighted material, the editors are indebted to the following publishers and individuals:

University of Wisconsin Press: For Douglas Gomery's "The Coming of Sound: Technological Change in the American Film Industry," which originally appeared under the title "The Coming of the Talkies: Invention, Innovation, and Diffusion" in Tino Balio, ed., *The American Film Industry* (Madison: University of Wisconsin Press, 1976); copyright © 1976 by The Regents of the University of Wisconsin System. The article printed here is the revised version from the forthcoming second edition of the Balio book.

Yale French Studies: For Douglas Gomery's "Economic Struggle and Hollywood Imperialism: Europe Converts to Sound"; Rick Altman's "The Evolution of Sound Technology"; Mary Ann Doane's "The Voice in the Cinema: The Articulation of Body and Space"; and Christian Metz's "Aural Objects," all of which first appeared in "Cinema/Sound," *Yale French Studies,* no. 60 (1980).

Barry Salt and the University of California Press: For Barry Salt's "Film Style and Technology in the Thirties," © 1976 by The Regents of the University of California; reprinted from *Film Quarterly*, 30, no. 1 (Fall 1976), 19-32, by permission of The Regents.

St. Martin's Press: For Mary Ann Doane's "Ideology and the Practice of Sound Editing and Mixing," from *The Cinematic Apparatus*, edited by Teresa deLauretis and Stephen Heath. © Macmillan and Teresa deLauretis and Stephen Heath, 1980, for the Center for Twentieth Century Studies, University of Wisconsin–Milwaukee, and reprinted by permission of St. Martin's Press, Inc.

Harcourt Brace Jovanovich: For "A Statement," by S. M. Eisenstein, V. I. Pudovkin, and G. V. Alexandrov, from *Film Form*, by Sergei Eisenstein; edited and translated by Jay Leyda. Copyright 1949 by Harcourt Brace Jovanovich, Inc. Renewed 1977 by Jay Leyda. Reprinted by permission of the publisher.

Grove Press: For V. I. Pudovkin's "Asynchronism as a Principle of Sound Film," from *Film Technique and Film Acting*, by V. I. Pudovkin; copyright © 1960, all rights reserved. Reprinted by permission of Grove Press, Inc.

Rudolf Arnheim: For the final pages of his essay "A New Laocoön: Artistic Composites and the Talking Film"; this essay was written in 1938 and republished in the 1957 American edition of Arnheim's book *Film as Art*, first published in German in 1932.

Dover Publications, Inc.: For Bela Balazs's "Theory of the Film: Sound," from *Theory of the Film: Character and Growth of a New Art* (New York: Dover Publications, 1970).

Oxford University Press: For Siegfried Kracauer's "Dialogue and Sound," from *Theory of Film: The Redemption of Physical Reality*, by Siegfried Kracauer. Copyright © 1960 by Oxford University Press, Inc. Reprinted by permission.

Robert Lamberton, Georges Borchardt, Inc., and Editions Seghers: For Jean Epstein's "Slow-Motion Sound," which originally appeared in Volume 2 of Epstein's *Ecrits* (Paris: Editions Seghers, 1975).

Robert Bresson: For his "Notes on Sound," which originally appeared in *Notes on Cinematography* (New York: Urizen Books, 1977).

Cahiers du Cinéma: For "Direct Sound: An Interview with Jean-Marie Straub and Danièle Huillet," which originally appeared in *Cahiers du Cinéma*.